The Extravagant

The Extra

CROSSINGS OF

vagant

MODERN POETRY AND MODERN PHILOSOPHY

ROBERT BAKER

University of Notre Dame Press · Notre Dame, Indiana

The author is grateful for permission to reprint poetry from the following:

The Poems of Emily Dickinson, Thomas H. Johnson, ed., Cambridge Mass.: The Belknap Press of Harvard University Press. Copyright © 1951, 1955, 1979 by the President and Fellows of Harvard College. Reprinted by permission of the publishers and the Trustees of Amherst College.

New and Collected Poems, 1952–1992 by Geoffrey Hill. Copyright © 1994 by Geoffrey Hill. Reprinted by permission of Houghton Mifflin Company. All rights reserved.

The Triumph of Love by Geoffrey Hill. Copyright © 1998 by Geoffrey Hill. Reprinted by permission of Houghton Mifflin Company. All rights reserved.

Collected Poems by Stéphane Mallarmé, translated by Henry Weinfeld, University of California Press. Copyright © 1994 The Regents of the University of California. Used by permission.

Toward the Poems of Mallarmé by (including translations) Robert Greer Cohn, expanded edition, University of California Press. Copyright © 1980 The Regents of the University of California. Used by permission.

George Oppen, *New Collected Poems,* copyright © 1965, 1968, 1975 by George Oppen. Reprinted by permission of New Directions Publishing Corp.

"Archaic Torso of Apollo," copyright © 1982 by Stephen Mitchell, from *The Selected Poetry of Rainer Maria Rilke,* by Rainer Maria Rilke, translated by Stephen Mitchell. Used by permission of Random House, Inc.

Arthur Rimbaud, *Collected Poems,* translated by Oliver Bernard. Penguin Books, 1962, rev. edition 1997. Copyright © Oliver Bernard, 1962, 1997. By permission of Penguin Books.

The Collected Poems of Wallace Stevens by Wallace Stevens. Copyright © 1954 by Wallace Stevens and renewed 1982 by Holly Stevens. Used by permission of Alfred Knopf, a division of Random House, Inc.

César Vallejo, "XLV" in *Trilce.* Translation copyright © 1992 by Clayton Eshleman. Spanish text © 1992 by Julio Ortega. Published in 2000 and reprinted by permission of Wesleyan University Press.

Copyright © 2005 by University of Notre Dame
Notre Dame, Indiana 46556
All Rights Reserved
www.undpress.nd.edu

Pubished in the United States of America

Library of Congress Cataloging-in-Publication Data
Baker, Robert, 1965–
The extravagant : crossings of modern poetry and modern philosophy / Robert Baker.
    p. cm.
Includes bibliographical references and index.
ISBN 978-0-268-02181-8 (CLOTH)—ISBN 978-0-268-02182-5 (PBK.)
1. Poetry, Modern—History and criticism. 2. Philosophy in literature. I. Title.
PN1161.B35   2005
809.1'9384—dc22

                                        2005002504

∞ *This book is printed on acid-free paper.*

For Joanna

Discus,
starred with premonitions,

throw yourself

out of yourself.

—Paul Celan

CONTENTS

Acknowledgments	xi
Abbreviations	xiii

INTRODUCTION
Passages of the Extravagant — 1

CHAPTER ONE
The Sublime in Kant, Wordsworth, and Lyotard — 48

CHAPTER TWO
Faustian Quest in Rimbaud, Nietzsche, and Bataille — 91

CHAPTER THREE
Apocalyptic Negativity in Kierkegaard, Dickinson, Mallarmé, and Derrida — 175

CONCLUSION
The Dialectic of Instrumental Society and Creative Negativity — 265

EPILOGUE
The Miracle of Place — 299

Notes	312
Bibliography	365
Index	380

ACKNOWLEDGMENTS

Any book involves debts beyond what an author can fully acknowledge. This is perhaps especially true of a book that attempts, as this one does, to synthesize a wide range of materials, and no doubt I'm indebted to many more readers, writers, and companions in conversation than I could possibly name in a page or two. The endnotes are meant to acknowledge the scores of critics and scholars who have helped me to find my way through histories of poetry and philosophy.

Essential to this book is the question of realities beyond clear or adequate representation in words, and in thinking of those whose more immediate support I wish to acknowledge here, I am again reminded of how basic this figure of the unfathomable is in our lives, not only in our solitudes but above all in our relations with others.

Jonathan Culler, Debra Fried, Roger Gilbert, Jonathan Monroe, José Piedra, and Jonathan Tittler, back in my years as a graduate student, taught me a great deal about literature and literary criticism. At the University of Montana my students have been engaged and curious, always happy to ask if I might like to clarify what I thought I was talking about. My colleagues here in the Department of English have been equally patient and supportive. Two of them, Chris Knight and Lois Welch, read an early draft of this book with great care, sympathy, and insight. Both have encouraged my work in all ways. Nellie Haddad also read an early draft and was tremendously helpful during an initial phase of guessing in the dark. David Klemm, taking on the manuscript before we had even met, read it with immense perceptiveness and imagination. Among the many others whose voices have been important to me during years of writing, I would like to thank in particular Sheila Black, Gerry Brenner, Casey Charles, Bryan Di Salvatore, Debra Earling, Ana Echevarría, Greg Glazner, Erik Herzog, Patrick Hutchins, Katie Kane, Dee McNamer, Ciaran O'Faolain, Ted Pearson, Bill Pekarske, Susie Pekarske, Tom Riggs, and Heather White. Two anonymous readers for the University of Notre Dame Press provided me with attentive, generous, and constructively critical readings of the book. If I have not always been able to work their broadest insights into this final version, it is not because I haven't wrestled with these insights time and again, a process I hope has left its mark in the texture of my arguments. Rebecca DeBoer was an altogether thoughtful, sympathetic editor in preparing the text for publication. Ingrid Muller copyedited my prose with savvy, alertness, and creative patience. I'm deeply grateful to Barbara Hanrahan, my editor at the University of Notre Dame Press, for her support, vision, sense of humor, and spirited resistance to cynicism.

Jonathan Culler, who directed my dissertation years ago, wryly quoting Nerval at moments when he thought he could perhaps save me from another blind alley in thought, has given his vast knowledge and clarity of mind to my work for a long time now. Roger Gilbert, a truly gifted teacher, read with unfailing energy an early draft of the book, offering pointed criticisms of everything from syntactic gaffes to interpretative follies, all the while encouraging me to keep at it. Many parts of this book involve questions I've been thinking through for years in conversation with Melissa Kwasny, briefly a student of mine in the past, ever since an inspiring teacher of mine. A few years ago, at a gray hour, I was fortunate to meet Peter Sacks, whose support has been invaluable. His wisdom is "further in summer than the birds," his twenty-mile walks figures of some "spectral power in thought" guiding him on walks in other measures. I'm luckier for having known each of these teachers. Their generosity has been extraordinary.

Above all I'm grateful to Joanna Klink. I could in no way express all that she has brought to my life and thought. Throughout years of conversation and debate she has given to this book her attention, boldness, vision, and presence of mind. Clairvoyant at the darkest crossroads, bearing always "the gift of shoulders," she has been everywhere along the way.

ABBREVIATIONS

CHAPTER ONE

Immanuel Kant

CJ *Critique of Judgment.* Trans. Werner S. Pluhar, with a foreword by Mary J. Gregor. Indianapolis: Hackett, 1987.
CPrR *Critique of Practical Reason.* Trans. and with an introduction by Lewis White Beck. 3d ed. New York: Macmillan, 1993.
CPR *Critique of Pure Reason.* Trans. Norman Kemp Smith. New York: St. Martin's Press, 1965.

Jean-François Lyotard

D *The Differend: Phrases in Dispute.* Trans. Georges Van Den Abbeele. Minneapolis: University of Minnesota Press, 1988.
I *The Inhuman: Reflections on Time.* Trans. Geoffrey Bennington and Rachel Bowlby. Stanford: Stanford University Press, 1991.
JG *Just Gaming.* With Jean-Loup Thébaud. Trans. Wlad Godzich, with an afterword by Samuel Weber. Minneapolis: University of Minnesota Press, 1985.
LAS *Lessons on the Analytic of the Sublime.* Trans. Elizabeth Rottenberg. Stanford: Stanford University Press, 1994.
LE *Libidinal Economy.* Trans. Ian Hamilton Grant. Bloomington: Indiana University Press, 1993.
P *Peregrinations: Law, Form, Event.* New York: Columbia University Press, 1988.
PC *The Postmodern Condition.* Trans. Geoff Bennington and Brian Massumi, with a foreword by Fredric Jameson. Minneapolis: University of Minnesota Press, 1984.
PF *Postmodern Fables.* Trans. Georges Van Den Abbeele. Minneapolis: University of Minnesota Press, 1997.
PW *Political Writings.* Ed. and trans. Bill Readings and Kevin Paul, with a foreword by Bill Readings. Minneapolis: University of Minnesota Press, 1993.

William Wordsworth

MW	*The Major Works.* Ed. Stephen Gill. New York: Oxford University Press, 1984.
Pre	*The Prelude: The Four Texts.* Ed. Jonathan Wordsworth. New York: Penguin, 1995.

CHAPTER TWO

Georges Bataille

AM	*The Absence of Myth: Writings on Surrealism.* Ed. and trans. Michael Richardson. London: Verso, 1994.
AS	*The Accursed Share.* 3 vols. Trans. Robert Hurley. New York: Zone Books, 1991.
E	*Erotism.* Trans. Mary Dalwood. San Francisco: City Lights, 1986.
G	*Guilty.* Trans. Bruce Boone, with an introduction by Denis Hollier. San Francisco: Lapis Press, 1988.
IE	*Inner Experience.* Trans. and with an introduction by Leslie Anne Boldt. Albany: State University of New York Press, 1988.
ON	*On Nietzsche.* Trans. Bruce Boone, with an introduction by Sylvère Lotringer. St. Paul: Paragon House, 1992.
TR	*Theory of Religion.* Trans. Robert Hurley. New York: Zone Books, 1992.
VE	*Visions of Excess: Selected Writings, 1927–39.* Ed. and with an introduction by Allan Stoekl. Trans. Allan Stoekl, Carl R. Lovitt, and Donald M. Leslie. Minneapolis: University of Minnesota Press, 1985.

Friedrich Nietzsche

BGE	*Beyond Good and Evil: Prelude to a Philosophy of the Future.* Trans. and with commentary by Walter Kaufmann. New York: Random House, 1966.
BT	*The Birth of Tragedy* and *The Case of Wagner.* Trans. and with commentary by Walter Kaufmann. New York: Random House, 1967.
GM/EH	*On the Genealogy of Morals* and *Ecce Homo.* Trans. and with commentary by Walter Kaufmann. New York: Random House, 1967.
GS	*The Gay Science.* Trans. and with commentary by Walter Kaufmann. New York: Random House, 1974.
SL	*Selected Letters.* Ed. and trans. Christopher Middleton. Indianapolis: Hackett, 1996.
TI/AC	*Twilight of the Idols* and *The Anti-Christ.* Trans. R. J. Hollingdale, with an introduction by Michael Tanner. New York: Penguin, 1990.
UM	*Untimely Meditations.* Trans. R. J. Hollingdale, with an introduction by J. R. Stern. New York: Cambridge University Press, 1983.
WP	*The Will to Power.* Ed. Walter Kaufmann. Trans. Walter Kaufmann and R. J. Hollingdale. New York: Random House, 1967.
Z	*Thus Spoke Zarathustra.* Trans. and with a preface by Walter Kaufmann. New York: Penguin, 1978.

Arthur Rimbaud

CP *Collected Poems.* Trans. and with an introduction by Oliver Bernard. New York: Penguin, 1962.
O   *Oeuvres.* Rev. ed. Ed. Suzanne Bernard and André Guyaux. Paris: Classiques Garnier, 1991.
SHI *A Season in Hell* and *The Illuminations.* Trans. Enid Rhodes Peschel, with a foreword by Henri Peyre. New York: Oxford University Press, 1973.

CHAPTER THREE

Jacques Derrida

C   "Circonfession." In *Jacques Derrida.* Paris: Seuil, 1991.
D   *Dissemination.* Trans. and with an introduction by Barbara Johnson. Chicago: University of Chicago Press, 1981.
FK "Faith and Knowledge: The Two Sources of 'Religion' at the Limits of Reason Alone." In Derrida and Vattimo, *Religion,* 1–78.
GD *The Gift of Death.* Trans. David Wills. Chicago: University of Chicago Press, 1995.
GT *Given Time: I. Counterfeit Money.* Trans. Peggy Kamuf. Chicago: University of Chicago Press, 1992.
HAS "How to Avoid Speaking: Denials." Trans. Ken Frieden. In *Derrida and Negative Theology,* ed. Harold Coward and Toby Foshay, 75–142. Albany: State University of New York Press, 1992.
MP *Margins of Philosophy.* Trans. Alan Bass. Chicago: University of Chicago Press, 1982.
MX "Marx and Sons." In Sprinker, *Ghostly Demarcations,* 213–69.
OAT "On a Newly Arisen Apocalyptic Tone in Philosophy." Trans. John Leavey Jr. In *Raising the Tone of Philosophy,* ed. Peter Fenves, 117–71. Baltimore: Johns Hopkins University Press, 1993.
OG *Of Grammatology.* Trans. Gayatri Chakravorty Spivak. Baltimore: Johns Hopkins University Press, 1976.
P   *Positions.* Trans. Alan Bass. Chicago: University of Chicago Press, 1981.
PC *The Post Card: From Socrates to Freud and Beyond.* Trans. and with an introduction by Alan Bass. Chicago: University of Chicago Press, 1987.
PIO "Psyche: Inventions of the Other." Trans. Catherine Porter. In *Reading de Man Reading,* ed. Lindsay Waters and Wlad Godzich, 25–65. Minneapolis: University of Minnesota Press, 1989.
SM *Specters of Marx.* Trans. Peggy Kamuf, with an introduction by Bernd Magnus and Stephen Cullenberg. New York: Routledge, 1994.
SP *Speech and Phenomenona.* Trans. and with an introduction by David B. Allison. Evanston: Northwestern University Press, 1973.
SPU *Spurs: Nietzsche's Styles.* Trans. Barbara Harlow. Chicago: University of Chicago Press, 1979.

WD   *Writing and Difference.* Trans. and with an introduction by Alan Bass. Chicago: University of Chicago Press, 1978.

Emily Dickinson

L   *Selected Letters.* Ed. Thomas H. Johnson. Cambridge: Harvard University Press, 1986.
P   *The Complete Poems.* Ed. Thomas H. Johnson. Boston: Little, Brown, 1955.

Martin Heidegger

AF   "The Anaximander Fragment." In *Early Greek Thinking,* trans. David Farrell Krell and Frank A. Capuzzi, 13–58. New York: Harper & Row, 1984.
BPP   *The Basic Problems of Phenomenology.* Rev. ed. Trans. and with an introduction by Albert Hofstadter. Bloomington: Indiana University Press, 1988.
BT   *Being and Time.* Trans. Joan Stambaugh. Albany: State University of New York Press, 1996.
ID   *Identity and Difference.* Trans. and with an introduction by Joan Stambaugh. New York: Harper & Row, 1969.
L   "Language." In *Poetry, Language, Thought,* 187–210.
LH   "Letter on Humanism." In *Pathmarks,* ed. and trans. William McNeill, 239–76. New York: Cambridge University Press, 1998.
OTB   *On Time and Being.* Trans. Joan Stambaugh. New York: Harper & Row, 1972.
OWA   "The Origin of the Work of Art." In *Poetry, Language, Thought,* 15–88.
PLT   *Poetry, Language, Thought.* Trans. and with an introduction by Albert Hofstadter. New York: Harper & Row, 1971.
PR   *The Principle of Reason.* Trans. Reginald Lilly. Bloomington: Indiana University Press, 1996.
QCT   *The Question Concerning Technology and Other Essays.* Trans. and with an introduction by William Lovitt. New York: Harper & Row, 1977.

Søren Kierkegaard

CI   *The Concept of Irony with Continual Reference to Socrates.* Ed. and trans. Howard V. Hong and Edna H. Hong. Princeton: Princeton University Press, 1989.
CUP   *Concluding Unscientific Postscript.* Trans. David F. Swenson and Walter Lowrie. Princeton: Princeton University Press, 1968.
EO   *Either/Or.* 2 vols. Ed. and trans. Howard V. Hong and Edna H. Hong. Princeton: Princeton University Press, 1987.
EUD   *Eighteen Upbuilding Discourses.* Ed. and trans. Howard V. Hong and Edna H. Hong. Princeton: Princeton University Press, 1990.
FSE   *For Self-Examination* and *Judge for Yourself.* Ed. and trans. Howard V. Hong and Edna H. Hong. Princeton: Princeton University Press, 1990.

FT	*Fear and Trembling* and *Repetition*. Ed. and trans. Howard V. Hong and Edna H. Hong. Princeton: Princeton University Press, 1983.
PC	*Practice in Christianity*. Ed. and trans. Howard V. Hong and Edna H. Hong. Princeton: Princeton University Press, 1991.
PF	*Philosophical Fragments* and *Johannes Climacus*. Ed. and trans. Howard V. Hong and Edna H. Hong. Princeton: Princeton University Press, 1985.
PV	*The Point of View for My Work as an Author: A Report to History*. Trans. Walter Lowrie, with a new preface by Benjamin Nelson. New York: Harper & Brothers, 1962.
SLW	*Stages on Life's Way*. Ed. and trans. Howard V. Hong and Edna H. Hong. Princeton: Princeton University Press, 1988.
SUD	*The Sickness unto Death*. Trans. Alastair Hannay. New York: Penguin, 1989.

Stéphane Mallarmé

C	*Correspondance: Lettres sur la poésie*. Ed. Bertrand Marchal, with a preface by Yves Bonnefoy. Paris: Gallimard-Folio, 1995.
CP	*Collected Poems*. Trans. and with a commentary by Henry Weinfield. Berkeley: University of California Press, 1994.
L	*Selected Letters*. Ed. and trans. Rosemary Lloyd. Chicago: University of Chicago Press, 1988.
Liv	*Le "Livre" de Mallarmé*. Ed. Jacques Scherer. Paris: Gallimard, 1977.
O	*Oeuvres complètes*. Ed. Henri Mondor and G. Jean-Aubry. Paris: Gallimard, 1951.
SPr	*Selected Prose Poems, Essays, and Letters*. Trans. and with an introduction by Bradford Cook. Baltimore: Johns Hopkins University Press, 1956.

INTRODUCTION

Passages of the Extravagant

THE EXTRAVAGANT

Wittgenstein concludes his *Tractatus Logico-Philosophicus* with an elegant reminder of the limits to our knowledge: "What we cannot speak about we must pass over in silence." There are boundaries to what we are able to speak about clearly, just as there are boundaries to what we are able to experience. Yet, as Stanley Cavell emphasizes in a discussion of Emerson's "Experience," our sense of limits, of what boundaries we are able or unable to cross, will be shaped by the judgments we have come to make concerning the scope of our experience:

> I hear Kant working throughout Emerson's essay on "Experience," with his formulation of the question, "Is metaphysics possible?" and his line of answer: Genuine knowledge of (what we call) the world is for us, but it cannot extend beyond (what we call) experience. To which I take Emerson to be replying: Well and good, but then you had better be very careful what it is you understand by experience, for that might be limited in advance by what we know of human existence, i.e., by our limited experience of it.

Cavell, speaking for Emerson, speaks in the voice of the romantic response to Kant and, more broadly, to the entire Enlightenment project of critique, science, the conquest of nature, and the rational reconstruction of society. Any number of modern writers, philosophers as well as poets, have responded to various post-Enlightenment definitions of our limits in a similar spirit. Some forty years before the appearance of Wittgenstein's text, Zarathustra decries the death of longing, wonder, and creative action in a world of rationally organized pointlessness, a world represented by blank "last men" who lack any capacity to justify or renew their own existence: "'What is love? What is creation? What is longing? What is a star?' thus asks the last man, and he blinks.... 'We have invented happiness,' say the last men, and they blink." There may be more in experience than is dreamt of in post-Enlightenment philosophy. And this excess, this unknown place to which Zarathustra calls us, can perhaps be found only through metamorphic search at the borders of our experience. Or it may be disclosed in moments of visitation, as in Wordsworth, or in curves of visionary de-figuration and re-figuration, as in Rimbaud, or in disclosive departures at the edge of ruin, as in Dickinson, or in reaching articulations of the nothing through which we drift, as in Mallarmé. Probably, as René Char affirms, it requires a passage through the shadow of death: "To make a poem is to seize a nuptial beyond, which is found well within this life, intimately attached to it, yet close to the urns of death. We must build and dwell outside ourselves, on the border of tears and in the orbit of famines, if we wish for something uncommon to be produced, solely for us."[1]

This book is a study of what I will call passages of the extravagant—passages of disclosive wandering—in modern poetry and engagements with these passages in modern Continental philosophy. Biblical rather than Homeric in spirit, these passages seek not a return to a lost household so much as a crossing toward a new heaven and a new earth, or seek, above all, the power itself to make things new. They are thus passages characterized, first, by a pointed criticism of the conventional boundaries of experience established by the dominant social, scientific, and philosophic frameworks of capitalist modernity. A blithe disregard of limits, of course, persuades no one. Thus genuine passages of the extravagant are characterized, further, by a wrestling with the very limits they aim to traverse and, in one way or another, to transform. This sort of wrestling involves, among other things, an internalization of the ironic stance that forms an important strand of enlightened modernity. It involves, too, an acknowledgment of the unsurpassable limit of death, a riddling dark explored by several of the poets and writers I engage in this study. All of these passages, sounding limits they at the same time subvert, seek a metamorphosis of our experience, a widening of our sense of the possible. "I dedicate this book to the improbable, that is to say, to what is."[2]

What I'm calling the extravagant is akin to what our culture has often called the sublime. The reason I've chosen not to use the latter term as a general rubric is that it tends to bring to mind a strong connection with certain names (for example, Kant) and certain fields (for example, high romantic poetries). The term "sublime," then, may not be the most apt term with which to characterize, in a word, this range of adventures, since in chapter 1 I explore different conceptions of the sublime in Kant, Wordsworth, and Lyotard, and in chapter 2 different paths of Faustian quest and crisis in Rimbaud, Nietzsche, and Bataille, and in chapter 3 different dynamics of apocalyptic negativity in Kierkegaard, Dickinson, Mallarmé, and Derrida. That said, the term "extravagant" could also serve, I think, as a general term with which to designate the field of modern culture that Jonathan Arac appears to have in mind when he speaks of "a differentiated history of the sublime."[3] The fields I explore in the main chapters of this book are important fields of any such history. My concern is to study a differentiated history of the extravagant in modern poetry and philosophy from the late eighteenth century through the present.[4]

The term "extravagance," formed of roots meaning "to wander beyond," is one I borrow from Thoreau's *Walden*. An important theme in this text is the opposition between sleeping and waking, desperation and renovation. "The mass of men lead lives of quiet desperation. What is called resignation is confirmed desperation." "To be awake is to be alive. I have never yet met a man who was quite awake. How could I have looked him in the face?" This opposition is recalled again in Thoreau's meditation on extravagance in the concluding chapter:

> It is a ridiculous demand which England and America make, that you shall speak so that they can understand you. Neither men nor women nor toadstools grow so. As if that were important, and there were not enough to understand you without them. As if Nature could support but one order of understandings, could not sustain birds as well as quadrupeds, flying as well as creeping things, and *hush* and *who,* which Bright can understand, were the best English. As if there were safety in stupidity alone. I fear chiefly lest my expression may not be *extra-vagant* enough—may not wander far enough beyond the narrow limits of my daily experience, so as to be adequate to the truth of which I have been convinced. . . . I desire to speak

somewhere *without* bounds; like a man in his waking moment, to men in their waking moments; for I am convinced that I cannot exaggerate enough even to lay the foundation of a true expression. Who that has heard a strain of music feared then lest he should speak extravagantly any more for ever? In view of the future or possible, we should live quite laxly and undefined in front, our outlines dim and misty on that side; as our shadows reveal an insensible perspiration toward the sun. The volatile truth of our words should continually betray the inadequacy of the residual statement. Their truth is instantly *translated;* its literal monument alone remains. The words which express our faith and piety are not definite; yet they are significant and fragrant like frankincense to superior natures.[5]

This passage weaves together a number of themes that we will encounter throughout this book. Linking the extravagant to both hyperbole, a throwing beyond, and metaphor, a carrying across, two tropes that set in play the power of turning words, Thoreau testifies to an extravagant desire to travel beyond conventional existential and linguistic boundaries. One question he raises is whether the wandering he evokes is an existential wandering that can only be adequately conveyed through a linguistic wandering, or whether it is in the first place a linguistic wandering that is then able to bring about an existential wandering, or whether it is perhaps both at once: this sort of ambiguity is characteristic of the writing of the extravagant. Thoreau underlines, further, that this disclosive wandering, while occurring on different scales, always involves a palpable break from leveled boundaries of experience and meaning, a break said to be inseparable from an awakened relationship to the openness of the future. Turning toward the open and the unforeseeable, the extravagant is a motion unloosed from common perceptual, experiential, linguistic, and social bonds. This is one of its fundamental bearings as well as one of its fundamental predicaments.[6]

Most importantly perhaps, Thoreau's meditation unfolds an opposition between common sense and uncommon truth: if the former belongs to established orders of dulled perception, narrow habit, and sleeping existence, the latter is found in elusive orbits of heightened perception, metamorphic passage, and awakened existence. "The substantive disagreement with Heidegger, shared by Emerson and Thoreau," Cavell writes near the end of his study of *Walden,* "is that the achievement of the human requires not inhabitation and settlement but abandonment, leaving."[7] One must abandon, first of all, one's attachment to an impeded, anxious self of habit locked in a restricted economy of experience. The discovery of the extravagant, therefore, involves a motion of conversion. Common sense, a lack of vision or translative power, is a kind of inertia, a death-in-life, while uncommon truth is a release of vision that transforms the subject, bears the subject toward other latitudes. In this respect Thoreau reaffirms a romantic metaphysic—one taught with particular force by Blake, Shelley, Emerson, and Nietzsche—according to which the extravagant "turns" of poetic invention are prior to, and recurrently disruptive of, the leveled "literalizations" of theology, philosophy, and common sense. Common sense is surpassed by an errant significance without which we are not awake, alive, but cramped, dying, already dead. The extravagant is the pulse of awakened life, the renovative force and uncommon reach of which are not represented in clear and distinct concepts so much as indirectly conveyed through the volatile play of words that wander. The extravagant is translocative. "What distinguishes poetry from automatic speech is that it rouses us and shakes us into wakefulness in the middle of a word. Then it turns out that the word is much longer than we thought, and we remember that to speak means to be forever on the road."[8]

There is a quiet prophetic valence in Thoreau's words. Speaking of faith as well as extravagance, he presents a secularized, naturalized analogue of the dynamic of conversion, a metamorphosis that involves a turning of one's entire being. This displaced religious dynamic tends to be found, in one form or another, wherever the extravagant is found in modern poetry. One could call it a "conversional" dynamic. That, however, is an unhappy term, so I'll follow Northrop Frye in his appropriation of the word "kerygmatic" to describe this dynamic that resonates in poetic language at its highest pitch. "This [the primary concern of 'how do I live a more abundant life'] is the central theme of all genuine kerygmatic, whether we find it in the Sermon on the Mount, the Deer Park Sermon of Buddha, the Koran, or in a secular book that revolutionizes our consciousness."[9] This kerygmatic dynamic, then, is inseparable from any ambition to write poems that will be neither well-wrought urns nor beautiful imitations so much as force fields of transformative power, composed and extended in a spirit of faith. It is this concern that guides the outrageous satirical prophet who, in Blake's early work *The Marriage of Heaven and Hell*, affirms that "if the doors of perception were cleansed everything would appear to man as it is: infinite." It animates the demonic visionary of Rimbaud's *Une saison en enfer*, whose tormented lover at one point wonders if his companion has discovered "the secrets for changing life," while this visionary himself is reported to have declared that "love is to be reinvented," perhaps under the aspect of that luminous force of Eros and Deliverance that sweeps across the world in Rimbaud's "Génie." And it is this concern that is voiced again—and provided with a striking headless emblem—in Rilke's "Archaic Torso of Apollo":

> We cannot know his legendary head
> with eyes like ripening fruit. And yet his torso
> is still suffused with brilliance from inside,
> like a lamp, in which his gaze, now turned to low,
>
> gleams in all its power. Otherwise
> the curved breast could not dazzle you so, nor could
> a smile run through the placid hips and thighs
> to that dark center where procreation flared.
>
> Otherwise this stone would seem defaced
> beneath the translucent cascade of the shoulders
> and would not glisten like a wild beast's fur:
>
> would not, from all the borders of itself,
> burst like a star: for here there is no place
> that does not see you. You must change your life.

This "torso suffused with brilliance from the inside," of course, is among other things a figure for the kind of poem Rilke would like to write, for the kind of power, akin to a power recovered from the mystery of ruins, that he would like his poems to embody and impart: a power to strike the reader like a star, to radiate the reader with an erotic aura, to stare at the reader with the force of a prophetic command or a call to conversion. This is the kerygmatic power to bring about a metamorphosis of life. It is the power that Thoreau evokes as the extravagant power of crossing boundaries. Adventures of the extravagant in modern poetry, while various in their turns, always involve this search for an awakening, a freeing, a dislocation of perspective, a passage toward other realms of life, a transformative wandering at once evoked and performed by language. It is significant that in a striking passage in *Spring and All,* Williams, a poet not usually located in this sort of tradition, writes: "So most of my life has been lived in hell—a hell of repression lit by flashes of inspiration, when a poem such as this or that would appear. What would have happened in a world similarly lit by the imagination." Such illuminations tend to be momentary turnings or crossings, after which one is left again in the gray, waiting and searching. Implicit in this modern poetic orientation, then, is not only a secular analogue of conversion but also a secular analogue of faith. One searches for another light, another opening, uncertain if it will come again. Montale, skeptical voice in search of a crossing, patient voice of a continual "waiting for the miracle," opens his second book with the words: "You have no eyes for any life / But that shimmering you alone can see. / You lean out toward it / from this window, now unlit."[10]

One guiding argument of this book is that the sounding of the extravagant characterizes broad fields of modern poetry from the romantic through the modernist period. Another is that it animates broad fields of modern Continental philosophy from the middle of the nineteenth century on. Before sketching the larger contours of these arguments, however, I would like briefly to recall the traditional philosophic stance toward poetic extravagance. For the well-known story of the ancient quarrel between philosophy and poetry has in recent years been recounted and reconsidered, yet again, in contradictory ways.

POETRY AND PHILOSOPHY: ANCIENT QUARREL,
ABIDING INTERANIMATION

Plato, as everyone knows, would like to exclude poets from his wise and just republic, and he would like to do so for two essential reasons. First, he claims that poets tell false stories or, as this argument is developed at the end of the dialogue, that they compose merely imitations of imitations, remaining at two removes from the truth. Since few of us share Plato's metaphysic, we can perhaps translate this line of thought into more familiar terms by saying that, with this objection, Plato expresses his unease with the ghostly quality of fictive language, with the power of fictive language to present as "there" what in fact is "not there." Second, he claims that poets stir unruly passions (notably fear and pity) in their listeners, appealing to irrational desire, inviting citizens of the republic to stray from the rational care of their souls and the proper fulfillment of their civic duties. Friends of the improper and the exorbitant, poets fabricate ghostly fictions and incite illicit passions. It is clear, then, that Plato's battle against the poets is of a piece with his battle against the teachers of rhetoric. For poets and sophists alike practice both an art of figurative language, language that wanders from the proper meanings of words, and an art of persuasive language, language of power that moves listeners at "non-rational" levels beyond the relatively stable semantic level that governs everyday communication and rational discussion. Dialectic, the method of patiently surpassing false and partial conceptions, must subordinate not only myth but also poetry and rhetoric to its own articulation of truth. This is the philosopher's project. In theory at least, if not in Plato's practice, it is resolutely opposed to the poet's inventive extravagance.[11]

This ancient quarrel, as is well known, has persisted throughout the modern period. Any number of philosophers have tried to situate poetry in either an irrelevant or a subordinate place within a larger project of finding the truth, appropriately modifying the terms of Plato's original polemic to suit their altered philosophic frameworks. At the same time, however, various romantic poets with speculative bents of mind, the ironic and prophetic Nietzsche, and many Continental philosophers working in the broad wake of Nietzsche have sought to revise the positions and the plot of this ancient quarrel, at times arguing that the errant inventions of poetry are constitutive of the clear schemes of philosophy, at times welcoming the wandering of poetry into the writing of philosophy, at times orchestrating cross-communications that unsettle our very definitions of poetry and philosophy. To recall the terms of Nietzsche's early work *The Birth of Tragedy*, a Dionysian spirit of creative transfiguration has been made to reverberate within the Apollonian house of enlightened method.

The question of the relationship between poetry (or, more broadly, art) and philosophy has been addressed in a number of books in recent years. Both Arthur Danto and Mark Edmundson claim that modern philosophers have continued, if occasionally in subtler ways than their giant ancestor, the attempt to regulate the wayward passions and impertinent departures of art.[12] Edmundson argues that Plato's distrust of poetry is in fact wholly alive not only in modern philosophy but also in contemporary literary criticism, no less in its worldly "historicist" modes than in its esoterically "theoretical" modes, while Danto argues that philosophers ever since Plato have repeated Plato's founding gesture of defining philosophy through a theoretical "disenfranchisement" of art. Traditionally, Danto claims, there have been two especially effective forms of this disenfranchisement: first, the "ephemeralization" of art (the Kantian tactic: art is only play, an indeterminate exercise of psychic faculties that, once they get back to work, will set out to discover the truth) and second, the sly "takeover" of art (the Hegelian tactic: art is a noble but youthful and finally superseded station on the way to a mature conceptual articulation of the truth). Danto adds an intriguing turn to his argument by suggesting that modernist art, through its lively acrobatics of self-reflexivity, has perhaps played the philosopher to itself and so been a little complicit with its own theoretical disenfranchisement.[13]

Appearing at about the same time as these books by Danto and Edmundson, however, were two books that made almost the exact opposite argument. Both Jürgen Habermas and Allan Megill claim that major currents in modern Continental philosophy have been decisively shaped by the adventures of modern art, in particular modern literature.[14] Both see Nietzsche as a crucial "turning point," the provocative postromantic philosopher looming over those Continental philosophers of the last century who, in a variety of ways, have critically interrogated the guiding aims and rules of the philosophic canon. Habermas argues that the critique of reason variously articulated in a tradition running from Nietzsche through Derrida is animated by a romantic and avantgardist appeal to a Dionysian "other" of reason that, however characterized or invoked, can never itself provide coherent "grounds" for the very critique it is made to serve. According to Habermas, then, the philosophers in this tradition are guilty of a "performative contradiction," namely, that of presenting rational arguments in the name of some force or alterity that is said to surpass the sphere of rational argumentation. They are also guilty, Habermas claims, of relying on a one-sided, excessively dystopian account of modernity, for which reason they remain blind to the genuine gains involved in the Kantian differentiation of modern rationality into distinct spheres governed by distinct rules of argumentation, and at the same time tend to exaggerate the "world-disclosing" function of language at the expense of the "problem-solving" function of language. In a similar way, Megill situates the projects of Nietzsche, Heidegger, Foucault, and Derrida in a philosophic field that he traces back to German romanticism, above all to the romantic critique of the disjunctions, both social and psychological, generated by the modern project of an instrumental conquest of a disenchanted nature. Further, like Habermas, Megill argues that these philosophers appropriate not only the romantic critique of enlightened reason but also the romantic faith in the creative or disclosive (as distinct from the representational) power of language—hence he characterizes their projects as phases in a long tradition of "aestheticism." Another important strand of Megill's argument is that this romantic tradition is inseparable from the "crisis" rhetoric and "historicist" perspective that, emerging with the romantic response to both the limits of the Enlightenment and the upheavals of the French Revolution, persists throughout the entire modern period, occasionally turning apocalyptic, especially in the late nineteenth and the early twentieth centuries, a turn clearly marked in the projects of both Nietzsche and Heidegger.

It is true that Danto, Edmundson, Megill, and Habermas write with different concerns and from different perspectives: Danto elucidates an "anti-art" bias at work in the entire philosophic tradition; Edmundson explores the strengths as well as the limits of some severe versions of this bias at work in contemporary literary studies; Megill and Habermas set out to clarify and critize major currents in modern Continental philosophy. It is nevertheless significant that, within a few years of one another, there have appeared lucid, probing, suggestive books that, at least in a broad sense, pair off into contradictory assessments of the relationship between poetry and philosophy in our culture. Do philosophers and literary critics, suspicious of art, continue the Platonic effort to regulate art's improper departures from ordinary communication and proper argumentation? Or, rather, have philosophers, enchanted by these departures, become philosophic poets? It would seem that the vexed question of the relationship between poetry and philosophy remains unresolved in our time. And the contradictory assessments of this relationship that have appeared in recent years indicate, at the very least, that these boundaries have indeed been made insecure. One might even propose that an important feature of modern culture, from the French Revolution on, is this creative and disruptive communication between art and philosophy. An abiding quarrel has turned out to be an abiding interanimation.

One of my concerns in this book is to examine this interanimation. While I write with great sympathy for Edmundson's "defense of poetry," my argument, in a sense, will be closer to those of Habermas and Megill than to those of Danto and Edmundson. For I share a sense that modern Continental philosophy has been broadly influenced by modern literature, in particular by what I've characterized as passages of the extravagant in modern poetry. Throughout the modern era, it is true, artists have drawn on philosophers just as the latter have drawn on the former—one need only call to mind the importance for many artists of, say, Kant, Nietzsche, James, Bergson, Freud, or, more recently, any number of post-structuralist thinkers. Yet I agree with the claim that, on the whole, the winds of influence have tended to blow more strongly from art to philosophy than from philosophy to art. My project will nevertheless differ from those of Habermas and Megill in at least four ways.

First, both Habermas and Megill make broad claims about romantic and avantgardist art without engaging specific works of art, while in this study I place poets and philosophers in close communication with one another in order to elucidate some of the similar paths they've pursued in their ambivalent engagements with modernity. Poets are not simply "myth-makers" who come along to seduce irresponsible philosophers, as both Megill and Habermas tend to suggest. They are writers who *think* and *engage the world* in their poems, which is a primary reason why they've had much to say to a number of Continental philosophers over the last two centuries. A thoughtful departure from the rules of modern philosophy, or a reflective opening to modern poetry, is hardly a flight from the essential concerns of philosophy. For modern poetry, as Harold Bloom has underlined in a defense of the romantic tradition in particular, is opposed not to the promise of reason but to the reductiveness of rationalization:

> The great enemy of poetry in the Romantic tradition has never been reason, but rather those premature modes of conceptualization that masquerade as final accounts of reason in every age. It is not reason that menaces the shaping spirit, but the high priests of rationalization, the great men with the compasses who have marked out circumferences, from Descartes, Bacon, Newton, and Locke down to subtler limiters of the imaginative horizon in Hegel, Marx, Freud, and their various revisionist disciples. Romanticism, in what seems its central tradition, at least in our language, is a revolt not against orderly creation, but against compulsion, against conditioning, against all unnecessary limitation that presents itself as being necessary.[15]

Second, while Habermas and Megill clearly locate the source of those currents in modern Continental philosophy that trouble them, they mischaracterize, I think, those currents themselves. Like Habermas and Megill, I emphasize the ample extent to which passages of the extravagant in modern poetry, and meditations on the extravagant in modern philosophy, are displaced articulations, secularized and at times naturalized, of older religious dynamics and discourses. Habermas and Megill are suspicious of these passages and meditations for just this reason, owing to just this genealogy. Yet Habermas, too reductively, tends to characterize these currents in modern culture as little more than nostalgic conjurations of the premodern or mystical flights from the work of reason and the unfinished task of modernity. And both Habermas and Megill, to my mind, exaggerate the presence within these currents of the dream, famously entertained by a few German romantics, of fashioning a "new mythology" able to heal the divisions of a disenchanted, divided, instrumentalized modern world. At stake in these currents in modern poetry and philosophy, I argue, is neither some conjuration of a Dionysian festival, nor some dream of a new mythology, nor simply a hyperbolic faith in the "world-disclosing" power of language, though writers in this tradition do occasionally turn in these directions, and, of course, they do emphasize and often activate the transformative potential of language. The primary issue, however, is the exploratory, unpredictable rearticulation in modern culture of dynamics that were once described in religious vocabularies of transcendence, conversion, and renovation, that is to say, dynamics of widened freedom, awakened power, and metamorphic passage. These are dynamics that, often linked to the modern sublime, I've broadly characterized as dynamics of the extravagant. And, among other things, they are pitched expressions of what Charles Taylor has called "radical freedom," perhaps the modern ideal par excellence, and one that brings with it large predicaments as well as cogent counterideals.[16]

This is to say as well that I characterize poetry, philosophy, and the relationship between the two differently than Habermas and Megill do. In my view, both Habermas and Megill underestimate the cognitive power of poetry—the capacity of poetry to address, according to its own conventions, issues of genuine philosophic import—and so, at the same time, overestimate the extent to which philosophic articulations of poetic extravagance depart from the guiding tasks of philosophy. Twentieth-century Continental philosophies are indeed influenced by passages of the extravagant in modern poetry, yet they are still recognizably philosophic discourses. If, as I believe, Habermas is too quick to interpret a philosophic conversation with modern art as an abdication of philosophy (or of reason itself), Jean-Luc Nancy's measured consideration of the demands involved in any such conversation can be heard as a cogent rejoinder to Habermas:

> The risk of seeming to appropriate through "literature" what would be lost in "philosophy." At least since Nietzsche, and up until all of us today—all those who dare philosophize—there has been no philosophical writing exempt from this risk: Bergson as much as Heidegger, Deleuze as much as Derrida. In certain respects, the history of contemporary philosophy is the history of this risk, in all the diversity of its variations—which means, in all the diverse ways in which freedom has come to implicate itself as a writing of philosophy (style, genre, character, address, audience, company, proximity, translations, untranslatabilities, words, metaphors, fictions, positions of enunciation, and so on and on: all that renders the "philosophical genre" hardly recognizable and yet perfectly identifiable in the concept, analysis, demonstration, systematicity, self-grounding, and self-questioning that were always its own).[17]

Habermas and Megill establish an *antithesis* between modern poetry and philosophy and then underline the weakness of philosophic discourses of the extravagant, whereas I would propose a *parallel* between modern poetry and philosophy and then underline the reach of philosophic discourses of the extravagant.

Finally, in tracing different fields and phases of a modern tradition of the extravagant, I would like to thematize, in each of my main chapters, an important feature of this tradition that remains largely neglected by the four authors I've mentioned above. Adventures of the extravagant, in recasting older dynamics of renovation in the decidedly altered circumstances of modernity, inevitably collide with the gray rock of all those reality principles that organize modern liberal, utilitarian, technocapitalist societies. One outcome of this collision is the internalization in these adventures, as a kind of inner counterpoint, of a forcefully ironic or skeptical perspective. Another is the frequent transformation of these adventures into nocturnal soundings of loss, despair, disorientation, and collapse: the baffled voyage darkward, time and again, turns out to be the genuine voyage outward. "Avalanche, veux-tu m'emporter dans ta chute?" (Baudelaire). And yet another outcome of this collision—and the feature of this history that I believe has been insufficiently thematized—is the emergence over time of *an increasing emphasis on the force of a disclosive negativity*. An emphatic de-reifying movement has always formed a part of certain religious discourses, especially of those developed in marginal traditions of apophasis and mysticism. Perhaps, then, one should not be surprised to find that currents of the extravagant in modern poetry and philosophy, having emerged as displaced, fractured, unstable rearticulations of earlier discourses of renovative metamorphosis, at certain moments come to trace an indirect return to those "de-ontologizing" discourses developed in the margins of religious orthodoxies. At any rate, many adventures in modern poetry and philosophy, in blowing open wooden conceptual idols and fixed representational schemes, begin to sound like ghostly versions of some vanished negative theology (one need only call to mind, for instance, the adventures of Dickinson, Mallarmé, Blanchot, and Derrida). Indeed, the languages of unmaking and undoing, of dislodging and decentering, of negativity and indeterminacy seem to have become important languages in a broad range of artistic and philosophic discussions over the last century. This is a significant long-term tendency that I would like to thematize and interrogate throughout this book, in part because it is my sense that this curiously expanded reverence for the negative may have gradually backed us into a predicament in which we devote our energy to celebrating our fear of our own constructive and transformative powers. Have we come to hear in the negative the last echo of divine absence? Have we come to hear in the indeterminate the last pulse and promise of genuine freedom? It is the way this trend comes to be elaborated in certain twentieth-century philosophic discourses of the extravagant that leads me to share some of Megill's and Habermas's doubts about the ethical and political claims set forth in these discourses.[18]

LARGER CONTEXTS: THE CULTURE OF MODERNITY AS A CULTURE OF CRISIS

At this point I would like to sketch some of the larger historical coordinates and philosophic perspectives that inform my approach to these modern adventures of the extravagant and their changing contours over time. It is clear that passages of the extravagant move countercurrent to a modern world often perceived as bleakly instrumentalized. Yet, in one of the contradictions typical of modernity, these passages of the extravagant at the same time register and engage a modern world often perceived as a zone of unceasing crisis and perpetual transition. One of the most prominent stories of crisis in modern culture, in fact, turns out to be the story of a highly instrumentalized world gone mad.

It is a commonplace that modernity has generated a culture of crisis. Matei Calinescu, in the introduction to his survey of "aesthetic modernity," writes that "aesthetic modernity should be understood as a crisis concept involved in a threefold dialectical opposition to tradition, to the modernity of bourgeois civilization (with its ideals of rationality, utility, progress), and, finally, to itself, insofar as it perceives itself as a new tradition or form of authority." Similarly, Habermas, in the introduction to his survey of the "philosophical discourse" of modernity, writes that "modernity can and will no longer borrow the criteria by which it takes its orientation from the models supplied by another epoch: *it has to create its normativity out of itself.* Modernity sees itself cast back upon itself without any possibility of escape. This explains the sensitiveness of its self-understanding, the dynamism of the attempt, carried forward incessantly down to our time, to 'pin itself down.'" For Calinescu, the voice of crisis in modern art has its source above all in the oppositional stance that art assumes toward both society and tradition, while for Habermas the voice of crisis in modern philosophy has its source, first, in the fractured relationship between philosophy and a tradition that has lost its authority, and second, in the radical instability involved in the effort to generate coherent grounds, norms, and frameworks out of a contradictory modern world that is itself in continual transformation. Marshall Berman, in fact, drawing on Marx's account of capitalism in the dizzying first section of *The Communist Manifesto*, has characterized the entire experience of modernity as an unceasing crisis generated by the dynamism of the industrial capitalist economy itself. "In the first part of the *Manifesto*," Berman writes, "Marx lays out the polarities that will shape and animate the culture of modernism in the century to come: the theme of insatiable desires and drives, permanent revolution, infinite development, perpetual creation and renewal in every sphere of life; and its radical antithesis, the theme of nihilism, insatiable destruction, the shattering and swallowing up of life, the heart of darkness, the horror. Marx shows how both these human possibilities are infused into the life of every modern man by the drives and pressures of the bourgeois economy." Both crisis and extravagance, according to this account, are currents set in motion by the mundane workings of the modern capitalist economy.[19]

Calinescu, Habermas, and Berman, then, all tend to describe the "project of modernity" as an unstable interplay of repeated projects of ambitious construction and repeated projects of ambitious destruction. Modernity, they argue, defines itself as precisely the power to define itself, that is, to define itself in opposition to the inherited models of tradition in the name of those possibilities found on the edge of the present. Freedom is the god, creative self-assertion the way, convention the enemy, change the rhythm, criticism of authority the imperative, and a suspicion of received structure (when not of structure itself) a lively impulse. From the French Revolution on, indeed, a Proteus at once ironic and inventive seems to have been one of the dominant spirits presiding over modernity, his authority matched only by that of a utilitarian Mammon and, too, by that of an elegiac Mnemosyne nostalgic for lost realms of vital wholeness thought to have been swept away with the vanishing of the premodern world. Utopian expectation and elegiac nostalgia turn out to be close companions in modern culture.[20]

Calinescu, Habermas, and Berman, to put this another way, provide generalized accounts of a range of enduring crises that have defined cultural modernity. One of these is a metaphysical crisis that can be sloganized as "the death of God," an event variously described as the waning of faith in any transcendent ground or horizon, the rational disenchantment of an instrumentally mapped world, or, less dramatically, the basic reorientation of human energies from primarily transcendent concerns to primarily immanent, historical, "humanist" concerns. Another crisis, emerging side by side with this metaphysical one, is a political crisis that can be sloganized as either "the death of traditional authority" or "the sovereignty of the people," an event manifest in the upheavals of the French Revolution and in the manifold dramas of political conflict that have occurred in its polymorphous wake. It is significant that the innovative artistic and philosophic projects of both the romantic and the modernist periods register, in analogous ways, the apocalyptic hopes and disappointments generated by thoroughly unstable contexts of revolution, war, and pervasive social disorientation. Both of these contexts involve a heightened sense of groundlessness, of a tottering past and present, and a heightened sense of utopian possibility. The kind of disorientation experienced in these contexts is inseparable, too, from what might be called a "crisis of the lifeworld" generated by the perpetual technological transformations of modern capitalism from the late eighteenth century on. And to this brief recollection of well-known currents of crisis should be added the "crisis of historicism" occurring in the late nineteenth and the early twentieth centuries. This crisis produces an atmospheric pressure specific to the modernist and avantgardist period, a pressure that stirs, among other things, a rethinking, at times in terms of Nietzsche's account of nihilism, of the crisis of the erosion of the transcendent.[21]

Two of these defining experiences of crisis, I believe, are linked in an especially forceful way with a major transmutation in modern traditions of the extravagant over the last century—the heightened fascination with the movement of the negative—which I've briefly described above. One of these is the crisis of historicism that makes itself so sharply felt in modernist and avantgardist art. Another is the perception of an increasingly mechanized modern world on the verge of turning into a vast iron cage: this anxious reading of the modern world, already articulated in romantic critiques of modernity, has been elaborated in revised and occasionally hyperbolic terms throughout our century. It is a reading inseparable from dominant notions of art throughout the modern period.

Historicism could be described as, among other things, a capacious response to both the metaphysical crisis (the death of God) and the political crisis (the specter of social revolution) that I mentioned above. For nineteenth-century historicism, in the broadest sense, involves not only a school of historiography, and not only the rise of teleological philosophies of history in the romantic period, but also the general story of progress that becomes a dominant cultural faith during the nineteenth century, whether in a liberal, vaguely positivist form or in any number of anarchist, socialist, and communist revolutionary forms. This story of progress responds, first, to the crisis of the death of God, replacing the meaningful patterns once supplied by a transcendent framework of salvation with the meaningful patterns now supplied by an immanent framework of progressive historical (and, at the individual level, existential) development. The relativist implications of this faith in progress are, at least for a time, kept at bay by its aggressively Eurocentric bias. In just this sense, too, as Immanuel Wallerstein has argued, the faith in progress, in its liberal version, responds to the political crisis set loose by the French Revolution, for the threat of social conflict comes to be managed, if at times precariously, through a broad political program that promises the gradual expansion of the franchise and of educational opportunity, the gradual integration of the "sovereign people" in a nation defined in racist and sexist terms, and the gradual but "inevitable" material and political progress of the social body as a whole. The story of inevitable progress, Wallerstein claims, is among other things a political program around which both liberals and conservatives rally from about 1848 on.[22]

For a time, then, a historicist narrative of progress functions as an effective response to both a metaphysical and a political crisis. Yet contestations of this narrative appear almost immediately and by the turn of the century attain an explosive force. An apocalyptic spirit comes to inhabit a wide range of aesthetic and political movements of the early twentieth century. The breadth and complexity of this crisis can be schematically mapped by briefly recalling (in reverse chronological order) three "emblematic" voices of this period. Breton, in his poems and manifestoes of the twenties, declares a vehemently "nonconformist" stance toward all the institutions of bourgeois society. Drawing on anarchist and visionary currents of earlier moments in the history of French romantic rebellion—including those of Proudhon, Lautréamont, and Rimbaud—he turns his energies of revolt entirely against the social structures and ideologies that have come to replace the divinity with which earlier writers in this tradition still found it meaningful to wrestle. Crisis is to be exacerbated, provoked, for the sake of decisive metamorphosis in every sphere of society. "If one would only take the trouble to *practice* poetry." This surrealist project doubtless remains in communication with the politics of revolutionary transformation and so with a certain version of radical progress, yet it does so with a deal of strain, as Breton's conflicts with his communist contemporaries attest. Anarchovisionary revolution is projected as the only way beyond a rotting society. On the opposite end of the political spectrum, in a conservative voice of mourning rather than a radical voice of defiance, Eliot, in his poems from "Prufrock" through "The Hollow Men," registers an equally severe loss of faith in both traditional religious frames and their modern secular substitutes. The voice of despair that eloquently murmurs in "Gerontion" evokes not only a Christianity that has gone to pieces in the whispered neuroses of isolated decadents but, too, a story of progress that has foundered in unqualified disillusion. It is this voice that is scattered into the multiplicity of desperate, broken, disoriented voices we hear in Eliot's version of the modern urban wasteland, a social hell of sheer alienation, where any power of renewal is felt only in its painful absence. The last station along this way of loss, so to speak, is the desolate nowhere inhabited by Eliot's "hollow men," later and more exhausted versions, as it were, of the industriously empty "last men" described by Zarathustra forty years earlier. And Nietzsche, of course, is an early and immensely influential voice in any map of this "modernist" crisis of the liberal story of development and progress. He brings fully to light the "relativist" or "perspectivist" implications at play in all the philosophic projects of the historicist nineteenth century. He generalizes the death of the Christian god into the death of any transcendent foundation and, at the same time, encounters the shadow of nihilism, a shadow that he understands as both the threat of a wasteland *and* the possibility of a renovated tragic vision of life to be brought forth through a creative transvaluation of all inherited values. And, not least importantly, he composes a sweeping narrative of the cultural history of the West that—though in fact far more ambiguous than is always recognized—has nonetheless often been read in our century as a critical narrative of decline set in opposition to a hollow narrative of progress. The influence of this philosophic rewriting of historical progress as historical decline (or at least as severe historical crisis) has been enormous.[23]

Nietzsche's incisive questioning of the meaning of the modern scientific enterprise in general and his critique of dominant trends of modernity are shaped by a romantic concern with powers (not least, creative powers) that exceed the frames of science, business, post-Kantian philosophy, and liberal humanism. And in the wake of Nietzsche these romantic concerns have repeatedly been attached to post-Nietzschean narratives of decline set in opposition to liberal narratives of progress or marxist narratives of eschatological revolution. The narrative of an increasingly instrumentalized modernity tending toward an iron cage, in particular, has turned out to be one of the most prominent narratives of gathering disaster in twentieth-century social theory, critical philosophy, and avantgardist aesthetics.

The story of a modern cage of highly organized unfreedom has its origins in romanticism, specifically, in the romantic concern to extend the Enlightenment's valorization of freedom while critically surpassing the Enlightenment's confidence in empiricist, mechanist, and instrumental models of understanding. Yet, from the earliest English and German romantics, through the antiutilitarian aestheticist and dandyistic voices of mid-nineteenth-century France, through Nietzsche, the critique of "scientific" reason in the name of "higher" values thought to be manifest in art—whether these values be associated with spiritual contemplation or with creative power—remains on the whole an existential rather more than a political critique. This is still partly the case even in Weber's influential characterization (doubtless based in part on his reading of Nietzsche) of modern reason as a mode of "formal rationalization" detached from any substantive reason or any substantive body of ideals. First published in 1905, Weber's famous description of the cage of formal rationalization that Western subjects have come to inhabit is worth citing at length, for it is an early version of a description that ever since has been rewritten many times:

> Since asceticism undertook to remodel the world and to work out its ideals in the world, material goods have gained an increasing and finally an inexorable power over the lives of men as at no previous period in history. Today the spirit of religious asceticism—whether finally, who knows?—has escaped from the cage. But victorious capitalism, since it rests on mechanical foundations, needs its support no longer. The rosy blush of its laughing heir, the Enlightenment, seems also to be irretrievably fading, and the idea of duty in one's calling prowls about in our lives like the ghost of dead religious beliefs. Where the fulfillment of the calling cannot directly be related to the highest spiritual and cultural values, or when, on the other hand, it need not be felt simply as economic compulsion, the individual generally abandons the attempt to justify it at all. In the field of its highest development, in the United States, the pursuit of wealth, stripped of its religious and ethical meaning, tends to become associated with purely mundane passions, which often actually give it the character of sport.
>
> No one knows who will live in this cage in the future, or whether at the end of this tremendous development entirely new prophets will arise, or there will be a great rebirth of old ideas and ideals, or, if neither, mechanized petrification, embellished with a sort of convulsive self-importance. For of the last stage of this cultural development, it might well be truly said:

20 • THE EXTRAVAGANT

"Specialists without spirit, sensualists without heart; this nullity imagines that it has attained a level of civilization never before achieved."[24]

This story of an increasing "colonization" (as Habermas puts it) of every sphere of social and psychic life by the operations of instrumental reason has had a two-hundred-year life in modern culture. If English and German romantics, French dandies and symbolists, and Nietzsche all inform Weber's story, Weber's story appears to have informed at least two distinct yet curiously parallel philosophic traditions in our century. It forcefully resonates, first, in an important tradition of twentieth-century Hegelian marxism: in Lukács's theory of capitalist "reification" (a re-Hegelianizing of Marx's theory of "commodification"), Marcuse's theory of "one-dimensional society," and Adorno's theory of the "logic of identity" and the "totally administered world." And, too, it seems to resonate, if far more obliquely, in an important twentieth-century tradition of the philosophic history of philosophy, for what Weber characterizes as a specific mode of rationalization at work in modern capitalist, industrial, scientific, bureaucratic societies appears to return, otherwise coded, in a line of high-altitude philosophic narratives of decline and error: in Heidegger's account of the forgetting of Being carried to a nihilist extreme by "the logic of enframing" that dominates "the age of the worldview," Levinas's account of a Western history of ontology governed by a reductive "economy of the same" indifferent to the infinite alterity of the other, and Derrida's account of a history of "the metaphysics of presence" based upon a motivated aversion to difference. In this broad field of theoretical accounts of the modern instrumental cage, one could also include Bataille's theory of a "restricted economy" of social life driven by the utilitarian imperatives of production and accumulation, Foucault's narrative of a modern "carceral system" organized around mechanisms of discipline and surveillance, and Lyotard's account of a totalizing theoretical reason complicit with the imperatives of a "techno-cybernetic" social system. One could surely add other stories to the list.[25]

I recall these well-known themes and names in twentieth-century social theory and critical philosophy for three reasons. First, I would like to underline the obvious but important fact that modern culture, from the age of romanticism through the present, has been ceaselessly haunted by the nightmare of a totally instrumentalized world, a totally functionalized social and psychic life. This is a remarkably persistent theme in modern culture. Second, twentieth-century versions of the story of the iron cage differ from their nineteenth-century precursors in at least one important respect, namely, in the way their critical perspectives tend to involve less an existential accent (a concern with the way the dominance of instrumental reason damages the creative potential of a human being) than a political accent (a concern with the way a voracious technocratic reason, organizing a society at once atomized and homogenized, functions as a force of social and political domination). And third, a guiding countertheme that almost invariably accompanies the story of the iron cage is that of art as a site of creative resistance to the operations of this cage. Art is the ray of hope slanting across the panoptic prison. To be sure, in the thinkers I've just mentioned, the specific ways in which this critical surpassing of the prison is said to be promised by art are as various as the specific ways in which the prison itself is described and interpreted. Yet the emphasis on art as a critical counterforce, a reaching promise in the midst of a mechanized wasteland, is prominent in almost all of them.[26]

It is my sense that a complex communication among three important modern themes—the crisis of historicism, the related tendency to replace sweeping narratives of progress with sweeping narratives of loss, decline, or disaster, and the variously elaborated theory of the cage of instrumental reason—has much to do with the increasing fascination with disclosive, invocatory, or simply wayward negativity that occurs in a range of twentieth-century poets and philosophers. Passages of the extravagant have always, from the romantic period on, contested the boundaries set in place by the dominant orientations of liberal, scientific, capitalist modernity. They have always contested one-dimensional models of subjectivity, knowledge, and discourse. They have always traced paths of visionary, metamorphic, prophetic, apocalyptic, or simply exploratory wandering beyond these models. Yet certain modernist poets and philosophers from the late nineteenth century on, and above all over the last century, have explored the play of an errant negativity in an emphatic way, as though only a writing guided by this emphasis could continue to resist the pressures of an increasingly mechanized world and its increasingly functionalized or "petrified" bodies and minds. This, as I've indicated, is one of the stories I wish to trace and scrutinize in this book.

Of course, if the story of the functionalist cage were to turn out to be a one-sided account of modernity, then this tradition of extravagant negativity would have to be elucidated from perspectives other than those which writers in this tradition imply or declare as their own guiding perspectives. Many thinkers, including those I mentioned at the outset of this section, have in fact characterized modernity as a world of perpetual transition, differentiation, mobility, and plasticity. Is modernity a cage or a chaos? Is it perhaps both at once?

This is a question to which I occasionally return throughout this book and address in greater detail in the conclusion.

LARGER TRAJECTORIES: INTERANIMATIONS OF MODERN POETRIES AND MODERN PHILOSOPHIES

In the preceding section I've sketched some of the larger contexts in which modern passages of the extravagant take place. Here I wish to sketch my understanding, first, of the way defining adventures of romantic and modernist poetry unfold and second, of the way prominent discourses of modern Continental philosophy come to engage these adventures.

It should be clear at this point that I'm working with a version of the secularization thesis, according to which romantic poetries and their predicaments emerge out of efforts to reappropriate for immanent human orientations those powers that are thought to have been alienated in traditional religious frameworks. Theology, as Feuerbach puts it, is to be translated back into the creative anthopology at its source. The old myths and powers, as Wordsworth puts it, are to be rediscovered in the energies and visions of the human mind. This sort of project becomes far more polemical or Faustian in "oppositional" writers like Blake and Nietzsche, for what appears in Feuerbach and Wordsworth as an attempt to translate traditional Christian frames into measured humanist frames appears in Blake, and with a decisive "naturalist" turn in Nietzsche, as an effort to overthrow "transcendent" gods, as well as their social and internal agents, in the name of a prophetic, visionary, or metamorphic transhumanism not immediately compatible with any sort of liberal humanism. And, too, in romantic poetries shaped outside the context of a politically progressive Protestantism, like those of nineteenth-century France, this oppositional orientation tends to become vehemently heightened and at the same time attached to a range of gnostic, occultist, Satanist, or anarchist orientations (an interplay still quite alive in interwar surrealism and its theoretical aftermath). The death of God, as Octavio Paz underlines and as Rimbaud, Nietzsche, and many others exemplify, is first of all a romantic and an existential theme—experienced as a drama of loss and hope—before it becomes a philosophic theme ultimately culminating in a variety of post-Nietzschean antifoundationalist discourses.[27] It is also a linguistic issue, a drama of changing figures. René Char, in a compressed Nietzschean poem, "Threshold," suggests not only that this floodlike abandonment is lived at the same time as a floodlike opening but, too, that our words themselves have been torn by their passage through this destructive and generative event:

> When the barrier of man gave way, pulled in by the giant rift of the abandonment of the divine, words in the distance, words that were unwilling to be lost, tried to resist the exorbitant thrust. It was there the dynasty of their sense was determined.
>
> I've run to the end of this diluvian night. Planted in the trembling dawn, my belt filled with seasons, I await you, oh my friends who are about to come. Already I divine you behind the blackness of the horizon. My hearthstone inexhaustibly wishes your houses well. And my cypress stick laughs with all its heart for you.[28]

Thus the "exorbitant" threshold from which a range of modern poets speak: a recognition of collapse, a premonition of rebeginning. It is as though every word had been fissured, leaving us to speak in echo and expectation.

Probably the best-known presentation of this sort of secularization thesis is M. H. Abrams's *Natural Supernaturalism: Tradition and Revolution in Romantic Literature,* a magisterial account of English and German romanticism. Abrams, in remarkable detail, develops the thesis proposed in the title of his book: romantic poetries, at once traditional and revolutionary, translate supernatural frames of experience into natural—or, more exactly, humanist—frames of experience. It has been objected that Abrams presents this project of translation as a smoother affair than the history of romantic and postromantic poetry shows it to have been: such a project, the objection runs, has not been pursued without far more losses, collapses, bewildering impasses, and skewed resignifications than Abrams acknowledges. I agree with this objection. At the same time, I think Abrams has exactly characterized the hyperbolic romantic wager: the effort to sustain, in secularized terms, religious dynamics of awakened freedom, renovated power, and extravagant metamorphosis that have little place in the dominant social and discursive structures of the modern world. "The ever-hooded, tragic-gestured sea / Was merely a place by which she walked to sing. / Whose spirit is this? we said, because we knew / It was the spirit that we sought, and knew / That we should ask this often as she sang" (Stevens). The history of romantic and postromantic poetry is, in part, the continually renewed drama of a collision between this bold project of translation and its steep impossibility. It is this recurrent collision that generates many of the innovations, both substantive and formal, of modern poetry.[29]

It is a working hypothesis of this book—one I hope to substantiate at least in part through my readings of Wordsworth, Rimbaud, Dickinson, and Mallarmé—that romantic and modernist poetries are dialectically interwoven with one another; or, put another way, that modernist poetries are inventions shaped in response not only to changing social contexts but also to both inherited romantic bearings and inherited predicaments generated by the exorbitance of those bearings. Even a cursory survey of some shared features of romantic and modernist poetries suggests a dialectical relationship of this sort. The romantic concern to "open the doors of perception" to reveal the infinite (Blake)—or, more modestly, to remove from our eyes the "film of familiarity and selfish solicitude" to reveal the ciphers of nature (Coleridge)—returns in the modernist concern to "renew" our perception of worldly presences by "defamiliarizing" our perception of literary patterns. The romantic valorization of "form as proceeding" over "shape as superinduced" (Coleridge), a faith in the power of processual patterning to resist abstract routines of thought and response, is reinvented in the modernist period as a conception of the poem as either a polyvalent construct humming with a distinctive stylistic signature, a resonantly mapped field of action, or a volatile space of exploratory meandering. Equally important in both periods is a heroic conception of the artist as an oppositional figure whose task is to sound forces of otherness and powers of vision or invention irreducible to conventional schemes of knowledge. And guiding the poetries of both periods, too, is a commitment to the "kerygmatic" dynamic that I briefly characterized above. Creative freedom, disclosive defamiliarization, processual form, heroic opposition to an instrumentalized modernity, the indirect sounding of alterity, and the search for a literary analogue of the kerygmatic word of renewal—these are but a few of the important bearings that traverse the entire period running from the origins of the romantic period through the last phases of the modernist period.

Modern poetry, then, through a range of displacements and reinventions, participates not only in an unlikely project of translating earlier religious curves of metamorphosis into secular frames of reference but also in the distinctly modern project of continual self-criticism and self-transformation. These are two major sources of its creative instability. And the fundamental issues that are continually sounded anew in modern poetries, it would seem, are those of creative *process*, visionary or inventive *power*, and evocative or dislocative *otherness*. These are the primary concerns of the oppositional adventures of modern poetries.

I WOULD LIKE to elaborate on these generalizations by sketching two sweeping stories of poetic invention with which poets and critics of the most diverse inclinations have often characterized these adventures. One of them is a story of creative process as the substance of any act of invention. Another is a story of the searching indirections that point toward forces coursing through any structure of representation. These two orientations, passing through various changes as they travel from the romantic period through the present, are intertwined with one another; frequently, in fact, they walk hand in hand. Still, because they tend to produce different poetic and theoretical ramifications, it is worth tracing the emphases specific to each of them.

It may help if I provide each of these orientations with a title and a slogan. I would call the first of them that of the poem as *action or process:* knowing is a kind of doing. I would call the second of them that of the poem as *gifted visionary:* the knowing that really matters happens where metamorphic powers roam beyond conventional models of knowing. Both of these orientations, and particularly the second, generate a third orientation which has been of particular importance over the last century, namely, that of the poem as *unruly demon:* the knowing that really matters happens where negativity shatters conventional models of knowing. Poems composed in the first of these traditions tend to foreground powers that pilot, extend, and modify specific acts of knowing and presentation. Poems composed in the second and third of these traditions tend to foreground powers that provocatively surpass—or, at times, polemically upend—conventional structures of knowledge and representation. In all of them the shuttle of force and representation, the play of Dionysus and Apollo, is variously engaged in ways resistant to the dominant social frames and cognitive models of modernity.

The first of these orientations, emerging out of a romantic concern with disclosive process, is inseparable from the modern "de-substantializing" of the soul. Whether or not the subject is a simple substance, Kant teaches, we cannot say, but we can affirm that the subject is a power (a movement that moves itself, so to speak, or, in Nietzsche's naturalist vocabulary, a will to power). Modern literature and philosophy have unfolded this theme in a variety of ways. In the domain of modern poetry, romantic "meditative" poets explore the imaginative processes of a subject passing through encounters with fields of natural otherness, innovative modernists the constructive activities of an inventor of polyphonic fields resistant to routinized habits of understanding, and polemical avantgardists the unpredictable forces released in charged performances of textual meandering and open-eyed impertinence. If all of these adventures involve different intentions, investments, and practices, they nonetheless manifest two broadly shared assumptions about the kinds of tasks modern poems should accomplish: first, that a poem should effect a metamorphosis of words, not least through a reshaping of the formal devices inherited from literary tradition; and second, that a poem should manifest processual forces of responding, searching, thinking, inventing, and writing that remain inadequately addressed in other disciplines of knowledge, above all because such forces are irreducible to clear and distinct representation. A heightened concentration on process, whether in a "visionary," "meditative," "constructivist," or simply "errant" and "prankish" mode, shapes the spirit as well as the form and texture of a range of modern poetries.

Doubtless one of the most enduring of these is the poetry of situated meditation that emerges in the romantic period. A typical "plot" in this kind of poetry involves a subject who explores a natural or social "landscape" as though it were a force field of energies mysteriously guiding him or her through an experience of searching, self-shaping, and self-surpassing. This sort of poetry, as Robert Langbaum has nicely put it, counters the "empiricism" of objective science with the "empiricism" of concrete experience, in this way bearing testimony to powers of dynamic response and judgment without which the schemes of positive knowledge readily become but abstract structures felt as opaque pressures by a passive subject. The concern, as Wordsworth affirms in *The Prelude,* is to enact the vital movement at play in "knowledge rightly honored with that name— / Knowledge not purchased with the loss of power." A poem of situated meditation is thus a compressed version of a quest poem, for it traces paths of self-formation, intricate trails of discovery, whereby perceptual and evaluative perspectives emerge and come to be shaped and textured. This sort of meditative poetry clearly speaks to a "novelistic" age that conceives of the subject less as a substance, an essence, than as a pliant source and, at any given moment, a provisional outcome of those responsive and creative powers which the subject has developed through engagements with a range of unpredictable situations he or she has passed through. As Abrams points out, Wordsworth's *Prelude,* a capaciously meandering "instance" of this type of poetry, reads like both a *Bildungsroman* and a *Künstlerroman* in blank verse.[30]

This poetry of meditation, further, implies a distinctive understanding of poetic form, one that Coleridge characterizes with the notion of "organic" or "motivated" form. Donald Wesling, in a brilliant triad of books, has theorized the ambitions and accomplishments of a long adventure of modern poetic innovation that can be traced back to this major romantic premise.[31] Rescuing Coleridge's notion from the poor reputation that has accompanied it in recent years, Wesling clarifies the way the notion of "organic" form designates, above all, a dialectical understanding of the fractured relationship between the conventions of literary history and the imperatives of poetic making in an age committed to "processual" theories of subjectivity and creativity. The privileging of *natura naturans* over *natura naturata*, in short, involves less a metaphysic of nature (though surely that is a vital dimension, in particular, of German romantic poetry and philosophy) than a theory of psychic energy, creative action, and poetic process. Romantic poets, conceiving a poem to be not an object, an imitation, or a piece of pointed instruction but rather a seismograph of the activity of a subject "formed" or "transformed" in time, encounter literary history as a potential obstacle to be creatively refashioned from within. This produces a serious anxiety for poets working in a culture that, from the French Revolution on, has tended to associate convention with either unfreedom or death—an association Coleridge explicitly makes in an important passage in which he distinguishes between "form as proceeding" and "shape as superinduced," that is, between form as a creative act marked by the demands of a concrete situation in the present and form as an echo of literary tradition inadequate to those demands.[32] An impossible yet productive ambition that romantic poets pass on to later writers is the ambition to write poems that, in every detail of their form, will testify to a searching engagement with the forces of a predicament in the present, not to a dependence on the rules of a tradition (an institution). This ambition exerts extreme pressure on the prosodic plane, for it implies that the rhythmic signature of a poem, presented as the embodiment of particular perceptual turns and existential decisions, will be a primary test of the quality and the reach—animated or faded, deft or dull, quickened or reified, free or buried—of the thinking enacted in the poem. This notion of poetic making is a major source of the "prosodic revolution" that begins in the middle of the nineteenth and extends across the entire twentieth century.[33]

The romantic practice of situated meditation and processual form is at once extended and transformed in the elastic "field poetic" that, in various ways, emerges in modernist and avantgardist poetries of the first half of the twentieth century. The poem—or often, in a distinctly literal sense, the page itself—comes to be conceived as an open space of exploratory action in multiple directions. In the Continental avantgarde this sort of practice emerges, among other places, in Apollinaire's playful "simultaneist" fields, in Reverdy's and Huidobro's "cubist" constructs, and in the general surrealist practice of weaving through the space of the poem as through the space of an urban phantasmagoria. These projects are clearly informed by a number of earlier romantic projects, including Rimbaud's elliptical prose poems, Nerval's occultist explorations of multiple planes of reality, Laforgue's melancholy theater of ironic masks, and Mallarmé's spaciously "scored" *Un Coup de dés*. The roaming spirit of romantic voyage passes into both an urban space and a formal space. Divinatory wandering becomes task and texture at once. Indeed, this strong connection with earlier romantic bearings would seem to mark one major difference between this avantgardist poetic and the "constructivist poetic" developed in a number of antisymbolist North American poetries at about the same time. In Pound's understanding of the poem as a multidimensional "vortex," for example, or in Williams's decidedly this-worldly conception of the poem as a well-spaced "field of action," there occurs a break with earlier romantic and symbolist poetries.[34]

For a constructivist poem, stepping back from the task of representing an inner space, foregrounds the searching compositional activity of a subject positioned as the orchestrator (or, as Williams liked to think of it in whimsical moments, the driver) of the poem. The poem is shaped as a field whose precisely measured acts of presentation are made to bear the sorts of expressive forces that, in other kinds of poems, are borne by dramatic speech, parabolic resonance, metaphoric disclosure, roomy conceptual play, the evocation of inwardness, and so forth. This, it is true, is probably to ask too much and so would seem to mark a limit to this type of poem. Yet it is simply necessary to recognize that this poetic strategy is always pursued *alongside* quite traditional poetic strategies (though advocates of poems written in this tradition tend to occlude this fact in highly misleading ways). It is a question of emphasis and orientation. It is this shift of emphasis that in the modernist period is often characterized in terms of the "autonomy" of the "non-mimetic" work of art: the energies and processes of formal virtuosity or technical innovation are lent a weight, a significance, that poets in the romantic tradition give to the energies and processes of imaginative action or visionary quest.

It is unsurprising, then, that critics who engage the inventions of poets like Williams tend to cite sooner or later either Wittgenstein's account of "meaning as use" or any of the similar themes that James and Dewey develop. A poet like Williams shows little concern either to ratify or to upend traditional models of knowledge and representation: he seems intent, rather, on changing the language game, inviting us to engage poems from perspectives that do not rely on strict oppositions between force and representation, or between an idealized representation of subjectivity and an ironic representation of subjectivity, or between the materiality of signifiers and the ideality of meaning. The point is to invent idiosyncratic curves of linguistic action that demand reenactment, curves that ask to be evaluated in terms akin to those in which we evaluate other modes of purposive action, other modes of active doing, in the world. The test of such curves, as Charles Altieri has argued in a number of books, lies in the power of the poet to manifest and make audible, in the concrete presentational acts of the poem, elusive qualities of attention and orientation that exceed direct representation. The task is to witness and adjust while composing, inventing a force field wherein precision occasions levitation, pattern tends toward trope, and an act of composition turns into a scored drama of expressive action. "I want," as Robert Creeley puts it, "to give witness not to the thought of myself—that specious concept of identity—but, rather, to what I am as simple agency, a thing evidently alive by virtue of such activity. I want, as Charles Olson says, to come into the world. Measure, then, is my testament. What uses me is what I use and in that complex measure is the issue."[35]

The manifold *processual* orientation I've just sketched is distinct from—yet, at the same time, is wholly at play within—the manifold *extravagant* orientation I wish to sketch next. This latter tradition, like the former traveling from the romantic period through the present, has often been theorized as a tradition of the sublime. Here I would like to sketch briefly some of its guiding bearings in very broad terms.

There emerges in the romantic period a tension between a "humanist" poetic of psychic wholeness and a "transhumanist" poetic of metamorphic departure. One might even say that the eighteenth-century distinction between the beautiful and the sublime loosely corresponds, from the romantic period on, to a difference between a "meditative" art of spirits in formation and an "extravagant" art of spirits in transformation (the latter occasionally turning into an art of spirits in disorientation). A guiding imperative of poetries written in this second tradition is that a poem manifest, in heightened ways, powers and currents of metamorphosis that are felt to be entirely ignored by the dominant philosophic, scientific, and even poetic models of the time. The wanderings, energies, and promises of religious romance are to be revived under decidedly irreligious circumstances. In fact, in reading poems in this tradition, one sometimes feels that an earlier conflict between reason and faith has been reimagined as a secular conflict between reason and the dark or radiant "other side" of reason, however this other side comes to be evoked or articulated. "How could we live without the unknown before us?" (Char). Such poems set out to effect a sweeping reorientation of conventional models of knowledge. Shamanistic in spirit, they venture elsewhere, occasionally risking an articulate shipwreck of the self, for "poetry will no longer take its rhythm from action: it will be *ahead*" (Rimbaud). They set out to sound regions of sheer transition and disclosive othering, finding passages beyond the familiar, the known, the schematized, and the bound, traveling like "a man lured on by a syllable without any meaning, / A syllable of which he felt, with an appointed sureness, / That it contained the meaning into which he wanted to enter, / A meaning which, as he entered it, would shatter the boat and leave the oarsmen quiet / As at a point of central arrival, an instant moment, much or little, / Removed from any shore, from any man or woman, and needing none" (Stevens). As these eerie lines suggest, among the major risks of these adventures are a vertigo of solipsism, a loss of reality, a veer toward nihilism, and so, finally, a return to the despair from which one sought to depart in the first place. Thus a major drama of these adventures lies in the effort to take the measure of these risks, to find a way past them, without simply abandoning the initial impetus of metamorphic departure.

According to one suggestive formula, variously pondered from Kant to Lyotard, this art of the extravagant seeks to present the unrepresentable, or more exactly, a collision between the unrepresentable and consciousness. One notable thing about the unrepresentable, however, is that, since no one knows exactly what it is, it can be located almost anywhere: in the haunting absence revealed by the withdrawal of the divine, the enigmatic resonance of the natural world, the sheer force of material otherness, the luminous drift and call of Being, the shadow the infinite casts across the finite (a shadow glimpsed in recent years falling across finite chains of signifiers), the voice of an uncanny guest in the self that is not the self, the death one can anticipate and pretend to walk into, the lost streets the mind is sent to when dream and desire open errant paths across words, or the unlikely haunts words disclose when they are turned through one another in wholly unexpected ways.

It would seem to be what Nietzsche called "the desire to be different, to be in a different place," whether up or down, that makes itself heard with particular force in the various poetries written in this tradition.[36] Like the speaker of Apollinaire's "Zone," they frequently explore an experience of sheer spaciousness, a roaming multiplication of life or a roving dispersal of the self. "I am afoot with my vision" (Whitman). "It seemed to me that to every being several *other* lives were owed" (Rimbaud). They often privilege the magnifications and disproportions of hyperbole, amplify the image-making powers of language, follow the lure of the incongruous, trace associative trails and unfolding digressions that take long excursions from narrative and thematic coherence, and, from Rimbaud and Lautréamont through poets as diverse as Perse, Breton, Césaire, Neruda, Vallejo, and Aleixandre, among others, display cumulative, incantatory rhythms that recall the iterative rhythms and rolling syntactic parallelisms of Whitman. Yet, if a kind of sweeping aeration of words is often an important dynamic in these poetries, so too is a kind of gnomic compression of words, a bending of words back upon themselves, as though a fathoming of bent words could release a portion of their buried invocatory power. "It will flame out, like shining from shook foil" (Hopkins). "As Lightning on a Landscape / Exhibits Sheets of Place— / Not yet suspected—but for Flash— / And Click—and Suddenness" (Dickinson). Thus is the reach of wonder retrieved. Indeed, a frequent aim in these poetries is linguistic phosphorescence, the transformation of words into prisms that, appearing to take on something of the reified quality of the world around them, cut through the flattening of language endemic to modern societies, words made into things thus becoming words that move like currents again. Rimbaud, no doubt, is one of the finest practitioners of this sort of "alchemy" of the deviant word, a spacious "transmemberment of song," to lift a figure from Hart Crane, a poet who seems to have learned much from his French precursor in the search for premonitions that point beyond a broken world. "It is not in the premise that reality / Is a solid. It may be a shade that traverses / A dust, a force that traverses a shade" (Stevens). At the source is the riddle, a mystery of time, provoking the riddling guesses that promise (in the words of a medieval kabbalist) to untie the knots of the soul.[37]

THESE GUIDING ORIENTATIONS, traced in schematic terms, animate a multiplicity of adventures that foreground energies of creative *process,* dramas of visionary and metamorphic *power,* and evocations of variously approached fields of *otherness.* At work in a range of different poetries, traversing the entire modern period, they animate those poetries of the twentieth century that often strike readers as strange, elliptical, multiperspectival, polyvalent, or bafflingly indeterminate. For in part these poetries are innovative unfurlings (or, one might say, dialectical exacerbations) of the resistant processual dynamics of romantic poetries. George Steiner, describing a type of "tactical" difficulty often found in poems, writes:

> We are not meant to understand easily and quickly. Immediate purchase is denied us. The text yields its force and singularity of being only gradually. In certain fascinating cases, our understanding, however strenuously won, is to remain provisional. There is to be an undecidability at the heart, at what Coleridge called the inner *penetralium* of the poem (there is a concrete sense in which the great allegories of ingress, of pilgrimage to the centre, such as the *Roman de la rose* and the *Commedia*, compel the reader to reenact, in the stages of his reading, the adventure of gradual unfolding told by the poet). There is a dialectical strangeness in the will of the poet to be understood only step by step and up to a point.[38]

Steiner persuasively recalls the affinities between ancient rituals of initiation and certain poems that disclose their significance only as a reader steps through the turns of their unfolding ways. "If you do not enter the dance, you do not understand the event." However, this account can be more precisely historicized, for Steiner's thinking in this passage draws not on Guillaume de Lorris, Jean de Meun, or Dante so much as on romantic and modernist poetries of exploratory process. Modern poetries demand a reenactment of their compositional processes insofar as they are designed to resist and surpass abstract habits of reading, reified models of understanding, and routinized modes of response: seismographs of minds in action, they demand that they be understood, hence undergone, from the inside. And as modern societies grow increasingly instrumentalized, modern poetries invested in these values, placed under pressure, grow increasingly deviant or defamiliarizing in their styles of resistant patterning. Therein lies one important dimension of the dialectic of romantic and modernist poetries.[39]

Further, this sort of processual patterning, I've claimed, is in modern poetries set in motion for the sake of sounding powers of invention, dynamics of metamorphic departure, and fields of otherness that elude conventional structures of knowledge and representation. In other words, the initiation by process, in particular in poetries of the extravagant, involves an indirect passage toward forces that tend to baffle, when not to dislocate, both the stable subject and the conventional models of representation that organize this subject. This sort of passage is thus one important source (there are surely several others) of those features of modernist works that have led critics to speak of these works as expressions of a "crisis of the subject" and a "crisis of representation."[40] At stake in these works is a critical exploration not only of the relationship between subjectivity and representation but, more broadly, of the relationship between force and representation. And it is in this region of explorations, above all, that twentieth-century Continental philosophy enters into a ranging conversation with romantic as well as modernist and avantgardist art. How, in an increasingly instrumentalized world, are we to engage and articulate those forces that at once condition, traverse, and exceed the representations we make, whether of "outer" or "inner" events? How are we to bring to words, without at the same time effacing or disfiguring, those fields of otherness that provoke, inhabit, unsettle, and elude the relatively clear and distinct themes we come to compose in words? These are among the guiding questions that Continental philosophy, opening itself to the challenges of modern art, has continually asked throughout our century.[41]

A range of twentieth-century Continental philosophy indeed reads as though it were a persistent attempt to invent supple theoretical languages for the wanderings of romantic, modernist, and avantgardist writing: the differentiated tradition of the extravagant—while certainly registered in important nineteenth-century philosophers like Kierkegaard, Nietzsche, and, in a rather more ambiguous way, Marx—has exerted an especially forceful pressure on the field of Continental philosophy over the last century. This field unfolds like a wide, complex, internally divided meditation on the "sublime," a many-sided effort to articulate those forces of otherness that disrupt conventional models of representation. Contesting the nihilist implications of traditional metaphysics, modern epistemology, and a modern scientific enterprise that has but thinly examined its own basis, Nietzsche affirms the will to power of the tragic artist and a renovative participation in the destructive and generative forces at play in the eternal recurrence of the same. In opposition to a restricted economy of utility and production, Bataille invokes postreligious experiences of sheer expenditure. Adorno, drawing on Nietzsche as well as Weber, developing Lukács's account of capitalist reification in terms of a dominative logic of identity, discerns in the negativity of modernist art an indirect promise of some nonrepressively "mimetic" relationship to textures of the nonidentical. Heidegger, reconceiving the cage of instrumental reason as the nihilist fate of a metaphysical logic of enframing in an epoch forgetful of Being, calls his readers to a meditative "releasement" toward the silent, drifting, lighting voice of Being. Rewriting Heidegger's deconstruction of ontotheology, Derrida seeks a bending path toward an otherness beyond (and secretly in) philosophic reason, an alterity now conceived not as the disclosive movement of Being but as the irrecuperable play of temporal *différance*. The later Lyotard, drawing on a number of these thinkers, comes to evoke a haunted destitution of the subject in an indeterminate drift as the last hope of some resistance to a totalizing technocratic rationality. I've recalled only some of the most prominent discourses of this type in our century. The insomnia of a reductive instrumental reason, objectifying everything and everyone it encounters, would seem to be the primary antagonist against which these various philosophic discourses that draw on modern art have been composed. And it is some not yet schematized otherness that is then variously explored in an effort to attain critical distance from a functionalist social system grown to devastating proportions. The ear and the mind turn toward a palpable absence calling from elsewhere. A good deal of twentieth-century Continental philosophy, in this sense, appears to have been written in the light of modern poetry and in the shadow of Weber's account of a modern world decisively shaped by long-term trends of scientific disenchantment, capitalist commodification, instrumental rationalization, and bureaucratic organization.[42]

One could put this another way. In the romantic period the sublime tends to be conceived as a threshold turned toward forces on the other side of positive representation and scientific knowledge. Over the last century, I think, there have been two especially important elaborations of this theme: first, the invention of a multiplicity of conceptual frames that read like sophisticated analogues of earlier romantic conceptual frames designed to trace the polemical tension between art and reason, poetic power and scientific knowledge, extravagant reach and common sense; and, second, the invention of a multiplicity of diagnostic perspectives from which the evocation of transrational forces or elusive fields of alterity can be strongly inflected with ethical and political accents. The romantic "sublime" or "extravagant," variously recast and on occasion lent a "textual" emphasis in the modernist period, is thus recast yet again in these diverse philosophic discourses written in close communication with innovative currents in twentieth-century art.

It would be foolish, of course, to claim that the philosophic discourses to which I've just alluded are all the same. They are clearly not, and the specific differences among them, including some severe oppositions, are doubtless as important as the affinities. That said, I think it is still worth stepping back from these discourses to measure the extent to which, on the whole, they are shaped in response to modern literary passages of the extravagant. It is not only that these philosophic discourses are thematically informed by both romantic and modernist passages of the extravagant. It is that the spirit and the practice of these passages appear to have traveled, at least on occasion, into the very texture of these discourses. Thus, for instance, the philosophers to whom

I've just alluded tend to write in prophetic, apocalyptic, or oracular tones. They display a striking knack for gnomic formulations (or aphoristic and riddling flashes of insight) of the sort we readily expect to find in poetic texts. Paradox tends to be a prominent trope in their writings. And thematically as well as tonally their projects incline toward hyperbole, a bias marked not least in the common tendency among these philosophers (especially pronounced in Nietzsche, Heidegger, Adorno, and Derrida) to construct sweeping diagnostic narratives of the entire history of Western thought. A pulse of the extravagant, then, is at work at the rhetorical as well as the thematic level of the texts these philosophers compose. Exploring a variously thematized "other" or "otherness" of instrumental reason, conventional models of representation, and functionalist social structures, they explore at the same time rhetorical modes other than those prescribed by conventional philosophic and communicative practice.

These issues have been addressed by J. M. Bernstein in an essay in which he presents an Hegelian interpretation of the well-known debate between Habermas and various French post-structuralists. According to Bernstein, if Habermas defends a renewal of the unfinished project of modernity, a project of establishing freedom in terms of a universal, procedural, quasi-transcendental, internally differentiated, and regulative framework of reason, various poststructuralists, akin in this respect to Heidegger and Adorno before them, produce a "discursive analogue" of artistic modernism, a practice of writing that seeks to sustain the promise of freedom through an exploratory critique of reason open to those fields of otherness that resist conceptual schemes. Bernstein calls this latter sort of practice "philosophical modernism":

> Philosophical modernism's totalizing critique eschews procedural rationality and universality, conceiving them as figures of domination, its extraordinary discourses presumptively leaving behind the claim of enlightened rationality for the sake of an apparently blind, normless particularism. Habermas, in contrast, wants to salvage the claims of enlightenment through the reconstructive sciences, operating as an analogue of transcendental reflection and legislation. A choice between these extremes—philosophical modernism's immanence and particularism, and Habermas's transcendence and universalism—is less than inviting. Can we not recognize in these extremes of universal and particular a fateful dialectic at work? A sundering of the very comprehensive reason for which Habermas takes himself to be spokesman? Can we not recognize in philosophical modernism's particularity a substantiality that has forgotten that it is also

subject? Can we not recognize in Habermas's ideal speech situation a subjectivity that has forgotten its substantiality? Are these two extremes not two halves of an integral freedom to which, however, they do not add up? Can we not recognize ourselves in the dialectical belonging and separation of these conflicting positions?[43]

Working from a Hegelian perspective informed by Adorno's negative dialectics, Bernstein casts light on the "modernist" resistance to straightforward exegesis that characterizes—if only, in fact, to a limited extent—many projects in the field of "philosophical modernism." He thus illuminates as well the intimate relationship between these projects and the adventures of modernist art, clarifying the way these different versions of "modernism," through their various modes of exploratory indirection and reinvention, attempt to lend voice to fields of alterity that tend to be excluded or silenced by the dominant procedural and instrumental frames of modern society. Not least importantly, he suggests how we can conceive of the debate between Habermas and various "modernist" and "post-structuralist" thinkers as a vital "dialogue" rather than the simple "either-or" to which it is so often reduced (first of all, alas, by Habermas himself).

Bernstein's is ultimately the sort of dialectical approach that I adopt toward the traditions I study in this book. Yet I understand it to be an approach that, in order to earn its cogency and become a voice in a genuine conversation, must be set in tension with all the dynamics in modern poetry and philosophy that resist it. There appears to be at work in Bernstein's essay an aesthetic of the beautiful developed in a tradition running from Kant, Schiller, and Coleridge through Lukács, Marcuse, and many others: an aesthetic that conceives of art as the promise of a reconciliation of the universal and the particular, the intelligible and the sensible, freedom and nature. This philosophic aesthetic does justice to what one might call the "sacramentalist" nostalgia animating many fields of modern art and philosophy, the longing for a coming together of conceptuality and actuality, the space of thought and the manifold material textures of our lives. But this is only a part of a larger story. Important adventures in modern poetry and philosophy, evading any lure of reconciliation in a wholly broken world, are irreducible to the terms of this aesthetic of the beautiful. And while such adventures are indeed guided by what Hegel calls the unhappy consciousness, they exert a forceful pressure on any dialectic that would comprehend them by seeking to conceptualize *exhaustively* the social grounds of the divisions and longings to which they testify. In their often "apocalyptic" hope and unpredictable wandering, adventures of the extravagant in romantic, modernist, and post-structuralist writing may involve less a concern to affirm the irreducibility of any precisely articulated "particularity" to a merely subsumptive "universality" than a concern to explore powers and force fields that elude any secure representational economy of universal and particular. These adventures, if they seek reconciliation, do so only on the far side of their guiding horizons of creative freedom and metamorphic wandering. An aesthetic of the beautiful, not reaching far enough toward the strange, may simply miss these adventures, while a dialectical thinking of the extravagant, if it is to be more than a subtle refusal of that which it claims to recognize, must fully open itself to the way these adventures are meant to contest and transform our familiar terms and boundaries.[44]

For large fields of modern literature occur in a weather of the sublime or the extravagant. Jean-Luc Nancy is but one of many critics who have underlined this point:

> One may be tempted to imagine that our epoch is rediscovering the *sublime*, its name, concept, or questions. But clearly, this is by no means the case, for one never returns to any prior moment in history. The sublime is not so much what we're going back to as where we're coming from. Ever since Boileau's translation and commentary upon Longinus, aesthetics, or the thought of art—but also thought insofar as it is provoked by art—has not ceased to pursue, either explicitly or implicitly, the question of the sublime. One could demonstrate this without difficulty throughout the entire modern and contemporary history of art, aesthetics, and philosophy. The sublime properly constitutes our *tradition* (in aesthetics at the very least, but then this restriction already entangles us in some of the questions which are today tied to the sublime).[45]

This passage, as I read it, refers to those currents of the broad tradition of the extravagant that I've sought to sketch in this introduction—a tradition that includes a sounding of the sublime in a relatively specific sense, while extending beyond it to include a range of other bearings, including, among others, the mythopoetic, the visionary, the Faustian, the metamorphic, the apocalyptic, or, later, the errant, the dislocative, the deconstructive, the indeterminate.

Yet the unfolding of this long tradition has involved far more than the task of putting "presence in question" (to recall the title of the book introduced by Nancy). There is a risk that, in engaging earlier performances and thematizations of the sublime from our contemporary situation, we will find in them little more than the guiding terms of our own predicaments and interrogations: interrogations that, as the essays in the volume introduced by Nancy make clear, tend to involve some version of either a post-Nietzschean or a post-Heideggerian critique of representation, critique of reason, and critique of the subject. There is a risk, in other words, that we will concentrate on important continuities in this tradition while ignoring equally important discontinuities, thereby finding merely anticipations of, rather than challenges to, the guiding questions and perspectives of our own situation. Or, to turn this skeptical thought the other way, there is a risk, too, that we will neglect important continuities in this tradition simply because they fail to translate readily into the terms of the guiding questions and perspectives of our own situation. Although I can hardly claim in this book to provide the sort of comprehensive narrative that reminders like these call for, I would like at least to provide a nuanced contribution to any such narrative. In orchestrating three different conversations among poets and philosophers of the last two centuries, my intention is to bring to light concealed but defining continuities as well as neglected but defining discontinuities, to elucidate persistent orientations as well as decisive transformations, and to explore not only the challenges posed by contemporary discourses of the extravagant but also the challenges posed by earlier discourses of the extravagant.

Romanticism undertakes the impossible, yet surprisingly productive, translation of religious passages of the extravagant into secular passages of the extravagant. The collisions and despairs these passages generate are multiple and ample: indeed, the fall back to despair, to a shore where one is "baffled, balk'd, bent to the very earth" (Whitman), is the most frequent outcome of these passages, though this despair itself is then frequently troped, turned again, in purgatorial crossings toward a farther station of hope. And out of these translations, collisions, and despairs emerge the multiple reinventions, the further displacements, of both passages of the extravagant in modernist poetries and discursive elaborations of these passsages in twentieth-century critical philosophies. The enigmatic promise of unclosed negativity comes to be variously explored in the most recent phase of this adventure, as though dynamics of undoing and unmaking, deconstructing and decentering, were the last and errant measures of certain postreligious dynamics our culture has at once abandoned and, in the end, refused to abandon. This entire adventure is splendid in its refusal to compromise with the flattened routines, the many masks of death-in-life, of a programmatically utilitarian, instrumental, thinly therapeutic modernity. It is an adventure whose current phase, however, perhaps risks leaving us in a desperate space of ghostly possibility, one lacking the hints, textures, or concrete premonitions of less evasively sketched horizons. Perhaps something has been lost in the most recent phase of this tradition of weavings, unweavings, and reweavings of the extravagant. And yet, it is true, a puzzled sense of loss has always accompanied the modern adventure of the extravagant. "Was music once a proof of God's existence? / As long as it admits things beyond measure, / That supposition stands. // So let the ear attend like a farmhouse window / In placid light, where the extravagant / Passed once under full sail into the longed-for."[46]

TRADITIONS OF THE EXTRAVAGANT: SUBLIME ENCOUNTER, FAUSTIAN QUEST, APOCALYPTIC NEGATIVITY

In the chapters that follow I study three major traditions of the extravagant: the experience of the sublime (chapter 1), the Faustian quest for visionary metamorphosis (chapter 2), and the sounding of apocalyptic negativity (chapter 3).

In the first chapter I examine different conceptions of the sublime developed in Kant, Wordsworth, and Lyotard. My decision to place Lyotard in this constellation is determined by the fact that he is one of the few well-known philosophers of our century who has explicitly elaborated his thought in relation to both Kantian and modernist versions of the sublime. In all three of these writers the sublime is understood to involve an initial movement of being dislodged from oneself through an encounter with an unrepresentable alterity. After this shared point of departure, however, there are large differences. Both Kant and Wordsworth, tracing what we now recognize as a canonical "high romantic" version of the sublime, understand this initial unsettling of the subject to be followed by a forceful recovery of the subject, an awakening of inner powers that might well have remained buried were it not for the initial dislocation. Yet they interpret this recovery in different ways: if Kant discerns in it an analogue of the power of moral freedom, Wordsworth discerns in it an experience of imaginative power that he anxiously understands to be potentially subversive of the common domain of everyday ethical bonds and relationships. Wordsworth, then, at the performative level of *The Prelude*, shows himself to be more keenly alert than Kant to the risks of solipsism involved in any lonely search for awakened power, any valorization of sublime freedom. And thus, I think, he teaches a caution we would do well to adopt in measuring not only the *analogies* but also the *tensions* between modes of existential self-formation and modes of ethical relationship.

Similar analogies and tensions are at play in the field of twentieth-century Continental philosophy. In the second half of this chapter I study them by examining the work of one influential post-structuralist thinker, Lyotard, elucidating the quite different accounts of the modernist sublime that he develops at different points in his trajectory. Throughout the sixties and seventies he develops a "Nietzschean" or "avantgardist" account, one that associates the sublime with the inventive power manifest in innovative works of art: our vocation, as revealed by the sublime, is to become nomadic inventors of unfamiliar languages and perspectives that subvert conventional representational codes and social practices. Yet, in the eighties and nineties, while abandoning Nietzsche as a guide and frequently drawing on Kant and Wittgenstein, Lyotard develops a "Heideggerian" account of the sublime, one that retains the first moment of the Kantian or Wordsworthian sublime, the dislocation of the subject, while canceling the second moment, the reawakening of the subject whose hidden powers have been called to life through an encounter with a force of otherness. The subject of a sublime encounter, momentarily freed from the internalized imperatives of a functionalist social system, is understood to be turned adrift in an openness to alterity that stirs no countermovement of self-assertion or awakened power. In this Heideggerian story, then, our vocation, as revealed by the sublime, is to become subdued subjects open to an indeterminate alterity that can never, without violence, be comprehended by a concept. It is this drift of the deposed subject open to the indeterminate that, for the later Lyotard, signals the ethicopolitical promise of the sublime.

This revised thematization of the sublime, emblematic of the sort of revision one finds in a great deal of twentieth-century Continental philosophy, is also emblematic of a number of unresolved problems at play in this field. At the end of the chapter I attempt to bring to light a few of these problems, concentrating in particular on the way the authorial voice one hears in Lyotard testifies not to a deposed subject but to a coherent, powerful, at times oracular subject. What takes place in Lyotard's discourse, as in many discourses in twentieth-century Continental philosophy, is an *idealization* of a deposed subjectivity that is in contradiction with the kind of powerful subjectivity animating the discourse itself. The sublime still guides a discourse concerned with finding an exit from an instrumental society: this marks a fundamental continuity between the romantic, the modernist, and the post-structuralist sublime. Yet, in philosophic meditations like Lyotard's the sublime, though only rarely named as such, is reconceived as an undoing of the synthesizing subject that, by undermining any recovery of a Kantian, Wordsworthian, or Nietzschean sort, opens the subject toward the clearing of Being, the texture of the nonidentical, the play of alterity, the call of the other, the openness of the indeterminate, or some other haunting "place" beyond the boundaries of conventional social and discursive practice. In these later philosophic meditations, in fact, any such recovery of the subject is conceived, at least implicitly, as the reassertive movement of a subject that, in this movement, would repeat the subsumptive operations of the functionalist network in which it has been programmed to operate as a productive power. The horizon of genuine freedom comes to be understood as the open drift of the negative. And it is in this sense that important currents of twentieth-century Continental philosophy indicate that we have become immensely suspicious of our own experiences of awakening, frightened by our own moments of release, repelled by the very discourse of the sublime that we nevertheless remain drawn to. No longer trusting our own powers, we now appear inclined to thematize our awakenings as destitutions for the sake of a sublime other, and a sublime other often conceived in ethical terms. Yet this revised thematization of the sublime, I argue, involves a dangerous confusion of a displaced religious longing for metamorphic freedom (or, put another way, for an exodus from a functionalist prison) with the difficult, yet ultimately mundane, demands of ethical and political relationship. It is my sense that we've hardly resolved or surpassed some difficult questions raised by a tradition of the sublime that we inherit from the romantic period. Wordsworth's complex performative exploration of the sublime, I think, poses a critical challenge to both Kant's and Lyotard's less troubled, less nuanced meditations on the relationship between the sublime and the ethical.

In the second chapter I bring together Rimbaud, Nietzsche, and Bataille, three writers whose explosive projects I characterize as adventures of Faustian quest and crisis. Without calling on the myth of Faust in any strict sense, I argue that all three of these writers, in their inclination to risk demonic destruction for the sake of radical metamorphosis, belong to a romantic tradition of antinomian revolt (or, as this occasionally expresses itself, especially in France, of romantic Satanism). The sought horizon, for all three, is a metamorphic surpassing of the nihilist flatness whose menace they perceive both in themselves and in the social structures of the world they inhabit. In seeking this horizon, all three affirm volatile dynamics of "going under" and "crossing over" (as Zarathustra puts it) that have been of great importance in the twentieth-century avantgarde: alchemical dissolution and visionary transfiguration (in Rimbaud), critical destruction of inherited idols and creative transformation of the emptiness exposed when these idols are destroyed (in Nietzsche), and ecstatic ruin and vertiginous freedom (in Bataille). Yet my argument is that this tradition of Faustian quest undergoes a mutation in Bataille parallel to the mutation that the tradition of the romantic and modernist sublime undergoes in Lyotard. While in Rimbaud and Nietzsche, as earlier in Blake or later in Breton, the "destructive" or "negative" and the "constructive" or "transfigurative" moments of this adventure are held together in dialectical tension, in Bataille the constructive moment, the concern with a reimagined horizon of life, is entirely abandoned for the sake of a pure affirmation of the moment of ruin, the rapturous undoing of the everyday self and its location in the world of work, production, development, and coherent representation. Further, both Rimbaud and Nietzsche, recognizing the risk of nihilism involved in their own exorbitant efforts to overcome nihilism, at important points in their quests revise their initial Faustian impulse, whereas Bataille, far from acknowledging this sort of peril, affirms rapturous crisis itself as the sole path toward radical freedom. Setting an atheistic "mysticism" in opposition to a kind of "hypertrophied Hegelianism" drawn from Alexandre Kojève, Bataille reconceives demonic quest *as* demonic crisis: emphatic ruin becomes metamorphic freedom. The movement of ruin, a passage through sheer negativity, becomes the movement of a groundless freedom "beyond" the limits of practical life itself.

Bataille thus revises the Faustian quest for radical metamorphosis in a decisive way, erasing that creative, constructive, or projective force that Blake figures as the Poetic Genius, Rimbaud as the *Génie* of his great prose poem by that name, Nietzsche as the overman or the philosopher of the future, and Breton as *la parole intérieure* or a power of imagination concealed in repressed regions of the psyche. Surrealism—with its "anarchist" and "irrationalist" emphasis on the unconscious, the incongruous image, the revelatory chance encounter, and so forth—can be understood as a dialectical response to a social system that Breton and Max Weber alike characterize as an iron cage taking over psychic life itself. Bataille carries this tendency further in his insistence that any constructive power of the sort figured by Blake's Poetic Genius can only become, in the end, a servant of the damaged instrumental world organized around practices of domination and self-domination. Or, put another way, from Bataille's perspective, earlier poetic and philosophic passages of critical dissolution and metamorphic refiguration appear themselves to have become bound to the very "iron cage" and "mechanized self" they have sought to surpass. He thus understands the promise of freedom to lie in volatile energies of irrecuperable negativity. There are telling affinities between Bataille and the later Lyotard: despite all their other differences, both valorize a motion of sheer negativity, a motion of sheer destitution, detached from any complementary motion of creative construction. The play of sheer revolt, on the one hand, and the drift of indeterminate negativity, on the other, tend to become ends in themselves.

Given the idiosyncratic character of some of Bataille's own concerns, it is perhaps surprising that his exorbitant voice has resonated in a range of twentieth-century "oppositional" poetries and philosophies. Yet a voice akin to his can be distinctly heard in a number of recent "postmodernist" discourses, particularly in those that affirm the liberatory force of disjunction, indeterminacy, disruptive play, and so forth. And variously routed through semiotic and psychoanalytic vocabularies, his voice has resonated widely in French poststructuralist thought. What remains in the name of resistance in these fields of thought, it often seems, is a kind of demon of negativity undoing the schemes of a vast network of normalization—a network emblematically mapped for our time in Foucault's *Discipline and Punish*. As this Faustian tradition unfolds in time, then, the dialectic of critical destruction and visionary refiguration is thinned down into a celebration of the disruptive force of errant negativity. Again, as in the case of Lyotard's revision of the sublime, this appears to be the sign of a desperate resistance to the limits of an instrumentalized modern world felt to have gradually subsumed earlier paths and visions that were once believed to contest those limits.

Finally, in the third chapter, I turn my attention to four writers who undertake apocalyptic soundings of abyssal negativity, arguing that Kierkegaard, Dickinson, Mallarmé, and Derrida, despite all their differences, are alike in the way they voyage into a boundless negativity that conditions, unsettles, and eludes our schemes of positive representation. Kierkegaard's emphasis on "keeping the wound of the negative open" and Derrida's description of himself as "the last of the eschatologists" mark two defining coordinates of this chapter: between these points Dickinson and Mallarmé, writing at about the same time as Nietzsche, measuring the motion of disclosive ruin, discover both a nihilist abyss (or the shadow thereof) and a vertiginous "unmooring" of subjectivity and language. This constellation of writers is likely to appear more eccentric than the constellations I orchestrate in the first two chapters. Yet one of my concerns in this chapter is to demonstrate that the *unmooring of subjectivity* from inherited metaphysical frames, typically associated with romanticism and forcefully registered in both Kierkegaard and Dickinson, and the *unmooring of language* from pretextual grounds, typically associated with modernism and forcefully registered in both Mallarmé and Derrida, are events far more closely intertwined with one another than our conventional periodizing narratives suggest. Dickinson and Mallarmé are thus pivotal figures in this chapter. At once "romantic" and "modernist," roamingly speculative and intently skeptical, both of them, like Nietzsche, articulate this interplay of a vertiginous wandering of inwardness and a vertiginous wandering of signification. Further, like Kierkegaard, Nietzsche, and Derrida, they are writers of a decidedly apocalyptic bent of mind.

Another of my concerns in this chapter is to explore the persistence as well as the transformations of this sort of apocalyptic bearing throughout modern culture. Alternately glowing and fading according to changing historical circumstances, resonating with particular force in both the romantic and the modernist periods, it is a bearing that has informed, in different ways, the thinking of a number of major philosophers, including Marx, Nietzsche, Heidegger, and Derrida, as well as the adventures of a number of major poets, including Blake, Dickinson, Mallarmé, Rimbaud, Breton, and Montale. Yet it is a bearing that tends to be concealed by the polemical Heideggerian and Derridean metanarrative of a history of ontotheology or logocentrism. The latter is not the only metaphysic of Western culture. The romance of exodus has ancient roots. It is fundamentally prophetic and, under certain circumstances, apocalyptic. And on the whole it tends to unsettle "foundationalist" modes of thought. But where the apocalyptic version of exodus is recast in modern passages of the extravagant, it typically takes shape in languages that, insofar as they recall the movement of exodus in a world lacking any clearly foreseen promised land, evoke a riddling movement toward an indeterminate opening, a paradoxical practice of "going where you cannot go" (to borrow Angelus Silesius's words) or, as Derrida has recently characterized this passage, a "messianic" expectation emptied of any concrete "messianism."

The turn toward the negative that I trace in the other chapters of this book, then, necessarily unfolds in a distinctive way in this current of the extravagant, for it is in the very nature of an apocalyptic perspective to concentrate on the disclosive force of unbound negativity. Yet in Derrida, I argue, there occurs, first, a *change of affect* in the exploration of the groundless negativity wherein we drift.[47] The rending wound of the negative voiced in Kierkegaard and Dickinson, the anguish of nothingness evoked in Mallarmé and Nietzsche, the tragic humor sounded in Kafka and Beckett tend to give way in Derrida (or at least in the Derrida of the sixties and seventies) to a lucid voice of irony and liberation. This change of affect, further, is intimately linked to a *change of emphasis* in the thinking of apocalyptic negativity. Rimbaud and Nietzsche hold together in dialectical tension the "destructive" and the "constructive" moments of their metamorphic quests, while Bataille largely abandons the latter in order to affirm a vertigo of dislocation as the movement of freedom; similarly, Dickinson and Mallarmé bring together an art of sounding the nothing wherein we drift and an art of constructing fictions of speculative reach, while Derrida tends to turn away from the mystery of fiction in order to trace (under the sign of paradox) a movement of unraveling as the opening of a wholly indeterminate expectation. The apocalyptic bearing grows rarefied. Derrida's decisive emphasis, in this tradition, on the deconstructive "spacing" of signification is analogous to Lyotard's decisive emphasis, in the tradition of the sublime, on the drift of a destitute subject open to the indeterminate, and to Bataille's decisive emphasis, in the tradition of Faustian quest, on the undoing of the subject formed by a functionalist society and its correlative structures of representation.

The experience of the sublime, the Faustian quest for visionary metamorphosis, and the apocalyptic sounding of boundless negativity: these are the major adventures of the extravagant that I study in this book. They all emerge as displaced articulations, in a modern weather of postmetaphysical skepticism, of earlier religious discourses. They generate ample predicaments, largely because they trace paths and pulses very much at odds with the dominant social structures and discursive frames of secular, utilitarian, technocapitalist modernity. They voice a range of crossings beyond the normative boundaries of modern social and psychic life. And, over time, they tend toward a thinking of (when not a hymn to) the promise of revelatory negativity, dislocative indeterminacy, the decentered, the dislodged, the undone, the de-reified, the errant. It is this trend that reaches a provisional culmination, as it were, in projects like those of Lyotard, Bataille, and Derrida.

The larger narrative shaping each chapter, then, is one that traces how important poets and philosophers in this broad tradition of the extravagant, in particular from the modernist period through the present, have explored the force of the negative in an emphatic way. It is as though writers in this tradition had increasingly come to feel that only a thinking guided by this decisive emphasis on the negative—thus guided, as well, by an evasion of orientations inherited from earlier moments of the tradition in which they write—could contest the boundaries of an increasingly flattened world and its increasingly flattened bodies, minds, and words. The larger interpretative argument shaping each chapter is that *a dialectic of instrumental reason and creative negativity* has been at work throughout modern culture. As the dominant instrumental structures of capitalist modernity have increasingly penetrated every realm of social and psychic life, producing a range of dehumanizing effects studied by just about every modern social theorist, the poetries and philosophies that have critically resisted these trends have repeatedly been pressured to negate and surpass, in one way or another, those "positive contents" of earlier voices in their traditions which, under these circumstances, have readily lost (or at least seemed to lose) their initial contestatory and visionary power. And so these adventures, moving in a sort of spiral of protest, anxiously turning away from inherited practices of writing perceived to have been colonized by instrumental schemes, have gradually unfolded into paradoxical discourses of the negative or riddling practices of the errant.

One concern I raise throughout this study is that this pronounced turn toward a celebration of the negative, while perhaps sustaining the possibility of another renewal of the long tradition of metamorphic passage, may have gradually backed us into a corner from which we are unable to project countervisions that go beyond rarefied invocations of horizons of otherness we can barely even begin to sketch. It is as though our hope had begun to hover in a void.

A related issue, which I address at length in the conclusion, is that the tradition of the extravagant may be waning in the changing field of contemporary postmodern consumer society. There would seem to be an important measure of truth in Fredric Jameson's claim that in the contemporary West the modern project of the "conquest" of nature has at last been "completed" by high-tech capitalism.[48] One response to this unprecedented condition, on the part of many poets and philosophers, has been an effort to explore fields of otherness not yet subsumed by the dominant instrumental structures of modernization: fields of strangeness that, insofar as they startle or bewilder the subject, still promise some passage beyond a pervasively instrumentalized world of regulated subjects and discourses. And among the most prominent thematizations of such fields over the last half century have been the wayward *materiality of language* and the wayward *negativity of signification*. These, it seems to be felt, are the intertwined mysteries that still promise to jar us from our flattened place in a functionalist network beyond our control, still hold powers of the sort once thought to be held by the mystery of Nature, the openness of Being, the call of the open road, the force fields of the changing city, and the vast echoes left by the vanishing of the divine, or by the migratory reaches of passion, dream, visionary quest, intimations released from the unconscious, and variously retrieved fragments of myth, among other things. Yet these late, refracted, attenuated displacements of the tradition of the extravagant in recent poetries and philosophies, I think, have become quite difficult to distinguish from the disjunctive play of codes and images that simply characterizes everyday life in contemporary high-tech, hypermediatized society. The thoroughly instrumentalized world of modernity—described by so many modern philosophers and social theorists as an iron cage or a disciplinary network of one sort or another—appears to have continued to expand and yet, at the same time, to have become the thoroughly disjunctive, weirdly dispersive world of contemporary "consumer capitalist" society. In my concluding chapter, therefore, I argue that these recent and influential spin-outs of the tradition of the extravagant are unlikely, in the absence of a more ambitious speculative turn, to guide us beyond our current predicaments.

CHAPTER ONE

The Sublime in Kant, Wordsworth, and Lyotard

My concern in this chapter is to examine different conceptions of the sublime developed in Kant, Wordsworth, and Lyotard. I place the latter alongside two romantic writers not least because he is one of the few prominent philosophers of our time who has explicitly elaborated his thought in relation to romantic as well as modernist soundings of the sublime. Yet perspectives that are explicitly articulated in Lyotard's thought, I believe, are implicitly or indirectly at work in the thought of a range of twentieth-century Continental philosophers.

In romantic art and philosophy, of course, the concept of the sublime belongs to a discourse of power highly conditioned by a context of insurgent individualism. In both Kant and Wordsworth, emblematic romantics in this respect, the power associated with the sublime is understood to involve a twofold movement, a dialectic of forces: an unsettling of the subject brought about by an encounter with a forceful otherness, followed by a counterassertion of the subject based on a discovery of inner powers that might well have remained hidden were it not for the initially disruptive encounter. Yet Kant and Wordsworth interpret this forceful recovery of the subject in different ways: while Kant discerns in it an analogue of the power of moral freedom, Wordsworth discerns in it a revelation of imaginative freedom that, he fears, may be subversive of the domain of everyday ethical relationship. Wordsworth, it is true, attempts to interpret the sublime in ethical terms, yet the performative testimony of *The Prelude*, as distinct from its thematic claims, testifies to an anxious recognition that any passage from the solitary weather of the sublime to the relational weather of the ethical is far more complex than Kant and Wordsworth alike wish to claim.

Lyotard's thinking is initially close to, but eventually far from, these canonical romantic lines of thought: between the seventies and the nineties, Lyotard develops two quite distinct accounts of the sublime. The first of these is a Nietzschean account that, while it recalls the romantic valorization of creative power, is spelled out in terms of the technical élan displayed in modernist art: the sublime, according to this account, involves a manifestation of uncommon powers of invention, a sounding of the unforeseeable, an iconoclastic production of eccentric languages and perspectives that elude both conventional social structures and unifying theoretical models. Later, however, Lyotard abandons this Nietzschean approach and in its place develops a Heideggerian meditation on the sublime, according to which the sublime involves not a display of inventive "power" so much as a disclosure of an "indeterminate" otherness that "deposes" the Kantian or Nietzschean subject of active or creative power. Thus does Lyotard cut the romantic sublime in half, so to speak, retaining its first moment, the decentering of the subject, while discarding its second moment, the recovery of the subject. Nietzschean power gives way to Heideggerian receptivity and Levinasian destitution. Yet it remains unclear whether in this Heideggerian version of the sublime the awakened power of the subject has truly vanished or, rather, simply been disavowed, concealed in a discourse thereby obscurely at odds with itself. It also remains unclear whether this Heideggerian version of the sublime is, finally, any less haunted by the shadow of solipsism than are traditional romantic versions of the sublime. Indeed, it may be that this shadow haunts any philosophic orientation that closely links the ethical and the sublime. It is partly for this reason that in the conclusion to this chapter I argue that Wordsworth's anxious "performance" of the sublime throughout *The Prelude*—a performance whose inner tensions remain resonantly unresolved—poses a critical challenge to both Kantian and Lyotardian "thematizations" of the sublime.

I will frame my comparisons of these writers in terms of two important issues explored by each of them: first, either a performance or an account of an "experience" of the sublime, and second, a meditation on the ethical and political "implications" of this experience. Emerson, always an advocate of transport, once wrote: "People wish to be settled; only so far as they are unsettled is there any hope for them."[1] The question is how people come to be unsettled and, further, what kind of hope they understand this being unsettled to disclose.

KANT

Kant, as is well known, arrives at the *Critique of Judgment* by an indirect path, that is, in the hope of resolving certain difficulties that he has posed for himself in other places. His primary concerns, spelled out in the first and second *Critiques*, are the self-critical autonomy of both theoretical reason and practical reason. The first *Critique* sets out to debunk rationalist metaphysics, on the one hand, and skeptical empiricism, on the other, a two-pronged operation whereby the ghostlier demarcations of critical idealism emerge. It is self-reflexive reason that determines the bounds and the objects of possible experience, just as it is self-reflexive reason, in the form of the moral law addressed to the subject of intelligible freedom, that determines the will. Thus the first *Critique*, tracing the limits of reason, denying uncritical knowledge in order to make room for rational faith (CPR, 29), marks out a "vacant place" (CPrR, 50) where, in the second *Critique*, the necessary postulates of practical reason will be lodged. These postulates are not all the same. The postulates of God and the immortality of the soul, despite Kant's efforts to attenuate the implications of his own critical project, remain wholly in the realm of hope or faith. The postulate of freedom, on the other hand, is said to be at once the condition and the implication of the enigmatic "fact" of the moral law (CPrR, 4, 29, 43). Throughout the second *Critique*, at any rate, Kant repeatedly emphasizes that he is providing no extension of our theoretical comprehension but only a clarification of "postulates" necessary "from a practical point of view" (CPrR, 140). Although we cannot theoretically know the inner nature of things in themselves, much less the inner nature of God, the soul, and freedom, we can rationally assure ourselves of our moral freedom, rationally affirm our moral independence of empirical laws. Kant's project in the first two *Critiques*, as Robert Pippin has emphasized, is thus emblematic of one of the defining ambitions of cultural modernity in general: "[Kant's] project is more consistent than any other with modernity's general self-understanding as an origination in history, a beginning not bound or conditioned by tradition or religious authority, finally free and independent, and so fully self-conscious about its own possibility."[2]

Yet the costs of this revolutionary critical project are as notable as its achievements. First, as Kant's early readers immediately recognized, there returns in Kant's critical idealism something of the skepticism he claims to have dispelled. For when Kant argues that we can only theoretically know things as they appear *for us*, according to the a priori conditions of our intuition and our understanding, and not things as they are in themselves, he seems, as Pippin nicely puts it, "to give to the skeptic with one hand what was taken away with the first."[3] We are left, in other words, with a kind of "transcendental" variation on Hume's "empiricist" skepticism. It is as though the critical power of reason, once radicalized, generated a spinning irony that reason could never surpass without forgetting itself, a self-reflexive irony that has indeed haunted modern philosophy ever since Kant, most recently in the paradoxes at play in any version of discursive constructivism. In this respect, one might say, Kant's philosophy is emblematic of an "ontological alienation" constitutive of modernity.

Further, and closely linked to this problem, Kant's "two worlds" philosophy, heavily inflected with Protestant accents, not only retains, but even sharpens, the dualism of traditional Christian metaphysics. For, as Charles Taylor emphasizes, in defining moral freedom in terms of the subject's absolute independence from the inclinations of its natural being as well as the habits and norms of any particular community, Kant provides an exhilarating account of freedom that, however, implies at the same time a severe disjunction between the subject of moral self-determination and everything "other" to this subject, including its own body and dispositions, the community to which it belongs, and the natural world at large. This conflict has continued to trouble modern society from Kant down to the present. Radical alienation, a kind of ghostly solipsism, may turn out to be the obverse side of radical freedom.[4]

Kant, acutely aware of this predicament, wrestles with it throughout the second *Critique*, presenting his postulates of God and the immortality of the soul as practical presuppositions that promise, in a distance disclosed by rational faith, an ultimate surpassing of the disjunction between the intelligible and the sensible. Yet it is in the third *Critique* that he most fully engages this predicament. There he attempts to provide not the certainty of any theoretical or practical surpassing of this disjunction—a transition in these realms remains forbidden—but the philosophically justified promise of some ultimate surpassing of it. The reflective judgment of "purposiveness without purpose," a kind of judgment that dwells attentively beside an object without "determining" it according to a rule, constitutes this promise. The interest of the beautiful lies in the way it promises, through the harmonious play of the imagination and the understanding in "indeterminate" aesthetic judgments, an ultimate reconciliation of the sensible and the intelligible, the domain of the concept of nature and the domain of the concept of freedom, between which domains, according to the first two *Critiques*, there otherwise remains "an immense gulf" (CJ, 14–15). The beautiful, like a gleaming cipher, permits us rationally to hope, though not theoretically to know, that the conflict between nature and freedom, creaturely happiness and spiritual goodness, may be overcome on a far horizon that eludes the powers of theoretical cognition.[5]

It goes without saying that this schematic account hardly does justice to the detail and complexity with which Kant explores these issues throughout the third *Critique*. Yet my concern here is only to situate Kant's account of the sublime in terms of his larger project. And perhaps the first thing to say about this account is that its "place" in the third *Critique* is puzzling. For if the interest of the beautiful lies in the way it promises an ultimate reconciliation of the sensible and the intelligible, the interest of the sublime, to the contrary, lies in the way it indirectly reaffirms the transcendence of the subject of moral freedom. The sublime, setting in play not a quickening harmony of the imagination and the understanding but a relationship-in-dissonance of the imagination and reason, functions as an aesthetic sign of the supreme "vocation" or "destiny" of the intelligible subject—the subject that, irreducibly other than and superior to nature, legislates its own moral action. Thus the short "Analytic of the Sublime" threatens to disrupt the "conciliatory" project guiding the third *Critique* as a whole.[6] Perhaps it is for this reason that Kant, in introducing the question of the sublime, claims that "the concept of the sublime in nature is not nearly as important and rich in implications as that of the beautiful in nature" (CJ, 100). And yet, as Lyotard underlines (PC, 78–81), modern art has tended to be an art of the sublime.

Kant describes the "experience" of the sublime as a twofold dynamic, a movement in two phases: a dislocation followed by a recovery, a feeling of inadequate power that leads to an awareness of transcendent power.[7] The subject, confronted by a natural phenomenon of sublime "magnitude" or "might," discovers that, although its "imagination" is incapable of presenting this magnitude or might in a sensible intuition, its "reason" is capable of "conceiving" a scope or a force superior to it. This power of superior conception resides in the subject's nonnatural transcendence of all natural measures and forces:

> For although we found our limitation when we considered the immensity of nature and the inadequacy of our ability to adopt a standard propor-

tionate to estimating aesthetically the magnitude of nature's domain, yet we also found, in our power of reason, a different and nonsensible standard that has this infinity itself under it as a unit; and since in contrast to this standard everything in nature is small, we found in our mind a superiority over nature itself in its immensity. In the same way, though the irresistibility of nature's might makes us, considered as natural beings, recognize our physical impotence, it reveals in us at the same time an ability to judge ourselves independent of nature, and reveals in us a superiority over nature that is the basis of a self-preservation quite different in kind from the one that can be assailed and endangered by nature outside us. This keeps the humanity in our person from being degraded, even though a human being would have to succumb to the dominance of nature. Hence if in judging nature aesthetically we call it sublime, we do so not because nature arouses fear, but because it calls forth our strength (which does not belong to nature within us), to regard as small the objects of our natural concerns: property, health, and life, and because of this we regard nature's might (to which we are indeed subjected in these natural concerns) as yet not having such dominance over us, as persons, that we should have to bow to it if our highest principles were at stake and we had to choose between upholding or abandoning them. Hence nature is here called sublime merely because it elevates our imagination, making it exhibit those cases where the mind can come to feel its own sublimity, which lies in its vocation and elevates it even above nature. (CJ, 120–21)

The language of this passage, a hymn to the radical freedom of the supersensible subject, clearly echoes the language of the second *Critique*. The sublime is described as an indirect revelation that our authentic "vocation" is that of radical freedom, a negative disclosure that our true "destiny" is with "infinitude," to draw on a passage from Wordsworth's *The Prelude,* to which I'll return:

> In such strength
> Of usurpation, in such visitings
> Of awful promise, when the light of sense
> Goes out in flashes that have shown to us
> The invisible world, does greatness make abode,
> There harbours whether we be young or old.
> Our destiny, our nature, and our home,
> Is with infinitude, and only there—

> With hope it is, hope that can never die,
> Effort, and expectation, and desire,
> And something evermore about to be.
> (VI, 532–42)

For Kant, then, the sublime involves a dynamic whereby, paradoxically, nature in its greatest magnitude or its greatest force—Schiller, anticipating Nietzsche as well as major currents in modernist art, would add nature in its greatest incomprehensibility—leads the subject to intimations of an excess all its own, premonitions of an ultimate "insufficiency" of nature to the subject's own extravagant demands. In this respect there are important affinities between Kant and Wordsworth.[8]

To be sure, Kant does not permit this exalted subject to err beyond certain bounds in its "obscure sense of possible sublimity" (*Prelude*, II, 336–37), in its recognition, awakened by its efforts to present for itself the unpresentable, of its own supersensible powers extending beyond positive presentation. For Kant's entire account is shaped, sometimes overtly and sometimes tacitly, by the guiding themes of the second *Critique*. In his account of the sublime he describes an unstable movement between different faculties: he composes a quasi-narrative that tells of a passage from the painful failure of the subject's powers of presentation, to the exalted affirmation of the subject's powers of conception, to the indirect awareness of the subject's moral freedom. Yet this story is in large part borrowed from book 1, chapter 3, of the second *Critique*. There, as in the "Analytic of the Sublime," we learn of the superiority of the supersensible subject to the sensible ego, of the free subject of the law to the finite creature of nature. There, as in the "Analytic of the Sublime," a conceptual distinction embedded in Kant's "two worlds" philosophy is partly set in motion, turned into a quasi-dialectic whereby "humiliation" in a lower world, the sensible domain of self-love, is at the same time "elevation" in a higher world, the supersensible domain of freedom in obedience to the moral law:

> Pure practical reason merely checks selfishness, for selfishness, natural and active in us even prior to the moral law, is restricted by the moral law to agreement with the law; when this is done, selfishness is called rational self-love. But it strikes self-conceit down, since all claims of self-esteem which precede conformity to the moral law are null and void.... Since this law, however, is in itself positive, being the form of an intellectual causality, i.e., freedom, it is at the same time an object of respect, since, in conflict with

its subjective antagonists (our inclinations), it weakens self-conceit. And as striking down, i.e., humiliating, self-conceit, it is an object of the greatest respect and thus the ground of a positive feeling which is not of empirical origin. (CPrR, 76–77)

We know the moral law, and thus our authentic freedom, as an "inner and intellecutal compulsion" (CPrR, 33) that, in placing a painful constraint on the inclinations of our sensible being, awakens our supersensible being to its moral power: "the lowering (humiliation) of the pretensions to moral self-esteem on the sensuous side is an elevation of the moral, i.e., practical, esteem for the law on the intellectual side" (CPrR, 82). The moral law, imposing on the subject of nature, calls the subject of freedom to its genuine vocation.

Paul de Man once claimed that Kant's "Analytic of the Sublime" is not an argument but "a story, a dramatized scene of the mind in action."[9] Though I find the conceptual opposition between argument and story to be less pure than de Man implies, his observation is still suggestive in this context. And what I would emphasize is that the quasi-story of the "Analytic of the Sublime" is based on the quasi-story set forth in the second *Critique*. The two texts largely rely on the same plot: a conflict between the sensible and the supersensible in which the subject, in recognizing the limits of its sensible powers, is awakened to its supersensible powers. Yet the specific characters differ from one text to the other: the conflict in the second *Critique* between the strivings of the finite creature of self-love and the free power of the subject of the moral law returns, in the "Analytic of the Sublime," as a dissonance between the finite strivings of the imagination and the free power of reason. Indeed, this latter conflict, as we have seen, is elucidated precisely as an aesthetic analogue of the former conflict. These are both stories about a radically free subject able to make of its very limitations and failures an affirmation of its power to think the infinite, of its very fractures and dissonances an affirmation of its power to pursue a transcendent vocation.

In emphasizing these intimate connections between the second and the third *Critiques*, I've attended little to the complex issue of "presentation" in the third *Critique*, an issue that for good reason has recently received ample attention. Yet I've done so because it seems to me important to emphasize that, whatever we may find in Kant relevant to our contemporary concerns with the limits of representation, Kant himself is primarily concerned to demonstrate that our encounters with these limits operate, indirectly, as signs of a "destiny" beyond sensible or representational limits. We risk losing sight of this argument of Kant's insofar as we remove his third *Critique* from its place in Kant's larger project as well as its place in Kant's historical context.[10] For Kant it remains the case that a sublime experience radically unsettles the subject and, precisely in doing this, awakens the subject to its own elusive, hidden, unpresentable powers. The subject set beside itself, fractured, in a sublime encounter recognizes that it is strangely other than what it is, that it is not yet what its own powers call it to be.

Kant articulates a "moral" or "quasi-moral" version of the high romantic sublime. His short "Analytic of the Sublime" reiterates his theme of themes: the radical independence of the self-legislating subject of reason from natural and social pressures. In doing so, it makes clear the extent to which Kant's account in the third *Critique* of the "reconciliation" promised by aesthetic and teleological judgment is, in a sense, an elaborate variation on his account in the second *Critique* of the practical postulates of God and the immortality of the soul: a capacious defense of a rational faith that can only be situated in the realm of deferred promise lest it undermine the demand for the radical freedom of the subject. The shadow of alienated solipsism may still hover close to this project.[11]

WORDSWORTH

One encounters in the field of romantic poetry a productive conflict between a valorization of wholeness and a valorization of departure, between the quest for a renewed self of harmoniously interactive powers and the quest for a transported self of metamorphic powers discontinuous with the habits of a coherent social self. The former could be called a poetic of reconciliation (or a poetic of the beautiful) and the latter a poetic of extravagance (or a poetic of the sublime). Kant's conception of the "indeterminate" aesthetic judgment, which promises an ultimate reconciliation between the sensible and the intelligible, Schiller's account of the "play instinct," which harmonizes a receptive power (the sense instinct) and a constructive power (the form instinct) and so promises to educate the individual for participation in a just and free society that will not repeat the violence of the Reign of Terror, Coleridge's notion of the nonrepressively "synthetic" imagination, which "brings the whole soul of man into activity," Keats's story of the soul forming itself through imaginative encounters with suffering in a worldly "vale of soul-making," and Wordsworth's uneasy effort to bring his moments of uncanny transport into consonance with the demands of discursive judgment and the habits of social existence—these are all versions of a romantic humanist ideal of activating and harmonizing, without erasing, the differentiated faculties or forces within the subject that, theoretically sketched by Kant at the end of the eighteenth century, are felt throughout the romantic period as internal divisions linked to larger social divisions. On the other hand, the ecstatic seer of Coleridge's "Kubla Khan," the enthusiastic Blakean prophet who seeks to jar his readers into a perception of the infinite, the spellbound singer of Novalis's *Hymns to the Night* who reaches toward death as toward the angel of his transfiguration, the demonic quester of Rimbaud's "Drunken Boat" and *Illuminations* who voyages through metamorphoses of self and language, and the Wordsworthian visionary who approaches "the invisible world" as "the light of sense / Goes out in flashes"—these are all figures of a transhumanist ideal of radical transport that is not immediately compatible with any conventional humanism. They sound a call for a passage beyond the terms of the given, a metamorphic departure from the bounds of the familiar.[12]

These passages could be characterized as literary expressions of what Charles Taylor, in his account of modern philosophy and social theory from Kant through the present, calls "radical freedom." For the *philosophes* of the Enlightenment, advocates of Bacon, Newton, and Locke, freedom is based on a bringing together of critical and instrumental reason: the task is to dissolve the contraints of traditional authority, expand scientific knowledge, master nature, and construct a free and prosperous society on the basis of rational principles and empirical studies. For Kant, while he is surely an advocate of this modern project, freedom is above all moral freedom: the power of the intelligible subject to legislate its own action independently of all natural forces and social pressures external to the subject. Yet for romantic poets, in particular those who pursue the adventure of the extravagant, freedom is above all imaginative freedom: the power of the subject, unfettered from received authority, to reimagine itself as well as the horizons of the world it inhabits. Thus Blake's emblematic cry in *Jerusalem*: "I must Create a System, or be enslav'd by another Mans / I will not Reason & Compare: my business is to Create." If for Kant one is free when determining one's own moral action, for a romantic poet one is free when transforming one's being through creative action. Further, insofar as the romantic "imagination" promises a renovation or transformation of one's being, it only partially resembles the "imagination" of Kant's third *Critique*. To be sure, it is associated in part with a receptive capacity, or with a capacity to present sensible forms to intuition, yet above all it is understood as a constructive, visionary, revelatory power, the all-in-all of the human mind, a power to discover paths of departure. The difficult question, then, is whether or not the subject thus transported in imaginative freedom can return again to the texture of everyday existence. The failure to return is solipsism—one of the major anxieties of romantic poetry—or, at an extreme edge, the risk of psychic free fall. This drama of "departure and return" is perhaps nowhere more anxiously played out than in Wordsworth's *Prelude*, a text that resonantly embodies the major romantic conflict between a valorization of recovered wholeness and a valorization of metamorphic departure.[13]

It is from this perspective, further, that one should approach the romantic fascination with wider fields or forces of "otherness" with which imaginative power is often felt to be aligned. "The sense of identity with a larger power of creative energy meets us everywhere in Romantic culture," Northrop Frye writes in an essay whose very title, "The Drunken Boat: The Revolutionary Element in Romanticism," is meant to recall the evocations of sweeping currents of "otherness" in both Shelley and Rimbaud.[14] These wider currents of creative energy, as Frye notes, are occasionally perceived as demonic, in particular in those poets, including Shelley and Rimbaud, who experience their imaginative freedom as inseparable from a revolt against dominant social conventions. Yet, too, these wider currents of otherness are on occasion perceived as powers that, like secret guides, rescue the imagination from a movement that might otherwise careen toward a solipsistic vertigo, in particular in those poets, including Wordsworth and Novalis, who experience their imaginative freedom at a remove from the energies of social rebellion. Whether these wider fields of otherness are perceived as demons or guides, whether they are associated with a buried Force of revolt, an elusive Spirit of nature, or, in Heidegger's later variation on this theme, a Presencing of Being that illumines and withdraws from beings, they always bear the promise of an uncommon movement of imaginative reach, a creative release from the "dull vapours of the little world of self" (Shelley).

Just as there is clearly a displaced Protestantism at work in Kant's philosophy of moral freedom, so there is clearly a displaced Protestantism at work in the romantic poetry of imaginative freedom: Kant recasts Protestant moral frameworks in secular terms, while romantic poets in the German, English, and North American traditions recast Protestant dramas of spiritual renovation in secular (or perplexingly quasi-secular) terms, as Northrop Frye, M. H. Abrams, Harold Bloom, and Geoffrey Hartman, among others, have shown in detail.[15] Bloom, for example, in his great essay "The Internalization of Quest-Romance," argues that English romantic poets "internalize" earlier literary romances of redemption, rewriting the traditional "exterior" movement from a fallen nature to a redeemed nature as an "interior" movement from a blocked self of defensive anxiety to a creative self of imaginative power. Yet, as Abrams demonstrates in the opening chapters of *Natural Supernaturalism,* this sort of internalization of a Christian romance of metamorphic renewal had already, well before the emergence of romanticism, been carried out in various left-wing traditions of Inner Light Protestantism (and at least partially in *Paradise Lost*), and these Protestant traditions themselves appear to have been in communication with esoteric traditions of the "inward voyage" that have meandered through Western culture ever since the Hellenistic period. It is the secularization of these earlier romances of redemption (the radicalization of older movements of internalization) that characterizes the unstable adventures of high romantic poetry.[16]

An unbroken translation of a Christian romance of redemption into a secular frame of reference may well be impossible. In romantic poets, at any rate, the translation tends to remain ambiguously, resonantly, perplexingly incomplete—one need only think of the difficulty of spelling out the exact sense in which Blake is a Christian. But a failure to recognize this project, as well as the immense ambitions and predicaments it generates, is likely to lead to a misreading of romantic poetry, for example, to an account of romantic poetry as *nothing more than* the ideology of the practical bourgeois subject that it inevitably becomes on one level. Yet on another level romantic poetry is an attempt to send a storm through this everyday ego of an individualist and instrumentalist society. According to a traditional Christian account of the person, there is a fallen natural being consisting of a body and a consciousness or an identity, and, on a radically different level, a holy spirit that, at those moments when it arrives, transfigures the natural being or, in a formulation of internalized apocalyptic, annihilates the natural being and renovates it in a wholly other realm of divine action: thus is the natural being born again, awakened to powers beyond the programs of the fearful selfhood. "When the good is near, when you have life in yourself, it is not by any known or accustomed way. . . . You take the way from man, not to man," as Emerson puts it in quasi-secular terms, anticipating Nietzsche's hyperbolic teaching of the creative overman.[17] Wordsworth, as we will see, when he speaks of those moments of greatest imaginative awakening, tends to speak of an experience of "visitation" or even "usurpation," as though he felt that at such moments something other than himself had suddenly swept through him. Thus are the Christian tropes set in motion anew (the holy spirit tending to become the creative imagination). Yet, if a

Christian vision of the dynamics of renovation presupposes a Christian metaphysic, it is anything but clear how it can be translated without substantive loss into a post-Christian, Newtonian, mechanical universe of matter and force. As I argued in my introduction, such a translation, variously explored, nonetheless constitutes the hyperbolic romantic wager. It is of course a wager that puts enormous weight on the promises felt in moments of imaginative release and creative power. It is a wager, too, that repeatedly provokes in romantic poets the fear that they have strayed into a zone of delusion, solipsism, and nihilism. A major drama of romantic poetry lies in the effort to evade this risk of delusion or solipsism and, at the same time, to evade any concession to a wholly empiricist or instrumental psychology, the contemporary versions of which are the multiplicity of Freudian, post-Freudian, and therapeutic psychologies embedded in the common sense of twentieth-century society—psychologies that, as romantic poets can only read them, risk becoming rationalizations of the defensive ego enclosed in despair.

Wordsworth's *Prelude* is a vast meditative performance of this romantic drama. The poem, as Abrams notes, has affinities not only with the novel of education and novel of artistic self-formation but also with the Christian spiritual autobiography.[18] The poet's primary concern is to trace the wandering formation of his imagination in time, a project that involves, among other things, layered recollections of defining phases in his past, a pivotal exploration of his surpassing of a major crisis in early adulthood, and evocative meditations on moments of exceptional imaginative awakening that, from early childhood through adulthood, arrive in the poet's lifelike visitations that reveal to him his true vocation. But these moments of awakening tend to occur differently at different points in his life, for Wordsworth's drama of the imagination is a distinctively temporal drama, an expansive exploration of the meandering paths of loss and return, enigmatic experience and enigmatic recollection. But the revelatory experiences of the child and those of the adult, for all their differences, display at least one important feature in common: they arrive as visitations of an otherness in the self, a strangeness in the quotidian. Wordsworth's imagination, in a word, is released under the aspect of visitation, occasionally named with the even stronger word "usurpation" (VI, 534; XIII, 51). This is the primary mode of the Wordsworthian sublime.

The sublime encounters that the child has with the natural world are experienced as collisions of obscure forces within and obscure forces without. Wordsworth, Hartman writes, finds nature to be "not an 'object' but a power and a presence" (WP, 42). The incipient poet encounters neither the empiricist's network of atomized sensations, nor the Kantian's manifold of objects of possible experience, but the existential phenomenologist's field of shifting contours and depths, a textured realm of presences bearing strange resonances. For this child, as Hartman says, nature is the paraclete (WP, 50). The natural world at its most forceful secretly educates him by provoking in him a release of imaginative energies he can scarcely understand, a drama splendidly evoked in the ninth stanza of the "Intimations" ode, where the poet expresses his thanks, not for the simple delights of childhood, but for the vital searchings of a growing mind, "those obstinate questionings / Of sense and outward things, / Fallings from us, vanishings, / Blank misgivings of a Creature / Moving about in worlds not realized, / High instincts, before which our mortal Nature / Did tremble like a guilty thing surprized" (MW, 301). Thus in the first book of *The Prelude* the famous account of the perplexed child who, having felt himself mysteriously pursued by a mountain after borrowing a boat, discovers in himself "unknown modes of being":

> There in her mooring-place I left my bark,
> And through the meadows homeward went with grave
> And serious thoughts; and after I had seen
> That spectacle, for many days my brain
> Worked with a dim and undetermined sense
> Of unknown modes of being. In my thoughts
> There was a darkness—call it solitude
> Or blank desertion. No familiar shapes
> Of hourly objects, images of trees,
> Of sea and sky, no colours of green fields,
> But huge and mighty forms that do not live
> Like living men moved slowly through my mind
> By day, and were the trouble of my dreams.
> (I, 415–27)

A strangeness without elicits a strangeness within. The haunted child encountering a haunted nature (cf. I, 490–501), "moving about in worlds not realized," is the figure of the emerging poet. Visitation is the way, the awakening promise, a gift demanding that the puzzled steward render a creative accomplishment in return (I, 270–71; cf. XI, 331–33).

Encounters of this sort do not entirely vanish in the adult poet—the "Ode: Composed Upon an Evening of Extraordinary Splendor" poignantly attests to a later experience of this sort—yet they do wane. The fear of this loss is of course one of the primary preoccupations of Wordsworth's best poetry, his response to the waning of these encounters, to the diminishing of his powers, forming the substance not only of his great "crisis" lyrics but also of large parts of *The Prelude*. And this response, in both the lyrics and *The Prelude*, consists above all of voyages into the depths of memory, of a searching openness to resonantly layered places of the past or (in the peculiar sense of this expression) returning "spots of time." As the child's powers are awakened by a natural world with which he collides, so the adult's powers are awakened by "spots of time" that come upon him like forces of resurrection. The greatest evocations of such "spots of time" are surely the marvelously weird recollections presented in book XI of *The Prelude*, the first of which tells of a childhood encounter with a murderer's name carved in grass and a girl bearing a pitcher upon her head while making her way against the wind (XI, 278–344). It is the "visionary dreariness" of this scene that, in returning to the adult, awakens in him powers he fears would otherwise be lost:

> So feeling comes in aid
> Of feeling, and diversity of strength
> Attends us if but once we have been strong.
> Oh, mystery of man, from what a depth
> Proceed thy honours! I am lost, but see
> In simple childhood something of the base
> On which thy greatness stands—but this I feel,
> That from thyself it is that thou must give,
> Elst never canst receive. The days gone by
> Come back upon me from the dawn almost
> Of life; the hiding-places of my power
> Seem open, I approach, and then they close;
> I see by glimpses now, when age comes on
> May scarcely see at all. . . .
>   (XI, 325–38)

Despite the affirmation of the necessity of giving in order to receive, the passage would seem to imply that imaginative power cannot be simply released by an act of will, for, like a Proustian epiphany, it comes as a gift, a lost dawn unexpectedly crossing an evening of the mind. Elsewhere, in the Snowdon passage, this renovative force buried in the ordinary self is indirectly figured as a "fracture," a "breach," and a "deep and gloomy breathing-place" (XIII, 29–66), while in the famous hymn to the imagination in book VI it is directly figured as an "abyss" (a word used in the 1850 edition) that arrives like a "visiting" of "awful promise" and, indeed, "usurps" the ordinary self of common perception:

>   Imagination—lifting up itself
> Before the eye and progress of my song
> Like an unfathered vapour, here that power,
> In all the might of its endowments, came
> Athwart me! I was lost as in a cloud,
> Halted without a struggle to break through;
> And now, recovering, to my soul I say
> "I recognize thy glory." In such strength
> Of usurpation, in such visitings of
> Awful promise, when the light of sense
> Goes out in flashes that have shown to us
> The invisible world, does greatness make abode,
> There harbours whether we be young or old.
> Our destiny, our nature, and our home,
> Is with infinitude, and only there—
> With hope it is, hope that can never die,
> Effort, and expectation, and desire,
> And something evermore about to be.
>   (VI, 525–42; cf. II, 321–41)

Geoffrey Hartman, whose illuminating account of *The Prelude* I will turn to shortly, has read this passage as a rare (and perhaps the only) moment in which Wordsworth wholly acknowledges and affirms his indirect quest for an "apocalyptic" imaginative autonomy unloosed from all natural boundaries and social bonds. It should also be noted that this hymn—composed, as Wordsworth composed this entire recollective passage of the Crossing of the Alps, some thirteen years after the event—is implicitly a hymn to the power of returning "spots of time." That, as we have seen, is the mode in which Wordsworth experiences extravagant imaginative release—the mode of a visitation that leaves the everyday self "lost as in a cloud," jarred by an uncanny "hiding-place" of power (cf. XI, 329–35), whether this visitation be the strangeness of a natural presence that haunts the child, or the strangeness of a returning "spot of time" that haunts the adult.[19]

Yet Wordsworth fears this kind of imaginative extravagance even as he desires it, and Hartman has taught us to recognize the way this ambivalence governs the entire adventure of *The Prelude*. It is an adventure in which Wordsworth seeks an affirmation of his imaginative freedom at the same time as he strives to anchor his imaginative freedom in both a natural world of common presences and a human world of common relationships. Hartman suggestively describes this oscillating drama of departure and return as an uneasy conflict between "apocalypse" and "akedah," a quest for sublime freedom and a quest for relational bonds:

> The episodes that conclude Book IV show the farthest point reached by the poet in becoming aware of his own powers (of imagination) without disowning nature. I shall call them and similar episodes *akedot* (singular, *akedah*), from the Hebrew word meaning a bond or tying. Some such term is needed to discriminate conveniently between two types of experience, one of which separates from, and one of which joins to nature. For the former the term "apocalypse" is often used. Wordsworth's own phrase, "spots of time," combines (for his own good reasons) the idea of both akedah and apocalypse, and so does not help at this point: one should respect, besides, his particular use of the term, and not generalize it avidly. It is of interest, however, that the episodes designated by it, though among the most apocalyptic experienced by Wordsworth, are his strongest supports for the idea of akedah, or of the marriage of imagination with nature. A true though rather simple view of the structure of *The Prelude* would be gained by showing how the poet continually displaces or interprets apocalypse as akedah. (WP, 225)

Hartman immediately adds that the Snowdon passage, appropriately framed as the climax of the poem, is the most striking instance of this effort to interpret an apocalyptic imaginative freedom as a reciprocity of imaginative power and natural power (WP, 226). Nature, the mysterious guide that lures the poet beyond itself (WP, 42–45), ultimately lures him to an awakening of imaginative extravagance that, for Wordsworth, implies the risk of an abyssal falling away from both nature and society. His response, elucidated in detail by Hartman, is to affirm his free imaginative power and, at the same time, to temper this power by emphasizing its embeddedness in both the natural and the human world, that is, by "naturalizing" and "humanizing" it. Thus are the uncanny visitations of imaginative awakening situated, anchored.[20]

Many readers have found Wordsworth's efforts to naturalize the imaginative freedom he discovers to be thoroughly persuasive; after all, these efforts constitute the originality, the distinctive meditative substance, of much of *The Prelude*. "An unresolved opposition between Imagination and Nature," writes Hartman, "prevents [Wordsworth] from becoming a visionary poet" (WP, 39). And yet, as Hartman makes clear, Wordsworth could not have become any other sort of poet, could not have become, say, a visionary poet in the Blakean mode. His meandering project is to articulate a bond between his imagination and a world of natural presences wherein his imagination has developed and, in mazes of time, attained an anchored freedom. In the unfolding of this dialectic, resonant not least because occasionally drifting on the verge of fracture, lies one of Wordsworth's greatest accomplishments—one he concisely reaffirms at the opening of the penultimate book of *The Prelude* and forcefully reenacts in the Snowdon passage of the final book.

But far fewer readers have been persuaded by Wordsworth's efforts to "humanize" or "moralize" the imagination. The project of binding the solitary departures of imaginative awakening to the everyday world of human community forms the burden of much of book VIII and that portion of book XIII which follows the Snowdon passage. In book VIII the poet, concerned to show how "love of nature leads to love of man," begins by presenting a series of recollections of his encounters with shepherds etched against the landscape in sublime solitude:

> A rambling schoolboy, thus
> Have I beheld him, without knowing why
> Have felt his presence in his own domain
> As of a lord and master, or a power,
> Or genius—under nature, under God,
> Presiding—and severest solitude
> Seemed more commanding oft when he was there.
> Seeking the raven's nest and suddenly
> Surprised with vapours, or on rainy days
> When I have angled up the lonely brooks,
> Mine eyes have glanced upon him few steps off,
> In size a giant, stalking through the fog,
> His sheep like Greenland bears. At other times,
> When round some shady promontory turning,
> His form hath flashed upon me glorified

> By the deep radiance of the setting sun;
> Or him have I descried in distant sky
> A solitary object and sublime
> Above all height, like an aërial cross
> As it is stationed on some spiry rock
> Of the Chartreuse for worship.
>
> (VIII, 390–410)

Like the other passages in which Wordsworth evokes serene and giant shepherds, this one has telling affinities, in figure and diction, with the visionary transports of both the Crossing of the Alps and the Snowdon passages. The shepherds are perceived as revelations of imaginative amplitude and spiritual dignity. That each of these shepherds is but an idealization or a type—an "abstraction" or an "impersonated thought" (VIII, 646)—is clear enough. More important is that each is a projected type of Wordsworth himself, a striking emblem of the sort of self-sufficient power of the visionary alone in the natural world that Wordsworth himself has experienced in all those moments when he has felt most alive and free, his soul "naked as in the presence of her God" (IV, 142), as though the awakened poet were a kind of isolated visionary shepherd. Indeed, at one point in the poem, when the poet is reflecting on his detachment from human life prior to his arrival at Cambridge, he explicitly compares himself to a solitary shepherd gazing from a promontory: "Hitherto I had stood / In my own mind remote from human life— / At least from what we commonly so name— / Even as a shepherd on a promontory / Who lacking occupation looks far forth / Into the endless sea, and rather makes / Than finds what he beholds" (III, 543–49). In an important sense, then, Wordsworth's admirable efforts to construct a bridge leading from a naturalized apocalyptic imagination to a humanized or moralized imagination never quite get beyond the first planks. The efforts remain entirely in the solitary weather of the sublime. There may in fact be no firm bridge for this poet who acknowledges that in his youth he was "taught to feel (perhaps too much) / The self-sufficing power of solitude" (II, 77–78). The performative testimony of *The Prelude*, as distinct from its thematic claims and hopes, thus attests to Wordsworth's anxious recognition that visitations of imaginative power may to some degree turn out to be antithetical to the domain of ordinary human relationship (this being one of the major issues animating Keats's creative wrestling with Wordsworth, or ultimately with himself, in a number of poems and letters, most notably in "The Fall of Hyperion").[21]

The poet of *The Prelude*, however, encounters not only giant shepherds but on occasion giant figures of a very different sort. The Discharged Soldier of book IV and the Blind Beggar of book VII are figures who connect the drama of imaginative self-formation unfolded in *The Prelude* to the drama of suffering explored in the *Lyrical Ballads* and elsewhere in Wordsworth's poetry: in all those patient meditations that bear witness to the sorrows and burdens of characters like the Old Cumberland Beggar, the Old Man Travelling, the Brothers, Michael, and the Leech Gatherer, among others. It is true that Wordsworth no more shows in these poems than in *The Prelude* that "love of nature" leads to either "love of humankind" or sympathy for battered figures of this sort. It is also true that these figures, like the shepherds, are often perceived by Wordsworth as emblems of his own spiritual bearings. Indeed, while the Blind Beggar seems to embody some limit of destroyed energy that simply stuns this prophet of imaginative power, figures like the Discharged Soldier and the Leech Gatherer appear to him as the vast subdued counterparts, so to speak, of the giant shepherds. For if the latter emblematize the glory of realized power, of imaginative amplitude and spiritual independence, the former emblematize the dignity of stoic resilience in the valley of fallen power, appearing to the startled poet as representatives of some saving fortitude, however thinned, akin to that affirmed in the conclusion to the "Intimations" ode or in "Peele Castle." Therein lies the "admonishing" power of these weathered characters: the question that they frame in quiet words is what to make of a diminished thing. Yet, that Wordsworth finds in these characters emblems of his own spiritual drama does not mean that the poems in which they appear are not at the same time genuine expressions of sympathy. It is a mistake to see these two perspectives as simply opposed to one another; the life of the soul and the life of relationship are more complex than that. Wordsworth's "other voice"—a troubled voice of sympathy with outcasts, misfits, the suffering, and the decaying—is in fact a voice that, as Stephen Gill underlines, was to be immensely important to later Victorian novelists such as Elizabeth Gaskell and George Eliot.[22]

It is my sense that the pressure of this world of suffering makes itself felt, however obliquely, throughout the *The Prelude*. Indeed, it would seem to be the pressure of this world that stirs the poet's anxious efforts to persuade himself that his solitary imaginative adventure bears some essential link with the struggles and sympathies of a common world of relationships. Or, put another way, the concern that has led various contemporary critics to denounce Wordsworth is present first of all in Wordsworth himself: a concern with the distance between a solitary search for awakened power, on the one hand, and a precarious world of human doings, sufferings, sympathies, and relationships, on the other. This concern is present throughout Wordsworth's poetry, largely as a question never persuasively answered, a difficulty never resolved. In that sense, at least, his poetry remains true to our divided lives, our broken world.

For Kant the sublime, involving an awakening of the subject to its power to think the infinite, is an aesthetic sign of the radical freedom that permits the subject to determine its own moral action. For Wordsworth the sublime, involving an awakening of the subject to its abyssal imaginative power, is a concrete experience of radical creative (rather than moral) freedom: a creative freedom, however, that threatens to disrupt the communal domain of moral relationship in an everyday (rather than a Kantian) sense of the moral. Wordsworth conceives of the moral in a lay sense, so to speak, rather than a Kantian or transcendental sense, and thus he fears that imaginative extravagance, insofar as it involves a dislocation of the self from the habits of a situated social self, may effect a severing of the bonds between the self and a social world of basic habits, sympathies, and norms. There is thus a conflict between Wordsworth's and Kant's conceptions of the sublime. It is a conflict inseparable from, though not reducible to, their different conceptions of the ethical. I will return to these questions at the end of this chapter.

LYOTARD

"Taste promised [the subject] a beautiful life; the sublime threatens to make him disappear," Lyotard writes near the end of his chapter on Kant's "dynamical" sublime in *Lessons on the Analytic of the Sublime* (144). Throughout the chapter Lyotard argues that for Kant the sublime is not an indirect manifestation of the subject's moral freedom so much as a radical unsettling of the coherent subject defined by its capacity to produce temporal and cognitive syntheses. The chapter concludes:

> In reality it [sublime feeling] is a question of two very similar but heterogeneous feelings. For the imagination, this "departure" is made regressively, in the fear of losing the minimal power that thinking has of synthesizing givens (its own included) by succession. For reason, on the other hand, the departure is made (and always already made) in a leap, in the exaltation of recovering the maximal power that thinking has of beginning a series

of givens without being bound to it. The first "no time" threatens the faculty of knowledge, the second "no time" establishes the faculty of pure desire. Thus it is very difficult to classify Kantism among philosophies of the subject, as is sometimes done. (145–46)

Though I remain unconvinced by Lyotard's attempt to show that Kant's account of the sublime traces a "deconstruction" or "destitution" of the subject, his book on Kant surely provides a suggestive articulation of his own conception of the sublime, according to which the sublime involves a certain "disappearance" of the subject.

This account of the sublime is a relatively late turn in Lyotard's thought. It is a turn we will better understand, I think, if we clearly follow the winding path whereby Lyotard eventually comes to it. From the seventies through the nineties, as he drifts away from an initial marxist phase, his thought develops in two distinct phases that correspond to two distinct conceptions of the sublime. In the seventies and the early eighties, Lyotard conceives of the sublime in terms of uncommon powers of invention, his thought in this period guided by both Nietzsche and the disruptive practices and ideologies of modernist art.[23] This perspective is articulated in Lyotard's well-known essay "Answering the Question: What Is Postmodernism?", a polemical essay that, parallel in important respects to the lines of thought presented in *The Postmodern Condition*, is given a political elaboration in *Pagan Instructions* and *Just Gaming*. Yet in the late eighties Lyotard, while continuing to think of modernist art as the preeminent site of the sublime, comes to conceive of the sublime less in terms of the inventive power of the subject than in terms of a destitution of the subject. This perspective, marked by Lyotard's turn away from Nietzsche and toward Kant and Wittgenstein as well as Heidegger and Levinas, is articulated in the talks collected in *The Inhuman* and *Postmodern Fables*. One could characterize *The Differend* as a hinge connecting these two phases of his thought, a meditative text that marks the transition whereby the wild Nietzschean of the seventies turns into the sober post-Kantian and quasi-Heideggerian of the late eighties and the nineties. The shifting tones of Lyotard's texts are themselves marks of this shift in perspective, an earlier voice of kinetic revolt yielding to a later voice of ruminative, if at times oracular, melancholy.[24]

In "Answering the Question: What Is Postmodernism?", originally published in 1982, Lyotard identifies the sublime with "modern art" in general, by which he clearly means the modernist or experimental art of the last one and a half centuries (78–81). And he theorizes this modernist sublime by drawing directly on Kant, describing the sublime as a presentation of the unpresentable, or as a presentation of the fact that the unpresentable exists:

> I shall call modern the art which devotes its "little technical expertise" (son "petit technique"), as Diderot used to say, to present the fact that the unpresentable exists. To make visible that there is something which can neither be seen nor made visible: this is what is at stake in modern painting. But how to make visible that there is something which cannot be seen? Kant himself shows the way when he names "formlessness, the absence of form," as a possible index to the unpresentable. He also says of the empty "abstraction" which the imagination experiences when in search for a presentation of the infinite (another unpresentable): this abstraction itself is like a presentation of the infinite, its "negative presentation." He cites the commandment, "Thou shall not make graven images" (Exodus), as the most sublime passage in the Bible in that it forbids all presentation of the Absolute. Little needs to be added to those observations to outline an aesthetic of sublime paintings. (78)

At this point in his trajectory Lyotard discerns in the sublime, first, the sort of unpredictable inventiveness characteristic of the modernist art of the first half of the twentieth century. He reads this inventiveness, further, as testimony to an "absolute" or an "infinite" that eludes positive representation or clear and distinct conceptualization: not a transcendent absolute, it is clear, but a kind of immanent absolute of the irreducible play of difference, akin perhaps to the "infinite disorder of prayers" of which Breton speaks in one of his poems.[25] Concluding his essay with an echo of Apollinaire's "La Jolie Rousse"—"I am here to judge the long debate between tradition and invention / Between Order and Adventure"—Lyotard sets the way of adventure, affirmed by the sublime inventions of modernist art, in opposition to the way of order, affirmed by the philosophic projects of Habermas and others who, in Lyotard's aggressive formulation, emit "mutterings of the desire for a return to terror":

> Finally, it must be clear that it is our business not to supply reality but to invent allusions to the conceivable which cannot be presented. . . . We have paid a high enough price for the nostalgia of the whole and the one, for the reconciliation of the concept and the sensible, of the transparent

and the communicable experience. Under the general demand for slackening and appeasement, we can hear the mutterings of the desire for a return of terror, for the realization of the fantasy of seizing reality. The answer is: Let us wage war on totality; let us be witnesses to the unpresentable; let us activate the differences and save the honor of the name. (81–82)

For the Lyotard of "Answering the Question," then, the unpresentable would seem to be but an alternative term for the unforeseeable and the unexpected: for the creative play of differences that disrupt and elude inherited as well as projected models for representing either a unified subject or a unified social totality. "Without invention nothing is well spaced," Williams writes in *Paterson*, and it is the unfamiliar "spacings" and exploratory differentiations of modernist art that Lyotard valorizes in "Answering the Question." The adventures of modernist art invent a multiplicity of languages and perspectives that, often incompatible with one another and decidedly disruptive of conventional codes of conduct and representation, alter our sense of the real and widen our sense of the conceivable. Lyotard, approaching modernism from this perspective, and concerned less with any specific modernist artist or movement than with the general modernist unsettling of realist modes of representation, routes a Kantian conception of the sublime through a celebratory reading of the errant doings of modernism. Our vocation, to recall a Kantian term, is to be extravagantly inventive. One could say just as well that Lyotard routes a Kantian conception of the sublime through a Nietzschean reading of modernism. One need only call to mind a few of Nietzsche's major themes—a critique of the faith in a universal model of truth, an exposure of the perspectival condition of all systems of knowledge, a denunciation of the nihilism of modern society and modern science no less than of Platonism and Christianity, and an affirmation of the creative will to power—and set these themes alongside Lyotard's account of the modernist sublime in order to recognize the coherence and plausibility of a Nietzschean reading of modernism. It is this kind of Nietzschean reading that Lyotard spells out in "Answering the Question." Nietzsche serves as the guide to a description of the modernist sublime as the unruly "activation" of differences resistant to theoretical subsumption.[26]

In the seventies and the early eighties Lyotard develops this Nietzschean reading of modernist art as a politics as well. *Just Gaming*, a book of dialogues published in the same year as *The Postmodern Condition*, is a brief presentation of this avantgardist politics. While the text bears marks of a transition in Lyotard's thought from Nietzschean and modernist to Kantian and Wittgensteinian themes, the former still remain dominant, as both Alan Schrift and Philippe Lacoue-Labarthe have underlined.[27] A guiding premise of *Just Gaming*—one quickly to become a platitude in discussions of postmodernism—is that the great metanarratives of progress, prosperity, freedom, socialism, and knowledge have all collapsed. So too have all rationalist political theories, whether those based on a universal "model" of justice or those based on a universal "autonomous" subject (JG, 31). Perhaps an old "liberal" distinction between fact and value remains, however, for a "rational politics" is said to be neither possible nor desirable (27–28, 75, 82), as a prescriptive statement can never be derived from a descriptive statement except through violence (17, 45, 59). Rather, any prescriptive statement, and so any ethics or politics, is understood to be inevitably "left hanging in mid air" (45), adrift in a field of improvised responses and inventions, though a rationalist, unsettled by the open-ended play of contingent differences, may illegitimately attempt to silence or subsume this play (62, 75, 99). Lyotard's conception of a practical reason that has overcome any nostalgia for a foundational or universal model of justice, then, is a variation on his conception of the experimental practices of modernist art. This is the philosophic position he calls "paganism" (perhaps in an allusion to Weber's famous account, in "Science as a Vocation," of modernity as the disenchanted domain of a ceaseless struggle among multiple "gods," or ultimate values, none of which can be rationally grounded):

> But I wanted to add that when I speak of paganism, I am not using a concept. It is a name, neither better nor worse than others, for the denomination of a situation in which one judges without criteria. And one judges not only in matters of truth, but also in matters of beauty (of aesthetic efficacy) and in matters of justice, that is, of politics and ethics, and all without criteria. That's what I mean by paganism. (16)

The "groundless ground" of this modernist politics, unsurprisingly, turns out to be Nietzsche's creative will to power, or the experimental imagination at play in modernist art:

> It [this ability to judge without criteria] bears a name in a certain philosophical tradition, namely Nietzsche's: the will to power. It is obvious that for someone like Kant (the expression "ability to judge" is Kant's), the ability

to judge is left mysteriously hanging. With respect to the moral law, Kant says of the will, in the *Critique of Practical Reason,* that it is an unfathomable principle. In a way, there is nothing to say about it, that is: in truth. But, without it, there would be no experience of obligation and no problem of justice. Here is the answer then: The ability to judge does not hang upon the observance of criteria. The form that it will take in the last Critique is that of the imagination. An imagination that is constitutive. It is not only an ability to judge; it is a power to invent criteria.[28] (17)

This modernist politics, however, bears implicit prescriptions of its own that at many points in the text become explicit. In the second half of the text, in particular, Lyotard attempts to connect this politics of creative invention, also dubbed a "philosophy of opinions" (JG, 75), to a Kantian "regulative Idea" of justice (75–78). This regulative Idea, which informs *The Postmodern Condition* and "Answering the Question" the same as it informs *Just Gaming,* demands that justice be thought "not under a rule of convergence but under a rule of divergence" (95). It is in fact an Idea that brings together two related Ideas: guided by the Idea of "the multiplicity of justices," one is to encourage a proliferation of heterogeneous language games, while guided by the Idea of "the justice of multiplicity," one is to discourage the subsumption of any of these language games under another (totalizing) language game claiming legitimacy beyond its specific domain (100). Injustice, in short, is the reduction of difference, the closure of the differential play of linguistic improvisation. "Here one would have to ask whether a language game that becomes excessive, that falls into what I was calling *pléonexia,* the 'wanting to have too much of it,' that is, precisely when such a language game begins to regulate language games that are not the same as itself, isn't such a language game always assisted by the sword?" (99). Lyotard's presentation of a modernist politics thus concludes with the same call to "wage war on totality," to "activate the differences," with which his presentation of a modernist aesthetic, "Answering the Question," concludes.

There are a number of problems with this politics, two of which I would like to emphasize here. First, despite his insistence on the difference between a constitutive concept and a regulative Idea, Lyotard hardly clarifies how his regulative Idea of "the justice of multiplicity" *differs in function* from, say, Habermas's regulative Idea or counterfactual horizon of a situation of undistorted communication. In fact, Lyotard and his interlocutor, Jean-Loup Thébaud, both recognize this difficulty at the end of their dialogue: in setting forth "a prescriptive of universal value" (100) that is clearly based on a theoretical ideal, namely "the justice of multiplicity," Lyotard finds himself in a position (or a performance) prohibited by his own arguments in the text. A second problem with this modernist politics is that it risks becoming a vacant formalist celebration of linguistic innovation in itself as a good. Fredric Jameson, in his perceptive foreword to the English translation of *The Postmodern Condition*, addresses this issue.

It is worth recalling Jameson's major criticisms of Lyotard's arguments in *The Postmodern Condition*, for they are criticisms that Lyotard, to some extent, appears to have adopted himself. One of these is that Lyotard, in his account of postmodern science as an inventive search for instabilities that unsettle the imperatives of efficiency and productivity largely guiding research in contemporary capitalist societies, relies on a highly problematic (not to say naive) transference much like that which transposes "aesthetics" into "politics" in *Just Gaming*, in this case a "transference" of the "older ideologies of aesthetic modernism, the celebration of its revolutionary power, to science and scientific research itself" (xx). This leads to Jameson's second criticism, namely, that the rhetoric of innovation and differentiation, far from establishing a critical vantage point on capitalist society, happens to be a cultural discourse largely of a piece with the ceaseless quest for innovation essential to capitalist production itself: "The dynamic of perpetual change is, as Marx showed in the *Manifesto*, not some alien rhythm within capital—a rhythm specific to those noninstrumental activities that are art and science—but rather is the very 'permanent revolution' of capitalist production itself: at which point the exhilaration with such revolutionary dynamism is a feature of the bonus of pleasure and the reward of the social reproduction of the system itself" (xx).

Lyotard, within a few years of the essays on the postmodern that have remained his most widely read texts in this country, seems to have arrived at a similar suspicion of a "complicity" between capitalist and modernist imperatives of innovation. Though he continues to celebrate the unfamiliar passages of modernist art, he reconceives the dynamics and the implications of these passages. Throughout the seventies and the early eighties, as we have seen, Lyotard rewrites a Kantian conception of the sublime in terms of Nietzschean and modernist motifs. From the late eighties on, however, he rewrites a Kantian conception of the sublime in terms of motifs variously lifted from Kant and Wittgenstein as well as Heidegger, Levinas, and, to a lesser extent, Adorno and Derrida. This swerve is clearly marked in the essays collected in *The Inhuman* (1988).

The earlier Lyotard discerns in the sublime a manifestation of the inventive powers of a subject that, subverting dominant social and cultural conventions, departs for the unforeseeable. The later Lyotard, searching for any cultural event resistant to the operations of a blindly one-dimensional social system, discerns in the sublime a certain "opening" of the human being toward a dimension of its own "inhuman" being that is radically different in kind from the "dehumanization" effected by the functionalist networks organizing modern societies:

> The suspicion they [the "talks" collected in this volume] betray (in both senses of this word) is simple, although double: what if human beings, in humanism's sense, were in the process of, constrained into, becoming inhuman (that's the first part)? And (the second part), what if what is "proper" to humankind were to be inhabited by the inhuman?
> Which would make two sorts of inhuman. It is indispensable to keep them dissociated. The inhumanity of the system which is currently being consolidated under the name of development (among others) must not be confused with the infinitely secret one of which the soul is hostage. To believe, as happened to me, that the first can take over from the second, give it expression, is a mistake. The system rather has the consequence of causing the forgetting of what escapes it. (I, 2)

This passage from the introduction to *The Inhuman* is, among other things, a retraction of the kind of uncritical "transposition" at work in both *The Postmodern Condition* and *Just Gaming*. A straightforward advocacy of inventive powers and innovative experiments will no longer do. Nietzsche will be abandoned as a guide.[29] From this point on, Lyotard will conceive of the sublime as that which bears witness to an irreducible "indeterminacy" of one sort or another: "With the advent of the aesthetics of the sublime, the stake of art in the nineteenth and twentieth centuries was to be witness to the fact that there is indeterminacy" (101). The "unpresentable" is now understood as the "indeterminate."

What kind of "indeterminacy" is this? In the introduction to *The Inhuman* Lyotard locates this "indeterminacy" in the "indeterminate" substrate of the child upon which social imperatives are imprinted:

> What shall we call human in humans, the initial misery of their childhood, or their capacity to acquire a "second" nature which, thanks to language, makes them fit to share in communal life, adult consciousness, and reason? That the second depends on and presupposes the first is agreed by

everyone. The question is only that of knowing whether this dialectic, whatever name we grace it with, leaves no remainder.

If this were the case, it would be inexplicable for the adult himself or herself not only that s/he has to struggle constantly to assure his or her conformity to institutions and even to arrange them with a view to a better living-together, but that the power of criticizing them, the pain of supporting them and the temptation to escape them persist in some of his or her activities. I do not mean only symptoms and particular deviancies, but what, in our civilization at least, passes as institutional: literature, the arts, philosophy. There too, it is a matter of traces of an indetermination, a childhood, persisting up to the age of adulthood. (3)

In this surprising retrieval of a Rousseauian and Wordsworthian theme, the child is imagined as a presocial substrate, a prerational or prerationalized nature, whose unfathomable indetermination (a kind of primary otherness) would remain the basis and the promise of any later openness to an "outside" of systems of socialization. One is reminded of Wordsworth's conception of the relationship between the child, lost in time, and the adult who hasn't entirely died under the imperatives of rationalization and socialization: though shades of the prison house begin to close upon the growing boy, as if his whole vocation were endless imitation, in the embers of the adult is "something that doth live," something indeterminate, if we are to believe Lyotard. Curiously, however, this theme of the secret promise of the child does not appear again in the essays gathered in *The Inhuman*. Its importance in the introduction, then, would seem to lie in its emblematic suggestiveness: the sublime, for Lyotard at this point, bears witness to an indeterminate otherness that eludes both the imperatives of socialization as such and the operations of the coherent subject constructed by these imperatives, the Kantian or Nietzschean subject of active synthetic powers.[30]

But the thought of the "indeterminate" that Lyotard begins to explore in *The Differend* and continues to elaborate in the essays gathered in *The Inhuman* is more complex than this story of the child suggests. Lyotard's guiding concern in *The Differend*, as in *Just Gaming*, is to underline the irreducible heterogeneity of language games, or, as they are named in this text, phrases, phrase regimens, and genres of discourse. When a phrase occurs, when a phrase is put into circulation, we cannot but "link on" to it with another phrase, yet a "wrong" occurs insofar as we link on to the phrase in a phrase regimen or genre of discourse that, implicitly or explicitly, regulates or subsumes the initial phrase in a phrase regimen foreign to it. If a "litigation" involves a dispute in which both parties share a language, a "differend" involves a dispute in which the language of one party subsumes (and so disregards) the language of another party:

> I would like to call a differend the case where the plaintiff is divested of the means to argue and becomes for that reason a victim. If the addressor, the addressee, and the sense of the testimony are neutralized, everything takes place as if there were no damages. A case of differend between two parties takes place when the "regulation" of the conflict that opposes them is done in the idiom of one of the parties while the wrong suffered by the other is not signified in that idiom. (D, 9)

There is thus a kind of "sublime" difference between phrase regimens, an "indeterminacy" that is "groundless" inasmuch as there is no genre of discourse that can without violence claim to adjudicate among all phrase regimens. To this "indeterminacy" we are called to respond not in an established phrase regimen but with new kinds of phrases, new ways of linking on to phrases:

> The same goes for every differend buried in litigation, no matter what the subject matter. To give the differend its due is to institute new addressors, new significations, and new referents in order for the wrong to find an expression and for the plaintiff to cease being a victim. This requires new rules for the formation and linking of phrases. No one doubts that language is capable of admitting these new phrase families or new genres of discourse. Every wrong ought to be able to be put into phrases. A new competence (or "prudence") must be found. (12–13)

One recognizes the reiteration, in a notably subdued tone, of the "modernist" or "Nietzschean" politics developed in *Just Gaming*. At the same time, however, Lyotard's thought takes a significant turn in *The Differend*—a turn clearly motivated by his effort to escape the sort of Nietzschean philosophy of the will (or, indeed, any sort of philosophical anthropology) that informs his projects of the seventies. This effort generates some of the peculiar features of *The Differend*. For one thing, discourse is often described in an oddly anthropomorphic way. When Lyotard argues that phrases, insofar as they institute different "universes" of addressors, addressees, referents, and senses, variously position persons who in this respect are constituted by the unpredictable play of phrases (49, 139), we are on familiar ground, for structuralism, psychoanalysis, and constructivist historicism all similarly argue that subjects are constituted, or unstably positioned, by the array of discursive webs in which they are caught up. But when Lyotard begins to speak of phrases that offend phrases, things do begin to sound a touch strange (85, 136–38). Further, in the section titled "Presentation," the "occurring" of phrases is lent a forceful "independence" of and "priority" to the human beings positioned by phrases. The philosopher who guides this line of thought is clearly Heidegger. Lyotard argues that the "happening" of each phrase is a "presentation" that ineluctably eludes any retrospective "representation" of that "presentation" in a cognitive or theoretical phrase (72–85). In this sense, each phrase, in occurring, is an elusive presentation that opens the possibility of a temporal manifold, as well as the possibility of representation and communication in general, even as it withdraws from representation. Each happening or presentation of phrases is a sublime opening of the domain of representation and communication in general. It is this unfamiliar bringing together of Kant, Wittgenstein, and Heidegger that shapes Lyotard's account of the sublime presentations of modernist art in the essays collected in *The Inhuman*.[31]

For the guiding thought of sublime indeterminacy in *The Inhuman*, then, set forth with particular clarity in the meditations on Barnett Newman's paintings and sculptures (78–107), is the thought of a quality of "happening" or "spacing" (to borrow a Derridean expression) that cannot be adequately framed, appropriated, or synthesized by the subject. The indirect presentation of this unpresentable indeterminacy, Lyotard argues, does not manifest the subject's unfettered powers of conception and invention but rather dismantles or deposes the subject, momentarily releases consciousness from the imperatives of a coherent social identity. This is said to be the experience stirred by the indeterminate "here and now" of Barnett Newman's paintings and sculptures of the fifties:

> This *now* [the *now* of the present instance] is one of the temporal "ecstasies" that has been analyzed since Augustine's day and particularly since Edmund Husserl, according to a line of thought which has attempted to constitute time on the basis of consciousness. Newman's *now* which is no more than *now* is a stranger to consciousness and cannot be constituted by it. Rather, it is what dismantles consciousness, what deposes consciousness, it is what consciousness cannot formulate, and even what consciousness forgets in order to constitute itself. What we do not manage to formulate is that something happens, *dass etwas geschieht*. Or rather, and

more simply, that it happens ... *dass es geschieht*. Not a major event in the media sense, not even a small event. Just an occurrence.³² (90)

One notes again the Heideggerian and Levinasian motifs: the modernist "unforeseeable," so to speak, has been replaced by the Heideggerian "unenframeable" and the Levinasian "unsynthesizable." A sublime presentation indirectly discloses the "indeterminacy" of a "happening" which eludes and in some sense undoes the subject that synthesizes both the temporal-spatial manifold and its own experience (to put the matter in the terms of a deconstructive postphenomenology), or a "happening" which escapes the vast network of functionalist systems that organize a one-dimensional society (to put the matter in the terms of a critical sociology). The "vocation" revealed by the sublime turns out to be that of opening oneself to an irreducible indeterminacy that, in dislodging one from the demands of a unifying subjectivity and the imperatives of everyday social practice, and in thus reminding one that one is other than a social identity, turns one toward an authentic dwelling in the othering of time wherein events and phrases elusively happen, are elusively presented.³³

It should be underlined that this account of both the "experience" and the "meaning" or "interest" of the sublime is accompanied by—or, rather, presupposes—a dystopian account of contemporary systems of capitalist development no less extreme than the similar accounts to be found in both Heidegger and Adorno. It is worth citing at length one of Lyotard's "programmatic" statements on this "question concerning technology":

> The striking thing about this metaphysics of development is that it needs no finality. Development is not attached to an Idea, like that of the emancipation of reason and of human freedoms. It is reproduced by accelerating and extending itself according to its internal dynamic alone. It assimilates risks, memorizes their informational value and uses this as a new mediation necessary to its functioning. It has no necessity other than a cosmological chance.
>
> It has thus no end, but it does have a limit, the expectation of the life of the sun. The anticipated explosion of this star is the only challenge objectively posed to development. The natural selection of systems is thus no longer of a biological, but of a cosmic order. It is to take up this challenge that all research, whatever its sector of application, is being set up already in the so-called developing countries. The interest of humans is subordinate in this to that of the survival of complexity.

And finally, since development is the very thing which takes away the hope of an alternative to the system from both analysis and practice, since the politics which "we" have inherited from revolutionary modes of thought and action now turns out to be redundant (whether we find this a cause for joy or a matter to be deplored), the question I am raising here is simply this: what else remains as "politics" except resistance to this inhuman? And what else is left to resist with but the debt which each soul has contracted with the miserable and admirable indetermination from which it was born and does not cease to be born?—which is to say, with the other inhuman. (I, 7)

This "politics," a desperate gesture born of demoralization, strikes me as notably thin. It would seem to be not a politics, in fact, so much as a speculative justification of an aesthetic individualism, a romantic pursuit of existential authenticity, though Lyotard is disinclined to acknowledge this. I will return to this issue, from a different angle, in the conclusion to this chapter. At this point my concern is with the way Lyotard rewrites, yet again, Kant's account of the sublime.

What occurs in Lyotard's account of the sublime during this phase of his thought, I think, is the following: the first moment of the Kantian sublime, the moment in which the subject is provoked into a recognition of its finitude, made aware of the limits of its imaginative power, is *retained,* while the second moment, the moment in which the subject is awakened to its transcendent power of conception, called to its vocation as a free subject of moral self-determination, is *canceled.* The sublime unsettling of the subject becomes the whole story, an unsettling now conceived as a haunted openness to some "indeterminacy" that undoes the syntheses of ordinary consciousness, some elusive "happening" that momentarily releases the subject from the self-assertive will of a Cartesian, Kantian, or Nietzschean subject. In a sublime encounter with the indeterminate the subject is imagined to drift outside itself and, as it were, to stay there: to drift, if only for a dilated moment, beyond any Kantian or Nietzschean counterassertion of its own active and creative powers. And thus the ethical vocation indirectly disclosed in such an experience (implied rather more than argued in Lyotard's account) is the task of a heightened openness to the other, while the political vocation indirectly disclosed (though on occasion, as we have seen, conceived as already at work in the sublime presentation itself) is the task of a resistance to dehumanizing systems of functionalist efficiency. For the later Lyotard, then, it is Heidegger and Levinas as much as Kant and

Wittgenstein who replace Nietzsche as philosophic guides to an adequate account of both the dynamics and the ethical and political implications of the modernist sublime. It is as though Lyotard had come to embrace Heidegger's critique of Nietzsche—and so, implicitly, of his own earlier writings—and then radically reconceived the modernist sublime in accordance with this altered perspective.

I would argue, further, that Lyotard presents in quite clear terms lines of thought that, in various ways, inhabit the entire field of what could be called the twentieth-century philosophic discourse of the sublime: a field that would include, among others, Adorno, Heidegger, Blanchot, Levinas, Derrida, and Lyotard himself. For in the diverse philosophic projects of these thinkers the sublime, though rarely named as such, tends to return in an indirect way, but now conceived as a movement of undoing that, insofar as it dislocates the enclosed ego and undermines any self-assertive countermovement of a Kantian or Nietzschean sort, opens the subject toward the clearing of Being, the texture of the nonidentical, the play of alterity, the force of the other, the openness of the indeterminate, or some other "place" beyond the boundaries and imperatives of conventional social and discursive practice. If, with the exception of Lyotard, the specific term "sublime" tends to be avoided by these philosophers, this would seem to be owing to its intimate historical connection with Kant's conception of the sublime. For Kant's account of the sublime includes a countermovement of self-assertion or awakened power that in these later philosophies tends to be conceived (implicitly or explicitly) as the countermovement of a subject that, precisely in this movement, would repeat the subsumptive operations of the functionalist network in which it has been programmed to operate, not least as a productive power and an efficient synthesizer. The subject that forcefully recovers from the shock of its unsettling is, from this perspective, a subject that simply returns to its proper role in a social system governed by the flattening reduction of difference, the pervasive appropriation of otherness (or, to cast this in the psychoanalytic terms of Weiskel's account, a subject that passes through a properly reenacted oedipal drama of crisis and resolution). In this sense, as I argued in my introduction, these influential philosophic discourses appear to have been written in the shadow of Weber's gloomy account of the iron cage of a demonically instrumentalized modernity. The horizon of freedom is revealed through a dislocation from this cage and a corresponding drift of Heideggerian receptivity.[34]

But can this account of the issues at stake open a "place" for the way the sublime is experienced and interpreted in Wordsworth as well as many other romantic and modernist poets? I'm not sure it can. Wordsworth speaks from a perspective not contained by this "debate" between earlier modern philosophies of an instrumental or synthesizing subject and recent Continental philosophies of a deposed or decentered subject—even though the latter, significantly, have drawn extensively on the exploratory adventures of both romantic and modernist art.

PASSAGES AND QUESTIONS

How are we unsettled? What is it that we find, or think we find, or hope we find when we are unsettled, shaken from our enclosed selves? Do we enter a realm of uncanny awakenings, a realm of uncanny destitutions, or both?

Kant reads the dissonant experience of the sublime as ultimately a sign of the subject's transcendent vocation as a subject of moral freedom. This account is inseparable from Kant's dualist conception of moral freedom as a power of self-determination set in opposition to both natural inclinations and particular human communities.

Wordsworth differs from Kant, first, in that he reads the uncanny experience of the sublime not as a sign of the subject's moral freedom but as a revelation of the subject's imaginative freedom. This kind of "revision" of Kant, whereby imaginative freedom is conceived as the source of all freedom, is characteristic of romantic poetry and returns later in Nietzsche's concept of the creative will to power. Yet this means that Wordsworth also differs from Kant in that for him the experience of the sublime, rather than simply reaffirming a moral vocation, transports the imagination into a solitude that threatens to subvert a stable social self and so to subvert a moral vocation understood in a conventional, rather than a Kantian, sense. Herein lies a fundamental difference between Kant and Wordsworth: Kant's conception of the ethical, if universalist, is also individualist, while Wordsworth's conception of the ethical could be loosely called conventionalist. Though Wordsworth nowhere articulates anything like an ethical theory, all of his writings indicate that he thinks of the ethical primarily as a domain of common norms, habits, and sympathies that operate as relational bonds within a given community: bonds, then, that restrain our existential freedom and temper our imaginative extravagance. Hence the tension between a longing for imaginative extravagance (Hartman's "apocalypse") and a search for relational embeddedness (Hartman's "akedah") to which Wordsworth testifies throughout *The Prelude*.

Wordsworth, to some extent akin to Lyotard in this respect, presents the sublime as a visitation that produces (as Hartman puts it) a discontinuity in the self. But for Wordsworth, in this respect akin to Kant, this dislocation of the self from the cramped boundaries of the everyday ego, experienced as a sweeping across the self of otherwise hidden power, is at the same time a metamorphosis of the self in a widened zone of being. Yet this movement is anxiously perceived to disrupt the anchored self of everyday ethical habits and relationships. One of Wordsworth's major responses to this anxiety—one that organizes the shape of *The Prelude*—is to recuperate his sublime experiences of uncanny awakening as animating moments within a larger dialectical narrative of self-formation. The dislocative awakenings and their strange amplitudes are in this way woven into the texture of a coherent self. Yet, as we have seen, this dialectic of self-formation does not wholly persuade Wordsworth himself that he has genuinely returned from the weather of solitary illumination to the weather of everyday ethical relationship. A path of self-formation, while doubtless of importance to our ethical lives, does not necessarily dovetail with an ethic of obligation or an ethic of relationship. Self-formation in solitude is just that, a solitary adventure, and solitude is not the primary place of ethics. Thus Wordsworth's anxiety remains always in his path. It is a path that, insofar as it conceives of the ethical as a mundane and quotidian affair, poses a challenge to those philosophic discourses that conceive of the ethical as a sublime affair.

In *The Sovereignty of Good* Iris Murdoch presents an incisive critique of a long Kantian tradition in modern ethics. It is perhaps no accident that this book was written by a philosopher who wrote novels. For one of Murdoch's concerns is to criticize the blind emphasis that a long tradition of moral philosophy has placed on the heroic will of the isolated individual:

> We are still living in the age of the Kantian man, or Kantian man-god. Kant's conclusive exposure of the so-called proofs of the existence of God, his analysis of the limitations of speculative reason, together with his eloquent portrayal of the dignity of rational man, has had results which might possibly dismay him. How recognizable, how familiar to us, is the man so beautifully portrayed in the *Grundlegung*, who confronted even with Christ turns away to consider the judgment of his own conscience and to hear the voice of his own reason. Stripped of the exiguous metaphysical background which Kant was prepared to allow him, this man is with us still, free, independent, lonely, powerful, rational, responsible, brave, the hero of so many novels and books of moral philosophy. The

raison d'être of this attractive but misleading creature is not far to seek. He is the offspring of the age of science, confidently rational and yet increasingly aware of his alienation from the material universe which his discoveries reveal; and since he is not Hegelian (Kant, not Hegel, has provided Western ethics with its dominating image) his alienation is without cure. He is the ideal citizen of the liberal state, a warning held up to tyrants. He has the virtue which the age requires and admires, courage. It is not such a long step from Kant to Nietzsche, and from Nietzsche to existentialism and Anglo-Saxon ethical doctrines which in some ways closely resemble it. In fact Kant's man had already received a glorious incarnation nearly a century earlier in the work of Milton: his proper name is Lucifer.[35]

Murdoch indicates her unease with the way this tradition locates the source of all value in the alienated will. Yet her primary objection is that the rational individual of this tradition of ethical thought is "alien" and "implausible" (SG, 10), in other words, that this individual is naively and melodramatically imagined in a way that has little to do with the way we live (or fail to live) the ethical dimension of our lives. For we do not, Murdoch argues, relate ethically to others on the basis of decisions made in a sublime solitude, whether that of an interiority in relation to a rational law or that of an interiority in relation to a transcendent command. Rather, we relate ethically to others on the basis of norms we have inherited and are continually in the process of weighing, habits we have acquired and are continually in the process of revising. Murdoch, who at times reads like a kind of post-Freudian Platonist, understands ethics to be inseparable from the continual reeducation of our "eros" and "attention," the continual reorientation of our "desires" and "energies." Ethics, then, can be described as a practical art that, requiring a capacity for intuitive responses and agile divinations, remains mundane through and through, a quotidian path, not a sublime height. One might want to object that in a century like ours, in which isolated individuals have been placed under extreme pressure by all sorts of violent governments, the image of what Murdoch calls "Kantian man" remains noble and painfully relevant. There is cogency in this objection. Yet it is an objection to which Murdoch has a cogent response: while it is always possible, of course, that an individual under pressure will be undone by pain and fear, it is also true that an individual is likely to act in a crisis in a way consonant with the *kind of person* which that individual has become through time, along a path of gradually formed ethical norms, habits, perspectives, forms of attention:

If we ignore the prior work of attention and notice only the emptiness of the moment of choice we are likely to identify freedom with the outward movement since there is nothing else to identify it with. But if we consider what the work of attention is like, how continuously it goes on, and how imperceptibly it builds up structures of value round about us, we shall not be surprised that at crucial moments of choice most of the business of choosing is already over. This does not imply that we are not free, certainly not. But it implies that the exercise of our freedom is a small piecemeal business which goes on all the time and not a grandiose leaping about unimpeded at important moments. The moral life, on this view, is something that goes on continually, not something that is switched off in between the occurrence of explicit moral choices. What happens in between such choices is indeed what is crucial. (SG, 37)

This is a sobering passage. Murdoch, I think, in criticizing a long Kantian tradition of moral philosophy, presents a powerful defense of Wordsworth's implicit conception of the ethical as a social domain of basic norms and relational bearings: a domain, hence, whose relation to the extravagant adventures of a lonely individual, or to the quiet adventures of a solitary path of self-formation, is likely to remain always unstable, the task of relating these different domains, then, coming to light as a task always to be taken up anew. Murdoch's criticism of this Kantian tradition, further, would seem to pertain just as well to the variation on Kantian ethics that one encounters in Levinas. For Levinas, in tipping Kant upside down, in turning the active hero of responsibility into the passive martyr of responsibility, remains within the solitary realm of the sublime: the "other" whom he claims to bring into this domain—a transcendent "other" exerting a divinely annihilative force upon the natural self—is no less remote than Kant's "moral law" from the concrete ethical tasks we are called to undertake, and the concrete human beings we come to encounter, in our daily lives.[36]

WHERE DOES LYOTARD stand in relation to these questions? Between the seventies and the nineties he articulates two different accounts of the sublime, a Nietzschean and a Heideggerian account, and the exact way in which he makes this shift is a crucial question raised by his work.

In the seventies and the early eighties, as we have seen, Lyotard's account of the sublime, while amply informed by the vocabulary of Wittgenstein and speech act theory, is guided above all by a Nietzschean reading of modernist art (and supplemented by a bohemian ethos of nomadic iconoclasm). The sublime is read as a manifestation of the subject's power of invention, its capacity to bring into being languages, perspectives, and criteria of judgment that did not exist prior to the play of creative action itself. A sublime work is a sounding of the unforeseeable. This Nietzschean elucidation of the experimental adventures of modernism is unmistakably rooted in a romantic valorization of creative power, inventive power that discloses unforeseen horizons, though now a romantic vocabulary of imagination and psychic transformation has been displaced by a modernist vocabulary of technical élan and formal experimentation (Nietzsche, a theorist and performer of both *power* and *style,* can readily be turned into the hinge of this translation from a romantic to a modernist rhetoric). Yet Wordsworth and Lyotard, in this Nietzschean phase of his trajectory, differ in the way they understand the ethical and political implications of any such manifestation of creative power. If for Wordsworth the awakening of such power threatens to disrupt the realm of ordinary norms and habits, for Lyotard it is precisely this creative disruption of ordinary norms and habits that bears an ethical and political promise (thus, an ironist might say, is a modernist bohemianism recoded as a philosophic ethics). The Kantian analogy between a sublime aesthetic experience and a sublime moral vocation—felt by Wordsworth to be no less a tension than an analogy—is in this way retained by Lyotard.

In the late eighties and the nineties, however, Lyotard passes through a philosophic reorientation that leads him to revise his earlier reading of modernism. The departure from conventional modes of representation characteristic of modernist art is now read less as a manifestation of inventive power than as a presentation of an indeterminacy that, unsynthesizable, deposes the appropriative subject constructed by a thoroughly instrumentalized society. The sublime is conceived as the sign not of a Nietzschean "will to power" but of a Heideggerian "letting be." For Lyotard, this kind of testimony to the indeterminate, insofar as it resists the imperatives of a technocratic society and its correlative subjects of instrumental cognition and action, clearly bears an ethical as well as a political valence.

There are two questions I would like to address to this later discourse of Lyotard's. The first has to do with the ethical and political implications that Lyotard ascribes to the presentation of sublime indeterminacy. Is the event that Lyotard describes as a "deposing" of consciousness any less problematically linked to the ethical (not to mention the political) than are the events that Wordsworth evokes as moments of sublime awakening? After all, Wordsworth, like most nineteenth-century romantics and their modernist descendants, also understands the sublime to be a departure from the imperatives of theoretical cognition and the habits of the everyday subject of instrumental action. Further, as Wordsworth dialectically recuperates his uncanny visitations of creative power within a narrative of self-formation, so Lyotard dialectically recuperates his uncanny visitations of indeterminate presentations within a discursive meditation on their significance. What I mean to suggest is that Lyotard's later discourse of the sublime, largely borrowed from Heidegger, is a discourse of existential self-formation, a meditation on a mode of existential dwelling in relation to an elusive "there is" whereby the world appears, and hence a meditation whose relation to the ethical and the political, as Wordsworth performatively reveals throughout *The Prelude,* remains far more troubled than Lyotard implies. The later Heidegger evokes a mode of existential dwelling, a meditative openness to the mystery of the fourfold and the temporal mystery of the "non-representable" difference between beings and Being. But for Heidegger himself this path seems to have remained remote from any ethical or political concern for other persons: "The one point I would urge in dealing with Heidegger," John Caputo writes, "is that he tends to be a little more interested in letting jugs and bridges be and to let it go at that, and he never quite gets around to letting *others* be, to our being-with others as mortals, to the fellowship or community of mortals." Caputo immediately adds that, since Heidegger himself does not make this turn, "we will do it for him."[37] One issue I have sought to underline in this chapter is that Wordsworth, while thoroughly concerned with making this kind of turn, resonantly testifies to its complexity. *The Prelude,* at the performative level, thus teaches a caution we would do well to adopt, I believe, in thinking through the "analogies" *and* the "tensions" between modes of existential dwelling and modes of ethical relationship.

Another question I wish to raise is whether the event that Lyotard describes as a "deposing" of consciousness is, finally, as far as Lyotard suggests from a romantic or modernist event of awakened creative power. Put another way, does the later Lyotard's account of the sublime express a "fact" or a "desire"? One can hardly evade a recognition of the fact that Lyotard, if he *thematizes* a deposed consciousness, manifestly *writes* as a self-assertive and often polemically oracular consciousness. It is possible, then, to approach Lyotard's Heideggerian account of the sublime less as an account immediately inviting either assent or dissent than as an account demanding elucidation from another perspective, specifically, a perspective that would question the meaning of a will to disavow one's own self-assertive or synthetic power, a will to idealize a destitute consciousness that may be remote indeed from one's own experience of subjectivity. It may be that the figure of a destitute consciousness is the figure that a longing for sublime departure tends to take in an age of rampant functionalist systems and their dominant models of instrumental reason and conduct. This might also allow one to elucidate the ease with which Lyotard, while deploying a Kantian and Wittgensteinian vocabulary, moves from a Nietzschean to a Heideggerian reading of the modernist sublime. The search for a path beyond a one-dimensional society and its correlative models of the instrumental subject would provide the deeper continuity beneath the striking discontinuity. Nietzsche and Heidegger would be different sides, as it were, of a shared late romantic response to the nihilism of a functionalist society working to reduce human beings to efficient robots.

TO NO SMALL extent, as Charles Taylor argues in his *Hegel and Modern Society*, we still dwell in a cultural climate generated by the ambivalent response of romantic writers to the project of the Enlightenment. As I've underlined earlier in this chapter, modern culture is significantly shaped by a tension between the ideal of "radical freedom" and the ideal of "expressive wholeness," a search for extravagance and a search for relationship, a path of sublime departure and a path of nostalgic return, or what Hartman, in elucidating Wordsworth's poetry, calls "apocalypse" and "akedah." If the beautiful is typically associated with reconciliation or return, the sublime is typically associated with exodus or departure.

Blake writes as a prophet of the sublime way of visionary departure. This orientation is naturalized by Nietzsche and plausibly aligned by Lyotard with the experimental adventures of modernist art. Without the visionary action of the prophetic Los, Blake teaches, we are trapped in a nihilism of mechanical reason and the death-in-life of the unhappy selfhood's blind rancors and aggressions. Without the unpredictable action of the inventive Joyce, the Lyotard of the seventies teaches, we are trapped in a nihilism of technocratic reason and the death-in-life of the instrumental ego's blind erasures of difference.

Heidegger would seem to write as a sage of a radically different orientation of romanticism. Yet, at the same time, though he studiously avoids the term "sublime," he quietly reimagines this other orientation as itself the way of sublime othering: the way of a heightened receptivity to a mystery that, always beyond us as well as always near us, promises to alter our mode of being in the world insofar as we patiently turn toward it.[38] With only the creative action of a productive Los, Heidegger teaches, without a quieting of the will (or what

Wordsworth calls a "wise passiveness") that opens us to the self-concealing clearing of Being (or what Wordsworth calls "the light of things"), we are trapped in a nihilism of "the logic of enframing" and the solipsistic violence of the heroic will. Without the indeterminate presentations of avantgarde painting that depose consciousness, the Lyotard of the late eighties teaches, we are trapped in a nihilism of technocratic reason and the reduction of alterity effected by the active subject programmed to synthesize everything it encounters.

Wordsworth, oscillating between an imaginative extravagance he cannot live without and a relational embeddedness he cannot live without, unfolds his spacious and troubled adventure between the extremes of a long romantic and postromantic tradition. It is worth noting that Lyotard shifts from an extreme Nietzschean perspective to an extreme Heideggerian perspective without pausing, it would seem, to consider the far more troubled "middle ground" from which a Wordsworth writes. This is perhaps the ambiguous place where most of us dwell.

What the thinkers in this long poly-tradition share is a conviction that the instrumental stance of the empirical ego is an anxious, defensive mask for a creature no longer truly alive. The sublime is then variously conceived as the promise of a departure from the hell of this death-in-life. Where the thinkers in this poly-tradition differ, of course, is in their account of the "nature" or the "dynamics" of this departure: does it involve an uncanny awakening to metamorphic powers that alter and widen one's being, or does it involve a quieting of powers that opens one to some strangeness that haunts while remaining other to one's being?

It is clear that it is the latter thought that fascinates some of the most important Continental philosophers of the last century, from Adorno and Heidegger, in their very different ways, through Blanchot, Levinas, Derrida, and the later Lyotard, among others. Important currents of twentieth-century Continental philosophy, in other words, indicate that we have grown suspicious of our own experiences of awakening, frightened by our own moments of released power, repelled by the very discourse of the sublime that we remain magnetically drawn toward, a discourse that, perhaps for this very reason, has in recent years been recoded as an ethical discourse of messianic openness to the other. No longer trusting our powers, are we now inclined, like the mystics of diverse religious traditions, to thematize our awakenings as destitutions for the sake of a sublimely transcendent other? Do we thus confuse a language of sublime self-dispossession—one of our culture's oldest languages of religious transcendence—with the language of ethical relationship? Do we thus confuse our desire for a renovative passage out of hell with the difficult yet mundane demands of an ethical relationship? I fear the answer to these questions may be yes: that we do not understand ourselves insofar as we have not clarified the "genealogy" of some currently prominent discourses of great power by which we are clearly fascinated.

A full account of why these discourses have recently been rearticulated in such striking ways would, I imagine, require telling a history of the twentieth century. For one would have to bring into a discussion of these discourses a clarification of the complex historical context in which they have emerged, a context that includes, among other events, the immense shadow cast on European culture by the increasing commodification and instrumentalization of all spheres of society over the last century, the hell of destruction into which Europe descended between 1914 and 1945, the devastating violence of the Holocaust, and the enormously destructive wars between imperialist and anti-imperialist powers of the early postwar period. It may indeed be a while before the most sensitive and alert minds of Europe can again begin to trust any promise in a renovation of our constructive powers. Their current distrust of any promise of that sort surely poses a challenge to some of the most important artistic and philosophic orientations of European modernity. Yet this distrust will cease to be a challenge as soon as it becomes (as, in fact, it is already becoming) a new dogma of routine invocations.[39]

CHAPTER TWO

Faustian Quest in Rimbaud, Nietzsche, and Bataille

The theme of creative destruction and destructive creation, whose origins lie in ancient apocalyptic thought, has been revived again and again throughout the modern period. And from Marlow through Mann, whether directly or indirectly, it has often been accompanied by the myth of Faust.

This myth hovers around the extravagant adventures of Rimbaud, Nietzsche, and Bataille. It is a myth that tells of a quest for demonic, superhuman powers, powers permitting one, for example, to change life through visionary metamorphosis (Rimbaud), to bring into being an exceptionally creative existence on the other side of a long history of nihilism (Nietzsche), or to attain an ecstatic release from the structures regulating social identity and social purpose (Bataille). The myth, further, associates the discovery of such powers with an antinomian passage beyond conventional moral codes, a searching out of extreme borders of experience, an impatience with what passes for the reality principle among the weary and the unimaginative, a willingness to risk a shipwreck of the self, and a nocturnal descent, in one way or another, to an abyss where some creative light beyond our chronically dim clarity is thought to abide. "Dans une magnifique demeure cernée par l'Orient entier," Rimbaud writes in "Vies," "j'ai accompli mon immense oeuvre et passé mon illustre retraite. J'ai brassé mon sang. Mon devoir m'est remis. Il ne faut même plus songer à cela. Je suis réellement d'outre-tombe, et pas de commissions [In a magnificent residence surrounded by the entire Orient I completed my immense *oeuvre* and spent my illustrious retirement. I stirred up my blood. My duty has been remitted. It need not even be thought of anymore. I am really from beyond the grave, and without commissions]" (O, 265; CP, 247). Nietzsche and Bataille often speak in similar terms. These three writers present themselves as explorers whose authority resides at least in part in their having traveled to extremes. The Faustian quest is guided by the now glowing, now darkening Book of Excess, one that teaches, according to a proverb of hell recorded by Blake, that "the road of excess leads to the palace of wisdom."[1]

Yet it may be that an unceasing dynamic of destructive creation is the very pulse of modernity itself. In the opening section of *The Communist Manifesto*, Marx describes modern capitalism in just these Faustian terms:

> The bourgeoisie has disclosed how it came to pass that the brutal display of vigour in the Middle Ages, which Reactionists so much admire, found its fitting complement in the most slothful indolence. It has been the first to show what man's activity can bring about. It has accomplished wonders far surpassing Egyptian pyramids, Roman aqueducts, and Gothic cathedrals; it has conducted expeditions that put in the shade all former Exoduses of nations and crusades.
>
> The bourgeoisie cannot exist without constantly revolutionising the instruments of production, and thereby the relations of production, and with them the whole relations of society. Conservation of the old modes of production in an unaltered form was, on the contrary, the first condition of existence for all earlier industrial classes. Constant revolutionising of production, uninterrupted disturbance of all social conditions, everlasting uncertainty and agitation distinguish the bourgeois epoch from all earlier ones. All fixed, fast-frozen relations, with their train of ancient and venerable prejudices and opinions, are swept away, all new-formed ones become antiquated before they can ossify. All that is solid melts into air, all that is holy is profaned, and man is at last compelled to face with sober senses his real conditions of life, and his relations with his kind.[2]

This is the central text in Marshall Berman's interpretation of modernity in *All That Is Solid Melts into Air*. Bringing together Goethe and Marx, in particular *Faust* and *The Communist Manifesto*, Berman argues, first, that both these writers characterize capitalist modernity as a process of perpetual upheaval, and second, that both emphasize the enormous extent to which modern *socioeconomic* dynamics of development and modern *existential* or *psychological* dynamics of development are intertwined with one another. According to this account, an anxious celebration of developmental plasticity, an ambivalent fascination with destructively creative transformation, is the basic dynamic of modern capitalism *and* of modern culture. We are inspired and elated, as it were, by the same Faustian dynamics that frighten and disorient us. Yet, though Marx occasionally appears troubled by the potentially nihilist implications of the transformative dynamics he describes, he nonetheless maintains his faith in the power of critical reason and cooperative action to steer the demonic chaos of capitalism toward a clarified realm of communism. Other Faustian visionaries of the modern era, including those discussed in this chapter, have found any such faith and project not only implausible but, in some respects, blind.³

Rimbaud, Nietzsche, and Bataille, then, like many important voices of the last two centuries, are "modern antimoderns" in at least the sense that they draw on the energies unleashed by the very modernity they contest, those vertiginous forces of destructive creation evoked by Marx in *The Communist Manifesto*. Yet where Marx sees a chaos, Rimbaud, Nietzsche, and Bataille see a cage. Where Marx advocates a political program of rational, secular, and cooperative communist revolution, Rimbaud, Nietzsche, and Bataille advocate metamorphic projects of transrational, quasi-religious, and largely anarchist revolution. And while Marx writes as a voice of the Enlightenment, confident in the power of rational human action to pilot the "demonic" energies of modernity toward a coherent outcome, Rimbaud, Nietzsche, and Bataille write as voices of the romantic critique of the Enlightenment, critical of the reification of the human person effected by the proliferating "rationalized" structures of modernity. Their contestation of the world they inhabit thus resonates with a wildness at odds with the rational revolutionary spirit of Marx. A *dérèglement de tous les sens,* in one fashion or another, is conceived by all three as the path of any transformation that would disclose a genuinely widened horizon of existence. Rimbaud's path of apocalyptic destruction and visionary invocation, Nietzsche's path of joyous negation and creative transvaluation, Bataille's path of destructive expenditure and awakened sovereignty: these are all dynamics of "going under" and "crossing over," to recall one of Zarathustra's figures, that express a similar experience of revolt and metamorphosis. The fetters of organized unfreedom are to be shattered in order to release buried creative energies; indeed, the shattering itself tends to be felt as the beginning of the creative crossing. "I love those who do not know how to live, except by going under, for they are those who cross over" (Z, 15).

Rimbaud, Nietzsche, and Bataille, in other words, tend to imagine transformative passages beyond the very bounds and terms of modernity. Their exorbitance in this regard is manifest not least in their shared allegiance to a solar metaphysic of boundless energy. The poems of Rimbaud's *Dernier Vers*, at times hauntingly hermetic, appear to express a longing for some passage into sheer luminosity. "Âme sentinelle, / Murmurons l'aveu / De la nuit si nulle / Et du jour en feu [Sentinel soul, / Let us whisper the vow / Of the night so nothing / And the day on fire]" (O, 160; CP, 217), he writes in one of his most beautiful poems, evoking a metamorphic fire at the core of things. Zarathustra, having begun his quest by likening his "overflowing" abundance to that of the sun, concludes it by emerging from his cave "glowing and strong as a morning sun that comes out of dark mountains" (Z, 327). Bataille theorizes a "general economy" based on a solar excess streaming over the planet, thereby recasting in cosmic terms Zarathustra's conception of the "gift-giving virtue" that spends itself freely out of a life-affirming will to power: "The origin and essence of our wealth are given in the radiation of the sun, which dispenses energy—wealth—without any return" (AS, 1:28). It is as though these writers were drawn toward a metaphysic of transformative energy that each lived as a kind of intuitive experience of the world: one need only think of Rimbaud's experience of his body and mind alike as zones of theatrical unfolding, Nietzsche's sense of life as the recurrent rising and setting of the will to power, and Bataille's perception of the world as an unclosed field of energies communicating with one another beyond any "restricted economy" of utility. Each in his own way sets an intuition of "the pure streaming of infinite life," as Rimbaud invokes this sort of power in an early poem (O, 41; CP, 73), against the reifying structures of the modern social and economic order.

At the same time, however, each evokes the pressure exerted by those structures that block any play of metamorphic power. Figures of constriction and mutilated life appear in their writings as frequently as do figures of expansion and renovated life. "Verily, my friends," Zarathustra says, sounding a motif closely echoed in Rimbaud and Bataille, "I walk among men as among the fragments and limbs of men. This is what is terrible for my eyes, that I find man in ruins and scattered as over a battlefield or a butcherfield. And when my eyes flee from the now to the past, they always find the same: fragments and limbs and dreadful accidents—but no human beings" (Z, 138). All three, therefore, affirm that a movement destroying the structures that have ruined us—structures at once internal and external—is inseparable from a movement unloosing buried powers. A destructive voyage through the dark, a Faustian version of the "dark night of the soul," is imagined as the path leading to a creative light and an altered horizon. This is of course a familiar mythic and religious pattern, one of particular importance in apocalyptic, gnostic, and mystical traditions.

Another important affinity among these writers, then, lies in the way they articulate their paths of revolt and metamorphosis in terms of displaced religious dynamics, above all dynamics of self-transcendence and creative crossing. Few readers fail to recognize this sort of dynamic in Rimbaud's apocalyptic quest. Most recognize it in Bataille's atheistic mysticism of departure in the void. Yet readers of Nietzsche, often taking his denunciations of Christianity as though they were the last word on the matter, tend seriously to underestimate the displaced "heterodox Protestantism" animating his project in a way akin to the way it animates that of Blake (who spells out Nietzsche's critique of orthodox Christian morality as nihilist *ressentiment* a hundred years before Nietzsche). That Rimbaud, Nietzsche, and Bataille all repudiate orthodox Christian metaphysics, and reinterpret traditional accounts of religious transcendence, is hardly surprising, for the revolt against any fixed authority external to the reach of creative power, and the reimagining of transcendence, are guiding currents of the romantic tradition in which they participate. But they are no more inclined than Blake to abandon the baffling call of transcendence, of creative self-surpassing. The linguistic energy of their texts derives not least from just this tension, a continual wrestling that generates a range of quasi-Christian, anti-Christian, and extra-Christian tropes.[4]

It is true that one pays for such extravagance. As the entire romantic tradition shows, Faustian adventures of this sort inevitably lead to crises, variously experienced as a loss of creative power (and so a return to the ruin one had inititally sought to surpass), a fear of solipsism, a free fall of self-destruction, or an exhausting collision with a network of "reality principles" both natural and social. Rimbaud, Nietzsche, and Bataille, at various points in their trajectories, directly engage the limits and fears with which they collide. Rimbaud and Nietzsche, in fact, both write texts that can be characterized as romantic "crisis texts": *Une Saison en enfer* and, in a very odd way, *Thus Spoke Zarathustra*. Bataille, on the other hand, having traced a mutation in this tradition of Faustian quest by reimagining crisis *as* transcendence, explores his collision with the limits of historical actuality in a quite different way; he undertakes the unlikely project of weaving together a Hegelian marxist theory of historical development and a displaced religious theory of rapturous negation of the given.

The quests and the crises explored by Rimbaud, Nietzsche, and Bataille, in their further articulations, have been among the most influential currents in "avantgarde" poetry and philosophy over the last century (above all in France). An understanding of the stakes of such later projects, then, would seem to demand an understanding of these earlier adventures of revolt and metamorphosis. In this chapter I would like to illuminate some of the important affinities among these three Faustian writers and then to clarify the way Bataille, while drawing on themes sounded in both Rimbaud and Nietzsche, significantly departs from them. His swerve, marking a decisive change in cultural weather, has had a greater resonance in postwar French thought than is always recognized on this side of the Atlantic.

RIMBAUD

The apocalyptic imagination, in its many expressions, always proposes at least two visions: first, a vision of "two worlds," a visible fallen world of the present and a hidden redemptive world to come, and second, a vision of destructive renovation, a dynamic that promises at once to sweep away the fallen world and to reveal the renovated world. The variously elaborated "internalizations" of this apocalyptic model—whether in gnosticism, mysticism, or Inner Light Protestantism—tend to temper (when not to dismiss) the model's historical vector while retaining its dynamic of destructive renovation and so its emphatic valorization of the motion of creative crossing: a motion that transports the subject from a condition of ruin to a condition of newness. It is this motion that Rimbaud variously enacts throughout his adventure. He is a voyager seeking to discover a gnostic amplitude on the plane of immanence. Thus the exceptional flights of élan, as well as the exceptional rendings, of his writings.[5]

While Rimbaud pursues his quest in multiple ways, there are perhaps two defining "poles" of dynamic passage in his poetry. The first, for which he is best known, could be characterized as metamorphic multiplication and self-multiplication. The best guide to this mode may be a striking assertion in *Une Saison en enfer:* "A chaque être, plusieurs *autres* vies me semblaient dues [To me it seemed that to every being several *other* lives were owed]" (O, 233; CP, 334). A second pole of passage, explored most poignantly in the so-called *Derniers Vers* of 1872, could be characterized as the passionate evanescence of the self in light. The best guide to this mode may be another remarkable assertion in *Une Saison:* "Enfin, ô bonheur, ô raison, j'écartais du ciel l'azur qui est du noir, et je vécus, étincelle d'or de la lumière *nature* [At last, oh happiness, oh reason, I removed from the sky the blue which is darkness, and I lived, a spark of gold of the light of nature]" (O, 232; CP, 333). At one extreme of his experience, then, Rimbaud explores theatrical, expansive, metamorphic multiplications of himself and the things and places he encounters, while at another extreme he evokes a kind of translation of the self into the sweep of light. His abiding antagonist is the pressure of the given, including the "given" self, felt as an unbearable mudlike fixity: "Ah! la poudre des saules qu'une aile secoue! / Les roses de roseaux dès longtemps dévorées! / Mon canot, toujours fixe; et sa chaîne tirée / Au fond de cet oeil d'eau sans bords,—à quelle boue? [Ah! the pollen of the willows that a wing shakes! / The roses of the reeds long since eaten away! / My boat still held fast; and its chain tugged / To the bottom of this borderless eye of water—to what mud?]" (O, 178; CP, 202).

Achieving a gradual extrication from this sort of mud is no part of Rimbaud's ambition. He seeks a pitched departure from it, as though only an apocalyptic pulse could bear him toward a hidden force of the infinite blowing through the finite. Jean-Pierre Richard has well described this sense in which Rimbaud is the poet of creative passage par excellence:

> At the origins of the world, then, there was a bird-spring [oiseau-source]. But even before these origins, what "mother" reality, what folded wing, what infra-source? . . . Paradox of a new *cogito*—one thinks me, therefore I become—which constitutes the key to the entire Rimbaldian adventure. The mystery Rimbaud's poetry interrogates is precisely that of this passage, of this advent of the same toward the other, by virtue of which movement the night passes into the day, the past into the future, nothingness into being. It is the mystery of creation.
>
> Let us see in the *Illuminations,* then, an effort, perhaps the most complete undertaken by any modern writer, to live humanly this mystery.[6]

This mystery of creation, of the creative sweeping through the created, is called by Rimbaud "la vie infinie" in both an early hymn to the marriage of sun and earth, "Soleil et chair," and a later hymn to a force of renovation, "Génie." To attempt to find this mystery with the intensity with which Rimbaud does is to open oneself to passages of sheer bewilderment, as many of his poems and a number of his talismanic words for creative release (*dégagement, envol, voler, en avant*) indicate clearly enough. At times beside himself, at times projecting himself beyond his circumstances, at times swept beyond any context, he continually turns in search of a force of departure. "La vie fleurit par le travail, vieille vérité: moi, ma vie n'est pas assez pesante, elle s'envole et flotte loin au-dessus de l'action, ce cher point du monde [Life flowers through work, an old truth: as for me, my life isn't heavy enough, it takes flight and drifts far above action, that cherished point of the world]" (O, 218; CP, 311). Rimbaud's signature quickness is the pulse of this search, that of a poet enacting a drama of metamorphic premonition, always, like the seven-year-old poet alone in his dark room, "pressentant violemment la voile! [violently anticipating sails!]" (O, 97; CP, 127). It would seem that the premonitions of another life are to be found everywhere, in the body, in the mind, in the surrounding world, in other persons. But as Rimbaud indicates on various occasions, they perhaps begin in the haunted texture of language. "A noir, E blanc, I rouge, U vert, O bleu: voyelles, / Je dirai quelque jour vos naissances latentes [A black, E white, I red, U green, O blue: vowels, / I shall someday tell your latent births]" (O, 110; CP, 171).

WHILE THE "VOYANT" letters of May 1871 can hardly be taken as precise threads promising to lead one through the labyrinth of Rimbaud's poems, they do spell out at least three basic lines of thought shaping his poetry. One of these is the marriage of Bakunin and Faust, the interweaving of the impetus of anarchist revolt and the impetus of visionary transformation. An apocalyptic impatience reverberates in all of Rimbaud's work, making itself variously heard in visions of sheer destruction, fantasies of sudden departure, and bitterly ironic mockeries of both the world around him and his own passions. This conception of the intimate relationship between destruction and metamorphosis resonates with the romantic Satanism circulating throughout nineteenth-century French culture, Satanism in this context functioning as a trope for "enlightened" political and cultural opposition to a broad array of conservative and reactionary forces in French society and for an existential affirmation of imaginative freedom. "Satanic revolt," in other words, is the analogue in French romantic writing—lasting all the way through and beyond surrealism—of what in English-language romantic writing tends to be cast as a "revolt against sky gods" and all their worldly and internalized representatives.[7]

A second imporant theme of Rimbaud's "voyant" letters is the criticism of "subjective" and "modern" poetry in the name of "objective" and "ancient" or "future" poetry. This sort of evaluative opposition is hardly unusual in romantic and modernist culture, expressing as it does an anxious frustration with the "merely subjective" that is variously voiced by a range of poets running from Keats through Mallarmé and Eliot, among many others. The accent Rimbaud places on this hierarchy is a concern with visionary, transpersonal revelation. Thus the project of "un long, immense et raisonné *dérèglement* de *tous les sens* [a long, immense, and reasoned *disordering* of *all the senses*]"—where "sens" suggests at once perceptual senses, discursive meanings, and spatial directions—is conceived not as an end in itself, but as a means of disclosing an expansive harmony, a widened field of vision (O, 348; CP, 10). Dissolution is but a phase of freedom, disclosure, and linguistic transformation. "One must still have chaos in oneself to be able to give birth to a dancing star," as Zarathustra later affirms (Z, 17), it being clear that the bringing to birth of a dancing star is the task. Tellingly, the figures that Rimbaud provides to exemplify his famous assertions that "On me pense" and "Je est un autre" are figures of pieces of matter awaking to find themselves musical instruments (O, 346, 347; CP, 6, 9). As passing through discordance is the chosen path of these letters, so becoming harmony is their projected horizon.[8]

What kind of harmony is this? It doesn't appear to be anything especially stable. "Un coup de ton doigt sur le tambour décharge tous les sons et commence la nouvelle harmonie [A blow of your finger on the drum releases all sounds and begins the new harmony]," a hymnal voice affirms in "À une raison" (O, 268; CP, 249). While Rimbaud's shifting, at times cryptic, understanding of *l'harmonie* may finally drift beyond the borders of clear conceptual retrieval, one can at least begin to approch this mystery by noting the way it is closely linked in the "voyant" letters with two of the major cults of French romanticism, the cult of universal analogy and the cult of synaesthetic transport. Another important theme in these letters is the distinctive inflection Rimbaud gives these romantic ideals. Setting beside one another a couple of suggestive passages in the second "voyant" letter brings this out:

> Car JE est un autre. Si le cuivre s'éveille clairon, il n'y a rien de sa faute. Cela m'est évident: j'assiste à l'éclosion de ma pensée: je la regarde, je l'écoute: je lance un coup d'archet: la symphonie fait son remuement dans les profondeurs, ou vient d'un bond sur la scène. [For I is an other. If the brass wakes up a trumpet, it's not its fault. To me this is evident: I witness the unfolding of my thought: I watch it, I listen to it: I make a stroke of the bow: the symphony begins to stir in the depths, or bounds onto the stage.]

100 • THE EXTRAVAGANT

[Le poète] est chargé de l'humanité, des *animaux* même; il devra faire sentir, palper, écouter ses inventions; si ce qu'il rapporte de *là-bas* a forme, il donne forme; si c'est informe, il donne l'informe. Trouver une langue.... Cette langue sera de l'âme pour l'âme, résumant tout, parfums, sons, couleurs, de la pensée accrochant la pensée et tirant. Le poëte définirait la quantité d'inconnu s'éveillant en son temps dans l'âme universelle.

[(The poet) is responsible for humanity, even for the *animals;* he must create inventions that can be smelled, touched, heard; if what he brings back from *over there* has form, he delivers form; if it is formless, he delivers the formless. To find a language.... This language will be of the soul for the soul, gathering everything, fragrances, sounds, colors, thought latching onto thought and pulling. The poet would define the amount of the unknown awakening in the universal soul in his time.] (O, 349–50; CP, 9–12)

There are surely political valences at work in these passages, echoes of nineteenth-century utopians' dreams of a new society promising "the new harmony, the new love, and the new men" (O, 268; CP, 249), "the joy of the new work" (O, 277; CP, 260), and "the fraternal awakening of all choral and orchestral energies" (O, 293; CP, 295). And probably there are occultist valences at work as well, echoes of the hermeticist vision of a universe in which *tout se tient.* Yet it is above all the romantic vision of resonant "analogy" or "correspondence" and synaesthetic transport that Rimbaud echoes in these passages. In fact, he all but cites Baudelaire directly. The adoration of the supple, the undulant, the synaesthetic amplitude of interwoven senses "having the expansion of infinite things," as Baudelaire writes in a famous sonnet, is expressed everywhere in Baudelaire's verse and prose. It is this sort of expansive transport that Rimbaud associates with synaesthetic harmony. What, then, is distinctive about his allegiance to this romantic ideal? First, as these passages hint, and as all his poetry demonstrates, Rimbaud lends this vision a *concrete dynamism* all his own. As he writes in the same letter, "la poésie ne rhythmera plus l'action; elle *sera en avant* [poetry will no longer take its rhythm from action; it *will be ahead*]" (O, 350; CP, 13). He is concerned less with the quiet, evocative distances of reverie than with the volatile, sweeping passages of synaesthetic voyage.[9] Further, Rimbaud understands this vision to involve, in an emphatic sense, an experience of *palpable metamorphosis:* metamorphosis of language, of perception, and of self. In perhaps the most remarkable lines of these letters, Rimbaud speaks of "witnessing the unfolding of his thought," watching and listening to it as it traverses him, as though he perceived his own thought to arrive apparitionally from another region of force (an experience more fully and dramatically evoked, it would seem, in the carnival of "Villes II" [O, 276–77; CP, 259–60]). This experience of *éclosion*—unfolding, birthing, emerging—is surely one meaning of the assertion *je est un autre*. Synaesthetic harmony, for Rimbaud, involves above all metamorphic *éclosion*.[10]

"Harmonic ecstasy" (O, 305; CP, 283), then, is the way. The visionary boat of "Le Bateau ivre," prior to its final cry of nostalgia and collapse, manifests the outward sweep so characteristic of Rimbaud's poetry. His elliptical fields of language display a "mouvement perpetuel," to recall the title of Aragon's first book of poems, or exemplify what Emerson once called "the centrifugal tendency in man." These poems unfold premonitions traveling "en avant" of the self, of practical action, of things in the world. Indeed, one of their striking features is the *anticipatory* way of inhabiting the world to which they testify, their author always leaning over the edges of things, exploring himself and the world around him as a field of nascent forces only a step away, as though he longed to touch a zone of sheer emergence, arriving dawn, "cette heure indicible, première du matin [that unspeakable hour, the first of the morning]" (O, 353). One of the clearest poems in the *Illuminations*, "Aube," is a swift narrative describing a child's unlikely pursuit of a summer dawn, a quest to embrace a moment of pure incipience. The poem bears affinities not only with "Conte" but also, in a subtler way, with "Après le déluge," a parable that evokes a luminous postapocalyptic freshness of things (at least for the brief spell preceding the return of an apocalyptic longing to wash the world clean again with another flood). In this brief hour of rebeginning, the simple motions of a child's arms, as if quickly traversing space, resonate with the amplitude of distant towers and weather vanes: "Une porte claqua, et, sur la place du hameau, l'enfant tourna ses bras, compris des girouettes et des coqs des clochers de partout, sous l'éclatante giboulée [A door banged, and, in the village square, a child waved his arms, understood by weather vanes and steeples everywhere, under the thundering downpour]" (O, 253; CP, 234). It is possible, these poems suggest, to be multiply elsewhere, sounding other places, while walking here, "debout dans les rages et les ennuis [standing in rages and vexations]" (O, 308; CP, 290). Such voyages in premonition—involving passages through other lives, distant spaces, disclosive turns of language—are the animating dynamic of the *Illuminations*. By turns riddling, theatrical, hymnal, ironic, desperate, and apocalyptic, their fluent substance is the manifold drama of metamorphosis.

Below I want first to explore this drama of the *Illuminations*. Then I will look, if only in passing, at the elusive drama of the *Dernier Vers* of 1872, one of Rimbaud's attempts to address a crisis brought about by his initial creative impetus. And finally I would like to engage, in greater detail, *Une Saison en enfer*, a crisis text in which the Faustian poet's metamorphic élan is ultimately retained, in a substantially qualified way, on the other side of a season of ruthless criticism.

IN RIMBAUD'S POETRY, as Jacques Rivière wrote long ago, "every place becomes the place for *something else*." This is one way to characterize what, in the first instance, is a formal challenge posed by the *Illuminations*, texts that draw heavily on the ancient art of the riddle, the incongruous saying of one thing in the clothes of a very different thing.[11]

Yet, beyond the riddle, there are many other forms Rimbaud clearly draws on—and occasionally parodies—in the *Illuminations*. It is my sense that most (though not all) of these poems fall loosely into one or more of four predominant modes of composition, provided that one understand these modes not as rigid schemes but as loose patterns readily combining with one another in a variety of ways. One of these is the parable that recalls the enchanted atmosphere of the fairytale: "Conte" and "Aube" are clear examples of this mode. Another is the theatrical or carnivalesque phantasmagoria, the presentation of a landscape, a cityscape, or the self as a magical theater of shifting masks and metamorphoses: "Parade," "Les Ponts," "Villes II," "Nocturne vulgaire," "Promontoire," and "Bottom," for example, as well as the autobiographical poems "Enfance" and "Vies," are shaped along these lines. Yet a third mode is the hymn or hymnal revelation, the celebratory, often apostrophic turning toward a magnetic presence that arrives in the poet's field of attention with a transformative force: "Being Beauteous," "A une raison," and "Génie" are resonant poems in this mode, though it is partially found as well in "Matinée d'ivresse," "Villes II," portions of "Phrases," "Veillées," and "Barbare," among others, and it is this sort of sublime encounter that is evoked, though framed by a narrative, in both "Conte" and "Aube." And a fourth mode is the spiritual autobiography or (as Lawler aptly calls it) the portrait of the artist, the dramatization of the poet's various lives, roles, journeys, studies, passions, hopes, and despairs. In some sense, of course, all the *Illuminations* can be read as spiritual autobiographies, yet this is nonetheless a distinct mode of its own, most clearly developed in the great autobiographical stories of self-multiplication, "Enfance," "Vies," and

"Jeunesse," and in a number of enigmatic poems of anguished self-exploration, including "Angoisse," "Métropolitain," "Barbare," "Dévotion," and "Soir historique." What the enchanted parable, the visionary theater of multiplying masks and scenes, and the epiphanic hymn all share is a fascination with palpable spaces of premonition, protean fields of metamorphosis. "I believed in all enchantments," the poet tells us in the story of his journey through hell (O, 228; CP, 326). The spiritual autobiographies explore the reachings and fallings of a poet entirely devoted to voyaging through these places of metamorphosis, these "other lives."[12]

Rimbaud's theatrical phantasmagorias are protean and carnivalesque in the extreme. The critic who has most carefully illuminated this dimension of Rimbaud's art is James Lawler, who, in his *Rimbaud's Theatre of the Self*, takes Rimbaud's fascination with the power of masks as his point of departure: "Beginning in 1871 and continuing through *Une Saison en enfer* and the *Illuminations*, [Rimbaud] creates a drama that rejects the fixated self. 'Acrobat' or 'priest,' 'beggar' or 'bandit,' the list of personas is wide by which he engenders himself and, as he says, 'quarrels with appearances.' ... The self occupies the stage in a portrayal of poetry as aleatory lifework and calling."[13] Indeed, it often seems as though Rimbaud discerned in everything he encountered—not least in other texts he encountered—a potential mask to wear, live through, and shed on his way to another place, as though every passing being and every passing word were a metamorphic route leading beyond itself, opening out elsewhere.

The three-part poem "Vies" (O, 264–65; CP, 245–47) can be read as an emblematic poem in this regard. It is a poem with a relatively clear pattern of repetitions and variations. In each of the three parts the artist presents himself as a wanderer, one who has journeyed through multiple spaces, including the ancient East, modern bohemia, and various rural and urban locations of Europe. In each he describes himself, more specifically, as a wanderer in search of knowledge: ancient and sacred knowledge in the first part, knowledge of the ways of the world in the second, historical, artistic, and scientific knowledge in the third. In each part he concludes by underlining his immoderate bent for oppositional, destructive, self-destructive action. And, finally, in each part he presents himself as a different type of artist: an extraordinary dramatist in the first part, an orphic musician of cosmic love in the second, and a kind of grand alchemist or Faustian mage in the third. This Faustian mage, an artist of artists, perhaps transumes the previous roles. He is not only the maker of an "immense oeuvre" but also an epic and orphic hero who, having roamed the world in his searches, has ultimately roamed through the space of death. One recognizes in this mythopoetic portrait of the lives of the artist the dynamic of disordering and release played out on a plane of the multiplied self. It is as though the poem were an exemplary parable of what it means to live out the poetic of a Faustian quester abandoned to a continual metamorphic fluency.[14]

This metamorphic practice animates not only Rimbaud's sweeping self-multiplications but also his roving passages through a kind of elastic and multiplied spatiality. Never wholly himself, always becoming another, he is always, as well, turning and traveling elsewhere. The third part of "Vies" begins with these catalogue-like lines:

> Dans un grenier où je fus enfermé à douze ans j'ai connu le monde, j'ai illustré la comédie humaine. Dans un cellier j'ai appris l'histoire. A quelque fête de nuit dans une cité du Nord j'ai rencontré toutes les femmes des anciens peintres. Dans un vieux passage à Paris on m'a enseigné les sciences classiques. [In an attic where I was shut in at the age of twelve I came to know the world; I illustrated the human comedy. In a cellar I learned history. At some nocturnal festival in a northern city I met all the women of the old painters. In an ancient alley in Paris I was taught the classical sciences.] (O, 265; CP, 247)

This compressed sweep, evoking a rapid traversal of multiple spaces, is characteristic of Rimbaud's poetry. And, despite all the differences of pace and tone, it brings to mind a near contemporary of his across the ocean, Whitman, another wanderer whose poems display this sort of spacious *translocative* dynamic:

> Voyaging to every port to dicker and adventure,
> Hurrying with the modern crowd as eager and fickle as any,
> Hot toward one I hate, ready in my madness to knife him,
> Solitary at midnight in my back yard, my thoughts gone from me a
>   long while,
> Walking the old hills of Judaea with the beautiful gentle God by my side,
> . . . .
> Backing and filling, appearing and disappearing,
> I tread day and night such roads.[15]

Appearing and disappearing, treading day and night roads ramifying into other roads, Whitman and Rimbaud are the presiding spirits of many later poetries of metamorphic wandering through rural, urban, and global space. Distinctive to the way Rimbaud undertakes this adventure, as all his readers have observed, is the rapidity with which his language moves, the swiftness with which he appears and disappears, turns from one mask to another, pitches from one emotion to another, crosses from one place to another. Like light in space—"c'est la mer allée / avec le soleil"—he departs as he arrives. He is a mobile multiplicity, and so he finds the loosened spaces he traverses to be. It is this sort of whirl of space, movement, impulse, and figure that is traced in poems like "Villes II" and "Promontoire."[16]

No doubt some of these theaters of metamorphosis are more hallucinatory than others. Poems like "Parade," "Les Ponts," and "Villes II" are perhaps those the author of *Une Saison* has in mind when he says that he "habituated [himself] to pure hallucination" (O, 230; CP, 329). In the play of masks, at times turning delirious, Rimbaud finds a well-nigh "sacred" power of transformation (O, 269; CP, 251). The actors to whom the orchestrator calls our attention in "Parade" are said to practice "magnetic or hypnotic stagecraft" (O, 261; CP, 242), and it is this sort of bewitched stagecraft that Rimbaud would practice in his illuminations. "J'ai seul la clef de cette parade sauvage [I alone hold the key to this wild pageant]," he affirms in the last line of "Parade": Caliban, Prospero, and Ariel at once, he composes scenes intended to carry out a metamorphic operation on himself, the places we encounter, and the words that bear our premonitions of other lives. It is for this reason, I think, that many of his dramas of self-multiplication and whirling space are incantatory and hymnal. For Rimbaud, the masks, energies, and metamorphoses of the theater, the opera, the music hall, and the carnival are in their expansive play a cipher of *la vraie vie*, the life we might come to live if all the hidden forces at our side were disclosed.

The world as an enchanted theater, then, would be a world where strange powers might always arrive in the wings. The invocatory turning toward such arrivals is a frequent mode in the *Illuminations*. Geoffrey Hartman, discussing the "archaic" mode of sublime poetry and the "epiphanic consciousness essential to it," writes:

> The traditional type [of hymnal lyric] was transmitted by both Greek and Hebrew religious poetry, and throughout the late Renaissance and eighteenth century, by debased versions of the Pindaric or cult hymn. [This] epiphanic structure evokes the presence of a god, or vacillates sharply between imagined presence and absence. Its rhetoric is therefore a crisis-rhetoric, with priest or votary, vastation or rapture, precarious nearness

or hieratic distance ("Ah Fear! Ah frantic Fear! I see, I see thee near!"). As these verses by William Collins suggest, epiphanic structure proceeds by dramatic turns of mood and its language is ejaculative (Lo, Behold, O come, O see).[17]

Such a description places one immediately in the atmosphere of Rimbaud's *Illuminations,* with their charateristic rhetoric of quickened syntactic glides, sharp oscillations of tone, unexpected and sometimes cryptic cries, multiple apostrophic turns. For all the strangeness of these poems, many of them do belong to a tradition of the invocatory hymn, whether in an entirely direct way, as in "Being Beauteous," "A une raison," and "Génie," or in a partial and fragmentary, yet equally resonant, way, as in "Phrases," "Villes II," and "Fleurs," among many others. The composer of the *Illuminations* at times displays a willful effort to induce an apparition (as in "Matinée d'ivresse"), at times a calm preparation for a coming revelation (as in "Veillées"), at times an ecstatic witnessing to a startling arrival (as in "Génie"), at times a desperate, apocalyptic cry for transport (as in "Barbare"), at times variations on these and other modes of visionary attention and expectation. These diverse approaches are alike in their incantatory reach across thresholds, animated as they are by an impulse to summon, address, or touch some force on the edge of the ordinary, some apparition that, like the "Vision in the making" of "Being Beauteous," arrives as a promise of bodily and imaginative renewal (O, 263; CP, 244).[18]

Thus, in the brief and wry "Antique" (O, 262; CP, 243), the speaker addresses, describes, and sends on its way a musical "fils de Pan," a hermaphroditic creature emerging in his peripheral vision like a mystery of erotic forces crossing the night. Something of this playful address returns, though with greater force and mystery, in "A une raison," a hymnal address to a kind of divine "raison" that is felt to hover on a threshold of presence and absence, to promise a new love, harmony, and power, and to be at once arriving and departing: "Arrivée de toujours, qui t'en iras partout [Arrived from always, you will depart everywhere]" (O, 268; CP, 249). And on occasion this sort of invocatory turn is multiplied in a polyphonic whirl like that unfolded in "Villes II" (O, 276–77; CP, 259–60), a poem that begins with an implicit cry of "behold" and, after an immersion in a phantasmagoric cityscape, concludes with an *éclosion* wherein hymnal celebration, carnivalesque metamorphosis, geographical displacement, and, at the end, elegiac prayer are woven together in a compressed proliferation. It is as though a force of metamorphosis, like a god of old, had arrived and withdrawn.

Faustian Quest in Rimbaud, Nietzsche, and Bataille • 107

Rimbaud, in the greatest of his hymns, "Génie" (O, 308–9; CP, 289–91), affirms this sort of visible-invisible force precisely in its inevitable arriving and departing. Ecstatic and lucid, a kind of song of the winter solstice, it is above all a hymn of visionary opening:

> Il est l'affection et le présent puisqu'il a fait la maison ouverte à l'hiver écumeux et à la rumeur de l'été, lui qui a purifié les boissons et les aliments, lui qui est le charme des lieux fuyants et le délice surhumain des stations. Il est l'affection et l'avenir, la force et l'amour que nous, debout dans les rages et les ennuis, nous voyons passer dans le ciel de tempête et les drapeaux d'extase.
>
> Il est l'amour, mesure parfaite et réinventée, raison merveilleuse et imprévue, et l'éternité: machine aimée des qualités fatales. Nous avons tous eu l'épouvante de sa concession et de la nôtre: ô jouissance de notre santé, élan de nos facultés, affection égoïste et passion pour lui, lui qui nous aime pour sa vie infinie . . .
>
> Et nous le rappelons et il voyage . . . Et si l'Adoration s'en va, sonne, sa promesse sonne: "Arrière ces superstitions, ces anciens corps, ces ménages et ces âges. C'est cette époque-ci qui a sombré!"
>
> Il ne s'en ira pas, il ne redescendra pas d'un ciel, il n'accomplira pas la rédemption des colères de femmes et des gaietés des hommes et de tout ce péché: car c'est fait, lui étant, et étant aimé.
>
> O ses souffles, ses têtes, ses courses: la terrible célérité de la perfection des formes et de l'action!
>
> O fécondité de l'esprit et immensité de l'univers!
>
> Son corps! le dégagement rêvé, le brisement de la grâce croisée de violence nouvelle!
>
> Sa vue, sa vue! tous les agenouillages anciens et les peines *relevés* à sa suite.
>
> Son jour! l'abolition de toutes souffrances sonores et mouvantes dans la musique plus intense.
>
> Son pas! les migrations plus énormes que les anciennes invasions.
>
> O Lui et nous! l'orgueil plus bienveillant que les charités perdues.
>
> O monde! et le chant clair des malheurs nouveaux!
>
> Il nous a connus tous et nous a tous aimés. Sachons, cette nuit d'hiver, de cap en cap, du pôle tumultueux au château, de la foule à la plage, de regards en regards, forces et sentiments las, le héler et le voir, et le renvoyer,

et, sous les marées et au haut des déserts de neige, suivre ses vues, ses souffles, son corps, son jour.

[He is affection and the present because he has made the house that is open to the foaming winter and the murmur of summer, he who has purified drink and food, he who is the charm of fleeting places and the superhuman delight of stations of pause. He is affection and the future, force and love that we, standing in rages and vexations, see passing in the stormy sky and the banners of ecstasy.

He is love, perfect and reinvented measure, marvelous and unforeseen reason, and eternity: beloved machine of fatal powers. We have all known the terror of his concession and of ours: oh rapture of our health, élan of our faculties, selfish affection and passion for him, him who loves us for his infinite life.

And we call him back and he voyages... And if Adoration goes away, rings, his promise rings: "Away with these superstitions, these old bodies, these families and these ages. It is this epoch that has sunk!"

He will not go away, he will not descend again from a heaven, he will not accomplish the redemption of women's angers and men's gaieties and all that sin: for it is done, because he is, and is loved.

Oh his breaths, his heads, his passages: the terrible velocity of the perfection of forms and of action!

Oh fecundity of the spirit and immensity of the universe!

His body! the deliverance dreamed of, the shattering of grace met with new violence!

His vision, his vision! all the old kneelings and pains *lifted* at his passing.

His day! the abolition of all resounding and moving suffering in more intense music.

His step! migrations more enormous than the ancient invasions.

Oh He and we! pride more benevolent than the lost charities.

Oh world! and the clear song of new misfortunes!

He has known us all and loved us all. Let us know, this winter night, from cape to cape, from the tumultuous pole to the castle, from the crowd to the beach, from looks to looks, tired forces and feelings, how to greet him and to see him, and to send him away, and, beneath the tides and at the top of the deserts of snow, to follow his visions, his breaths, his body, his day.]

At once grounded and prospective, this hymn brings together all of Rimbaud's visionary horizons, gathering in a single field every pulse of metamorphosis found variously throughout his other writings: the apocalyptic sinking of Christian orthodoxy; the gnostic awakening to renovated spaces and faculties; the premonition of extraordinarily heightened powers; the participation in migratory distances; the élan of a perilous *bonheur* felt as a cosmic *fatalité*; the encounter with the flow of infinite life. In fact, as has often been noted, this poem reads like a radiant transumption of everything else Rimbaud wrote: it recalls the mystical *Derniers Vers* no less than the visionary adventures that the author of *Une Saison en enfer*, at least in one of his voices, is inclined to dismiss as "impossible" quests leading only to destruction. "Génie" thus reverberates as a hymnal counterstatement to any farewell to the sorts of ambitions recorded in Rimbaud's *carnet de damné*.

The voyaging Génie has been variously interpreted as a god, the guide of a utopian social ideal, a manifestation of "the divine spirit of poetry," and the threshold figure of a force that at once precedes and exceeds any figuration at all.[19] Yves Bonnefoy, placing this figure on the edge of the human realm, has finely measured its liminal quality:

> [The Génie] is a being far beyond our condition at present but whom it would be wrong, despite all, to consider a god. For if it is true that he reconsecrates the world, clears it of its opacity and restores it to desire..., this is no more than the highest act of which our human powers are capable; and if it is true as well that he reveals himself "in the stormy sky and the banners of ecstasy," above our horizon, we must understand that these are not the limits between transcendence and immanence but rather those within existence itself, in that part of life that has remained free and pure, in the sky of *illuminations* where the hope of the young Rimbaud took shape.[20]

One might say, then, that Rimbaud's Génie is an emanation of what Blake calls the Poetic Genius, the spark of creative power without which life readily ruins itself in *les rages et les ennuis*, in anxiety, erosion, anger, despair. The Blakean Orc that animates so many of Rimbaud's poems, the energy of revolutionary rage, is in this hymn swept into the Blakean Los, the spirit of prophetic vision, for in this song of opening an ardent impatience is balanced with a clairvoyant poise. The speaker commands us to greet, see, send off, and follow this appearing-disappearing figure. For one cannot *be* this sort of creative energy. Like the lightning Zarathustra invokes, it is that which jars and renovates one's being when it is released: "the deliverance dreamed of, the shattering of grace met with new violence!" One can only find it and lose it, be found by it and lost by it, time and again. It arrives and departs. "Arrived from always, you will depart everywhere." If it is found, in its coming-going passage, it is found only as a measure "reinvented" once again. It cannot be fixed or possessed. It is no refuge from pain, no escape from "new misfortune," though it bears the power of a clearing song in response to misfortune: "Oh world! and the clear song of new misfortunes!" It is an energy of emergence and passage, a force of opening, a power at play in the power of time.

Yet this figure, an immanent transcendence, a "necessary angel of earth" (Stevens), may ultimately elude even this sort of Blakean reading. Migrating from cape to cape, this Génie bears affinities with Apollo, the shining one, genius of radiant apparition, departing and returning bearer of light, source and measure of song. Roger Munier writes: "This is not a being, but neither can one say that it is not: it is an élan, the appearing-disappearing passage of a pure élan.... This would be like Being, then, since there is hardly any other word for it, but in a sense other than that which metaphysics gives it: Being not as concept or ground, but dynamically, poetically, as élan, as nothing other than élan."[21] The Génie is Rimbaud's imagining of the infinite: a pure unfolding, a force of opening and clearing and crossing. When he imagines this sort of force—imagines that he has touched a horizon of his premonition—he imagines the movement of light through space, as though he longed to become the distances of light itself.[22]

THIS LONGING IS expressed not only in "Génie" but also in a hymnal "charm" of 1872, "L'Éternité" (O, 160; CP, 217):

>   Elle est retrouvée.
>   Quoi?—L'Éternité.
>   C'est la mer allée
>   Avec le soleil.
>
>   Âme sentinelle,
>   Murmurons l'aveu

De la nuit si nulle
Et du jour en feu.

Des humains suffrages,
Des communs élans
Là tu te dégages
Et voles selon.

Puisque de vous seules,
Braises de satin,
Le Devoir s'exhale
Sans qu'on dise: enfin.

Là pas d'espérance,
Nul orietur.
Science avec patience,
Le supplice est sûr.

Elle est retrouvée.
Quoi?—L'Eternité.
C'est la mer allée
Avec le soleil.

[It is found again.
What?—Eternity.
It's the sea that has fled
With the sun.

Sentinel soul,
Let us murmur the vow
Of the night so nothing
And the day on fire.

From human regards,
From common concerns
You free yourself here
And fly as you will.

112 • THE EXTRAVAGANT

> Since from you alone,
> Embers of satin,
> Duty is breathed
> With no one saying: enough.
>
> Nothing of hope here,
> No *orietur*.
> Knowledge and patience,
> The pain is sure.
>
> It is found again.
> What?—Eternity.
> It's the sea that has fled
> With the sun.]

A question raised by these enigmatic songs of 1872, in particular those of "Comédie de la soif" and "Fêtes de la patience," is the question of the relationship between reaching affirmations like that of "L'Éternité" and the bitterness with which the poet repeatedly attempts to embrace a kind of stoic "patience" detached from both worldly and delirious ambitions. "Patience" is a word woven through these poems like a riddling thread. "J'ai tant fait patience / Qu'à jamais j'oublie; / Craintes et souffrances / Aux cieux sont parties, / Et la soif malsaine / Obscurcit mes veines [I've been patient so long / I've forgotten forever; / Fears and sufferings have left for the skies, / And the unhealthy thirst / Darkens my veins]" (O, 158; CP, 216). Are the "patience" and the "quest" of these poems at one with one another or, rather, opposed to one another in a lived contradiction? John Porter Houston, commenting on the poems of "Fêtes de la patience," writes: "By a dialectic shift [the poet's] acedia and discouragement cease to be a source of individual misfortune and become the means whereby he loses himself in the life of the seasons."[23] It is well to remember that these are among the poems that, in "Délires II," Rimbaud cites in describing his most exorbitant longings. "Je me traînais dans les ruelles puantes et, les yeux fermés, je m'offrais au soleil, dieu de feu [I would drag myself through stinking alleys and, eyes closed, offer myself to the sun, god of fire]" (O, 231; CP, 331). The poet of "Fêtes de la patience" and other songs of this period readily traces the "dialectic shift" Houston describes because the patience of these poems, though at times a patience of endurance, is at times a patience of fire. "Que je dorme! que je bouille / Aux autels de Salomon, / Le bouillon court sur la rouille, / Et se mêle au Cedron [Let me sleep! let me simmer / On the altars of Solomon, / The simmering runs over the rust / And mingles in the flow of the Kedron]" (O, 232; CP, 226). This is the patience of a desert father, a passion, a longing for departure. These kenotic songs, invoking a vanishing of the self in light and air, are animated by a "patience" not always far from the "impatience" animating other phases and modes (satire, voyage, incantatory metamorphosis) of Rimbaud's trajectory.

This impatience is among the exorbitant passions with which the Faustian poet wrestles in *Une Saison en enfer*. Destructive-creative impatience, in fact, is the most demanding of Rimbaud's demons: a revolutionary impatience with the social structures of his time; a disorienting impatience with himself; a gnostic impatience with finitude itself, with limits as such, lived out with great force, at great cost.

UNE SAISON MAY initially appear to express a pitch of negation equal to the pitch of affirmation expressed in "Génie." Yet this is a misreading. For the writer of *Une Saison* moves through an extreme crisis and works out a precarious recovery. It is true that this recovery is ambiguous, but that it *is* a recovery is often neglected only because the text is often read as an expression of decisions Rimbaud made not in 1873 but in 1875. *Une Saison*, further, is a text written not in the wake of a crisis but in the very midst of a crisis. Hence its volatility.

Une Saison, indeed, is unforgettable not least owing to its careening pitch. Rimbaud's initial anarchovisionary impulse was so hyperbolic that his subsequent crisis of faith could hardly have been less hyperbolic. This Faustian poet undergoes the collision between the promise of vision and the pressure of the real as a fall that sends him crashing through earth. Thus he casts his crisis as a journey through hell. The journey through the underworld, of course, has a deep mythic and literary background: Orpheus and Christ as well as the great heroes of epic all travel through the underworld and return alive (Odysseus's journey to Cimmeria is in fact alluded to in "Délires II" [O, 233; CP, 335]). Yet it is above all the myth of Faust that Rimbaud echoes in composing *Une Saison*.[24] According to the myth, one recalls, Faust is a man impatient with the limits of ordinary life, weary of learning, tired of books that (like science for Rimbaud) are too slow. He seeks not knowledge but gnosis, not gradual progress but actual power. Hence he begins the study of magic, occult lore, the mysteries of numbers, and so forth, all in a quest to acquire superhuman capacities. Alone, alienated from a society whose narrow ambitions he cannot share, he comes to make a pact with the devil, handing over his soul in exchange for demonic powers of divine proportions. Having thus allied himself with nocturnal regions of power and "buried in darkness the tree of good and evil" (as Rimbaud puts it in "Matinée d'ivresse"), he attains great powers, including the power to visit the underworld (not the Christian hell but the pagan underworld and, in Goethe's version, also the depths of night where the Mothers dwell). From this realm he brings back lovely visions. He becomes a voyant. But he is condemned, nevertheless, and at the end of his life is swallowed by hell. Goethe, it is true, revises the myth: his Faust, whose demonism God benevolently justifies as an errant expression of noble human striving, is at the last minute rescued from the clutches of Satan. Rimbaud, too, revises the myth in which he casts himself. He climbs out of hell, though unlike Goethe's Faust he does spend time there, and unlike Goethe's Faust he is forced to rely on his own forces to bring about a return to the world and a changed orientation. There are no angels, no eternal feminine, not even "a friendly hand" in the last chapter of *Une Saison*.

This myth provides the frame for a text that, in its essential features, closely follows the pattern of the romantic crisis poem.[25] This type of poem, recalling a familiar Christian curve of experience, confronts an existential and vocational crisis, explores how this crisis has come about, and often (though by no means always) traces some path of recovery. While dwelling above all in the condition of crisis, such a poem at least implies a temporal movement from an initial phase of creative expectation, through a disorienting phase of disillusion, to a later phase of reanimation. This later phase is usually voiced from a widened or autumnal perspective, one that embodies a revision of the initial creative impulse, though in many poems of this sort—including, for example, Browning's "Childe Roland to the Dark Tower Came," Whitman's "As I Ebb'd with the Ocean of Life," Baudelaire's poems of "spleen," and Mallarmé's poems of impasse—the only recovery attained is that implicit in the purgatorial writing out of the crisis itself. One kind of crisis often explored in this sort of poem is that of an anxious awareness of waning creative powers. Another is that of a startled recognition of lost contact with reality and so of damaged faith in the point of any creative project in a world where released imaginative energy often appears as childish fantasy, solipsistic evasion, or self-destructive flight from a range of social norms and reality principles. It is the second of these concerns—the awareness of having suffered a divorce from the real and from others—that is addressed by the poet of *Une Saison*. One could put it another way, transposing this sort of predicament into the terms in which Zarathustra encounters it. The initial Faustian quest, undertaken by both Rimbaud and Zarathustra, is a contestation of what Nietzsche calls passive nihilism: the smallness of a life no longer creatively engaged as challenge and promise but merely endured as block and routine. Yet the Faustian quester may discover that the adventure of extravagance is itself potentially nihilist insofar as its dynamic impatience with the given, taken to an extreme, risks a destruction of the given self (whether understood as "natural" or "social") as well as a ruin of those common limits that shape the realm of human relationship. The path through the predicament, seen from this perspective, becomes that of reimagining the initial creative élan, which has taken a swerve toward ruin, without yielding to the passive nihilism which that initial élan had promised to surpass.[26]

I've paused to dwell on this well-known pattern because I believe that its unmistakable presence in Rimbaud's *Une Saison* contradicts any reading of the text as a farewell to poetry. The prologue begins by expressing the experience of a devastating fall: "Jadis, si je me souviens bien, ma vie était un festin où s'ouvraient tous les coeurs, où tous les vins coulaient.... Je me suis enfui. Ô sorcières, ô misère, ô haine, c'est a vous que mon trésor a été confié [Once, if I remember well, my life was a feast where all hearts opened, where all wines flowed.... I fled. Oh witches, oh misery, oh hatred, it was to you that my treasure was entrusted]" (O, 211; CP, 299). And this sense of lost bearings is again voiced in the opening lines of "Matin," at a moment when the poet is about to attempt a decisive reorientation:

> N'eus-je pas *une fois* une jeunesse aimable, héroïque, fabuleuse, à écrire sur des feuilles d'or,—trop de chance! Par quel crime, par quelle erreur, ai-je mérité ma faiblesse actuelle? Vous qui prétendez que des bêtes poussent des sanglots de chagrin, que des malades désespèrent, que des morts rêvent mal, tâchez de raconter ma chute et mon sommeil. [Had I not *at one time* a lovely youth, heroic, fabulous, to be written on pages of gold—too lucky! Through what crime, through what error, have I deserved my present weakness? You who claim that animals sob with grief, that the sick despair, that the dead have bad dreams, try to recount my fall and my sleep.] (O, 239; CP, 342)

Une Saison is the poet's attempt to respond to these questions concerning the "crimes" and "errors" that have led him to his current "weakness." The prologue, a quick sketch of the issues engaged in the rest of the text, also voices the recognition that marks the fallen poet's point of departure: "Or, tout dernièrement m'étant trouvé sur le point de faire le dernier *couac!* j'ai songé à rechercher la clef du festin ancien, où je reprendrais peut-être appétit [Now, just recently having found myself on the point of uttering my last *croak!* I thought of looking for the key to the ancient feast, where I might perhaps recover my appetite]" (O, 211; CP, 300). Though this is immediately mocked in the next few lines—in the sort of sharp reversal characteristic of this text—the task of recovery is thus set forth.

The next four chapters of the text, closely intertwined with one another, present the poet's volatile meditations on the rages, ambitions, and experiments that have landed him in hell. In "Mauvais sang" he critically examines, if with a vehemence that is no small part of the problem, his apocalyptic impatience, his impetus of revolt. In "Nuit de l'enfer," continuing this line of thought, he explores the vastations he has brought upon himself through his rages, his experiments in hallucination, his "poisonous" faith in the magical surpassing of limits. "Nuit de l'enfer," the poet's proud denunciation of his own outrageous pride, thus communicates closely with "Délires II: Alchimie du Verbe," the poet's dazzling and derisory account of his adventures in visionary metamorphosis and luminous departure from the world. "Délires I," occupying a slightly eccentric position in the text, provides an account of the poet's failed attempt at a meaningful relationship with his lover. "Mauvais sang," "Nuit de l'enfer," and "Délires II" thus form a sustained movement that casts a well-focused light on "Délires I," for the former dramatize features of the poet's character and errant projects he has pursued that have much to do with the failure of love described in the latter (wherein the Infernal Bridegroom plays Faust to the Foolish Virgin's Margarete). However splendid his ambitions to reinvent love and to find the secrets for changing life (O, 224–25; CP, 320–22), the adolescent studied in "Délires I," a character given to outbursts of violence and fond of dwelling in a phantasmagoric world all his own, is impossible to live with, a truth not mitigated, he appears to recognize, by the fact that the Foolish Virgin he insults is a sentimental character difficult to live with as well. "Enfin sa charité est ensorcelée [In short, his charity is bewitched]," the Foolish Virgin accurately notes (O, 225; CP, 322). "L'Impossible," a hinge in the text, attempts a kind of "comprehensive" clarification of the four chapters preceding it. The poet underlines that his apocalyptic revolts and visionary flights have been expressions of a "religious" longing for an "impossible" realm of amplitude beyond history, time, finitude, the limits of life itself. The ambition to *change life* has drifted into an ambition to *escape reality*. There is the crux of his crisis, as exactly described by the Foolish Virgin in "Délires I": "A côté de son cher corps endormi, que d'heures des nuits j'ai veillé, cherchant pourquoi il voulait tant s'sévader de la réalité. Jamais homme n'eut pareil voeu [Beside his dear sleeping body, how many nights have I sat up for hours, trying to discover why he so desired to escape from reality. Never has a man had a desire equal to it]" (O, 225; CP, 322). The poet acknowledges this longing in his own voice in "L'Impossible." This chapter thus forms a transition between the poet's account of his destructive adventures, in the first four chapters, and his oscillating effort, in the last three chapters, to recover his bearings and sketch a new orientation on the other side of hell.

This schematic sketch of the plot of *Une Saison* is meant to indicate the extent to which the text unfolds as a drama of crisis, critical exploration, and reorientation. Though I don't have the space here to undertake a detailed reading of the text, I would like in what follows to draw attention to passages in the chapters of critical self-scrutiny that are essential to an understanding of the reorientation articulated in the last three chapters, and then to clarify the issues at stake in this reorientation.

Like "Délires I," "L'Impossible," and "L'Éclair," "Mauvais sang" is among other things an emphatic expression of the poet's refusal of the modern imperatives of work, production, science, patriotic identity, and faith in progress. This chapter may be the most difficult (because the most chaotic) chapter in the entire text. Yet Yves Bonnefoy has usefully observed that all the characters appearing in this chapter ultimately belong to one of three types: nobles (*seigneurs*), peasants (*paysans*), or outcasts (*autres*).[27] Where Wordsworth in the "Immortality" ode probes his crisis by composing a story about the origins of the soul in a divine light from which it has fallen, and then developing a gloomy theory of socialization as imprisonment, the poet of *Une Saison* probes his crisis by sketching a geneaology of the "inferior race" from which he has descended, and then presenting his experience of socialization as an unbearable imposition on his creative disquiet. "Il m'est bien évident que j'ai toujours été de race inférieure. Je ne puis comprendre la révolte. Ma race ne se souleva jamais que pour piller: tels les loups à la bête qu'ils n'ont pas tuée [It's perfectly obvious to me that I've always been of an inferior race. I can't understand revolt. My race never rebelled except to plunder: like wolves with the beast they haven't killed]" (O, 213–14; CP, 302). He imagines himself as belonging—though, as soon becomes clear, not entirely—to a "race" of never Christianized "peasants" whose revolts have always exhausted themselves in violent destructions and profanations. At the same time he associates this race of peasants with those who have attained their place in history with the arrival of modernity. "La race inférieure a tout couvert—le peuple, comme on dit, la raison; la nation et la science [The inferior race has spread everywhere—the people, as they say, reason; the nation and science]" (O, 214; CP, 303).[28] It is this modern world in which his race has at last attained a place, however, that he has always refused. "J'ai horreur de tous les métiers. Maîtres et ouvriers, tous paysans, ignobles. La main à la plume vaut la main à charrue.—Quel siècle à mains!—Je n'aurai jamais ma main [I loathe all trades. Masters and servants, all peasants, ignoble. The hand with the pen is worth the hand on the plow.—What an age of hands!—I'll never have my hand!]" (O, 213; CP, 301). This vexation is reiterated at the end of "L'Éclair." In opposition to this world, he has engaged in a process of apocalyptic destruction, visionary departure, becoming-other, and subversive re-identification, aligning his energies and fantasies with all the outlawed and the outcast, all the scorned and the subjugated: convicts, witches, vagabonds, the colonized, anyone outside the order of proper order. Much of this chapter, at times repeating and (as it were) upending the sort of "orientalist" discourse pervasive in French romantic literature, is a bewildering evocation of this mode of oppositional self-othering and self-multiplication.[29] And it is clear that the poet has always felt that his anarcholibidinal political dynamic and his anarcho-visionary poetic dynamic move to the same metamorphic rhythm, a voice that once promised an open road of freedom for those with sufficient courage to respond to its call:

> Sur les routes, par des nuits d'hiver, sans gîte, sans habits, sains pain, une voix étreignait mon coeur gelé: "Faiblesse ou force: te voilà, c'est la force. Tu ne sais ni où tu vas ni pourquoi tu vas, entre partout, réponds à tout. On ne te tuera pas plus qui si tu étais cadavre." [On the roads, on winter nights, without shelter, without clothing, without bread, a voice would clutch my frozen heart: "Weakness or force: there you are, it's force. You know neither where you are going nor why you are going: enter everywhere, respond to everything. They won't kill you any more than if you were a corpse."][30] (O, 216; CP, 307)

Yet the chapter concludes with the poet imagining himself first as a black African forced to undergo conquest and baptism, and then as a French soldier forced to march along the path of honor, both of which pictures strike him as farces. The exasperation is fierce by the end of the chapter. "La vie est la farce à mener par tous [Life is the farce to be lived by all]" (O, 219; CP, 312). Does the poet at least arrive at some understanding of his predicament? Or would it be more accurate to say that he spins himself through a kind of purgatorial exorcism? Perhaps both. It seems to me that he does finally attain a measure of critical insight, recognizing that his volatile reidentifications with those outside the order of modernity have been insufficiently lucid, and insufficiently creative, insofar as they have been driven by an excessively reactive violence: the violence of those "peasants" who, failing to understand revolt, exhaust their forces of rebellion in incoherent destruction and self-destruction. The poet thus articulates at least a partial clarification of the "enfant de la colère" who, through a disordering of himself and the world around him, had hoped to release a storm of buried powers. "Nuit de l'enfer," "Délires I," and "Délires II" are further explorations of adventures animated by this apocalyptic impatience.

In "Délires II" the poet provides an account of his visionary path, rapidly tracing different phases of his search for creative powers capable of "changing life" or releasing the "infinite life" concealed by the reified world. There are three phases of his quickly unfolded quest that he records and, it seems, derides as delusions: the alchemical phase of the early poems of *voyance*, the ambiguously stoic and mystical phase of the *Derniers Vers*, and the elusively curving phase (begun before the writing of this text and probably extending beyond it) of the invocatory *Illuminations*.[31] As other chapters of the text make clear, he mocks these adventures because, from his current perspective, they appear to have led him down a path of destruction. He asserts in this chapter that they have carried him to the edge of madness, ruining his relationship with himself, with others, and with everyday reality, leading him "to the ends of the world and of Cimmeria, land of darkness and whirlwinds" (O, 233; CP, 335). Further, in striking lines (O, 232–33; CP, 333–34), he spells out the gnostic impulse that has animated his quest for an infinite life beyond the life we know: a life of sheer metamorphic dispersal ("I became a fabulous opera") or, in a vision intimately if paradoxically linked to this one, a life of pure passage in light ("I lived, a spark of gold of the light of nature"). One recalls the "golden birds" invoked near the end of "Le Bateau ivre": "Est-ce en ces nuits sans fonds que tu dors et t'exiles, / Million d'oiseaux d'or, ô future Vigueur? [Is it in those bottomless nights that you sleep and are exiled, / Million golden birds, oh future Force?]" (O, 131; CP, 170). It is this spark of pure light, like the Genius of Light voyaging through space, that in "L'Impossible" is troped yet again as an Impossible East beyond the conditions of history. These and their kin throughout Rimbaud's poetry are figures, finally, for that quickening of sheer potential which he has sought to touch and live throughout his Faustian adventure. It is the wild hyperbole of this desire that the poet appears to leave behind in this chapter. "Cela s'est passé. Je sais aujourd'hui saluer la beauté [That's over. I know today how to greet beauty]" (O, 234; CP, 336).

And yet. The derision of "Alchimie du Verbe" is not as unambiguous as it may initially seem. At moments, as in the second of the passages cited above, the poet unexpectedly shifts into the present tense to clarify with great force a perspective that he had been dismissing a moment before as a deluded affair of the past. And, more generally, his extended self-criticism in this chapter soars with a pride and elation at odds with his general stance of mockery. No doubt self-denunciation, even self-annihilation, in particular for a writer devoted to a vision of destructive renovation, can be an exhilarating experience, and a good measure of self-mockery in the midst of sweeping affirmation is at play in many of Rimbaud's writings.[32] That, I think, is relevant to our reading of both this chapter and *Une Saison* as a whole. The tone of elation in this chapter, the sheer force of its writing, communicates a bearing—one suggesting a faith still alive in spite of all—that resonates in tension with the chapter's ironic tone and general thematic movement of self-criticism. The ambiguities of this chapter anticipate the ambiguities, or the severe oscillations, of the reorientation traced in the final chapter.

"L'Impossible" brings to a culmination the first half of *Une Saison*. It can be read as a parable, ragged at the edges, serving to focus a fundamental impulse animating all those adventures that have led the poet to hell. Thus he begins the chapter by at once recalling and mocking the prologue's opening cry of mourning for a lost freedom and fullness of youth. Nevertheless, though he mocks himself, he doesn't retract his severe judgments of the world (O, 235; CP, 337). At this point, yet again, he is drawn to the dream of escape, a dream that is explored, comprehended, and judged in the rest of the chapter. It is the dream of the Impossible, a lost place of sheer potential and luminous reach, imagined as an Eternal East of calm, clarity, amplitude, abiding wisdom (O, 236; CP, 338–39). This is the realm the poet has hoped to enter if only he could cross beyond the history of the West, beyond Christianity and modernity alike, and beyond, so to speak, his own poisoned efforts to get there. But now he recognizes, with sharp irony, that this dream is stirred not only by one of various tropes for a lost paradise beyond history but by a trope that in fact belongs to the very tradition he has sought to escape: "C'est vrai; c'est à l'Eden que je songeais! [It's true; it is Eden I was dreaming of]" (O, 236; CP, 339). At this point, perhaps, he realizes that "his vision is of something older than history."[33] The concluding lines voice a sudden reawakening followed by an abrupt fall back to suffering, a last gnostic leap followed by a decisive return to hell

(O, 237; CP, 340). From this point on he attempts to pick up the pieces and find a new path.

The last three chapters present his unstable effort to find this path. "L'Éclair" and "Matin" are soundings of two possible paths, neither of which proves adequate: the first a path of resignation, including reintegration into the modern order of work and sobriety, the second a path of calmly reawakened hope that risks, however, a drifting back toward the escapist dreaming he is trying to leave behind. The concluding "Adieu" traces a wavering effort to hold to a course that resists both the death-in-life of resignation and the self-destruction of sheer evasion.

The title of "L'Éclair" is bitterly ironic, suggesting that the only "illumination" left for this disillusioned visionary may be the flash of insight inviting him to join the modern regime of work, science, progress. "Le travail humain! c'est l'explosion qui éclaire mon abîme de temps en temps. "Rien n'est vanité; à la science, et en avant!" crie l'Ecclésiaste modern, c'est-à-dire *Tout le monde* [Human labor! this is the explosion that shines in my abyss from time to time. 'Nothing is vanity; to science, and forward!' cries the modern Ecclesiastes, that is to say, *Everyone*]" (O, 238; CP, 341). Yet he has no more changed his mind about the routines of this regime than, as "L'Impossible" makes clear, he has changed his mind about those it imprisons. His refusal of the initial flash of insight stirs, once again, thoughts of the old life of visionary wandering that he has already criticized:

> Ma vie est usée. Allons! feignons, fainéantons, ô pitié! Et nous existerons en nous amusant, en rêvant amours monstres et univers fantastiques, en nous plaignant et en querellant les apparences du monde, saltimbanque, mendiant, artiste, bandit,—prêtre!

> [My life is worn out. Let's go! let's deceive, let's do nothing, oh pity! And we will exist by amusing ourselves, by dreaming of monstrous loves and fantastic universes, by complaining, and by quarrelling with the world's appearances, clown, beggar, artist, bandit—priest!] (O, 238; CP, 341–42)

In this passage—as in the immediately following lines in which he expresses contempt for that part of himself still susceptible to the consolations of the orthodox faith of his childhood—the poet exposes the affinity between his own "role" as metamorphic visionary and the priest's "role" as proclaimer of a divine world beyond the given world. This is a severe judgment. Yet he is at a loss. In the conclusion to the chapter he voices a desperate revolt against the death he still perceives in the modern regime of work and utility, his pride forcefully reasserting itself, all the more movingly inasmuch as its insurgence at this point upends the idea of actually accepting the order of modernity with which the chapter at least appears to begin (O, 238; CP, 342). This first effort at recovery, then, is an unqualified failure: a turning that, turning straight into a wall, provokes the old responses of sheer revolt and fantasy.

"Matin" presents another effort at reorientation. It opens with an expression of disorientation that recalls the first line of the prologue, the poet regretting the loss of a fabulous childhood and wondering what "crime" and "error" have led him to his wrecked condition. He has done much to answer this question during his season in hell. In fact, his bewilderment at this point is in part a result of recognitions he has recently passed through, including the recognition that he has exhausted himself in seeking a freedom beyond history, and the recognition that he is nevertheless unwilling to betray himself by submitting to the modern regime of work and utility. He stands a moment on the edge of the abyss, still uncertain, though he has climbed out of the fires of hell. At this point he undertakes a turn toward the future—toward a distant but immanent New Jerusalem—that brings with it a rekindling of something of those hopes that had guided his initial quest, though now in a measured tone of quietly ascending interrogation (O, 239; CP, 343). Perhaps, however, his vision of the "new work" and "new wisdom" of the future, though invoked in a calm spirit of promise (or prayer) rather than a vehement spirit of departure (or revolt), risks a return to the art of roaming fantasy that the poet has struggled to overcome. In "Adieu," a third effort at reorientation, he will refuse to surrender to either sheer facticity or sheer premonition.

"Adieu," consisting of two parts, is well introduced by the last line of "Matin": "Slaves, let us not curse life." The poet, having stepped out of hell, seeks a restored communication with life. It is autumn, and it is an autumnal spirit that shapes this chapter, though a spirit ultimately turned toward an expectation of dawn. As the chapter opens, the poet is on a boat moving between hell and a modern city, or, as Henri Meschonnic has put it, he is traveling from one hell, that of his apocalyptic self-destruction, to another hell, that of the modern city in which he has known great suffering.[34] The approach to this city of poverty and ruin—itself a rather infernal city, flecked with fire and mud and presided over by a "ghoul queen" as severe as any Queen of Hell (O, 240; CP, 344)—fills the returning poet with fear and disgust, provoking in him the old response of visionary flight. In this case, however, in one of the unforgettable turns in *Une Saison,* the imaginative élan is suddenly shut down, the artistic gifts suddenly buried:

> —Quelquefois je vois au ciel des plages sans fin couvertes de blanches nations en joie. Un grand vaisseau d'or, au-dessus de moi, agite ses pavillons multicolores sous les brises du matin. J'ai crée toutes les fêtes, tous les triomphes, tous les drames. J'ai essayé d'inventer de nouvelles fleurs, de nouveaux astres, de nouvelles chairs, de nouvelles langues. J'ai cru acquérir des pouvoirs surnaturels. Eh bien! je dois enterrer mon imagination et mes souvenirs! Une belle gloire d'artiste et de conteur emportée!
>
> Moi! moi qui me suis dit mage ou ange, dispensé de toute morale, je suis rendu au sol, avec un devoir à chercher, et la réalité rugueuse à étreindre! Paysan!
>
> Suis-je trompé? la charité serait-elle soeur de la mort, pour moi?
>
> Enfin, je demanderai pardon pour m'être nourri de mensonge. Et allons.
>
> Mais pas une main amie! et où puiser le secours? (O, 240)

> [—Sometimes I see in the sky beaches without end covered with white nations of joy. A great golden ship, above me, waves its many-colored standards in the morning breezes. I have created all festivals, all triumphs, all dramas. I have tried to invent new flowers, new stars, new bodies, new languages. I believed I had acquired supernatural powers. Well! I must bury my imagination and my memories! A glorious fame as an artist and a storyteller swept away!
>
> I! I who called myself mage or angel, exempt from all morality, I am given back to the earth, with a duty to seek, and rugged reality to embrace! Peasant!
>
> Am I deceived? would charity be the sister of death, for me?
>
> Well, I will ask forgiveness for having fed on lies. And let us go.
>
> But not one friendly hand! and whence am I to draw help?] (CP, 344–45)

Thus the unstable threshold at which the first part of "Adieu" ends: an abrupt turning away from the visionary adventure, a stoic embracing of the real, a lucid attempt to cut through illusion and self-deception, a troubled recognition of solitude, and a poignant expression of doubt about the sort of "charity" of which this poet back from hell is capable. What duty or obligation does he intend to seek? In the concluding part of "Adieu" he provides significant hints, if no transparent statements, concerning the altered calling he hears.

In the severity of the new hour (O, 241; CP, 345), he affirms he has achieved a victory in having found his way back from hell. He commands himself to hold to the course of embracing the real and engaging the modern: "Il faut être absolument moderne. Point de cantiques: tenir le pas gagné [One must be absolutely modern. No hymns: hold on to the stride made]" (O, 241; CP, 346). These lines posit a stark opposition between the modern (the realm of work, science, rugged reality, peasant realism) and the hymnal (the realm of poetry, alchemy of the word, invocatory departure, visionary metamorphosis). Yet the repudiation of poetic flights that have shown themselves to be self-destructive evasions—refusals to settle for anything less than an absolute horizon of light, passage, and freedom—does not imply an unqualified repudiation of the creative force itself that animated those flights. In fact, this creative force, in yet another unexpected turn in this chapter, is reawakened in a motion of premonition that now, however, remains anchored to the real:

> Cependant c'est la veille. Recevons tous les influx de vigueur et de tendresse réelle. Et à l'aurore, armés d'une ardente patience, nous entrerons aux splendides villes.
>
> Que parlais-je de main amie! Un bel avantage, c'est que je puis rire des vieilles amours mensongères, et frapper de honte ces couples menteurs,—j'ai vu l'enfer des femmes là-bas;—et il me sera loisible de *posséder la vérité dans une âme et un corps*. (O, 241)

> [Meanwhile it is the eve. Let us receive all influxes of force and of real tenderness. And at dawn, armed with an ardent patience, we will enter the splendid cities.
>
> What was I saying about a friendly hand! One fine advantage is that I can laugh at the old false loves, and strike shame into those lying couples—I have seen the hell of women down there;—and it will be permitted to me to *possess the truth in one soul and one body*.] (CP, 346)

These are resonant lines to arrive at this point. The poet, though he has left behind the dreams of Faust, has not entirely buried his imagination, or his hope, or his creative anticipation of light and passage, whatever he may have said a moment ago. An acknowledgment of the weight of the real is not identical with a submission to the doctors of the law or a passive resignation to the given. This poet, in the early autumn of 1873, still knows this. "Vigueur" (vigor), one of his talismanic words for the force that opens passage, is brought into resonance with "aurore" (dawn), a word of expectation that itself embodies, like a cryptic promise, the word "or" (gold), another of his talismanic terms for force and possibility. The speaker, back from hell, poises himself on the edge of night and dawn, the given and the yet to come, stoic engagement with facticity and creative leaning in premonition. He has found a measure of "patience," but he has retained a rhythm of "ardor" as well, without which he might not even have managed to write his way out of hell. This conclusion thus echoes, revises, and affirms the contradictions in "Alchimie du Verbe" to which I drew attention above.

Intact on the other side of infernal crisis, Rimbaud has managed to bend his *ardent impatience* into an *ardent patience*. And this ardent patience, though near to, is yet different from the ardent patience or patience of fire (as I characterized it above) that animates the *Derniers Vers*. For the ardent patience of *Une Saison* is not a passion for a departure of the self into the mysteries of light and the whole but a living contradiction that holds to both the fact of "rugged reality" and the promise of "splendid cities," the limiting pressure of the real and the creative reach of premonition. This contradiction, as well as the altered relationship with the real and with others that it implies, would seem to be the "truth" that the poet, according to the last line of the text, now intends to embody as an existential and poetic bearing. For Rimbaud at this point, Yves Bonnefoy writes, "modernity is the 'peasant' knowledge of a reality that no miracle borders, of a harsh but salutary duality of the human condition, at once misery and hope. And the future will be a future not of pure possession or glory but of truth, the obsession with salvation or its vain denial having given way to this creative recognition: that we exist only in this desire that never triumphs and never surrenders, in our unceasing confrontation with finitude, as far from the credulous as from 'the people who die by the seasons.'"[35]

NIETZSCHE

One of Nietzsche's guiding questions is related to the question Wordsworth tends to pose as that of the relationship between "knowledge" and "power." Nietzsche tends to pose it as that of the relationship between "knowledge" and "value," where different values are understood as different evaluations made by different phases of the will to power, that is, by different phases of life itself (ascending or descending, affirmative or negative, active or reactive). In the "Attempt at a Self-Criticism," written in 1886 to preface a new edition of *The Birth of Tragedy*, Nietzsche affirms "the task which this audacious book dared to tackle for the first time: *to look at science in the perspective of the artist, but at art in that of life*" (BT, 19). Nietzsche, then, is concerned with the limits of scientific knowledge, in particular with the inability of scientific knowledge to respond cogently to questions concerning the *value* of any human activity (including the activity of seeking knowledge) or of human life in general. His question recalls the ancient question of the good life, though it is shaped in response to major coordinates of his own time, including Kant's critique of reason, Schopenhauer's philosophy of the world as will and representation, and the romantic critique of the limits of the project of the Enlightenment in the name of existential wholeness and creative freedom.[36]

This is a question, too, that Nietzsche often poses as the question of nihilism, a term that means many things for him. First, it means the devaluation of life implicit in traditional "metaphysical" projections of a transcendent world "beyond" our immanent world of time, finitude, and suffering. It also means, then, the negation or repression of creative forces that is organized by the "ascetic" moralities that accompany these traditional metaphysical models, moralities fueled by *ressentiment*, a spiritualized revenge against others and against life itself. And yet, at the same time, nihilism designates the sense of absurdity or meaninglessness that emerges with the collapse of traditional metaphysical and moral frameworks. The culture of modernity, the culture of the "last man" and the devaluation of traditional "higher values," is for Nietzsche no less nihilist than those traditions which it appears to have surpassed: it is in fact a hollow aftermath of those traditions, a passive completion of the will to nothingness long hidden in them as their creative secret. Finally—and this is one motif that connects the early *Birth of Tragedy* with the later works of the eighties—nihilism designates that sense of the emptiness of transient human life that the Nietzsche of *The Birth of Tragedy* calls "the wisdom of Silenus" and that, he argues, the Greeks creatively overcame first through the Apollonian invention of the Olympian gods and again through the tragic art of the classical dramatists. For Nietzsche, then, there is an important sense in which modernity, characterized by the collapse of traditional values and the erosion of any absolute faith in the reach of theoretical knowledge, brings about a reencounter with the nihilist wisdom of Silenus (BT, 97–98). In *Zarathustra*, a text that Nietzsche presents as a "tragedy" (GS, 274), Silenus returns, wearing the mask of "the soothsayer."

It is often said that *The Birth of Tragedy* and the *Untimely Meditations* belong to the youthful Nietzsche's romantic, Schopenhauerian, Wagnerian phase of thought: a phase he is then said to have left behind, first, in the ironic or "Voltairean" works of the seventies, and second, in the "mature" works of the eighties in which he develops all those major philosophic approaches for which he has become best known. There is obviously some truth in this map of Nietzsche's trajectory. Nevertheless, it oversimplifies the relations among different texts of his, and in particular it occludes the return in *Zarathustra* of important intuitions first explored in *The Birth of Tragedy*. Thus, before turning to the extravagant quest and enigmatic crisis of *Zarathustra*, I would like briefly to recall the major arguments of *The Birth of Tragedy*. For it will be my argument that *Zarathustra* is a strange recasting of the conception of tragedy and of tragic overcoming presented in Nietzsche's first book.[37]

ONE COULD DESCRIBE the general shape of *The Birth of Tragedy* by saying that it brings together two distinct types of argument: a theory of art, including an account of primary "artistic energies which burst forth from nature herself" (38), the Apollonian and the Dionysian; and a theory of the different historical processes whereby different artistic forms and philosophic stances emerged and declined in ancient Greece.

Drawing on Schopenhauer's philosophic categories, while contesting his account of tragedy, Nietzsche describes the Apollonian force as that which organizes the realm of illusions and appearances, a realm governed by the principle of individuation, and the Dionysian force as that which expresses an unfathomable flux that perpetually destroys and creates anew the web of individuated appearances, a groundless ground of destructive and creative energy. In this Schopenhauerian account, indeed, the reverberant force of the Dionysian is ultimately "the foundation of all existence," "the basic ground of the world" (143). It is in terms of the shifting interplay of these Apollonian and Dionysian artistic energies, Nietzsche claims, that one can elucidate the history of epic, lyric, and tragic poetry in ancient Greece.

Having set these metaphysical coordinates in place, Nietzsche examines three different processes of "overcoming" whereby, in turn, the Olympian art of epic poetry, the Dionysian art of tragic drama, and the Socratic practice of theoretical optimism emerged (Nietzsche interprets this last, however, not as a noble overcoming but as a base decline whereby art itself was negated). Eventually, too, he celebrates a fourth "overcoming" that happens to be taking place in nineteenth-century Germany: the rebirth of tragedy in the art of Wagner, a mythomusical "overcoming" of the nihilist abyss disclosed when the limits of reason have at last (thanks to Kant) been acknowledged.

Whence emerges the epic poetry whose calm, clarity, and "naiveté" had so struck Schiller? Nietzsche's way of probing this question is an early demonstration of what would remain a characteristic feature of his thought: he reads epic poetry as an outcome of a process. For the Apollonian clarity of epic poetry, Nietzsche argues, is the product of an overcoming of a recognition of the pointless suffering of transient existence, a recognition taught by the soothsayer in *Zarathustra* and associated with the energies of the Titans, the energies of Dionysus, and the "folk wisdom" or "Dionysian wisdom" of Silenus in *The Birth of Tragedy*. According to the story Nietzsche retells, Silenus, echoing a famous chorus in *Oedipus at Colonnus,* teaches King Midas that for humans the best is not to be born, and the second best to die soon. Once we have heard this "folk wisdom," Nietzsche writes, "it is as if the Olympian magic mountain had opened before us and revealed its roots to us. The Greek knew and felt the terror and horror of existence. That he might endure this terror at all, he had to interpose between himself and life the radiant dream-birth of the Olympians" (42). The epic fabric of Apollonian illusions preserves life by veiling the destructive forces of the Titanic underside of life: "Where we encounter the 'naive' in art, we should recognize the highest effect of Apollonian culture—which always must first overthrow an empire of Titans and slay monsters, and which must have triumphed over an abysmal and terrifying view of the world and the keenest susceptibility to suffering through recourse to the most forceful and pleasurable illusions" (43).

However, this achievement is precarious, for the Apollonian art of illusions does not engage and transfigure so much as veil the Titanic forces it has glimpsed, and in time these Titanic forces return to tear down the veil, now in the form of the Dionysian mysteries. Once again the tragic wisdom of Silenus makes itself heard: "The wisdom of Silenus cried 'Woe! woe!' to the serene Olympians. . . . *Excess* revealed itself as truth. Contradiction, the bliss born of pain, spoke out from the very heart of nature" (46). There is joy in these Dionysian states, insofar as they sweep the individual into a particpation in the destructively creative flux of nature, yet there is terror in these states as well, insofar as they reveal to the individual the pointless transience of all individuated beings and so of all human efforts. In this sense the Dionysian wisdom of Silenus is nihilist, inducing a sort of stunned passivity, a nausea very much like the nausea Zarathustra feels during his critical encounter with the thought of the eternal recurrence:

> In this sense the Dionysian man resembles Hamlet: both have once looked truly into the essence of things, they have *gained knowledge,* and nausea inhibits action: for their action could not change anything in the eternal nature of things; they feel it to be ridiculous or humiliating that they should be asked to set right a world that is out of joint. Knowledge kills action; action requires the veils of illusion; that is the doctrine of Hamlet. . . .
> Now no comfort avails any more; longing transcends a world after death, even the gods; existence is negated along with its glittering reflection in the gods or in an immortal beyond. Conscious of the truth he has once seen, man now sees everywhere only the horror or absurdity of existence; now he understands what is symbolic in Ophelia's fate; now he understands the wisdom of the sylvan god, Silenus: he is nauseated.[38] (60)

It is at this point that art arrives "as a saving sorceress" (60) to accomplish yet another overcoming of the Dionysian abyss of nihilism, for "art alone knows how to turn these nauseous thoughts about the horror or absurdity of existence into notions with which one can live: these are the *sublime* as the artistic taming of the horrible, and the *comic* as the artistic discharge of the nausea of absurdity" (60). Tragic drama and the comic satyr play (though Nietzsche has nothing further to say about the latter in this text) preserve life where Apollonian epic has been overwhelmed by a return of Titanic energies and, so, by a return of the threat of nihilist apathy.[39]

How, then, does tragic art accomplish this creative overcoming of nihilism? To say that it turns the horrible into the sublime is simply to repeat the question at one remove. How is this transformation brought about? What *happens* in this transformation? Nietzsche's answer to this question, while scattered throughout the text, appears to involve two lines of thought. First, he elucidates tragic drama as a bringing together of the Apollonian and the Dionysian wherein the Dionysian predominates. "For a long time the only stage hero [of tragic drama] was Dionysus himself," and "all the celebrated figures of the Greek stage—Prometheus, Oedipus, etc.—are mere masks of this original hero" (73). Tragic art is thus fundamentally a Dionysian art:

> [We] must understand Greek tragedy as the Dionysian chorus which ever anew discharges itself in an Apollonian world of images. Thus the choral

parts with which tragedy is interlaced are, as it were, the womb that gave birth to the whole of the so-called dialogue, that is, the entire world of the stage, the real drama. In several successive discharges this primal ground of tragedy radiates this vision of the drama which is by all means a dream apparition and to that extent epic in nature; but on the other hand, being the objectification of a Dionysian state, it represents not Apollonian redemption through mere appearance but, on the contrary, the shattering of the individual and his fusion with primal being. Thus the drama is the Dionysian embodiment of Dionysian insights and effects. (64–65)

Second, drawing on romantic "expressivist" theories of art, according to which art operates by expressing *natura naturans* rather than imitating *natura naturata,* Nietzsche proposes a "participatory" theory of tragedy: the ecstatic raptures experienced in the Dionysian mysteries—the individual's joyous participation in the primary flux of destructive creation—are transposed to the tragic stage where, at the same time, they are modulated by Apollonian clarities. The "sublime" dynamic of tragic art lies in this transformation of a horrified awareness of Dionysian destructive power into a joyous participation in Dionysian creative power:

Dionysian art, too, wishes to convince us of the eternal joy of existence: only we are to seek this joy not in phenomena, but behind them. We are to recognize that all that comes into being must be ready for a sorrowful end; we are forced to look into the terrors of individual existence—yet we are not to become rigid with fear: a metaphysical comfort tears us momentarily from the bustle of the changing figures. We are really for a brief moment primordial being itself, feeling its raging desire for existence and joy in existence. (104)

In this way tragic art, while communicating the abyssal wisdom of Silenus, at the same time stirs in the spectator a joyous participation in the destructive-creative play of the world. And this is the basis of the tragic, joyous affirmation that "even the ugly and disharmonic are part of an artistic game that the will in the eternal amplitude of its pleasure plays with itself" (141).[40]

Nietzsche's theory of art, then, is neither "mimetic" nor "moral" but "transfigurative" (140–41).[41] He believes the task of art is to engage and transfigure the real and, in so doing, to bring about an overcoming of apathy, nausea, nihilism, the dark wisdom of Silenus. Thus at one point he speaks of art as a "corrective of, and supplement for science" (93), and elsewhere as a "metaphysical supplement of the reality of nature, placed beside it for its overcoming" (140). It is only art, not logical science or positive knowledge, that can transfigure the nihilist wisdom of Silenus. And it can do so because it communicates a tragic yet joyous "participation" in the destructive-creative energies of the Dionysian flux. This would seem to be the "logic" behind the famous assertion that "it is only as an *aesthetic phenomenon* that existence and the world are eternally justified" (52).

But the noble, creative pessimism of tragic art is soon undone by the new demon of Athens: Socrates, dialectics, theoretical optimism, a radically new (though decadent) approach to the problems of existence. It is an approach averse to the unrestrained passions and mythic obscurities of the great tragic dramas. Hopeful philosophy, in this story, effects the going under of tragic art. "Consider the consequences of the Socratic maxims: 'Virtue is knowledge; man sins only from ignorance; he who is virtuous is happy.' In these three basic forms of optimism lies the death of tragedy" (91).

Yet all is not lost. A musical Socrates, a rebirth of tragedy in a philosophic or postphilosophic culture, may be possible. For theory, in pursuing its own logic, eventually encounters a limit it cannot surpass on its own terms, a border at which the ancient wisdom of Silenus once again becomes heard:

> But science, spurred by its powerful illusion, speeds irresistibly toward its limits where its optimism, concealed in the essence of logic, suffers shipwreck. For the periphery of the circle of science has an infinite number of points; and while there is no telling how this circle could ever be surveyed completely, noble and gifted men nevertheless reach . . . such boundary points on the periphery from which one gazes into what defies illumination. When they see to their horror how logic coils up at these boundaries and finally bites its own tail—suddenly the new form of insight breaks through, *tragic insight* which, merely to be endured, needs art as a protection and a remedy. (97–98)

It is this "turning" that presents nineteenth-century Western culture with its greatest challenge: "Here we knock, deeply moved, at the gates of present and future: will this 'turning' lead to ever-new configurations of genius and especially of the *Socrates who practices music?*" (98). While the young Nietzsche casts Wagner as the agent of a rebirth of tragedy in a post-Socratic culture—a culture that has undone its own grounds and so left itself on a Silenian border—it is clear that Nietzsche would come to feel that the invention of a *Socrates who practices music* was above all a task destined for him. The ideal of the agile philosopher-poet, an ideal important in German romanticism, would haunt Nietzsche for the rest of his philosophic life. And the tragic philosopher-poet he would create in Zarathustra is doubtless an analogue of the musical Socrates he evokes in his first book. "I had discovered the only parable and parallel in history for my inmost experience," he writes in his discussion of *The Birth of Tragedy* in *Ecce Homo*, "and thus became the first to comprehend the wonderful phenomenon of the Dionysian.... Before me this transposition of the Dionysian into a philosophical pathos did not exist: *tragic wisdom* was lacking" (EH, 271–73). *Zarathustra* was lacking.

ZARATHUSTRA IS A crisis text in more than one sense. First, as is well known, it emerged out of a crisis in Nietzsche's own life, taking shape at a moment of great personal suffering. Further, the text is the working out of a philosophic crisis or a crisis in thought. While the exact place and significance of *Zarathustra* in Nietzsche's trajectory continues to be debated, and while one must study his later texts of the eighties in order fully to understand its guiding concepts, one can at least say with confidence that the text enacts a "pivotal" passage in Nietzsche's philosophic trajectory, a turn from the "Voltairean" phase of the seventies, where Nietzsche plays the ironic naturalist intent on debunking all human pieties, to the "mature" phase of the eighties, where he develops all those major concepts and approaches that have had such an immense influence over the last century: the will to power, the eternal recurrence, the theory of perspectivism, the question of nihilism, the practice of critical genealogy, the exposure of the place of revenge in the history of religious, metaphysical, and moral thought, and the protodeconstructive undoing of the most cherished concepts and presuppositions of both traditional and modern philosophy. *Zarathustra*, in other words, marks the decisive emergence of that explosive philosopher whom most of us have in mind when we think of Nietzsche. Finally, the story of *Zarathustra* itself includes the dramatization of a crisis suffered and overcome, namely, the crisis of Zarathustra's encounter with the abysmal thought of the eternal recurrence.[42]

This major crisis in *Zarathustra*, while difficult to interpret, is not difficult to locate. Indeed, Zarathustra's wrestling with the thought of the eternal recurrence loosely breaks the text into two parts, dividing parts 1 and 2 from part 3, though more exactly the crisis begins in part 2 at that point where Zarathustra collides with the nihilist teaching of the soothsayer. Parts 1 and 2 are largely devoted to a presentation of Zarathustra's teaching, including his "destructive" criticisms of the nihilism of otherworldly metaphysics, ascetic moralities, and modern flatness, as well as his "constructive" sketches of a countermetaphysic of dynamic immanence, a counterethic of the will to power and creative sublimation, and a countervision of creative self-overcoming and radical renovation. The entire project is emblematized by the ideal of the overman and the hyperbolic valorization of creative power essential to this ideal. The creative self-overcoming that "crosses" toward the overman—that "creates and carries together into One what is fragment and riddle and dreadful accident" (139)—promises to enact the overcoming of nihilism in all its major forms past and present. However, Zarathustra's critical and prophetic teaching is in a sense disrupted by his encounter with the thought of the eternal recurrence. He seems never quite the same after he hears the dark wisdom of the soothsayer. Throughout most of part 3, while wandering back to his mountain alone, he talks to himself, occasionally talks to people he runs into (including sailors on his way back from the Blessed Isles and later the raging fool known as "Zarathustra's ape"), and finally, back on his mountain, talks with his animals. In brief, part 3 is characterized by important shifts in theme, mood, and setting. Something has happened to Zarathustra. And Zarathustra, curiously, never teaches his disciples the thought of the eternal recurrence, though it has been the enigmatic source of his nauseating crisis and his joyous recovery.[43]

Even a cursory sketch of the dramatic structure of *Zarathustra*, then, serves to highlight some major interpretive questions that any reading of the text has to address. What is at stake in the project of the overman? What is the meaning of the thought of the eternal recurrence and of Zarathustra's complex response to this thought? What is the relationship between the project of the overman and the thought of the eternal recurrence? Is the thought of the eternal recurrence, as many commentators have argued, the ultimate test of the overman, the trial serving to distinguish the overman, one who has genuinely overcome nihilism, from all the rest? Or rather, as far fewer commentators have argued, and as I'm inclined to argue, does the thought of the eternal recurrence lead Zarathustra to a crisis that forces him to revise his initial teaching of the creative overman? And, finally, what is the import, for our understanding of Zarathustra's teaching, of the dramatic pattern that I've briefly sketched above?[44]

Zarathustra descends from his mountain, arrives in a town on the edge of the forest, and immediately declares his mission to an uncomprehending crowd: "*I teach you the overman. Man is something that shall be overcome. What have you done to overcome him?*" (12). At the very end of part 1, as he prepares to depart from his disciples, he repeats this message: "*Dead are all gods: now we want the overman to live*" (79). In some sense, then, the task of the overman "encapsulates" Zarathustra's initial teaching. There is no need to place great emphasis on the specific term "overman." As others have noted, it is a term that only rarely appears in Nietzsche's work outside of *Zarathustra*, perhaps because Nietzsche quickly recognized the sorts of misreadings it invites, as would seem to be indicated by his remarks to that effect in *Ecce Homo* (261).[45] Yet the theme to which the term "overman" lends hyperbolic expression is one of the most important themes in Nietzsche's thought from first to last: the theme of self-overcoming through courageous self-criticism and creative self-transformation. There may be no more constant theme in all of Nietzsche's work. It informs, as we have seen, his early account of Greek tragedy as the artistic overcoming of nihilist insight; it informs his early reading of Greek culture in general in "On the Uses and Disadvantages of History for Life" (UM, 122–23); it shapes his early conception of the genuine philosopher in "Schopenhauer as Educator" (UM, 128–29); it is a recurrent theme in all his major works from *Zarathustra* on; and it is an ideal hilariously affirmed in the unforgettable *Ecce Homo*.[46]

The concept of self-overcoming is not exactly original. In fact, Zarathustra's conception of the human being as "a rope tied between beast and overman—a rope over an abyss" (Z, 14) is, in no small sense, a secular adaptation of Christian anthropology. According to the latter, each fallen human being, situated in nature, is called to a decision: either to realize a truly superhuman destiny, ultimately a redemption in Christ, or to sink to a subhuman death-in-life, ultimately an eternal exile from the divine. In Nietzsche, as in romanticism and later in existentialism, the post-Christian destiny of the individual is reimagined as an immanent existential "project" whose meaning is determined by the "situated" yet "free" individual's creative words and acts. But a defining mark of Zarathustra's vision of this path of self-creation is its Faustian hyperbole. As Tyler Roberts notes, Zarathustra presents the overman less as some ideal model of selfhood than as a powerful event that may *happen* to a self, a lightning-bolt that, in traversing the given self, effects the latter's decisive "going under" as well as its exceptional "crossing over" (Z, 14–16).[47]

Like other romantic writers, notably Rimbaud, Zarathustra underlines the destructive as well as the transfigurative effects of any radical release of creative power. And both the violence associated with the overman, and the extravagant project of creative renewal it demands, are marks of its Christian origins. The project of the overman is animated by a displaced individualist and apocalyptic Protestantism; alongside the denunciations of Christian metaphysics and Christian morality, it is a displaced vision of shattering renovation that Zarathustra teaches in the early phases of his ministry. Thus Zarathustra's vision, like the Christian vision, involves first of all *a premise of condemnation:* the human being qua given self is a ruined, bitter thing adrift in the despair of death-in-life, a living No even when it appears to say Yes. Zarathustra holds his own with the most vehement of the Christian teachers of contempt for the merely given self. However, Zarathustra's vision, again like the Christian vision, involves at the same time *a premise of possibility:* the human being qua creative being or renovated self, struck by currents of creative power, is transfigured, created anew, released from gravity, made capable of walking joyously though it find itself in the valley of the shadow of death. These religious tropes and dynamics in Zarathustra's teaching are refigurations, familiar to readers of romantic poetry, that signal the displaced substance shaping his vision as he initially undertakes his quest to overcome nihilism. An immanent release of creative power is to accomplish that renovative self-surpassing which, it was once felt, only the dazzling arrival of the Spirit could accomplish. Creative power, refigured by Nietzsche as "Dionysian," is at once the bridge and the crossing. There is in this vision an inexhaustible restlessness, as well as an apocalyptic impatience with the given, that recalls similar impulses in Rimbaud, despite the many philosophical and ideological differences between these two Faustian questers.[48]

Yet Zarathustra's teaching of this hyperbolic project is disrupted by the crisis he undergoes in encountering the thought of the eternal recurrence. It is a crisis from which he recovers, though his path to recovery, like the gradual emergence in the text of the thought itself, is perplexingly indirect.

There seem to be four major ways in which commentators on Nietzsche have interpreted this riddle of the eternal recurrence. First, it can be understood as a quasi-mechanistic theory of the universe, a cosmological theory. Though Nietzsche dallied with this perspective, on occasion sketching "proofs" in his notebooks, it appears always to have been of secondary importance to him. At any rate, he never published anything like a sustained argument in defense of this perspective.

A second way the eternal recurrence has been interpreted is as the figure of a particular "intuition" or "experience" of Nietzsche's that eludes conceptual clarity. One can read the figure in this way without necessarily ascribing to

Nietzsche any sort of mystical experience (though an experience of that sort may have been involved). Long ago, for instance, Walter Kaufmann suggested that this figure was less an idea than a riddling expression of a specific pathos Nietzsche experienced: "The eternal recurrence was to Nietzsche less an idea than an experience—the supreme experience of a life unusually rich in suffering, pain, and agony. He made much of the moment when he first had this experience because to him it was the moment that redeemed his life."[49] This would help to explain, at least, why Nietzsche, though he clearly considered the thought of the eternal recurrence to be immensely important, made so little effort to clarify it in philosophic terms.

A third way this figure is often understood is as an "existential imperative" or a "diagnostic test." This is the prevalent interpretation of the eternal recurrence in recent studies of Nietzsche, and there is ample textual support for it. It is an interpretation proposing that the eternal recurrence is less a theory or a concept than a kind of mythic image serving as a test of one's existential attitude, a challenge to one's basic stance toward oneself and toward life. For only those who had creatively overcome all revenge against time, all fear of death, all resentment toward finitude, all bitterness toward their own contingent path to the present could genuinely and joyously will the eternal recurrence of their lives. As Bernd Magnus has succinctly put it: "The attitude toward life captured in the doctrine of eternal recurrence is the expression of nihilism already overcome."[50] Magnus has developed a variation on this widely held view by emphasizing that, if one pushes hard on this thought of the eternal recurrence, it turns out that only the overman, not any human being, could authentically pass the test it poses (though the self-deceived and the pathological could appear to pass it). Hence the thought of the eternal recurrence becomes a diagnostic thought that, by projecting before us a contrastive horizon of postnihilist joy, sheds light back on our human, all-too-human condition.[51]

There is a fourth way of interpreting this thought that is rather less common than the ones I've just mentioned, namely, as a mythopoetic figure for the recurrent Dionysian rhythms of life, for the destructive-creative play of a ceaseless Dionysian flux, the "artistic game that the will in the eternal amplitude of its pleasure plays with itself" (BT, 141), a Dionysian "game" that, according to the Nietzsche of *The Birth of Tragedy*, reverberates in the heroic overcoming manifest in ancient Greek tragedy. Many passages in which the eternal recurrence is presented in *Zarathustra* recall the evocations of Dionysian flux found in Nietzsche's first book. For example:

"O Zarathustra," the animals said, "to those who think as we do, all things themselves are dancing: they come and offer their hands and laugh and flee—and come back. Everything goes, everything comes back; eternally rolls the wheel of being. Everything dies, everything blossoms again; eternally runs the year of being. Everything breaks, everything is joined anew; eternally the same house of being is built. Everything parts, everything greets every other thing again; eternally the ring of being remains faithful to itself. In every Now, being begins; round every Here rolls the sphere There. The center is everywhere. Bent is the path of eternity." (Z, 217–18)

Nehamas notes the way this passage echoes the "Dionysianism" that appears so frequently in Nietzsche's works from first to last.[52] And Magnus, Stewart, and Mileur, in exploring the way Zarathustra's conception of the eternal recurrence at times seems intimately linked to the mysteries of birth, have juxtaposed the "Gate of the Moment" parable in *Zarathustra* (Z, 158) with the following passage from *Twilight of the Idols*:

For it is only in the Dionysian mysteries, in the psychology of the Dionysian condition, that the fundamental fact of the Hellenic instinct expresses itself—its "will to life." *What* did the Hellene guarantee to himself with these mysteries? *Eternal* life, the eternal recurrence of life; the future promised and consecrated in the past; the triumphant Yes to life beyond death and change; *true* life as collective continuation of life through procreation, through the mysteries of sexuality. It was for this reason that the sexual symbol was to the Greeks the symbol venerable as such, the intrinsic profound meaning of all antique piety. Every individual detail in the act of procreation, pregnancy, birth, awoke the most exalted and solemn feelings. In the teachings of the mysteries, pain is sanctified: the "pains of childbirth" sanctify pain in general—all becoming and growing, all that guarantees the future, *postulates* pain.... For the eternal joy in creating to exist, for the will to life eternally to affirm itself, the "torment of childbirth" *must* also exist eternally.... All this is contained in the word Dionysus. (TI, 119–20)

This is a hymn to the Dionysian recurrence of life itself, not to the exact recurrence of specific identities that come to be and pass away within life.[53]

It is a hymn, too, that could well have appeared in Nietzsche's first book. And it is this parallel between the later figure of the eternal recurrence, whose first major presentation occurs in *Zarathustra*, and Nietzsche's earlier meditation on a Dionysian art that at once communicates and overcomes a Dionysian wisdom, that I would like to spell out in my reading of Zarathustra's crisis and recovery. For *Zarathustra*, I think, unfolds like a visionary return of certain guiding intuitions and preoccupations that Nietzsche first explored in *The Birth of Tragedy*. That *Zarathustra* is a "tragedy" is often noted; Nietzsche tells us as much (GS, 274). But often it is then suggested that the "tragedy" lies in Zarathustra's "failure" to communicate his vision to others or to realize his transformative projects. The text, read in this light, dramatizes a tragic collision between heroic aspiration and crushing limitation. Yet I doubt this is what Nietzsche has in mind in alluding to *Zarathustra* as a tragedy. One should note, at least, that "tragedy" in this sense has more in common with the sort of "ironic" collision between "the ideal" and "the real" explored in the European novel than with what Nietzsche himself considers to be the substance of tragedy.

My own sense is that there occurs in *Zarathustra* a transposition, into the terms of individual experience, of the same dynamic of overcoming nihilism through creative transfiguration that Nietzsche describes in *The Birth of Tragedy*. Zarathustra is at once the hero, the artist, and the spectator of his own tragic drama. *For he traverses on the plane of his own experience the same phases that, in that earlier work, are described on the plane of larger cultural dynamics:* the passage from a recognition of the nihilist wisdom of Silenus, which induces nausea, through a transfigurative overcoming of this nihilist wisdom, which generates a joyously affirmative state of being. Zarathustra's traversal of these phases is dramatized above all in "The Soothsayer," "On the Vision and the Riddle," and "The Convalescent."

The soothsayer is at once a mask of the Ecclesiast, a mask of Schopenhauer, and, most importantly, a mask of Silenus. He teaches the emptiness of all things, the repetitiveness of all efforts, the pointless transience of all beings in the destructive-creative motions of becoming. The soothsayer is a nihilist, and his teaching seriously wounds Zarathustra, stirring in him the first of two nightmarish visions that he recounts in this work. In this vision Zarathustra sees himself as a "night watchman and a guardian of the tombs upon the lonely mountain castle of death" (134). A wind shatters the gates of his "castle" and hurls the derision of death at him:

> And amid the roaring and whistling and shrilling the coffin burst and spewed out a thousandfold laughter. And from a thousand grimaces of children, angels, owls, fools, and butterflies as big as children, it laughed

and mocked and roared at me. Then I was terribly frightened; it threw me to the ground. And I cried in horror as I have never cried. And my own cry awakened me—and I came to my senses. (135)

This is the thought of Dionysian recurrence under the aspect of nightmare. One of Zarathustra's disciples, however, does not quite recognize this. He interprets the dream as a disguise in which the truth has simply been reversed: according to him, it is Zarathustra, "the advocate of life," who is the roaring wind blowing through all moldering tombs with his transvaluative teaching (135–36). Zarathustra, hearing this interpretation, looks at his disciple and silently shakes his head. Robert Pippin claims that the disciple "gets all this exactly wrong."[54] But things are more complex than that. In a later section, "On Old and New Tablets," Zarathustra appears to affirm the disciple's interpretation: "O my brothers, like a fresh roaring wind Zarathustra comes to all who are weary of the way; many noses he will yet make sneeze. Through walls too, my free breath blows, and into prisons and imprisoned spirits" (206). Zarathustra's ambiguous response to the disciple, then, signifies not that the disciple is simply mistaken so much as that his understanding remains partial. His vision, aligned with the extravagant hope of Zarathustra's initial teaching, lacks the Silenian perspective, the nihilist perspective, that Zarathustra has now attained as well.[55]

In "On the Vision and the Riddle" Zarathustra, having left behind his disciples, at last presents a parable of the eternal recurrence. He presents it first to a dwarf of gravity, a kind of inner demon, and then, in the retelling that we hear, to a group of sailors on the ship bearing him back from the Blessed Isles (these sailors remain oddly silent). The dramatic shape of this section closely parallels that of "The Soothsayer." In both sections either a poetic teaching or a parabolic vision (the soothsayer's teaching of the emptiness of all, Zarathustra's parable of the Gate of the Moment) is followed by a nightmarish vision (the dream where Zarathustra is a guardian of tombs mocked by death, the dream where Zarathustra stumbles upon a shepherd being choked by a snake). Later, in "The Convalescent," Zarathustra explicitly identifies himself with the figures that appear in both of these dreams (219). The dwarf, or "spirit of gravity," responds to Zarathustra by recasting the teaching of the soothsayer in a mocking way: "'O Zarathustra,' he whispered mockingly, syllable by syllable; 'you philosopher's stone! You threw yourself up high, but every stone that is thrown must fall'" (156). It was this intuition of the vanity of all efforts that filled Zarathustra with such despair when he heard the soothsayer. In this case, however, Zarathustra manages to slay the demon of despair by telling him the parable of the Gate of the Moment. Yet when he finishes the parable and the dwarf has vanished, he finds himself in a visionary landscape where he encounters a shepherd choking on the "serpentine" thought of the eternal recurrence: "A young shepherd I saw, writhing, gagging, in spasms, his face distorted, and a heavy black snake hung out of his mouth. Had I ever seen so much nausea and pale dread on one face?" (159). But finally, with Zarathustra's desperate encouragement, the shepherd bites off the snake's head and leaps up as "one changed, radiant, laughing," laughing as no human being has ever laughed before (160). The entire vision is Zarathustra's premonition of his own recovery from the nausea he has felt since he encountered the soothsayer.

"The Convalescent" begins with Zarathustra summoning his "abysmal thought": he will no longer evade his thought through riddling projections. But the direct encounter with this thought nearly kills him, sinking him into a kind of coma (216). As the allusion to the creation of the world suggests—the quasi-coma lasts seven days—Zarathustra, in this experience, seems to die and to revive to the world, as though he had undergone a passion, initiation, and rebirth. He has returned to the garden of the world. His animals then undertake the task of teaching him the "doctrine" of the eternal recurrence that he is to teach the world, drawing amply on mythopoetic figures evocative of the "Dionysian" rhythms of nature. While Zarathustra affectionately mocks their songs, he does assent, if not to their exact figures, at least to the issue they raise, in the one important speech on the eternal recurrence that he makes in this section:

> The great disgust with man—*this* choked me and had crawled into my throat; and what the soothsayer said: "All is the same, nothing is worth while, knowledge chokes." A long twilight limped before me, a sadness, weary to death, drunken with death, speaking with a yawning mouth. "Eternally recurs the man of whom you are weary, the small man"—thus yawned my sadness and dragged its feet and could not go to sleep. Man's earth had turned into a cave for me, its chest sunken; all that is living became human mold and bones and musty past to me. My sighing sat on all human tombs and could no longer get up; my sighing and questioning croaked and gagged and gnawed and wailed by day and night: "Alas, man recurs eternally! The small man recurs eternally!"
>
> Naked had I once seen both, the greatest man and the smallest man: all-too-similar to each other, even the greatest all-too-human. All-too-small, the greatest!—that was my disgust with man. And the eternal recur-

rence of even the smallest—that was my disgust with all existence. Alas! Nausea! Nausea! (219)

Yet even as he recalls it with such force, Zarathustra appears to have recovered from this nausea. By the end of the section, as his animals continue to play the joyous "chorus" to his tragic passage, he is curiously absent from them, "conversing with his soul" (221). And the last three sections of part 3 are joyous songs of affirmation that make clear that he has "overcome" his nausea. He has found a power of affirmation stronger than the recognition of the horror of Dionysian recurrence. "O my soul, I gave you the right to say No like the storm, and to say Yes as the clear sky says Yes: now you are still as light whether you stand or walk through storms of negation" (222). He sees in the "night-eye" of life "a golden boat . . . blinking on nocturnal waters" (224). He has reached a joyous state of *amor fati*. He is able to "carry the blessings of [his] Yes into all abysses" (165).

What has happened? How has Zarathustra managed to overcome the nausea with which the thought of the eternal recurrence, the Silenian wisdom of the soothsayer, filled him? It is clear that Zarathustra's overcoming of this nausea involves an overcoming of what he calls the eternal recurrence of the "small man" or the "smallness of man." Hence an understanding of his overcoming requires an elucidation of this figure. Further, Zarathustra's overcoming involves not a sudden change of mind, a simple reversal, but a passage that unfolds in time: a passage parallel to the passage from nausea to joy that, according to *The Birth of Tragedy*, is accomplished through tragic art. Hence an understanding of Zarathustra's drama requires a clarification of this parallel.

One transformation that occurs here, I believe, involves Zarathustra's recognition of the potential nihilism of his own hyperbolic effort to overcome nihilism. The "small man" that has filled him with "nausea" is, in one sense, the "small man" within himself that can never be entirely surpassed.[56] His nausea at the thought of this "small man," in other words, is based in a feeling of revenge toward the contingently given self. This is obliquely suggested by Zarathustra's first response to the dream that the soothsayer's teaching stirred in him. He attempts to recover from this dream, in "On Redemption," by setting forth his most brilliant and hyperbolic speech on the project of the overman. It is a speech in which he spells out both the "root" of all earlier forms of nihilism—the revenge against time, the will's aversion to time's "it was"—and the challenging path of creative self-transformation necessary to any genuine overcoming of nihilism:

> I led you away from these [nihilist] fables when I taught you, "The will is a creator." All "it was" is a fragment, a riddle, a dreadful accident—until the creative will says to it, "But thus I willed it." Until the creative will says to it, "But thus I will it; thus shall I will it."
>
> But has the will yet spoken thus? And when will that happen? Has the will been unharnessed yet from his own folly? Has the will yet become his own redeemer and joy-bringer? Has he unlearned the spirit of revenge and all gnashing of teeth? And who taught him reconciliation with time and something higher than any reconciliation? For that will which is the will to power must will something higher than any reconciliaton; but how shall this be brought about? Who could teach the will to will backwards? (141)

The overcoming of nihilism, then, demands not only an overcoming of the fear of death—though that is important—but also an overcoming of the fear of unfreedom, the hostility to one's contingent finitude, or, in Heidegger's great trope, one's "thrownness." And this overcoming, Zarathustra teaches, can be accomplished only by creatively transforming the contingent being one has become in time: only thus can one also affirm one's life.

However, there are puzzles and countercurrents in this speech. First, it is of interest that Zarathustra acknowledges here that he too is a "cripple" on the bridge of becoming (139). Further, at the conclusion of his speech, he seems to respond to his own words with bafflement: "At this point in his speech it happened that Zarathustra suddenly stopped and looked altogether like one who has received a severe shock" (141). Does Zarathustra, as Pippin suggests, suddenly recognize a certain "folly of the will" in his own project of the overman? Does he perhaps recognize the extent to which his own project involves a "religious" longing to transcend all limits? It would seem that Zarathustra, in acknowledging the "small man" within himself, in acknowledging the "crippled" self that he too is, recognizes that his project of creative self-transformation, if carried to an apocalyptic pitch, expresses such an extreme contempt for the given self that it risks becoming itself an expression of nihilism—perhaps even a nihilism, a folly of the will, not so far from the nihilism of the ascetic priest that Nietzsche illuminates in *On the Genealogy of Morals*. "The ascetic priest," Nietzsche writes in one of the most brilliant sections of that book, "is the incarnate desire to be different, to be in a different place, and indeed this desire at its greatest extreme, its distinctive fervor and passion" (GM, 120). To be sure, the project of the overman is motivated by "a desire to be different" projected along a horizontal or immanent plane, toward an unfolding future, rather than along a vertical plane, toward a realm beyond time. Nevertheless, Zarathustra appears to recognize that this project, if directed with boundless vehemence toward a "different place" in the future, may turn into a revenge against time, a nihilist contempt for the difficulties of a present shaped by the play of the past. In *Une Saison en enfer,* as I argued above, Rimbaud wrestles in a similar way with an apocalyptic impatience that risks becoming as nihilist as the nihilist flatness it would surpass. Both of these questers find their way toward an ardent patience.

This does not mean that Zarathustra, in his recovery, abandons his vision of creative self-overcoming and cultural transvaluation. It means that he revises it, reimagines it from an altered perspective that now brings together the project of creative transformation and the existential orientation of *amor fati.* "And I myself," Zarathustra asks as he awakes from his seven-day coma, "do I thus want to be man's accuser?" (218). The implicit answer is clearly no: the "accusers" of the world are those metaphysicians and moralists whose teachings Zarathustra wishes to overcome. Hence the overcoming of nihilism demands at one and the same time an affirmation of, and a transformation of, the vexing limitations of the given. "In *amor fati,*" as Jaspers puts it, "the seemingly incompatible meet: intensified activity aiming at future fulfillment joins loving acceptance of whatever happens. But conceptual expression of this fusion is possible only through paradoxes": paradoxes that point to an existential contradiction that Nietzsche himself lived and expressed in the last ten years of his life as a writer. The paradoxes themselves are easy enough to repeat. To perform them, to accomplish them in a creative life, is more difficult, involving a genuine overcoming of nihilism.[57]

Yet, there is another transformation that occurs in Zarathustra's recovery, another overcoming of nihilism, or perhaps an overcoming of nihilism on another plane. For in an important sense Zarathustra's nausea at the thought of the "small man" is a nausea at the thought of the "smallness of man" in general: "Naked I had once seen both, the greatest man and the smallest man: all-too-similar to each other, even the greatest all-too-human" (Z, 219). In part, then, Zarathustra's nausea is simply his disgust at the dark teaching of the soothsayer—the teaching that all human efforts, in the general sweep of the Dionysian flux, are but passing and pointless wrecks. This, as Nietzsche argues in *The Birth of Tragedy,* is the nihilism that both precedes the rise of nihilist metaphysics and returns with the collapse of nihilist metaphysics. It is the insight of "Dionysian man": "Conscious of the truth he has once seen, man now sees everywhere only the horror or absurdity of existence; now he understands what is symbolic in Ophelia's fate; now he understands the wisdom of the sylvan god, Silenus: he is nauseated" (BT, 60). This is exactly the condition of Zarathustra once he has heard the Silenian teaching of the soothsayer. I would emphasize that, for Nietzsche as for Zarathustra, this nihilism is not a mistaken view of things. To the contrary, it is an insight gained by cutting through the illusions—metaphysical, religious, moral, and scientific—with which we typically veil this Silenian truth from ourselves.

Of course, this insight is not the whole story. How does "Dionysian man" overcome his suicidal nihilism? How does he overcome his nausea and despair? How, in the language of *On the Genealogy of Morals,* does he preserve his will and even reanimate his will? How, in the language of *Zarathustra,* does he find not only reconciliation with time but something higher than any reconciliation? We should recall the answer that *The Birth of Tragedy* gives to this question: "Here, when the danger to his will is greatest, art approaches as a saving sorceress, expert at healing. She alone knows how to turn these nauseous thoughts about the horror or absurdity of existence into notions with which one can live" (BT, 61). For art is a *transfigurative supplement* to knowledge that, "placed beside [the reality of nature] for its overcoming," brings about an affirmative overcoming of the nihilism experienced at the limits of knowledge (BT, 93, 97–98, 141). This is the sublime accomplishment of tragic art. According to *The Birth of Tragedy,* as we have seen, this accomplishment is based in the way tragic art sweeps the spectator into a joyous "participation" in the creative power of the primary Dionysian play of the world. Traces of this "participatory" theory do return in *Zarathustra.* In his recovery, which allows him to sing a sacred Yes to everything, Zarathustra appears to resemble the child who, in "On the Three Metamorphoses," is evoked as a creative "self-propelled wheel" on the other side of the lion's pride, autonomy, and critical power: "the child is innocence and forgetting, a new beginning, a game, a self-propelled wheel, a first movement, a sacred Yes" (Z, 27), a participant in, rather than an antagonist of, the eternal Dionysian recurrence of life.[58]

Yet something else is at stake here. Zarathustra is at once the hero, the artist, and the spectator of his own tragic drama. He is also the teacher of the way of creative power and self-overcoming. The dominant point of view in *Zarathustra,* then, is that of the "artist" or the "creator," not, as in *The Birth of Tragedy,* that of the "spectator." Hence the transfigurative overcoming of nihilism in Zarathustra's drama is accomplished by and for the creator (Zarathustra himself) rather than for the spectator. What is Zarathustra's "art" that allows him to "supplement" and "transfigure" his nihilist insight? What, from this point of view, replaces the young Nietzsche's "participatory" theory of art? The answer, I think, is *a theory of troping* or, more broadly, *a theory of creative action*. Zarathustra must overcome his Silenian wisdom through a creative troping that at once retains that nihilist wisdom and affirmatively transfigures it. That is what he does: he refigures the nauseating "Silenian wisdom" of the soothsayer as the joyous "nuptial ring" of the eternal recurrence. Zarathustra, in other words, rather openly presents the eternal recurrence as a mythopoetic figure, a metaphysical guess, that supplements the nihilism apprehended at the borders of knowledge. This figure is not a concept, a theory, or a doctrine. And that is why Zarathustra mocks the various efforts that others make to turn it into a doctrine. For Zarathustra is a tragic poet who, in inventing a reaching figure in response to Silenian nihilism, has acknowledged and at the same time joyously overcome that nihilism. Others, if they cut through their illusions, recognize the abyssal truth of nihilism, and wish to overcome it, will have to invent their own figures. Hence Zarathustra's warning: "'This is *my* way; where is yours?'—thus I answered those who asked me 'the way.' For *the* way—that does not exist" (Z, 195).[59] Zarathustra warns us not to mistake his tropes (in this case the trope of the eternal recurrence) for his principles (in this case the necessity of both recognizing and creatively overcoming nihilism). *It is above all the act of creative refiguration that brings about both a self-overcoming and a transformed relationship to becoming as a whole.* Thus the teaching by exemplification of a Socrates who plays music, a philosopher who practices poetry.[60]

This is also the point, I think, of Zarathustra's curious discourse on "words" when he first awakens from his deathlike sleep in "The Convalescent":

> How lovely it is that there are words and sounds! Are not words and sounds rainbows and illusive bridges between things which are eternally apart? . . . Have not names and sounds been given to things that man might find things refreshing? Speaking is a beautiful folly: with that man dances over all things. How lovely is all talking, and all the deception of sounds! With sounds our love dances on many-hued rainbows. (217)

In this speech, according to a common reading, Zarathustra is concerned to underline either the inaccessibility of the crisis he has just passed through, or the wide difference between any abstract formulation of that crisis and his own lived experience of it. That is probably so. Yet it may be that Zarathustra wishes, above all, to indicate that it is only through the creative "turning" of language that one can "supplement," "transfigure," and so "overcome" the Silenian wisdom of the soothsayer. As it is put in *The Birth of Tragedy:* "Perhaps there is a realm of wisdom from which the logician is exiled? Perhaps art is even a necessary correlative, and supplement for science?" (93). It is in just this sense that "speaking is a beautiful folly: with that man dances over all things": dances in turned words—in their reaching, affirmative refigurations of the mystery of the whole—over the Silenian nihilism taught by the soothsayer, a nihilism to which Socratic theory may have no adequate response.[61]

Yet the troping in *Zarathustra* extends well beyond Zarathustra's troping. For the real artist of this tragic drama is of course Nietzsche. And the strange art of parts 1–3 of *Zarathustra* consists of the mapping of a one-character tragic drama, according to the theory of tragic drama presented in *The Birth of Tragedy,* onto a narrative pattern lifted from the Gospels. Part 4, from this perspective, is the one-act satyr play that follows the three-act tragic drama.[62]

Zarathustra is cast as a tragic hero, not in the sense that his mission fails, but in the sense that he is a "mask" of Dionysus (BT, 73), an overreaching hero who suffers a collision with abyssal forces and "goes under" or suffers a passion. Yet his suffering is at the same time a transfigurative passage of overcoming. There is a precedent in Greek tragedy for the suffering hero who lives to experience his own transfiguration, namely Oedipus, whose passage from immense suffering to "superterrestrial cheerfulness" and ultimate transfiguration is discussed in *The Birth of Tragedy* (67–69). Like Oedipus, Zarathustra is a hero whose gift for solving riddles turns out to be inseparable from his destiny of suffering. In some sense, then, Zarathustra passes through an entire tragic trajectory. Indeed, the rhetoric of "going under" and "overcoming" in *Zarathustra* appears to recall, in an indirect way, the description of tragic drama in *The Birth of Tragedy:* perhaps the peculiar term *Übermensch,* in the end, is but a whimsical renaming of the overreaching tragic hero.

At the same time *Zarathustra* is a creative parody of the Gospels. My point is not simply that the text is a countergospel intended to displace the Christian (as well as the Platonist) tradition, though that is perfectly evident. My point is that the text is closely patterned after the Gospels, is in fact a Dionysian refiguration of the Gospels.[63]

Like Jesus, Zarathustra withdraws to a mountain at the age of thirty to prepare himself for his ministry. Like Jesus, he assumes the stance and the rhetoric of a prophet, a charismatic sage whose abrupt words are meant to shock like bolts of existential wisdom. Like Jesus, he speaks in aphorisms, riddles, and parables, modes of speech intended to jar his audience out of their habitual modes of response so that they will begin to transform themselves.[64] Like Jesus, and like Socrates, he is a teacher who engages his listeners face to face, not a writer. Like Jesus, he gathers a band of disciples, alienates most of the "good" and "just" and "educated" people of his time, and shows himself to be alternately generous and impatient (not to say outrageous). And like Jesus, he is a kind of human storm bringing at one and the same time a judgment of condemnation, a call to a redemptive task that demands a "turning" of the entire being of anyone who would respond to this call, and a promise, rather vaguely evoked, of a future that, whatever else it may involve, clearly involves a disclosure of uncommon power, an astonishing renovation of the human being, and a new way of life. To be sure, Zarathustra is no Jesus, and not only because he teaches the death of God and the affirmation of a Faustian human pride. Yet he resembles that earlier apocalyptic teacher who "astounded" those he taught because "he taught them as one having authority, and not as their scribes" (Matthew 7.29).

Further, and at least as importantly, the schematic "plot" of *Zarathustra* is lifted from the schematic "plot" of the Gospels. There are two basic "planes" in the plot of the Gospels: first, an episodic narrative, organized around the wanderings, doings, and sayings of the charismatic hero, and second, an overarching narrative, organized around the teaching, the passion, and the resurrection of the hero. The plot of the Gospels, in a word, describes the curve of Jesus' ministry, his lonely suffering of death on the cross, and his triumphant resurrection. The plot of parts 1–3 of *Zarathustra* resonantly follows this model. It describes the curve of Zarathustra's ministry, his lonely suffering or "passion" of the thought of the eternal recurrence (Z, 239), and his triumphant self-renewal on the other side of a deathlike coma. The "comic" resurrection from the passion of death is replaced by a "tragic" or "artistic" recovery from the passion of the nihilist thought of the eternal recurrence. The promise of eternal life is replaced by a tragic affirmation of *amor fati*. In the 1886 preface to *The Gay Science* Nietzsche appears to tell us exactly what he has done: "'*Incipit tragoedia*' we read at the end of this awesomely aweless book. Beware! Something downright wicked and malicious is announced here: *incipit parodia*, no doubt" (GS, 33). He has composed a three-act tragic drama, the Dionysian drama of Zarathustra's abysmal going under and transfigurative crossing over, and "maliciously" imposed it upon the narrative pattern of the Gospels. The last words of *Ecce Homo* read: "Have I been understood?—*Dionysus versus the Crucified*" (335). With these words Nietzsche again describes, among other things, the refigurative vision accomplished in the very form of *Zarathustra*. The text is an exemplification of a creative affirmation of the past that is at the same time a creative transformation of the past. This sort of refiguration permits one to surpass both the nihilism of despair (sheer resignation to the given, the death-in-life of sheer passivity) and the nihilism of blind negativity or escapist fantasy (sheer destruction of the given, the death-in-life of sheer reactivity). In this way Nietzsche overcomes a crisis of nihilism.

NIETZSCHE WOULD HOVER along this border between critical reason and visionary quest for the rest of his life as a philosopher. In *Zarathustra*, a pivotal text, it is as though the Dionysian Nietzsche, the tragic visionary weaving together creative passage and *amor fati*, and the Socratic Nietzsche, the gay ironist concerned to expose the hydra-headed stratagems of self-deception and false assurance, were brought together in a dynamic conflict. Abiding and wrestling there, Nietzsche passed through a crisis in his own thought and found a capacious orientation that would animate him until the last days of 1888. As a critic, he would *belong* to his culture, ironically engaging it, mocking it with a finely tuned hammer, constructing arguments designed to jar it from its complacent reliance on eroded foundations and mystifying pieties. As a riddling poet, a visionary poet-philosopher, he would *depart* from his culture, inventing provocative counterperspectives, exploring spacious metaphysical guesses, traveling with a kind of strange joy through the Silenian space he imagined to be our ineluctable condition: an abyssal groundlessness that could only be overcome again and again through creative passages of tragic recognition and affirmative refiguration (the "measure" of Rimbaud's renovative Genius, we could recall in this context, must be "reinvented" again and again). In this way he could retain his exceptional Faustian mobility, his dynamic concern to sketch visions of what *la vraie vie* might be, without succumbing to the Faustian risk (ultimately but another sort of nihilism) of turning either the fantasy of pure departure or the exercise of pure negativity into a new idol.[65]

There is much, then, that Nietzsche and Rimbaud share: a Faustian courage; a bent for hyperbole; an apocalyptic vision of destructive renovation; a defiant longing for freedom from the prisons they perceive around them; an enormous valorization of creative power and vision; a sweeping post-Christian faith in vast horizons of metamorphosis; a fascination with masks as sources of both irony and power; and, in communication with a "modernist" practice they anticipate, a stylistic energy, virtuosity, complexity, and polyphony that conveys, as it were, some experience of bewildering openness, of metamorphic passage in multiple directions at once. Both, too, undergo a severe crisis during which they come to recognize the potential nihilism of their own Faustian efforts to surpass nihilism. And both, in different ways, articulate recoveries from their crises, working out revised perspectives that permit them to reanimate their transformative visions without falling out of communication with the world they inhabit.

Bataille, an eccentric voice in the modernist period, bends these adventures back toward the wholly demonic, making of vertiginous negativity the source of authentic freedom, setting a Faustian exorbitance in opposition to the limits of any context, given, altered, or reimagined.

BATAILLE

Bataille could no more abide his social context than Rimbaud and Nietzsche could abide theirs. Like his Faustian predecessors, he longed for a wild freedom, perceived in the operations of modernity an organization of mutilated subjects, and responded to this world by bringing together a passionate refusal and a search for the impossible.

"I abhor all trades. Masters and workers, all peasants, ignoble," wrote the Rimbaud who insisted he would never work (O, 213; CP, 301). "Life flowers through work, an old truth: as for me, my life isn't heavy enough, it flies away and drifts far above action, that cherished point of the world" (O, 218; CP, 311). "Action is not life, but a way of wasting some force, an enervation" (O, 233; CP, 334). Thus did he anticipate Bataille:

> I cannot exist entirely except when somehow I go beyond the stage of action. Otherwise I'm a soldier, a professional, a man of learning, not a "total human being." The fragmentary state of humanity is basically the same as the choice of an object. When you limit your desire to possessing political power, for instance, you act and know what you have to do. The possibility of failure isn't important—and right from the start, you insert your existence advantageously into time. Each of your moments becomes *useful*. With each moment, the possibility is given you to advance to some chosen goal—what's normally called living. Similarly, if salvation is the goal.

> Every action makes you a fragmentary existence. I hold onto my nature as an entirety only by refusing to act—or at least by denying the superiority of time, which is reserved for action.
>
> Life is whole only when it isn't subordinate to a specific object that exceeds it. In this way, the essence of entirety is freedom. (ON, xxvii)

Radical freedom and an "entirety" of existence demand a departure from the structured world of work, utility, discursive representation, any "project" at all. "Existence is elsewhere," as Breton declares in the last sentence of the first surrealist manifesto.

Nietzsche taught not simply that God was dead—that was a commonplace of his time—but that the enormous implications of this death had yet to be recognized: that the transcendent and the foundational had themselves collapsed, that we were adrift in a radical metaphysical insecurity, that in seeking to replace the transcendent with reason, or nature, or an array of other principles we were evading both the nihilist abyss and the uncanny freedom we had nonetheless begun to approach. Thus the words of Nietzsche's famous "madman," whose listeners cannot yet understand his urgency: "'I have come too early,' he said then; 'my time is not yet. This tremendous event [the death of God] is still on its way, still wandering; it has not yet reached the ears of men'" (GS, 182). Perhaps Bataille saw himself in this lucid madman.[66] For a period of some forty years, in a variety of forms, he argued that the modern West was still enclosed in the slumber from which Nietzsche's "madman" was trying to shake us, a slumber of rationalized "projects" wherein we exchanged our birthright of freedom for a servile security we naively mistook for freedom. With Faustian energy, Bataille set himself against this world of calculated projects, repeatedly tracing those movements that lead to a rapture of "non-sense" beyond practical utility and discursive justification, an ecstatic "sovereignty" discovered when the isolated, defensive, purposive ego is undone in a communion with unintelligible being:

> Death alone—or, at least, the ruin of the isolated individual in search of happiness in time—introduces that break without which nothing reaches the state of ecstasy. And what we thereby regain is always both innocence and the intoxication of existence. The isolated being *loses himself* in something other than himself. What the "other thing" represents is of no importance. It is still a reality that transcends the common limitations. So unlimited is it that it is not even a thing: it is a *nothing*. (IE, 26)

Bataille's project, then, is a paradoxical project of exploding project (IE, 46), a capacious study of those extreme experiences that pass beyond the "restricted economy" of work, prohibition, discursive reason, and self-preservation. Only such disruptive passages, Bataille claims, turn the isolated subject toward the limits of the possible, abandon the subject to a "general economy" of excess. "Hegel's construction is a philosophy of work, of 'project.' . . . The only obstacle in this way of seeing . . . is what, in man, is irreducible to project: non-discursive existence, laughter, ecstasy, which link man—in the end—to the negation of project which *he* nevertheless *is*" (IE, 80).

ONE OF THE traditions that Bataille draws on is a poetic tradition of Satanism and delirium running from Nerval, Baudelaire, Lautréamont, and Rimbaud through surrealism. Bataille is in fact closer to the surrealist project than he and some of his later commentators have always wished to recognize.[67] He draws amply on a postromantic and surrealist poetic of creative disordering, metamorphic passage, convulsive beauty, erotic transgression, demonic laughter, and errant sounding of *le hasard*. However, unlike Rimbaud and Breton, he considers these delirious modes of experience less as phases of disclosure (paths toward a renovated space of existence) than as the very movement of radical freedom. For Bataille (who strangely recalls some notably less ecstatic characters in Beckett) freedom is this vertigo itself:

> My difficulty: total loss of certainty, the difference between a sculpted object and fog (usually we imagine that it is dreadful). If I expressed joy, I would be off the mark: the joy which I have differs from other joys. I am accurate in speaking of fiascos, of collapses without end, of absence of hope. Yet . . . fiasco, collapse, despair are, in my eyes, light, laying bare, glory. (IE, 55)

"The concern for harmony," he adds, "is a great servitude. . . . Harmony is made manifest by the man engaged in project; he has found calm, has eliminated the impatience of desire" (IE, 56). It is this "impatience of desire" that Bataille wishes to save from the reified domain of worldly projects. And, in this sense, I would argue, one of Bataille's guiding impulses is a kind of *absolute lyricism*: a search for isolated moments of rending intensity that, he insists, can never be turned into dialectical moments of an existential project (of a life unfolding in time). This extreme and ultimately implausible dichotomy informs all of Bataille's thought. His speculative historical works read like those of a mystical lyricist who has oddly decided to compose a revised Hegelian marxist anthropology.

One can discern a similar slant in Bataille's approach to Nietzsche. Given the variety of forms in which Bataille works, he might well seem to be an eccentric version of the poet-philosopher Nietzsche poses as an ideal. Yet if he is a poet-philosopher, he nonetheless tends to abandon the lucid Socratic ironist that continues to speak in Nietzsche, and he entirely ignores the powerful creative legislator that Nietzsche (no doubt recalling Plato) presents as an ideal (BGE, 235–36). What Bataille finds in Nietzsche, rather, is a Dionysian mystic and a teacher of active nihilism. He reads Nietzsche not as a theorist of the will to power, not as a critical genealogist, but as a visionary prophet challenging us to acknowledge the "nothing" on which we drift once our inherited fictions of transcendence have collapsed. Bataille, it would seem, barely hears in Zarathustra the voice of critical transvaluation and creative self-overcoming. He is indifferent to the voice that, in "On Redemption," speaks of creatively gathering the fragments of one's being into a transformative project—any such existential project is, to Bataille's mind, but another illusion of a transcendent horizon inviting us to surrender the impatience of desire, the freedom of vertigo. What Bataille hears in Zarathustra is the siren song of a mystical foundering in the "nothing" that genuine sovereignty is: "'I am NOTHING': this parody of affirmation is the last word of sovereign subjectivity, freed from the dominion it wanted—or had—to give itself over things" (AS, 3:421; cf. ON, 123). Hence the crossing over of which Zarathustra speaks *is* this movement of foundering; there is no other shore, so to speak, beyond this "movement of collapse" (ON, 65). In this way—from an entirely de-reified postreligious perspective—Bataille turns Nietzsche into a Dionysian mystic and a radicalized surrealist. Vertiginous crisis is the movement of radical freedom. Thus the dynamic of Bataille's atheistic mysticism.[68]

This mystical and surrealist perspective in Bataille is inseparable from an equally extreme Hegelian marxist perspective. The latter, largely borrowed from Alexandre Kojève, serves as the perfect dramatic foil—a totalizing account of rational social development—against which the ecstatic movements are lived and thought. According to this metanarrative, one that bears some affinities with Adorno's, history is opened by the negation of both outer nature and inner nature (the animal within the human) effected through the social organization of labor, prohibition, and discourse. This primary negation of nature—of a natural realm that, from the human and historical perspective constituted by this negation, appears as violence and excess—opens both the promise of freedom and the fear of death. History, then, is the development of human societies that command their subjects to maintain themselves in and through negativity, to transform their world and themselves through purposive work, thereby sustaining an intersubjective realm of relative freedom. Yet the grim ruse of history, according to this narrative, is that the potentially free subjects constituted through projects of transformative work become the servile subjects of the very social structures or "second nature" they have constructed. "Servitude, inextricable downfall: the slave frees himself from the master through work (the essential movement of *The Phenomenology of Spirit*), but the product of his work becomes his master" (IE, 129; cf. AS, 1:57). The subjects of history, having constructed a world of things for the sake of freedom, become themselves mere things. The slaves who have at last become masters, at last wrested independence from necessity through work and the deferral of expenditure, turn out to remain slaves insofar as they have yet to surpass the fear, isolation, and self-preservative anxiety constitutive of their subjectivity. They become the anxious servants of those social structures that maintain their narrow projects and identities. Thus the promise of freedom, only minimally realized throughout premodern history, is yet again blocked in modern history as subjects become increasingly integrated into a thoroughly reified order of technocratic rationality and rationalized labor. Existence is mutilated.[69]

Genuine freedom thus requires a further negation of an increasingly rigid social positivity. Unlike Adorno, however, Bataille does not posit the possibility of a dialectical movement whereby reason, opening itself to the "non-identical" that eludes it, might surpass its own subsumptive operations. Bataille, rather, while *wholly accepting* Kojève's Hegelian narrative, at the same time *wholly contests* it. This important contradiction, embraced by Bataille with open eyes, underlies many of the other contradictions that appear throughout his *oeuvre*. Dialectical knowledge and the realm of projects are contested, not in the name of a transformed knowledge and a renovated realm of projects, but in the name of a mystical collision with nonknowledge and a volatile departure from the realm of projects. Bataille thus orchestrates, in one text after another, less a dialectic than an irresolvable dualist conflict between a totalizing Hegelianism and a lyrical Dionysianism, the latter ultimately having less to do with Nietzsche than with Bataille's rewriting of motifs variously drawn from surrealism, mysticism, negative theology, anthropology, and comparative religious studies.[70]

The dynamics of this conflict are strikingly explored in the fascinating series of texts written in the forties—*Inner Experience, Guilty,* and *On Nietzsche*— which Bataille hoped to gather in a general *Somme athéologique*. At once spiritual diaries, provocative confessions, and erratic theoretical sketches, soaked in the vocabularies of mysticism and negative theology, these "meditations" are primarily concerned with a variously traced movement from the known to the unknown, from practical action to exorbitant transgression, from a servile posture to a sovereign release, from the subject that synthesizes time in a developed project to the subject that loses itself in a flashing intensity. And one issue that emerges with particular force in these meditations is the relationship between Bataille's atheistic mysticism, or his secular appropriation of negative theology, and his conception of freedom as a decisive turning toward death (evidently a post-Christian and, as it were, trans-Hegelian conception). What Bataille admires in negative theology is the practice of definition through negation, the refusal to represent the transcendent as an "object" like other objects. He locates its failure, however, in the way it finally returns to a representation of the transcendent as a highest being beyond being, an ultimate "ground," a magnetic "end," founding the mystic's path of salvation. For the reinstatement of a positive transcendence again reduces the subject to a project, again subordinates the subject to a temporal, self-preservative dialectic guided by an organizing horizon. In this sense Bataille perceives no fundamental difference between a Christian and a Hegelian (IE, 25). Both posit an ultimate framework or horizon that justifies the realm of temporally unfolded human projects. Both restrict the subject to the servile order of calculation and self-preservation. Both turn away from Nietzsche's challenge to embrace nihilism ("Build your cities on the slopes of Vesuvius! Send your ships into uncharted seas!" [GS, 228]). Both flee from an encounter with the "uncharted seas" on which we drift, the "nothing" we are.

Both, thus, surrender the adventure of an abyssal freedom that, in abandoning servility, plays in the space of death. For if the obstacle to radical freedom is any posture of servility, any submission to social structures that sustain the subject in time, the primary obstacle underlying all the others would seem to be our fear of death, our anxious desire to maintain ourselves in time by risking only as much of ourselves as we can later draw a safe return on. "From the viewpoint of the sovereign man, faintheartedness and the fearful representation of death belong to the world of practice, that is, of subordination. In fact, subordination is always rooted in necessity; subordination is always grounded in the alleged need to avoid death" (AS, 3:222). This motif often emerges in Bataille's engagements with the ambitions of Hegel's dialectic:

> A comic little summary. Hegel, I imagine, touched upon the extreme limit. He was still young and believed himself to be going mad. I even imagine that he worked out the system in order to escape (each type of conquest is, no doubt, the deed of a man fleeing a threat). To conclude, Hegel attains *satisfaction,* turns his back on the extreme limit. *Supplication is dead within him.* Whether or not one seeks salvation, in any case, one continues to live, one can't be sure, one must continue to supplicate. While yet alive, Hegel won salvation, killed supplication, mutilated himself. Of him, only the handle of the shovel remained, a modern man. But before mutilating himself, no doubt he touched upon the extreme limit, knew supplication: his memory brought him back to the perceived abyss, *in order to annul it!* The system is the annulment. (IE, 43; cf. 80–81)

In searching for this freedom found only at the "extreme limit" of his being, beyond conceptual knowledge, Bataille occasionally draws on the weird fiction of the epitaph, pretending to speak from the measureless nowhere of death: "At the elusive extreme limit of my being, I am already dead, and I in this growing state of death speak to the living: of death, of the extreme limit. . . . The extreme limit is a window: fear of the extreme limit commits one to the darkness of a prison, with an empty will for 'penal administration'" (IE, 44–45; cf. G, 17). But simply killing oneself would of course defeat the purpose of the quest to surpass all purpose: the subject must survive if he or she is to experience the release of an abyssal "approach" to death. Bataille is quite aware of the direction in which this lyricism of death leads him. It leads him to describe the ecstatic moments he seeks as intuitive mimes of the movement of dying:

> If the consciousness which I have of my *self* escapes from the world, if, trembling, I abandon all hope for a logical harmony and dedicate myself to *improbability*—at first to my own and, in the end, to that of all things (*this is to play the drunk, staggering man who, in a movement of logic, takes himself for a candle, blows it out, and crying out with fear, in the end, takes himself for night*)—I can grasp the self in tears, in anguish (I can even prolong my vertigo to the vanishing point and only find myself in the desire for another—for a woman—unique, irreplacable, dying, in all things similar to me), but it is only when death approaches that I will know without fail what it is about. . . .

It is by dying, without possible evasion, that I will perceive the rupture which constitutes my nature and in which I have transcended "what exists." As long as I live, I am content with a coming and going, with a compromise.... The self-that-dies abandons this harmony: it truly perceives what surrounds it to be a void and itself to be a challenge to this void; the self-that-dies restricts itself to intuiting the vertigo in which everything will end (much later). (IE, 70–71; cf. 34–35)

The studious or delirious anticipation of death, occasionally accompanied by absurdist laughter (ON, xxix), is one of Bataille's most frequently traced paths toward an abyssal freedom beyond the limits of secure life. "Death is the only means of avoiding the abdication of sovereignty" (IE, 160).[71]

In his mystical meditations of the forties, then, Bataille in part writes variations on the long tradition of proleptic songs of death. One current of this tradition, wholly acknowledged in Bataille's texts, is that of Christian mysticism. The Christian mystic, continually dying, "muriendo de no morir," dissolving normative boundaries of the self, occasionally suffering an erotic ecstasy, reaches toward God. Bataille retraverses this experience while erasing from it any "positive" transcendence: he reaches not toward God but toward a "nothing" at the "limit" of his being. Another current of this tradition, rarely alluded to in Bataille's texts, is that of modern poetic voyages into the space of death, voyages that are at times proleptically elegiac, at times hymnal, at times both fascinated and resistant. Keats, Whitman, Dickinson, Baudelaire, Rimbaud, Mallarmé, Rilke, Stevens, Crane, and Lorca, among many others, have written great poems of this sort. It is a perplexing sort of voyage in a post-Christian world in which death, not a transcendent being or a transcendent order, has become the ultimate "limit" of human life. For a Christian mystic the lyricism of death has a clear logic: death is the door to the divine, the mysterious passage to the infinite. For a post-Christian poet, however, death becomes something else, perhaps a haunting cipher of the infinite, perhaps the stark and uncannily intimate challenge that most forcefully calls forth imaginative power, perhaps an enigmatic promise of ghostly departure and expansion that is resisted only through a movement of disenchantment. At any rate, whatever death has meant for other poets, Bataille seems to have perceived in it the seductive figure of an impossible surpassing of limits, a sweeping dilation of existence. "Existence recognizes that it is at the disposal of chance, provided that it can see itself on the same scale as the starry sky, or death. It recognizes itself in its magnificence, made in the image of a universe untouched by the stain of merit or intention" (VE, 231).[72]

ONE MIGHT HAVE guessed that Bataille, having in the forties turned so sharply into the realm of atheistic mysticism, would not easily find his way back to the broader anthropological, historical, and political themes addressed in his writings of the twenties and thirties. Yet so he did. The texts on which he worked during the last twenty years of his life, including *Erotism, Theory of Religion,* and *The Accursed Share,* undertake an ambitious speculative return to those broader themes. His focus in these texts tends to shift from mysticism to history, from private explorations of sovereign experience to public manifestations of sovereign experience, from personal contestations of the given to collective dialectics of production and expenditure. One finds in these texts a renewed concern to elaborate a Hegelian marxist philosophy of history—thoroughly revised, to be sure, by Bataille's theory of sovereignty and expenditure.[73]

While the three-volume work *The Accursed Share* deserves more space than I'm able to give it here, a schematic account of its arguments will, I hope, at least allow me to cast light on some important problems that emerge from the extreme dualism shaping Bataille's thought. The guiding metanarrative of this text is the revised Kojèvian-marxist narrative that I briefly described above. History is constituted by the negation of nature established through social structures that organize work, prohibition, discourse, and power. And history develops through the labor of the negative, that is, through purposive projects realized by subjects who, working upon their world, at once negate, preserve, and transform their world and themselves. Yet Bataille refuses the typical "utilitarian" bias of liberals and marxists alike, the well-nigh exclusive emphasis on these useful or, in Bataille's vocabulary, "restricted" dialectics of development.[74] He insists, rather, on the social and political significance of those collective expressions of "useless" expenditure, of "non-productive" sovereignty, traditionally manifest in the domains of the sacred and the royal (in all the displays and rituals of royalty, priesthood, religious mysteries, social carnivals, and so forth). Bataille, like any marxist, recognizes that the traditional manifestations of sovereignty have typically been alienations in the service of political hierarchy and ideological mystification. He too practices an ideology critique of false positivities. "Sovereignty is NOTHING, and I have tried to say how clumsy (but inevitable) it was to make a thing of it" (AS, 2:256). But he believes there is much else at stake in these traditional manifestations of extravagance, for he understands them to be distorted expressions of the sort of radical freedom otherwise blocked throughout history by the dominance of useful projects of work. If history is constituted by the negation of nature accomplished through human work as well as through the entire network of discourse, prohibition, and political hierarchy, the sacred, according to Bataille, has traditionally been experienced as a further negation, a liberating negation of the negation constitutive of the structured world of history. This involves not the formation of some new positivity (that is but a typical mode of alienation which reduces the sacred once again to a utile project) but rather a rapturous break with the world of things:

> Not only is the festival not, as one might think, a return by man to his vomit, but it *ultimately* has the opposite meaning. I said that the initial human negation, which created the *human* in contrast to the *animal*, had to do with the being's *dependence* on the natural given, on the body which it did not choose, but the break constituted by the festival is not at all a way of renouncing independence; it is rather the culmination of a movement toward autonomy, which is, forevermore, the same thing as man himself. (AS, 2:90–91; cf. AS, 1:55–59, AS, 3:339–43)

This kind of sovereign movement, according to Bataille, is a human birthright, an essential aspiration (however repressed or mutilated) of human beings in general. Thus we must "seek in the [traditional sovereign] structures we have destroyed not the answers that are now antiquated but, beyond them, the primary exigency that these answers evaded. We can now recognize that man is himself and that he *alone* is the sovereign value of man, but this means above all that man was the real content of the sovereign values of the past. There was nothing in God, or in the kings, that was not first in man, and without the alienation that reduces him I would rediscover in him what was enchanting in God or in the magnificence of the kings" (AS, 3:321; cf. 284–85). This is Bataille's revised Feuerbachian dialectic. It is shaped by a concern to recover premodern manifestations of the sacred not for existential projects in time but for lyrical departures from practical imperatives in general:

> What distinguishes sovereignty is the consumption of wealth, as against labor and servitude, which produce wealth. . . . Let us say that the sovereign (or the sovereign life) begins when, with the necessities ensured, the possibility of life opens up without limit. . . . Life *beyond utility* is the do-

main of sovereignty. We may say, in other other words, that it is servile to consider duration first, to employ the present time for the sake of the future, which is what we do when we work. (AS, 3:198)

The twofold task, then, is to free these movements of sovereignty from their traditional alienations—their traditional fixations in positive structures serving social utility and political hierarchy—and to revive them in modern societies that, owing to their blind productivism, tend to dismiss manifestations of sovereign excess as anachronisms permitted only in the safely circumscribed realm of art (AS, 3:315).

Is this possible, or desirable? Bataille reads the dominant movement of modern history as twofold. First, it is characterized by the negation—accomplished by the classical democratic political revolutions—of those traditional manifestations of sovereignty that, insofar as they were fixed in positive structures, were alienated from the mass of human beings who, however obscurely, seek true sovereignty. Second, it is characterized by the staggering expansion— effected by modern capitalism and the industrial revolution—of a restricted economy of work, production, and accumulation that, attaining a historically unprecedented sway, tends to reduce everyone to anxious servility. This twofold movement is the essential dynamic at work in the bourgeois-capitalist revolutions of the modern period. These revolutions destroyed those sites of sovereign excess essential to the feudal world and, at the same time, set in motion a Promethean economy of production and accumulation. But the groups that came to power in these revolutions, far from rethinking the meaning of the feudal manifestations of excess they had abolished, simply appropriated for themselves the vestiges of feudal sovereignty, integrating these "signs" into the productivist economy that serves their interests (the good bourgeois, thus, puts the "signs" of sovereignty to use in projects of getting ahead). Hence communism, though it is less an overcoming than an exacerbation of the dominant tendencies of capitalism, nonetheless remains the last hope of a possible emergence of radical freedom as well as a possible realization of social egalitarianism. "Today sovereignty is no longer alive except in the perspectives of communism. It is only insofar as the convulsions of communism lend life to it that sovereignty takes on a vital meaning in our eyes. Hence I will not seek the meaning of sovereignty directly, but rather that of communism, which is its most active contradiction" (AS, 3:261).

Communism is the "active contradiction" of sovereignty in at least two senses. It decisively carries to completion the negation of alienated expressions of sovereignty, a project from which the ruling classes of capitalist societies have retreated. Further, it exacerbates the instrumental imperatives of production and accumulation to such an extent that it tends toward the erasure of the human individual as such. Yet Bataille, embracing a madly hopeful logic of dialectical reversal, nonetheless discerns in this protoclassless and hyperproductivist communist society (a society at once highly industrialized and highly secularized) the promise of an ultimate renovation of useless expenditure under social conditions in which the experience of sovereignty could at last be authentically lived. For "sovereignty cannot be understood as a form that history would realize. If it appears in the perspective of history, this is because it was already given; history merely rids men of that which kept them from finding it" (AS, 3:302). Communism is to accomplish this clearing. Then the Dionysian festival, perhaps "an ahistorical mode of existence in which erotic activity is the expressive form" (AS, 2:189), could begin. Perhaps it would resemble the carnival of Rimbaud's "Villes II."

At times this sweeping narrative reads like a dialectical attempt to outstrip Hegelian dialectics. There are doubtless echoes in this narrative of the great marxist story of a dialectical passage from necessity to freedom, from mutilated human powers to liberated human powers, from reductive and alienated production to creatively reappropriated production, from an unjust distribution of social wealth to a just distribution of social wealth. At the same time, the marxist narrative is supplemented and finally transumed by Bataille's innovative story of a passage from mystified and alienated sovereignty to demythologized and recovered sovereignty, from servile production to sovereign expenditure, from the reductive reign of utility to the explosive kingdom of rapture. "Let us say that the sovereign (or the sovereign life) begins when, *with the necessities ensured,* the possibility of life opens up without limit" (AS, 3:198; my italics). Has Bataille, finally, written a utopian anarchist supplement to a Hegelian marxist narrative? Could his narrative, with minor revisions, be aligned with the utopian Hegelian marxism of, say, Marcuse? Is Bataille arguing that we should strive for a classless society in which, at last, we could undertake a rational organization of festivals of sovereign expenditure which, however, are by definition destructive of rational organization? Is this a cogent paradox? Or, rather, would the rational organization of sovereign excess inevitably become the betrayal, the instrumental travesty, of everything Bataille associates with sovereignty? "What is sovereign can only come from the arbitrary, from chance. There ought not to exist any *means* by which man might *become* sovereign: it is better for him to *be* sovereign, in which case sovereignty cannot be taken away from him, but if he does not possess it, he cannot acquire it. . . . Nothing sovereign must ever submit to the useful" (AS, 3:226). So much for any dialectic of transition. And yet, does not Bataille, in at least some passages of *The Accursed Share,* place his surrealist antinomianism in tension with the pressures of larger historical dynamics?[75]

Bataille never resolves these contradictions. If projects of becoming and horizons of development belong to the servile, if the servile are servile precisely because they commit themselves to such projects and horizons, then sovereignty, finally, would seem to be an experience that cannot occur *within* the realm of history—an experience that can only be found in a negation of historical limits that slides toward an abyssal non-sense. Historical life, then, turns out to be the dim "condition of possibility," as it were, of the dislocations that free one from historical life. "Of course, sovereignty—in a practical sense, the use of resources for nonproductive ends—cannot be given as the goal of history. I even maintain the contrary: that if history has some goal, sovereignty cannot be that goal, and further, that sovereignty could not have anything to do with that goal, except insofar as it would differ therefrom" (AS, 3:281). This insistence makes it difficult for Bataille to sketch a possible transition from a society of sheer instrumentalism to a society of awakened sovereignty. Because he defines sovereignty as the explosive negation of all ends, the antinomian risking of all projects and identities, he can hardly do otherwise than evoke sovereignty as the "beyond" rather more than the "end" of history. *His narrative, finally, sketches less a practical "transformation" of historical life than a rapturous "exit" from historical life.* His impetus toward freedom is vehement. Had he lived in the second century, he might have been a friend of the wildest of the Gnostics. "This existence that I am is a revolt against existence and is indefinite *desire"* (ON, 187).

But this extreme dualism is difficult to translate into a cogent social theory. Habermas rightly claims, I think, that the severe dichotomies at work in Bataille's project cannot be set in motion in any sort of coherent dialectic or convincing vision of transformative process:

> If sovereignty and its source, the sacred, are related to the world of purposive-rational action in an absolutely heterogeneous fashion, if the subject and reason are constituted only by excluding all kinds of sacred power, if the other of reason is more than just the irrational or the unknown—namely, the *incommensurable,* which cannot be touched by reason except at the cost of an explosion of the rational subject—then there is no

possibility of a theory that reaches beyond the horizon of what is accessible to reason and thematizes, let alone analyzes, the interaction of reason with a transcendent source of power. Bataille sensed this dilemma but did not resolve it.[76]

There is some irony in this. Bataille, the restless thinker of all that wrecks coherent thought, tends to organize his own thinking in terms of severely dichotomous abstractions. One need only bring to mind the vast diversity of human activities, both practical and intellectual, that Bataille sweepingly subsumes under the single abstract concept of "project." From this perspective, the entire fallen world, the entire world of human history, appears as a vast cage without nuances, and there is no possibility, whether on the individual or the collective plane, of an existential or historical dialectic whereby enigmatic moments of release could be brought into meaningful communication with the unfolding of a life in time.[77] Yet, too, it is just here that Bataille's hypertrophied Hegelianism, which impedes him on the theoretical level, is at least contradicted by his own performance as a writer. And thus does he sound anew, in a lyricism of searching bewilderment, a contradiction sounded many times before in the writings of his great mystical and negative theological precursors. For though "in theory" Bataille tends to deny the possibility of a meaningful communication between rapture and project, between the night of nonsense and the day of knowledge, "in practice" his passionate, jagged texts are shuttling explorations that roam through just this cross-lit realm between the known and the unknown. Bataille's deepest impulse is toward a rapturous religious freedom, an impossible crossing of all limits. But no quest for freedom, however wild, can be wholly detached from the realm of human projects and discourses (including discursive conjectures of half-knowledge) where the promise of freedom is pursued, lived, guessed, and thought. Bataille's eccentrically "significant" writings, despite his own starkly dualist theories, testify to that.

PASSAGES AND QUESTIONS

The three Faustian writers I've discussed in this chapter are nothing if not extreme. They all pursue a path of destructive creation in quest of metamorphosis. They all risk an experience of foundering on their way toward freedom. They all live their thought with uncommon intensity. They all write with exceptional provocative force. Bataille insists that only those who have risked themselves as he has will hear in his paradoxical discourse something other than a quixotic effort to outwit Hegel on Hegel's terrain (IE, 116). Nietzsche asserts that not everyone has a right to his prophetic thought (BGE, 53). Rimbaud draws the reader through metamorphic spaces that he continually mocks, erases, displaces yet again, leaves behind as he departs for another of his missing lives. These Faustian questers compose texts that are like baffling lures wired with what Nietzsche, describing his own rhetoric, calls "the magic of the extreme" (WP, 396). The dramatist of Rimbaud's "Vies I" defiantly asks: "What is my nothingness compared to the stupor that awaits you?" (O, 264; CP, 246).[78]

To note only these affinities of risked delirium, however, would be misleading. Rimbaud risks shipwreck for the sake of metamorphic vision, of finding an unknown "language of the soul for the soul," of bringing about a renovative clearing like that evoked in "Génie" and "Éternité." Nietzsche risks shipwreck for the sake of metamorphic transvaluation, of finding a visionary philosophic perspective that at once recognizes and surpasses the nihilist challenge he believes we have come upon. Bataille, on the other hand, risks, or rather intends, shipwreck for its own sake: it is the shipwreck itself, the sinking of the coherent subject, that is conceived as the event of radical freedom and ecstatic communion with the mystery of being.

Bataille thus marks a profound change in cultural weather. In his texts the Faustian adventure of demonic negativity is purified, so to speak, filtered through an uncompromising negative atheology, cleansed of any positive residues, washed of any traces of creative projects that would seek to change life or invent transformed horizons. Such projects and horizons are now understood to belong, by definition, to the fallen realm of servitude with which the experience of radical freedom decisively breaks. No doubt there is much in Bataille that resists this deepest tendency of his thought. One might say that he contests his own exorbitant demon of contestation, wrestles with his own dualist extremism, throughout the "philosophy of history" texts of the postwar period. And yet it would seem that he never quite abandons this dualist extremism. It is as though a strong part of him wished to say: let the fallen world have its reasons, hopes, memories, and projects while we, bold mystics of nothingness, seek an abyssal freedom found only through repeated transgressions of that fallen world; let others, the anxious subjects who sustain themselves in the restricted economies of historical life, concern themselves with wandering abroad in time, transforming the world, changing life, accomplishing a transvaluation of values, or what have you, while we, ecstatics of zero, pursue rapturous communions with the abyss of being. This is not the only voice in Bataille.

Yet it is, I think, the dominant one. And so the freedom Bataille invokes is finally at risk of becoming an empty freedom, a freedom not at all of this world, a freedom that happens precisely nowhere.

AT THE BEGINNING of this chapter I recalled Marx's evocation, in *The Communist Manifesto*, of the Faustian dynamics of capitalism itself. But Marx often speaks in another voice as well, one akin to the voices of a Blake, a Rimbaud, or a Nietzsche. In the *1844 Manuscripts* and *The German Ideology* in particular, but also in *Capital,* he describes the way capitalist modernity organizes social and psychic division, the fragmentation of life, and the alienation of human beings from their own powers, wreckings that can only be overcome, he argues, through a revolution that will permit, for the first time in history, the emergence of the "totally developed individual," the individual "cultivating his gifts in all directions":

> In communist society, where nobody has one exclusive sphere of activity but each can become accomplished in any branch he wishes, society regulates the general production and thus makes it possible for me to do one thing today and another tomorrow, to hunt in the morning, fish in the afternoon, rear cattle in the evening, criticise after dinner, just as I have a mind, without ever becoming hunter, fisherman, shepherd, or critic. The fixation of social activity, this consolidation of what we ourselves produce into an objective power above us, growing out of our control, thwarting our expectations, bringing to naught our calculations, is one of the chief factors in historical development up till now.[79]

This famous utopian passage clearly reveals the romantic humanist vision that, as a number of writers have pointed out, shapes the thought of the young Marx (and I would claim, contra Althusser and his followers, the mature Marx as well). Indeed, this romantic perspective, at once critical and utopian, has been the perspective from which most (though not all) of the prophetic projects of modern culture have been undertaken. Visionaries like Blake, Rimbaud, and Nietzsche contest the order of damaged lives that Marx perceives in capitalist modernity—an order characterized by Max Weber as a spreading "iron cage"— in the name of genuine freedom, renovated wholeness, a transformative unfolding of creative powers.[80]

Bataille, then, a peculiar postromantic voice, marks an innovative moment in what I've called the dialectic of instrumental reification and creative negativity at work in the culture of modernity. As capitalist commodification and technocratic rationality have increasingly extended their sway over every zone of social life, producing a range of dehumanizing effects, the major artistic, philosophic, and political discourses that have resisted these processes have, it appears, repeatedly been driven to negate and surpass, in one way or another, those "positive contents" of earlier voices in their traditions which, under these circumstances, have lost their initial contestatory force. Bataille, troubled by a lost "entirety of existence" in modern social life, shows little interest in the contestatory "humanist" discourses (whether of the naturalist or the idealist sort) that traverse modern culture. His interest lies in the emphatically "postreligious" contestatory discourses of this period. And he spells out a critique of these discourses that, emptying them of their "positive" horizons, allows him to define a postreligious mode of radical freedom as a volatile rupture with all "positivity," both in fact and in thought. He composes a mysticism of ecstatic negation and rapturous transgression, locating freedom in passages of studiously sought delirium "wholly other" to, though at the same time "wholly dependent" upon, the practical realm of worldly projects.

The significance of Bataille's provocative discourse, I think, can be further illuminated if it is set in a larger historical perspective. Thus I would like to conclude with a brief narrative that begins with Blake, passes through Rimbaud and surrealism, and returns to Bataille.

Blake's *The Marriage of Heaven and Hell* is a pertinent text to bring into this field of questions. It could be read as a powerful, comic expression of romantic Satanism—though that would be an incomplete and finally mistaken reading. It could also be read as a powerful, comic defense of radical antinomianism— a reading that, if also incomplete, would not be as far from the truth. Blake explores in this text a pitched conflict between the realm of the Devil and the realm of the Angel. The "revolutionary" realm of the Devil represents buried energies of erotic and creative power, or, in Nietzsche's vocabulary, active forces and affirmative expressions of the will to power: they are energies largely associated with the figure of Orc (or the fallen Luvah) in Blake's later works. The "despotic" realm of the Angel represents repressive, moralizing, rationalizing, and mechanizing counterenergies, or, in Nietzsche's vocabulary, reactive forces and nihilist expressions of the will to power: they are energies largely associated with the figure of Urizen (in his fallen form) in Blake's later works. The "good" angels teach reductive reality principles and repressive moral laws in order to bind those primary energies that they characterize as "evil." These buried "satanic" energies, since they inevitably disrupt the "angelic" realm the moment they are released, initially manifest themselves as negative and destructive forces. Yet for Blake this antinomian explosion is hardly enough. Having studied *Paradise Lost* with care, it was clear to him that Satan's energy of revolt, while magnificent in some respects, remained scarred by its constitutive relationship to Jehovah. Social and psychic fragmentation have produced this conflict, which therefore cannot be overcome in the broken terms of this conflict itself. The Devil alone, the force of satanic revolt, the explosive energy of revolutionary upheaval, will ultimately serve but a consolidation of repressive law if this force is not *creatively transformed* through an alliance with the spark of the Poetic Genius: a power largely associated with the prophetic figure of Los in Blake's later works. Without this power of creative transformation, the volatile negativity of repressed energy is likely to play itself out in futile gestures, time and again returning to the prison with which it will remain secretly complicit, as is shown by the readiness with which, throughout history, Orc tends to become Urizen, the prophet a priest, the revolutionary either a violent despot or a resigned cog in the machine, the visionary, like Jesus, an ambiguous figure betrayed by a church founded in his name. Only the metamorphic power of Los can at once actively gather the rebellious energies of Orc (which thereby cease to be merely the disruptive forces of negativity and become instead the animating fires of creative freedom) and actively redeem the binding forces of Urizen (which thereby cease to be the damaging limits of a reason decayed into rationalization and become instead the bounding lines of creative freedom). From Blake's perspective—and too, I think, from Rimbaud's, at least at important points in his trajectory, and from Nietzsche's—to locate in the Devil alone the principle of freedom is an error in political no less than in artistic and pyschological terms. It is for this reason, I think, that in Blake's later works the implicit bearings of the Devil are developed and clarified. As Blake's vision is unfolded, that is, the Devil of *The Marriage of Heaven and Hell* turns into two figures that, though related to one another, yet remain distinct from one another: Orc or the fallen Luvah, a figure of natural rebellion, and Los or the fallen Urthona, a figure of visionary transformation (the Poetic Genius of *The Marriage*). On the following page I've sketched a "map" of Blake's text.[81]

As this map is meant to show, Blake's prophetic satire, while engaged in the artistic and political conflicts of his time, presents both an anticipatory

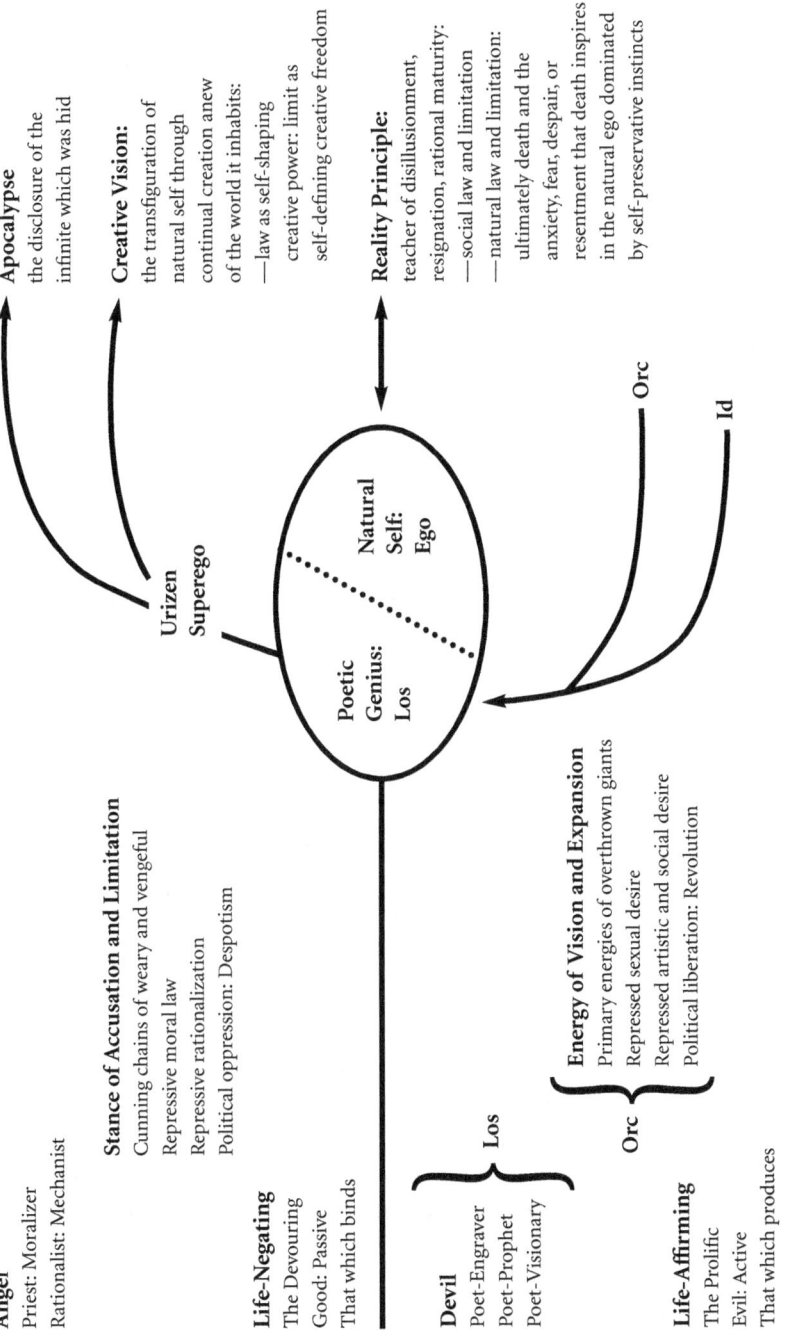

sketch and an anticipatory criticism of Freud's later model of the psyche. And much is riding, of course, on whether one accepts a Freudian criticism of Blake, according to which the Poetic Genius is but an illusion of the ego, or a Blakean criticism of Freud, according to which that Freudian criticism is itself but a reactive expression (posing as maturity) of disappointment, loss of power, death of vision. The crucial question is whether or not there is in the self a creative power—a power to initiate vision and action, a power to transform the scarred self and the broken world it inhabits—which is not wholly reducible to a damaged effect of those forces that have shaped the self: a power that would be not a substance or an agent but a potential, a movement, having no reality outside its transformative manifestations (hence the ease with which a power of this sort could be variously troped as "Poetic Genius," "Imagination," "Power," "Invention," and "Writing," among other things). If the Blakean spark of metamorphic vision is abandoned, as in Freudian and post-Freudian therapeutic models of the self, the unhappy ego is left to undertake a continual practice of shoring itself up as it defends itself against the conflicting forces of law and revolt, order and energy, stoic compromise thus emerging as an ideal (one that, as Blake makes clear, has political as well as psychological consequences). And if the therapeutic model is as popular in our time as the Anglican model was in Blake's, this is largely because these two models, for all their differences, are alike in their grimly accurate account of the way most of us live most of the time, most of us having little notion of what it might mean to enter the dynamic of creative vision, or metamorphic anticipation, to which writers like Blake, Rimbaud, and Nietzsche testify. Hence, naturally, we prefer to characterize such writers as "delirious" rather than to acknowledge their characterization of us as largely "dead." Hence, too, the inevitability with which such writers appear to the societies they address as wildly "idealist" and erratically "antinomian." Yet, however this inevitable conflict is played out, revised, and reimagined in the long run, it would seem that if these dynamic challenges to our dominant models of psychic and political life were to disappear, we might find ourselves enclosed in the death-in-life that Zarathustra perceived in the spiteful "last men" who could respond to his words only with mockery.

It is clear that an apocalyptic Devil animates Rimbaud's writings. Anarchic revolt is a resonant impulse throughout his trajectory. Yet at the same time Rimbaud reaffirms a Poetic Genius, a light of creative power and metamorphic vision, most resonantly figured by the sweeping "génie" of his great hymn by that name. The renovative "autre" that he hopes to find once the enclosed "je" has been jarred open is this sweeping power of luminous expansion. And it is this energy that animates the spacious metamorphic passages and premonitions of the *Illuminations*. Rimbaud does not abandon this creative élan but holds it in lucid conflict with the ineluctable pressure of limit, in the last chapter of *Une Saison* and in many of the most moving (because most fractured) of the *Illuminations*.

The surrealist adventure revives both the antinomian and the prophetic energies of writers like Blake, Rimbaud, and Nietzsche in a changed historical context. Fredric Jameson has observed that French surrealist writers find in the run-down sections of early twentieth-century Paris an analogue of what earlier romantic writers found in natural landscapes: an auratic realm whose objects, appearing to be peculiarly charged with hidden promises, readily jar consciousness from its fixed routines and so release repressed powers. The fading zones of an older urban landscape, not entirely buried beneath the faceless grid of an emergent corporate capitalist urban landscape, are perceived as realms of latent phantasmagoric power:

> These objects—the places of objective chance, or of preternatural revelation—are immediately identifiable to us as the products of a not yet fully industrialized and systematized economy. This is to say that the human origins of the products of this period—their relationship to the work from which they issued—have not yet been fully concealed; in their production they still show traces of an artisanal organization of labor while their distribution is still predominantly assured by a network of small shopkeepers. Advertising, in the dimension so familiar to us, is scarcely developed at all; indeed, the very ads themselves, whether *affiche*, the sandwich man of Ulysses, or that crude painting on a vacant wall which was Gertrude Stein's first introduction to the secret prestige of oil paints, can still be apprehended as objects of fascination in their own right. Thus what prepares these products to receive the investment of psychic energy characteristic of their use by Surrealism is precisely the half-sketched, uneffaced mark of human labor, of the human gesture, on them; they are still frozen gesture, not yet completely separated from subjectivity, and remain therefore potentially as mysterious and as expressive as the human body itself. By the same token, they remain linked forever to a determinate stage in our socio-economic development. This we can see more clearly who look back upon that stage, already completed and now historical, with a nostalgia which is that of the suburb for the traditional city on its way to extinction.[82]

This interpretation of the surrealist adventure from the "objective" side corresponds closely with an interpretation of it from the "subjective" side. Romantic imagery, Northrop Frye has shown, is characterized by a movement "downward, into the profounder depths of consciousness," a movement expressed not least in the romantic fascination with caves, tombs, and underground chambers of every sort (a fascination strongly marked in Rimbaud's poetry).[83] For in an increasingly instrumentalized world, the sources of contestatory and creative power are felt to reside in those elusive regions of the psyche that have still escaped the "binding" forces of reification and disciplinary socialization. An emphatic furthering of this "downward" movement occurs in the surrealist adventure: as "nature" comes to be found in the fading and not wholly "rationalized" regions of an older city, so creative "power" is found to have descended into the deeper and less "rationalized" regions of the psyche. Thus the importance in surrealism of all those tactics and principles spelled out in Breton's prose and poetry, including vehement nonconformism, anarchic doodling, convulsive beauty, shocking illumination, the incongruous image of "marvelous" strangeness, the revelatory play of "chance" crossings, and so on. The forces of the unconsious are called forth to roam through the haunted landscape of the city and the haunted texture of language. Yet surrealism does not simply abandon a romantic affirmation of a constructive imaginative power. Breton, misreading Freud, at times sounds almost Blakean:

> We are still living under the reign of logic: this, of course, is what I have been driving at. But in this day and age logical methods are applicable only to solving problems of secondary interest. The absolute rationalism that is still in vogue allows us to consider only facts relating directly to our experience. Logical ends, on the contrary, escape us. It is unnecessary to add that experience itself has found itself increasingly circumscribed. It paces back and forth in a cage from which it is more and more difficult to make it emerge. It too leans for support on what is most immediately expedient, and it is protected by the sentinels of common sense.... It was, apparently, by pure chance that a part of our mental world which we pretended not to be concerned with any longer—and, in my opinion, by far the most important part—has been brought back to light. For this we must give thanks to Sigmund Freud. On the basis of these discoveries a current of opinion is finally forming by means of which the human explorer will be able to carry his investigations much further, authorized as he will henceforth be not to confine himself solely to the most summary realities. The imagina-

tion is perhaps on the point of reasserting itself, of reclaiming its rights. If the depths of our mind contain within them strange forces capable of augmenting those on the surface, or of waging a victorious battle against them, there is every reason to seize them—first to seize them, then, if need be, to submit them to the control of our reason.[84]

In this passage, however, the constructive imagination of a Blake has been revised. For the imagination that Breton invokes, while still bearing projective force, has been driven further downward toward the realm of Blake's revolutionary Devil or Rimbaud's anarchic phase of *dérèglement*. This shift in emphasis can be understood as a dialectical response to a social system that, in the words of both Breton and Weber, develops by extending an instrumental "cage" that increasingly comes to colonize psychic life itself. Nevertheless, in surrealism this downward movement, making itself heard as anarchic revolt, remains in tension with a return movement, making itself heard as imaginative utopianism. This sort of tension is found everywhere in Breton, Éluard, and other surrealists.[85]

It is this current of "Icarian" utopianism that Bataille distrusts in surrealism. Having earlier emphasized Bataille's affinities with the surrealists, I would at this point emphasize his differences with them.[86] He spells out his criticisms of surrealism, in particular of Breton, in his early essay "The 'Old Mole' and the Prefix *Sur* in the Words *Surhomme* and Surrealist" (VE, 32–44) and in numerous other places in his writings. One of his critical claims is that the surrealists remain enclosed in a "literary" sphere detached from concrete political and existential realities (VE, 41; cf. IE, 49). This criticism is of limited force, however, not only because it is a criticism that Bataille often makes of literature in general, but because it is a criticism that the surrealists themselves make of literature. "May you only take the trouble to practice poetry," Breton writes in the first manifesto, declaring his concern to break down the boundaries between art and life.[87]

Bataille's second major criticism of surrealism is more significant. He claims that the surrealists, out of touch with authentic revolutionary dynamics, are little more than conventional "idealists," Icarian dreamers of an "immaterial" world of spiritual values above the "molish" world of filthy material forces and improper heterogeneous energies:

> Subsequently surrealism has recognized the legitimacy of the organizational endeavors and even the principles of Marxist communism, seeing

> therein the only means to bring about an indispensable revolution in the real world. But the surrealists continue persistently to express their basic predilection for values above the "world of facts" with such banal formulas as "revolt of the Spirit," etc. (VE, 33)

> More precisely, since surrealism is immediately distinguishable by the addition of low values (the unconsious, sexuality, filthy language, etc.), it invests these values with an elevated character by associating them with the most immaterial values. (VE, 39)

It is easy enough to misunderstand Bataille's criticism. The issue, as he underlines in the second of the passages above, is not the extent to which writers include "low values" in their works. After all, many early readers found surrealist works "shocking" in this sense, and these matters are at any rate decidedly labile, as the exhaustion in our own time of the valence of "scandal" in the arts indicates. Further, simply to replace a "high" positive value made to figure unbound energies with a "low" positive value made to figure unbound energies would betray Bataille's project. The issue, rather, is the nature of authentic revolutionary energy or, put another way, the question of the recuperability or irrecuperability of forces of antinomian negativity. All of Bataille's writings testify to his distrust of any effort to recover the negativity of excess for a constructive task in the realm of useful projects. All is to be risked and, so to speak, left suspended in a zone of risk. This is the basis of Bataille's dispute with surrealism.

Bataille, then, while elaborating a Hegelian marxist philosophy of history, at the same time relaunches the Faustian adventure of demonic negativity with a genuine difference: the erasure of that creative or constructive power that Blake figures as the Poetic Genius, Rimbaud as the renovative "Génie," Nietzsche as the overman, the philosopher of the future, the visionary of *amor fati,* or the creative child born of the critical lion, and Breton as a force of imagination concealed in repressed regions of the psyche. Bataille abandons any such power to the mutilated Angelic-Urizenic world of servile masters, situating all "sovereign" contestatory power in the satanic world of hidden explosive energies, buried antinomian impulses. Blake's transformative Poetic Genius remains wholly alive, if in different ways, in the apocalyptic-renovative visions of Rimbaud, Nietzsche, and Breton. From Bataille's perspective, however, this Genius cannot but become a dim Icarian functionary of the order of reductive systems. The insurgent Devil alone manifests the non-true truth of metamorphic negativity and rapturous expenditure. Sheer revolt against meaning and project—against practical life itself—becomes the principle of freedom. Bataille thus marks a sea change in the tradition in which he composes his song of undoing.

BATAILLE'S REWRITING OF creative transcendence and radical freedom as virtually identical with the subversive force of irrecuperable negativity would seem loosely (and, given Bataille's own obsessions, rather surprisingly) to anticipate a number of contemporary discourses of postmodernism, in particular those that gather together the themes of disjunction, indeterminacy, disruptive play, and so forth. And, variously routed through semiotic, psychoanalytic, and literary critical vocabularies, it has reverberated widely and forcefully in French post-structuralist theory. Blanchot, Kristeva, Derrida, and Foucault, among others, all owe debts of diverse sorts to Bataille's project. Blanchot was a contemporary of Bataille's, it is true, and each of these writers owes the other debts, yet it seems to me that, from the forties on, Blanchot largely elaborates motifs drawn from Bataille, unfolding these in a climate of affect (the melancholy of a haunted theologian of death) quite different from that of Bataille (the anguished joy of a mystic of the abyss of being). Kristeva's influential *Revolution in Poetic Language* reads like a rewriting of Bataille in the vocabularies of semiotics and psychoanalysis. Derrida, in a number of his major essays of the sixties and seventies, weaves motifs drawn from Bataille into his paradoxical thematization of an unthematizable play of *différance*: "*Différance* is not. It is not a present being, however excellent, unique, principal, or transcendent. It governs nothing, reigns over nothing, and nowhere exercises any authority. It is not announced by any capital letter. Not only is there no kingdom of *différance,* but *différance* instigates the subversion of every kingdom." This sounds very much like Bataille's paradoxical account of an abyssal negativity that escapes all discursive recuperation.[88] And the Bataille who appears in Foucault's essay "Preface to Transgression" is the heroic mask of a contestatory energy that, one comes to surmise, stands as the reverse image of that seamless carceral system described a decade later in *Discipline and Punish*. This sort of riven synthesis of a hypertrophied Hegelianism (as I characterized it above) and a post-Nietzschean fascination with anarchic negativity is a pervasive feature of post-structuralist thought. It is a riven synthesis that, though hardly deriving from Bataille alone, powerfully echoes him. Blake's dialectical figure of an *apocalyptic marriage* of heaven and hell, two hundred years later, turns into post-structuralism's paradoxical figure of a *synthetic divorce* of heaven and hell.[89]

Adventures that move in Bataille's wake, however, encounter difficulties akin to those Bataille encountered. One of these is the difficulty of turning a discourse that has abandoned a faith in the creative or projective power figured by Blake's Poetic Genius into either a philosophy, a poetics, or a politics capable of surpassing the disruptive play of errant negativity. Bataille's discourse of demonic negativity brings together a Hegelian marxist philosophy of history, on the one hand, and both a displaced mystical discourse of ecstatic departure and an exacerbated Faustian dynamic of destructive creation, on the other. Yet the whither of this sort of discourse, in its many brilliant rearticulations over the last forty years, is not always clear. In a bleak period of triumphant corporate capitalism, pervasive technocratic reification, and reductive therapeutic psychology, a negative atheology of any sort has the tremendous virtue of knocking holes in the wall, obliquely pointing to spaces beyond the given, sustaining a kind of negative hope, the possibility of possibility. That's hardly nothing. But there is force in Zarathustra's question: "Free *from* what? . . . But your eyes should tell me brightly: free *for* what?" (Z, 63). Perhaps we have become less daring than those whose languages we continue to echo at a distance. Can we dwell in a space of possibility lacking the textures and contours of affirmatively and quasi-concretely projected horizons? Can we free ourselves from the prisons we inhabit without risking the exploratory sketches of premonition and expectation with which genuine crossings elsewhere begin? René Char, one of the greatest twentieth-century poets at work in the wake of Rimbaud, has written: "Le poème est l'amour réalisé du désir demeuré désir [The poem is the realized love of desire still remaining desire]."[90] This reads like a one-line commentary on Rimbaud's "Génie" and, too, on Blake's *The Marriage of Heaven and Hell*. Perhaps, all three of these poets suggest, we need the concrete realizations of love no less than the impatience of desire, need the palpable realizations of vision no less than the energies of negation, if we are to find some way toward an embodied freedom in those worldly places we are at once bound to inhabit and called to inhabit otherwise.

CHAPTER THREE

Apocalyptic Negativity in Kierkegaard, Dickinson, Mallarmé, and Derrida

If Hegel marks a crisis in philosophy, he does so not least by recasting philosophy as narrative, a shift in orientation that informs not only the entire Marxist tradition but also, in different ways, the projects of Nietzsche, Heidegger, Derrida, and all the philosophers influenced by these composers of sweeping philosophic narratives. Further, Hegel's turn to narrative, guided by a conception of truth not as what timelessly is but rather as what has come to be in time, places the thinking of constitutive negativity at the center of philosophy. Put another way, Hegel's project abolishes an independent or "alienated" realm of transcendence and registers, even as it evades, the collapse of ultimate grounds and ends, at once tracing and skirting the event we have come to call "the death of God," that long event stretching from the middle of the eighteenth century through the middle of the twentieth century. Hegel, it is true, rescues philosophy from the risks to which he exposes it, not (as anti-Hegelians carelessly claim) by reducing the messy play of differences to the schematic movement of contradictions and syntheses, but by holding on to a conception of Spirit realizing the Absolute in history that, from a later point in time, looks like an aftereffect of the metaphysical constructs of the past which in other respects he surpasses. In his ambiguous reliance on a kind of World Spirit, Hegel resembles the first two generations of European and American romantic writers. It is as though there were a short transitional period (stretching, one might say, from Kant on the far side to Darwin, Marx, Nietzsche, and Freud on the near side) during which it remained possible to imagine a shedding of monotheism that would not imply a shedding of traditional conceptions of an "absolute" order of truth and spirit.

From one point of view, then, Hegel can be read as a retreat from the radical character of Kant's critical project, an attempt to recover, in the name of reconciliation, those metaphysical assurances that Kant had suspended. From another point of view, however, Hegel can be read as a bold surpassing of those traditional elements (including the reliance on transhistorical categories of reason) that continue to inform Kant's critical project, a radical effort to think the destructive and creative movement of temporal negativity. This dimension of Hegel's project has reverberated widely in European culture over the last two centuries, many of the most important philosophic and artistic currents in the wake of Hegel having involved the thinking of an irreducible negativity, a groundless play of forces engaged by Nietzsche as both the question of nihilism and the promise of a new point of departure. The negativity that in Hegel makes an appearance only to be "resolved" in the thinking of self-realizing Spirit has, since him, been unloosed and sounded in a multiplicity of ways. Despite the repeated questioning of our faith in progress, for example, the "bad infinite" of historicism (whether old or new) has gradually become the common air of our culture, while philosophers working from "phenomenological" and "ontological" perspectives have continued to explore the thought of what Merleau-Ponty once called "militant finitude" and Derrida "the indefinite movement of finitude."[1]

Inasmuch as the thinking of abyssal negativity involves the thinking of the absence of foundations, it is inseparable from two prominent themes—one could also call them two prominent experiences—of modern culture. One of these, emerging with particular force in romantic poetry, is the *vertiginous freeing of subjectivity,* an exorbitant awakening of immanent creative power. This event is surely related to, though not identical with, that experience of "self-assertion" that Hans Blumenberg takes to be the defining stance of modernity from the Renaissance on.[2]

Intimately linked to this unmooring of subjectivity, though emerging slightly later in time, is an event that could be described as the *vertiginous freeing of language or signifying power,* the unmooring of signification from pretextual grounds. Significantly, Mallarmé, like Nietzsche, discovers this strange errancy at the same moment as he encounters nihilism, "the uncanniest of all guests at the door," and the dynamics of Dickinson's poetry are akin to those traced in the texts of her more famous Continental contemporaries. The exploration of language unhinged from grounds—as though one could hear it speaking by itself in a strange boundlessness—is an important aspect of Mallarmé's adventure that anticipates many later modernist adventures. Derrida's project, developed in close relation to literary modernism, articulates among other things a generalization of this discovery, a provocative unfolding of its implications.

Doubtless a part of Nietzsche's immense influence in our century has to do with the way he engages at one and the same time both of these "unmoorings": the visionary who celebrates a creative subject freed from transcendent norms (indeed freed from all external norms) is also the ironist who describes the subject as a fiction produced by wandering linguistic tropes. If it is true, then, that Nietzsche carries out a naturalization and historicization of the "constitutive" categories of Kant's critical idealism, it is equally true that he carries out a linguistification of these categories, thereby pointing toward the "linguistic turn" of a great deal of twentieth-century philosophy. Yet to discern in this linguistic turn *only* a repetition of Kantian critical idealism, with language or discourse rather than the transcendental subject playing the constitutive role, is to leave out of the story the disruptive movement (marked above all by the long-distance conversation between Mallarmé and Nietzsche) whereby the subject is "unmoored" as the play of language unfolds with an "unmoored" life of its own. It is a movement whose implications we are still trying to sort out.[3]

These unmoorings, further, bring with them the sort of perpetual instability and open-endedness implied by the recognition of radical negativity. A thinking that, as Kierkegaard's Climacus says, "constantly keeps the wound of the negative open" (CUP, 78)—insofar as any securing of the negative in the positive is understood to produce illusion and self-deception—generates an *anticipatory openness* to the abyssal that echoes the dynamic of negative theology. This kind of echo frequently and perhaps inevitably haunts any heightened thinking of negativity, and in this regard one should not be surprised by the emergence of the "messianic" as a major motif in a number of Derrida's texts over the last twenty years. Kierkegaard's paradoxical Christian discourse, a passionate negative theology raised to an extreme pitch, describes the knight of faith as an individual lying out over a deep of seventy thousand fathoms.

"Deity," Climacus writes, "is present as soon as the uncertainty of all things is thought infinitely" (CUP, 80), and perhaps only then, he suggests. Dickinson's uncanny voyages into the boundless space of death and psychic ruin, where all things seem riddled by "the distance on the look of death," hover in an aura of baffled expectation. Mallarmé's tracings of empty rooms, tombs, and tomblike spaces, where "nothing will have taken place but the place" except perhaps the constellation formed by these very tracings, repeatedly evoke a present absence, an absently present "rose dans les ténèbres," which, like the impossible Book, arrives only as a shadowy premonition. And Derrida's accounts of a movement of *différance* that escapes any clear presentation, articulated under the sign of paradox, variously emit prophetic, apocalyptic, and messianic sounds that may be inevitable the moment one begins to speak of an alterity that, though it *is* not, promises the "subversion of every kingdom" (MP, 22). Indeed, Derrida himself has observed that any discourse of radicalized negativity, whatever its intentions, leaves itself open to appropriation by a negative theology: "From the moment a proposition takes a negative form, the negativity that announces itself need only be pushed to the limit for it to begin at least to resemble an apophatic theology. . . . The name of God would then be the hyperbolic effect of that negativity or of all related negativity in a given discourse" (HAS, 76). It is clear that this sort of language and its provocative effects continue to fascinate our culture. Kierkegaard, Dickinson, Mallarmé, and Derrida are similar in the way they emphatically sound this force of negativity, generating a resonant openness to the absent, the unforeseeable, perhaps simply the abyssal.

Of course, the four thinkers I'm bringing together in this chapter are very different from one another, and thus the constellation formed in this chapter is likely to appear more eccentric than those formed in the first two chapters. Nevertheless, despite their immense religious, philosophic, and stylistic differences, all four of these writers pursue the adventure of the negative to an extreme (all of them, too, share a hyperbolic bent and a pronounced fondness for paradox). If Kierkegaard and Dickinson remain within a Christian framework, they do so in decidedly eccentric ways, their texts frequently skirting the thought of nihilism, while, if Mallarmé and Derrida write from an atheistic perspective, they do so in ways no less eccentric, their texts frequently curving toward a non-place where negative theological echoes are set resonating. And if the withdrawal of a Hidden God to an infinite distance is registered by Kierkegaard and Dickinson as an exorbitant movement of inwardness, while the demise of a theistic metaphysic and the vanishing of secure grounds are explored by Mallarmé and Derrida as an enigmatic release of the errancy of signification, these different emphases, as I've briefly suggested above, cross through one another, a crossing manifest with particular force in the texts of both Dickinson and Nietzsche. Further, these different adventures of the negative all produce openings toward the absent that are variously riddling, allusive, disruptive, and apocalyptic. It is as though something ancient were oddly sustained in these texts, echoed and left to drift off balance, some pulse of the impossible that still haunts an increasingly secularized and instrumentalized modern culture.

Perhaps in this respect the so-called end of philosophy, one of whose versions is the art of thinking our groundlessness, communicates with the beginning of philosophy, one of whose versions is the art of thinking our death and our longing for transcendence. In the abyss of negativity, it would seem, there echoes a silence that beckons like a promise, akin perhaps to a call Keats heard in the song of a nightingale, Whitman in the song of a thrush. It sounds like a call of departure that comes from nothing.

KIERKEGAARD

Kierkegaard's resonance in the last century has been extensive. His influence on twentieth-century existentialist philosophy, in particular on Heidegger's *Being and Time,* has of course been immense. His "romantic" discourse of radicalized inwardness as a critical response to the objectifying, impersonalizing trends of modernity echoes an array of similar responses throughout the modern period. In developing these lines of thought, his primary philosophic antagonist is Hegel, and, as one of the early efforts to articulate a criticism of metaphysics in general through an attack on Hegelianism in particular, his project anticipates similar anti-Hegelian polemics throughout our century (above all in the field of French post-structuralist theory). And his criticism of the subsumptive constructs of metaphysics in the name of the ethicoreligious "existing individual" prefigures important philosophic currents that extend well beyond existentialism. His account of the solitary individual's relationship to God, for example, a relationship exorbitantly situated in a space beyond history, objectivity, theoretical reason, and representation itself, is far closer to Levinas's account of the ethical subject's relationship to the other than Levinas himself ever acknowledges.[4]

Prescient, too, is Kierkegaard's understanding of the link between an effective critique of metaphysics and a self-conscious art of writing. His agile invention of masks, his hiding of a mobile authorial perspective behind an array of eccentric pseudonyms, his entire theory and practice of "indirect communication" or "maieutic artistry" take to an extreme a performative questioning of the relationship between philosophy and writing that has been carried out with comparable urgency by a number of philosophers in his wake, including Nietzsche, Heidegger, Wittgenstein, and Derrida, among others. One of the great philosophic ironists, Kierkegaard, like Nietzsche, seems always to be rethinking his relationship with Socrates. How are we to interpret the indirect communications of a writer who, while incisively criticizing the orientation of romantic irony, at the same time draws on all the tactics of irony to articulate a religious orientation of hyperbolic inwardness in relation to an absently present divinity? From his early "aesthetic" writings through his late "religious" writings, Kierkegaard weaves a meditation on the relationship between the ironic mobility of a teaching by indirection and the extravagant inwardness of a life in faith.

ALL OF KIERKEGAARD'S tactics and polemics are designed to serve his guiding theme of teaching what it means to exist in perpetual ethicoreligious striving. "But the genuine subjective existing thinker is always as negative as he is positive, and *vice versa*. . . . He is conscious of the negativity of the infinite in existence, and he constantly keeps the wound of the negative open" (CUP, 78). It is this inwardly striving individual that Kierkegaard would like to awaken from the abstract routines of speculative metaphysics, complacent Christianity, and, more generally, what Climacus calls the "increasingly unreal" character of the age (CUP, 283). "In the midst of all our exultation over the achievements of the age and the nineteenth century, there sounds a note of poorly conceived contempt for the individual man; in the midst of the self-importance of the contemporary generation there is revealed a sense of despair over being human" (CUP, 317). Thus, according to Climacus, the task is to teach, first, what it means to exist as a human being, and then, what it means to become a Christian:

> It became clear to me that the misdirection of speculative philosophy, and its consequent assumed justification for reducing faith to the status of a relative moment, could not be anything accidental, but must be rooted deeply in the entire tendency of the age. It must, in short, doubtless be rooted in the fact that on account of our vastly increased knowledge,

men had forgotten what it means to EXIST, and what INWARDNESS signifies.... I now resolved to go back as far as possible, in order not to reach the religious mode of existence too soon, to say nothing of the specifically Christian mode of religious existence, in order not to leave difficulties unexplored behind me. If men had forgotten what it means to exist religiously, they had doubtless also forgotten what it means to exist as human beings. (CUP, 216; cf. 223)

Perhaps Kierkegaard's most powerful presentation of this project appears in the *Philosophical Fragments* and the *Concluding Unscientific Postscript*, in part because it is in these texts that Kierkegaard, speaking through Climacus, attains a full clarity concerning those "spheres" of existence that he had begun to explore in his earlier works. His conception of the aesthetic sphere of existence remains fairly consistent throughout his trajectory. It is regularly characterized as a mode of existence that treats others as things rather than persons, valorizes reflective possibility (and so irony) over resolute commitment, oscillates between enjoyment and disappointment, drifts upon an undercurrent of boredom and melancholy, and embodies an ultimate truth of despair—thus Kierkegaard's damning account of modern (secular) individualism. Remaining fairly consistent, too, is his conception of the religious sphere, which is regularly characterized as a mode of existence that, while necessarily passing through the sphere of ethical resolution, practices renunciation in an increasingly intensified inwardness in relation to the absolute, thus stirring a deepening of both suffering and guilt.[5] Yet Kierkegaard's conception of the ethical sphere of existence is less stable. In early works like *Either/Or* and *Fear and Trembling*, the ethical is characterized as a spiritual orientation guiding action in the world, an integration of the self achieved through a "choice" of oneself as an individual committed to binding ideals, resolved to assume "responsibility" for the whole of the self in time, both who one has been and who one is to become: indeed this "resolution" is precisely the constitution of the ethically coherent self gathered out of aesthetic dispersion. Yet in these works the ethical is also characterized as a decision to adopt communal norms that raise the individual from the idiosyncratic, the erratic, and the hidden into the universal, the constant, and the disclosed, and in this sense it bears strong Hegelian accents (Judge William, for instance, while fond of the Kantian term "duty," tends to speak in a distinctly Hegelian voice). However, as the polemic against Hegel is heightened, in *Stages on Life's Way* and in the *Fragments* and the *Postscript*, these Hegelian accents wane and the ethical comes to be conceived as a transitional phase (SLW,

476) that either remains in the hollow drift of aesthetic self-dispersal, and so in despair, or else realizes itself in the integrative striving of ethicoreligious inwardness (SLW, 435). It is owing to this increased emphasis on inward action that some commentators have spoken of a "return to Kant" in Kierkegaard's thought: an insistence on the primacy of the ethical, a concentration on the qualitative orientation of the will (a concentration that careens, unnecessarily, into a dismal solipsism in book 2, part 2, chapter 3 of the *Postscript*), a dramatization of the always incomplete striving of the ethical individual, and, in general, a sort of recasting of Kant's rational ethics of continual striving in relation to the moral law within as a Christian existential ethics of continual striving in relation to the divine infinite "negatively present" in the subject (CUP, 52). To be sure, Kierkegaard at no point accepts Kant's conception of ethical autonomy. He insists, against Kant, that any ethics, if it refuses the lure of self-deception, cannot but come to ruin in the experience of guilt and despair. "The God of the religious way of life appears not in ethical victory, but only in the shipwreck of freedom on the shoals of guilt."[6] The authentic ethical individual, therefore, must ultimately surrender his or her sense of inner power to an absolute power that, "not of this world," can only be negatively experienced in the passion of faith. In both *Stages on Life's Way* and the *Postscript*, the ethical sphere is thus reconceived as the ethicoreligious sphere of inward striving in faith, the highest task for the concretely existing individual, set in opposition to both the aesthetic mode of existence (an empty dispersal of the self existing in time) and the impersonality of metaphysical speculation (an abstract evasion of the self existing in time). Hegel is decisively opposed while Kant is emphatically rewritten in Christian terms.[7]

The genuinely existing ethicoreligious individual, then, "conscious of the negativity of the infinite in existence," inhabits an always unsettled negative dialectic of subjectivity and ideality, existential effort and the religious absolute. Climacus's concern throughout the *Postscript* is to describe this dialectic in detail and to underline its difficulty, the difficulty of striving to realize the ideal within existence. It is from this perspective that he arrives at his provocative insistence on the subjective character of ethical and religious truth. Truth, he claims, involves not an objective system considered abstractly, or in its correspondence to exterior reality, but the relationship maintained by an existing individual to an ideality that he or she strives to assimilate to a concrete life in time. Truth thus requires not disinterested judgment but earnest appropriation. It is a question not of "what" but of "how":

> In the ethico-religious sphere, the accent is again on the "how." But this is not to be understood as referring to demeanor, expression, or the like; rather it refers to the relationship sustained by the existing individual, in his own existence, to the content of his utterance. Objectively the interest is focussed merely on the thought-content, subjectively on the inwardness. At its maximum this inward "how" is the passion of the infinite, and the passion of the infinite is the truth. But the passion of the infinite is precisely subjectivity, and thus subjectivity becomes the truth. (CUP, 181)

And in almost the same breath—at this point unsurprisingly—Climacus asserts the identity of "truth" and "faith":

> Here is ... a definition of truth: an objective uncertainty held fast in an appropriation-process of the most passionate inwardness is the truth, the highest truth attainable for an existing individual.... But [this] definition of truth is an equivalent expression for faith. Without risk there is no faith. Faith is precisely the contradiction between the infinite passion of the individual's inwardness and the objective uncertainty. If I am capable of grasping God objectively, I do not believe, but precisely because I cannot do this I must believe. If I wish to preserve myself in faith I must constantly be intent upon holding fast the objective uncertainty, so as to remain out upon the deep, over seventy thousand fathoms of water, still preserving my faith. (CUP, 182)

The truth of faith, so to speak, is the passion with which an existing subject maintains itself in the wounding dialectic between its own finitude and the infinite ideality it strives to assimilate in inwardness, continually suffering this contradiction between the finite and the infinite, the temporal and the eternal, the necessary and the possible (see SUD, 43–44). The negativity of becoming, for Climacus, is the negativity of a finite individual's uncertain but passionate relationship to an absently present transcendence. Faith only *anticipates* a positive infinite, for the existing individual inwardly experiences this infinite as the negativity of a relationship in dis-relationship.

Neither Climacus nor Kierkegaard is the polemical antirealist or skeptic that both may superficially appear to be. In the *Fragments* and the *Postscript*, Climacus, while asserting that all our "objective" knowledge about nature and history is inevitably "approximative," shows no interest in contesting conventional "correspondence" theories of truth *in their proper domains*. His primary concerns are other. First, following Kant, he insists on the primacy of ethics and underlines that the reality of ethical experience is distorted insofar as it is approached in objective terms. "All knowledge which does not inwardly relate itself to existence, in the reflection of inwardness, is, essentially viewed, accidental knowledge. . . . But [this] means that [essential] knowledge has a relationship to the knower, who is essentially an existing individual, and that for this reason all essential knowledge is essentially related to existence" (CUP, 176–77). Many of Climacus's provocative assertions, in a word, become less provocative the moment one recognizes that he tends to use the word "truth" where most of us, according to semantic and pragmatic conventions, would use the word "truthfulness" or, to recall a term later important in existentialist discourses, "authenticity." At stake is the ethicoreligious integrity of the self. Further, and again following Kant, Climacus makes the bolder claim that our only access to religious truth is through ethical experience, not through philosophic, scientific, or historical knowledge. "The ethical is [the individual's] complicity with God" (CUP, 138). It is in this sense that every genuine Christian is a "contemporary" of Christ, the decision of faith involving a decisive turning of the spirit, a transformative movement of the individual alone with the absolute, to which the propositions of philosophic knowledge, historical research, and religious tradition are irrelevant (PC, 62–66). According to this line of thought, religious truth, the passion and uncertainty of religious faith, is discovered only through that inwardness which strives to realize the claims of infinite ideality. "Christianity," Climacus states in one of his characteristic flights of hyperbole, "protests every form of objectivity. . . . it is subjectivity that Christianity is concerned with, and it is only in subjectivity that its truth exists, if it exists at all; objectively, Christianity has absolutely no existence" (CUP, 126). "Christianity," he asserts elsewhere, is not an "objective doctrine" but an "existential communication" addressing ethicoreligious imperatives to the existing individual (CUP, 339). Religious faith is sustained, as it were, in the passionate effort to live the truth of religious faith (CUP, 37–38; cf. FSE, 67–69).[8]

Yet what are we to make of the romantic accents audible in this discourse of ethicoreligious striving? The emphases on passionate striving, heroic subjectivity, the movement of inwardness in relation to infinite ideality, the fraught relation between the concrete individual and impersonal social routines: all these recall similar emphases in a great deal of romantic writing. Despite his lucid criticisms of the predicaments of the aesthetic individual, then, might not Kierkegaard's "striving" ethicoreligious individual have important affinities with the "questing" romantic poet, or even with the romantic ironist whose vertiginous negative freedom is scrutinized in Kierkegaard's doctoral thesis, *On the Concept of Irony?*[9] In his study of irony, Kierkegaard distinguishes between Socratic irony and romantic irony: the former, Kierkegaard argues, negates basic elements of a social formation perceived as no longer viable, while the latter negates the positivity of any finite context or of "actuality in general" (CI, 271). Romantic or absolute irony, then, marks an experience of negative freedom attained through a "sacrifice" of the finite as such. "Irony *sensu eminentiori* is directed not against this or that particular existing entity but against the entire actuality at a certain time and under certain conditions.... It is not this or that phenomenon but the totality of existence that it contemplates *sub specie ironiae*. To this extent we see the correctness of Hegel's view of irony as infinite absolute negativity" (CI, 254; cf. 271–75). In fact, in *The Concept of Irony*, Kierkegaard, as if sketching a first draft of Judge William's critique of the aesthetic individual in *Either/Or*, largely reiterates Hegel's critique of the ironist as an "abstract" or unrealized type of subjectivity. The ironist, in negating everything for the sake of a negative freedom, in thus turning the self into a mere pivot of restless negativity, fails to attain the resolute selfhood and concrete wholeness of the realized ethical and social individual. Kierkegaard, in an important sense, never abandons this line of thought. In his view the ethicoreligious individual always remains, on one level, a resolute ethical individual situated in a given social world.[10]

Yet how would Kierkegaard respond to the suggestion that, nevertheless, Climacus's conception of a specifically *religious* inwardness curiously resembles the romantic ironist's practice of "infinite absolute negativity"? "Deity ... is present as soon as the uncertainty of all things is thought infinitely" (CUP, 80). How is this religious inwardness that recognizes the vanity of the finite for the sake of the infinite different from the ironic inwardness that negates the finite for the sake of an indeterminate freedom? Kierkegaard himself, as though writing with uncanny foresight, addresses just this question in his book on irony:

> Finally, insofar as irony, when it realizes that existence has no reality, pronounces the same thesis as the pious mentality, irony might seem to be a kind of religious devotion. If I may put it this way, in religious devotion the lower actuality, that is, the relationships with the world, loses its validity, but this occurs only insofar as the relationships with God simultaneously affirm their absolute reality. The devout mind also declares that all is

vanity, but this is only insofar as through this negation all disturbing factors are set aside and the eternally existing order comes into view. (CI, 257–58)

Thus Kierkegaard's response to the suspicion voiced above—that the romantic ironist returns in Climacus's account of the religious individual who, while remaining in the midst of the finite, strives to renounce the finite for the sake of the infinite—would presumably be a straightforward declaration of faith: a claim that an ethicoreligious individual's relationship to God in the passion of faith involves a radically different sort of "negativity" than the romantic ironist's relationship to the empty freedom of infinite negativity. The ethicoreligious individual relates his or her existence to an absently present transcendence, not simply to the open-endedness of immanent becoming. An understanding of Kierkegaard's apparently "romantic" discourse of religious inwardness thus requires an understanding of both his negative theology and his polyvocal practice of indirect communication. I will return to the latter at the end of this section. The former is spelled out most fully in the *Fragments* and the *Postscript*.

IN CLIMACUS'S ECCENTRIC theology, as is well known, the Mystery of the Incarnation is refigured as the Offense of the Paradox, while the Faith that exceeds and completes reason is refigured as the Absurd that ruins reason. The paradoxical object of faith magnetizes the paradoxical passion of thought. Thus the well-known opening lines of the third chapter of the *Fragments*:

> But one must not think ill of the paradox, for the paradox is the passion of thought, and the thinker without the paradox is like the lover without passion: a mediocre fellow. But the ultimate potentiation of every passion is always to will its own downfall, and so it is also the ultimate passion of the understanding to will the collision, although in one way or another the collision must become its downfall. This, then, is the ultimate paradox of thought: to want to discover something that thought itself cannot think. This passion of thought is fundamentally present everywhere in thought, also in the single individual's thought insofar as he, thinking, is not merely himself. (PF, 38)

Louis Mackey has pointed out that this entire chapter of the *Fragments* can be read as a counter-Hegelian discourse decisively determined by Hegelian discourse:

Chapter III of the *Philosophical Fragments,* on the absolute paradox, may be read as an attempt to conceive the Augustinan doctrine of the relation of faith and reason in terms of a Hegelian conception of reason. It argues that reason is fulfilled in faith; that is perfectly Augustinian. But it adds that the fulfillment of reason is the undoing of reason—the crucifixion of the understanding. That is to take "reason" in an idealistic sense.[11]

As other commentators have observed, however, it may finally be Kant rather than Hegel who is the most significant unnamed presence in the passage from the *Fragments* cited above and, more generally, in Climacus's negative theology.[12] In the first *Critique,* Kant examines the intrinsic tendency of reason to overshoot the bounds of possible experience, to move from the conditioned to the unconditioned. "Human reason," he writes in the opening sentence of the preface to the first edition, "has this peculiar fate that in one species of its knowledge it is burdened by questions which, as prescribed by the very nature of reason itself, it is not able to ignore, but which, as transcending all its powers, it is also not able to answer" (CPR, 7). Kant's concern is to show that this transcendent domain is beyond the bounds of theoretical cognition. Any effort to attain positive knowledge of this realm merely leads the understanding into contradictions and, at worst, the errors of superstition and fanaticism, or in reaction to these, the errors of skepticism and indifference. We can *think* but cannot *know* freedom, God, and the immortality of the soul. Kant then argues that freedom, God, and the immortality of the soul, although they cannot be "objects" of theoretical knowledge, since the latter is limited to the domain of empirical experience, are nonetheless necessary "postulates" of practical reason. And these postulates are not in contradiction with the findings of theoretical reason, Kant claims, insofar as it has been demonstrated, first, that there must be a realm of things-in-themselves (the unconditioned) without which there could be no realm of appearances (the conditioned) for the understanding to know, and further, that this supersensible realm, although necessarily thought by reason, remains beyond the sensible domain of the proper employment of theoretical reason. "I have found it necessary," Kant writes in a famous assertion, "to deny *knowledge* in order to make room for *faith*" (CPR, 29). Kierkegaard, as Ronald Green has shown in detail, wholly follows Kant up to this point.

In their thinking of the religious, then, where do Kant and Kierkegaard differ? There are fundamental points of conflict. First, the incarnate God, essential to Kierkegaard's thinking of the religious, is of no importance to Kant's ethical or religious vision. Further, as I've noted above, Kierkegaard refuses the Kantian ideal of ethical autonomy. While he teaches a qualified ethical autonomy, presenting it as a necessary "stage on life's way," he insists that the ethical subject inevitably founders in a despair that can only be overcome through a passionate surrender of the self to the power and promise of an absently present God. From this experience derives a specifically religious type of suffering:

> This suffering has its ground in the fact that the individual in his immediacy is absolutely committed to relative ends [or to what Kant would call the ends of self-love]; its significance lies in the transposition of the relationship, the dying away from immediacy, or in the expression existentially of the principle that the individual can do absolutely nothing of himself, but is as nothing before God; for here again the negative is the mark by which the God-relationship is recognized, and self-annihilation is the essential form for the God-relationship. (CUP, 412)

Nevertheless, according to the paradoxes of faith, this self-annihilation or inward suffering is also the highest joy, for, as Frater Taciturnus puts it, "the religious is the sphere of fulfillment, but, please note, not a fulfillment such as when one fills an alms box or a sack with gold, for repentance has specifically created a boundless space, and as a consequence the religious contradiction: simultaneously to be out on seventy thousand fathoms of water and yet to be joyful" (SLW, 476–77).

Frater Taciturnus's words reveal, too, a third fundamental difference between Kant and Kierkegaard, namely, the place of "passion" in their conceptions of religion. Whatever Kant's intentions, his ethical theory has usually been read less as an elucidation of how we find the religious through the ethical than as a rewriting of the religious as a wholly secular and rational ethic of human autonomy. Kant's reduction of religion to morality, whereby faith becomes a sober postulate granted to the moral individual, is from Kierkegaard's point of view not faith at all. For Kierkegaard, faith without passion is a travesty, since faith is nothing if it is not the highest passion, the passion of the infinite sustained over a deep of seventy thousand fathoms. "Christianity," Climacus writes, "wishes to intensify passion to its highest pitch" (CUP, 117), for "truth is precisely the venture which chooses an objective uncertainty [namely the existence of God and the possibility of an eternal happiness] with the passion of the infinite. . . . Without risk there is no faith. Faith is precisely the contradiction between the infinite passion of the individual's inwardness and the objective uncertainty" (CUP, 182). Where Kant wishes to restrain the exorbitant inclination of thought, Kierkegaard, in a complex movement, wishes at one and the same time to encourage the passion of this inclination and wholly to suspend its search for positive knowledge.

It is this dimension of Kierkegaard's thought that might seem to approach the sort of inner-light "enthusiasm" to which Kierkegaard himself is no less averse than Kant (Kierkegaard, despite his distance from the sometimes complacent Judge William, shares the latter's distrust of mysticism as a flight from the difficult task of realizing the infinite *within* the worldly contexts of the finite [EO, 2:243–51]). Yet a distinctive feature of Kierkegaard's "dialectic" of inwardness, as Adorno has observed, is that it is "objectless" in the ordinary sense of "object" and so tends toward a mystical dialectic:

> Kierkegaard bestows the term "dialectics" on the movement that subjectivity completes both out of itself and in itself to regain "meaning." This cannot be conceived as a subject-object dialectic since material objectivity nowhere becomes commensurate with inwardness. This dialectic transpires between subjectivity and its "meaning," which the dialectic contains without being merged with it, and which does not merge with the immanence of "inwardness." The affinity between this dialectic and the mystical dialectic does not escape Kierkegaard.[13]

Perhaps this sort of approach to a mystical dialectic is inevitable if one radicalizes, at one and the same time, a movement of hidden inwardness and a negative theology of the Hidden God, a heightening of inward passion and a prohibition against any representation of the divine. The negativity of a passionate inwardness then becomes the mark of a torn reaching toward a felt transcendence. "In the infinite passionate interest for his eternal happiness," Climacus writes, "the subject is in a state of the utmost tension, in the very extremity of subjectivity, not indeed where there is no object, which is the imperfect and the undialectical distinction, but where God is negatively present in the subject; whose mode of subjectivity becomes, by virtue of this interest, the form for an eternal happiness" (CUP, 52). Does a passage like this justify the claim that Climacus rewrites Christianity as a wildly subjectivist and irrationalist faith? That Climacus's Christianity is emphatically subjective is clear enough. Yet, at the same time, Climacus, insisting on the Kantian prohibition against cognitive claims concerning the transcendent, underlines the subject's *negative* relationship to the divine. Probably the most important words in the passage just cited are the words "where God is negatively present in the subject": the inwardness of faith, according to Climacus, is always lived as a *fractured* relationship to the transcendent, a relationship in the dark. All of book 2, part 2, chapter 4, of the *Postscript* is a detailed elucidation of the suffering, the guilt, and, for the Christian, the awareness of sin involved in the passion of this fractured relationship to the absolute. The passion of faith is lived as an intensification of this relationship in dis-relationship. "In the relationship which underlies the dis-relationship, in the immanence barely suspected which underlies the divisive dialectic," Climacus writes, describing the non-Christian Religiousness A, whose dynamics Christianity radically intensifies, "the man holds onto the happiness, suspended as it were by the finest thread" (CUP, 477). Climacus's and, I think, Kierkegaard's distinctive conception of faith, then, could be said to involve this *simultaneous approach to and avoidance of an inner-light mysticism*, this holding fast, in an irresolvable contradiction, both the passion of the infinite and the negativity of a fractured relationship in the dark. "Faith is precisely the contradiction between the infinite passion of the individual's inwardness and the objective uncertainty" (CUP, 182).[14]

This conception of faith requires a kind of passionate balancing in the abyss. It also requires a capacity to dwell in the discrepancy between passionate inwardness and social outwardness. This discrepancy, based in a movement of faith incommensurate within any social or linguistic expression, has an ironic structure. And it is at this point that the question of the relationship between Kierkegaard's ironic mode of presentation and his concern to teach the hyperbolic passion of faith is posed in its most riddling fashion. While the question of the "place" from which Kierkegaard himself speaks in the maze of masks he has composed will never be fully answered, it is a question we can never avoid taking up yet again. Irony and hyperbole, mask and faith, seem to touch, even to come together, at some enigmatic point in this maze.

PERHAPS THE EASIEST way to make sense of Kierkegaard's play of masks is to read his entire *oeuvre* as a vast novel lending representation to multiple characters, lives, discourses, and perspectives interwoven with one another in a complex whole whose truth consists not of any one of these perspectives but rather of the multiple ways in which they qualify one another. As Kenneth Burke has pointed out, the trope of irony and the path of dialectic are intimately linked to one another.[15] In Plato's dialogues, where irony and dialectic are brought together in a highly self-conscious way, dialectic is presented, in one sense, as a mode of thought that moves through multiple perspectives in a kind of conversational journey wherein "truth" consists less of any one of these perspectives than of the entire journey: truth, inseparable from the process of its emergence, is discovered through the interplay of partial perspectives whose significance is fully elucidated only as they come to be situated within the wider horizon developed through the dialogical journey itself.[16] Hegel would conceive of the movement of history as the space of this unfolding dialogue of truth. In this sense, one can recognize in the polylogic, multiperspectival modern novel an "ironic" and "dialectical" mode of thinking realized in an "aesthetically" concrete form of presentation. And this would seem to explain, at least in part, Kierkegaard's attachment to a novelistic mode of teaching. It is a mode that permits him not only to draw attention to the concrete implications of shaping a life in terms of different spiritual bearings or abstract ideals—be they aesthetic, ethical, or religious—but also to study the way these different bearings "ironically" qualify one another within a larger "dialectical" pattern. As many commentators have noted, Kierkegaard, to a significant extent, does transpose a Hegelian rhythm of dialectical development to the plane of the existing individual, thus exploring the way the individual is able to move from one "stage of life" to another, traversing a path along which each stage, eventually colliding with its limits and so pointing beyond itself, comes to be at once canceled and retained (in a qualifed or sublated way) in the next stage.[17]

Yet there is more at stake in Kierkegaard's play of masks than this dialectical vision of existential development. Both the Socratic and the romantic ironist, as Kierkegaard understands them, practice an indirect mode of communication, expressing a genuine inwardness by speaking through a mask that, paradoxically, signals the impossibility of any full outward expression of the very inwardness thereby communicated. Kierkegaard orchestrates a play of masks (wherein "Kierkegaard" himself may ultimately become but another mask) in order to carry out a similar project of the indirect communication of inwardness. "Whatever is profound loves a mask," Nietzsche writes in *Beyond Good and Evil,* adding in a later section of the same book:

> The hermit does not believe that any philosopher . . . ever expressed his real and ultimate opinions in books: does one not write books precisely to conceal what one harbors? Indeed, he will doubt whether a philosopher

could *possibly* have "ultimate and real" opinions, whether behind every one of his caves there is not, must not be, another deeper cave—a more comprehensive, stranger, richer world beyond the surface, an abysmally deep ground behind every ground, under every attempt to furnish "grounds." Every philosophy is a foreground philosophy—that is a hermit's judgment: "There is something arbitrary in his stopping *here* to look back and look around, in his not digging deeper *here* but laying his spade aside; there is also something suspicious about it." Every philosophy also conceals a philosophy; every opinion is also a hideout, every word also a mask.[18]

Kierkegaard shares this understanding of genuine philosophic or religious writing. He, too, believes that "whatever is profound"—for example, the inward passion of faith—inevitably hides behind a play of masks, a dance of ironic words that are at once mere "surfaces" and indirectly conveyed "caves" of thought. And thus, to recall an issue I raised above, he would seem to erase the possibility of "outwardly" distinguishing between the passionate inwardness of a religious individual and the restless inwardness of a romantic ironist. For both of these perspectives involve a recognition that authentic inwardness can never be unambiguously "expressed" or "represented" in the daylit realm of outwardness. Should we believe Climacus when he tells us, repeatedly, that he is not a Christian but merely a "humorist" concerned to clarify for himself what it would mean to become a Christian? Or should we guess, rather, that his declared detachment, nutty digressiveness, comic prolixity, and perplexing hyperbole are but the ironic masks through which he at once hides and communicates his genuine Christian faith? Is there any way of answering this question in the theater Kierkegaard has constructed? Kierkegaard and his various pseudonyms set out to stir, through ironic indirection, a hyperbolic venture of faith. And this oscillation between the hyperbole of faith and the irony of presentation can be resolved, it would seem, only through the decisive venture of faith itself, not through any literary analysis or philosophic judgment—and that, indeed, is an essential "point" of Kierkegaard's teaching. Irony and hyperbole, mask and faith, are well-nigh seamlessly woven together in this project.[19]

In fact, all of Kierkegaard's thought inclines toward hyperbole as well as irony. His Christianity, Paul Ricoeur writes, "is so extreme that no one could possibly practice it. The subjective thinker before God, the pure contemporary of Christ, suffering crucifixion with Him, without church, without tradition, and without ritual, can only exist outside of history."[20] How are we to read Kierkegaard's errant, extravagant retropings of traditional Christian figures and themes? Is there any way, finally, to unravel the interplay in his texts between ironic provocation and hyperbolic performance? Louis Mackey has spelled out one plausible way of stabilizing this oscillating rhetoric:

> But the fact remains that Kierkegaardian Christianity is imbalanced and excessive. And the decisive fact, still outstanding, is that Kierkegaard knew it and meant it that way. To all such friendly apologetics [attempts to excuse or to recode Kierkegaard's language], as well as to all the proper protests of his accusers, Kierkegaard would reply that *Training in Christianity, Fear and Trembling,* the *Fragments,* the *Postscript,* and all the rest were but "correctives" recommended to the complacent debility of "the present age." The works of Anti-Climacus in particular are a volley of thoughts that wound from behind, aimed at "revival and increase of inwardness" among Christians, not at a theological synthesis for the benefit of the professors of Christianity.... What Anti-Climacus writes is not theology or criticism but rhetoric designed to introduce his reader into the presence of the "sign of contradiction" and to evoke a decision.[21]

This is a persuasive reading of Kierkegaard's rhetorical excesses, and, as *The Point of View of My Work as an Author* makes clear, it is how Kierkegaard himself came to understand his rhetorical tactics. Everything excessive and imbalanced in Kierkegaard, then, can be read as a "defamiliarizing" tactic motivated by his decision to be a gadfly, a Christian Socrates in a context of complacency in which Christianity was presented as a doctrine, an abstract set of beliefs, rather than a way of life demanding self-transformation in fear and trembling, a transfigurative relationship to God experienced in solitude. "If truth is spirit," Climacus writes, "it is an inward transformation, a realization of inwardness; it is not an immediate and extremely free-and-easy relationship between an immediate consciousness and a sum of propositions" (CUP, 37). Contesting any such "free-and-easy" divorce of knowledge from inward action, Climacus sets out "to create difficulties everywhere" (CUP, 166). Hyperbole, then, is but one of his modes, an especially provocative one, of Socratic irony.

Yet Mackey's reading, I think, does not quite exhaust the meaning of hyperbole in Kierkegaard. Hyperbole is so essentially woven into the texture of his Christianity that finally it seems to be less the rhetorical tactic of a Christian Socrates than a performative expression of that passionate faith that Kierkegaard understands to be the essence of an authentic religious inwardness. In the *Fragments,* as we have seen, Climacus declares that "paradox is the passion of thought" and that "the ultimate potentiation of every passion is always to will its own downfall" (PF, 37). Recalling the etymological root of hyperbole in "to throw above or beyond," one could say that Kant, in the first *Critique*, characterizes reason as intrinsically hyperbolic, intrinsically impelled to transcend the empirical bounds within which alone it can properly function. Kierkegaard wholly agrees with this account. Subjectivity, awakened from the sleep of finite immediacy and superficial routine, experiences the "wound of the negative" as the mystery of its relationship to the wholly other that transcends it (CUP, 74–86). And from this experience of the negative emerges the passion of faith, a hyperbolic movement of the inwardness that, situated in the finite and haunted by death, reaches toward the infinite in passionate anticipation. Yet, since Kierkegaard also adopts the Kantian prohibition against claims to knowledge concerning the transcendent, perhaps one should describe the hyperbole of his thought as primarily a mode of negative hyperbole (involving the paradox that ruins reason, the absurdity that demands a paradoxical leap of self-surrender, the intensification of inwardness that requires decisive self-renunciation, the transformation of the subject in relation to an absolute that, negatively present in inward suffering, implies an ultimate negation of existence, and so forth). The venture of faith sustains a relationship to a Hidden God "negatively present" in the subject of hidden inwardness. This passion of faith, then, is a venture of negative hyperbole, a renunciation of the finite on the part of the finite creature who, precisely in this renunciation, reaches toward the infinite, suffering the relationship in dis-relationship, the expectation of eternity, in a movement of abyssal longing. There is an apocalyptic pulse in Kierkegaard's presentation of Christian faith. Ultimately, perhaps, all the ironic masks are but indirect signs of this genuinely extravagant pulse.

WHILE KIERKEGAARD PRESENTS his primary targets as the abstractions of Hegelianism, the spiritless evasions of routinized Christendom, and the impersonalizing trends of modernity, his entire project is also an eccentric Christian response to the rise of atheism in the nineteenth century. Hegel's account of Christianity as the bearer of an implicit truth at last made explicit in his own philosophy—a kind of prototruth only fully illuminated by being translated from its merely "figurative language" into the fully developed concepts of Hegelian philosophy—can be read as a polite way of saying that orthodox Christianity is simply false. A number of Hegel's immediate followers, having understood him to have implied just that, set out to make explicit what he had left implicit. Kierkegaard, who had read Feuerbach, would seem to have understood Hegel in the same way. An ironist might say that his response was to embrace the enemy's criticisms (the claim, for instance, that Christianity is an absurdity impossible to accept on rational grounds) and to turn them into defining features of a Christian truth to be discovered only through the voyage inward. "The path of mystery leads inward" (Novalis echoing Augustine).[22] One could also say, with or without irony, that his response was to risk turning Christianity into a romantic dialectic of inwardness and ideality, a quest of passionate subjectivity sustained over a deep of painful yet exhilarating uncertainty.

What would happen if one maintained all the drama of Kierkegaardian faith, all the negativity of a passionate venture in uncertainty, all the intensified inwardness in relation to an absolute discovered only through this abyssal inwardness, while letting waver the bridge of faith itself? One might find oneself in the weather of Emily Dickinson's poetry. The affinities between Kierkegaard and Dickinson are numerous. Both lend voice to a passionate yet fractured relationship to a Hidden God. Both draw from the Protestant tradition the resources for an epic adventure of subjective voyage. Both explore an exorbitant inwardness to the point of vertiginous solipsism (and, unlike many romantic writers of their period, neither seems troubled by this). Both, in sounding the wound of infinite longing and in practicing a kind of demonic introspection, turn themselves into dazzling psychologists of extreme, unstable, disorienting states of thought and feeling. In just this zone of experience, both illuminate paradoxical psychic curves wherein despair and elation, suffering and joy, collapse and transcendence are found to be bafflingly intertwined with one another. Both find that hyperbole, negation, and paradox are essential to the expression of their extravagant desire, their experience of a longing that can be satisfied by no finite object or horizon. As bold explorers of abyssal insecurity, both find death to be a familiar defamiliarizing teacher. And both carry to an extreme pitch a Christian "sacrificial" economy of desire wherein loss is gain, renunciation possession, the abyssal ruin of the finite the abyssal disclosure of the infinite. The motion of negativity, as it were, becomes the truth, the way, and the life—the life of a passionate renunciation of self or the life of an ecstatic anticipation of death. "The existing subject is eternal," Climacus writes, "but *qua* existing temporal. The elusiveness of the infinite now expresses itself through the possibility of death at any moment" (CUP, 76), a thought very close to the pulse of Dickinson's psychic life.

To be sure, Kierkegaard and Dickinson differ in many ways, and not least in their relationship to the fundamentals of Protestant Christianity. Dickinson, while voicing an exorbitant Christian psychic economy, abandons any conventional Christian faith, retaining only a troubled belief in the existence of a Hidden God. She explores an apocalyptic economy of desire and an apocalyptic drama of imagination at a specific moment in the waning of the Christian tradition. It is this tension that determines many of the distinctive qualities of her poetry. It also, curiously, turns her into a kind of protomodernist writer.[23]

DICKINSON

In a discussion of the "transitional" context in which Dickinson wrote, Allen Tate observes that she "was born into the equilibrium of an old and a new order. Puritanism could not be to her what it had been to the generation of Cotton Mather—a body of absolute truths; it was an unconscious discipline timed to the pulse of her life."[24] The resources of the old order, including its vocabulary and its typological schemes, operate as "an unconscious discipline" in a poet who, at the same time, alertly explores the new order with all the energy of her more decisively "post-Christian" contemporaries like Emerson and Whitman. Dickinson's poetry, then, would seem to be an exact, if idiosyncratic, map of that secularizing "displacement" of individualist Protestantism which is an essential dynamic in the emergence of English and North American romantic poetry. And Dickinson is often characterized as a high romantic poet in just this sense. Her celebration of imaginative transport at all costs, her affirmation of the divinity within as the source of creative power, her exploration of an unstable inwardness heightened to the point of vertigo, and her fascination with radical dislocations lived as sublime ecstasies: all these features of her poetry signal her participation in a broader field of romanticism. Her decidedly errant romanticism may be the major precursor of the weaving "transmemberment of song" we later find in Hart Crane's poetry.

At the same time, Dickinson is sometimes characterized, with good reason, as a kind of peculiar modernist poet *avant la lettre*. Her cryptic, elliptical mode of composition that often defies the reader, her tendency to "cede the initiative to words" (Mallarmé) in poems whose figural movements spin outward in surprising "raids on the inarticulate" (Eliot), and her recurrent exploration of a consciousness stunned by its encounter with vast emptiness: these features of her poetry signal her participation in a broader field of what we often think of as modernism. Indeed, there appears to be an intimate, if complex, link in her poetry, as in Mallarmé's, between a certain hermeticism, an obscure tropic play, and a recurrent evocation of nothingness. Though she is rarely mentioned in the same breath as famous continental contemporaries of hers like Nietzsche and Mallarmé, this, I think, is a mistake, for Dickinson explores the shadow of nihilism with the same seriousness and reach as Nietzsche in his major texts from the 1870s on and Mallarmé in his great poems and letters from the 1860s on. And like Nietzsche and Mallarmé, Dickinson, in encountering an abyssal groundlessness, discovers at the same time the baffling errancy not only of subjectivity but also of language. She is articulately adrift.

When all of that is said, it remains true that Dickinson is a poet thoroughly embedded in a Christian tradition. Often she sounds like a subtle "devotional" poet, writing in inherited Christian terms of love and loss, death and immortality, the lonely individual and a remote God, the difficulty of faith in a world battered by pain. Most important in this regard is her appropriation of traditional "figural" or "typological" patterns of interpreting experience. As all of her finest critics have underlined, she draws heavily and innovatively on these patterns, tracing the contours of her own psychic experience in the "epic" or "heroic" terms provided by Christian typology. Christian typology involves a decidedly dynamic conception of the relationship between experience and signification, for it posits that an event in history discloses its full meaning only in the unfolding of time and, ultimately, in the ruin of time. In fact, typology bears within it an "apocalyptic" vector that, I will argue below, is the dimension of typology most resonantly set in play in Dickinson's poetry, a poetry whose guiding impulse is an emphatic revelatory or apocalyptic movement. Much of her distinctiveness as a poet, at any rate, would seem to reside in the creative crossing of these very different currents: an innovative recasting of Christian typological schemes, a romantic celebration of imaginative power and psychic transport, and a modernist practice of elliptical composition that evokes the strange errancy of language discovered as inherited grounds waver or collapse.[25]

The complexity of this crossing of currents is manifest, in particular, in Dickinson's many poems of abyssal transport. Perhaps the clearest sign of her closeness to a high romantic poetic is her Emersonian worship of power. "There seems a spectral power in thought that walks alone," she writes in a letter to Higginson, adding, "When a little Girl I remember hearing that remarkable passage and preferring the 'Power,' not knowing at the time that 'Kingdom' and 'Glory' were included" (L # 330). "If I feel physically as if the top of my head were taken off, I know *that* is poetry," she is reported to have said in another Emersonian affirmation (L # 342), one that underlines her identification of poetry with sheer power, and sheer power with extravagant transport. Yet there is the question, for in Dickinson's poems, as every reader knows, transport is often figured less as deliverance or transcendence than as abyssal fall or vertiginous ruin. In fact, though she is in fundamental respects closer to a Christian imaginative universe than Emerson, she is in other respects further from any Christian or post-Christian "idealism" than he. It is in this peculiar sense that she seems to travel beyond her context in a way that Emerson, at least in some respects, does not.

In many of her riddling poems, at any rate, she discovers eerie transport in abyssal voyage. Thus the curve of one of her most famous poems:

> I felt a Funeral, in my Brain,
> And Mourners to and fro
> Kept treading—treading—till it seemed
> That sense was breaking through—
>
> And when they all were seated,
> A Service, like a Drum—
> Kept beating—beating—till I thought
> My Mind was going numb—
>
> And then I heard them lift a Box
> And creak across my Soul
> With those same Boots of Lead, again,
> Then Space—began to toll,
>
> As all the Heavens were a Bell,
> And Being, but an Ear,
> And I, and Silence, some strange Race
> Wrecked, solitary, here—
>
> And then a Plank in Reason, broke,
> And I dropped down, and down—
> And hit a World, at every plunge,
> And Finished knowing—then—
>   (P # 280)

The fictive occasion of the poem is ambiguous. While it is clear that the phases of a funeral are being described (or the phases of a wake, a funeral, and a burial), each of these phases exerting an increased pressure on the speaker (on her brain, mind, and soul), it is not clear whether the speaker is a grieving survivor, suffering a loss so painful that it induces psychic breakdown, or whether she is herself passing through death, suffering the exile of death.[26] I incline toward the second reading, largely because the speaker seems to be voicing the experience of dying from the inside, yet surely the poem holds out both possibilities, and suffering and despair are usually experienced by Dickinson as a kind of dying anyway. "Looking at Death, is Dying" (P # 281). The first three stanzas evoke a solitary consciousness under extreme pressure, while the last two stanzas, the sublime dislocation in the poem, evoke a mind falling through its own floor, a psychic collapse of staggering proportions. The last stanza, more exactly, is a kind of painful coda to the collapse, an evocation of the definitive vastation of knowledge, consciousness, bodily coherence, and time. Whether this is a poem of despair or a poem of proleptic death, then, it is a powerful instance of Dickinson's uncanny art of "dying in Drama" (P # 531). "'Tis Dying—I am doing— but / I'm not afraid to know" (P # 692).

    The most enigmatic images in the poem, no doubt, are the palpable abstractions of the fourth stanza. Perhaps few poems have so weirdly evoked the immeasurable loneliness of death, the appalling solitude of the passage from being to nonbeing, figured in this poem as a shattering fall from the harmony of being to the silence and exile of sheer wreck. The startling images of the fourth stanza, however strange, do recall the figures of Christian apocalyptic. The resonant tolling of space between the Heavens and Being would seem to allude to the harmony established in the beginning between the Creator (or the Creative Word) and the Creation. It is this harmony that holds chaos, the abyssal waste, at bay. The wreckage, solitude, and silence of death, then, are imagined as a radical exile from this harmony of Creator and Creation, a return to primordial chaos at the moment the Creative Word withdraws its sustaining power, abandoning the creature to ruin. The stanza thus brings together, in a way characteristic of Dickinson's poetry, traditional Christian figures and figures of boundless nothingness that (though themselves reminiscent of Christian apocalyptic) undermine the promise embodied by those traditional figures. Death is imagined as a voyage nowhere, a bottomless fall through a space where no redemptive gleam flickers. Apocalyptic ruin, transposed to the plane of the individual, discloses not radiant eternity but infinite nothingness.

    Yet to remain at this level would be to ignore the performative force of the poem, to neglect the apparent contradiction between the "content" of the poem, its presentation of sheer suffering followed by a devastating loss of self, and the "spirit" of the poem, its evocation of a kind of uncanny transport and even exhilaration. "'Tis so appalling—it exhilarates— / So over Horror—it half Captivates," as Dickinson writes in another poem (P # 281). "I felt a funeral in my brain" celebrates the wildness of departure even as it registers a lucid terror at the thought of death, as though decisive ruin had become delirious release, as though the conventional orientations on the spirit's compass had been set spinning.[27] As in Browning's "Childe Roland to the Dark Tower Came," or in a number of Baudelaire's poems, a voyage into nothingness and a release of vision are brought together in a disorienting way. God, heaven, and immortality may have vanished in the dark, but death remains the teacher, and indeed the muse, stirring motions of transport, dislocative awakenings. Like Keats, Whitman, and Stevens, Dickinson discovers in an acute awareness of death a heightened pulse of life; like Baudelaire and Mallarmé, on the other hand, she seems in no particular hurry to return to the world she occasionally leaves behind, inclining rather to hover in a bewildered sounding of death, as if drifting through a place of mystery. While there is little sense in calling Dickinson "morbid," there is no question that her poems express a distinctive relationship to death, a relationship that involves above all the imagining of intensely felt psychic curves as disclosive anticipations of death.[28] It is as though Dickinson lived the negativity of experience as a ceaseless, bottomless disclosure of the infinite. The boundless possibility in which she dwells is closely linked to the play of a negativity that, as we will see, she reads under the aspect of apocalypse, or more exactly, to reinflect an expression of Derrida's, of "apocalypse without apocalypse," revelation without revelation, abyssal apocalypse. She articulates this dynamic vision through her idiosyncratic rewriting of Christian typological hermeneutics.

CHRISTIAN TYPOLOGY WAS an element of Dickinson's cultural context. According to the ancient rule, typology posits that "in the Old Testament the New Testament is concealed, and in the New Testament the Old Testament is revealed."[29] It is this diachronic figural model that Dickinson's Puritan ancestors had transposed to the setting of their new journey in the wilderness, thereby lending a sense of epic scope to historical and even personal events that might otherwise have seemed ordinary or hopeless. As Cynthia Griffin Wolff writes, "An Old Testament hero might be seen as anticipating not only some crucial moment in Christ's life as described in the New Testament but also crucial moments in any individual Christian's life. . . . There was, then, a continuum of heroic and antiheroic possibilities that extended uninterruptedly from the ancient biblical past into mid-nineteenth-century Massachusetts."[30] Adopting this figural model while lending it an emphatic "internal" cast, Dickinson invents, in David Porter's expression, a "typology of private affairs," one that allows her to present the contours of personal experience with all the enigmatic reach and epic resonance of biblical narrative.[31] Of particular importance in Dickinson's poetry, further, is the apocalyptic pulse that she borrows from this figural model. According to traditional typology, not only are New Testament events antitypes or fulfillments of Old Testament types, they are themselves types whose antitypes are to be revealed in eternity. "This suggests another clue to the origin of typology: it is essentially a revolutionary form of thought and rhetoric. . . . The full thrust of New Testament typology goes in two directions: into the future and into the eternal world, the two things coinciding with the apocalypse or Last Judgment."[32] It is this apocalyptic vector, I think, that is far more important to Dickinson than the practice of reading the events of personal life in terms of Old Testament types. To see the world—to experience specific perceptions and even the shifting pressures of one's inner life—from this apocalyptic perspective is to encounter a present that is ceaselessly whirling toward eternity. It is to apprehend any present event as but the insecure hint of a "fulfilled" event elsewhere, to apprehend the present itself as but a perpetual motion of erasure pointing toward a distance at once alluring and obscure. All things are perceived to hover in an aura of elsewhere, or, in the darkened terms in which Dickinson tends to rewrite this pattern, to gleam in a shadow of nowhere. The distance of the infinite, as it were, is felt to be inherent both in things and in oneself, a distance that becomes darkened when skepticism fractures any faith in a positive eternity to be disclosed, at which point the enigmatic vanishing of the finite is perceived to reveal but a resonant blankness, a sort of abyssal circumference. This is the apocalyptic dynamic that Dickinson's imagination sounds time and again, a typological thrust forward she never abandons, though it repeatedly bears her into a boundlessness as appalling as it is exhilarating. It is boundlessness that magnetizes her: "[T]hank you for the Beauty," she writes in a late letter, "thank you too for Boundlessness—that rarely given and choicest Gift" (L # 953).

Robert Weisbuch is the critic who has most sensitively explored this dynamic in Dickinson's poetry. He argues that in her poetry, as in certain "interiorizing" traditions as old as the origins of Christian theology, the typological model is individualized, personal "death" replacing the ultimate "end" of historical typology: "Personal death replaces Christ as the prime antitype; and personal states of consciousness, ecstatic or painful, replace historical events as the foreshadowing types. The self becomes type and antitype, its own future fulfillment."[33] Weisbuch persuasively shows how in Dickinson's poetry heightened states of consciousness, figured as anticipations of death, are made to resonate with the mysterious vastness of death. I would hardly wish to contest this interpretation, for it certainly illuminates an important dimension of Dickinson's typological poetic, yet I would like to complement it with a slightly different reading. It is my sense that Dickinson, while indeed "personalizing" typology, often figures death in a way quite similar to the way it is figured in traditional typological or apocalyptic patterns, namely, not as the end itself, but rather as the sublime ruin that discloses the invisible end. The negativity of the finite, or at its ultimate pitch the ruin of time itself, is not the end but rather the door to the end, the process whereby the unfathomable end is sublimely disclosed. One reason Dickinson's poetry is so unsettling, I think, is that she frequently aligns her psychic energy with the destructive and disclosive movement of sheer negativity, as though she were an *ecstatic agent* as well as a *suffering patient* of an apocalyptic force. This would seem to be the source of all those paradoxical yokings of despair and elation in her poetry. "All things swept sole away / This—is immensity," she writes in a late, telling two-line jotting (P # 1512). Dickinson is fascinated by the disclosive ruin of the finite, including the ruin of the finite self, even though her fractured faith often discerns in that ruin only an empty vastness, not a taste of eternity. "At Half past Seven, Element / Nor Implement, be seen— / And Place was where the Presence was / Circumference between" (P # 1084). This is the movement that I've characterized above as apocalypse without apocalypse.[34]

It is this skewed figural dynamic that is sounded in Dickinson's "wintered" poem about the experience of a certain slant of light:

> There's a certain Slant of light,
> Winter Afternoons—
> That oppresses, like the Heft
> Of Cathedral Tunes—
>
> Heavenly Hurt, it gives us—
> We can find no scar,

But internal difference,
Where the Meanings, are—

None may teach it—Any—
'Tis the Seal Despair—
An imperial affliction
Sent us of the Air—

When it comes, the Landscape listens—
Shadows—hold their breath—
When it goes, 'tis like the Distance
On the look of Death—
                                (P # 258)

Cast in Christian terms, the poem speculatively explores an acute perception of an ephemeral (if curiously distended) natural event that is suffered as an interior passion, an inward suffering of significant scars. In this speaker's figural imagination, that is, the perception of angled light becomes "typic," an intuition of "something other" than what it literally is. While in part this "something other" involves a premonition of death, "an Omen in the Bone / of Death's tremendous nearness" (P # 532), in part it involves a premonition of unreachable significance, "a Druidic Difference [that] / Enhances Nature now" (P # 1068). The suffering, the inner wound of temporal difference, is felt as the generative source of this mysterious significance. "Heavenly Hurt, it gives us— / We can find no scar, / But internal difference, / Where the Meanings, are—." And in this way the poem recalls the Christian pattern of suffering and transfiguration, passion and transcendence, though at the same time it fractures this Christian dialectic, the ambiguous conclusion leaving it suspended in shadowed uncertainty. The last stanza evokes not a faithful anticipation of eternity but a puzzled fascination with the ambiguous "distance" on the visage of death. It is a "distance" in which an aura of transcendence and an aura of nothingness are brought together. And this suspended conclusion is all the more startling for the way the "Distance / On the look of Death" evokes less a promise of transcendence than the uncanny face of a corpse, uncanny because the "look" of a corpse is at once concretely *here* and infinitely *elsewhere*, starkly *present* and unfathomably *absent*. The poem studies a piercing perception in terms of a typological pattern that it unfolds to a threshold of bewildered doubt and bewildered reach, a threshold of nothingness apprehended as the vastness of a sort of negative transcendence.

This peculiar "Distance / On the look of Death" is what Richard Wilbur, in a marvelously perceptive essay, has called the "occult circumference" toward which "all things are straining and flying" in Dickinson's poetry.[35] Wilbur notes that Dickinson's point of departure would seem to be the experience of a loss so fundamental that no finite object could possibly assuage it. "The Missing All—Prevented Me / From missing minor things" (P # 985; cf. P # 959). This is Dickinson's pointed expression of what Emerson and Stevens call our existential "poverty," an emphatic sense of the limits of our finitude that, in Dickinson, is inseparable from an exorbitant longing for the boundless. Dickinson's primary response to this lived contradiction, as Wilbur underlines, is a particularly intense version of the Christian "sacrificial" economy of desire whereby loss becomes gain, death life, and the negativity of the finite the promise of the infinite.

> Renunciation—is a piercing Virtue—
> The letting go
> A Presence—for an Expectation—
> Not now
>
> (P # 745)

> The Admirations—and Contempts—of time—
> Show justest—through an Open Tomb—
> The Dying—as it were a Height
> Reorganizes Estimate
>
> (P # 906)

> To disappear enhances—
> The Man that runs away
> Is tinctured for an instant
> With Immortality
>
> . . . .
> Securest gathered then
>
> The Fruit perverse to plucking,
> But leaning to the Sight

> With the ecstatic limit
> Of unobtained Delight
> (P # 1209)

One could cite Dickinson's poems almost at random for expressions of her allegiance to this economy of creative negativity or productive loss. Wilbur characterizes her drama thus:

> Emily Dickinson elected the economy of desire [as opposed to what Wilbur calls the economy of appetite], and called her privation good, rendering it positive by renunciation. And so she came to live in a huge world of delectable distances. Far-off words like "Brazil" or "Circassian" appear continually in her poems as symbols of things distanced by loss or renunciation, yet infinitely prized and yearned for. So identified in her mind are distance and delight that, when ravished by the sight of a hummingbird in her garden, she calls it "the mail from Tunis." And not only are the objects of her desire distant; they are also very often moving away, their sweetness increasing in proportion to their remoteness. . . .
>
> To the eye of desire, all things are seen in a profound perspective, either moving away or gesturing toward the vanishing point. Or to use a figure which may be closer to Miss Dickinson's thought, to the eye of desire the world is a centrifuge, in which all things are straining or flying toward the occult circumference. . . .
>
> At times it seems that there is nothing in her world but her own soul, with its attendant abstractions, and, at a vast remove, the inscrutable Heaven. On most of what might intervene she has closed the valves of her attention, and what mortal objects she does acknowledge are riddled by desire to the point of transparency.[36]

I've cited this passage at length because, to my knowledge, no critic has so suggestively elucidated the significance of all those figures of distance, vastness, circumference, vanishing, and "miles of stare" that we encounter in Dickinson's poetry. What I hear in this passage, whether or not Wilbur exactly intends it, is that Dickinson responds to her experience of the "Missing All" not only by adopting the way of creative renunciation but also—and this is what is strangest in her poetry—by aligning her imagination with the disclosive movement of transience, vanishing, ruin, sheer negativity. She inhabits an apocalyptic space without a strongly held faith in any positive outcome. And thus her poems, operating as though they were creative mimes of disclosive negativity itself, repeatedly voyage into a blank or indeterminate infinite. One of her letters includes the question: "Don't you know that 'No' is the wildest word in Language?" (L # 562). Perhaps for Dickinson it is also the truest word in language. "Circumference" in her poetry is a figure not of the bound but of the errantly unbound, of a boundlessness evoked by the falling away of things, of self, and of words. "All things swept sole away / This—is immensity—" (P # 1512). "I touched the Universe— // And back it slid—and I alone— / A Speck upon a Ball— / Went out upon Circumference— / Beyond the Dip of Bell" (P # 378). It is this imaginative dynamic, I think, that animates the riddling volatility of Dickinson's figures.

A comparison between Wordsworth and Hegel, on the one hand, and Dickinson and Kierkegaard, on the other, may be helpful at this point. Wordsworth and Hegel (or at least a certain Hegel) are powerful voices of a *measured humanist* dialectic of loss and gain. While both acknowledge that loss is the inner texture of life, both affirm the possibility of a genuine restitution of loss (indeed a restitution with interest) through a dialectic of remembrance and interiorization: therein lies the promise of a coherent widening and deepening of the subject. Dickinson and Kierkegaard, on the other hand, are powerful voices of an *exorbitant apocalyptic* dialectic of loss and gain. Both understand loss to be a rift in experience so fundamental that no act of creative remembrance could possibly repair it: hence only a further movement into the sorrow of negativity and an extravagant anticipation of the infinite—whether in Kierkegaard's absurd "leap" of faith or, even more insecurely, in Dickinson's "baffled" suspension over an abyssal infinite—are able to bear the finite self beyond despair. This explains why Dickinson, though she is a great poet of loss, is *not* a poet of nostalgia or of the sort of creative recollection variously explored in writers like Wordsworth, Proust, and Woolf. As Robert Weisbuch exactly puts it, for a typological imagination like Dickinson's, "the present is defined by a projected future rather than a retrojected past."[37] Dickinson, as though impelled to vie with time itself, "riddles" objects and "riddles" words with her own creatively destructive or destructively creative longing for the infinite. "My Business is Circumference."

This apocalyptic dynamic is enacted and thematized with particular clarity in the some forty "sunset" poems Dickinson wrote. Like Mallarmé, she tends to imagine sunset, "the Western Mystery" (P # 266), under the aspect of apocalypse, the play of destruction and disclosure. And she occasionally tropes the poet as a creator or an imitator of sunset (as, for example, in P # 307 and P # 308), an imitator of, a dynamic participant in, the drama of ruin and revelation.[38]

This drama often leaves the speaker adrift in a space of widened and puzzled expectation, as in the poem in which she likens the vanished sun to a vanished circus:

> I've known a Heaven, like a Tent—
> To wrap its shining Yards—
> Pluck up its stakes, and disappear—
> Without the sound of Boards
> Or Rip of Nail—Or Carpenter—
> But just the miles of Stare—
> That signalize a Show's Retreat—
> In North America—
>
> No Trace—no Figment of the Thing
> That dazzled, Yesterday,
> No Ring—no Marvel—
> Men, and Feats—
> Dissolved as utterly—
> As Bird's far Navigation
> Discloses just a Hue—
> A plash of Oars, a Gaiety—
> Then swallowed up, of View.
>   (P # 243)

The departure of the sun is figured as the departure of the shining tents and marvels of a circus, a disappearance that leaves behind a breathtaking, palpable emptiness, "just the miles of Stare— / That signalize a Show's Retreat— / In North America." This figure is further elaborated in the second stanza and then, in an unexpected turn, unfolded into yet another figure: the sunset-circus has vanished as a distant bird in flight, at the moment of its disappearance from our view, discloses a suggestive hue, though this rowing bird's charmed departure for the infinite, the last line suggests, may turn out to be a flight into a voracious abyss. Unfolding out of one another in a gliding motion, the figures suggest that sheer transience is the source of a disclosive widening of consciousness ("death is the mother of beauty"). Indeed, what I would emphasize about this poem is that it is untraced by nostalgia. Its presiding affect, rather, is a kind of quietly puzzled elation, as though the poet wished not to recover in memory the lost objects the poem evokes but rather to share in the power of their departure, to participate in the enigmatic reach of their vanishing in a trans-horizontal distance. In the drama of the "Western Mystery," as Dickinson writes in another poem, "Merchantmen—poise upon Horizons— / Dip—and vanish like Orioles!" (P # 266). While "I've known a Heaven, like a Tent" evokes the disappearance of things, the becoming absent of the finite, it is nevertheless not elegiac so much as hymnal, a searching celebration of vanishing itself—a vanishing into which the poet leans with such longing that she sees her own longing staring back at her as "miles of stare" in a felt absence of continental scope. For a moment, as it were, she dwells in the distance on the look of death.[39]

The poem, then, is a presentation of disappearance and a disclosure of the movement itself of disclosure. Probing the movement of disclosive vanishing, the poem mimes in its figural gliding the creative force of negation, as though it were exemplifying a Mallarméan poetic of "dissolved as uttered" ("dissolved" is a recurrent and important word in Dickinson's poetry). The motion from figure to figure is like the motion of revelatory negativity.

It is this creative motion that is carefully studied in a sunset poem that imitates, stanza by stanza, the "power of the negative" at work in the falling of dusk:

> They called me to the Window, for
> "'Twas Sunset"—Some one said—
> I only saw a Sapphire Farm—
> And just a Single Herd—
>
> Of Opal Cattle—feeding far
> Upon so vain a Hill—
> As even while I looked—dissolved—
> Nor Cattle were—nor Soil—
>
> But in their stead—a Sea—displayed—
> And Ships—of such a size
> As Crew of Mountains—could afford—
> And Decks—to seat the skies—
>
> This—too—the Showman rubbed away—
> And when I looked again—

Nor Farm—nor Opal Herd—was there—
Nor Mediterranean—
                          (P # 628)

The poem is a serene performance of presentation and withdrawal, of evocation as erasure and erasure as evocation. Keeping pace with the cosmic Showman's erasures, the poet becomes a ventriloquist of time, the voice of a negativity that uncovers a vast, haunted, haunting emptiness. The emotional and speculative weather of the poem is complex, bringing together a sense of loss, a probing perception of disappearance and dilation, a well-nigh hypnotic recognition of the paradoxical presence of absence, and a poised affirmation of transience as the groundless ground of imaginative reach. Once again, the governing spirit of the poem is not elegiac so much as quietly hymnal, the poet seeming to be at once fascinated and baffled by the disclosive power of negation, her own as well as the cosmic Showman's. Yet the vastness disclosed by this power remains empty, unfilled by any positive vision, the poem thus hinting that the infinite may be but the sweeping distance evoked by this ceaseless foundering of the finite. All things are vanity, the second stanza suggests, destined to undergo a dissolution that reveals yet another domain of the finite itself destined for dissolution. It is as though the poet were measuring her infinite longing against the infinite void of temporal negativity. One could read the poem as a revision, at once dark and affirmative, of the opening paragraphs of Emerson's "Circles."[40]

Evoking the way things grow gradually less distinct as the sun disappears, the poem unfolds as a process of creative negation. The process begins with the withdrawal of the primary referent, the "sunset" itself for which the speaker was called to the window, and in the opened place of that withdrawal the first figures emerge, those of the farm and the single herd. These figures, too, are immediately withdrawn, "dissolved," and in the motion of their negation further figures emerge, those of enormous ships adrift on an almost cosmic sea. And then these figures too are negated, "rubbed away," leaving behind only a palpable emptiness, a poignantly vacant "there," in which the non-presence of three objects (the felt absence of the three figures evoked in the earlier play of creative negation and emergence) is declared. The poem concludes with these resonantly present absences. It is as though the poem were telling a story about the creative power of negation, about the departure into figural space generated by the falling away of finite reference. Negativity is explored as the inner force of psychic reach and linguistic figuration. "Destruction was my Beatrice,"

Mallarmé writes in a famous letter (C, 349), voicing a thought with which Dickinson is intimately acquainted. In this poem she presents the dying of natural light as the uncovering of amplitude. "There is a finished feeling / Experienced at Graves— / A leisure of the Future— / A Wilderness of Size" (P # 856).

The culminating perfection of the poem lies in the marvelous "Mediterranean" of the last line. In its etymology, it sounds a pun on the terrestrial domain that appears sea-like in the third stanza of the poem. As a place name, its specificity heightens the paradoxical play of presence and absence in the last stanza. It is a figure whose blue-green surface glimmers in the dark in which it absently appears, whose geographical distance from this New England "there" brings a felt strangeness into the midst of this dark, whose evocative six-syllable unfolding (in a poem otherwise consisting solely of monosyllabic and disyllabic words) resonates like a tangible amplitude in this vacant space from which all things have been swept away. Like Mallarmé's absently present "rose dans les ténèbres," it is at once there and not there, the mysterious mark of a "sumptuous destitution" (P # 1382), a charm attached to "illocality" (P # 963), a hint of both the palpable vastness of uncovered absence and the dazed longing that leans toward the infinite through the ruin of the finite.

The effect of this word "Mediterranean," the way its peculiar thingness arrives out of nowhere to jar the reader, is characteristic of Dickinson's poems, whose textual materiality tends to be foregrounded with great force. As is well known, the materiality of a text becomes strangely concrete as soon as a text disrupts a coherent "illusionistic" space, or, put another way, as soon as the syntactic and semantic "deviations" of a text exceed the limited play permitted by the conventions of realist writing and ordinary communicative practice. Dickinson's characteristic rhetorical practices—the tropic errancy, the occasional confusion of tenor and vehicle, the elliptical syntax, the frequent suspension of the verb in an ambiguous infinitive-subjunctive tense, the quirky punctuation and capitalization, and so forth—all serve to place her poems in a zone where figural strangeness and textual concreteness become exactly proportionate to one another. "They called me to the window" reads like a calm, slow-motion display of this dynamic of creative negation and revelatory deviation that, often in a far wilder fashion, organizes Dickinson's poetry. The tropic departures of her poetry, I have argued, are animated by an apocalyptic imagination that discerns in the foundering of the finite the disclosure of a negative infinite, at once anxiously suffers and actively participates in this movement of foundering, and thus, like a showman-sunset erasing the things of the world, tends toward a creative ruin of stable reference for the sake of a tropic play that ceaselessly alludes to a distant, if hauntingly indeterminate, elsewhere. "'Tis Compound Vision— / Light—enabling Light— / The Finite—furnished / With the Infinite—" (P # 906).

The imaginative dynamic that shapes Dickinson's apocalyptic "sunset" poems, then, is fundamentally the same as that which shapes her poems of the revelatory ruin of the self, as one of her brief "metapoems" suggests:

The Soul's distinct connection
With immortality
Is best disclosed by Danger
Or quick calamity—

As Lightning on a Landscape
Exhibits Sheets of Place—
Not yet suspected—but for Flash—
And Click—and Suddenness
(P # 974)

This is a compressed "allegory" not only of the disclosive reach of lightning-like figures in Dickinson's poetry but also of her longing for lightning-like revelations on the edge of ruin. Her longing, her expectation, is as abyssal as her skepticism. She walks abroad beyond herself, beyond boundaries, risking vertigo and wreck. She dwells not only in possibility but, like her vanishing birds, in the distance of departure. "Because in going is a Drama / Staying cannot confer" (P # 1349). Because in going is a drama of boundless sheets of place:

A nearness to Tremendousness—
An Agony procures—
Affliction ranges Boundlessness—
Vicinity to Laws

Contentment's quiet Suburb—
Affliction cannot stay
In Acres—Its Location
Is Illocality—[41]
(P # 963)

DICKINSON DID NOT need to read Johannes Climacus to understand the importance of "keeping the wound of the negative open" in order to sustain a relationship to the infinite. "Deity . . . is present as soon as the uncertainty of all things is thought infinitely" is a sentence Dickinson could well have written. And many of her poems could be paraphrased in terms like those which organize Climacus's thought. Nevertheless, while many of her poems hover close to the religious world of Climacus, they evoke rather different imaginative adventures. For she tends to experience the infinite "uncertainty of all things" less as a decisive relationship to the divine than as a disclosure without disclosure, a passage, in bewildered expectation, toward an empty infinite. She voyages "further in summer than the birds," yet, having travelled there, finds an ambiguous "distance on the look of death," or a mesmerizing post-sunset "there" from which all things have been swept away (except the cryptic word of an absent glimmer), or a "Chaos—stopless—cool— / Without a Chance, or Spar— / Or even a Report of Land— / To justify—Despair" (P # 510). "Chaos" and "stopless," we learn, rhyme. Everything is foundering always, "stoplessly," therein lying a bottomless source of pain, a mysterious source of vision.

Dickinson's "passion of the infinite," further, animates a poetic practice in which the errancy of language is unloosed in a creatively destructive play of figures. And in this respect she has affinities with Mallarmé that, to my knowledge, have never been examined (no doubt because in many respects, of course, these two poets *are* very different writers working in very different contexts). Both are driven by a forceful desire for transcendence countermeasured by a forceful skepticism. Both turn renunciation into a kind of first principle that opens the realm of what Dickinson calls "possibility" and Mallarmé "virtuality." Both, in pursuing this path, foreground the creative power of linguistic negation, exploring in poem after poem the magnetic resonance of things absently present or presently absent. Well practiced in imagining their own death and absence, both conceive of poetry as an art demanding articulate voyages into the shadows of ruin. Both are intimate with a disorienting, though ultimately creative, despair. The intuition of a sea of negativity upon which we insecurely drift is an intuition that haunts and generates many of the poems of both (at one point during his crisis of the 1860s, Mallarmé planned to write two major books, one of which was to consist of "sumptuous Allegories of the Void" [C, 367], and a study of Dickinson's poetry, rather than Poe's, might have taught him much in this regard). And both, opening a path toward modernism, discover an intimate link between their experience of abyssal negativity and their exploration of an errant unmooring of language from stable reference. The modern poet, Mallarmé writes in a famous passage, must "cede the initiative to words," becoming the impersonal operator of the poem. While I cannot imagine Dickinson writing that—there is no "elocutionary disappearance of the poet" in her poems—she nonetheless seems to have approached in her volatile figural play a conception of poetic language that in important respects parallels that of Mallarmé.

Yet at just this point resides one of their major differences. Mallarmé, in part because he sharpened his skepticism to the point of convinced atheism, in part because he produced his poetry in a late romantic cultural context in which art had come to be conceived as a sublime substitute for a vanished religion, constructed in both his poems and essays a fully developed poetic "project" and "theory" of a sort that Dickinson chose to leave implicit. Decisively detached from a Christian context, yet still troubled by the old metaphysical dramas, Mallarmé observed the unanchored "independence" of language rise up before him, in all its strangeness, as a question demanding ceaseless attention in his poetry. The "uncertainty of all things thought infinitely" came to include, as it were, language in general and the operations of poetic language in particular. Literary modernism found itself embarked on the sea of *Un Coup de dés*.[42]

MALLARMÉ

The prose poem "Le Démon de l'analogie" (O, 272–73; CP, 93–94), though it may have been written a year or two before Mallarmé's extended crisis of 1866–1871, anticipates the fully developed poetic that would emerge out of that crisis. The poem begins with the speaker experiencing, as he leaves his apartment, the sensation of a wing gliding over the cords of an instrument. This sensation is immediately replaced by a voice pronouncing an "absurd" phrase: "La Pénultième est morte." A field of associated images (formed of a number of Mallarmé's obsessions, including the wing, the feather, the stringed instrument, the palm, and the sound and the sense of nullity or negation) quickly gathers around this phrase as the speaker strolls through the streets. A short time later he finds himself gazing at his own reflection in a shop window and recognizes with astonishment that the shop is full of old instruments hung on the wall, palms placed on the floor, and feathers buried in the shadows. He has been initiated into the mystery of *correspondances*. The "rhyming" play of words has predicted the contingent events of life. The speaker flees the scene with an obscure sense that he has been bizarrely elected, that he is henceforth condemned to mourn "l'inexplicable Pénultième."

This wry, absurdist tale of poetic calling communicates with many currents of Mallarmé's *oeuvre* as a whole.[43] Here I would like to underline but two of these. First, the poem evokes the creative errancy of words at play among themselves, forming associative patterns that cast a strange light back on the texture of the real. It is not that the speaker of this poem has "ceded the initiative to words" so much as that the floating words, "lambeaux maudits d'une phrase absurde [acccursed scraps of an absurd phrase]," have taken the initiative on their own and called the speaker to a task that, in this poem, still remains a touch obscure to him. The words, in visiting the speaker, bring with them a life—or rather a death and a power—of their own. Indeed, the poet's peculiar calling is inseparable from an acute experience of negativity and a relationship to death. The poet's first "recognition" in the poem, born of a concentration on the play of sound and sense, is a recognition of "the negative" concealed in the penultimate syllable of the word "pé-nul-tième": "Je fis des pas dans la rue et reconnus en le son *nul* la corde tendue de l'instrument de musique [I took a few steps in the street and recognized in the sound *nul* the taut string of the musical instrument]." The riddling phrase itself announces a death, though the exact nature of this death remains unclear, and at the end of the story the poet is left with a feeling that he is "condemné à porter probablement le deuil de l'inexplicable Pénultième [condemned probably to mourn for the inexplicable Pénultième]." His visitation by a "demonic" domain where drifting words weave unexpected patterns is obscurely linked to an encounter with death. All of Mallarmé's later work would involve, among other things, a sounding of this relationship between the palpable irreality of fiction and the close, if ungraspable, nothingness of death.

"Le Démon de l'analogie" thus anticipates Mallarmé's disorienting, though ultimately creative, experience of "le Rien qui est la vérité [the Nothing that is truth]" (C, 298; L, 60). In passing through the crisis of the years 1866–1871, a crisis at once poetic and metaphysical, Mallarmé develops a multidimensional poetic based above all on a deepening meditation on the nature of fiction, the nature of verse or the principle of rhyme, and the impersonality of the poet (his conception of artistic impersonality emerging not only out of his "lived" experience of nothingness but also out of his "artistic" experience of the ideality of fictive transposition and the echoing play of verse). In what follows I would like to explore this multidimensional poetic. In fact, one might do well to speak rather of an interplay among multiple poetics: a poetic of the invention of "glorious lies" or supreme fictions; a poetic of the surpassing of chance in the intricately composed poem or, ultimately, in the totalizing Book in which the world is to culminate; and a poetic of the meditative sounding of death. All of these bearings are brought together in Mallarmé's mobile and searching adventure.

AS HIS LETTER to Cazalis of April 28, 1866, indicates, Mallarmé encountered nihilism while working on the "Ouverture ancienne" of *Hérodiade,* the experience of writing this poem having borne him toward an experience of nothingness. "Malheureusement," he writes to his friend, "en creusant le vers à ce point, j'ai rencontré deux abîmes, qui me désespèrent [Unfortunately, in carving out the lines to this extent, I've come across two abysses, which fill me with despair]" (C, 297; L, 60), one the abyss of cosmic nothingness, the other the abyss of his own hollow lung. It is from this experience that one of Mallarmé's guiding conceptions of poetry emerges, a conception of poetry as a fictive ghost, a "glorious lie" projected upon a senseless universe:

> Oui, *je le sais,* nous ne sommes que de vaines formes de la matière,—mais bien sublimes pour avoir inventé Dieu et notre âme. Si sublimes, mon ami! que je veux me donner ce spectacle de la matière, ayant conscience d'elle, et, cependant, s'élançant forcenément dans la Rêve qu'elle sait n'être pas, chantant l'Ame et toutes les divines impressions pareilles qui se sont amassées en nous depuis les premiers âges, et proclamant, devant le Rien qui est la vérité, ces glorieux mensonges! Tel est le plan de mon volume Lyrique, et tel sera peut-être son titre, La Gloire du Mensonge, ou le Glorieux Mensonge. Je chanterai en désespéré! (C, 298)

> [Yes, *I know,* we are merely empty forms of matter, but we are indeed sublime for having invented God and our soul. So sublime, my friend, that I want to gaze upon this spectacle of matter, fully conscious that it exists, yet launching itself madly into the Dream that it knows does not exist, singing the Soul and all the divine impressions of that kind that have accumulated within us from the earliest ages and proclaiming, in the face of the Nothing that is the truth, these glorious lies! That's the plan of my lyric volume and that might also be its title, The Glory of the Lie, or The Glorious Lie. I shall sing as one in despair!] (L, 60)

Mallarmé's "glorious lie" resembles, in some respects, Stevens's "supreme fiction." "To find the real, / To be stripped of every fiction except one, // The fiction of an absolute—Angel, / Be silent in your luminous cloud and hear / The luminous melody of proper sound."[44]

In the earliest phase of his crisis, then, Mallarmé adopts a stoic stance and a conception of poetry as a tragic, affirmative, ultimately pointless practice of fictive venturing in the void, or, to put the matter in more reassuring terms, a conception of poetic fiction as a self-reflexive practice of coping with all that ultimately defies comprehension. Does Mallarmé, as he works his way through his extended crisis, come to abandon this seemingly straightforward conception of poetry? In fact, this conception persists, alongside others, throughout Mallarmé's trajectory. Many of his great poems written both during and after the crisis of 1866–1871 affirm it. "Quand l'ombre menaça de la fatale loi," for instance, evokes a poetic light cast across the dark of infinite space, a light produced through the interior "folding" of the "wing" of an ancient dream of transcendence. "Toast funèbre," a meditation on the blank of death in a universe with no transcendent surround, affirms that the deftly measured words of the poet, one who has found "pour la Rose et le Lys le mystère d'un nom [for the Rose and the Lily the mystery of a name]" (O, 55; CP, 45), will endure in the aftermath of his disappearance. This is a theme in a number of the "Tombeaux." Further, important passages in "La Musique et les Lettres," a lecture delivered at Cambridge and Oxford in 1894, recall, in a decidedly intricate manner, the early letter to Cazalis:

> Nous savons, captifs d'une formule absolue, que, certes, n'est que ce qui est. Incontinent écarter cependant, sous un prétexte, le leurre, accuserait notre inconséquence, niant le plaisir que nous voulons prendre: car cet *au-delà* en est l'agent, et le moteur dirais-je si je ne répugnais à opérer, en public, le démontage impie de la fiction et conséquemment du mécanisme littéraire, pour étaler la pièce principale ou rien. Mais, je vénère comment, par une supercherie, on projette, à quelque élévation défendue et de foudre! le conscient manque chez nous de ce qui là-haut éclate.
>
> A quoi sert cela—
> A un jeu.
>
> En vue d'une attirance supérieure comme d'un vide, nous avons droit, le tirant de nous par de l'ennui à l'égard des choses si elles s'établissaient solides et prépondérantes—éperdument les détache jusqu'à s'en

remplir et aussi les douer de resplendissement, à travers l'espace vacant, en des fêtes à volonté et solitaires. (O, p. 647)

[Captives of an absolute law, we know, certainly, that only what exists exists. Yet it would be absurd to choose such a pretext as the basis for refusing all illusion, denying the very pleasure that we seek. The *beyond* is our means to that pleasure, the motor or the instrument, I might almost say, were it not repugnant to me to carry out in public the impious disassembling of fiction and so of the literary mechanism, in order to display its principal piece, or nothingness. But I admire how, by a ruse, we project, upon some prohibited height of thunderbolts, the conscious lack within us of what explodes in brilliance above.
What does this serve—
A game.
For just as we have the right to elicit emptiness from ourselves, hampered as we would feel if things were to establish themselves as too solid and preponderant, so do we act, desperately, that a superior attraction, as from a void, may draw us out of those heavy things and yet endow them with a splendor, scattered across a vacant space, in willful and solitary celebrations.] (SPr, 48)

The word "supercherie" (ruse or trick) in this passage echoes the word "mensonge" (lie) in the early letter to Cazalis. A fiction, spun out of a creative nothingness within, corresponds to an abyssal nothingness without that the fiction is projected across. The ghost of fiction is unfolded in the hollow of death. The apocalyptic drama of *Un Coup de dés* expansively reaffirms this theory of fiction. Contingent fictions, including supreme conjectures concerning constellations of beauty and order, are composed out of a shipwreck in the abyss. Therein lies the "jeu suprême" (supreme game) with all its "doute" (doubt) (O, 74; CP, 80).[45]

Yet this sort of theory of fiction is more complicated, more troubled, than it may initially appear. While it affirms the free power of invention, as though anything were possible now that the gods had departed, it also proposes a severe truth claim. Mallarmé speaks of "le Rien qui est la vérité [the Nothing that is the truth]" (C, 298; L, 60). For a poet like Mallarmé, or Keats, or Rilke, or Stevens, then, a genuine poetic fiction must do more than evoke a projected constellation, a fictive *as if*: it must also explore the relationship between fictive invention and tragic emptiness, between the act of poetic making and the irreducible pressure of death. It must, as Keats suggests, present not only the temple of delight, an enchanting fiction, but also the inner shrine of melancholy, a shadowed truth inhabiting all temples and fictions, as, in "Ode on a Grecian Urn," an abandoned town, a distant desolation, is discovered secretly to trace the pastoral beauty that would disguise this cold unpastoral truth of all urns. Similarly, as I argued in chapter 2, Zarathustra presents the affirmative fiction of the eternal recurrence as a vision valid only insofar as it embodies, at the same time, the dark "Silenian wisdom" of the soothsayer. Or, again, in Mallarmé's "Toast funèbre," the elegized poet, Gautier, is praised for his creation of fictive gardens that alter the way we dwell in the gardens of the world, yet the elegist himself composes a *tombeau,* a poetic tomb, inscribed with his meditations on the "solemn agitation" of words within the vast reaches of dust and space. Any fiction that matters, then, any fiction that is to be more than a mere fiction, must engage that which resists our fictive ventures. A distinctive feature of Mallarmé's adventure is the persistence, depth, and subtlety with which he explores this relationship for some thirty years. He finds in the "present absences" of poetry at once the reach of ideality and the nearness of nothing. His letters and essays no less than his poems attest to an abiding fascination with the extent to which fictive ideality, which from one point of view would seem to transcend the annihilative force of death, from another point of view turns out to be strangely inhabited and, as it were, worked by death. *Hérodiade,* the "sonnet en -yx," the sonnets of the *Triptyche,* "Toast funèbre," and *Un Coup de dés,* among many other texts of his, are searching meditations on death. From Socrates on, of course, the thinking upon death has been proposed as a path of wisdom. From this perspective, the theory of poetry as the invention of supreme fictions turns out to be a search for truth or, at least, an initiatory sounding of the truth of death that, in a post-Christian world, shadows, traces, unsettles, and ultimately eludes all our discourses of truth.[46]

YET THIS ORIENTATION of Mallarmé's would seem to be in sharp contradiction with an orientation equally important to him, namely, his conception of poetry as a patient effort (acknowledged, at last, to be an impossible dream) to surpass *le hasard,* to transmute or "to fix" the errant play of chance. For Mallarmé, chance is identical with pointless contingency, specifically, the pointless contingency of things, of words, and of the self.[47] Fundamental to Mallarmé's project, from the poems and letters of the late 1860s through the essays and poems of his last two decades, is the elaboration of a theory of the poetic transfiguration of chance in each of these domains. The fictive "transposition" of the thing into an evocative pattern of "ideas" is to transfigure the contingency of things. The exact patterning of words in a field of "reciprocal reflections" is to transfigure the contingency of words. And the metamorphosis of the poet into an "impersonal" operator invisibly at work in the poetic field is to transfigure the contingency of the self. One readily recognizes the traditional dualisms at work in this theory. Indeed, it is clear that this poetic of transmutation—guided by a threefold meditation on fiction, on verse (or "rhyme" in a generalized sense), and on impersonality—involves an attempt to turn poetry into a substitute for a vanished religious model of transcendence. It is probably this project for which Mallarmé is best known. Hence I would like to outline it, if all too quickly, before stepping back to ask how it relates to Mallarmé's practice of composing meditations on death.[48]

It is in developing this extravagant project that Mallarmé forms a second of his major conceptions of poetry, a conception related, though not reducible, to the "symbolist" theme of suggestion or evocation. "*Nommer* un objet," Mallarmé remarks in a late interview, "c'est supprimer les trois quarts de la jouissance du poème qui est faite du bonheur de deviner peu à peu; le *suggérer*, voilà le rêve [To *name* an object is to suppress three fourths of the pleasure of a poem, the delight of which is formed by guessing or divining little by little; to *suggest* the object, there is the dream]" (O, 869; SPr, 21). Similar statements appear in both "Crise de vers" and "La Musique et les Lettres" (O, 365, 645; SPr, 40, 45). Yet this practice of "transposition" involves not simply a movement of interiorizing idealization, and not simply an art of indirect evocation, but above all an act of patterning whereby the evoked object or theme is set oscillating in a relational field. "L'acte poétique consiste à voir soudain qu'une idée se fractionne en un nombre de motifs égaux par valeur et à les grouper; ils riment [The poetic act consists in seeing, suddenly, an idea disperse into a number of equivalent motifs that are at the same time gathered together; they rhyme]" (O, 365; SPr, 39). This understanding of poetry as a radicalized *play of analogies*, a shimmering *articulation of relationships*, is set forth in a number of Mallarmé's later essays:

La Nature a lieu, on n'y ajoutera pas; que des cités, les voies ferrées et plusieurs inventions formant notre matériel.

Tout l'acte disponible, à jamais et seulement, reste de saisir les rapports, entre temps, rares ou multipliés; d'après quelque état intérieur et que l'on veuille à son gré étendre, simplifier le monde. ("La Musique et les Lettres," O, 647)

[Nature takes place, one will add nothing to it but the cities, railroads, and other inventions forming our material.
 The only act possible, forever, is to grasp the relationships, among times, rare or multiplied, according to some interior state, in order to expand or simplify the world as one wishes.] ("Music and Literature," SPr, 48)

Les qualités, requises en ce ouvrage, à coup sûr le génie, m'épouvant un parmi les denués: ne s'y arrêter et, admis le volume ne comporter aucun signataire, quel est-il: l'hymne, harmonie et joie, comme pur ensemble groupé dans quelque circonstance fulgurante, des relations entre tout. ("Quant au livre," O, 378)

[The qualities required for this work, including no doubt genius, are frightening for me, one among the destitute: but let us not halt there, and let us assume that the volume bears no signature, for thus it is: the hymn, harmony and joy, like a pure ensemble, gathered in a fulgurant circumstance, of the relationships among everything.] ("Concerning the Book," SPr, 24–25)

This ideal of poetry as an articulation of relationships is quite different from the ideal of poetry as a glorious lie projected upon a senseless universe. Yet these two conceptions, whatever their exact connection, do accompany one another throughout Mallarmé's adventure. Indeed, they are held side by side, paragraph by paragraph, in the essay "La Musique et les Lettres" (O, 647; SPr, 48–49). It is as though Mallarmé perceived in the mystery of relationality—in the play of implicit, fleeting, elliptical communications *between* words—a kind of mysteriously articulate "nothingness" akin to the silent "nothingness" he apprehended as the pointless void upon which fictions are projected. And it is the evocative power of this relational play in language ("the near disappearance in vibration" of the empirical fact "by means of the play of the word") that Mallarmé associates with the unfolding of the ghostly "idea" that transfigures the contingency of things (O, 368; SPr, 42).[49]

It would seem, then, that this second of Mallarmé's major conceptions of poetry is intimately linked to his experience of verse or rhyme; one might even infer that the former is essentially derived from the latter.[50] "Le livre, expansion totale de la lettre, doit d'elle tirer, directement, une mobilité et spacieux, par correspondances, instituer un jeu, on ne sait, qui confirme la fiction [The book, complete expansion of the letter, should directly draw from it a spacious mobility, through correspondences, thereby instituting a game, who knows, that confirms the fiction]" ("Quant au livre," O, 380; SPr, 26–27). For Mallarmé's dismay with *le hasard* has its source not least in his dismay with the flatness of words in their condition of mere givenness. "Un désir indéniable à mon temps," he writes in "Crise de vers," "est de séparer comme en vue d'attributions différentes le double état de la parole, brut ou immédiat ici, là essentiel [An undeniable desire of my time is to separate, in view of their different qualities, the twofold condition of the word, on the one hand brute or immediate, on the other essential]" (O, 368; SPr, 42). In the same essay, however, he makes clear that this project of transmuting the word is motivated less by an antinaturalist idealism than by a dream of overcoming the disjunction of sound and sense that happens to be inherent in language. As he whimsically puts it, "A côté d'*ombre,* opaque, *ténèbres* se fonce peu; quelle déception, devant la perversité conférant à *jour* comme à *nuit,* contradictoirement, des timbres obscur ici, là clair [Compared to *ombre,* opaque, *ténèbres* darkens but slightly; what deception, faced with the perversity that, contradictorily, confers on *jour* a dark timbre, on *nuit* a clear one]" (O, 364; SPr, 38), though he adds that were this sort of disjunction not characteristic of language, no poetry would exist at all, for poetry consists precisely in the "game" of trying to surpass this pervasive disjunction, in the effort to compose a relational field wherein echoing sound and exploratory thought are harmonized with one another. Thus the famous account of the principle of verse in "Crise de vers":

> L'oeuvre pure implique la disparition élocutoire du poète, qui cède l'initiative aux mots, par le heurt de leur inégalité mobilisés; ils s'allument de reflets réciproques comme une virtuelle traîné de feux sur des pierreries, remplaçant la respiration perceptible en l'ancien souffle lyrique ou la direction personnelle enthousiaste de la phrase. (O, 366)

> [The pure work implies the elocutionary disappearance of the poet, who cedes the initiative to words, which are mobilized by the collisions of their differences; they are illuminated by reciprocal reflections like a virtual streak of fire over precious stones, replacing the tangible respiration of the ancient lyric breath or the enthusiastic personal direction of the phrase.] (SPr, 40–41)

The hidden angles of words are to be raised from oblivion, as it were, an operation promising to effect the transformation of words from their "natural" condition, where they are worn and dimmed, to their "poetic" condition, where they flicker like virtual lights of strange reach. Mallarmé conceives of poetry as an art of generalized rhyme—and does so, significantly, at the same moment in time at which another student of echo, Gerard Manley Hopkins, develops a theory of poetry as an art of generalized parallelism.[51]

Through these practices, further, the contingent poetic maker is to disappear into the relational field that he or she has composed, becoming the impersonal orchestrator of the poem, a kind of "absent presence" around which relational threads are woven. In a letter of 1866 Mallarmé speaks of himself as a "sacred spider" poised amid the "webs" he has spun (C, 316; L, 67). Over twenty years later, describing the impersonal reach of the horizonal Book that is to trace the relationships among everything that exists, he writes: "Impersonnifié, le volume, autant qu'on s'en sépare comme auteur, ne réclame approche de lecteur. Tel, sache, entre les accessoires humains, il a lieu tout seul: fait, étant. Le sens enseveli se meut et dispose, en choeur, des feuillets [Impersonal, the volume, insofar as it is separated from the author, requires no approach from the reader. Thus, among our ordinary human props, it takes place entirely alone: made, being. The buried meaning moves and disposes itself, in a choir, among the pages]" (O, 372). This is the third fold of the threefold transmutation proposed by this poetic: the contingent self is to vanish in the impersonal "choir" sounded as the meaning "buried" between the words and the pages of the text—as though concealed in a space of sheer relationality—begins to move with all the mystery of a Spirit brooding over the face of the waters or rising from the open tomb of the Book.

It is significant that, at one moment in "Crise de vers," Mallarmé moves step by step, in the space of a single page (O, 366; SPr, 40), from an account of the power of fictive transposition ("évocation dites, allusion je sais, suggestion..."), to an account of the mystery of versification ("l'oeuvre pure implique la disparition élocutoire du poète"), to an account of the spacious internal harmony of the impersonal poem ("une ordonnance du livre de vers point innée ou partout, élimine le hasard; encore la faut-il, pour omettre l'auteur"). This is the path, we are told in the same paragraph, that leads to "the magical concept of the *Oeuvre*" (O, 367; SPr, 41), to what in the so-called autobiography is called "un livre qui soit un livre":

Quoi? c'est difficile à dire: un livre, tout bonnement, en maints tomes, un livre qui soit un livre, architectural et prémédité, et non un recueil des inspirations de hasard, fussent-elles merveilleuses. . . . J'irai plus loin, je dirai: le Livre persuadé qu'au fond il n'y en a qu'un, tenté à son insu par quiconque a écrit, même les Génies. L'explication orphique de la Terre, qui est le seul devoir du poëte et le jeu littéraire par excellence: car le rhythme même du livre alors impersonnel et vivant, jusque dans sa pagination, se juxtapose aux équations de ce rêve, ou Ode. (C, 586)

[What? it's hard to say: a book, quite simply, in many volumes, a book that would be a book, architectural and premeditated, and not a collection of chance inspirations, however marvelous they might be. . . . I'll go even further, I'll say: the Book, persuaded that ultimately there is only one, attempted (if unknowingly) by everyone who has ever written, even by Geniuses. The orphic explanation of the Earth, which is the sole duty of the poet and the literary game par excellence. For the very rhythm of the book, impersonal and alive then, even in its pagination, will be juxtaposed with the equations of this dream, or Ode.] (SPr, 15)

It is this sweeping dream—the receding horizon of the threefold poetic of transmuting the empty play of chance into the gathering play of prismatic harmony—that ends in shipwreck, beneath a subjunctively composed constellation, in *Un Coup de dés*.

AT THIS POINT I return to a question I posed earlier: what is the relationship, in Mallarmé's work as a whole, between this "post-Christian" poetic of transcending chance and the equally prominent "tragic" poetic of meditating on (or orphically descending into) death? I would begin a response to this question by underlining again the ambiguous or twofold meaning of "impersonality" in Mallarmé's poetic. "Impersonality" in his project bears at once a "technical" and an "experiential" (not to say "metaphysical") meaning. This is an ambiguity to which Blanchot has drawn attention:

La tension contre le hasard signifie: tantôt le travail de Mallarmé pour achever, par la technique propre du vers et des considérations de structure, l'oeuvre transformatrice de la parole;—tantôt une expérience de caractère mystique ou philosophique, celle que le récit d'*Igitur* a mise en oeuvre avec une richesse énigmatique et partiellement réalisée.

[The struggle against *le hasard* means: at times the attempt to bring to completion, through the technical and structural operations of verse, the transformative work of the word; at times an experience of a mystical or philosophical character, that which the story of *Igitur* stages and, with an enigmatic richness, partially realizes.]⁵²

Igitur, the story of a mystical self-annihilation, at once lucid and mad, was written in the midst of Mallarmé's crisis and, according to Mallarmé's own account, as an attempted "cure" or "resolution" of the crisis (C, 451–52; L, 89–90). It corresponds closely not only to important passages in *Hérodiade* but also to the mystical sense of vocation expressed in a number of the letters of 1866–1871, as in the peculiar letter to Cazalis of May 14, 1867:

> Je viens de passer une année effrayante: ma Pensée est pensée, et est arrivée à une Conception Pure. Tout ce que, par contre-coup, mon être a souffert, pendant cette longue agonie, est inénarrable, mais, heureusement, je suis parfaitement mort, et le région la plus impure où mon Esprit puisse aventurer est l'Éternité, mon Esprit, ce solitaire habituel de sa propre Pureté, que n'obscurcit plus même le reflet du Temps.
> ... Mais comme cette lutte [avec ce vieux et méchant plumage ... Dieu] s'était passé sur son aile osseuse, qui, par une agonie plus vigoureuse que je ne l'eusse soupçonné chez lui, m'avait emporté dans des Ténèbres, je tombai, victorieusement, éperdument et infiniment—jusqu'à ce qu'enfin je me sois revu devant ma glace de Venise, tel que je m'étais oublié plusieurs mois auparavant. (C, 342)

> [I've just spent a terrifying year: my Thought has thought itself and reached a Pure Conception. All that my being has suffered as a result during that long death cannot be told, but, fortunately, I am utterly dead, and the least impure region where my Spirit can venture is Eternity, my Spirit, that solitary accustomed to its own Purity, which is no longer darkened even by the reflection of time.
> ... But as that struggle (with that old and wicked plumage ... God) had taken place on his bony wing which, in death throes more vigorous

than I would have suspected with him, had carried me into the Shadows, I fell, victorious, desperately and infinitely—until at last I saw myself again in my Venetian mirror, such as I was when I forgot myself several months earlier.] (L, 74)

In this same letter Mallarmé speaks of his plans for the *oeuvre* of a lifetime's labor, at this point projected as a set of three verse poems of "unprecedented beauty" and four prose poems concerning "the spiritual conception of the void." "After having found the Void," he writes in an earlier letter, "I have found the Beautiful" (C, 310; L, 65).

Every reading of Mallarmé's poetry at least implies a reading of his "experience" of the years 1866–1871, for his mature poetic, including his ambiguous notion of impersonality, emerged out of this experience. Letters like the one from which I've just cited would seem to justify those who claim that Mallarmé resolved his crisis—largely a crisis of the death of God, a crisis of nihilism—by adopting, if not exactly Hegelianism, at least some sort of esoteric postreligious vision of the universe as a drama of the absolute unfolding in language through the movement of negativity. The poet, according to this vision, could articulate the ideal patterns of this drama insofar as the contingent self was negated in order to be raised into the impersonal linguistic realm of the absolute. This would be the "metaphysical" basis of Mallarmé's poetic of the transmutation of chance into relational ideality. That Mallarmé was, at the very least, strongly drawn toward this sort of vision is unquestionable.

Nevertheless, there are problems with this account of Mallarmé's trajectory. Perhaps the most serious of these, as Charles Mauron has emphasized, is that Mallarmé's crisis persisted with great intensity for three years (1866–1869), and to a significant extent for five years (until he moved from the provinces to Paris in 1871), that is to say, his crisis lasted throughout the very years in which he was describing in letters his vision of a great *oeuvre* of the absolute that would require a labor of twenty years.[53] Whatever Mallarmé discovered in these years, it did not serve as an "idealist resolution" to his crisis of despair. All the more significant, then, is the fact that, after a period of apparent calm in the 1870s, all the obsessions and speculations of the late 1860s returned in the poems and essays of the last two decades of his life (a return perhaps stirred by the death of his son in 1879). *Hérodiade* is a poem that came back to haunt him in his last years. And the dark texts of the crisis years—including the "sonnet en -yx," *Igitur,* and, in all likelihood, the *Triptyche*—are extremely close to the later *Un Coup de dés* and to the short poems that move in the margins of this final throw of the dice.

It is my sense, then, that Mallarmé in fact *never resolved the crisis* that he entered during the initial writing of *Hérodiade* but rather *continued to inhabit this crisis,* to write out of it, to sound it in poems of irresolvable paradox. Beauty and Void in the letters of the late 1860s are related to one another not according to the dialectical logic of an esoteric Hegelianism but according to a tragic logic of paradox. And they are related in this way because Mallarmé, like Nietzsche, does not permit himself to flee the shadow of nihilism, the thought of groundless negativity, though neither does he permit himself to sink in despair over it. He invents a supreme fiction of transcending an abyssal "nothing" while continually measuring the way this "nothing," a palpable absence, surrounds and inhabits his supreme fiction. His poems thus bring together, in a perpetual oscillation, a "post-Christian" poetic of the transfiguration of *le hasard* and a "tragic" poetic of the voyage into *le néant*. In *Un Coup de dés,* the brilliant final expression of this vision, the constellation subjunctively evoked in the last pages would seem to be not a figure of an eternal realm of beauty and order but a figure of the poem itself: the poem that, in its polyphonic unfolding, explores the relationship between the affirmatively tragic search for supreme fictions and the abyssal surround within and against which all searches for pattern, and all lives, are ventured and shipwrecked.[54]

The "sonnet en -yx" (O, 68–69; CP, 69), a poem that thirty years later would be recast with cosmic scope in *Un Coup de dés,* is one of Mallarmé's most haunting articulations of this vision:

> Ses purs ongles très haut dédiant leur onyx,
> L'Angoisse, ce minuit, soutient, lampadophore,
> Maint rêve vespéral brûlé par le Phénix
> Que ne recueille pas de cinéraire amphore
>
> Sur les crédences, au salon vide: nul ptyx,
> Aboli bibelot d'inanité sonore,
> (Car le Maître est allé puiser des pleurs aux Styx
> Avec ce seul objet dont le Néant s'honore).
>
> Mais proche la croisée au nord vacante, un or
> Agonise selon peut-être le décor
> Des licornes ruant du feu contre une nixe,

Elle, défunte nue en le miroir, encor
Que, dans l'oubli fermé par le cadre, se fixe
De scintillations sitôt le septuor.

[Her pure nails very high up dedicating their onyx,
Anguish, this midnight, holds up, lamp-bearing (lamp-bearer),
Many an evening dream burned by the Phoenix
That no funeral amphora gathers

On the credenzas, in the empty salon: no ptyx,
Abolished knickknack of sonorous emptiness (inanity),
(For the Master has gone to dip tears from the Styx
With this sole object with (through) which Nothingness honors
   (adorns) itself).

But near the vacant casement (turned) to the north, a gold (something)
Is dying according perhaps to the decoration
Of unicorns kicking fire against a nixie,

She, defunct nude (or cloud) in the mirror, while
In the oblivion bounded by the frame is fixed
Of scintillations at once the septet (the Great Bear).][55]

The poem presents an abandoned room that, through enigmatic gleams in a tomblike mirror, enters into relationship with a constellation of the night sky. This inside-outside pattern, marked by the six rhymes in x, is crossed by a threefold pattern that sets in parallel an upper realm of sky, a terrestrial realm of the empty room, and a lower realm of the underworld to which the Master has journeyed (a threefold pattern that loosely returns in *Un Coup de dés* as a parallelism between the upper realm of sky, the marine realm of shipwreck, and the submarine realm of abyssal dark). All three of these realms, further, are traced by patterns, marked by the eight rhymes in *or*, that are analogues of one another: the constellation in the night sky, the scintillations "fixed" in the mirror of the empty room, and the knickknack of sonorous emptiness, the mysterious *ptyx*, that the Master has carried with him to the Styx. The poem thus evokes three zones of emptiness and, within each of them, a pattern of light or sound that illuminates the emptiness. Pattern is that with which "le Néant s'honore": with which the Void honors itself, adorns itself, and, to follow the pun, sounds itself. "After having found the Void, I have found the Beautiful" (C, 310; L, 65). Anguish, death, and emptiness, on the one hand, and fictive pattern, on the other, are held together in their interwoven contradiction with one another, the poem suggesting that poetry or art (an "abolished knickknack of sonorous emptiness") may be but an articulation of the folds of negativity, a measuring of the hollow of death (in *Un Coup de dés* the abyss appears to generate its own creative wing only to encompass it again in the end). The hour is midnight, the mystical hour of *Igitur,* and this interplay of nothingness and pattern in an eerie wide quietness, an abandoned room akin to an empty tomb, is inseparable from the drama of the poet's proleptic passage into death.[56]

That the poem measures the depths of Mallarmé's crisis of the 1860s is evident. "J'ai l'esprit calme," Mallarmé writes in a letter of 1867, "l'agonie terrible, ou la naissance, (ce qui est une même chose) de la Pensée est finie, et une mort magnifique a succédé [My spirit is calm: the terrible agony, or birth (which is the same thing) of my Thought is finished, and a magnificent death has succeeded]" (C, 358). The poem evokes both this experience of creative kenosis and the poetic of the transfiguration of contingency that Mallarmé unfolds out of it. One notes, first, that the poem is an evocative display of the sort of fictive transposition that, through negation, shapes a field of relational traces, a pattern of palpable absences. An art of erasure forms a field of "vibratory disappearances": the sun has vanished, leaving behind a cosmic anguish holding the scattered ashes of day's dreams; the Master has departed for the Styx, leaving behind an empty room; the ptyx, absent from the credenzas, is itself but a "knickknack of sonorous emptiness"; the nixie (a kind of nymph) on the frame has vanished in the oblivion of the mirror wherein the constellation is reflected. I've but scratched the surface of this poem's manifold parallels, antitheses, and gliding echoes. Initially titled "Sonnet allégorique de lui-même [Sonnet allegorical of itself]," shaped by a nocturnal "demon of analogy," it is a text of vertiginous *correspondances,* a striking enactment of Mallarmé's generalization of the principle of rhyme, his faith in the power of words to generate fictions through their manifold echoing with one another. A riddling question the poem poses is that of the source of the unexpected "or" that begins to gleam in the first line of the sextet, a flicker of hope in emptiness, prepared by the turn on "mais" at the beginning of the line. Perhaps this gleam is but the fire of the unicorns carved on the mirror frame. Perhaps it is but an effect of celestial light falling upon the mirror. Yet it is hard to avoid the surmise that it is derived above all from the rhymes in *or* themselves, from the echoing *décor* of the verbal composition, a pattern of sound stirring an arrival of light. In the beginning was the rhyme, an echo in emptiness. Mallarmé's own account of the poem—anticipating his later discussion of "ceding the initiative to words" in "Crise de vers"—would seem to support this guess: "J'extrais ce sonnet . . . d'une étude projetée sur *la Parole:* il est inverse, je veux dire que le sens, s'il en a un, (mais je me consolerais du contraire grâce à la dose de poësie qu'il renferme, ce me semble) est évoqué par un mirage interne des mots mêmes [I'm extracting this sonnet . . . from a projected study on the Word: it is inverse, I mean that the meaning, if it has one (but I would console myself, were the contrary the case, thanks to the dose of poetry it encloses, it seems to me), is evoked by an internal mirage at play among the words themselves]" (C, 392; L, 86–87).[57] Finally, this "ceding of the initiative to words," this "elocutionary disappearance of the poet," is figured in the poem by the Master's disappearance from the room. The poem traces a creative death of the self that is at once "experiential" and "technical." This oscillating, self-reflexive poem reads like a first draft of Mallarmé's fully developed poetic of the transfiguration of *le hasard* through the threefold practice of fictive transposition, radicalized rhyme, and authorial impersonalization.

Yet, at the same time, this poem, like *Un Coup de dés* thirty years later, holds fast to the thought that "un coup de dés jamais n'abolira le hasard." It keeps the wound of the negative open, as in Climacus's negative theology, or suspends itself in a place of baffled reach, as in Dickinson's poetry. It is a sounding of the silence of death. The cryptic word "ptyx" is one sign of this. It is a Greek word that Mallarmé seems to have chosen for its place in the rhyme scheme even before he knew what it meant. Originally meaning "fold" and by metonymic extension "shell," in this poem it is set in apposition to an absent "funeral amphora," an urn taken back to the desolation it would commemorate, and then redefined as a "knickknack of sonorous emptiness," presumably a figure for this poem itself and for the work of art in general. And this peculiar object, like the Master or Poet, is absent from the room because the latter has taken it with him to the region of nothing where, so to speak, it may authentically honor the nothing that sounds through it. Akin to "Un pur vase d'aucun breuvage / Que l'inexhaustible veuvage [The pure vase of no potion / But inexhaustible widowhood]" (O, 54; CP, 9), to a mandolin "au creux néant musicien [musician of the hollow nothing]" (O, 74; CP, 43), the "ptyx" figures the poem in which it absently appears as a runic "word" foreign to our ordinary language—"a total word, new, strange to the language, and, as it were, incantatory," as we read in "Crise de vers" (O, 368; SPr, 43)—and, at the same time, as an articulate fold of nothing, a reverberant shell of negativity. From this perspective, it would seem, the creative kenosis of the poet serves not to unveil an absolute ideality that transcends pointless contingency but rather to bear the poet further into the "Ténèbres Absolues" (C, 349; L, 77), to guide him further toward a measure of the death that exceeds our measures. The poem, a lucid throw of the dice, is a meditation on death, fiction, and the relationship between the two. That it is a *tombeau* of a peculiar sort is further emblematized by the vanquished "nixe" buried in the oblivion of the mirror (as the "ptyx" is "buried" in the underworld to which the poet has carried it) wherein the constellation, yet another figure of the poem, is reflected. The poet who has become "un maître" is called to "draw tears from the Styx" or, as we read in the earlier "Le Démon de l'analogie," to mourn the death of "l'inexplicable Pénultième." He is writing his own "inexplicable" death. "La mort triomphait dans cette voix étrange [death triumphed in this strange voice]" (O, 70; CP, 71), as Mallarmé writes in his elegy on Poe, describing his own art.

The "sonnet en -yx" thus brings together, in a field of echoing paradox, two of the major orientations of Mallarmé's poetry: the supreme fiction of transfiguring chance in a constellation of intricately traced echoes and relationships, and the tragic movement of voyaging articulately into the unfathomable space of death. The poem oscillates between these perspectives without resolution.

It is significant that the "sonnet en -yx" reads like a sort of "initiatory" poem. The voyage into the space of death, the term *Maître* itself, the dark room suggesting at once an empty tomb and the secret chamber of a mystery rite, the religious vocabulary of the first stanza, the hermetic "ptyx," the figures out of legend on the mirror frame, the enigmatic arrival of an unspecified gleam in the dark: all these things evoke an atmosphere of ritual or initiation.[58] The poem recalls Nerval's "El Desdichado," whose speaker, "the dark, the widowed, and the unconsoled," dwelling in a tomb, claims that he has "twice, conqueror, traversed the Acheron." It also seems to recall, like Nerval's poem, the myth of Orpheus's descent to Hades through the power of his song. Surprisingly, however, Orpheus is not an important figure in Mallarmé's writings (notwithstanding the famous claim that the Book would be "the orphic explanation of the earth"). Yet the poem brings to mind another myth of trial and initiation, namely, the myth of Psyche. According to the myth, one recalls, Psyche, having been separated from Eros, is put through a series of trials by Venus. The last of these is a journey to Hades to gather in a small box a portion of Proserpine's beauty. All goes well until, ignoring a warning, Psyche opens the box to observe the beauty of the world of shades: far from finding anything tangible, she finds only a Stygian sleep that, sweeping over her, leaves her on the border of death. She has encountered "no potion but inexhaustible widowhood." She has stepped into the core of nothing. Eros, having calmed antagonisms in the upper world, returns to revive Psyche with a drink of ambrosia; Psyche is made immortal and translated to Olympus; the two are reunited. One imagines that the story of a beauty that turns out to be a vapor of death would have fascinated Mallarmé. "O femme," Hérodiade says, "un baiser me tûrait / Si la beauté n'était la mort [Oh woman, a kiss would kill me / If beauty were not death]" (O, 44; CP, 29). Unlike Psyche, who is rescued from Death by Love, the poet of the "sonnet en -yx" remains awake and alone in the midst of this interpenetration of beauty and nothing. He has voyaged into the space of death and lingered there, mourning amidst shadows, drawing tears from the Styx, a lucid resident of nothing, as though this nothing were the source of beauty, the tragic underside of fictive ideality. Fiction is inhabited by the death it appears to transcend. Perhaps the Mallarméan initiation promises a capacity to write from this uncannily close nowhere without wishing it away in dreams of transcendence ("la mort triomphait dans cette voix étrange"). Death, or, as Derrida would say, the differential "spacing" of temporality, is at once the generative condition and the inevitable ruin of presence, self-presence, and representation. Death "speaks" in the relational play constitutive of ideality. "The relationship with *my death* (my disappearance in general)," Derrida writes in his essay on Husserl, "thus lurks in this determination of being as presence, ideality, the absolute possibility of repetition. The possibility of the sign is this relationship with death. The determination and elimination of the sign in metaphysics is the dissimulation of this relationship with death, which yet produced signification" (SP, 54). Derrida, so to speak, disrupts Hegelian dialectics and Husserlian phenomenology with Mallarméan tragic paradox.

ONE OF MALLARMÉ'S finest meditations on fiction is the short prose piece "Mimique" (O, 310). While this meditation is cast as a commentary on Paul Margueritte's pantomime booklet *Pierrot assassin de sa femme*, it is primarily an articulation of Mallarmé's own understanding of fiction. It reads like a marvelous commentary, in particular, on "L'Après-midi d'un faune."

> Voici—"La scène n'illustre que l'idée, pas une action effective, dans un hymen (d'où procède le Rêve), vicieux mais sacré, entre le désir et l'accomplissement, la perpétration et son souvenir: ici devançant, là remémorant, au futur, au passé, *sous une apparence fausse de présent*. Tel opère le Mime,

dont le jeu se borne à une allusion perpétuelle sans briser la glace: il installe, ainsi, un milieu, pur, de fiction."

[This—"The scene illustrates but the idea, not any actual action, in a hymen (out of which flows Dream), tainted with vice yet sacred, between desire and fulfillment, perpetration and remembrance: here anticipating, there recalling, in the future, in the past, *under the false appearance of a present*. Thus does the Mime operate, whose act is confined to a perpetual allusion without breaking the mirror (or the ice): he thus installs a medium, a pure medium, of fiction."][59]

An arabesque of paradox, this passage evokes the allusive and elusive atmosphere of Mallarmé's dreamy faun, who dwells in just this sort of oscillatory climate stretched between desire and fulfillment, perpetration and remembrance, weaving a milieu of fiction whose relationship to the milieu of experience remains as puzzling to him as it does to the reader. Like the mime, further, the faun is, among other things, a figure of the wandering of writing and the wandering of desire. "Did I love a dream," the faun asks himself, recognizing that his recollections may be but fictive translations of the silence in which he finds himself alone, just as the mime's improvisatory writing, Mallarmé suggests, is akin to an orchestra's translation of a silent background or a poet's translation of a silent ode. Fiction is constitutively related to this silence, to what, in other places, Mallarmé variously calls nothing, absence, death, and the void. In "Mimique" the art of pantomime is said to be the "genre situé plus près de principes qu'aucun [the genre situated closer to principles than any]." In "La Musique et les Lettres" the "principle" of fiction is said to be a kind of "nothing" (O, 647; SPr, 48).[60]

"Mimique" is Derrida's point of departure in the first part of his two-part essay on Mallarmé, "The Double Session" (D, 173–286). One of Derrida's concerns is to present Mallarmé's textual practice as an exemplary instance of the release of writing from any subordinate relationship to a pretextual order of reference, be this order understood as logos, nature, reality, truth, or creative subjectivity (D, 205–11, 219). No pretextual ground, Derrida argues in terms less familiar in 1970 than they are now, governs the act of writing but rather the act of writing produces, as effects, gliding meanings. One could perhaps say that in the first part of this essay Derrida rewrites Mallarmé's early modernist notion of the "autonomy of fiction," an unanchored exploration of the unknown, as an avantgardist notion of the "autonomy of writing," a wandering of words producing the unforeseeable. Writing, the play of material signifiers, displaces fiction, the play of ideal relationships. While it is true that this displacement already occurs in Mallarmé, Derrida's specific emphases may risk a slight thinning of Mallarméan paradox, a slight stepping away from Mallarmé's preoccupation with the inseparability of the reaching play of fiction and the initiatory sounding of death. It certainly involves a change of affect, the combination of tragic pathos and wry musing characteristic of Mallarmé giving way to an avantgardist tone of subversive play and liberatory promise characteristic of Derrida (at least in his writings of the sixties and seventies).

While in the second part of "The Double Session" Derrida initially appears concerned less with Mallarmé than with the limits of thematic criticism, he returns to Mallarmé in a provocative reading of important "words" in Mallarmé's text that have often been studied as essential "motifs" or "themes." Concentrating specifically on *blanc* (white or blank) and *pli* (fold), terms with decidedly self-referential valences, Derrida argues that no thematic criticism can comprehend the play of these terms in Mallarmé's text, not because they bear an inexhaustible semantic depth, but because they designate among other things the very movement of textual "spacing" or "relating" that, in opening the space of any ideality, at once conditions and exceeds any gathered meaning, any thematic recuperation (D, 245–85). *Blanc* and *pli* in Mallarmé's text, like *hymen* and *voile*, turn out to be alternatives for *différance*. In this part of the essay, then, Derrida not only traces the limits of thematic criticism but also recodes Mallarmé's highly self-reflexive "art of analogy" as an open-ended "play of dissemination." The demon of analogy becomes the demon of dissemination. Post-structuralist errancy and the spirit of avantgardist subversion replace high modernist self-reflexivity and the spirit of heroic artistry. In Mallarmé, as we have seen, this self-referential practice involves not only a studious technique but also a spiritual discipline. It is inseparable from a conception of poetry as a well-nigh religious vocation demanding an "impersonalizing" movement through a pattern of echoes designed to sound the blank of death. Derrida's reading of Mallarmé appears to set aside this sort of "postreligious" preoccupation in the name of an emancipatory "decentering" of the subject no longer bound to "logocentric" models of truth and mimesis.

Nevertheless, it remains true that Derrida is closer to Mallarmé's guiding preoccupations than these observations suggest. Both are tireless students of the movement of signification and the "espacement de la lecture" (O, 455; CP, 121). Both explore the concept of "relationality" to the point at which it begins to fracture, opening onto a hollow, as though it were the most paradoxical of concepts. Almost kabbalistic in their attention to the specific character of writing, in the ordinary sense of this term, both discern in textual relationality not a patterning of constituted meanings so much as the movement that constitutes meanings always already turning elsewhere. The words of an accomplished poem, Mallarmé writes, "se reflètent les uns sur les autres jusqu'à paraître ne plus avoir leur couleur propre, mais n'être que les transitions d'une gamme [reciprocally reflect one another until they seem no longer to have their own color but to be solely transitions in a scale]" (C, 329–30; L, 69). Meaning comes and goes between the lines. And both, though in quite different vocabularies and entirely different ideological contexts, find in the wavering "mimed presence" of fiction, or of ideality in general, the ghostly "absent presence" of nothing, death, differential force, irreducible negativity. Derrida, indeed, can be said to have spent the last forty years obeying one of the oldest imperatives in the canon of philosophy, namely, to think upon our death, to fathom the truth (painfully obvious, ultimately unfathomable) that in life we are in death. *Un coup de dés jamais n'abolira le hasard. Un coup de dés jamais n'abolira la différance.* A throw of the dice, a venture of thought, "plume solitaire éperdue [solitary desperate feather]" (O, 468; CP, 136), will never abolish shipwreck in death. Yet thought is drawn to venture there, again and again, a wing or a sail in the dark, gliding while sinking. "And, in the isolation of the sky, / At evening, casual flocks of pigeons make / Ambiguous undulations as they sink, / Downward to darkness, on extended wings."[61]

DERRIDA

Derrida's texts form a labyrinth whose multiple entrances lead, if not to a center, at least to an organizing sheaf of arguments. Key terms or quasi-concepts like "différance," "writing," "pharmakon," "hymen," "supplementarity," and "trace," among others, all lead back to one another and, in most cases, can readily, or almost, be substituted for one another (thus does the demon of analogy enter the house of philosophy). I would like to begin by stepping through three meanings of the term "writing" in Derrida's discourse, for this term carries one quickly and clearly into the guiding issues at stake in his project. What is the significance of the seemingly paradoxical claim, famously proposed in the great texts of the sixties, that writing precedes speech? What motivates the decision to disrupt a "logocentric" tradition of the "metaphysics of presence" in the name of a movement dubbed "arche-writing"?

There can be no doubt that Derrida chooses the term "writing" in part because he wishes to associate his project with a literary avantgarde running from Mallarmé through Sollers. His essays on these two writers, published side by side in *Dissemination,* make this link clear. "If we had the time," Derrida says in the interview "Implications," "we could ... ask ourselves too why the irreducibility of writing and, let us say, the subversion of logocentrism are announced better than elsewhere, today, in a certain sector and a certain determined form of 'literary' practice" (P, 11). The essay on Mallarmé that I schematized above indicates the major lines of "subversion" that Derrida finds in this field of avantgardist writing. One of the most important of these is the unloosing of the practice of writing from any obedience to a pretextual order of reference. Derrida, further, links this literary avantgarde with Nietzsche's perspectivism. In *Of Grammatology* he writes:

> Nietzsche, far from remaining *simply* (with Hegel and as Heidegger wished) *within* metaphysics, contributed a great deal to the liberation of the signifier from its dependence or derivation with respect to the logos and the related concept of truth or the primary signified, in whatever sense that is understood. Reading, and therefore writing, the text were for Nietzsche "originary" operations (I put that word within quotation marks for reasons to appear later) with regard to a sense that they do not have to transcribe or discover, which would not therefore be a truth signified in the original element and presence of a logos, as *topos noetos,* divine understanding, or the structure of a priori necessity. (OG, 19)

The same claim is made about Mallarmé in "The Double Session." This yoking of a "modernist" Nietzsche and a "modernist" Mallarmé is an important move shaping Derrida's project.

On another level, the one for which Derrida is best known in this country, the overturning of the traditional hierarchy of speech and writing is meant to illuminate the nature of language in general. On this level the term "writing" functions as a defamiliarizing concept in a "theory of language." In saying that speech is already writing (OG, 7) or that "language ... is first writing" (OG, 37), Derrida wishes to show that all those features of "secondariness" traditionally ascribed to "writing" in order to subordinate it to an imagined "full presence" of speech—materiality, distance or difference from the speaker, distance or difference from the present, drift in time, and so forth—are in fact already defining features of speech (OG, 6–73). Language, whether spoken or written, is a differential system of instituted marks and, as Saussure teaches despite his occasional repetition of traditional prejudices, could not function otherwise. The myth of speech as the transparent medium of a consciousness present to itself cannot withstand a scrutiny of the differential structure of language. The subject, whether speaking or writing, is always already eccentrically "inscribed" in a field of differential marks (OG, 68–69; MP, 15). Language, like all that is traced by language, drifts. Any word, sliding from one place to another, potentially begins to mean otherwise.

Yet it would be partial to characterize Derrida as a theorist of language concerned to bring out the deconstructive implications of structuralist linguistics. He concentrates on the traditional opposition of speech and writing because he perceives therein a "symptomatic" and, in a complex way, not "unmotivated" decision repeated throughout the history of philosophy.[62] As is well known, he reads the traditional denigration of writing as a symptom of the desire for a stable presence, a "transcendental signified," that, located outside the play of signification, would promise an ultimate end to this play. In "Structure, Sign, and Play in the Discourse of the Human Sciences," perhaps his best-known presentation of this line of thought (WD, 278–93), he characterizes the history of philosophy as a single, if internally fissured, history animated by a search for an atemporal foundation determined as a full presence unmarked by textuality, difference, and death (WD, 279–80). Taken to this point but no further, then, Derrida's argument would seem to be a post-Nietzschean "constructivist" argument of the sort currently pervasive in our culture. The notorious statement that *il n'y a pas de hors-texte* (OG, 158, 163) would be a polemical version of the claim that we have no access to an extralinguistic reality (whether transcendent, objective, or subjective) not always already traced by the differential play of signification. There is no escape from the centerless "Nietzschean" game of errant acts of signification.[63]

No doubt this "constructivist" current is forcefully present in Derrida, guiding the "deconstruction" of what Richard Rorty calls a tradition of "foundationalism" and what Derrida, following Heidegger, calls a tradition of "ontotheology" or the "metaphysics of presence." Yet this current is not the whole story. For in the traditional hierarchy of speech and writing Derrida perceives not only a "symptom" of the desire for a pure extralinguistic foundation but, more basically, a "symptom" of the evasion of the thought of difference, in particular of temporal difference. It is as though he found in the history of the "metaphysics of presence" a recurrent failure to think the irreducible othering of time, the abyssal spacing of death even in the realm of ideality.[64] On this level, then, the concept "arche-writing" designates, in a rather elusive way, the primoridal movement of time, the differential "spacing" of temporalization: "arche-writing, movement of *différance*, irreducible arche-synthesis, opening in one and the same possibility, temporalization as well as relationship with the other and language, cannot, as the condition of all linguistic systems, form a part of the linguistic system itself and be situated as an object in its field" (OG, 60). Or again:

> Arche-writing, at first the possibility of the spoken word, then of the "*graphie*" in the narrow sense, the birthplace of "usurpation," denounced from Plato to Saussure, this trace is the opening of the first exteriority in general, the enigmatic relationship of the living to its other and of an inside to an outside: spacing. The outside, "spatial" and "objective" exteriority which we believe we know as the most familiar thing in the world, as familiarity itself, would not appear without the grammè, without differance as temporalization, without the nonpresence of the other inscribed within the sense of the present, without the relationship with death as the concrete structure of the living present. (OG, 70–71)

This, to put it mildly, is neither the language of the romantic ironist, reflexively negating each proposition set forth, nor the language of the post-Nietzschean constructivist, insisting that every claim we make about the world (about time, death, or the concrete structure of the living present, for example) is but an effect of an open field of discursive practices. In fact, this is the kind of language that, prior to Heidegger and Derrida's imposition on our culture of a particular definition of "metaphysics," might well have been characterized as "metaphysical." It is a language that provides a general description of time, space, life, death, signification, and certain "fundamental" or "originary" structures of being and becoming. Derrida, I will argue below, is among other things a post-Heideggerian philosopher of time, his thinking in this domain having been forcefully shaped by a critical engagement with major Heideggerian questions.

How, then, are these different strands of the concept of "writing" or "arche-writing" related to one another? The first and the second of the strands I've sketched—the Mallarméan, or modernist, strand and the Nietzschean, or constructivist, strand—readily come together in Derrida's project. The emphasis on the unmooring of writing from pretextual grounds, and the emphasis on the perspectival interpretation of an always already discursively traced domain of the real, are mutually implicated elements of an ironic current in Derrida that I've broadly characterized as constructivist. Yet the relationship between this ironic "post-Nietzschean" current in Derrida and the quite different current that I've characterized as "post-Heideggerian"—the description of presence as always already divided from itself in the abyssal play of time—would seem to remain obscure.

The question of this relationship is at once openly posed and, to my mind, not clearly resolved in the programmatic essay "Différance." In this essay, it is true, Derrida is in part simply concerned to situate his project in relation to a modern philosophic field of the *thinking of difference* (MP, 7): Hegel, Husserl, Nietzsche, Freud, Saussure, Heidegger, Bataille, and Levinas (one notes the resonant absence of Marx) are all named as major "coordinates" in this eclectic field. Yet it is a critical reading of Saussurean linguistics, on the one hand, and an ambiguous wrestling with Heidegger's conception of the ontic-ontological difference, on the other, that appear to overshadow all the other theoretical fields named. Saussure is extensively engaged throughout the first half of the essay, while Heidegger, in particular his meditation on the Anaximander fragment, is closely engaged in the last six pages of the essay. Thus, again, a major question the essay raises is that of the relationship between the movement of signification and an enigmatic movement said to be "older" than the ontic-ontological difference (MP, 22). This crucial question also hovers over the entire first part of *Of Grammatology* and many of Derrida's other essays of the sixties and seventies: what is the relationship between the play of time and the play of signification, between "the indefinite movement of finitude" (WD, 248) and "the indefinite referral of signifier to signifier" (WD, 25)? Perhaps this sounds like asking for an account of the relationship between *différance* and *différance*. That, I think, is one of the major questions raised by Derrida's writings of this period.

While Derrida, like Kierkegaard and Nietzsche, is a decidedly "polyvocal" philosopher, happy to speak from different places in different essays or even within the same essay, I will argue that there are nonetheless two primary philosophic perspectives from which he tends to theorize the relationship I've just sketched as a question. One of these is a traditional perspective of transcendental argument: albeit a perspective crossed by a subversive account, adopted from Bataille, of Hegelian dialectics as a restricted economy inscribed within a general economy (an economy of "the unity of life and death" [WD, 248]) whose abyssal negativity at once conditions and exceeds any recuperative dialectic of meaning. Whether by accident or design, this approach seems to be especially marked in a number of the essays gathered in *Writing and Difference*. Another of Derrida's approaches to the question I've posed, however, draws largely on Heidegger's narrative of the history of philosophy as a history of the determination of being as presence, hence as a history characterized by the nonthinking of the temporal movement of Being whereby "beings" emerge from a disclosive "clearing," or whereby "presence" emerges from a disclosive "presencing," or whereby "presence" and "time" alike emerge from a more primordial movement of "It gives" (*Es gibt*). This approach seems to be especially marked in *Of Grammatology*, "Différance," and a number of the essays gathered in *Margins of Philosophy*. At this point I would note that if Derrida is able to move fluently between these different perspectives, it is not least because, despite their differences, these perspectives share a common point of departure, namely, a sweeping narrative of the history of philosophy according to which modern philosophy, in particular, is conceived as an instrumental economy of reason unable to think the "originary" movement of time and alterity. Levinas, who like Derrida draws on Heidegger only then to criticize Heidegger himself, calls this instrumental economy an "economy of the same." Derrida occasionally speaks this language too.

Below I want first to sketch the way Derrida repeats and unsettles a language of transcendental argument by weaving through it a variation on Bataille's subversive Hegelianism. Then I will engage, at greater length, the way Derrida revises Heidegger's thinking of the temporal movement of Being and Heidegger's narrative of the history of philosophy by rewriting them in terms of important Nietzschean themes. Having traced these guiding perspectives in Derrida's project, I would like to step back and raise the question of their relationship to Derrida's reading of a certain "modernist" literary tradition in which Mallarmé is at once an emblematic and an eccentric figure.[65]

DERRIDA HAS ACKNOWLEDGED the importance of Bataille to his project. In the interview "Positions," he alludes to Bataille's concept of a "general economy" and, in a footnote later added to the conversation, writes: "Here I permit myself to recall that the texts to which you have referred (particularly '*La double séance*,' '*La dissémination*,' '*La mythologie blanche*,' but also '*La pharmacie de Platon*,' and several others) are situated *explicitly* in relation to

Bataille, and also explicitly propose a reading of Bataille" (P, 105–6 n. 35). All the more significant, then, is Derrida's description of *différance,* in another interview, as a concept designating "the most general structure of economy": "I would even say that it is *the* economical concept, and since there is no economy without *différance,* it is the most general structure of economy, given that one understands by economy something other than the classical economy of metaphysics, or the classical metaphysics of economy" (P, 8–9). Bataille's account of a general economy of abyssal negativity that at once conditions and exceeds any Hegelian economy of sublated negativity is rewritten by Derrida as a general economy of *différance* that inevitably undoes any foundationalist discourse, secretly ruins any ontotheological discourse.

Yet Derrida's relationship to Bataille remains oblique, in large part because Derrida shows little interest in the sort of ranging "philosophical anthropology" that Bataille pursues in all his writings. Thus Derrida's one major essay on Bataille, "From Restricted to General Economy: A Hegelianism without Reserve" (WD, 251–77), is difficult to interpret clearly. For in this essay Derrida, at least initially, appears to lend his approval to Bataille's Hegelian account of the historical formation of a desire for mastery through the transformative activity of labor, the gradual surpassing of bondage, the preservation of the subject in the face of death, and the recuperation of meaning in the face of the non-sense of radical negativity. According to Bataille's narrative, which I discussed in chapter 2, history is constituted through the negation of "natural immediacy" effected by the establishment of all those regulated structures we know as social labor, social prohibition, political hierarchy, and social discourse (this last being more or less equated by Bataille with "discursive reason" as such). What Bataille calls a "sovereign experience" involves both a radical departure from these utilitarian structures and a nonconceptual turning toward a "participatory" relationship with the groundless play of life and death. Bataille adopts a Hegelian marxist account of labor and discourse as processes whereby social subjects maintain and transform themselves in and against negativity: yet he adopts this account only to put it in question, to disclose its limits, to explore a range of ecstatic "exits" from its restricted economy. A large portion of Derrida's essay on Bataille is devoted to a reading of Bataille's meditations on the possibilities of escaping the dark reversals implicit in Hegel's account of the restricted dialectic of master and slave (WD, 254–62). Yet where Bataille at this point speaks of various *lived experiences* that transgress a restricted economy of dialectically regulated negativity, Derrida speaks exclusively of parodic *textual practices* that set a restricted economy of meaning "sliding" toward a general

Apocalyptic Negativity • 241

economy of non-meaning (WD, 256–60, 267–68). Derrida, that is, appears to step back from—without explicitly criticizing—Bataille's philosophical anthropology in order to concentrate on the more limited question of a dialectical economy of meaning and its relationship to an abyssal economy of non-meaning. How are we to read this move? Is Derrida lending assent, implicitly, to Bataille's Hegelian marxist narrative? Or, rather, is he choosing to remain silent on this question in order to concentrate on "transcendental" issues?

Derrida's silences in this essay (and elsewhere) are perplexing. They indicate that though the concept of a "desire for presence" or a "desire for mastery" powerfully informs his thought, he would like *not* to rely in any direct way on an interpretation of such a "desire" that can be readily found in the works of any number of modern philosophers. Yet the concept of a "desire for presence" or a "desire for mastery"—like any concept designed to illuminate the unthematized motivations of "reason" or a "philosophic tradition"—at least *implies* an account of this "desire" as either a natural essence, a transcendental structure of experience, or a historical formation. Derrida, in his essay on Bataille, avoids *explicitly* aligning himself with any of these positions, though it would seem that *implicitly* he writes from the standpoint of a transcendental phenomenology. He repeats Bataille's account of the abyssal relationship between a restricted economy and a general economy while maintaining a studious distance from any philosopical anthropology, any Hegelian marxist narrative, or any Heideggerian narrative.[66]

To put this another way, Derrida, even in a reading of a philosopher as "improper" as Bataille, tends to remain attached to a "transcendental phenomenology," albeit a transcendental phenomenology in which the "problematic of the sign" has been deconstructively accentuated. The reading of Husserl in *Speech and Phenomena* moves on this plane. The quite early essay "Force and Signification" includes a transcendental account, in terms of an economy of *force*, of what a short time later would come to be called an economy of *différance*: "Hegel demonstrated convincingly that the explication of a phenomenon by a force is a tautology. But in saying this, one must refer to language's peculiar inability to emerge from itself in order to articulate its origin, and not to the *thought* of force. Force is the other of language without which language would not be what it is" (WD, 27). And in "Violence and Metaphysics" Derrida criticizes Levinas's account of an ethical relationship to the other—a relationship said to be "anarchically" prior to any cognitive relationship to the other in the order of representation—by arguing that the "transcendental violence" that opens the realm of representation is the very condition of possibility of any ethical relationship at all: "That I am also essentially the other's other, and that I know I am, is the evidence of a strange symmetry whose trace appears nowhere in Levinas's descriptions. Without this evidence, I could not desire or respect the other in ethical disymmetry.... For this transcendental origin, as the irreducible violence of the relation to the other, is at the same time nonviolence, since it opens the relation to the other. It is an *economy*" (WD, 128–29). A certain violence toward alterity, according to this argument, has its basis not only in a long history of social domination, or in a form of cognition conditioned by that long history, or in the impersonal structures of social existence in general, but also in the spatial polarity of inside and outside instituted with the order of representation. This is a "transcendental violence" that opens the possibility of "ethical non-violence": the latter is a promise requiring our "vigilance" within a wider, groundless "economy of violence" (WD, 117; cf. OG, 139–40). Often, then, Derrida hovers within traditional modes of transcendental argument.[67]

Yet he hovers there, of course, eccentrically. In *Speech and Phenomena* a "relationship to my death" is shown to be constitutive of transcendental ideality (SP, 54). What is called a *general economy* in both "Implications" and the essay on Bataille is called an *economy of violence* in the essay on Levinas from which I've just cited. This economy is described (though not named) as an *economy of force* in the early essay "Force and Signification." And in both *Of Grammatology* and "Différance" this economy is, rather strikingly, called an *economy of death*:

> Spacing as writing is the becoming-absent and the becoming-unconscious of the subject. By the movement of its *dérive* the emancipation of the sign constitutes in return the desire of presence. That becoming—or that *dérive*—does not befall the subject which would choose it or would passively let itself be drawn along by it. As the subject's relationship with its own death, this becoming is the constitution of subjectivity. On all levels of life's organization, that is to say, of the *economy of death*. All graphemes are of a testamentary essence. And the original absence of the subject of writing is also the absence of the thing or the referent. (OG, 69; cf. 246)

It becomes clear, then, that this variously named "economy of death" is what Derrida elsewhere calls "spacing," "différance," and "arche-writing," among other things.[68]

In this way Derrida undermines the sort of transcendental reflection that he at the same time reiterates. For this general economy of death conditions and exceeds, traverses and unsettles, the subject that would grasp it in reflection or the restricted economy of meaning that would comprehend it in discourse. And this general economy can no more be conceived on the basis of presence (or the present) than it can be conceived on the basis of a constitutive subjectivity (or a consciousness present to itself). The concept of a general economy designates the equiprimordial movements of time and alterity: "the indefinite movement of finitude, of the unity of life and death, of difference, of original repetition, that is, of the origin of tragedy as the absence of a simple origin" (WD, 248; cf. SP, 52, 86; OG, 246). Thus, to return to the question I posed earlier, one way Derrida theorizes the relationship between the movement of time and the movement of signification is by describing an unclosable "general economy" wherein language, while establishing an apparently secure order of representation within which the subject finds itself inscribed, is always already inhabited by the differential force of primordial temporality that at once inhabits and exceeds it. "Force is the other of language without which language would not be what it is" (WD, 27). This *force* is *time:*

> Space is "in" time; it is time's pure leaving-itself; it is the "outside-itself" as the self-relation of time.... The going-forth "into the world" is also primordially implied in the movement of temporalization. "Time" cannot be an "absolute subjectivity" precisely because it cannot be conceived on the basis of a present and the self-presence of a present being. Like everything thought under this heading, and like all that is excluded by the most rigorous transcendental reduction, the "world" is primordially implied in the movement of temporalization. As a relation between an inside and an outside in general, an existent and a nonexistent in general, a constituting and a constituted in general, temporalization is at once the very power and limit of phenomenological reduction. (SP, 86)

Derrida, in this sense, practices a quasi-transcendental thinking of time as an "unconditioned" movement (or, since this movement is always already both "conditioned" and "unconditioned," a paradoxically "quasi-unconditioned" movement) that he believes to have been insufficiently thought in the history of philosophy.

244 • THE EXTRAVAGANT

YET DERRIDA'S DEBTS to both Husserl and Bataille are finally less important than his debts to both Nietzsche and Heidegger. For his radical thinking of time would seem to emerge, above all, out of a complex, quasi-Nietzschean rewriting of Heidegger. While there are various ways of characterizing the "turn" in Heidegger's trajectory—a general shift in emphasis from the priority of *Dasein* to the priority of *Sein*—it remains the case that his entire philosophic path, from *Being and Time* on, involves an attempt to think "*time* . . . as the horizon of *being*" (BT, 392; cf. 16–17). If Being is intrinsically intertwined with time, always already a movement of disclosure, then it cannot be adequately thought in terms of a simple present, a simple presence, or a simply present being. The first task for thought is thus to "de-structure" a "history of ontology" that has always determined Being on the basis of presence (BT, 17–23; cf. BPP, 22–23). The forgetting of Being, or the forgetting of the difference between Being and beings, is above all a forgetting of the disclosive movement of Being. In Heidegger's essay on the Anaximander fragment, this unthought difference between Being and beings is described as the unthought difference between "presencing" (a variation on what Heidegger elsewhere calls "unconcealing" or "clearing") and "what is present." At issue in the Anaximander fragment, Heidegger writes, is "the presencing of what is present. But to be the Being *of* beings is the matter of Being." This leads to an account of Being as the movement of presencing from which the present and present beings emerge:

> The grammatical form of this enigmatic, ambiguous genitive indicates a genesis, the emergence of what is present from presencing. Yet the essence of this emergence remains concealed along with the essence of these two words. Not only that, but the very relation between presencing and what is present remains unthought. From early on it seems as though presencing and what is present were each something for itself. Presencing itself unnoticeably becomes something present. Represented in the manner of something present, it is elevated above whatever else is present and so becomes the highest being present. As soon as presencing is named it is represented as some present being. Ultimately, presencing as such is not distinguished from what is present: it is taken merely as the most universal or the highest of present beings, thereby becoming one among such beings. The essence of presencing, and with it the distinction between presencing and what is present, remains forgotten. *The oblivion of Being is oblivion of the distinction between Being and beings.*[69] (AF, 50)

The history of metaphysics, then, is the history of an "objectifying" mode of thought that, in thinking Being in terms of either a foundational Being, a highest Being, or, in the modern period, a constitutive subject, and in thinking truth in terms of either representation or correspondence, fails to think not only the difference between Being and beings but also the intrinsic temporal movement of Being and of truth that belongs to this difference. Heidegger would turn our attention to a presencing that is not a ground so much as an enigmatic occurrence that opens the possibility of any thinking of grounds. This enigmatic occurrence, Heidegger suggests in a later essay, is the movement or "play" of Being *as* Abyss: "Every founding and even every appearance of foundability has inevitably degraded being to some sort of a being. Being *qua* being remains ground-less. Ground/reason stays from being, namely, as a ground/reason that would first found being, it stays off and away. Being: the *a*-byss" (PR, 111).

In the beginning was time. And truth, a happening that is at once a disclosing and a concealing, emerges out of a groundless movement that thought can never comprehend in representation. Is this the twofold story, paradoxical in its formulation, that Heidegger wishes to tell? Does Being "give" itself equiprimordially with time? Or is Being "given" by an originary drift of time? In "On Time and Being," a lecture delivered sixteen years after the essay on the Anaximander fragment, Heidegger holds out the latter possibility only to withdraw it:

> True time is the nearness of presencing out of present, past, and future—the nearness that unifies time's threefold opening extending.... Time is not the product of man, man is not the product of time. There is only giving in the sense of extending which opens up time-space....
>
> Thus true time appears as the "It" of which we speak when we say: It gives [*Es gibt*] Being. The destiny in which It gives Being lies in the extending of time. Does this reference show time to be the "It" that gives Being? By no means. For time itself remains the gift of an "It gives" whose giving preserves the realm in which presence is extended. (OTB, 16–17)

Time, then, is said to be "given" with Being in a more primordial movement that Heidegger, later in the lecture, calls *Ereignis:* "What determines both, time and Being, in their own, that is, in their belonging together, we shall call: *Ereignis,* the event of Appropriation. *Ereignis* will be translated as Appropriation or event of Appropriation. One should bear in mind, however, that 'event' is not simply an occurrence but that which makes any occurrence possible" (OTB, 19). Is it possible to speak in any clear way of this groundless "giving" that bears such resonant theological echoes?[70] This "giving" would seem to be the obscure movement that, in opening Being and time and any thought of Being and time, at the same time eludes any conceptual determination. Is Derrida's concept of *différance* but another "quasi-concept" with which to allude to this differential "other" of all thought that nonetheless "traces" all thought? Are these but so many different names, finally, for the mystery of temporal alterity and the mystery of the way it traverses language? I think so. We dwell and drift, and so the words we speak drift, in the shadows and crossings of time. "It is not in the premise that reality / Is a solid. It may be a shade that traverses / A dust, a force that traverses a shade."[71]

It is Heidegger's essay on the Anaximander fragment, not his lecture "On Time and Being," that Derrida engages in the last six pages of "Différance."[72] An important claim Derrida makes is that *différance* is "older" than the ontic-ontological difference:

> And yet, are not the thought of the *meaning* or *truth* of Being, the determination of *différance* as the ontico-ontological difference, difference thought within the horizon of the question *of Being,* still intrametaphysical effects of *différance*? . . . Since Being has never had a "meaning," has never been thought or said as such, except by dissimulating itself in beings, then *différance,* in a certain and very strange way, (is) "older" than the ontological difference or than the truth of Being. When it has this age it can be called the play of the trace. The play of a trace which no longer belongs to the horizon of Being, but whose play transports and encloses the meaning of Being: the play of the trace, or the *différance,* which has no meaning and is not. Which does not belong. There is no maintaining, and no depth to, this bottomless chessboard on which Being is put into play.[73] (MP, 22)

There are three points I would like to make about this passage. First, it is not clear, to my mind, that what Derrida calls *différance* is "older," more primoridal, or more originary than what Heidegger variously calls "unconcealing," "clearing," "presencing," the "play" of abyssal Being, or the "giving" of Being and Time in a groundless *Ereignis* or "event." Second, the words "meaning" and "truth" in this passage are left to resonate ambiguously. It is true that Heidegger speaks of the "truth" and the "meaning" of Being, yet it is also true that he does so in a way that breaks with a traditional philosophic use of these words, for he speaks of a "truth" of Being that is adrift in time, an unfolding unmoored from any determining ground or end, an originary "disclosive" movement that, like the movement Derrida names *différance*, opens the very possibility of any "representation" of the real or of any "judgment" of truth and untruth.

Third, Derrida's slightly gnomic claim that the play of the trace "does not belong" is indeed significant, a mark of his rewriting of Heideggerian lines of thought from within a Heideggerian perspective. However startling his breaks with traditional determinations of truth and meaning, Heidegger, following Hölderlin, remains firmly attached to the notion of an original, prereflective, nonconceptualizable, secretly abiding "belonging" of *Sein* and *Dasein*—"the human being is the shepherd of Being" (PM, 252)—a "belonging" that he nostalgically imagines to have been experienced authentically in pre-Socratic Greek culture and that, he likes to hope, may be discovered anew, in some unforeseeable way, at the end of our nihilist age of the oblivion of Being. This motif runs through all his thought. Inseparable from what Derrida has pointedly called "an entire metaphorics of proximity" (MP, 130), it is a motif that Derrida, whose guiding "metaphors" are very different, has always criticized.

One might naively ask: Why does it matter whether or not *différance* is "older" than the ontic-ontological difference described by Heidegger? It matters in part because Derrida's entire project is decisively shaped by what he calls "Heidegger's uncircumventable meditation" (MP, 22; cf. P, 9–11). While Derrida remains ironically attached to the language of transcendental phenomenology, and while he readily shuttles into the kind of subversive Hegelian discourse developed by Bataille, his essential *point of departure* is neither Bataille's critical account of a restricted economy of meaning, nor any Hegelian marxist account of a spreading grid of reification, but rather Heidegger's account of a history of "onto-theological" philosophy wherein the abyssal temporal movement of Being has remained unthought. He repeats Heidegger's narrative while at the same time enclosing Heidegger himself within his own distinctive displacement of it.[74]

In a review of Derrida's *Specters of Marx*—in fact an illuminating reading of Derrida's entire trajectory—Fredric Jameson has precisely described this "double-movement" that characterizes Derrida's relationship to Heidegger. I cite two passages that appear at some distance from one another in the essay:

> But as an intellectual operation, it was always a crucial necessity for deconstruction to move Heidegger, and in particular Heidegger's view of the

history of metaphysics, centrally into the canon of philosophical reading, to impose Heidegger's problematic inescapably within contemporary philosophy: if only in order, in a second movement, to be able to draw back from Heidegger's own positions and to criticize the essentially metaphysical tendencies at work in them as well.

Not only does it [the deconstructive text] not wish to generate a new philosophical system in the old sense . . . ; it does not lay claim to a "distinctive voice" or an "original set of perceptions." . . .

What saves the day here is the central formal role of the Heideggerian problematic, which assigns a minimal narrative to the entire project, and thus converts an otherwise random series of philosophical texts and fragments into an implicitly grand history: one of metaphysics within philosophy itself. This is the sense in which one might argue that Rorty's project, which effectively destroys philosophy itself as a history and a discipline (and leaves its Samson-like destroyer in the self-trivialized role of an aesthete and a belletrist, when not a merely liberal political and cultural critic and commentator), is more radical than Derrida's, which manages to rescue the discipline in this backdoor Heideggerian manner and thereby to invest its own texts with a certain dignity as moves and positions within a larger theoretical project: after which Heidegger himself . . . can be thrown to the winds and deconstructed as so much metaphysics in his own right.[75]

Derrida, oddly, responds to this reading of his project by evading it:

When Jameson writes that "what saves the day here is the central formal role of the Heideggerian problematic, which assigns a minimal narrative to the entire project," or, again, when he affirms that Rorty's aestheticism . . . is, as aestheticism, more radical than mine, because I arrange "to rescue the discipline secretly in this backdoor Heideggerian manner . . . ," etc., I would merely recall that my mistrust of this "minimal narrative" and Heideggerian axiomatic has been abiding, frequently emphasized, and legible. Everywhere. I even have the unpardonable pretension of thinking that among attentive readers of Heidegger (I cannot say whether there are many of them, but I am trying to be one), I do not know any more reticent than I am in this regard. I will not, then, allow myself to be trapped in the alternative "aestheticism/Heideggerianism."[76]

In these sentences Derrida responds to exactly half of Jameson's argument. Jameson, as the passage I've cited above makes clear, is perfectly aware that Derrida has time and again articulated his "mistrust" of Heidegger's narrative of the history of metaphysics. His claim is that this "mistrust" acquires its significance only through a simultaneous decision to establish Heidegger's narrative as what Derrida himself has called an "uncircumventable meditation" (MP, 22). There seems to be no way that Derrida can plausibly deny this. His simultaneous *adoption* and *critique* of Heidegger's "problematic" is indeed "legible" everywhere in his text.[77]

Jameson's description of Derrida's "ambivalent" relationship to Heidegger reads like a gloss, in particular, on the curiously convoluted shape of Derrida's essay "The Ends of Man" (MP, 109–36). In this essay Derrida presents two arguments that, though they superficially appear at cross-purposes with one another, in fact define the place from which he speaks. On the one hand, he contests the humanist appropriation of Hegel, Husserl, and Heidegger by French existentialist philosophers, drawing attention to everything in these three thinkers that resists any such appropriation. Having made this argument, however, he turns around and draws attention to the ways these thinkers do remain enclosed in a humanist tradition: yet in a humanist tradition now defined, not in conventional terms, but in terms Derrida has adopted from Heidegger's account of the history of metaphysics and the fundamental complicity between metaphysics and humanism. At this point Derrida turns Heidegger's thought against Heidegger himself and, in a reading of the "Letter on Humanism," demonstrates that Heidegger remains embedded in the very tradition he deconstructs. "And if Heidegger has radically deconstructed the domination of metaphysics by the *present,* he has done so in order to lead us to think the presence of the present. But the thinking of this presence can only metaphorize, by means of a profound necessity from which one cannot simply decide to escape, the language that it deconstructs" (MP, 131).

In his reading of the "Letter on Humanism," Derrida concentrates on the dominant "metaphorics of proximity" in Heidegger's text. "And the choice of one or another group of metaphors," Derrida underlines, "is necessarily significant" (MP, 131). Indeed it is. For it is above all through a radically different "group of metaphors" that Derrida has rewritten Heidegger's philosophic adventure, composed an innovative repetition of Heidegger's narrative of the history of philosophy. Where Heidegger speaks of clearing, presencing, and *es gibt,* Derrida speaks of writing, spacing, and *différance.* Where Heidegger speaks of nearness and proximity, the primordial belonging of *Dasein* to *Sein,* Derrida speaks of errancy and dissemination, the abyssal drift of Being and our irreducible exile from presence. Where Heidegger speaks of the proper and the event of appropriation, Derrida speaks of the improper and an originary expropriation. Where Heidegger speaks solemnly of the epochs of Being that have been "sent" in the history of Being, Derrida speaks whimsically of the errant "sending" of postcards whose destination is always open to the drift of the contingent. Where Heidegger seeks to "retrieve" a hidden word of Being, Derrida affirms the multiple words with which we name a temporal movement bearing no essential name. Where Heidegger evokes the way Being addresses us, lays a claim upon us, calls us to our essence as guardians or shepherds of Being, Derrida evokes our wandering in an abyssal play, an abyssal Becoming, from which Being itself emerges. Heidegger's nostalgic metaphorics of *proximity* is displaced by Derrida's anticipatory metaphorics of *errancy.* Heidegger's rural, idyllic language of a *meditative turning toward Being* is displaced by Derrida's cosmopolitan, nomadic language of a *joyous wandering in différance,* "a wandering without return," as he says (WD, 294).[78]

A passage near the conclusion of "The Ends of Man" signals this displacement Derrida carries out—as well as one of its major sources—quite clearly:

> We know how, at the end of *Zarathustra,* at the moment of the "sign," when *das Zeichen kommt,* Nietzsche distinguishes, in the greatest proximity, in a strange resemblance and an ultimate complicity, at the eve of the last separation, of the great Noontime, between the superior man (*höhere Mensch*) and the superman (*Übermensch*). The first is abandoned to his distress in a last movement of pity. The latter—who is not the last man—awakens and leaves, without turning back to what he leaves behind him. He burns his text and erases the traces of his steps. His laughter then will burst out, directed toward a return which no longer will have the form of the metaphysical repetition of humanism, nor, doubtless, "beyond" metaphysics, the form of a memorial or a guarding of the meaning of Being, the form of the house and of the truth of Being. He will dance, outside the house, the *aktive Vergesslichkeit,* the "active forgetting" and the cruel (*grausam*) feast of which the *Genealogy of Morals* speaks. No doubt that Nietzsche called for an active forgetting of Being: it would not have the metaphysical form imputed to it by Heidegger.[79] (MP, 135–36)

Apocalyptic Negativity • 251

My argument, then, is that Derrida rewrites Heidegger by weaving an emphatic Nietzschean perspective into a Heideggerian meditation on time (a Heideggerian thinking of Being as a disclosive movement always already at play in the open drift of time) and a Heideggerian narrative of the history of philosophy (a history of the metaphysics of presence). This Nietzschean perspective can readily be interwoven with other perspectives frequently audible in Derrida's texts of the sixties and seventies, including the voice of an adventurous literary avantgarde and the voice of a transgressive Hegelianism along the lines of Bataille's project. It is, I think, this inventive bringing together of a Heideggerian field of thought, on the one hand, and the Nietzschean and avantgardist currents of a specific cultural field in postwar France, on the other, that largely characterizes Derrida's innovative project as it emerges in the sixties. Heidegger, repeated, is radically reinflected. The thought of *belonging to Being* is turned into the thought of *errancy in Becoming:* thus the path of Derrida's movement away from Heidegger, toward Nietzsche, within a Heideggerian account of the history of metaphysics.[80]

Heidegger's orientation is strongly marked by a romantic concern with healing our alienation from being as a whole. He seeks a revived openess to, a renovated belonging to, the disclosive resonance of "nature" or "being" (in the large sense that poets like Wordsworth and Hölderlin give these terms):

> The granting that sends in one way or another into revealing is as such the saving power. For the saving power lets man see and enter into the highest dignity of his essence. This dignity lies in keeping watch over the unconcealment—and with it, from the first, the concealment—of all coming to presence on this earth.... Only when man, as the shepherd of Being, attends upon the truth of Being can he expect an arrival of a destining of Being and not sink to the level of a mere wanting to know. (QCT, 32, 42)

Beyond the nihilist ruin of the history of ontotheology, which culminates in the technological domination of the earth and human beings, Heidegger seeks a renewed relationship with the movement of Being. Beyond, yet secretly within, the forgetful history of metaphysics there gleams the possibility of a true relationship to the mystery of presencing. "Is there any rescue? Rescue comes when and only when danger *is.* Danger *is* when Being itself advances to its farthest extreme, and when the oblivion that issues from Being itself undergoes reversal" (AF, 58).

Derrida's project, on the other hand, is strongly marked by a romantic concern with extravagant quest (a concern recast in Nietzsche and the twentieth-century avantgarde). The task for thought is not to restore a broken relationship with Being, not to retrieve a buried meaning of Being, but to voyage across a Nietzschean sea of the infinite:

> There will be no unique name, even if it were the name of Being. And we must think this without *nostalgia*, that is, outside of the myth of a purely maternal or paternal language, a lost native country of thought. On the contrary, we must affirm this, in the sense in which Nietzsche puts affirmation into play, in a certain laughter and a certain step of the dance. (MP, 27)

Beyond the "repressions" at work in the history of the metaphysics of presence, beyond the "anxious" evasion of the play of difference (WD, 279), Derrida evokes, in the apocalyptic tones of Nietzsche, a trans-humanist affirmation: "the Nietzschean affirmation, that is, the joyous affirmation of the play of the world and of the innocence of becoming, the affirmation of a world of signs without fault, without truth, and without origin which is offered to an active interpretation. *This affirmation then determines the noncenter otherwise than as loss of the center.* And it plays without security" (WD, 292). Beyond, yet secretly within, the history of metaphysics there gleams an errancy, a promise of freedom, that exceeds all reassuring myths of foundation and closure. It is the call of a passage toward the unforeseeable.

These differences are of course important. Derrida has translated Heidegger in genuinely innovative ways (and thus, among other things, he has re-articulated much that is vital and provocative, while critically sifting through much that is ideologically rotten, in Heidegger). Yet equally important, I think, are at least three concerns that Heidegger and Derrida share. First, they both undertake a radicalized thinking of the mystery of time, a thinking they both take to be inseparable from an exploration of the way any discourse of truth is always already caught up in a groundless play of disclosure and concealment, within which play any "foundationalist" or "representationalist" scheme can only come to be relatively stabilized. Second, they both engage in a deconstruction of the history of philosophy conceived as a sequence of "ontotheological" projects that, in determining Being as presence, have failed to think the abyssal movement of time, signification, and the interplay between time and signification. And third, both, if in different ways, draw on Zarathustra's apocalyptic vision of "going under" and "crossing over." The deconstruction of the history of metaphysics is to disclose an unforeseeable horizon. An apocalyptic and eschatological pulse marks the weaving line running from Nietzsche through Heidegger and Derrida. "As something fateful, Being itself is inherently eschatological," Heidegger writes in his meditation on the Anaximander fragment (AF, 18); as something ineluctable, *différance* is disruptively trans-eschatological, Derrida all but writes in a famous account of the play of time and signification (see MP, 22). Nietzsche, Heidegger, and Derrida all lend voice to a displaced apocalyptic rhetoric that has its roots in ancient apocalyptic and, behind that, in biblical prophecy. I will return to this issue in the concluding section of this chapter.[81]

AT THE END of the first chapter of *Of Grammatology*, Derrida describes Hegel as "the last philosopher of the book and the first thinker of writing" (OG, 26). One can readily imagine him describing Mallarmé in similar terms. "The original opening of interpretation," he writes in an essay on Jabès, "essentially signifies that there will always be rabbis and poets. And two interpretations of interpretation" (WD, 67): the nostalgia of the rabbi and the wandering of the poet, a Hegel of the totalizing book and a Hegel of the movement of writing, a Mallarmé of the architectural book and a Mallarmé of the generalization of rhyme, a Rousseauistic quest for the lost origin and a Nietzschean affirmation of the absence of origins (WD, 292), a Heideggerian meditation on the destined meaning of Being and a Heideggerian meditation on the abyssal drift of Being. In his reading of Mallarmé in "The Double Session," Derrida, expressing an important change of emphasis in the thinking of radical negativity, concentrates on the poet of writing, the mime who discloses the play of dissemination in the house of ideality. Yet perhaps what is most demanding and enigmatic about Mallarmé's poetry, finally, lies in the way it brings together both an art of the book and an art of writing, both a search for fictive pattern and a sounding of ruin.

While all four of the writers I've discussed in this chapter "keep the wound of the negative open," exploring the revelatory falling away of the finite, Mallarmé differs from the others in that his poems bear only a subdued eschatological pulse. There is a strange "stillness" that hovers around his poems, in the margins and between the lines, as though the author of these floating "laces" and vacant "cups" had been permanently marked by his encounter with ruin (O, 54, 74; CP, 3, 80). In his stoic "toasts" to voyage (O, 27, 72; CP, 3, 76), as in his final masterpiece, shipwreck is recognized from the beginning as the inevitable end. And yet, as his most brilliant disciple would write, "il faut tenter de vivre." Mallarmé persists in his effort to articulate the relationship between all our tracings of pattern and the surround of ruin wherein we voyage. Not the least moving quality of his poetry, perhaps, lies in its interweaving of this lucid tragic vision with a worldly spirit of wry urbanity, mobile grace, and elegant stoicism. The pale but smiling "Vasco" of "Au seul souci de voyager" (O, 72; CP, 76), knowing the ruin of night and despair into which he sails, yet holding to the course of his far, if futile, voyage, is among the finest of the various masks Mallarmé has composed for himself. And in this sense—though it may initially sound counterintuitive to say so—Mallarmé is perhaps closer to Beckett than to either Heidegger or Derrida. Like Beckett, he finds himself at once baffled and serene in the face of impasse. Like Beckett, another stoic who finds in the unfolding of syntax a source of calm, he composes patiently measured articulations of ruin. Like Beckett, he often sounds as though he were echoing a tradition of "spiritual exercises" demanding a meditation on death. And, like Beckett, he enacts in his writings a pliant art of sustaining one's poise while falling through dark. These two writers, despite all their unmistakable differences, bear intriguing affinities with one another.[82]

The quiet nocturnal tone of writers like Mallarmé and Beckett is absent from Derrida's essays of the sixties and seventies (including the essay on Mallarmé published in *Dissemination*). Even writers like Bataille and Nietzsche, perhaps closer to Derrida's own theoretical bearings, are selectively echoed in these essays: the surrealist eros and the existentialist anguish of Bataille, like the nausea and the anguish of Zarathustra during his passage through a crisis of nihilism, tend to vanish. In Derrida's explorations of abyssal negativity, one hears above all the song of a liberatory dance. His influential essays of the sixties and seventies, then, express not only a *change of emphasis* but also a *change of affect* in the philosophic encounter with the nothing through which we drift.[83] A passage in "The Ends of Man" signals this change of affect in a subtle but telling way:

> The attention given to system and structure, in its most original and strongest aspects, that is, those aspects which do not immediately fall back into cultural or journalistic gossip, or, in the best of cases, into the purest "structuralist" tradition of metaphysics—such an attention, which is rare, consists neither (a) in restoring their classical motif of the system, which can always be shown to be ordered by *telos, aletheia,* and *ousia,* all

of which are values reassembled in the concepts of essence or of *meaning;* nor (b) in erasing or destroying meaning. Rather, it is a question of determining the possibility of *meaning* on the basis of a "formal" organization which in itself has no meaning, which does not mean that it is either the non-sense or the anguishing absurdity which haunt metaphysical humanism. (MP, 134; cf. P, 86)

The groundlessness that Derrida evokes in this passage, in "post-Saussurean" terms, is not all that far, finally, from either Nietzsche's notion of a groundless play of forces, or Bataille's notion of a nonsensical abyss of negativity that conditions and disrupts meaning, or even Sartre's notion of the "absurd" lack of any metaphysical foundation for a project of meaning. It would seem that the primary difference that Derrida articulates is rather a difference in the attitude adopted toward this abyssal groundlessness. The "death of God," in the broad sense that Nietzsche lends this expression, is now to be experienced not as both a nocturnal crisis and a creative promise but rather as solely an ironic demystification (though the latter itself turns out to be a kind of creative promise). The wry, haunted stoicism sounded in Mallarmé, the interplay of anguish and joy or the intertwining of apocalyptic hope and *amor fati* explored in Nietzsche, the tragic humor voiced in Kafka and Beckett are displaced, as it were, by a wholly detached lucidity and often by the joyous laughter of a certain voice in Nietzsche (see, e.g., WD, 292, and MP, 27, 135–36). Therein lies both a change of affect and a change of emphasis.

Whence these changes? How do the unmistakably tragic motifs traced in Derrida's thought come to be sounded in such emphatically liberatory tones? In part, it would seem, this interweaving of a tragic exploration and a liberatory tone is but an expression of the tendency in modern culture, particularly pronounced in existentialist and postexistentialist philosophies, to experience the destruction of idols as a movement of freedom. Derrida draws on both avantgardist and Nietzschean rhetorics of hyperbole in invoking this path of critical freedom. It is Nietzsche who teaches, more forcefully than any other modern philosopher, that the shedding of our illusions of any authorized foundation or end, or of any ultimate transcendence or truth, is worth all the risks it involves (though Nietzsche himself, at the same time, underlines the severity of these risks). In part, too, this fading of a tragic accent in Derrida's meditations on abyssal negativity may signal, indirectly, that we have simply passed into a later stage in the long collapse in modern culture of any vital religious or metaphysical tradition: perhaps nihilism, at least as a metaphysical question, has lost its power to startle us, to haunt us.[84]

Yet, above all, these changes of emphasis and affect would seem to express a forceful, if indirect, response to a particularly heightened perception—one common to late-twentieth-century culture—of a spreading "iron cage" of instrumental social organization. Perhaps I can clarify this suggestion by addressing to Derrida's discourse the vulgar (though at the same time basic) question that Nietzsche liked to address to everything he read: what is it in many of us that *wants* this discourse to be a persuasive account of the way things are? In 1975, about a decade after Derrida emerged in France as a provocative philosopher, Foucault published *Discipline and Punish: The Birth of the Prison*. The subtitle of this dystopian book, of course, is grimly ambiguous: by the end of the book the birth of the modern prison has become a synecdoche for the birth of modern "disciplinary" society, a society in which human beings are relentlessly "produced" as docile, obedient, normalized, highly productive robots. Every time a screw appears to have been loosened somewhere in the system through an act of reform, Foucault insistently demonstrates, a dozen other screws have been set more firmly in place. There is no exit from this industrious network of panoptic normalization, compared to which Weber's iron cage looks like an English garden. Whether or not the story Foucault's book tells is true, it evokes a nightmare that doubtless haunts many of us in a modern world that often seems to be, at one and the same time, ever more bewildering, ever more organized, ever more madly scheduled, ever further beyond our capacities for meaningful intervention. Reading Derrida, after such a nightmare, can only be a relief: every time a screw is tightened, he teaches no less insistently than Foucault teaches the opposite, another screw has begun to come loose. There is a drift that drifts through things. Undoing, the opening of an opening, is possible. The center (and all its operative structures) cannot hold—not entirely, at least, thanks to the mystery of *différance*. With the aid of a deconstructive push, an errant turning toward the other, the promise of an exit may emerge. And who would not prefer errancy in the abyss of time to death-in-life in the well-organized hell of disciplinary production? Deconstruction invites us to cross the "Desert of the Promise" (WD, 66) for the sake of freedom. It belongs to a tradition, at once ancient and modern, of the myth of exodus. As Derrida affirms in "Circonfession," with a Kierkegaardian irony that tells a truth of some sort, "I will always have been eschatological, so to speak, in the extreme, I am the last of the eschatologists" (CC, 74).[85]

PASSAGES AND QUESTIONS

In this chapter I've sought to show that, in modern culture, the Kierkegaardian practice of "keeping the wound of the negative open" is inseparable from a radical unmooring both of subjectivity and of language from traditional metaphysical grounds. This dual unmooring is one of the defining "events" of modern culture. Kierkegaard and Dickinson explore an exorbitant inwardness in relation to an increasingly hidden God felt (or, one might say, guessed) as absently present in the suffering and longing of negativity. In Dickinson's poetry, this dynamic comes to be traced as at once a volatile errancy of the subject and a volatile errancy of language. The foundering of the finite that for Kierkegaard calls the subject to a hyperbolic venture of faith, a passionate inwardness reaching over a deep of seventy thousand fathoms, for Dickinson calls the subject to a haunted reaching over a similar, if darkened, sea-like deep. In this boundless space words themselves begin to wander and, at times, to depart in free fall. And it is this sort of abyssal opening and this sort of linguistic wandering that both Nietzsche and Mallarmé, writing from a post-Christian perspective, explore in ways that reverberate throughout the poetry and philosophy of the twentieth century. The *romantic* unmooring of subjectivity and the *modernist* unmooring of language, set in motion by the collapse of traditional metaphysical foundations, are events far more intimately intertwined with one another than is suggested by many of our current commonplaces about romanticism, modernism, and postmodernism. These unmoorings, among other things, animate a variegated tradition of modern adventures of the negative.[86]

These unmoorings, further, generate an anticipatory openness toward a variously riddling, empty, obscure, magnetic horizon of the yet to come. The adventure of the negative, in all four of the writers I've discussed in this chapter, tends to be unfolded as a movement of abyssal voyage, and it tends to bear an apocalyptic and eschatological pulse. Even in Mallarmé, whose poems frequently hover in a sort of wavering stillness, there is a trace of this pulse, if only in that reach into the open, however dark, that occurs whenever, in Angelus Silesius's words, "you go where you cannot go."[87] Derrida's discourse of the "ruin of presence" can be read as an inventive turn in a long tradition of prophets and poets who—whether in despair, elation, or both at once—have explored the "ruin of the finite" as bafflingly disclosive, enigmatically promising. "Not only is there no kingdom of *différance* but *différance* instigates the subversion of every kingdom" (MP, 22). This sort of language, as some of Derrida's perceptive readers noted early on, belongs not only to a tradition of modern poetry but also to a tradition of prophetic or apocalyptic expectation within both Judaism and Christianity. The crossing of freedom, according to a tradition reaching back to the biblical prophets, begins with the shattering of the many idols of our bondage, the most hardened of which is doubtless the petty ego centered upon itself. It is a tradition that in modern culture has been reinvented, above all, in passages of the extravagant in romantic and modernist poetry and in critical philosophies written in communication with these passages. And these passages, often voyages of the negative, frequently evoke a movement of exodus, or rather, in a postmetaphysical world lacking pillars of fire and clearly sketched horizons, a movement of the puzzled anticipation of exodus. This movement often sounds like an invocation of some opening toward which we are able to reach only in riddles. Kierkegaard calls it the passion of the infinite. Dickinson figures it as a participation in the mystery and the distance of vanishing. Mallarmé explores it as a virtual death of the poet passing through a ghostly play of words in echo. Derrida characterizes it as the ruin of the present obliquely disclosing the impossible. They are all going where they cannot go. For that (among other reasons) we were given words.

THESE UNMOORINGS I'VE described are inseparable from the question of nihilism as it emerges in the wake of the Enlightenment. Hence Nietzsche is a pivotal figure in this story. In chapter 2 I sketched at least four meanings that the term "nihilism" bears in his thought. Here I wish to recall but two of these: nihilism designates the loss of meaning that occurs with the collapse of traditional metaphysical models while, at the same time, it designates the desperate flight from worldly existence (existence in time) that generated these models in the first place.

These issues are perhaps most fully explored in *Thus Spoke Zarathustra* and *On the Genealogy of Morals*. In the latter, Nietzsche, examining the relationship between religion and philosophy, describes the traditional philosopher as a gloomy creature derived from the ascetic priest: "the ascetic priest provided until the most modern times the repulsive and gloomy caterpillar form in which alone the philosopher could live and creep about" (GM, 116). The philosopher, then, has retained a good deal of the ascetic priest. And the ascetic priest, Nietzsche argues, is an expression of life, in a struggle against death, paradoxically turning against life itself in a desperate effort to preserve life, that is, to salvage a point for living, if only the vital point of "meaning" in the midst of suffering: "the meaninglessness of suffering, *not* suffering itself, was the curse that lay over mankind so far—*and the ascetic ideal offered man meaning!*" (GM, 162). In other words, "life wrestles in and through it [the ascetic ideal] with death and against death; the ascetic ideal is an artifice for the preservation of life" (GM, 120; cf. GM, 62–63). The point for living, then, turns out to be the "elsewhere" that, the ascetic priest hopes, will one day redeem life from its present misery: "the ascetic priest is the incarnate desire to be different, to be in a different place, and indeed this desire at its greatest extreme, its distinctive fervor and passion" (GM, 120). The history of religion and philosophy, from this point of view, is the history of a creative nihilism serving to avert a suicidal nihilism.[88] Unfolding a thought later essential to both Heidegger's and Derrida's projects, Nietzsche characterizes the history of religion and philosophy as a continual effort to find a transcendent "ground" and "end" to existence, an abiding foundation beyond the rending of temporal finitude and the agonistic play of interpretation. What this history evades is the tragic movement of Dionysian Becoming. The overcoming of nihilism, therefore, demands a critical overcoming of this long evasion and a creative passage toward an affirmatively tragic vision of life. This is the path Zarathustra traverses. At the end of the second essay of the *Genealogy,* indeed, Zarathustra is named as the advocate of a vital counterideal to the "ascetic ideal" that informs "priestly" religion and philosophy (GM, 96), while near the end of the third essay Homer is set against Plato as a voice of this counterideal (GM, 153–54). An affirmative transfiguration of existence in time, a creative spirit of *amor fati,* is the way beyond the history of metaphysical flights from time.

Yet Nietzsche, to borrow a line from Derrida, likes to "speak several languages and produce several texts at once" (MP, 135). And his understanding of the relation between the history of religion and philosophy, on the one hand, and his own project of overcoming this history, on the other, is more complex than the sketch above suggests. As he makes clear in the *Genealogy,* the history of metaphysics, whatever its basis in fear and evasion, has been truly creative. For if the long "internalization of man" (GM, 84) has produced in us an illness, an inward reactivity of the sort later studied in detail by Freud, it has at the same time produced in us a spiritual depth and power that might not have emerged in any other way: "the existence on earth of an animal soul turned against itself, taking sides against itself, was something so new, profound, unheard of, enigmatic, contradictory, and *pregnant with a future* that the aspect of the earth was essentially altered" (GM, 85; cf. GM, 33). In the *Genealogy,* then, Nietzsche develops a dialectical figure of thought (though this often goes unrecognized): our present is said to embody the promise of a future that, potentially, will at once negate, retain, and surpass our present. The only way to a greater health or a more abundant life, Nietzsche suggests, is through a creative activity that at once assumes and transforms our complex history of repressive inwardization.

A dialectical movement of this sort is dramatically presented in *Zarathustra*. As I sought to show in chapter 2, Zarathustra comes to recognize, at the very moment he has made his most powerful speech on the dynamic of creative self-overcoming, that something of the ascetic priest is present in himself, that the ancient religious vision of voyaging toward a different place animates his own apocalyptic vision of going under and crossing over (Z, 137–42). Seeking to destroy all previous biblical interpretations of life, Zarathustra finds himself proposing yet another variation on them. His apocalyptic rhetoric of going under and crossing over belongs, in important respects, to the biblical tradition he would like to destroy. Yet he recognizes at the same time that to abandon this vision is to risk sinking into the passive nihilism that he discerns in the blank, spiteful, industrious "last men" who mock his longings. There is a nihilism of dull resignation as well as a nihilism of reactive evasion. Nietzsche, like Zarathustra, if read beyond a set of polemical slogans, teaches that there is no simple path between these poles. Creative *amor fati*, a bearing able to navigate this tension, sustaining both the élan of creative crossing and the spirit of tragic affirmation, is a bearing to be renewed again and again in a creative life, not a bearing either simply given or attained once and for all.[89]

THERE WOULD SEEM to be various reasons why Heidegger's and Derrida's philosophic projects have been so influential. They resonate with the "anti-instrumental" or "de-reifying" themes shaping the art and philosophy of the last two centuries. They resonate, too, with the "antifoundationalist" and "anti-essentialist" themes pervasive in contemporary thought. And they involve critical engagements with Nietzsche's thinking of nihilism. Heidegger and Derrida are among the most original thinkers to have wrestled with Nietzsche's provocative explorations of nihilism, the history of philosophy, and the possibility of overcoming metaphysics.

How do Heidegger and, in his wake, Derrida respond to Nietzsche's multidimensional thinking of nihilism? The originality of Heidegger's rewriting of the history of philosophy lies not least in his decision to situate the modern philosophy of the subject—from Descartes through Kant and the long aftermath of German idealism—within the tradition of metaphysics. Substance becomes subject, Heidegger argues, but this only radicalizes the "nihilist" oblivion of Being characteristic of the tradition of "substance" philosophy. Nietzsche's prophetic teaching of the will to power—at once the apotheosis and the explosion of humanism—is but a desperate voice at the end of the line. This innovative story allows Heidegger to interpret Nietzsche's thought as not a critical overcoming but rather a nihilist completion of the history of metaphysics: a history now characterized less as a dream of escaping finitude and temporality than as a ruinous forgetting of the mystery of Being. Derrida, while he follows Heidegger in enclosing the modern philosophy of the subject in metaphysics, turns Nietzschean themes of abyssal becoming and perspectival interpretation against Heidegger himself.

Both of these accounts of the "metaphysics of presence" draw on Nietzsche's interpretation of religion and philosophy. Yet both tend to occlude some of the complexities at play in the latter. As I noted above, Heidegger and Derrida, in very different ways, echo Zarathustra's rhetoric of going under and crossing over, or, put another way, Nietzsche's project of the destruction of idols (later to become deconstruction) and the transvaluation of values (later to become the overcoming of metaphysics). Yet this ambitious project, as Zarathustra recognizes at a turning point in his drama, is itself a displaced apocalyptic project that borrows from the biblical tradition it seeks to surpass. And it is this ancient, enduring, multivalent biblical tradition that Heidegger and Derrida echo no less than Nietzsche does. Heidegger and Derrida, that is, deconstruct "the metaphysics of presence" in part by drawing on different versions of a variously displaced religious tradition whose matrix, at once distant and abiding, at once distant and multiply translated in time, is the myth of exodus. It is a myth that, throughout history, has been variously cast in prophetic, apocalyptic, eschatological, and gnostic or "inner light" terms. It has been at least as influential in the history of Western culture as the metaphysics of presence. And, while it has often been linked to the conceptual networks of Greek philosophy, it is not identical with them. *The desire to be different or to be in a different place* is not always, and not necessarily, the same as *the desire to secure a pure presence or to find an unchanging ground* (though orthodoxy tends to insist on this conflation). The myth of promise is not always, and not necessarily, the myth of foundation. It is not clear that either the Jewish tradition, or the Christian tradition, has been primarily or solely a foundationalist quest. At their most vital moments, at least, or at their dynamically heterodox moments, both of these traditions have been a search for a Promised Land, a Restored

Jerusalem, a Kingdom of Heaven, a New Jerusalem, a redemptive turning, an awakening of spirit in a movement of crossing.[90]

THE MYTH OF exodus, the shaping story of both the Jewish Bible and the Christian Bible, is one of the oldest myths of Western culture. The prophets of Judah, interpreting the experience of exile and return as a repetition of the national myth of enslavement in and exodus from Egypt, gave this myth the shape it now has in the Bible and, at the same time, articulated a certain "individualizing" of the myth that would be variously elaborated within both the normative Jewish and the normative Christian traditions of the Common Era. "In every age," as an ancient rabbi said, "man must see himself as if he himself went out of Egypt."[91] During the intertestamental period, on the margins of Jewish culture, apocalyptic emerged as a kind of exacerbated and otherworldly rewriting of Jewish prophetic discourse. "If European philosophy can be described as a series of footnotes to Plato, as Alfred North Whitehead put it, Jewish apocalypticism, and substantially also Western apocalypticism, may be conceived as footnotes to the apocalyptic visions of Daniel and the drama of redemption described in Exodus."[92] The apocalyptic translation of earlier prophetic discourse forcefully shaped the eschatological teaching of Jesus. And early Christians, effecting yet another displacement, transposed this teaching into Christological terms strongly influenced by the "interiorizing" and "gnosticizing" dynamics of Hellenistic mystery religions. For two thousand years, in these and other forms, a distant prophetic current, though often forced underground, though often driven beyond the boundaries of orthodoxy, has remained a vital current in Western culture. The call of a crossing over, a call of promise, returns again and again, whether in an outward "historical" mode or in an inward "quasi-gnostic" mode. As there is always a place of unfreedom, a condition of exile, a time of despair before an empty tomb, a world in decay, a life at a loss, so there is always a longing for this call, felt as the wound of the negative, "in wounds pledged once to hope—cleft to despair" (Hart Crane). Often, it is true, as Kierkegaard and others have made clear, this wound has to be startled open again, since often, in protecting ourselves, we destroy ourselves, enclose ourselves in a dimness we mistake for light.

In the modern period, with the waning of traditional metaphysical models and the fading of faith in a promised elsewhere, this vision of crossing over has been recast in a range of displaced and fractured modes, particularly in the wanderings of modern poetry. Further, as I hope to have shown in this chapter, it has often been reinvented in errant adventures of the negative, abyssal voyages in the dark. This apocalyptic bearing also animates, in very different ways, the thought of three of the most influential iconoclasts of the nineteenth century, Kierkegaard, Marx, and Nietzsche. And through these philosophers, and through multiple voices in romantic and modernist poetry, the variously displaced myth of exodus then travels into ample domains of twentieth-century Continental philosophy. This, I think, is the vital background of numerous twentieth-century "philosophic critiques of philosophy"—including those of Bloch, Adorno, Heidegger, Bataille, and Derrida, among others—that transmit (translate yet again) resonant, if elusive, religious echoes. The story of a history of the metaphysics of presence, like any sweeping story, is necessarily selective. It doesn't tell the whole story of the history of Western metaphysics. The myth of exodus—a polemical, often desperate, almost inevitably open-ended "metaphysic" of the passage from an erosion of life in unfreedom toward a renovation of life in freedom—has always accompanied the metaphysics of presence. It is still with us, in very powerful ways, though it has gradually come to be sounded primarily in languages that echo negative theology or, rather, glide toward negative atheology. Perhaps these riddles of the negative are our slanted prayers, our minimalist passages of the extravagant, in gray hours of doubt and bewilderment. Montale, in the opening poem of his great sequence of "Motets," recalls in fractured echoes both the lost pilgrim of *The Inferno* and some darkened troubadour searching for the lost sign of a crossing:

> Lo sai: debbo riperderti e non posso.
> Come un tiro aggiustato mi sommuove
> ogni opera, ogni grido e anche lo spiro
> salino che straripa
> dai moli e fa l'oscura primavera
> di Sottoripa.
>
> Paese di ferrame e alberature
> a selva nella polvere del vespro.
> Un ronzío lungo viene dall'aperto,
> strazia com'unghia ai vetri. Cerco il segno
> smarrito, il pegno solo ch'ebbi in grazia
> da te.
>   E l'inferno è certo.

[You know: I must leave you again and I can't.
Like a well-targeted shot, every effort,
every cry, unsettles me, even the salt
breeze overflowing
from the quays that make Sottoripa's
springtime so dark.

Land of ironworks and masts
forested in the dust of evening.
A long humming comes from open space,
scratches like a fingernail on glass. I search for the lost
sign, the only pledge I had
of your grace.
                    And hell is certain.][93]

    We dwell in echoes. Yet have people not always, in all times and places, sought to find their way amid a range of echoes? "And when the evening was come, he was there alone. But the ship was now in the midst of the sea, tossed with waves: for the wind was contrary. And in the fourth watch of the night Jesus went unto them, walking on the sea" (Matthew 14.24–25). So the ancient Israelites crossed a water of ruin on their way to freedom, guided by the same creative force that, in speaking, had originally brought into being a creation against the waters of chaos. So Jesus crossed a water of death on his way to a coming renovation, recalling a miraculous passage of one of the earliest of the ancient prophets, Elijah. And so, perhaps, we dwell in another wilderness, an industrial *selva oscura*, searching again, as always, among the long and varied echoes of such crossings, reaching in the dark, as if to go where we cannot go.[94]

CONCLUSION

The Dialectic of Instrumental Society and Creative Negativity

PASSAGES OF THE EXTRAVAGANT,
PASSAGES OF THE NEGATIVE

In this book I've sought to illuminate important currents of a broad tradition of passages of the extravagant in modern poetry and philosophy. Passages of the extravagant are passages of disclosive wandering that tend to be postbiblical in spirit, seeking not a return to a lost home so much as a renovative crossing elsewhere, a metamorphic translation. And these passages, displaced and rearticulated religious dynamics, emerge in modern culture above all in the adventures of modern poetry from the romantic period through the aftermath of the modernist period.

Modern philosophy, too, has continually wrestled with earlier religious traditions that have shaped its guiding questions. In fact, as Derrida has noted, a number of influential modern philosophic projects can be read as nondogmatic echoes of religious discourses they at once repeat and evade:

> If one takes into account certain differences, the same can be said [as has just been said for Jan Patocka's work] for many discourses that seek in our

> day to be religious—discourses of a philosophical type if not philosophies themselves—without putting forth theses or *theologems* that would by their very structure teach something corresponding to the dogmas of a given religion. The difference is subtle and unstable, and it would call for careful and vigilant analyses. In different respects and with different results, the discourses of Levinas or Marion, perhaps of Ricoeur also, are in the same situation as that of Patocka. But in the final analysis this list has no clear limit and it can be said, once again taking into account the differences, that a certain Kant and a certain Hegel, Kierkegaard of course, and I might even dare to say for provocative effect, Heidegger also, belong to this tradition that consists of proposing a non-dogmatic doublet of dogma, a philosophical and metaphysical doublet, in any case a thinking that "repeats" the possibility of religion without religion.[1]

One could surely add other names to the list Derrida provides. Modern philosophy, like ancient philosophy, comes to self-consciousness in an ambiguous twilight, at once dusk and dawn, reworking a range of questions shaped by earlier religious traditions it can never simply leave behind. Further, modern critical philosophies in which these displaced religious discourses make themselves heard, in particular from the middle of the nineteenth century on, have usually been those which have been in close communication with modern poetries. For romantic and modernist poetries are the preeminent force fields in which displaced religious dynamics have been explored in modern culture.[2]

Throughout this book, then, I've been working with a version of the "secularization" or "reoccupation" thesis, according to which modern poetries emerge out of efforts to recast in terms of immanent human orientations the sorts of powers and dynamics once articulated in religious terms of transcendence, awakening, conversion, renovation, spiritual metamorphosis. Hence the importance in these poetries of what in the introduction, drawing on Rilke and Frye, I characterized as a "kerygmatic" imperative: "you must change your life." Hence the search in these poetries to bring about a metamorphosis of language that at once manifests and provokes a metamorphosis of existential orientation. And hence the emphasis in these poetries on the ways in which an exploration of creative *process,* a release of visionary or inventive *power,* and a sounding of variously evoked fields of *otherness* promise a surpassing of the normative social and psychic boundaries of an increasingly instrumentalized modern world. The search is for passages opened by "the transhumance of the word" (René Char).

Hence, too, the endless predicaments and darkened turns of poetries in this tradition. For no translation of "supernatural" into "natural" or "human" dynamics of metamorphosis can occur without a range of collisions and crises: the dove of eros and rebeginning, as Stevens writes in a late poem, "howls / Of the great sizes of an outer bush / And the great misery of the doubt of it."[3] Perhaps this sort of translation is finally impossible, and poetries of the extravagant, in numerous skewed ways, can but draw the impossible a touch nearer the possible. For these poetries inevitably encounter—with fewer resources, so to speak, than were available in earlier times and places—the limits of our finitude and mortality. They inevitably collide with all those reality principles that organize modern liberal, utilitarian, instrumental societies. They necessarily internalize, often in volatile ways, the skeptical stance characteristic of post-Enlightenment modernity. And, indeed, a return to despair, followed by a purgatorial passage through despair, is one of the curves most frequently traced in these poetries—poetries that begin by seeking a surpassing of the "quiet desperation" that, according to Thoreau, shrouds our lives when a power of metamorphic passage fades from them. Lacking this élan, we are only the scattered ruins Zarathustra sees around and within him. The restless drama of continual displacement, crisis, and reinvention characteristic of modern poetry emerges, to a large extent, out of the unceasing collision between this provocative project of translation and its sheer unlikeliness in the world of capitalist modernity. It is thus a project continually taken up anew from another place, another perspective, under increasingly unpromising circumstances.

Modern Continental philosophies seem to have been drawn to these passages of the extravagant—provoked into an effort to translate yet again their already translated dynamics—for a variety of reasons. First, these poetries are emphatic expressions of what is perhaps the preeminent, if perilous, modern ideal, namely, what Charles Taylor has called "radical freedom," perhaps *the* promise of modernity, and one that, at least if the major novelists of the last two centuries are to be believed, our society has realized in only partial and highly ambiguous ways.[4] Further, seeking a movement and a power of metamorphosis, these passages of the extravagant reaffirm the modern ideal of freedom while criticizing the way critical reason and creative freedom tend, in modern society, to become subordinate to mechanical reason and instrumental social organization. It is significant, then, that critical philosophies begin to borrow from these passages in particular as the nineteenth-century historicist faith in science, progress, and the rational reconstruction of society comes to erode— a gradual process of dissolution that leads, in the wake of Nietzsche, to the apocalyptic sensibility traversing European culture throughout the first half of the twentieth century. Finally, as traditional metaphysical models slowly wane throughout the modern period, these poetries of the extravagant, having always pursued the unpredictable drift of language into the darkest reaches of our experience, are found to have already voyaged far through fields of otherness beyond our conventional frames of positive knowledge. They sound not only the nothing wherein we drift but also enigmatic places and forces that promise an indirect surpassing of the limits of an increasingly functionalized world. These are among the major bearings these poetries share with the field of twentieth-century critical philosophies, a field that, for this reason, often reads like a multidimensional meditation on various forces or events irreducible to conventional models of representation. The concern shared by poetries and philosophies in this tradition has been to find concealed forces of freedom, unsuspected horizons of life, elusive places of significance promising a resistance to what we and our world have become. When asked to linger where he has arrived, René Char writes, the poet "responds that he belongs to the country *just to the side*, to the sky that has just gone dark."[5]

Ever since the French Revolution, of course, the trends repeatedly contested by these passages have only continued to expand their sway over every sphere of the modern world. And this would seem to be the primary reason why these passages, in both poetry and philosophy, gradually tend toward an emphasis on the promise of errant negativity or disjunctive indeterminacy. In this book I've thus argued that a dialectic of instrumental schematization and creative negativity has been at work throughout modern culture. Before again taking up in general terms the unfolding of this dialectic in modern culture, perhaps I should briefly recall the arguments I've made in each of these chapters.

In the first chapter I've brought together Kant, Wordsworth, and Lyotard, exploring the way the sublime has been variously conceived from the romantic through the modernist period and the latter's aftermath in post-structuralist thought. Across the entire span of this tradition, the sublime has been understood to involve a strange encounter that momentarily dislocates the subject from the imperatives of theoretical cognition and the habits of the everyday self of instrumental action. Kant and Wordsworth, elaborating versions of a familiar "high romantic" sublime, understand this initial dislocation to stir a subsequent recovery, a countermovement of awakened power. Yet Wordsworth, I've argued, is more attentive than Kant to the potential solipsism involved in this sort of solitary discovery of creative power. *The Prelude* poignantly shows that there is no untroubled link between the experience of awakened power (a power discovered along a path of existential self-formation) and the call of duty or response (a call heard in the common domain of ethical and political relationship). Lyotard, in the first of the two phases of his work that I've traced, elaborates an unmistakably late romantic or Nietzschean account of the "modernist" or "avantgardist" sublime, one that associates the sublime with the creative power manifest in innovative works of art—works that bring into being languages and perspectives that at once disrupt and exceed the normative frameworks of the contexts in which they appear. The romantic theme of creative power is thus retained while being routed through a modernist vocabulary of technical élan and formal inventiveness. Yet, in a later phase of his work, Lyotard abandons Nietzsche and, in his place, draws variously and at times indistinctly on Adorno, Blanchot, Levinas, and, above all, Heidegger, elaborating an account of the modernist sublime that retains the initial moment of the romantic sublime, the decentering of the subject, while canceling the second moment, the recovery or reassertion of the subject. The sublime, in this account, is understood to involve an encounter that, in deposing the subject without stirring any countermovement of a Kantian or Nietzschean sort, leaves the subject quietly open to an indeterminate alterity. This subdued turning toward the drift of the indeterminate is conceived as the precarious promise of genuine freedom and genuine openness to fields of otherness in a society that, it is feared, operates by gradually colonizing all difference, programming its subjects to function as efficient schematizers of all that we encounter. Yet Lyotard's severe shift from a Nietzschean to a Heideggerian account of the sublime involves a decided neglect of the sort of troubled, ambiguous, ambivalent path *between* these two perspectives that a poet like Wordsworth explores. It is almost as though Lyotard had "overreacted" to the dynamic hyperbole of his earlier Nietzschean or avantgardist phase of thought. And in this sense, I've argued, the later Lyotard's thought is characterized by a failure to engage a fundamental *tension* that has always been at play in the exploration of the sublime, the tension between an interest in creative power and freedom, on the one hand, and an interest in ethical obligation or responsiveness, on the other. Lyotard backs himself into a position in which he is unable to thematize or avow, and so unable to take responsibility for, his own interest in creative power. The quite reasonable fear of the longing for such power—given the vastations that released powers have produced over the last century—seems to have led him to the less reasonable (as well as less imaginative) concealment of both the reality and the implications of that longing.[6]

In the second chapter I've examined three writers who, in their vision of creative destruction and destructive creation, belong to a romantic tradition of Faustian revolt guided by a search for a transformative widening of the boundaries of our experience. Rimbaud, Nietzsche, and Bataille, in pursuing this quest, affirm volatile dynamics of destruction and metamorphosis, variously conceived as anarchist disorientation and visionary disclosure (in Rimbaud), critical demystification and creative transformation (in Nietzsche), and vehement dislocation and ecstatic freedom (in Bataille). But this tradition undergoes a severe mutation in Bataille parallel to the mutation that the tradition of the romantic and modernist sublime undergoes in Lyotard. In Blake, as later in surrealism, the disruptive energies of the Devil or Orc are dialectically swept up into the creative energies of the Poetic Genius or Los. In Rimbaud, the dislocative forces of alchemical *dérèglement* are dialectically gathered into the visionary forces of metamorphic *harmonie*. In Nietzsche, the "destructive" practice of smashing idols is dialectically linked to the "constructive" practice of projecting transformative counterhorizons. In Bataille, however, the second moment of these Faustian quests almost entirely vanishes: demonic ruin becomes, in itself, the movement of freedom. Fearing that earlier romantic and modernist passages of destruction and transformation have themselves become complicit with the flattened world of instrumentally organized practices and discourses, Bataille understands creative transcendence and radical freedom to be virtually identical with the subversive energies of irrecuperable negativity (negativity that cannot be "put to work" in any sort of transformative project). Blake's antinomian Devil becomes, so to speak, the whole story. Yet this exacerbated story of rapturous dislocation, I've argued, expresses a kind of desperate fading or thinning of the far more expansive dialectical visions developed at earlier points in this tradition. And a voice akin to Bataille's, as I underlined at the end of chapter 2, can be clearly heard throughout the field of contemporary thought, both in many post-structuralist theories and in various postmodernist discourses. Yet, again, these recent Bataille-like discourses tend to evade the provocative, ranging, multidimensional challenge of thinkers like Blake, Rimbaud, Nietzsche, and many writers in their wake. It is as though the volatile play of errant negativity had become our late and reduced ideal.

Finally, the third chapter has brought together four apocalyptic writers who, well practiced in "keeping the wound of the negative open," explore a groundless negativity that conditions, unsettles, and exceeds our schemes of positive knowledge and clear and distinct representation. I've placed these four writers within a single constellation in part to show that the unmooring of subjectivity from traditional metaphysical frames, typically associated with romanticism and registered in the exorbitant inwardness explored by Kierkegaard and Dickinson, and the unmooring of language from pretextual grounds, typically associated with modernism and registered in the enigmatic movement of writing explored by Mallarmé and Derrida, are in fact events far more intimately connected with one another than many of our commonplaces about romanticism, modernism, and postmodernism suggest. It is the waning of traditional metaphysical models, the unmooring of both subjectivity and signification consequent upon this waning, and the displaced religious longing for metamorphic passage beyond the limits of secular modernity that connect, in a long arc forming one of the major dramas of modern culture, the "romantic" and the "modernist" emphases of this tradition. Indeed, Kierkegaard, Dickinson, and Mallarmé, like Rimbaud and Nietzsche, are exact seismographs of that transitional moment in modern culture where romanticism, while resonantly abiding, turns into modernism.

These intertwined unmoorings animate a range of modern adventures of apocalyptic negativity. The apocalyptic translation of the myth of exodus, as I've underlined at different points throughout this book, traverses all of modern culture, at times in volatile political modes, often in internalized, quasignostic, or inner-light modes. All four of the writers I study in this chapter lend voice to this apocalyptic bearing in modern culture. And the dialectic of instrumental reason and creative negativity that I trace in other chapters of the book, then, necessarily unfolds in an oblique way in this tradition of the extravagant, for it is in the very nature of an apocalyptic bent of thought to concentrate on the disclosive force of unbound negativity. Yet in Derrida's work, I've argued, there occurs a subtle but telling change of affect in the exploration of the nothing through which we drift, a change marked above all by the absence in his writings of the tragic accents so audible in earlier explorers of abyssal negativity, including Kierkegaard, Dickinson, Mallarmé, Rimbaud, Nietzsche, Bataille, Kafka, and Beckett, among others. Derrida replaces this tragic mood with an ironic and liberatory mood. And this change of affect appears to be linked as well to a change of emphasis in Derrida's thinking of negativity. Kant and Wordsworth understand the sublime to involve a double movement, a forceful dislocation of the subject followed by a forceful reawakening of the subject, whereas Lyotard retains the first moment, the dislocation, while canceling the second moment, the reawakening. Rimbaud and Nietzsche pursue Faustian quests in which the destructive and the constructive bearings are dialectically held together, whereas Bataille abandons the second of these bearings to the world of one-dimensional projects, decisively affirming the former (a movement of ecstatic ruin) as the movement of radical freedom. In a similar way Dickinson and Mallarmé bring together both a practice of sounding a groundless negativity and a practice of constructing fictions of speculative reach, whereas Derrida tends to turn away from horizons of ideality (of conceptual or fictive space) in order to emphasize the movement of an errant negativity opening a wholly indeterminate expectation. The adventure of the negative reaches a kind of rarefied extreme in the "messianism without content" (SM, 65) elaborated in Derrida's project.

The experience of the sublime, the Faustian quest for radical metamorphosis, and the apocalyptic sounding of abyssal negativity, then, are the three major currents of the tradition of the extravagant that I've examined in this book. Passages of the extravagant, in each of these currents, emerge as displaced articulations of earlier religious discourses in a world of postmetaphysical skepticism and pervasive instrumental social organization. What is sought in these passages, in all their diversity, is a metamorphic surpassing of the conventional boundaries of experience established by the dominant social structures and discursive frames of secular, empiricist, utilitarian, technocapitalist modernity. Repeatedly, however, given the dominant trends of the modern world, these passages lead to severe collisions and crises, in response to which they are later revised, recast, and yet further displaced. From this process emerge the defining discontinuities in this tradition. Over time, thus, the romantic valorization of creative freedom, imaginative power, and visionary metamorphosis turns into the modernist valorization of formal inventiveness, self-reflexive difficulty, elliptical composition, and multiperspectival complexity. And still later, in what I've characterized as the last phase or theoretical aftermath of modernism, these modernist orientations turn into the post-structuralist fascination with the disruptive materiality of language, the errant "spacing" of signification, and the wandering play of the negative in general. It is the unfolding of this dialectic that I've traced in each of the main chapters in this book. As the dominant instrumental structures of capitalist modernity have increasingly penetrated every zone of social and psychic life, producing an array of dehumanizing effects studied by every modern social theorist, the poetries and philosophies that have critically resisted these trends have repeatedly been pressured to negate and surpass, in one way or another, those earlier voices and visions in their traditions that have lost (or at least seemed to lose) their initial contestatory and transformative power. And so these adventures, "sprouting erasures" (John Ashbery), repeatedly turning away from inherited practices of writing perceived to have been subsumed by instrumental schemes, have over time turned into paradoxical discourses of the negative or riddling practices of the disjunctive.

Our currently prevalent discourses of undoing and unmaking, dislodging and dislocating, deconstructing and decentering are late, troubled soundings of the promise of freedom and fullness of life in a world that, from Weber through Foucault, has often been perceived as a spreading cage of functionalist rationalization. And, too, as I've sought to show, they are late, wayward soundings of displaced religious dynamics that our culture has at once abandoned and, ultimately, refused to abandon. For these variously displaced dynamics, from the romantic period through the present, have animated many of our culture's most powerful voices of dissatisfaction with the obstacles to our freedom and the wreckings of life we find around and within us. In our current allegiance to the dislocative promise of the negative, however, we may have finally backed ourselves into a serious predicament: a faith in the disruptive unaccompanied by a faith in the creative, a power to unsettle the leaden structures of our world divorced from a power to project counterpremonitions, or counterhorizons, of sufficient depth and texture to draw us a little beyond ourselves and our many practical, linguistic, and subjective prisons. A ghostly rhetoric of the negative seems to have become a late, baffled, desperate song of hope.

ROMANTIC MODERNISM CONTRA INSTRUMENTAL MODERNIZATION

At this point I would like to step back and attempt to situate this modern dialectic of instrumental reason and creative negativity in a larger context. My concern is with the way different currents in the broad tradition of the extravagant have gradually come to involve less a twofold dynamic of critical dislocation and exploratory refiguration than a loosely anarchic dynamic of open-ended dislocation.

To a large extent, as Charles Taylor argues in his *Hegel and Modern Society,* modern culture has been profoundly shaped by the ambivalent response of romanticism to the Enlightenment. Romantic writers reaffirm the Enlightenment ideal of critical freedom from external authority and, in this sense, they wholly participate in the spirit of the French Revolution. At the same time, however, they criticize both the post-Enlightenment tendency to replace premodern forms of external authority with insidious modern forms of external authority—one recalls those wheels that, for Blake, figure a mechanical reason coming to dominate social and psychic life—as well as the social atomization and psychic fragmentation generated by the emergence of industrial capitalist modernity. Thus modern culture, in the wake of romanticism, has been significantly shaped by a tension between the ideal of "radical freedom" and the ideal of "expressive integrity," a longing for creative independence and a longing for existential wholeness, a Kantian emphasis on individual self-legislation and a Hegelian emphasis on social reconciliation, or, as I occasionally characterized this tension in my discussion of Wordsworth in chapter 1, a search for creative departure and a search for relational embeddedness. Wordsworth's poetry, indeed, is emblematic in the way it hovers in the midst of these larger cultural tensions. Yet many modern poetries, in particular those I've characterized as passages of the extravagant, while they bear a utopian valence pointing toward a horizon of restored psychic and social wholeness, initially manifest, in their metamorphic crossing of common boundaries, a movement of imaginative freedom. Therein lies a source of their great power and of many of their predicaments.

These contradictory responses to the conditions of modernity continue to shape the artistic, political, and philosophic discourses of the first half of the twentieth century. While a poet like Breton experiences a prison of instrumental repression and routinization and so affirms a countervision of metamorphic freedom, a poet like Eliot experiences a wasteland of rending atomization and alienation and so affirms (or sighs for) a countervision of social reconciliation and existential wholeness. And, as Richard Sheppard underlines, the most influential modern sociologists after Marx, Emile Durkheim and Max Weber, closely echo these contradictory responses to modernity explored in romantic and modernist literature:

> It is . . . worth pointing out that sociology, which grew out of the experience of modernity, found itself in exactly the same situation as literature and the arts. . . . Like the writers and artists [of this period], sociologists around the turn of the century were grappling with two experiences and ways of understanding modernity. At one pole of the debate, Emile Durkheim . . . analyzed modernity in terms of the feeling of entropic chaos, anomie, which was induced by modernity's destruction of traditional communities and which Elsen explicitly connects with Rodin's *La Porte de l'Enfer*. At the other pole, Max Weber saw modernity turning into a "de facto

unbreakable shell," "a shell which is hard as steel," "a shell for the new serfdom," "a steel shell of modern industrial labor," and "a shell of that bondage which is to come."[7]

Already in the modernist period, however, the Weberian story, quickly re-elaborated in very different ways in Lukács's *History and Class Consciousness* and Heidegger's *Being and Time*, begins to acquire the prominence it has held throughout the last century. Yet perhaps this primacy of the Weberian story is already implicit in the ambivalent romantic response to industrial capitalist modernity. For romantic thinkers—whether "humanists" like Schiller or "apocalypticists" like Blake—tend to interpret the experience of social disintegration and psychic fragmentation as itself, ultimately a condition brought about by the hypertrophy of instrumental reason characteristic of modernity: the dominance of a formalizing rationality detached from a broader vision of a fully realized life, or, as this plays itself out on the existential plane, the dominance of a debased reason whose "mind-forg'd manacles" govern the defensive stance of the everyday ego. Romantic writers, in their fear that everything and everyone on the planet will be reduced to objectified means in an anonymous system of production, are prescient. And the issue, finally, is not "reason" itself, whatever the philosophers may have to say about this, since "reason" in a broad sense is usually considered a potential to be recommended in the conduct of life, but rather what the hypertrophy of a functionalist rationality has done to life in a global system in which (as Immanuel Wallerstein puts it) production for the sake of an endless accumulation of capital is the foremost priority. This system organizes the world more fully at present than it organized it two hundred or even a hundred years ago.

At any rate, Weber's story, often attached to either Marxist or Nietzschean themes, becomes the dominant story that informs many influential poetries and critical philosophies in the wake of romanticism. Robert Pippin has concisely captured this defining shift in modern culture whereby a romantic ambivalence toward the *contradictions* of modernity slides toward a modernist opposition to the *cage* of modernity: "Heidegger . . . continues the great shift in philosophically inspired criticism of modern culture that began with Nietzsche; away from the Hegelian problems of alienation and fragmentation, the lack of any 'ethical place' *within* modernized societies, to a different though connected concern with mass culture 'absorption,' herd mentality, conformism, homogenization; with the absence of any ethical place *outside* such routinized wholes."[8] I would add to Pippin's observation that major early voices of the shift he describes include, in addition to Nietzsche's, those of Kierkegaard, Emerson, Rimbaud, and Mallarmé, among others. And all of these writers, significantly, draw heavily on critical bearings developed in earlier romantic projects. The shift occurring in the poetries and philosophies of the extravagant in the middle of the nineteenth century, then, is an important development in the dialectic of instrumental society and creative negativity traversing modern culture. The romantic responses to the dominant orientations of enlightened capitalist modernity are, at this point, put under great stress. Kierkegaard's mobile, ironic, digressive writing is motivated by a concern to startle readers who, he fears, "have forgotten what it means to exist as human beings." Rimbaud, experiencing modern society as a reductive system of disciplinary labor, repeatedly invokes, in volatile language, an apocalyptic renovation of the world under the open sky of freedom, suggesting that words themselves have to be swept open if psychic freedom and existential wholeness are to be found. "It seemed to me that to every being several *other* lives were owed." He, and many in his wake, depart in search of these other lives and languages.

This exacerbated romantic orientation animates the entire field of modernist and avantgardist culture. The crisis of historicism grows acute around the turn of the century. The destruction brought about by the First World War, on the one hand, and what Perry Anderson has aptly called "the imaginative proximity of revolution," on the other, produce an apocalyptic climate of fear and expectation, collapse and promise. And the second industrial revolution, while stirring utopian hopes, at the same time heightens fears of the sort expressed in Weber's narrative of a spreading iron cage. This interwar climate of crisis is the generative matrix of a great deal of twentieth-century art and philosophy.

Modernist poetries, then, articulate further displacements of romantic poetries of the extravagant under circumstances increasingly at odds with any such projects. They also retain the romantic concern to explore creative processes irreducible to conventional frames of positive knowledge or direct representation (indeed this concern comes to guide modernist novels as well). Modernist poems, more emphatically than romantic poems, demand a patient reenactment of their processes of patterning—they must be undergone from the inside—insofar as they are meant to suspend and then transform abstract habits of reading and reified forms of understanding, in short, to jar the mind to life and reach again through a "dislocation" (as Eliot puts it) of familiar patterns of making sense. There is thus no simple break between romantic and modernist poetries. What occurs, rather, is that basic romantic orientations and compositional dynamics are put under pressure, turned through all those unfamiliar, elliptical, occasionally obscure bendings of form and sense characteristic of modernist literature. In the shaping of these texts, it is clear, inherited literary forms of representation are distrusted almost as much as dominant social forms of representation. "Literary technique in modernist writing is, as it were, put on high alert in response to what other techniques or technologies have already done to life and language."[9] What is feared is that other social technologies have flattened both life and language, emptied words of their capacity to testify to vital depths of experience, as well as hidden fields of otherness, irreducible to the mapping of things in a network of functions. Defamiliarization is put in the service of criticism and transformation: the implicit or explicit claim—one ultimately derived from romantic poetics—is that you must "change your language" if you would "change your life."[10]

A guiding question explored in these poetries, then, is how, in an increasingly functionalist society, we might retrieve and disclose those forces that, be they "inner" or "outer," exceed the conventional linguistic frames with which we attempt to articulate them. And it is here that Continental philosophy, over the last century, has sustained an intimate conversation with romantic, modernist, and avantgardist art. The critical philosophies of the last century, highly influenced by both Nietzsche and Weber, tend to generalize the late romantic and modernist "crisis" sensibility into a vast narrative of social unfreedom against which is set the precarious promise of freedom and transformation manifest in modern art. And thus a broad field of twentieth-century Continental philosophy comes to read like a many-sided effort to invent theoretical languages analogous to the metamorphic wanderings of romantic, modernist, and avantgardist literature. Nietzsche, Heidegger, Marcuse, Adorno, Bataille, Blanchot, Derrida, Lyotard, and Foucault, among others, all belong to this complex field that I sketched in my introduction. The nightmare of a totally mechanized world, first making itself heard in romantic poetries, also haunts these later discourses, as does a faith in art as a site of resistance to a network of one-dimensional reason threatening to reduce things and persons to cogs within a system of production. And though Habermas, from a neo-Kantian perspective, would like to stigmatize these philosophies as either irrationalist flights from modernity or contradictory performances unable to reflect on their own argumentative status, these discourses (with the exception, I think, of the fatalist myth of Being composed by the later Heidegger) remain attached to the modern project of critical reflection, critical argument, and critical understanding of the conditions and possibilities of freedom. Philosophy at its best, from Plato on, has always engaged both what can be said in clear discursive terms and what, exceeding our discursive terms, can be articulated only through indirections akin to the searching indirections of myth, religion, and poetry. It is the tendency to erase or to disqualify these sorts of indirections—and the reaches of experience to which they point—that these philosophies, like modern literary passages of the extravagant from which they borrow, contest. And they do so in the name of modern ideals of freedom, critical reflection, and the possibility of a renewed relationship to an ultimately unfathomable whole from which we sense we have fallen away.

It is nevertheless true that philosophies and poetries written in the aftermath of modernism have grown exacerbated in the extreme. A major fear animating these discourses would seem to be clear: a fear of the destruction of freedom in a technologically developed social world in which, for the first time in history, a genuine realization of freedom for all is possible. The fear is that the very conditions that permit this realization perversely operate, instead, to integrate subjects ever more fully into a society that severely impedes this possibility. Thus the destructive irrationality of a highly rationalized social system.

The fear, in other words, is that the subject of reflective or creative freedom, even in the most privileged realms of modern society, has come to be absorbed by larger instrumental dynamics of social and economic organization. The way the dialectic of instrumental reason and creative negativity unfolds, then, is closely linked to the way the tension between what Charles Taylor has called "private romanticism" and "public utilitarianism" develops in modern society. Taylor, in a passage worth citing at length, underlines that modern Western societies have largely taken shape in terms of a *de facto* compromise between romantic quest in the private sphere and instrumental organization in the public sphere:

> But the Romantic strain has been contained, as it were, in modern Western civilization. The major common institutions reflect rather the Enlightenment conception in their defining ideas. This is obviously true of the economic institutions. But it is as true of the growing rationalized bureaucracies, and it is not much less so of the political structures, which are organized largely to produce collective decision out of the concatenation of individual decisions (through voting) and/or negotiation between groups. The major collective structures of advanced industrial society appear at best as instruments of production or decision (at worst, as threatening oppressors), whose value must ultimately be measured in what impact they have on the plight of individuals. The influence of Romantic ideals

The Dialectic of Instrumental Society and Creative Negativity • 279

has largely been on the definition of individual fulfillment, for the sake of which these larger structures operate.

Modern civilization has thus seen the proliferation of Romantic views of private life and fulfillment, along with a growing rationalization and bureaucratization of collective structures, and a frankly exploitative stance towards nature. Modern society, we might say, is Romantic in its private and imaginative life and utilitarian or instrumentalist in its public, effective life. What is of ultimate importance in shaping the latter is not what its structures express, but what they get done. The bent of modern society is to treat these structures as a neutral, objectified domain, to be reorganized for maximum effect, although this may be held in check or even periodically overridden by powerful collective emotions, principally nationalism, which have their roots in the Romantic period. But the day-to-day predominance of these collective structures over private Romanticism is evident in the exploitation of Romantic images of fulfillment to keep the wheels of industry turning, for instance in much contemporary advertising.[11]

An implicit claim in this passage, I think, is that the dream of achieving ethical and expressive wholeness in social life, as projected by thinkers like Hegel and Marx and various political movements in the twentieth century, has at least provisionally faded as a vital ideal in our culture, in large part, one suspects, because in many of those societies over the last century in which this project has been attempted it has been imposed from above, and so misrealized as totalitarian violence. Another implicit claim, one that marxist cultural critics have liked to emphasize, is that the most powerful voices in modern art, in particular in poetries of the extravagant, are profoundly complicit with—even as they resist, volatilize, transform, or strive to sweep open—the flattened individualism of everyday life in modern society. Hence, if voices like these lose contact with substantive force fields of strangeness beyond the individual, they are likely to be quickly absorbed, in the very details of their thinking and practice, by the society they would criticize.

This issue, I think, is closely linked to a third implicit claim in the passage of Taylor's I've cited. For the last sentence of this passage suggests that the compromise between individual romanticism and social instrumentalism has always been unstable and precarious. To begin with, the private individual who might creatively resist instrumental imperatives comes to be increasingly organized by them, integrated into the functionalist network that spreads across every sphere of society, hence potentially emptied of sources and recesses of experience that might exceed the routines of that network. While the "private-public" distinction remains firmly in place in contemporary society, being necessary to the functioning of the latter, the gradual assimilation of the life and mind of the "private" individual to larger dynamics of "public" instrumentalism is entirely compatible with the formal and legal maintenance of this distinction. Just this tendency, in fact, has been a major theme in the writings of a number of critical philosophers and social theorists over the last century and a half, from Kierkegaard and Nietzsche, through Marcuse and Adorno, down to Habermas and Foucault, among many others. The colonization of the life-world by technocratic and market imperatives—and so the penetration of the concrete individual by larger instrumental dynamics—appear to be powerful trends of capitalist modernity.

These trends, further, are inseparable from another trend that may weaken the distinction, or at least the force of the distinction, between individual romanticism and social instrumentalism. It is clear that an eccentric, alienated, often isolated interiority, formed by an idiosyncratic texture of concrete experience set off from dominant social patterns, was an important source of modern oppositional poetries and philosophies. Yet this individual locus of experience was never in itself an oppositional force: its oppositional force lay in the way it at once emerged out of and opened onto creative processes, unexpected sources of power, and enigmatic fields of otherness in some sense "outside" the dominant social and discursive frames of a highly instrumentalized world. The inner strangeness of the individual was a potential bridge, as it were, to the outer strangeness of forces not yet subsumed by the defining structures of an always expanding capitalist system. It is possible that these force fields of strangeness have themselves, in various ways, been subdued insofar as the structures of modernization have continued to penetrate them. It is at any rate a perception of this sort, I think, that partly explains what I've called the emphatic turn in recent years toward discourses of the negative. It is as though the search for the strange—for metamorphic forces that bewilder and release—had been driven by the one-dimensional society it contests into ever more evasive and rarefied forms of resistance.

A brief recollection of some of the prominent ways in which these force fields of otherness have been evoked in modern passages of the extravagant may help to clarify this issue. One of these force fields is that which I've emphasized throughout this book, namely, the resonance of earlier religious patterns of experience in a secularized world in which, over time, religious and metaphysical models slowly erode and gradually lose their hold on both psychic and practical life. These displaced religious dynamics animate those passages of the extravagant in modern poetry and philosophy that have been variously prophetic, apocalyptic, mythopoetic, occultist, radically metamorphic, or simply errant and exploratory, among other things. They remain audible throughout the first half of the twentieth century. Only in recent decades, it would seem, have they begun to undergo a kind of final dying.[12]

These displaced religious dynamics, further, have often been linked to a range of different ways of exploring and thematizing force fields of otherness in modern culture. One of these zones of otherness, at least in European culture, was the aristocratic milieu that, in large part owing to its loaded mystifications, could for a time provide a site of resistance to the growing dominance of commercial and instrumental stances toward experience. It was a site on which artists readily drew until its final destruction at the end of the Second World War. Linked to this, it would seem, is the way many artists adopted a kind of pseudo-aristocratic stance around the middle of the nineteenth century, Baudelaire's dandyism or Mallarmé's hermetic withdrawal being early expressions of a tradition that would last well into the twentieth century, whether in visionary elitists like Yeats, Pound, and Montale, or in evasive dandies like Valéry, Duchamp, and Max Jacob. And, perhaps surprisingly, in the avantgardist milieu this tradition would even mesh in curious ways with the very different tradition of the *poète maudit* and an entire bohemian subculture. These sorts of aristocratic, pseudo-aristocratic, and bohemian subcultures within a utilitarian market society seem to have provided a certain "outside," a vantage point of opposition, throughout this period. In diverse ways, too, they seem to have allowed for an eccentric, but nonetheless charged, relation to otherwise fading cultural resources of the past. The past itself, one recalls, was a vital source of otherness throughout the modernist period, whether in the explorations of layers of lost time in writers like Proust and Woolf, or in the mythopoetic retrievals of poets like Pound and H. D., or in the general modernist and avantgardist fascination with a range of lost, heterodox, and "premodern" or "primitive" traditions.[13]

Yet surely the most forceful and frequently evoked domain of otherness to which displaced religious dynamics have been linked throughout the modern period is "nature," whether externally or internally encountered. There is the "wild" nature so important in the emergence of the romantic sublime, conceived by Schiller as the obscure splendor of the "incomprehensible," later by Nietzsche as the joyous enigma of Dionysian becoming, and still later by Bataille as the sheer power of Being understood as both a play of solar excess and an abyss of negativity. There is the preindustrialized (or not yet wholly industrialized) rural world so important in the meditative "scenic" poetries of the romantic period and later in a whole line of "pastoral" or "nature" poetries all the way down to our own time. There are all the old and worn objects bearing the pressure of human contact that so fascinated Neruda and Alberti, akin to the run-down areas of an older modern city that so magnetized Breton and his companions, akin to the forgotten letters and half-heard voices next door that have so haunted John Ashbery, fields of "outward" material strangeness eliciting an "inward" psychic strangeness in much the way the natural world stirred an inward power in the solitary Wordsworth walking abroad on country paths. The surrealists also mark a decisive moment in the history of modern thematizations of "inner" nature: a history running from the romantic celebration of creative passion and transrational power, through the symbolist fascination with the indirect disclosures of dream and intuition and polyphonic verbal suggestion, through the surrealist exploration of an anarchic and utopian "inexhaustible murmur" hidden in the depths of the psyche, the release of which promises to transfigure both language and the world. The practices linked to this surrealist project, readily detached from the project itself, later live an eclectic second life in poetries of exploratory wackiness that emerge throughout the second half of the twentieth century. And a broad range of twentieth-century Continental philosophers, deeply influenced by these romantic and modernist traditions, compose visions of well-nigh mythopoetic resonance, seeking to turn our attention to the buried texture of the nonidentical, or the luminous drift of Being, or a haunting indeterminacy that calls us to our authentic dwelling in time.

Further, in a paradoxical turn in this tradition taken far by figures like Mallarmé and Beckett, modern writers and philosophers have explored an abyss of negativity that can never be gathered in a coherent representation. The nothing and nowhere of death, after all, cannot be comprehended in even the finest scientist's scheme. Nor can this nothing, at least insofar as it remains distinct from violence (or the gothic), be captured and exchanged on the market by even the savviest entrepreneur. There, so to speak, is something, a nothing, that cannot be put to use in any system. Mallarmé composes ghostly fictions that paradoxically sound the unfathomable nothing that inhabits them. Rilke praises a motion of falling, guided by "our intimate companion, Death," whereby the earth passes into the invisible. Neruda, in his elegiac poems of the twenties and thirties, explores a weather of dilapidation as if undergoing a sort of transdescendence. In his early work Heidegger imagines death as the uncanny horizon that permits a groundless human being to achieve authentic individuation. Bataille and Blanchot open their nocturnal meditations toward what they call, in a telling expression, "unemployable negativity." Thus an echo of religion, evoking like all religions a transcendence of mere utility, returns in various discourses of haunting absence, as if to persuade us that here, at least, in relation to nothing, we have not yet become *simply* things:

> The palm at the end of the mind,
> Beyond the last thought, rises
> In the bronze decor,
>
> A gold-feathered bird
> Sings in the palm, without human meaning,
> Without human feeling, a foreign song.
>
> You know then that it is not the reason
> That makes us happy or unhappy.
> The bird sings. Its feathers shine.
>
> The palm stands on the edge of space.
> The wind moves slowly in the branches.
> The bird's fire-fangled feathers dangle down.[14]

Have these force fields of otherness vanished, then, or somehow lost that power of bewilderment and awakening they were felt to transmit in earlier periods? It seems clear that the aristocratic and bohemian subcultures of the past have disappeared—marginal locations of that sort, though still present throughout the sixties, have gone from the world or, in the case of bohemian countercultures, been captured by the world of consumerism. And, as I've already noted, the enigmatic pressures of earlier religious frames and dynamics of experience also seem to have waned considerably, to have lost a large measure of their power to startle or to haunt consciousness, as Gadamer suggests in the passage I've cited above, or, when they do persist, to appear above all, if not solely, in hazy New Age texts (recalling, curiously, the vogue for theosophy and the occult around the turn of the last century), or in highly rarefied discourses of the other (as in Levinas, Blanchot, and Derrida, among others), or, if we turn to the popular domain, in moralizing fundamentalisms whose reactionary political programs are thoroughly calculating in the most high-tech

284 • THE EXTRAVAGANT

modern fashion. The many sorts of "pastoral" or meditative "nature" poetries that continue to be written in our time, however, and the many ecological writers who for decades have been insisting that our relationship with the natural world is now an urgent social and political as well as an abiding existential and artistic question, suggest that the otherness of the natural world has not, in any simple way, lost its animating pull on our psychic life. Yet it may be that our relationship with the green world, nevertheless, has gone through some peculiar mutation over the last several decades, a period during which a completion of "modernization" has done away with older lifeworlds that for a long time coexisted alongside the "modernized" lifeworld. "One is tempted to speak in this connection," Fredric Jameson writes, "of a new and historically original penetration and colonization of Nature and the Unconscious: that is, the destruction of precapitalist Third World agriculture by the Green Revolution, and the rise of the media and the advertising industry." While Jameson tends to exaggerate in presenting his dialectical forecast of the present, he has surely touched on a change of enormous significance in this respect; many artists and philosophers of the last several decades, at any rate, seem to have gone about their work partly in response to the transformation that Jameson has characterized as the conquest of nature at last "completed" by contemporary high-tech capitalism.[15]

One response to this unprecedented condition in the wake of modernism has been an effort to explore fields of otherness not yet subsumed by the dominant instrumental structures of modernization. Thus, for example, aleatory and formula-based modes of composition meant to open the domain of art to the wind of chance, if already explored in the modernist period, have guided various artists throughout this period (one thinks of Zukofsky and Cage and all those influenced by them, though the most striking expression of this current may be that dialectical reversal whereby the surrealist celebration of anarchic spontaneity and "objective chance" turns into the Oulipean concern to release the unpredictable through wholly formalized modes of composition). Yet it would seem that the most prominent thematizations of otherness over the last half century have been the wayward *materiality of language* and the wayward *negativity of signification*. These, it seems to be felt, are the intertwined mysteries that still promise to jar us from our place and function in a network beyond our control, still hold powers of the sort once thought to be held by the numinous manifold of nature, the disclosive openness of being, the renovative weather of the open road, the enigmatic regions of a changing city, and the haunting echoes of the withdrawal of the divine, or by the unpredictable reaches of passion, dream, metamorphic vision, unconscious force, and rescued fragments of myth, among other things. While one could cite any number of writers in this context, Julia Kristeva's *Revolution in Poetic Langugage,* which echoes Bataille and surrealism while spelling out a revisionist approach to modern literature, strikes me as especially emblematic of this widespread turn in recent thought.[16]

Kristeva's theoretical approach, to put it in schematic terms, posits a layering within language of a symbolic realm, the order of representation or the domain of structured ideality, and a semiotic realm, the material texture of language wherein unconscious drives or energies make themselves heard. These energies disruptively traverse the symbolic order, opening the latter to the play of wandering transformations. Though Kristeva speaks of the dialectical interplay between these two levels, her own cast of thought, both in this book and in others, tends toward a decisive emphasis on the way a play of force on the semiotic level volatilizes the space of representation on the symbolic level. Framing her whole discussion in the vocabularies of semiotics and psychoanalysis, drawing motifs from anarchism, surrealism, and Bataille, she reinterprets romantic and modernist literature as a long adventure whose true source of otherness turns out to have been the creative force of the unconscious making itself felt in the surprising textures and wayward indirections of innovative acts of writing. The order of representation is taken to be guilty until proved innocent, or more exactly, guilty until purged by the trial of a dislocative negativity that rarely comes to rest in a patterned horizon of meaning. Blake's Orc tends to displace Blake's Los, Rimbaud's demon of disordering to displace Rimbaud's *génie* of renovation, Mallarmé's textual glides to displace Mallarmé's exploratory fictions, Breton's anarchism to displace Breton's utopianism, Stevens's ironic erasures to displace Stevens's conjectural refigurations, Montale's deserts of negation to displace Montale's prayers of reach. The unruly material slippages of language, the elliptical spacings of signification explored in unfamiliar literary texts, are cast as the places and movements of an enigmatic otherness still promising a departure from the cage of an instrumentally mapped world and its correlative structures of congealed meaning. Alterity is found anew in the fleeting word. "After you, my beautiful language," as Breton once put it, recalling both Rimbaud and Mallarmé, yielding the initiative to the distances of words, yet meaning something different by that, finally, from what it has come to mean among recent theorists of the materiality of language and the errancy of signification. We are now called to wander where patterns are always going apart in open drift. A textualized Bataille returns as the presiding ghost of this late, refracted phase of modernism.[17]

POSTMODERNISM AND THE FADING OF THE EXTRAVAGANT

Up to this point, both in this chapter and in this book as a whole, I've said very little about the question of a "postmodern" society or culture. My concern has been to elucidate a many-sided tradition of the extravagant in poetry and philosophy that travels from romanticism through the last phase of modernism. Post-structuralist theory in general, I've sought to show, is a late articulation of romantic and modernist as well as avantgardist orientations. Thus I'm inclined to distinguish sharply between "postmodernism," as it has been variously characterized in recent years, and "post-structuralism," as I've characterized it in this study. Emphasizing complex and fractured continuities extending from the romantic period through the present, I've tried to clarify influential poetries and philosophies that, though their resonance is perhaps fading in contemporary culture, may at least have much to tell us about where our culture is, insofar as we are able to recognize in them where our culture is no longer. The story told in this book perhaps belongs primarily, though not solely, to the period lasting from 1789 through the late 1960s and early 1970s.[18]

At this point, however, I need to address the question of a distinctive postmodern social and cultural field, if all too briefly and schematically, for I would like to try to clarify the way certain residual modernist (including post-structuralist) bearings wind through this field like peculiar currents easily lost in a vast electronic theater. Andreas Huyssen, whose mapping of the postwar field in Europe and especially in the United States I loosely follow here, has soundly argued that the diverse orientations of postwar culture must be clearly situated, and clearly distinguished from one another, rather than simply subsumed under a general category of the postmodern. For these orientations emerge in very different ways, out of very different contexts, and articulate a range of quite different projects and horizons.[19]

One important dimension of postwar culture lies in the emergence, alongside important late modernist and existentialist projects, of neo-avantgarde movements in various countries. The countercultures of the fifties and sixties, that is, are less expressions of what has come to be called postmodernism than either marginal revivals or late reworkings of the polemical, inventive, prankish, and on the whole romantic avantgarde that first appeared throughout Europe during the first three decades of the twentieth century. In the United States, for example, as Huyssen underlines, the conditions for the emergence of this sort of disruptive movement (including, not least importantly, the presence of an established tradition of high art perceived to play some role in the legitimation of a leaden and illegitimate society) did not really obtain until the institutional canonization of modernism in the decade following the Second World War. Only at that point, in the fifties, could a volatile avantgarde, concerned to contest the divorce between art and life and the domestication of creative energies in established institutions, truly take off. And take off it did, reviving the romantic and later dada and surrealist longing to place art and life in intimate communication with one another, and so recasting a whole range of romantic (as well as modernist) themes, including, among others, the spirit of experimental invention, the power of unfettered imagination, the freedom of the open road, the force of creative eros, the reach of disclosive attention, and the divinatory play of intuition and collage. Many of the adventures of these early postwar decades cannot easily be assimilated to that distinctive postmodernist climate which emerges in the flickering high-tech landscape that comes into being in the late sixties and early seventies.

Yet surely the most important dimension of postwar society and culture—one often bearing a fraught relation to the postwar countercultures or neo-avantgardes—lies in the global emergence of new kinds of "antisystemic" movements (to borrow a term from Immanuel Wallerstein). These movements, as is well known, resonantly animated one another in a kind of spreading wave-like pattern—beginning with postwar decolonizing movements and wars for national liberation and quickly extending to civil rights movements, feminist movements, and democratizing movements of many different kinds—until they peaked on a global scale in the late sixties and early seventies and then waned in the aftermath of reaction that has shaped the last thirty years of history. While some of these movements (notably feminism) have made extraordinary gains and sustained their power in the face of the last thirty years of reaction, others (notably the civil rights movement in this country and national liberation movements around the globe) have suffered severe setbacks throughout this period. Whatever their gains and losses in the social and economic sphere, however, these movements have radically transformed the landscape of contemporary culture. And many of the artistic works aligned with these movements involve presuppositions and projects that bear a complex, slanted relationship to the presuppositions and projects of dominant Euro-American modernist, avantgardist, or postmodernist movements in the arts and philosophy. Indeed, not the least forceful effect of these movements has been the charged, unruly, transformative rethinking of "culture" in general to which they've given rise over the last three decades. It is as though these movements had called the globe to a long education in the activity of engaging multiple traditions and multiple criteria of interpretation and evaluation. That, barring reaction even more violent than what we've already seen, appears to be the future of thought in a world whose nations will increasingly be formed of multiple peoples, languages, cultures, and traditions.[20]

Postmodernism, then, in the sense it has been given by many of its most prominent theorists, would seem above all to designate a distinctive cultural field in the first world that, while anticipated by various currents at play in the sixties, belongs primarily to a historical condition that can be located with some precision: the condition that emerges with the fading of the utopian horizons of these earlier political and cultural movements of the fifties and sixties and, at the same time, the triumphant reorganization of multinational capitalism around a range of new technologies, new extensions of the mass media, and new strategies of drawing everything and everyone into the circuit of commodification and consumerism. The "society of the spectacle," as Guy Debord presciently named it some thirty-five years ago, emerges "when the commodity attains the *total occupation* of social life. Not only is the relation to the commodity visible but it is all one sees: the world one sees is its world."[21] As Jameson and others have noted, this explains why postmodernism as a "cultural dominant" first appears (and first becomes an ideology) in the United States, a nation that, during this period, becomes at once "modernized" and "commodified" to a historically unprecedented degree, the effort to extend this process to the rest of the globe—and the many efforts to resist it—forming a crucial drama of contemporary history. The emblematic artist of this dominant, then, would be Andy Warhol, the savvy and cynical entrepreneur who received his artistic education in the world of advertising.[22]

No doubt the finest critical theorist of postmodernism in this sense is Fredric Jameson, who, in an initial move, characterizes postmodernist culture by contrasting it with modernist culture, mapping out a series of oppositions that are by now well known: modernism is to postmodernism as anxiety is to affectlessness (or, in an unstable inversion, to hysterical affect), depth to surface, critical parody to blank parody, hermeneutic recovery to textual commentary, paranoid or alienated interiority to schizoid or dispersed subjectivity, and an experience of the pressure of the past to a waning of any experience of the past (the latter now lost in a maze of multiplying images).[23] At least as important as these broad characterizations, however, are two of Jameson's bold, startling periodizing claims. One of these, to which I referred above, is that postmodernity is a condition in which the modernization process has been brought to a "completion" that, perfectly familiar because everywhere around us, yet curi-

The Dialectic of Instrumental Society and Creative Negativity • 289

ously unfamiliar because entirely unprecedented, might almost be characterized as uncanny. In the first world, from the late sixties on, earlier premodern or semimodern modes of production and their corresponding lifeworlds have been overtaken by the expanding movement of capitalist modernization. Hence our relationship to the natural world wherein we and our histories take place, the enigmatic whole wherein we are born and die, may be going through a mutation difficult even to think concretely. Another of Jameson's bold periodizing claims involves a reinterpretation of the common observation that in contemporary culture the borders between "high" and "popular" art are frequently blurred. Jameson's more sweeping claim is that this sort of blurring is itself a consequence of a broader, severely contradictory twofold dynamic, namely, the massive expansion of the cultural sphere in general (a change involving genuine democratizing effects) and, at the same time, the tendential subsumption of *all* cultural activity, in every social sphere, by the logic of the market (a change involving notable leveling effects).[24] It does appear that the dynamics organizing activity in the contemporary art, literary, and academic worlds have become difficult to distinguish from those organizing contemporary society at large. And it may be, as Jameson underlines, that no decisive "outside" to the zone of these dynamics is to be found anymore, that they've become the parameters of our lives, that any of our critical accounts of this society are thus at risk of simply disappearing into the vast cybernetic theater from which they momentarily emerge. The very place and function of culture in social life, therefore, may be passing through a transformation we've only begun to imagine.[25]

It is in this peculiar climate that lively currents of the artistic and political movements of the first two decades of the postwar period still make themselves felt. And it is through this climate, too, that post-structuralist lines of thought, as well as contemporary literary adventures refracting earlier modernist and avantgardist bearings, travel in a variety of ways. The two turns in certain fields of contemporary culture that I briefly characterized above—the emphasis on the dislocative materiality of language and the fascination with the errant movement of signification—are, in my view, residual, recoded, highly refracted avantgardist preoccupations sounded anew in this radically transformed social field.

The guiding concerns of contemporary "experimental" or "oppositional" poetries throughout Europe and the Americas (akin to some, though by no means all, of the concerns one encounters in post-structuralist theories) are often expressed in terms of three loosely interwoven themes: the theme of errant desire, the theme of foregrounded textuality, and the theme of indeterminacy, where "indeterminacy" has less to do with the meaning of this term in deconstructive theories than with a flexible concept of either semantic polyvalency or thematic, narrative, and expressive discontinuity.[26] The foregrounded "compositional process" becomes the defamiliarizing marker of practices designed to volatilize discursive codes that, because they inevitably tend to grow "automatized," as the Russian formalists liked to say, always threaten to dull our attention to the ways we might rearticulate them and thereby reimagine our relationship to the places we inhabit. An art of lively unmaking opens the kind of loosened discursive space required if one is to weave unfamiliar turns out of the colliding discursive codes that organize our lives. The primary task is to keep the signifying energies in motion, evading the emergence of a gathered pattern of meaning, permitting the words to whirl against and away from any such pattern, thereby time and again (to borrow a distant expression from Edmund Burke) "hurrying the mind out of itself." The fear appears to be that developed thematic and figural orchestration, even of a complex and multidimensional sort, may spell the deadening of the composer no less than of the composed. An open-ended play of linguistic negativity is conceived as both a force of critique and a pulse of freedom. In these poetries of the errant, then, as in the writings of Kristeva or the later Barthes, the modernist and, in particular, avantgardist tradition is reconceived as a long adventure whose secret of creative resistance, in an age of totalizing instrumentalism and commodification, turns out to have been the promise of freedom sustained by the play of errant negativity. We walk in the dark of a thousand false lights, unclear of where and who we are, but still alive, occasionally beside ourselves, insofar as we are sent abroad in an indeterminate meander of words, a wayward drift of sounds. The poem becomes a hovering maze of misdirections. Poetic and theoretical orientations of this sort articulate a late and desperate turn in the dialectic of instrumental reason and creative negativity unfolding across modern culture. Indeed, these orientations might be characterized as passages of the dispersive arriving at the end of a long tradition of passages of the extravagant from which—across multiple displacements whose origins have been erased or forgotten—they loosely derive. The metamorphic horizon, when not the act of reconfiguration itself, tends to be left behind. Knocking holes in a wall of impoverished sense felt to be surrounding us, these passages affirm our potential to wander through a space of linguistic drift, akin to a twilit demon of otherness, calling us elsewhere.[27]

Recent poetries of the errant and the theoretical discourses that accompany them readily bring to mind the roots of lyric in riddle, charm, sound play, or, more generally, semantic defamiliarization. Northrop Frye long ago provided a fine description of the generative tension in lyric poetry between the pressure of this sort of play and the counterpressure of what he wryly called "the plausibility-principle":

> What we think of as typically the poetic creation . . . is an associative rhetorical process, most of it below the threshold of consciousness, a chaos of paronomasia, sound-links, ambiguous sense-links, and memory-links very like that of the dream. Out of this the distinctively lyrical union of sound and sense emerges. Like the dream, verbal association is subject to a censor, which (or whom) we may call the "plausibility-principle," the necessity of shaping itself into a form acceptable to the poet's and his reader's waking consciousness, and of adapting itself to the sign-meanings of assertive language well enough to be communicable to that consciousness.[28]

This passage, mildly revised, could be made to serve as a highly compressed version of the "neo-avantgarde" theory of literature that contemporary poets and theorists have variously elaborated in the vocabularies of, among other things, anarchism, semiotics, psychoanalysis, critical theory, nominalist empiricism, and a sort of left-wing reader-response theory. The major difference, of course, is that these recent writers display rather less respect than Frye for the "plausibility-principle" that governs our everyday practices of making sense of ourselves, of others, and of the world at large. The proportion between "play" and "plausibility" has undergone a mutation. For it is clear that there is at work in many neighborhoods of contemporary culture a suspicion that our inherited practices of making sense have been colonized almost beyond recovery by a network of instrumental schemes. In a critical discussion of mass culture written at an earlier point in time, Horkheimer and Adorno made much of the difference between the externally imposed "order" of art produced for profit and the internally generated "coherence" of art born out of a genuine search for meaning: "The so-called dominant idea [of a work of the culture industry] is like a file which ensures order but not coherence. The whole and the parts are alike; there is no antithesis and no connection. This pre-arranged harmony is a mockery of what had to be striven after in the great bourgeois works of art."[29] What seems to have taken place in the aftermath of modernism, in the unfolding of the perspectives I've sketched above, is that the difference still maintained by Horkheimer and Adorno has become for many writers blurred, if not erased. Earlier forms of complex coherence—including those internally generated, fractured, polyphonically orchestrated patterns characteristic of romantic and modernist writing—are themselves suspected of anxiously imposing a factitious order on unruly impulses and materials and, so, of remaining complicit with the functionalist society and the routinized self they claim to surpass. Hence the studious evasion or dislocation of such complex patterns is undertaken as a practice of de-reifying resistance. It is as though various zones of contemporary culture were guided by a lively suspicion that a "plausibility principle" in any guise had been debased by a giant machine of instrumental reduction. Agility of movement in multiple directions at once—be it traced with melancholy, whimsy, fire, irony, or what have you—becomes a broken figure of exiled freedom, as it were, and an anxious, if acrobatic, *promesse de bonheur*.

The figuring of poetry as a kind of "music" in symbolist poetics involved at least two distinct (if often intertwined) analogies: first, an analogy between the evocative indirections of poetry and the ineffable reaches of music, and second, an analogy between the polyphonic structure of an intricately orchestrated poem and the polyphonic structure of an accomplished musical composition. Mallarmé was the finest theorist of both of these analogies that were to exert such an ample influence on twentieth-century literature (as Edmund Wilson showed long ago in *Axel's Castle*). The first of these analogies was to inform a range of twentieth-century poetries. The second was to inform, in particular, the "polyphonic," or (in Wilson's term) "symphonic," constructions of a range of major modernist novelists and poets, including, among others, James, Proust, Joyce, Woolf, Rilke, Valéry, Stevens, Eliot, Pound, H. D., Zukofsky, Montale, Guillén, Cernuda, Vallejo, and, late in the day, yet still working in this line, however strangely, Beckett. It is the transformation in modernism of this second major current of the symbolist conception of "musical structure" that, it seems, has come to be treated with the sort of distrust previously reserved for less complicated modes of thematic patterning.[30]

Not the least intriguing thing about contemporary poetries of the errant is the way they recall prominent features of the postsymbolist, early-avantgarde, or (in the broad sense in which Marcel Raymond uses the term) *fantaisiste* poetries that emerged in Europe around the turn of the last century, particularly, but not solely, in France—poetries whose wayward, acrobatic, improvisatory, often melancholy turnings would make themselves heard in surrealist writings and later in a range of neo-avantgarde adventures over the last century. The absurdist meanders of a Max Jacob, the elliptical weavings and calligrammic tracings of an Apollinaire at his most whimsical, the playful mystifications and roving misdirections of a Philippe Soupault, for example, sometimes seem to have come back to life in our own time, most notably perhaps in New York School poetries and their many recent echoings, and most brilliantly in John Ashbery's poetry in particular, where tactics like these are richly crossed with the meditative bearings of a tradition running from Wordsworth through Stevens and Bishop. Earlier poets in this *fantaisiste* mode wished to defend the free mobility of the spirit against the instrumental mappings of science, positivism, business, and the everyday domain of orderly life and orderly sense. Jarry's pataphysics was the promise in the air; existence was elsewhere, calling from vanishing margins; *la vraie vie* was to be found in the dreaming gaps between proper paths of sense; the clown of words alone was free, alive in zaniness, wise in folly, while all the rest were dupes. The revival of these wayward bearings in our own time seems to express a concern to defend the free mobility of the spirit against what is perceived as the analogue of these instrumental mappings in the literary and cultural realm in particular. Not only the world, but we ourselves and our ways of talking and making sense, so to speak, are too much with us. We want diversion, space in which to breathe, and so are drawn to rove through slanting fields of deviant phrases, riddling detours, evocative deletions, indeterminate turnings. "Words turn on the mischief of their telling."[31] Thus does the demon of imaginative analogy, become the demon of mobile impertinence and textual dispersal, continue its long revolt, in studious and erratic ways, under changed circumstances.[32]

It is no accident, then, that these adventures of the dispersive, in their anarchist bent, tend to read like dexterous inversions of the dystopian map of a madly instrumentalized modernity drawn by Foucault in *Discipline and Punish*. Foucault, as is well known, presents modernity as a vast disciplinary regime in which individuals are insidiously constructed as docile-utile bodies and efficient-normalized producers. In his detailed study of displinary mechanisms at work in the barracks, factories, schools, hospitals, and prisons of modern France, he attempts to show that the mechanisms Marx observed in the modern factory, in particular the subjection of the worker to the industrial apparatus, pervade all spheres of modern society in a single "carceral continuum" of disciplinary normalization. No sphere of society and no realm of discourse are untainted by the operations of this system, by what Foucault in his next book calls the total organization of "bio-power." And as though developing strong hints culled from writers like Marcuse and Adorno, Foucault insists that even the lonely "individual," conceived as a source of resistance in so many liberal and romantic discourses, is itself but an "effect" or a "result" of this disciplinary network, which operates less through obvious mechanisms of repression than through subtle mechanisms of productive regulation that, among other things, persuade the individuals wired to this network that they are in fact realizing their natural potentials through polished techniques of training and development (as, in some sense, they are). Knowledge is technical power, Bacon said with hope at the beginning of modernity; knowledge is normalizing power, Foucault says with horror at the end of the twentieth century. There appears to be no escape, and indeed Foucault's entire narrative seems to emanate from a kind of nowhere, or perhaps from a detached stoic who, like Spinoza, knows that freedom is the recognition of necessity.

On passing occasions, however, Foucault does suggest possibilities of resistance or evasion. One of the most telling of these appears near the end of the first volume of *The History of Sexuality*. This book, unlike the next two books in this series, reads like a coda or a supplementary chapter to *Discipline and Punish*. We are now told that our sexual life has been regulated no less insidiously than every other aspect of our life. The great ruse in this domain turns out to have been the implantation in our consciousness (this seems a proper way to put it) of a belief in an essential sexual identity buried in the natural being of each individual. Foucault thus attempts, throughout this book, to criticize what he calls "the repressive hypothesis" and its corresponding politics of emancipation, a politics that has traditionally called for an overturning of social and cultural institutions of repression and so an uncovering of authentic sexual identities. Yet, though he seems to promise an alternative to this hypothesis, in the end Foucault provides but a variation on it. And what turns out to have been repressed, in this modified version of the repressive hypothesis, is not an inner sexual identity but an untapped potential for polymorphous erotic play. Our potentially multiple bodies, pleasures, knowledges, and discourses—not our secret identities—have been repressed by the regulatory system of biopower:

> So we must not refer a history of sexuality to the agency of sex; but rather show how "sex" is historically subordinate to sexuality. We must not place sex on the side of reality, and sexuality on that of confused ideas and illusions; sexuality is a very real historical formation; it is what gave rise to the notion of sex, as a speculative element necessary to its operation. We

must not think that by saying yes to sex, one says no to power; on the contrary, one tracks along the course laid out by the general deployment of sexuality. It is the agency of sex that we must break away from, if we aim—through a tactical reversal of the various mechanisms of sexuality—to counter the grips of power with the claims of bodies, pleasures, and knowledges, in their multiplicity and their possibility of resistance. The rallying point for the counterattack against the deployment of sexuality ought not to be sex-desire, but bodies and pleasures.[33]

An anarchic carnival of multiplied pleasures and knowledges is invoked in opposition to the prison of normalized production, normalized discourse, and normalized subjectivity. We are called to shake off the disciplinary or instrumental imperatives we've internalized—now including, it is clear, those orientations developed in earlier humanist discourses that were once believed to resist such imperatives. A similar call, at the level of textual practice, is often made by contemporary poets and philosophers writing out of the avantgarde traditions of the last century. Charles Bernstein, for instance, in a playful account of the centrifugal force he would like poetic activity to exert on traditional forms of literary patterning, writes:

> Not "death" of the referent—rather a recharged use of the multivalent referential vectors that any word has, how words in combination tone and modify the associations made for each of them, how 'reference' then is not a one-on-one relation to an 'object' but a perceptual dimension that closes in to pinpoint, nail down (*this* word), sputters omnitropically (the in in the which of who where what wells), refuses the build up of image track/projection while, pointillistically, fixing a reference at each turn (fills vats ago lodges spire), or, that much rarer case . . . of "zaum" (so-called transrational, pervasively neologistic) . . . in which reference, deprived of its automatic reflex reaction of word/stimulus image/response roams over the range of associations suggested by the word, word shooting off referential vectors like the energy field in a Kirillian photograph.[34]

Thus another call, from another domain, for a centrifugal carnival of roaming pleasures and multiplying significations. This, I've argued, is the most recent phase of the long dialectic of instrumental reason (or, ultimately, instrumental social organization) and creative negativity traversing modernity.

Foucault and Bernstein may sound like distant, agile, nominalist descendants of the anarchic Rimbaud who, with desperate and visionary passion, felt that "to every being several *other* lives were owed." They call for a release of multiplied perspectives, an unfolding of nomadic movements of signification, as though proposing a late, refracted version of the romantic affirmation of the superiority of the organic to the mechanical, of the textured amplitude of a creative life to the dim narrowness of an instrumentally mapped life. Is this another promise of freedom and spaciousness of life, then, set in opposition to the routines and codes of a one-dimensional society? Perhaps. Yet Foucault and Bernstein (as I read them) hardly believe that things are quite so clear or simple. What if this one-dimensional society is at the same time a society that generates continual processes of differentiation in all realms of work, play, and knowledge? What if this instrumental system of highly regulated routines is at the same time a machine that generates the distinctly modern ideal held by Kierkegaard's aesthetic dandy or romantic ironist, namely, the ideal of unlimited plasticity and mobility in all realms of personal and social life? Is this not the most pervasive ideal (or fantasy) of contemporary consumer society in particular? And what if this homogenizing capitalist system, drawing everything and everyone into the circuit of commodification, is at the same time a system that produces both actual and simulated fields of multiplying heterogeneities? We would then need a more dialectical vision of modernity than any story of an iron cage or a panoptic network is able to provide—perhaps a vision akin to that which Marshal Berman, imaginatively following the Marx of *The Communist Manifesto,* elaborates in *All That Is Solid Melts into Air.* The power of Marx's "modernist" vision, Berman shows, lies in the way it dialectically brings together both a "solid vision" and a "melting vision," both a sense of the "nightmare that weighs on the minds of the living" and a sense of the dynamic whereby "all that is solid melts into air," both a study of those structures that damage and impede the development of human powers and a study of those processes that sweep everything and everyone away in a groundless movement that seems beyond our control. The iron cage is a dynamic chaos as well. This immense contradiction, Berman argues, has to be addressed in any substantive thinking of social and cultural modernity.[35]

Not the least provocative claim of Jameson's interpretation of postmodernity, in any case, is the claim that a carnival of errant flows has already arrived: unfortunately, he says, it happens to be the cultural delirium produced in the first world by the disorienting realities of global multinational capi-

The Dialectic of Instrumental Society and Creative Negativity • 297

talism. We have grown so adapted to our alienation and our fragmentation, Jameson suggests, that we no longer even recognize them: we take delight in them.[36] From this point of view, the many dismantlings of the "ideology of the subject" prominent in contemporary culture would be but seismographic expositions of the scattering of the subject actually effected by postmodern society. The sort of narrative developed by Foucault, despite its emphasis on "decentralized" networks of power, would turn out to be a detailed variation on the narratives developed earlier by Marcuse and Adorno, a "Weberian" critical theory no longer entirely adequate to the transformed conditions of our time (which would not be to say that it isn't partially adequate, for it certainly is, as the grim proliferation in recent years of practices of video and computer surveillance indicates clearly enough). And the multiplied or dispersed subject evoked in so much contemporary art and theory would point less to a subject potentially released from a one-dimensional capitalist network than to a subject already integrated into that network in a historically original way. I would like to believe that Jameson, a brilliant dialectician and hence a clairvoyant hyperbolist, describes less the world we currently inhabit than a future possibility, a place we may be headed toward, but a place we might avoid. For his bleak forecast is that of a world in which, paradoxically, the individual thoroughly assimilated to the imperatives of one-dimensional society would at the same time be the individual dispersed across the multiplying codes, images, and routines of this society. The culmination of an individualist market society in that case would be the emergence of a market society of wired individualists at once disciplined and incoherent, finely trained and finely scattered. It would hardly look like a world of liberation, or a world of a creatively widened life. It would look like the ruin of potentially free individuals in a flattening, nihilist space of dazzling images and pointless wheels of production. "These with a thousand small deliberations / Protract the profit of their chilled delirium, / Excite the membrane, when the sense has cooled, / With pungent sauces, multiply variety / In a wilderness of mirrors" (Eliot). Postmodern capitalist society would turn out to be an odd hell indeed, a version of Eliot's wasteland transposed to a high-tech, hypermediatized society, whose final victory over its dazed subjects, perhaps, would lie in its having persuaded us that our turns of complicity were turns of resistance. It might be enough to send one searching again for a voice of thunder, however heard, however translated, or, perhaps, for a missing wing of night, however conjured:

    Y si así diéramos las narices
en el absurdo,
nos cubriremos con el oro de no tener nada,
y empollaremos el ala aun no nacida
de la noche, hermana
de esta ala huérfana del día,
que a fuerza de ser una ya no es ala.

    [And if in this way we bang head-on
into the absurd,
we'll cover ourselves with the gold of having nothing,
and will hatch the yet unborn wing
of night, sister
of this orphan wing of day,
that by dint of being one no longer is a wing.]37

EPILOGUE

The Miracle of Place

Are we losing a world, ourselves, our relationships, a meaningful and open horizon that calls us further? Is it not always so? "It is one of the peculiarities of the imagination that it is always at the end of an era."[1] I've made clear, I think, my sense that postmodernist culture, at least insofar as it involves the "cultural dominant" described by Jameson and others, is unlikely to bear us anywhere except further into the intricate instrumental network that the poetries and philosophies explored in this book have always resisted. But I've also suggested that adventures in the broad tradition of the extravagant, having gradually unfolded into a range of paradoxical discourses of the negative and riddling practices of the dispersive, may have reached a certain end of the line, a far margin from which texts of evocative erasure and acrobatic dislocation are mailed to the world as though they were melancholy letters of desperate, thinned, exiled freedom. I would like to believe that these late pulses of a long tradition at least sustain the possibility of another renewal of the speculative art of metamorphic passage. I imagine they do.[2]

Fortunately, as Hans Enzensberger underlines, creative action is highly unpredictable: "it is inherent in the process of creation that there is no way to predict its results." And, of course, in this book I've described only one tradition in modern culture—if a many-sided and extremely influential one—leaving a broad range of important poetries, fictions, and philosophies outside my narrative. Sources of renewal, of transformed bearings, may emerge from any number of relatively foreseeable and wholly unforeseeable places. "The position of those who saddle modernity with its past, like a mortgage," Enzensberger writes, "as if everything great had already been done and the only possibility left were to copy, exploit, imitate, or capitulate, is not clever but contemptible. 'Everything has been done already' is the maxim of cowardice."[3]

However, by suggesting that on the whole the adventures traced in this book may have gradually backed themselves into a corner, I've perhaps backed myself into a corner. So it may be appropriate to conclude with a brief word concerning at least a few of the various orientations in poetry and philosophy that, to my mind, are among the most reaching of recent decades. Those I have in mind voice not exactly a negation but certainly a counterpoint to the tradition of the extravagant studied in this book. More importantly, I think, they articulate a vital countercurrent to the general climate of postmodernist culture, in part by sustaining or reworking in complex ways a forceful modernist orientation.

Gillian Rose, J. M. Bernstein, and Robert Pippin are among those philosophers who in recent years have made an ambitious effort to develop anew a sophisticated postmetaphysical Hegelian dialectic, one distinct not only from the dismissive caricatures of Hegel found in all those philosophies that set him up as the supreme metaphysician of the monologic spirit, but also from the entire nondialectical, nonspeculative historicist current in modern culture that, in some sense, derives from Hegel. There is thus a probing worldliness, complexity, and historical scope in the interpretative narratives developed by these philosophers. Each, in different ways, tries to steer a path between, on the one hand, a metaphysic of spirit and a narrative of progress that cannot withstand the ironic and darkened historical self-understanding of our time, and on the other, a reduction of Hegel to any of a number of nominalist historicisms (old as well as new) that are at a loss to elucidate not simply the entanglement but also the distinction between power and reason. This sort of dialectic works toward a supple comprehension of the whole range of contradictions shaping modernity. And so, for example, it neither simply identifies with, nor simply dismisses, the many efforts in the tradition of the extravagant to disclose an "other" of the spreading instrumental "cage" of capitalist modernity. It seeks, rather, to unfold a conceptual narrative able to grasp both the potentials and the limits, both the utopian bearings and the desperate turns, at play in this tradition. It should be clear, then, that philosophers like Rose, Bernstein, Pippin, and, of course, Charles Taylor have informed, from a distance, my own less ambitious (more plainly historicist and hermeneutic) narrative in this book.[4] One of my differences with these thinkers may lie in the greater emphasis I place on the presence in this tradition of displaced religious dynamics that, bent through a range of indirections, have haunted and animated its most powerful voices: they are voices, then, that tend to be extreme (at times perilously so, yet valuably so too) in their search for vision and freedom. Yet the thought of these late Hegelian philosophers is capacious enough to bring these voices into a conversation with the perspectives necessary for a many-sided interpretation of modernity, including a philosophic comprehension of our decidedly everyday problems of violence and injustice. Critical theorists in the Frankfurt School tradition, as Bernstein understands and extends their work, "fuse a concern for justice with a concern for 'meaning,' or, said otherwise, following on from an understanding of the young Marx or the Marx of *Capital* conjoined with Nietzsche (mediated through Weber), they perceive a connection between the problem of domination and the problem of nihilism, where the terms 'domination' and 'nihilism' themselves recall the dual provenance of critical theory in social science and philosophy." These two predicaments, the weight of injustice and the fog of pointlessness, complexly condition one another in the modern world.[5]

However, since throughout this book I've tended to read philosophers in the light of poets rather more than I've read poets in the light of philosophers, it seems well to conclude with two poets. George Oppen and Geoffrey Hill, I believe, are two of the most distinctive English-language poets of the last half century, akin in stature and in seriousness, say, to Paul Celan in postwar German-language poetry, or to René Char and Yves Bonnefoy in postwar French poetry, or to José Ángel Valente in postwar Spanish poetry. And it may be only a coincidence, but it may be significant that Oppen seems to associate the term "extravagance" with capitalist waste.[6] Yet Oppen and Hill, I think, do not simply oppose the poetries I've traced in this study so much as they resist them in a kind of resonant counterpoint. Further, for all their immense differences of background, intention, and style, they are both poets who work against the grain of the dominant trends defining the different postwar contexts in which they write.

I would underline, first, that both are poets who express a searching *worldliness* in just about every substantive (noncynical) sense of this term. Akin in this regard to poets as otherwise different from them and from one another as T. S. Eliot, César Vallejo, Gwendolyn Brooks, or Adrienne Rich, they seek to lend voice to a broken human world, a potentially shared, if actually divided, world of fragile and often failed relationships, begun and discontinued conversations, initiated and derailed projects, precarious hopes and steep despairs, a world where, as Vallejo writes, "pain grows thirty minutes a second, step by step."[7] Like Vallejo, too, they seem to experience the world not as an iron cage but as a battered terrain of continual war or, at times, as a vast hospital of disintegrating patients. While there are hymnal passages in both (Hill's greatest work, in fact, may be his *Mercian Hymns,* a sequence marked by a visionary humor worthy of Blake), it is nonetheless true that they tend to write from despair, or from the edge of despair, with hope patiently sustained through the measured testimony, word by word, line by line, silence by silence, of a persisting capacity for living response and meditative reach:

> Cars on the highway filled with speech,
> People talk, they talk to each other;
>
> Imagine a man in the ditch,
> The wheels of the overturned wreck
>
> Still spinning—
> I don't mean he despairs, I mean if he does not
> He sees in the manner of poetry.
> (CP, 198)

Both, then, while testifying to their own sense of isolation, are philosophic poets, not afraid of carrying a complex movement of thought through to a provisional conclusion, and concerned in particular to articulate a questioning, self-questioning understanding of historical life: of the bridges, wreckings, and possibilities of human communities in time. Hill, delving through familiar and unfamiliar historical materials, seeking to recall to our lives the weight of the past and in particular of the dead, expresses this concern above all through a wounded elegiac and commemorative bearing, one placed under great pressure by the purgative force of self-scrutiny to which he subjects it.[8] Oppen, while often working in an elegiac mode, in particular in his recollections of those whom he encountered in his own experience throughout the twenty-five years during which he wrote no poetry, voices this concern with historical life above all through an extended meditation on the enormous predicaments of the present, on the saving pull of the future, and, linked to this, on the meaning of "covenant," a promise of relationship to be realized in time, involving "A devoutness // Toward the future / Recorded in this city" (CP, 120). "I know that no one would live out / Thirty years, fifty years if the world were ending / With his life" (CP, 40–41). Oppen, in fact, often expresses a sort of last-ditch faith in children, the simple and startling presence of the future in the present, or the living promise in the present that another generation might finally begin the long deferred project of "rescuing" one another from violence, poverty, isolation, and despair (CP, 47–49, 51, 52–54, 166, 234). Hill concludes one of his intent, critical, self-critical poems with an abrupt prayer to Love: "O Love, / You know what pains succeed; be vigilant, strive / To recognize the damned among your friends."[9] And though Oppen would not address this particular figure of Love—he is a naturalist who tends to speak, rather, of an immanent Eros—the spirit and passion of these lines could be set above his poetry as well as Hill's. "Crusoe // We say was / 'Rescued.' / So we have chosen" (CP, 166). The forming of responsible bridges in time as well as place is the broken promise of history we are called to realize: it is, as Oppen puts it, "the meaning / Of being numerous" (CP, 166).

Yet both of these poets, too, in different ways, weave across their concern with historical life a reaching openness to a metaphysical dimension of experience. Hill is a troubled, passionate Christian, at times bringing to mind a Pascal or a Kierkegaard, whose faith is sustained by being made to endure through rendings of guilt and doubt. Oppen, a wholly secularized Jewish writer, at times echoing the evocation of the luminous gift of being in the later Heidegger, at times echoing the evocation of the flowing "erosion" of nature or the "fatal rock" of the outer world in a long line of North American romantic writers (CP, 155–56, 179), voices both an experience of fear in response to the ceaseless flow of things and an almost pre-Socratic experience of wonder in response to the disclosive movement of what comes to be, "the open / Miracle // Of place" (CP, 156), the "mystery . . . that there is something for us to stand on" (CP, 159). The tension in both of these poets between a darkened historical vector and a speculative metaphysical vector, or between what Oppen sometimes calls the "horizontal" and the "vertical," lends their poetries a scope that sounds provocatively strange in the midst of our thoroughly flattened and commodifed world. Both Oppen and Hill, that is, while grounded in contemporary contexts as well as broader depths of history, and while in an important sense writers of the moral imagination, concerned to clarify the "limits" without which relationships become impossible, at the same time explore a "metaphysical" intuition of the bewildering "disproportion" between the finite person and the immensity of the universe: for Hill (as for Pascal or Kierkegaard) at once a nothing of infinite space and a hint of an infinite God, for Oppen (as for Heidegger or Merleau-Ponty) at once a nothing of infinite transience and a miracle of perpetual emergence and openness. "Surely infiniteness is the most evident thing in the world," Oppen writes (CP, 184), yet easily, he reminds us again and again, we forget this, grow oblivious to it, though it is there, the "obvious" itself (CP, 185, 211), "this in which the wild deer / Startle, and stare out" (CP, 99), "the initial light" (CP, 217), "'the picturesque / common lot' the unwarranted light // Where everyone has been" (CP, 225–26). Hill speaks of a mystery of "the unsustaining / wondrously sustained" disclosed in occasional visions "where grace has surprised us" (C, 4).

In our contemporary context it is perhaps especially significant that one can hardly read either of these poets without finding words like "authenticity" and "integrity" distinctly present in one's mind. Both of them, concerned to find what Oppen calls "a substantial language / Of clarity, and of respect" (CP, 156), or what Hill calls a "diligence / and attention, appropriately understood / as actuated self-knowledge" (TL, 63), commit themselves to a "testimonial" poetic pitched at a level so demanding it turns almost "prophetic" in its bearing. A poem is to enact, in every pulse of sound and silence forming its pattern, an exemplary movement of spirit finding a self-reflexively tested, fathomed response to the situation or preoccupation calling for attention.[10]

It is, Oppen writes in a late poem, "difficult to know what one means / —to be serious and to know what one means" (CP, 208). A "serious" testimonial poetic like Oppen's or Hill's, in its effort to voice a realized movement of response and reach, surpasses the simple expression of a self (though its basis in a distinctive curve of experience is clearly audible) in the direction of a "transpersonal" or "ideal" horizon; it addresses a challenge to the reader by addressing it first of all to the poet or, to lift a Hegelian term out of context, articulates a "shape of spirit" that summons both poet and reader beyond our habitually stubborn carelessness and thoughtlessness. The poem becomes a meditative field, the place of a sort of "spiritual exercise," in which language is probed, listened to, put under great pressure so that the horizons words can potentially draw us to (and perhaps hold us to) may come to be disclosed. In an ironic and jaded time like ours, of course, when "ideal" is often reduced to "idealization" or "illusion," such a poetic and the horizons it projects are frequently ironized, debunked, or simply abandoned, since, as a lazy argument has it, they are untrue to our lives; yet, more precisely, as Kierkegaard would say, it is our lives that are untrue to them.

Further, as Robert Hass has pointed out, this sort of poetic, in a very loose sense, has been so often travestied or debased that one at least understands the temptation simply to abandon it or debunk it. In contemporary poetry, Hass notes, the display of minor tics of tone and personality often replaces the shaping in form of substantive bearings of spirit:

> Instead of being an instrument to establish person, tone has become an instrument to establish personality. And the establishment of distinctions of personality by peripheral means is just what consumer society is about. Instead of real differences emanating from the life of the spirit, we are offered specious symbols of it, fantasies of our separateness by way of brands of cigarettes, jogging shoes, exotic food. Once free verse has become neutral, there must be an enormous impulse to use it in this way, to establish tone rather than to make form. Because it has no specific character, we make a character in it. And metrical poetry is used in the same way. When it is strong, it becomes, as it did for Eliot and Pound in the twenties, a personal reaction against cultural formlessness. When it is graceful and elegant, it becomes, as it was in Herrick, a private fiction of civility with no particular relation to the actual social life we live.[11]

Significantly, these acute observations, which say more about certain neighborhoods of contemporary culture than entire books have said, come nowhere near the poetries of Oppen and Hill except, precisely, in the "constrastive" standards they propose. Tone and pace, in Oppen and in Hill, measure shapes of spirit. Language in their poems is at once keenly mistrusted, for the readiness with which it serves our automatized dullness, and carefully trusted, for the power it holds to bear us a little beyond ourselves. One first of all *hears*, responds to the sound of, these poets. It is, among other things, the sound of a thinking integrity, a force sufficient to carry the effort, patiently renewed from poem to poem, of working through grim circumstances toward difficult, tested, reaching, provisional clarifications. In a climate like the one we inhabit, enormously polluted as it is by packaged codes and reified pseudoclarities, a poet unable to achieve such a force in sound is, in a sense, left with a choice between two fairly limited options: the writing of a kind of withdrawn verse, marked by a retreat from our context and the condition of our language, or the writing of an ironically indeterminate verse that, marked by a lucid alertness to our context and the condition of our language, anxiously avoids the saying of anything forceful at all and so, whatever its critical or diagnostic valence, hovers at a sort of impasse, in the shy half-lit space of a watchful clown. It is not, I think, an easy time in which to write poetry.

Oppen and Hill make clear what we risk losing if we abandon the horizons of this sort of poetic. Hill, characterizing the ideal to which he holds his own practice, recalls its roots in romantic poetics: "Readers of the *Biographia Literaria* may note that Coleridge's concern is not so much with thought as with 'the mind's self-experience in the act of thinking' and that this 'self-experience' is most clearly realized by the process of 'win[ning one's] way up against the stream' or of observing how 'human nature itself [fights] up against the wilful resignation of intellect' to the dominion of common assumption and mechanical categorization."[12] Oppen, in one of his few published essays, expresses this ideal with forceful concision: "It is part of the function of poetry to serve as a test of truth. It is possible to say anything in abstract prose, but a great many things one believes or would like to believe or thinks he believes will not substantiate themselves in the concrete materials of a poem."[13] These statements illuminate the demands involved in this conception of poetry: a poem is understood to be a field of linguistic action where, by listening with heightened pressure to what we are saying, and not saying, we discover just what we do believe or are capable of believing, what we do feel or are capable or incapable of feeling, how our being responds, or fails to respond, or can respond, or is called to respond to the matter that has drawn our attention. It is a question, Hill writes, of a search for a just and responsive language:

> Even now, I tell myself, there is a language
> to which I might speak and which
> would rightly hear me;
> responding with eloquence; in its turn,
> negotiating sense without insult
> given or injury taken.
> Familiar to those who already know it
> elsewhere as justice,
> it is met also in the form of silence.
> (TL, 18–19; cf. 63)

"What do we believe / To live with," Oppen asks in the first poem he wrote after a silence of twenty-five years (CP, 52)—a period during which he was, among other things, working for the Communist Party, fighting in a war against fascism, and living in exile in Mexico, but writing no poems—and, in an important sense, all his poetry is a continual wrestling anew, in the texture of the language he patiently explores, with this question, from different perspectives, from the changing places of his life. "Oppen is willing to be startled, unsettled, even frightened by the word or the world. Line by line, he wins a place to stand, constructing statements fit to stand on."[14] His syntax, at once halting and convincing, enacts the patience with which he searches, pauses, tests, searches again. He talks with himself, questioning himself and his words and the situations he encounters, carefully turning through the contradictions of his life, as he would talk, in a field of attention, with others. "We must talk now. Fear / Is fear. But we abandon one another" (CP, 89; cf. 158). "The poem becomes conversation," Paul Celan once stated in a now famous speech—a pained, but not quite despairing, speech—and the affirmation is close in spirit, if in different ways, to both Oppen's and Hill's poetries.[15]

To discuss Oppen or Hill in depth would require another book. At this point, since my concern is but to call to mind two poetries that I take to be substantive countercurrents to the climate of our time, I wish only to turn a moment to the last poem of Oppen's sequence "A Narrative" (CP, 150–56). This sequence, though not as ranging as the great sequences Oppen would publish a few years later, "Of Being Numerous" and "Route," anticipates those later journeys. The concluding poem of the sequence, like the sequence as a whole, embodies the characteristic tensions of Oppen's work that I briefly sketched above: the effort of a solitary individual to understand a society he fears is going to pieces; the poised reach toward the transience and the openness of the natural world wherein our singular lives and communal histories take place and come to wreck; the quietly unfolded affirmation of the love without which we are swept toward darkness in our own isolated defensiveness; the holding together, in a voice at once firm and pliant, of fear, wonder, joy, perplexity, openness, care; and the precise and spacious measuring, in the unfolding of the poem, of a "substantial language" in which these orientations are weighed, gathered, trued against both experience and hope:

> River of our substance
> Flowing
> With the rest. River of the substance
> Of the earth's curve, river of the substance

Of the sunrise, river of silt, of erosion, flowing
To no imaginable sea. But the mind rises

Into happiness, rising

Into what is there. I know of no other happiness
Nor have I ever witnessed it. . . . Islands
To the north

In polar mist
In the rather shallow sea —
Nothing more

But the sense
Of where we are

Who are most northerly. The marvel of the wave
Even here is its noise seething
In the world; I thought that even if there were nothing

The possibility of being would exist;
I thought I had encountered

Permanence; thought leaped on us in that sea
For in that sea we breathe the open
Miracle

Of place, and speak
If we would rescue
Love to the ice-lit

Upper world, a substantial language
Of clarity, and of respect.

It would be only a slight exaggeration to say that Oppen's entire vision is implied in this poem. The substance of all, of both the surrounding world and our lives, is evoked as the ceaseless flowing of all that is: at once an endless erosion, a mystery of nothing, and an abiding openness of what is there, a recurrent miracle of place. There we find our fear, the experience of the downward pull of erosion, and our possible reach, the rising of the mind into what is happening. It is as though Oppen were recalling some distant shared root of religion, philosophy, and poetry in a manifold experience of fear, wonder, perplexity, and orientation coming to words, attaining a provisional clarity. Yet the erosion is unrelenting. The religious, philosophic, or lyric "rising" into the openness of "what is there" readily sinks and darkens, perhaps, if it remains the movement of a mind in isolation from others. Eurydice, recalled at the end of the poem, is dragged to the underworld in a moment of misfortune; Psyche, also recalled at this point, wanders through loss and trial until coming to founder in nothing. Ruin is everywhere and near. Work, eros, attention, and speech are our resources. It is in resistance to this steady erosion, then, that Oppen throughout his poetry expresses a weathered, barely sustained hope, despite all the failures, in a larger historical project of community and, at an immediate or existential level, a quiet but convinced faith in the conversation of relationship, the latter being the realm of experience predominant in this particular poem. Psyche without Eros, as Keats suggests at the end of "Ode to Psyche," is likely to find herself at a loss, less an inner wide quietness than a solipsistic cave of shadows. Oppen, who at times seems to have obliquely elaborated a myth of Eros and Thanatos echoing and revising that of the later Freud, conceives of eros and language, desire and speech, as intimately intertwined in the project of shaping a common place in which to live: in another poem, "Of Being Numerous," he speaks of our "desire" and our "need" as "our jubilation / Exalted and as old as that truthfulness / Which illumines speech" (CP, 183–84). A "substantial language," he affirms at the end of "A Narrative," is a language of clarity and of respect, of disclosure and of care, that at once acknowledges and resists the endless erosion of the "substance" in time that we are and inhabit. This sort of intent language—sounding in its patiently articulated turning through descriptions, affirmations, qualifications, conjectures, pauses, suspensions, and crossings a complex recognition of what exceeds us, what sustains us, and what ruins us—may be, for Oppen, a basic condition of genuine conversation, relationship, and, as an ideal horizon and a difficult project, community in time. "Belief? / What do we believe / To live with? Answer. / Not invent— just answer—all / That verse attempts. / That we can somehow add each to each other?" (CP, 52). Perhaps *verse*, like trope a solitary turning of word and spirit in time, born of fear and wonder, of longing for passage, is called further by *conversation*, a turning together of words and lives in time, born of fear and care, of longing for relationship. Vision and companionship, as we read in one of

Oppen's unforgettable love poems, unfold against the terrors that make us "companion to the earth":

> What distinction
> I have is that I have lived
> My adult life
> With a beautiful woman, I have turned on the light
> Sometimes, to see her
>
> Sleeping—The girl who walked
> Indian style—straight-toed—
> With her blond hair
> Thru the forests
>
> Of Oregon
> Has changed the aspect
> Of things, everything is pierced
> By her presence tho we have wanted
> Not comforts
>
> But vision
> Whatever terrors
> May have made us
> Companion
> To the earth, whatever terrors—
>
> (CP, 129)

There is a letter of Oppen's, written about the time he may have been writing "A Narrative," whose language closely echoes that of the last poem of the sequence. Oppen seems in general to have had mixed feelings about the counterculture of the fifties and sixties. He certainly supported the political revolt against the programs of a ruling class given to insanities of violence. In this letter, however, he expresses a concern that some currents of the counterculture, in their restless and occasionally extreme turning away from inherited forms of art felt to have become leaden or inadequate, risk producing but an echo, at a slight distance, of the empty and pointless flowing away that our lives are always at risk of becoming anyway. It is as though he had a glimpse of what we have since come to know as "postmodernism"—a culture that celebrates the play of all sorts of multiplying flows, disconnected intensities, dispersive semantic currents—and, speaking out of an older rhythm of experience, wondered if this might not prefigure a catastrophic paradox: a society that, coming into being at a late moment in history, having attained an unprecedented degree of economic and technological development, would at that point blindly return to the natural history (the senseless passing of countless unremembered generations) out of which, in some unlikely turn in the distance of prehistory, the built world of human history had once emerged. Against this possibility he affirms his search for a substantial language whose disclosive measures, contours, and horizons permit us to build a habitable human world, to find our bearings, "the sense / Of where we are," within the open and the dark of the unknown:

> The new wave movies, the electronic music, or rather the music depending on hazard, the "accidental" music, those of the paintings which are deliberately formless, the poetry which is automatic writing, more or less—they may indeed display the truth, the meaningless river which flows with ourselves and our talk. And it may be that this is what art will become, the narrative of nothing, or of the inhuman event of humans. But I ponder simple brutal self defense: If it is that river, that meaningless river in which we are, it is nevertheless talk by which we are alive. If we want to continue to invent life for ourselves and for our children and for our friends it might be worth one's whole effort to find the alternative, some seed of an alternative, to this art.[16]

NOTES

INTRODUCTION. PASSAGES OF THE EXTRAVAGANT

1. Wittgenstein, *Tractatus Logico-Philosophicus*, 74; Cavell, *Senses of Walden*, 126; Nietzsche, *Thus Spoke Zarathustra*, 17; Char, *Les Matinaux*, 193.
2. Bonnefoy, *L'Improbable*, 1.
3. Arac, *Critical Genealogies*, 139.
4. The conventional threefold periodization of "modernity" describes an early period lasting from the Renaissance through the eighteenth century, a second period lasting from the French Revolution through World War I, and a recent period lasting from World War I through the present (this periodization is clearly and concisely mapped by Marshall Berman in *All That Is Solid*, 16–17). Except in a few places where the context clearly indicates otherwise, the expressions "modern art" and "modern philosophy" in this book refer to the span of the second and third periods of this conventional periodization. But the whole question of a "postmodern" phase that has perhaps emerged over the last thirty or forty years is a question I defer until the concluding chapter.
5. Thoreau, *Walden*, 9, 83, 288–89.
6. For a suggestive discussion of this and other meditations on *extravagance* in both Thoreau and Emerson, see Poirier, *Poetry and Pragmatism*, especially 37–75. I've learned a great deal from this essay and, in general, from Poirier's various studies of an Emersonian tradition in North American writing. Harold Bloom, another critic writing out of this tradition, is to my knowledge the only critic of the last century to have made central to his own practice the unquestionably valid recognition that *hyperbole* is a major trope of the entire history of poetry. That the prominence of this trope in poetry has been so little thematized is itself perhaps occasion for reflection. Bloom often borrows Thoreau's figure of extravagance for his thinking of hyperbole: see, for example, his account of romantic extravagance in the introduction to *Ringers in the Towers*, 3–11, or his discussion of the play of Negation, Evasion, and Extravagance in "Wallace Stevens," in *Agon*, 246–51. For illuminating studies of the central place of hyperbole in Nietzsche's project, see Nehamas, *Nietzsche*, 13–41, and Magnus, Stewart, and Mileur, *Nietzsche's Case*, 138–55. I am particularly indebted to the second of these books, in which Magnus, Stewart, and Mileur draw on Bloom as well as Nehamas in a reading of Nietzsche and his broad influence in modern culture. "Hyperbole," they write, "is of course inflated language, and since what goes up must come

down, it follows from this, deflated language as well. But hyperbole is not just the language of heights aspired to and depths fallen to, it is also the language of detours, of errancy, extravagance, and even errantry. . . . As the text-producing trope, hyperbole has been variously (though largely unconsciously) characterized by contemporary theorists as errancy (de Man), transgression (Foucault), dissemination (Derrida), and daemonization (Bloom). In this larger context, Nehamas's argument [concerning hyperbole in Nietzsche's work] opens the way for a reading of Nietzsche which would grasp that the unconscious autobiography (that every philosophy is) is, in Nietzsche's case, an extended meditation on the hyperbole that makes his text and his philosophy possible" (139–40). One might also recall in this context the opening invocation of Mallarmé's "Prose (pour des Esseintes)": "Hyperbole! de ma mémoire / Triomphalement ne sais-tu / Te lever, aujourd'hui grimoire / Dans un livre de fer vêtu" (*Oeuvres*, 58). "Poetry," Stephen Owen writes, "may call to that part of us that hungers for straying" (*Mi-Lou*, 11). From a very different perspective, Gerald Bruns, in *Heidegger's Estrangements*, characterizes poetry as a wandering that strays from, and so unsettles, both philosophy and common sense.

7. Cavell, *Senses of Walden*, 138.

8. Mandelstam, "Conversation about Dante," 259. My attention was first drawn to this passage, and to the extraordinary essay in which it appears, by Meschonnic (*Critique du rythme*, 33).

9. Frye, *Words with Power*, 116; cf. 111, 128–29. Frye is concerned to distinguish between rhetorical, poetic, and kerygmatic language, in this respect loosely recalling Longinus's attempt to distinguish between rhetorical language that "persuades us" and sublime or elevated language that "transports us in wonder" (*On the Sublime*, 100). "In poetry," Frye writes, "anything can be juxtaposed, or implicitly identified with, anything else. Kerygma takes this a step further and says: 'You are what you identify with'" (116). The kerygmatic, then, tends to break through contemplative detachment. In any case, I would define the poetic as a mode of the rhetorical, and the kerygmatic as the poetic at its highest pitch. The issue I mean to underline is simply that the kerygmatic, in this borrowed sense, is a characteristic dynamic in modern poetries and a fortiori in modern poetries of the extravagant.

10. Blake, *Complete Poetry and Prose*, 39; Rimbaud, *Oeuvres*, 225–26; Rilke, *Selected Poetry*, 61; William Carlos Williams, *Collected Poems*, 1:116; Montale, *Occasions*, 1. Montale once wrote to a friend: "My genre is wholly a waiting for the miracle, and in this day and age, with no religion, miracles are very rarely sighted" (cited by Arrowsmith in his notes to *Occasions*, 173).

11. Plato, *Republic*, II–III (376d–403c) and X (595a–608b). I've sketched here a "canonical" Plato whose framework Nietzsche and a number of philosophers working in his wake understand themselves to be disrupting or complicating. In several important books over the years, Stanley Rosen, paying attention to what Plato does as well as to what he says, has illuminated a very different Plato, one who acknowledges that a dialogue between poetry and philosophy necessarily takes place *within* any philosophy that would not decay into a mere formalism: see especially Rosen's *Limits of Analysis* and *Quarrel between Philosophy and Poetry*.

12. Danto, *Philosophical Disenfranchisement*, and Edmundson, *Literature against Philosophy*.

13. I would also note in this context the opening chapter, as funny as it is lucid, of Stephen Owen's *Mi-Lou*. There are affinities between Owen's and Edmundson's approaches. Both of these critics make clear that the quarrel between poetry and philosophy readily takes the form of a debate between Platonists and Aristotelians concerning the nature of poetry—a debate, as Owen in particular orchestrates it, between the *puritanical* philosopher highly sensitive to the unruly passions at play in poetry and the *professorial* philosopher intent on demonstrating the cognitive and therapeutic virtues and so the genuine social usefulness of poetry. Yet, as Edmundson shows, it is a post-Marxist and post-Freudian version of Plato's severe stance that appears to have become the dominant stance of the contemporary professor of literature.

14. Habermas, *Philosophical Discourse,* and Megill, *Prophets of Extremity.* Megill draws attention to similar arguments set forth by Stanley Rosen in his antihistoricist polemic, *Nihilism.* Rosen develops this polemic in a different way, as a sharp critique of postmodernism and post-structuralism, in his later *Hermeneutics as Politics.* Vincent Descombes's *Basometer of Modern Reason* has some affinities with these works. Don Byrd's *Poetics* includes a critical account of the shaping presence of romantic themes in post-structuralist thought. Charles Altieri has criticized the way romantic orientations guide, in particular, post-structuralist readings of modernist art (see the long, lucid, and challenging footnote in *Painterly Abstraction,* 426–29 n. 5).

15. Bloom, *Ringers in the Tower,* 323–24. One of the weakest chapters in Habermas's *Philosophical Discourse* is the chapter on Nietzsche, in which Habermas establishes the basic terms of his further readings of philosophers who have worked within a broad post-Nietzschean field of Continental philosophy. It is a weak chapter, above all, owing to the way Habermas simply erases the "ironic critic" always in tension with the "riddling visionary" in Nietzsche's project, turning Nietzsche's multidimensional voice into a one-dimensional voice of irrationalism (see Dallmayr, "Discourse of Modernity," 68–74). Or, to make this point another way, there is at work in a large part of modern philosophy a tension analogous to the major creative tension at work in almost all of modern poetry, a tension, as Charles Altieri describes it, between "the claims of lyricism" and "the claims of lucidity" (*Painterly Abstraction,* 61–64).

16. See Taylor, *Hegel and Modern Society,* especially 1–23. I discuss this important book in chapter 1 and again in the conclusion. Taylor argues that the major counterideal in tension with the ideal of radical freedom is that of expressive wholeness, substantive participation in a natural and a social world where one is "at home" as well as "free." For another powerful, multidimensional meditation on this tension in modern culture, see the essays gathered in two books by Robert B. Pippin, *Modernism* and *Idealism as Modernism.*

17. Nancy, *Experience of Freedom,* 150.

18. For a fine study of various apophatic religious traditions, see Sells, *Mystical Languages.* For an insightful account of the "negative theological" motifs at play in Heidegger, Derrida, and Blanchot, see Dufrenne, "Philosophie non théologique." Derrida presents a ranging engagement with this question in "How to Avoid Speaking."

19. Calinescu, *Five Faces,* 10; Habermas, *Philosophical Discourse,* 7; Berman, *All That Is Solid,* 102. The paradoxical "logic" of a culture of perpetual crisis is also a major theme of Octavio Paz's brilliant survey of modern poetry, *Hijos del limo.*

20. For an account of "self-assertion" (or, to translate this into the Nietzschean terms it recalls, "will to power") as the defining stance of modernity, see Blumenberg, *Legitimacy,* 125–226; for a similar characterization of this basic stance of modernity, from a severely critical point of view, see Rosen, *Nihilism.* On the interweaving of the elegiac and the utopian throughout modern culture, see Hartman, *Fateful Question,* 71–73, 190.

21. On the shaping presence in romantic poetry of the apocalyptic hopes both raised and disappointed by the French Revolution, see Abrams, "English Romanticism," and Bloom, "Internalization." On some analogous contextual coordinates of modernist and avantgardist art, see Anderson, "Modernity." "European modernism in the first years of this century," Anderson writes, "flowered in the space between a still usable classical past, a still indeterminate technical present, and a still unpredictable political future" (326). For illuminating discussions of the late-nineteenth-century "crisis of historicism," see Thomas, *New Historicism* and "Preserving and Keeping Order." For an exceptionally ranging and penetrating account of the unstable course of historicist thinking in nineteenth-century German philosophy in particular, see Löwith, *From Hegel to Nietzsche.* And for a probing meditation on the intertwining of historicist perspectives and crisis rhetorics throughout the modern period, both in literature and in philosophy, see Megill, *Prophets of Extremity.*

22. See Wallerstein, "Liberalism and Democracy," in *End of the World,* especially 90–91, and the essays collected in *After Liberalism.* Wallerstein argues that the global upheavals of the late sixties and early seventies mark the general collapse of this program.

23. For a perceptive discussion of the coexistence in the modernist period of "traditionalist" and "antitraditionalist" or "schismatic" modes of apocalyptic vision and rhetoric, see Frank Kermode's chapter, "Modern Apocalypse," in *Sense of an Ending,* 93–124. For a fine reading of Eliot in the terms I've just sketched, see Schneider, *T. S. Eliot.* For a ranging overview of surrealism, including an account of the political debates that both animated and splintered the movement, see Nadeau, *History of Surrealism.* Karl Löwith, in *From Hegel to Nietzsche* and *Martin Heidegger,* provides subtle accounts of the complexities of Nietzsche's reception in the early part of the twentieth century. In the latter part of the century, significantly, a relativist historicism comes to be a dominant cultural frame—one usually cast in Nietzschean or Foucauldian terms of "social power"—even as any ground for this framework wanes and any horizon of promise it might sustain grows radically uncertain. Nietzsche's exposure of reason as a mask of domination, once a startling defamiliarization, turns into an academic commonplace. Lyotard's *Postmodern Condition,* then, with its well-known thesis of the post-1968 collapse of all (progressive) metanarratives, could be said to register the popularization of a crisis of historicism that once belonged to limited spheres of high culture. For a marxist approach to this question in concrete social and political terms, see the works by Wallerstein cited in note 22. At any rate, historicism, in its relativist guise, appears to have been powerful enough to survive its own crisis.

24. Weber, *Protestant Ethic,* 181–82.

25. For a detailed, suggestive reading of Heidegger's *Being and Time* (published in 1927) as an indirect response to Lukács's *History and Class Consciousness* (published in 1923), see Goldmann, *Lukács et Heidegger.* Cf. Richard Bernstein's thoughts on this connection in *New Constellation,* 100–101.

26. One major exception, it is true, would be Levinas, who sets in opposition to an ontological "economy of the same" not any promise manifest in art but rather the "an-archic" force of the face of the other that commands an infinite ethical responsibility: see *Totality and Infinity* and *Otherwise than Being*. One could nonetheless observe that Levinas's ethical discourse, insofar as it is shaped by Heidegger's philosophy, owes at least an indirect debt to the tendency to set the promise of art in opposition to the cage of instrumental reason. For Levinas develops his prophetic ethic in a series of moves that could be schematized as follows. First, he lifts his account of Western ontology, understood as a reductive economy of the same, from Heidegger's account of ontotheology as a forgetting of Being, an unthinking of the ontic-ontological difference, or an unthinking of the mysterious *Ereignis* that, like an absent god of drift, gives both Time and Being. Second, in the place of these unthought dimensions and events evoked in Heidegger's later philosophy, he sets the sublime face of the other who commands the infinite responsibility of the ethical subject constituted through this command. Third, having borrowed all that he needs, he encloses Heidegger's later philosophy itself in the history of ontotheology or the economy of the same. But he has borrowed a good deal from a deconstruction of ontotheology that was informed by a long meditation on the relationship between art and philosophy. Another major exception in this field, of course, would be Habermas. Habermas's theory of the "colonization of the lifeworld" by "functionalist" logics of anonymous social systems, while clearly derived from the Hegelian marxist thought of the Frankfurt School, is developed in a quasi-Kantian or "transcendental" mode (though from a communication-centered, rather than a subject-centered, perspective). Further, contesting the sort of turn toward the call of art that I've sketched here, Habermas discerns a counterforce to these instrumentalizing trends not in the promise of art but rather in the ideal horizon implicit in ordinary communicative practice; see *Theory of Communicative Action*, especially vol. 2, *Lifeworld and System: A Critique of Functionalist Reason*, 283–373. Perhaps Gadamer and Ricoeur, major thinkers in the hermeneutic tradition, could be said to hover creatively to the side of this field of debates, insofar as their philosophic approaches are entirely alert to the reductions of instrumental thought, deeply responsive to the cognitive power of art, and yet skeptical of the emphatically romantic or modernist turns in Nietzsche, Adorno, the later Heidegger, and various post-structuralist thinkers. This, unfortunately, is a question I'll not have space to address in this book.

27. Paz, *Hijos del limo*, especially 65–87. See, too, Calinescu, *Five Faces*, 61–63, and Heller, *Importance of Nietzsche*, 3–4.

28. Char, *Fureur et mystère*, 181.

29. Stevens, "The Idea of Order at Key West," in *Palm*, 97; see Harold Bloom's fine discussion of these lines in *Wallace Stevens*, 98–101. For a parallel reading of modern French poetry, see Raymond, *De Baudelaire au surréalisme*. Interpretations of the romantic project akin to Abrams's are developed in Frye, "Romantic Myth," Bloom, "Internalization," and Altieri, *Painterly Abstraction*. For a critical review of Abrams's book, written from Nietzschean and Derridean perspectives, though with no acknowledgment that these perspectives are themselves further displacements within a long romantic tradition, see Miller, "Tradition and Difference." One effective way to revise Abrams's "translation thesis," I think, would be to turn it into a literary version of the "reoccupation thesis" that Hans Blumenberg, in *Legitimacy*, presents in his ranging engagement with the entire question of a

"secularization" process in modern culture. Blumenberg, primarily concerned with modern philosophy and philosophy of history rather than with modern literature, argues that the excesses and the predicaments encountered in a good deal of modern philosophy derive from the way modern thinkers have tended to "reoccupy" traditional Christian "questions," "positions," and "expectations" without acknowledging the considerably diminished resources, so to speak, available to any post-Christian thinker. This thesis, in my view, characterizes the impossible wager of many romantic and postromantic poetries just as well as it does the impossible wager of many modern philosophies and philosophies of history. In modern poetries, it is true, the hyperboles (as well as the predicaments they generate) tend to be emphatically foregrounded, unpredictably displaced, and time and again recast against all odds. This literary drama belongs nevertheless to a larger drama of steep ambition and steep disillusion enacted throughout modern culture.

30. Wordsworth, *Prelude* (1805), V, 448–49; Abrams, *Natural Supernaturalism*, 74. For detailed and illuminating discussions of this sort of poetry, all of which I draw on extensively here, see Langbaum, *Poetry of Experience*, 9–37; Abrams, "Structure and Style" and *Natural Supernaturalism*, especially 74–83 and 123–29; and Altieri, *Painterly Abstraction*, 59–107. Altieri calls this sort of practice "the scenic mode." In *Self and Sensibility* he sharply criticizes contemporary versions of this mode.

31. Wesling, *Chances of Rhyme, New Poetries*, and *Scissors of Meter*. My schematic account of this tradition is wholly indebted to Wesling's path-breaking work. Wesling's work in turn draws deeply and inventively on Abrams's *Mirror and the Lamp*, in particular chapters 7 and 8 of this book, "The Psychology of Literary Invention: Mechanical and Organic Theories" and "The Psychology of Literary Invention: Unconscious Genius and Organic Growth."

32. Coleridge, "On Poesy or Art," 262. This passage is of great importance in Wesling's account of the "rise of insurgent prosodies" in the postromantic period (see *New Poetries*, 13, 70–85).

33. In Wordsworth, as Geoffrey Hartman puts it, the modern lyric "frees itself from the tyranny of point" and thus, at the same time, from the repeated as well as conclusive closure of sense that a poetry of point or epigrammatic wit tends to secure ("Beyond Formalism," 15). The open-ended poem becomes a major force in modern poetics. Whitman and Rimbaud, among many others, expand this search for patterns and journeys resistant to those received patterns that are felt to perpetuate the abstraction or alienation of language from its speakers, that is, from these speakers' concrete and historically variable processes of thinking and responding (see Cook, "Point, Closure, Amplitude"). At the same time, this suspicion of the conventional device frees the old devices for other lives: a traditional metrical scheme no less than a pattern of free verse may turn out to be an exact seismograph of the shifting pressures of the present. Pitched against abstraction, patterned unpredictability becomes the measure (as, in a sense, it always has been); Whitman, Hopkins, and the French inventors of the prose poem are tall characters in Wesling's story.

34. For an illuminating survey of important communications that do nevertheless take place between these different Continental, Latin American, and North American adventures, see Paz, *Hijos del limo*, 168–82. And for a suggestive account of the shaping presence of late romantic and, in particular, "occultist" themes in the modernist poetries of Yeats, Pound, and Eliot—H. D., inexplicably, is left out of the story—see Surette, *Birth of Modernism*. All of

these adventures, further, draw expansively on the "poetic of the mask" (or, as it is better known in the English-language tradition, the "dramatic monologue") elaborated in nineteenth-century late romantic or symbolist poetries. This many-sided tradition, running from the nineteenth through the entire twentieth century, is splendidly studied in Langbaum, *Poetry of Experience,* especially 75–108, Christ, *Victorian and Modern Poetics,* especially 15–52, and Hamburger, *Truth of Poetry,* especially 61–80 and 110–47. As Hamburger writes, "poetic form itself can act as a mask" (75), a formulation that subtly illuminates the way a "constructivist" poetic comes to emerge out of a "symbolist" or "mask-making" poetic. Among other broad and suggestive accounts of the dialectical emergence of modernist poetries out of romantic or symbolist poetries, I would mention at least Raymond, *De Baudelaire au surréalisme,* Gelpi, *Coherent Splendor,* and, with an emphasis on the break between romantic and modernist modes, Nicholls, *Modernisms,* and Altieri, *Painterly Abstraction.*

35. Creeley, "Sense of Measure," 15. "A poem," William Carlos Williams writes, "is a small (or large) machine made of words" (*Collected Poems,* 2:54). One does not ask of a machine what it represents, or what it un-represents, but what it does, whether or not it works, how it helps one to proceed or hinders one from proceeding, what kinds of activities it creates or extends. Such created or extended ways of proceeding, if we bring the metaphor back to the realm of purposive action, can be said to involve not meanings so much as lines of meaningfulness, not an order of *signifiés* so much as orientations in a field of *signifiance* (see Meschonnic, *Critique du rythme,* 65–115, and Byrd, *Poetics,* 22–24). Charles Altieri is probably the finest theorist of this sort of "constructivist" poetic: here I've drawn heavily on his "Objectivist Tradition," *Act and Quality,* "What Modernism Offers," *Painterly Abstraction,* and *Subjective Agency.* Modernist art, Altieri argues, replaces "the logic of the window and the narrative account with . . . the logic of the imaginative site. Whereas the logic of the 'window' correlates scenic properties with forms of significance or types that can be sustained by a mode of 'telling,' the logic of the 'imaginative site' substitutes formal elements for those scenic features, and establishes their significance by making *the composing energies exemplify possible dispositions of mind with which an audience is invited to identify*" (*Painterly Abstraction,* 395–96). Elsewhere Altieri writes of the objectivist "field poetic" in particular: "[B]ecause the 'real' is accomplished, not simply given in perception, acts of disclosure and formal composition demand all those energies which romantic poets often felt could only be expressed either in apocalyptic vision or in dramatizing one's awareness of the dilemmas inherent in pursuing that vision" ("Objectivist Tradition," 31). It is the bringing together of a heightened attention to the act of composition and a heightened attention to the things and energies of everyday life that characterizes the "objectivist" current in twentieth-century North American poetry—an important countercurrent to the long tradition of extravagant quest or exploratory wandering.

36. Harold Bloom has often made this point—see, for one instance among many, *Agon,* 59. Bloom likes to translate Nietzsche's expression as the "urge to be elsewhere." Nietzsche speaks of the ascetic priest's "desire to be different, to be in a different place," in *Genealogy of Morals,* 120.

37. Hence Zarathustra's words: "To you, bold searchers, researchers, and whoever embarks with cunning sails on terrible seas—to you drunk with riddles, glad of the twilight, whose soul flutes lure astray to every whirlpool, because you do not want to grope along a

thread with cowardly hand; and where you can *guess,* you hate to *deduce*—to you alone I tell the riddle that I *saw,* the vision of the loneliest" (156). Or, as a voice in Forrest Gander's recent *Science and Steepleflower* says, "No one comes prepared / for the meaning of the sentence. / Yet we compass. Sometimes. We see" (14). I've adopted the expression "aeration of the text" from Fredric Jameson's discussion of a poetic tradition running from Whitman through Hart Crane and surrealism (see *Marxism and Form,* 101). Whitman's own trope in this respect is "dilation": "I dilate you with tremendous breath, I buoy you up" (*Leaves of Grass,* 74).

38. Steiner, "On Difficulty," 35.

39. Adorno's *Aesthetic Theory* is probably the most brilliant interpretation of modernism from this perspective. J. M. Bernstein, drawing on Adorno to elucidate the foregrounding of "formal properties" and the consequent disruption of illusionistic space and thematic clarity in modernist art, writes: "As aesthetic ideas were increasingly drawn within the governance of enlightened reason, their capacity to inhibit interpretation and conceptual articulation weakened; traditional works, including premodernist autonomous works, were drawn level with language by an increasingly self-confident critical community. Modernist art hence had to disabuse art of its reliance on these ideas and turn inwards on to its own productive forms" (*Recovering Ethical Life,* 171). This, again, is one important dynamic animating the transition from a romantic rhetoric of imaginative power, through a symbolist rhetoric of indirect evocation, to a modernist rhetoric of technical élan. Richard Poirier, whose lively suspicion of this line of thought does not blind him to its forceful claims, writes: "The idea that innovation in the arts is a form of cultural heroism—this is perhaps the central mythology behind the modernist cult of difficulty. In *Ulysses,* no less than in *Women in Love,* whose preface announces that the 'struggle for verbal consciousness should not be left out in art,' intended eccentricities in design, as against those considered at the time more conventional, are meant to imply that life calls upon the writer to rescue it from its entrapments in cultural systems, secular, ecclesiastical, and literary. Literary technique in modernist writing is, as it were, put on high alert in response to what other techniques or technologies have already done to life and language" (*Renewal of Literature,* 112).

40. Eysteinsson, *Concept of Modernism,* 44–49. Eysteinsson provides a very illuminating account of important lines of force that lead from modernism in the arts to poststructuralism in theory. See, too, Butler, *Early Modernism,* especially 1–25 and 89–132.

41. Emblematic in this respect is one of Derrida's quite early essays, "Force and Signification" (1963), an unmistakably "Nietzschean" and "modernist" meditation on the questions I've just sketched, one that works with concepts of "force" or "difference" (not yet "différance") and "representation" or "meaning" hardly distinguishable from similar Nietzschean concepts (*Writing and Difference,* 3–30). Here is the place to underline that what is often foregrounded and thematized as "process" in modern oppositional poetries tends to be engaged and thematized as "force" (or some close variant thereof) in modern critical philosophies written in conversation with these poetries.

42. See Weber, *From Max Weber,* 129–58, 180–95, 196–244, 267–322.

43. Bernstein, *Recovering Ethical Life,* 160–61. Elsewhere in the same essay (173) Bernstein draws attention to a passage in *Negative Dialectics* in which Adorno spells out the "modernist" orientation guiding his own philosophic practice: "instead of reducing philosophy to categories, one would in a sense have to compose it first. Its course must be a ceaseless

self-renewal, by its own strength as well as in friction with whatever standard it may have. *The crux is what happens in it, not a thesis or a position—the texture, not the deductive or inductive course of one-track minds.* Essentially, therefore, philosophy is not expoundable. If it were, it would be superfluous; the fact that most of it can be expounded speaks against it" (*Negative Dialectics*, 33–34; my italics). Adorno thus characterizes philosophic composition in precisely the terms ("the heresy of paraphrase") in which modern culture tends to valorize literary writing. It is true that in this passage Adorno is echoing the preface to *The Phenomenology of Spirit*, yet it is also true that that he carries this dialectical conception of philosophic practice to an extreme, polemical, quasi-artistic level, that is, to what Bernstein suggestively characterizes as a "modernist" level. For another reading of post-structuralism as late modernism, see Huyssen, *Great Divide*, 206–16.

44. Cf. the way Harold Bloom, in a spirited defense of the movements of creative vision in English high romantic poetries, questions the interpretation of these movements as projects of reconciliation in any but a metamorphic sense: "Even Northrop Frye, the leading romance theorist we have had at least since Ruskin, Pater, and Yeats, says that 'in Romanticism the main direction of the quest of identity tends increasingly to be downward and inward, toward a hidden basis or ground of identity between man and nature.' The directional part of this statement is true, but the stated goal I think is not. Frye still speaks of the Romantics as seeking a final unity between man and nature, but Blake and Shelley do not accept such a unity as a goal, unless a total transformation of man and nature can precede unity, while Wordsworth's visions of 'first and last and midst without end' preserve the unyielding forms both of nature and of man" ("Internalization," 10; cf. 6). Bloom perhaps misreads the Blakean Frye's distinctive use of the term "nature"—in which case his criticism of Frye would be borrowed, as it were, from Frye himself—yet his point is still well taken. The question, indeed, is what we mean by "nature" or "natural otherness," that is, how we imagine this substance or basis of our embodied lives. Blake at once wholly affirms a release of human desires (as well as an expansion of all the senses) and wholly objects to any language of "fitting and fitted" (a language, in his view, of a fallen, a passive, or a resigned imaginative stance). See, too, Thomas Weiskel's keen reflections on the tendency of thinkers within marxist and *marxisant* traditions to adopt a Kantian aesthetic of the beautiful while ignoring an aesthetic of the sublime (*Romantic Sublime*, 45–46, 85). But there are exceptions, for example, T. J. Clark. On modern art and the unhappy consciousness of Hegel's *Phenomenology of Spirit*, see Clark, *Farewell to an Idea*, 329. Clark's is the most brilliant book I've read on modernist painting and, more broadly, on the relations between modernist art and radical politics. Unfortunately, it's a book I discovered far too late to be able to bring into my work here in any serious way.

45. Nancy, preface to *Of the Sublime*, 1. The fact that most twentieth-century philosophers avoid the term "sublime" itself is an important issue (and a telling sign) that I address in chapter 1.

46. Heaney, *Seeing Things*, 100. Heaney, in a luminous discussion of Shakespeare's Sonnet 60, writes: "Something visionary happens there in the fifth line ["Nativity, once in the main of light"]. 'Nativity,' an abstract noun housed in a wavering body of sound, sets up a warning tremor just before the mind's eye gets dazzled by 'the main of light,' and for a split second, we are in the world of the *Paradiso*. The rest of the poem lives melodiously in a world of discourse but it is this unpredictable strike into the realm of pure being that

marks the sonnet with Shakespeare's extravagant genius" (*Government of the Tongue*, 15). Heaney uses the term "extravagant" in a similar way in a brief discussion of Herbert's poetry at the end of his well-known essay "The Redress of Poetry": "The confirmations bestowed by proportion and pace and measure are undeniably essential to [Herbert's] achievement, and there is a fundamental strength about the way his winding forms and woven metaphors match the toils of consciousness; but it is when the spirit is called extravagantly beyond the course that the usual life plots for it, when outcry or rhapsody is wrung from it as it flies in upon some unexpected image of its own solitude and distinctness, it is then that Herbert's work exemplifies the redress of poetry at its most exquisite" (*Redress of Poetry*, 16). Heaney's own poetry has involved a long, complex meditation on this fundamental tension between respect for the "gravitational pull of the actual" (*Redress of Poetry*, 3) and an openness to what Heaney variously calls, among other things, the extravagant, the buoyant, the lightened, the marvelous, the unroofed.

47. I loosely adopt the expression "change of affect" from Fredric Jameson: see chapter 3, note 83.

48. Jameson, *Postmodernism*, especially ix, 36, and 307–10.

CHAPTER ONE. THE SUBLIME IN KANT, WORDSWORTH, AND LYOTARD

1. Emerson, "Circles," in *Essays and Lectures*, 413.
2. Pippin, *Modernism*, 46. My general understanding of Kant's project is indebted both to Pippin's account in this book (and in *Idealism as Modernism*) and to Charles Taylor's account in *Hegel and Modern Society*.
3. Pippin, *Modernism*, 53.
4. For a detailed argument that Kant does not establish the sort of severe dualism that he has often been understood to establish, see Guyer, *Experience of Freedom*, 335–94. For a persuasive argument that this is the way in which Kant has nevertheless been "read" throughout the modern period, see Taylor, *Hegel and Modern Society*, 1–23 and 76–84. Taylor argues that throughout the modern period the major ideal in tension with this ideal of "radical freedom" has been the ideal of "expressivist wholeness." One might say, a little schematically, that a tradition running from Hegel and Marx through twentieth-century Western marxism has spoken primarily for the latter, while a tradition running from Kierkegaard and Nietzsche through twentieth-century existentialism has spoken primarily for the former (see Taylor, *Hegel and Modern Society*, 135–69, for a somewhat different, and highly nuanced, sketch of this conflict in modern philosophy after Kant).
5. Our promise, Schiller subsequently writes, lies in the interanimation of our faculties set in motion in aesthetic play: "[M]an only plays when he is in the fullest sense a human being, and he is only fully a human being when he plays" (*Aesthetic Education*, 107). "The poet, described in ideal perfection," Coleridge writes, "brings the whole soul of man into activity" (*Biographia Literaria*, 2:12). It would be left to philosophers and poets in Kant's wake, including Schiller and Coleridge, to translate Kant's "transcendental" and "formalist" account of the beautiful into either anthropological, psychological, or on occasion metaphysical terms.
6. See Allison, *Kant's Theory*, 306–7.

7. Paul Guyer points out that there is a certain indeterminacy in Kant's own conception of aesthetic experience, a tension between his occasional emphasis on the "primacy of feeling" and his occasional emphasis on the "primacy of judgment," the latter being of particular importance in his account of the complex movements involved in the sublime (*Experience of Freedom*, 205–9).

8. See Schiller, "On the Sublime," especially 204–10. Geoffrey Hartman writes of the poet of *The Prelude:* "He recognizes that his home is with infinity. The recognition, however, frees him for the world it denies because he is now absolutely sure of imagination's autonomy. It has shown itself distinct from nature, as an unmediated, apocalyptic force. The visionary dreariness of the spots of time also foretells the insufficiency or even the destruction of nature" (*Wordsworth's Poetry: 1787–1814*, 216). This book of Hartman's will hereafter be cited in my text as WP.

9. de Man, "Phenomenality," 104.

10. See Guyer, *Experience of Freedom*, 191–92.

11. It is from the perspective of a double movement of challenge and recovery that one can most clearly discern the affinities as well as the differences between Kant's and Edmund Burke's accounts of the sublime. For one of the important themes that Kant transposes from Burke's sensationalist or physiological account of the sublime into his own idealist or transcendental account is that of this movement in two phases whereby a human power is discovered and awakened through an unsettling challenge to that power. Burke describes this dynamic in terms of an activity of "labour" that surmounts "difficulties" encountered: "Melancholy, dejection, despair, and often self-murder, is the consequence of this gloomy view we take of things in [a] relaxed state of body. The best remedy for all these evils is exercise or *labour;* and labour is a surmounting of *difficulties,* an exertion of the contracting power of the muscles.... Now, as a due exercise is essential to the coarse muscular parts of the constitution, and that without this rousing they would become languid, and diseased, the very same rule holds with regard to those finer parts we have mentioned; to have them in proper order, they must be shaken and worked to a proper degree" (*Philosophical Enquiry,* 135). Recalling the high valorization of textual "complexity" over the last century, one could readily translate this passage into the terms of a plausible "psychological" account of the modernist "textual" sublime. Nietzsche, too, often moves in this field of thought: "What is happiness?—The feeling that power *increases*—that a resistance is overcome" (*Twilight of the Idols,* 125). Thomas Weiskel, in *The Romantic Sublime* (83–103), characterizes this double movement of the Kantian or negative sublime as an oedipal drama: a threat to the self followed by a restorative reidentification of the self with an internalized model of authority. But it may be, he also suggests, that this drama is superimposed on an earlier pre-oedipal ambivalence, "a wish to be inundated and a simultaneous anxiety of annihilation" (105). In "The Notion of Blockage in the Literature of the Sublime," Neil Hertz, attending closely to Weiskel's study and to Angus Fletcher's study of allegory, suggests that the romantic sublime involves a translation of an earlier "rhetorical" notion of the sublime into an "experiential" or psychological notion, as well as a translation of questions of textual "difficulty" into questions of experiential "blockage"; both of these moves, he says, are "designed to consolidate a reassuringly operative notion of the self" (48).

12. These passages of the extravagant, then, are among other things expressions of what both M. H. Abrams and Harold Bloom have described as the creative "inwardization"

of the apocalyptic expectations raised and disappointed by the course of the French Revolution: see Abrams, "English Romanticism," and Bloom, "Internalization."

13. I've borrowed the expression "departure and return" from Tyler Roberts's suggestive discussion of a similar "problem" in Nietzsche's writings: see *Contesting Spirit*, especially 202–4. In romantic poetry, Northrop Frye writes, "the emphasis is not on what we have called sense, but on the constructive power of the mind, where reality is brought into being by experience" ("Drunken Boat," 207; cf. Frye, "Romantic Myth," 14–15).

14. Frye, "Drunken Boat," 209.

15. As we will see in the next chapter, French romanticism, at its most extreme a kind of gnostic anti-Catholicism, is a different (though closely related) story.

16. See Bloom, "Internalization," especially 5–13, *Visionary Company*, xiii–xxv, and the essays collected in *The Ringers in the Tower*. Cf. Frye, "Romantic Myth," especially 35–38. Bloom emphasizes that this internalized quest tends to involve not a realized horizon but primarily what he calls a *purgatorial process* of freeing imaginitive energy from the many repressions and anxieties that burden it: hence the importance of the "crisis poem" throughout the romantic tradition ("Internalization," 6–8, 11). Abrams writes: "[An] important and dramatic phenomenon [in the Christian tradition] was the tendency, grounded in the New Testament itself, to internalize apocalypse by transferring the theater of events from the outer earth and heaven to the spirit of the single believer, in which there enacts itself, metaphorically [or, in the language of Inner Light Protestantism, according to the spirit rather than the lettter], the entire eschatological drama of the destruction of the old creation, the union with Christ, and the emergence of a new creation—not *in illud tempus* but here and now, in this life" (*Natural Supernaturalism*, 47; cf. 55–56). Isaiah Berlin, though he overstates the irrationalist or anti-Enlightenment dimensions of romanticism, similarly underlines the way romantic writers draw on "pietist" or "inner light" movements of the seventeenth and eighteenth centuries (*Roots of Romanticism*, especially 36–45).

17. Emerson, "Self-Reliance" in *Essays and Lectures*, 271.

18. Abrams, *Natural Supernaturalism*, 74–94. Abrams traces the pattern of both Wordsworth's *Prelude* and Proust's *À la recherche du temps perdu* back to Augustine's *Confessions*.

19. Wordsworth makes the link between these two kinds of visitation quite clear in book 12. The lines immediately preceding the extended "spots of time" passage are these: "I had felt / Too forcibly, too early in my life, / Visitings of imaginative power / For this to last: I shook the habit off / Entirely and for ever, and again / In nature's presence stood, as I stand now, / A sensitive, and a creative soul" (XII, 250–56).

20. So too in "Tintern Abbey," a kind of compressed fore-echo of *The Prelude*, the poet, while weaving a restorative hymn out of an elegiac anticipation of death, affirms this ambiguous drama: "And I have felt / A presence that disturbs me with the joy / Of elevated thoughts; a sense sublime / Of something far more deeply interfused, / Whose dwelling is the light of setting suns, / And the round ocean, and the living air, / And the blue sky, and in the mind of man, / A motion and a spirit, that impels / All thinking things, all objects of all thought, / And rolls through all things. Therefore am I still / A lover of the meadows and the woods, / And mountains; and of all that we behold / From this green earth; of all the mighty world / Of eye and ear, both what they half-create, / And what perceive; well pleased to recognize / In nature and the language of the sense, / The anchor of my purest

thoughts, the nurse, / The guide, the guardian of my heart, and soul / Of all my moral being" (MW, 134).

21. Jonathan Wordsworth, in a discussion of book VIII of *The Prelude*, writes: "The shepherds chosen to show how the poet came to feel 'Love human to the creature in himself' do nothing of the kind. They are symbolic figures stalking giant-like through the mist, or glorified by radiance from the setting sun. . . . The shepherds take hold of the imagination because they are so removed from the human normality they are supposed to exemplify. They are not 'brothers of this world' but borderers on the verge of another" and so, in a sense, "are Wordsworth himself" (*Borders of Vision*, 282, 289). Many years ago, in *The Limits of Mortality*, David Ferry presented a similar argument in notably severe terms, claiming that there is indeed a misanthropic bearing at work in all of Wordsworth's poetry, a bearing at once marked and disguised by the poet's fascination with "aberrant" human characters, in whom he discerns, above all, uncommon emblems of his own uncommon mind (see especially 53, 104–11, and 142–43). For another argument of this sort, see Frances Ferguson's comments on "Tintern Abbey" in *Solitude and the Sublime*, 125–27.

22. Abrams ("English Romanticism," 112–19) speaks of Wordsworth's "other voice," arguing that this voice is grounded in the transvaluation of values of the Gospels. Gill writes, "[T]he George Eliot of *Adam Bede* and *Silas Marner* and other novelists . . . are the true heirs of Wordsworth in the Victorian period" (*William Wordsworth*, 24–25 and 426, n. 27). For a probing study of the sort of "sympathy" and "solidarity" Wordsworth voices in his poetry of the 1790s, see Bromwich, *Disowned by Memory*. And for a very thoughtful account, in particular, of the poet's encounter with the Blind Beggar of book VII of *The Prelude*, see Jonathan Wordsworth, *Borders of Vision*, 302–7.

23. In my discussion of Lyotard I take the terms "modernism" and "avantgarde" to be interchangeable. The distinctions between "modernism" and "the avantgarde," while important to any detailed account of the arts in this period, do not appear to be of much importance to Lyotard. Yet it should be borne in mind that modernist and avantgardist art are, for Lyotard, always associated with the decidedly "radical" aesthetic and political orientations characteristic of the Continental avantgarde in particular.

24. Lyotard (P, 32–36) has expressed his own dismay at the hyper-Nietzschean rhetoric of *Libidinal Economy* (1974), a book that seeks to outstrip Deleuze in a Deleuzian fashion. The book is an enthusiastic expression of Lyotard's "antisystem" or "invention-contra-representation" rhetoric of the seventies. If surrealism can be described as a practice of open-ended play wherein the eros animating textual wandering is set in opposition to the solidities of theoretical reason and practical calculation, Lyotard's direction throughout the seventies could be described as a kind of avantgardist (or postsurrealist) philosophy of avantgardism. "One must be a nomad," Picabia is reported to have said, "and pass through ideas as one passes through countries and cities" (see Breton, "For Dada, etc.," 206). This could serve as an epigraph to Lyotard's writings of the seventies.

25. Breton, "Mille et mille fois," in *Poems*, 33. On the tendency of post-structuralist thinkers to recast Nietzsche's obsession with "vertical" hierarchies as a concern with "horizontal" differences, see Schrift, *Nietzsche's French Legacy*, especially 22–23, 65–67.

26. In the last few pages of this essay Lyotard presents his "paradoxical" definition of the "postmodern": "In an amazing acceleration, the generations [of artists] precipitate

themselves. A work can become modern only if it is first postmodern. Postmodernism thus understood is not modernism at its end but in the nascent state, and this state is constant. . . . If it is true that modernity takes place in the withdrawal of the real and according to the sublime relation between the presentable and the conceivable, it is possible, within this relation, to distinguish two modes (to use the musician's language). The emphasis can be placed on the powerlessness of the faculty of presentation, on the nostalgia for the presence felt by the human subject, on the obscure and futile will which inhabits him in spite of everything. The emphasis can be placed, rather, on the power of the faculty to conceive, on its 'inhumanity' so to speak (it was the quality Apollinaire demanded of modern artists), since it is not the business of our understanding whether or not human sensibility or imagination can match what it conceives. The emphasis can also be placed on the increase of being and the jubilation which result from the invention of new rules of the game, be it pictorial, artistic, or any other. What I have in mind will become clear if we dispose very schematically a few names on the chessboard of the history of avant-gardes: on the side of melancholia, the German Expressionists, and on the side of *novatio*, Braque and Picasso, on the former Malevitch and on the latter Lissitsky, on the one Chirico and on the other Duchamp. The nuance which distinguishes these two modes may be infinitesimal; they often coexist in the same piece, are almost indistinguishable; and yet they testify to a difference on which the fate of thought depends and will depend for a long time, between regret and assay" (79–80). Though in my view this passage casts little light on postmodernism, it splendidly clarifies Lyotard's understanding of modernism as an artistic field that, if occasionally nostalgic for a lost order and a lost ground, is above all animated by a Nietzschean spirit of creative experimentation and incalculable adventure. It is this Nietzschean spirit of modernism that Lyotard characterizes in terms of the Kantian sublime: in terms of the subject's awakened powers of invention, conception, and possibility.

27. Schrift, *Nietzsche's French Legacy,* 104–9, and Lacoue-Labarthe, "Ou en étions-nous," 182–89.

28. Or again, when asked about the viability of an ethics or a politics that could never respond with irrefutable reasons to the question why, Lyotard answers with a description of the political field as a field of Nietzschean improvisations and avantgardist experiments: "I actually think that the question of the 'why,' in the strict sense of the term, never really gets answered. . . . This implies that the task is one of multiplying and refining language games. I mean that, ultimately, what does this thesis lead to? To a literature, in the best sense of the term, as an enterprise of experimentation on language games, to a general literature if one can put it this way" (49; cf. 60–62). This motif is further elaborated in *The Differend,* though in this later text the emphasis falls less on the aesthetic question of inventing new idioms than on the ethical question of responding attentively to irreducibly different idioms: "One's responsibility before thought consists, on the contrary, in detecting differends and in finding the (impossible) idiom for phrasing them. This is what a philosopher does. An intellectual is someone who helps forget differends, by advocating a given genre, whichever one it may be (including the ecstasy of sacrifice), for the sake of political hegemony" (D, 142).

29. Elsewhere in this book, too, Lyotard seems to echo Jameson's foreword to *The Postmodern Condition:* "Yet there is a kind of collusion between capital and the avantgarde.

The force of scepticism and even of destruction that capitalism has brought into play, and that Marx never ceased analyzing and identifying, in some way encourages among artists a mistrust of established rules and a willingness to experiment with means of expression, with styles, with ever-new materials" (I, 105).

30. This motif of the "indeterminacy" of the "child," however, does briefly return in two of the essays in *Postmodern Fables*, "Unbeknownst" (especially 194–97) and "Music, Mutif" (especially 218), and in an essay, "The Grip," included in *Political Writings* (148–58).

31. "Language speaks. Man speaks in that he responds to language," Heidegger writes in "Language" (*Poetry, Language, Thought*, 210). Lyotard seems to draw not only on this lecture but also on Heidegger's lecture "Time and Being." He attempts to distinguish his meditation from Heidegger's by claiming that the latter remains anthropocentric insofar as the *Ereignis* or Event of Appropriation is said to be "addressed" to "man," whereas his own meditation is free of any anthropocentrism insofar as the "There is" of a phrase is said to be not addressed to anyone but, rather, to situate an addressee as merely one of the situational instances it institutes (75). This is sound enough as a critique of Heidegger's notion of a destiny of Being "addressed" to "man," but it hardly marks a departure from a thoroughly Heideggerian weather of thought, a weather in which Lyotard moves in all his texts from *The Differend* on. Lyotard has transposed Heidegger's notion of *Ereignis* to the happening of phrases—a move already suggested in various texts of Heidegger's—while dispensing with Heidegger's story of a history of Being sending "postcards" to "man" (to recall Derrida's impish trope on this tale). Further, Lyotard *does* often sound a Heideggerian language of "authenticity," for example, in the passage from the introduction to *The Inhuman* that I cited above. What, if not "authenticity," is at stake in a passage like the following: "The suspicion they [the 'talks' collected in *The Inhuman*] betray . . . is simple, although double: what if human beings, in humanism's sense, were in the process of, constrained into, becoming inhuman (that's the first part)? And (the second part), what if what is 'proper' to humankind were to be inhabited by the inhuman?" (2). For a more sympathetic reading of Lyotard's attempt to distance himself from the Heidegger he echoes here, see Bennington, *Lyotard Writing the Event*, 127–29.

32. This response to Newman's paintings should be juxtaposed with the responses of alert critics who were closer to Newman's own orientations and to the specific context in which he worked: Lawrence Alloway has argued that Newman's work is rather closely aligned with traditional conceptions of the sublime (*Topics in American Art*, 31–51), while Harold Rosenberg has illuminated the productive puzzles raised by Newman's work in the context of postwar art in New York (*Anxious Object*, 169–74, and *Art on the Edge*, 50–59). Both Alloway and Rosenberg, in line with the dominant spirit of modern art, respond to Newman's paintings primarily from the artist's point of view. Lyotard, in shifting from a Nietzschean to a Heideggerian account of the sublime, shifts as well from an account based on the artist's point of view to an account based on the spectator's point of view. This limits the scope of his discussion.

33. Elsewhere, in a clear transposition of a Levinasian theme, Lyotard describes the experience of the subject unsettled in its encounter with a sublime indeterminacy as an experience of a "passability" prior to the opposition between passivity and activity (I, 116–18). Lyotard might object to the language of "authentic dwelling in time" in this para-

graph, yet, as I point out in note 31, I'm not at all persuaded that Lyotard has moved very far from the weather of Heidegger's meditations.

34. Lyotard, as I noted above, seems at least in part to accept Jameson's reiteration of Marx's vision of capitalism as itself the "permanent revolution" of ceaseless innovation. Yet he finally retains the "antisystem" perspective already developed in his earlier writings. On the whole, that is, he maintains his adherence to a reading of capitalist modernity as primarily "functionalist imprisonment" rather than primarily "perpetual upheaval," or, to put this more exactly, he understands the perpetual upheaval of capitalist modernity to be itself an effective ruse of a larger dynamic of functionalist imprisonment.

35. Murdoch, *Sovereignty of Good*, 80. In the next two paragraphs of my text this book is cited as SG.

36. Is this fair to Kant? Probably not. In the second of the passages just cited, it would seem, Murdoch means above all to criticize existentialist and "rational choice theory" versions of a post-Kantian tradition.

37. Caputo, *Radical Hermeneutics*, 266–67. See, too, Bernstein, "Heidegger's Silence? Ethos and Technology" in *New Constellation*, 79–141.

38. On the quiet, unannounced presence in Heidegger of the thought and the language of the romantic sublime, see Lacoue-Labarthe, "Sublime Truth." This essay includes, among other things, a brilliant reading of Heidegger's "Origin of the Work of Art."

39. For a thoughtful discussion of the impact of the crises of the thirties and forties in particular on the major post-structuralist thinkers of postwar France, see Descombes, "The French Crisis of Enlightenment," in *Barometer of Modern Reason*, 65–92. In *Oneself as Another*, 336–41, Paul Ricoeur sympathetically elucidates the way Levinas's prophetic ethic emerges through a *hyperbolic inversion* (the ethical subject painfully held hostage to the other) of a *hyperbolic presupposition* (the natural self relating to alterity of any sort in the mode of sheer subsumptive violence). It would be plausible, then, to read this ethic, and the meditative movement out of which it emerges, as a resonant "historical" allegory. The most powerful critique I've encountered of the Levinasian ethic currently in the ascendant in both the French and the Anglo-American academies is that which Gillian Rose spells out in a lucid and polemical series of books: see her *Broken Middle, Judaism and Modernity*, and *Mourning Becomes the Law*.

CHAPTER TWO. FAUSTIAN QUEST IN RIMBAUD, NIETZSCHE, AND BATAILLE

My translations of Rimbaud's poetry and prose in this chapter rely upon, though they often depart from, the translations by Oliver Bernard in *The Collected Poems*, and by Enid Rhodes Peschel in *A Season in Hell/The Illuminations;* both of these works are listed in the abbreviations preceding the text. For the sake of brevity and clarity, however, only Suzanne Bernard and André Guyaux's edition of the *Oeuvres* and Oliver Bernard's edition of the *Collected Poems* are cited throughout the text.

1. Blake, *The Marriage of Heaven and Hell*, in *Complete Poetry*, 35. Nietzsche, near the end of his writing life, claims that Faust's adventure, as represented by Goethe, is but a

pale anticipation of his own abyssal adventure, likening himself instead to Byron's Manfred: "I must be profoundly related to *Byron's* Manfred: all these abysses I found in myself; at the age of thirteen I was ripe for this work. I have no word, only a glance, for those who dare to pronounce the word 'Faust' in the presence of Manfred" (EH, 245).

2. Marx, *Communist Manifesto*, 58. The figure of the sorcerer who has lost control over the powers he has conjured up appears two pages later: "Modern bourgeois society with its relations of production, of exchange and of property, a society that has conjured up such gigantic means of production and of exchange, is like the sorcerer who is no longer able to control the powers of the nether world whom he has called up by his spells" (60).

3. For Berman's account of Marx, see *All That Is Solid*, especially 87–129; for his account of Marx's wrestling with nihilism in particular, see 94–105, 110–11, and 355 n. 9. For a marxist critique of Berman's reading of both Marx and modernity, see Anderson, "Modernity and Revolution." And for Berman's response to Anderson, see *Adventures in Marxism*, 153–69.

4. For a perceptive exploration of numerous parallels between Rimbaud's visionary adventure and those of other romantic writers, in particular Blake and Nietzsche, see Ahearn, *Rimbaud*.

5. On the basic elements of apocalypticism, see Collins, "Apocalypticism," especially 146. Harold Bloom has underlined in many places the immense importance of the experience of *transition* or *crossing* in gnostic currents of thought: "Gnosis, whether in Gnosticism or in Emerson, emphasizes that *transition* is more real than being" (*Agon*, 13). "Life only avails," Emerson writes in a famous passage, "not the having lived. Power ceases in the instant of repose; it resides in the moment of transition from a past to a new state, in the shooting of a gulf, in the darting to an aim" ("Self-Reliance," in *Essays and Lectures*, 271). This is a vision shared by Rimbaud.

6. Richard, "Poésie du devenir," 193.

7. On the romantic revolt against "sky-gods," see Frye, "Romantic Myth," 13–14, and "Drunken Boat," 204–5. Why did satanic revolt and occultist voyage attain in French romantic culture an importance they never attained in the romantic revolutions in other nations? An adequate answer to this question would presumably require a history of modern France, a history that would have to include an account of the place in French society of a Catholic Church largely committed to reaction from 1789 through 1945, as well as an account of the relative invisibility in nineteenth-century France of the individualist and politically progressive Protestant traditions that were creatively recast in German, English, and North American romanticism.

8. As Charles Russell puts it: "The implicit paradox in this poetic venture is that the passionate derangement of the self should lead to a vision of an impersonal harmony" (*Poets, Prophets, and Revolutionaries*, 52). Richard, in a similar vein, writes: "[I]n Rimbaud's hierarchy of creative gestures, then, let us place disordering [*dérèglement*] well below release [*dégagement*]" ("Poésie du devenir," 190–91). On the multiple meanings of "sens" in Rimbaud's famous formulation, see Ross, *Social Space*, 9.

9. This is the claim splendidly developed in James Lawler's reading of "Le Bateau ivre" as a dynamic or "kinaesthetic" response to Baudelaire's meditative and largely discursive "Voyage" (*Theatre of the Self*, 7–40). Lawler, in a similar way, shows how "Voyelles" dy-

namically transforms the evocative synaesthesia of Baudelaire's "Correspondances" (*Theatre of the Self*, 47–53).

10. It is this experience of *éclosion*, I think, that lies behind the passion for sheer *fluency* to which Rimbaud attests throughout his poetry. Some commentators have emphasized the many evocations in Rimbaud of liquidity, porosity, and fermentation (see, for example, Richard, "Poésie du devenir," and Jameson, "Rimbaud and the Spatial Text"), while others have emphasized the many evocations of light and fire (see, for example, Munier, *L'Ardente Patience*), while still others have emphasized the many evocations of music, harmony, and orphic orchestration (see, for example, Lawler, *Theatre of the Self*, and Bonnefoy, *Rimbaud*). It seems to me that all these readings are sound insofar as they acknowledge the equal soundness of the others. Rimbaud's passion for fluent motion, so to speak, cannot be reduced to a single element in his perceptual imagination. All that is wavelike, all that departs as it arrives, all that is perceived as at once a palpable presence and a metamorphic force in motion draws Rimbaud after it like a promise of renovative passage. This is his distinctive inflection of the ideal of synaesthetic transport.

11. Rivière, *Rimbaud*, 137. Cf. Kenneth Burke's account of metaphor in *A Grammar of Motives*, 503–5. Perhaps we could say that Rimbaud goes to the root of speculative play. "All we can say about these venerable texts," Johan Huizinga writes in a discussion of the Vedic hymns, "is that in them we are witnessing the birth of philosophy, not in vain play, but in sacred play. Highest wisdom is practiced as an esoteric *tour de force*" (*Homo Ludens*, 107). One enters the mystery by singing, praying, or riddling, versions of an abiding vocation of the human mind, reaching by guessing. "Elle est retrouvée. / Quoi?—L'Éternité. / C'est la mer allée / Avec le soleil [It is found again. / What?—Eternity. / It's the sea that has fled / With the sun]" (O, 160; CP, 217).

12. As regards the dates of composition of the *Illuminations*, I follow the current consensus, set forth by André Guyaux in the *Classiques Garniers* edition of Rimbaud's texts (O, 60–64), according to which the writing of the *Illuminations* "overlaps" the writing of *Une Saison*, some of the prose poems surely having been written as early as 1872, some of them probably having been written as late as 1874. Guyaux emphasizes, too, that there is no solid evidence (as distinct from many suggestive conjectures) for the dating of specific poems at specific times. On these questions see, too, Guyaux, *Duplicités de Rimbaud*.

13. Lawler, *Theatre of the Self*, 3–4; cf. 201–3. My account of Rimbaud's art of "self-multiplication" is greatly indebted to Lawler's brilliant study. On the carnivalesque in Rimbaud, see also the suggestive discussion in Kittang, *Discours et jeu*, 333–44.

14. As Lawler puts it near the end of his study: "Rimbaud on every occasion beginning with 'Le Bateau ivre' writes his last poem" (*Theatre of the Self*, 219). See, too, Lawler's fine reading of "Vies" as the "multiple self-dramatization" of a "self-ironist" (110–24).

15. Whitman, *Leaves of Grass*, 64–65.

16. Fredric Jameson, in "Rimbaud and the Spatial Text," argues that Rimbaud's distinctively mobile experience of space involves an exceptionally awakened "adolescent body" registering, in a kind of seismographic fashion, the immense changes in industrial structure, social space, and global space taking place in his time. Kristin Ross, complementing Jameson's argument in *Social Space*, similarly links the "swarming" dynamics of Rimbaud's texts to the rapidly changing social space of his era while emphasizing, in particular, their

affinities with the anarchocommunist currents brought to life in the Paris Commune. Curiously, neither of these critics mentions Whitman, though the North American context of Whitman's poetry (war, nationalist-imperialist expansion, the rapid building of railroads, the transition to full-blown industrial capitalism) is in some respects very similar to the French context of Rimbaud's. It is possible that Rimbaud may have come across some of the earliest French translations of Whitman, which first appeared in literary magazines in 1872; intriguingly, they were translations of his free verse into short prose paragraphs punctuated with dashes. On this possible connection, see Erkkila, *Walt Whitman*, 58–69.

17. Hartman, "Poem and Ideology," 126–27. In the essay from which I cite Hartman is concerned to show how Keats's "To Autumn" attains the sublime while quietly overcoming this traditional epiphanic mode of the sublime. If there is anything of Rimbaud in Keats, then, it is to be found not in this poem but rather in "Ode to Psyche" and "Ode to a Nightingale."

18. The rapid, compressed, sliding syntax for which Rimbaud has always been celebrated—"a whole new practice of plural substantives and of multiplied apostrophes," as Fredric Jameson puts it, "as well as a curious and innovative production of self-modifying verbs (*les fleurs de rêve tintent, éclatent, éclairent*)" ("Rimbaud and the Spatial Text," 77)— is splendidly exemplified in the compressed syntactic amplitude of "Being Beauteous." While this swift syntactic rhythm would seem in part to enact Rimbaud's urgent protean impulse, it would seem in part, as well, to enact his urgent invocatory impulse, as though the spirit of hymnal attention had entered into the very pulse of his syntax. This is nicely suggested by one of Jacque Rivière's characterizations of Rimbaud's style: "But what appears first of all in Rimbaud is a sort of attention: his syntax is like the attitude of one who wants not to let slip away that which is happening at his side" (*Rimbaud*, 186–87).

19. For these readings, see, respectively, Houston, *Rimbaud's Poetry*, 223–27, Suzanne Bernard (commentary in Rimbaud's *Oeuvres*, 494–95 and 538–39), Cohn, *Poetry of Rimbaud*, 390–97, and Munier, *L'Ardente Patience*, 421–28.

20. Bonnefoy, *Rimbaud*, 144.

21. Munier, *Ardente Patience*, 421–22. Munier's ten-page commentary on this poem is splendid. His detailed reading of "Alchimie du Verbe" (190–220) also explores issues relevant to a reading of "Génie."

22. While Wallace Stevens and Rimbaud have little in common, Stevens's visionary "River of Rivers in Connecticut," written in Stevens's late style of sober clairvoyance, evoking a spacious flow of life force as fateful as death, may be the best "commentary" on Rimbaud's ecstatic hymn that we are likely to find. It is worth citing the poem in its entirety here: "There is a great river this side of Stygia, / Before one comes to the first black cataracts / And trees that lack the intelligence of trees. // In that river, far this side of Stygia, / The mere flowing of the water is a gayety, / Flashing and flashing in the sun. On its banks, // No shadow walks. The river is fateful, / Like the last one. But there is no ferryman. / He could not bend against its propelling force. // It is not to be seen beneath the appearances / That tell of it. The steeple at Farmington / Stands glistening and Haddam shines and sways. // It is the third commonness with light and air, / A curriculum, a vigor, a local abstraction. . . . / Call it, once more, a river, an unnamed flowing, // Space-filled, reflecting the seasons, the folk-lore / Of each of the senses; call it, again and again, / The river that flows nowhere, like a sea" (*Palm*, 386–87).

23. Houston, *Rimbaud's Poetry*, 128. My discussion here is very much indebted to Houston's probing, detailed discussion of the *Derniers Vers*, in particular to his account of the sort of "mystical" drama of ascetic "disincarnation" and pantheistic "communion" often evoked in these poems (see especially 124–36).

24. In the letter of May 1873 to Delahaye in which he speaks of the "Livre païen, ou Livre nègre" on which he is working—almost certainly a first draft of "Mauvais sang"— Rimbaud asks his friend to send him a copy of Goethe's *Faust* (O, 355). Enid Starkie, whose lead I follow here, presents a very suggestive reading of *Une Saison* in terms of the Faust myth in her *Arthur Rimbaud*, 16–17 and 287–312.

25. On the basic dynamics of this type of poem, see Abrams, "Structure and Style," 224–29, and "Wordsworth's *Prelude* and the Crisis-Autobiography," in *Natural Supernaturalism*, 71–140 (especially 77 and 123), and Harold Bloom, " 'To Reason with a Later Reason': Romanticism and the Rational," in *Ringers in the Tower*, especially 326–28, and *Wallace Stevens*, 50–67.

26. John Porter Houston, in a commentary on Rimbaud's "Vies," draws attention to the way the provocative voice of this poem, in its outrageous sweep, becomes at the same time a kind of self-mocking laughter: "This autocritical process constitutes a kind of arraignment of poetry as Rimbaud understood it, for he was nurtured on romantic conceptions of the primacy of the imagination and the Word as forces in life. As he pushed these notions to an extreme and became absorbed above all in visionary modes of poetry, the tension he felt between the Word and the world, between the domains of imagination and real possibilities, seems to have become more acute and to have produced a tart, ironic undercurrent seldom completely absent from his verse. More than other poets, he apparently felt the conflict between the power of poetry and the crushing presence of ordinary experience to be a problem which could not be ignored even in the very texture of poems" (*Rimbaud's Poetry*, 236). This is finely perceived, and no doubt Rimbaud experienced this "conflict" between inwardness and outwardness more extremely than all but a very few other poets. But it should still be underlined, I think, that it is just this sort of conflict that generates not only the romantic crisis poem so common over the last two centuries but also the poetic of the ironic mask variously developed from about the middle of the nineteenth century on, whether in the dramatic monologues of Tennyson, Browning, and various modernists in their wake, or in the ironically dandyistic poetries of Baudelaire, Corbière, Laforgue, and various mask makers in their wake. Indeed, the poetic of the mask is one of the most important connections between romantic and modernist poetries. On these traditions, see Langbaum, *Poetry of Experience*, especially 75–108, Christ, *Victorian and Modern Poetics*, especially 15–52, and Hamburger, *Truth of Poetry*, especially 61–80 and 110–47.

27. Bonnefoy, *Rimbaud*, 113–25. I've borrowed a great deal from Bonnefoy's reading of this chapter.

28. A little earlier he writes, "J'entends des familles comme la mienne, qui tiennent tout de la déclaration des Droits de l'Homme [I mean families like mine, who owe everything to the Declaration of the Rights of Man]" (O, 213; CP, 302). But in "L'Impossible" he declares, "M. Prudhomme est né avec le Christ [M. Prudhomme was born with Christ]" (O, 236; CP, 339). These different identifications may produce a contradiction in the text, for according to the identification of Christianity and nobility, peasants like this poet are excluded

from Christianity, while according to the identification of Christianity and modernity, peasants like him are included in a modernity that is a continuation of Christianity.

29. For illuminating, richly contextualized discussions of these dynamics, see Ross, *Social Space*. See, too, Nicholls's brief but pointed reflections on these dynamics in *Modernisms*, 31–33. For a ranging study of "orientalist" rhetorics at work in French romantic literature, see Said, *Orientalism*, 166–94.

30. Where does this voice come from? Out of the shadow of death? Like *la voix* heard and addressed throughout Rimbaud's writings, it is riddling in the extreme. Yet, to my ear, it has affinities with the voice of the sea that the child-poet, passing through an initiation, hears in Whitman's "Out of the Cradle Endlessly Rocking": a voice at once murmuring to him the fate of inevitable ruin and calling him to a freedom of imaginative reach.

31. Difficult questions are raised, it is true, by the *absence* in this chapter of any citation of—or any direct reference to—the prose poems of the *Illuminations*. Nevertheless, it seems to me impossible to read "Alchimie du Verbe"—especially the part beginning "Je devins un opéra fabuleux" (O, 233; CP, 334) or, in the next paragraph, "A chaque être plusieurs *autres* vies me semblaient dues" (O, 233; CP, 334)—without inferring that at least some of the adventures of the *Illuminations* are being considered. For a more developed version of this judgment, see Blanchot, *Entretien infini*, 422–23.

32. In this regard I refer again to the fine observations by John Porter Houston that I've cited in note 26.

33. Rivière, *Rimbaud*, 103.

34. Meschonnic, *Modernité*, 126. Meschonnic also presents a fine account of the rather widespread misreading of the most famous line in this chapter ("Il faut être absolument moderne").

35. Bonnefoy, *Rimbaud*, 131–32. In a splendid essay on Rimbaud, René Char, though more inclined to the prophetic than Bonnefoy, shows a similar attunement to the experience of rending, or the truth of inevitable contradiction, voiced in Rimbaud's adventure: "We are advised: outside of poetry, between our foot and the stone it presses, between our look and the field it surveys, the world is null. The true life, the indisputable colossus, takes shape only on the slopes of poetry. Yet we haven't the sovereignty (or haven't anymore, or haven't yet) to dispose at our discretion of this true life, to quicken ourselves there, except in brief flashes akin to orgasms. And in the darkness that follows these flashes, thanks to the knowledge they have brought, Time—between the horrible void it secretes and a hope-presentiment that arises solely from us (and is but the next condition of sheer poetry and vision announcing itself)—Time distributes itself, flows away, but to our gain, half orchard, half waste" (*Recherche*, 110).

36. On the question of Nietzsche and the good life, see Rosen, *Limits of Analysis*, 209, and *Mask of Enlightenment*, and Pippin, "Morality as Psychology: Psychology as Morality: Nietzsche, Eros, and Clumsy Lovers," in *Idealism as Modernism*, 351–71. In his discussion of eros and the good life in Nietzsche, Pippin, among other things, suggestively elaborates a thought first proposed, I believe, by Walter Kaufmann—the thought that Nietzsche's "will to power" may be a recasting of Plato's "eros" (see Kaufmann, *Nietzsche*, 246–56).

37. In these claims I am close to John Sallis, *Crossings*, a detailed and illuminating reading of *The Birth of Tragedy*. In what follows I presuppose Sallis's reading of Nietzsche's

first book. Richard Schacht, in *Making Sense of Nietzsche*, 132–33, also notes some significant parallels between the theory of art presented in *The Birth of Tragedy* and the vision of creative self-overcoming developed in *Zarathustra* and other later works.

38. Nietzsche thought highly of this reading of Hamlet. Almost twenty years later, in *Ecce Homo*, he cryptically repeated it: "Is Hamlet *understood?* Not doubt, *certainty* is what drives one insane.—But one must be profound, an abyss, a philosopher to feel that way.—We are all afraid of truth" (246).

39. I've omitted from this brief sketch Nietzsche's account of the lyric. Its importance for his argument lies in the way it anticipates the tragic chorus out of which the tragic drama later emerges: "[L]yric poems," he writes at one point, "in their highest development are called tragedies and dramatic dithyrambs" (50). For the lyric poem, he argues, is not the expression of the individual lyric poet but rather a projection of "image sparks" generated by the primordial Dionysian will acting through the poet (48–56).

40. At this point in the argument Nietzsche recalls Heraclitus: "Thus the dark Heraclitus compares the world-building force to a playing child that places stones here and there and builds sand hills only to overthrow them again" (142).

41. These are the terms of Richard Schacht's insightful discussion of this issue in *Nietzsche*, 476–529, and in "Making Life Worth Living," in *Making Sense of Nietzsche*, 129–52.

42. For a brief but illuminating discussion of the philosophic crisis out of which *Zarathustra* emerged, see Hollingdale's introduction to his translation of *Thus Spoke Zarathustra*, especially 15–16.

43. The place or the significance of part 4 in Zarathustra's drama remains a puzzling question. Part of the problem is that we can't be entirely sure how Nietzsche conceived of its place. My own sense is that parts 1–3 form a coherent dramatic whole and that part 4 occupies an eccentric position with respect to this whole. Or, put another way, parts 1–3 would seem to be the "tragic drama" to which part 4 has been attached as the "comic satyr play." I will try to defend this reading more fully near the end of this section.

44. For an excellent discussion of *Zarathustra* as a crisis text that pivots around Zarathustra's crucial wrestling with the thought of the eternal recurrence, see Pippin, "Irony and Affirmation." I've learned a great deal from this essay that, among other things, carefully traces the dramatic structure of *Zarathustra*, and in some ways I closely follow Pippin's argument, in particular his claim that Zarathustra's struggle with the thought of the eternal recurrence forces him to revise his initial quest or initial teaching (see especially 52–55 and 69, n. 17). This revision, according to Pippin, involves above all Zarathustra's recognition that his own project is inevitably embedded in the very cultural context he wishes to surpass. Yet, while I think there is much to say for this argument, I also think that Pippin turns Zarathustra into a Hegelian historicist a touch too quickly. He does not explain why Nietzsche, if his primary concern is to reveal Zarathustra's dramatic recognition of the historical contingency and contextual embeddedness of his own project, chooses to orchestrate this recognition around the weird mythopoetic thought of the eternal recurrence. Surely there are clearer ways to illuminate the necessity of a historicist or Hegelian self-consciousness. At any rate, I consider my reading of *Zarathustra* to be, in some sense, a conversation with Pippin's essay. Incidentally, Pippin makes a much stronger case for certain Hegelian presuppositions operative in Nietzsche's thought in his study "Nietzsche's Alleged Farewell:

The Premodern, Modern, and Postmodern Nietzsche," in *Idealism as Modernism*, 330–50. Here I would like to note as well my debt to Stanley Rosen's critical interpretation of Nietzsche in *The Mask of Enlightenment* and in several other essays over the years—see *Limits of Analysis*, 190–215; *Quarrel between Philosophy and Poetry*, 183–203; and *The Ancients and the Moderns*, 189–234. Though Rosen and I are at odds concerning most issues in Nietzsche, I've found his work of immense value, in particular in its clarification of Nietzsche's engagement with major figures and positions of the Platonic, the Christian, and the modern traditions. At times Rosen argues that Nietzsche's fundamental metaphysical position—that all is ultimately a chaos of becoming—is entirely incompatible with his equally fundamental concern to measure (or rank) different values. At other times he argues that Nietzsche's thought is a radical culmination of the "world-making" or "historicist" current of modernity set in motion by Bacon and Descartes and accelerated by German idealist thinkers: a current whose nihilism, in Rosen's view, is at last brought to light, or made explicit, by Nietzsche. Rosen's reading of Nietzsche, then, has affinities with Heidegger's.

45. After *Zarathustra* Nietzsche seems to deploy alternative figures for this ideal, including "Dionysus," "Zarathustra" himself, and perhaps the "philosophers of the future" of *Beyond Good and Evil*. But the term "overman" does on occasion return (see, for example, AC, 126, and EH, 305).

46. Walter Kaufmann, in his *Nietzsche*, long ago underlined the persistence of this theme in Nietzsche's trajectory.

47. "Creation happens—it is as much, maybe more, an event than an intentional action," Roberts writes, recalling a major romantic conception of creative power (*Contesting Spirit*, 197). Roberts characterizes Zarathustra's passage toward *amor fati* in similar terms: "Zarathustra's affirmation is not the result of a calculating knowledge that determines it better to affirm than to deny, for it takes place only as the boundaries of the self are broken, as the self is overtaken by the 'Yes.' This 'Yes' is not something he controls, but something that occurs in him, an affirmation that strikes in lightning bolts that say 'Yes' and laugh 'Yes'" (189; cf. 125–29). Zarathustra's drama, thus, revives as well the romantic theme of "the one life within us and abroad," to recall Coleridge's words ("The Eolian Harp" in *Major Works*, 28), or of the way that "in creating we extend the very energy that's created us," to cite the words of a contemporary poet (Sobin, "That the Universe is Chrysalid," in *Bias of Sound*, 5).

48. Zarathustra's rhetoric, in a word, is an extravagant rhetoric of romanticism. There is nothing eccentric about Nietzsche's lifelong love of Emerson, Emerson representing an almost pure expression of a displaced Protestant type of romanticism. Implicit in this reading of *Zarathustra*, then, is my belief that it's nonsense to take Nietzsche's polemics against romanticism at face value. He seems to have disguised (from himself as well as many of his later commentators) his own debts to romanticism by defining the latter as Wagner plus Schopenhauer, with Carlyle occasionally tossed in for good measure. On Nietzsche's relationships to both romantic and modernist currents in the arts, see Nehamas, *Nietzsche*; and Magnus, Stewart, and Mileur, *Nietzsche's Case*. These are excellent, ranging books that have informed and provoked my thinking about Nietzsche in many ways. I'm indebted to them even when I differ with them.

49. Kaufmann, *Nietzsche*, 323.

50. Magnus, *Nietzsche's Existential Imperative*, 142. For a similar reading with different nuances, see Higgins, *Nietzsche's Zarathustra*, 159–202. Harold Alderman writes: "Whatever may constitute proper acceptance [of the idea of eternal recurrence], we know for certain that it does not consist of simply asserting the truth value of a proposition. The renewing element of the teaching of eternal recurrence lies beyond the propositional in the realm of visionary experience" (*Nietzsche's Gift*, 99).

51. See Magnus, "Deification of the Commonplace," especially 168–77. There is, in my view, at least one serious textual problem with Magnus's argument: Zarathustra does come to affirm the thought of the eternal recurrence, to affirm an attitude of joyous *amor fati*, yet he is not (by my reading) at any point presented as having become an overman. To anticipate a little, one of my concerns in the reading of Zarathustra's crisis that follows is to argue that it is a mistake to identify the meaning of the figure of the eternal recurrence—Nietzsche's "highest formula of affirmation" (EH, 295)—with some unimaginable state of superhuman self-surpassing.

52. Nehamas, *Nietzsche*, 145–47.

53. Magnus, Stewart, and Mileur, *Nietzsche's Case*, 107–19. These authors make clear (111) that this mythopoetic or "Dionysian" vision of the eternal recurrence provides the strongest "textual support" for Deleuze's interpretation of the eternal recurrence as the recurrence of becoming itself. "We misunderstand the expression 'eternal return,'" Deleuze writes, "if we understand it as 'return of the same.' It is not being that returns but rather the returning itself that constitutes being insofar as it is affirmed of becoming and of that which passes" (*Nietzsche and Philosophy*, 48). Deleuze's interpretation has seemed to many readers eccentric, distant from what Nietzsche had in mind, yet if one attends to the relative frequency with which, in those texts that Nietzsche *published*, the eternal recurrence is linked to "Dionysian" figures of recurrent rhythms of life, Deleuze's interpretation appears more plausible, a kind of conceptual explication of what Nietzsche chose to present in metaphor.

54. Pippin, "Irony and Affirmation," 53.

55. Higgins reads this nightmare as a sign that Zarathustra has become entrapped in the abstract "dogma" of his own formulations and so has strayed from the dynamic experiential ground to which those formulations point (*Nietzsche's Zarathustra*, 149). While I'm sympathetic to Higgins's general point concerning the importance to Nietzsche (and to Zarathustra) of a vital relationship between theoretical formulations and existential orientations, I think her specific account of Zarathustra's dream in "The Soothsayer" is mistaken. First, a reduction of the thought of the eternal recurrence to an abstract formulation is likely to cause not nightmares but either vague indifference or bemused curiosity. Second, Zarathustra's vision, I would argue, involves no "mistake." To the contrary, Zarathustra has glimpsed what both he and Nietzsche consider to be a fundamental truth: the Silenian truth—"the horror or absurdity of existence" (BT, 60)—that the Greeks overcame first through Apollonian epic and later through Dionysian tragedy. We should recall the young Nietzsche's account of "Dionysian man": "In this sense the Dionysian man resembles Hamlet: both have once looked truly into the essence of things, they have *gained knowledge*, and nausea inhibits action" (BT, 60; cf. EH, 246). The insight Zarathustra "sees" in his dream, then, is not untrue; it is incomplete, insofar as he has yet to bring about a transfigurative overcoming of this insight.

56. For a fine discussion of this issue, see Alderman, *Nietzsche's Gift*, 50–53 and 110–112.

57. Jaspers, *Nietzsche*, 368. For another fine discussion of the bringing together of "transformation" and "affirmation" in Nietzsche's thinking, see Stambaugh, *The Other Nietzsche*. My discussion of Zarathustra's overcoming of the potential nihilism of his own effort to overcome nihilism has affinities with both Pippin's discussion in "Irony and Affirmation," especially 54–57, and Maudmarie Clark's discussion in *Nietzsche on Truth*, 245–86. Yet Clark errs, I think, in reading the project of the overman; as almost entirely a project fueled by nihilist *ressentiment* and the affirmation of the eternal recurrence as almost entirely a replacement for that earlier ideal. Her discussion is weakened by her inattention to the place of creative action in Zarathustra's conception of the overman; in this regard Jasper's, Stambaugh's, and Nehamas's arguments provide important correctives to her argument.

58. Further, in "The Stillest Hour," Zarathustra's "stillest hour" tells him that, if he is to teach the eternal recurrence, he must first be "broken" and re-created as a "child" (145–47; cf. 162–63).

59. Perhaps the best exegesis of this passage is provided by Emerson in his account of the misreading of Jesus in normative Christianity: "Jesus said, in this jubilee of sublime emotion, 'I am divine. Through me, God acts; through me, speaks. Would you see God, see me; or, see thee, when thou also thinkest as I now think.' But what a distortion did his doctrine suffer in the same, in the next, and the following ages! . . . The idioms of his language, and the figures of his rhetoric, have usurped the place of his truth; and churches are not built on his principles, but on his tropes" ("An Address to the Senior Class in Divinity College," in *Essays and Lectures*, 80).

60. For an excellent discussion of Nietzsche's teaching by "exemplification," see Nehamas, "Who Are the Philosophers of the Future?"

61. This discourse on the "beautiful folly" of words thus recalls Zarathustra's earlier affirmation, in his sharing of the vision of the eternal recurrence with the sailors, of creative riddling: "To you, bold searchers, researchers, and whoever embarks with cunning sails on terrible seas—to you, drunk with riddles, glad of the twilight, whose soul flutes lure astray to every whirlpool, because you do not want to grope along a thread with cowardly hand; and where you can *guess*, you hate to *deduce*—to you alone I tell the riddle that I *saw*, the vision of the loneliest" (156). His characterization of words as "rainbows" further emphasizes the power he finds in creatively re-turned words, for in an earlier discourse he has borrowed the rainbow as the sign of a redemption from revenge: "For *that man be delivered from revenge*, that is for me the bridge to the highest hope, and a rainbow after long storms" (99).

62. For a fine reading of part 4 as a kind of "Menippean satire" patterned after Apuleius's *Golden Ass*, see Higgins, *Nietzsche's* Zarathustra, 203–32.

63. Magnus, Stewart, and Mileur, in *Nietzsche's Case*, chapters 2 and 3 (especially 47–52, 94–107, and 119–32), present a ranging and illuminating discussion of Nietzsche's as well as Zarathustra's many parodic and refigurative engagements with Jesus, the Gospels, and Christianity. My reading here owes a great deal to their work.

64. See Vermes, *Jesus the Jew*, 117, and Sheehan, *First Coming*, 72.

65. Tyler Roberts writes of Nietzsche's engagement with nihilism: "There are no easy or clear answers to Nietzsche's problem, because he offers no answers that promise a defini-

tive overcoming of nihilism. The will to the definitive overcoming of nihilism would merely reinscribe the metaphysics of mastery, as Blanchot recognizes. . . . Instead of offering a solution to nihilism, Nietzsche *responds* to nihilism. . . . Nietzsche finds joy at this boundary of Western culture and human life. Nihilism as meaninglessness now becomes a space in which creativity is possible, a space of freedom where the turn to affirmation can be accomplished: it becomes, as Nietzsche puts it in a note, 'a divine way of thinking.' This affirmation is not consolation but a difficult joy that takes shape in the tension between the renunciatory 'No' of nihilism and the 'Yes' of creativity" (*Contesting Spirit*, 187–88). Roberts refers to Blanchot's essay "Limits of Experience."

66. "Bataille speaks of Hegel; he becomes Nietzsche's madman" (Hollier, "Nietzsche's Absence," 66).

67. Bataille himself does occasionally acknowledge this: "Having spoken of André Breton, I should immediately have mentioned the debt I owe to Surrealism. If I've quoted anything to ill effect, it's against my own best interests. The reader for whom 'the letter' is less attractive than 'the spirit' will notice in my questioning the continuation of a certain moral interrogation that permeated Surrealism and, in the climate presupposed by my life, a perhaps not unfamiliar prolongation of Surrealist intolerance" (ON, 190). Bataille immediately goes on to spell out his differences with Breton. I will return to the question of these differences in the concluding section of this chapter. Bataille's writings on surrealism have been gathered by Michael Richardson in *Absence of Myth*. Richardson, in the introduction to this volume, provides a subtle account of Bataille's shifting relationship to the surrealists over the years.

68. Bataille occasionally speaks of the bias and the distinctive pathos that he brings to Nietzsche. "I am the only one who thinks of himself not as a commentator of Nietzsche but as being the same as he. Not that my thought is always faithful to his: it often diverges from it, especially if I consider the detailed developments of a theory. But that [my] thought is placed under the same conditions as was his" (AS, 3:367; cf. ON, xx–xxi).

69. "Man, having enslaved the elements, remains himself a slave," as Shelley puts it ("Defence of Poetry," 203). A distinctive feature of Bataille's philosophy of history is his conviction that Kojève's account of speculative knowledge—of the totalizing dialectical knowledge that at once elucidates and justifies this rationalization of the real and this realization of the rational—is entirely sound in its own "restricted" sphere. This is obviously a judgment with enormous implications. For it establishes a dialectical identity between the clear unfolding of discursive reason and a pervasively reified society in which subjects are turned into instruments of blind social production. And this, indeed, is where Bataille and Adorno decisively part ways. Adorno's "negative dialectics" is motivated by a refusal of this judgment that the pervasive instrumental rationality of capitalist modernity is either the "truth" or the "completion" of the substantive promise of reason—for Adorno it is, in fact, the expression of a violent betrayal of the promise of reason.

70. Bataille's perspective at times seems closer to Schopenhauer's dualism than to Nietzsche's philosophy. Thus, for example, in the introduction to *Erotism* he writes: "On the most fundamental level there are transitions from continuous to discontinuous or from discontinuous to continuous. We are discontinuous beings, individuals who perish

in isolation in the midst of an incomprehensible adventure, but we yearn for our lost continuity" (15).

71. Lionel Abel, in a fine essay on Bataille's relationship with Nietzsche, "Georges Bataille and the Repetition of Nietzsche," pointedly characterizes this extreme perspective from which Bataille writes: "Nietzsche, protesting against the fragmentation of the individual in the modern world, wanted a wider horizon, a larger theater, and while recognizing a contradiction between action and consciousness regarded consciousness rather than action as the evil for which remedies were to be found. But Bataille's animus is directed not against some specialized form of life, but against life because it specializes; not against some incomplete form of action, but against action because it renders incomplete. . . . Now the only norm antagonistic to life and commensurable with it is death. And, in fact, it is from the point of view of death that Bataille has restated Nietzsche's criticism of the incomplete man and his demand for a fuller and more satisfying life" (54). Derrida, in "From Restricted to General Economy: A Hegelianism without Reserve," in *Writing and Difference,* 251–77, presents a dizzying account of various "parodic" movements whereby Bataille points toward a "general economy" of negativity irreducible to the "restricted economy" of Hegelian dialectics. Michele Richman's *Reading Georges Bataille,* an excellent study of Bataille's debts to Durkheim and Mauss, also includes a good chapter on Derrida's relationship to Bataille.

72. Sartre, in "Nouveau Mystique," an essay on *Inner Experience,* emphasizes the depositivized "mystic" or "ecstatic" dimension of Bataille's adventure. On the way modern philosophers (especially from Nietzsche on) have tended to imagine death rather than a transcendent source as the ultimate limit of life and thought, see Löwith, *From Hegel to Nietzsche,* 207–8, and Rosen, *Mask of Enlightenment,* 124–25.

73. Probably the most important early essays in this direction—or those that have received the most attention—are "The Notion of Expenditure" and "The Pyschological Structure of Fascism" (VE, 116–29 and 137–60). I should note here that I wholly share the common judgment that Bataille's historical descriptions in *The Accursed Share*—in particular those of the character of Soviet society and the character of the Marshall Plan—are seriously flawed. The historical descriptions, in a word, are turned into types. The text nonetheless presents a provocative speculative theory that it is worth engaging as just that—a theory, one whose major concepts or types, if occasionally passed off as historical referents, can be readily grasped as abstract types.

74. Vincent Descombes, in an illuminating discussion of Bataille, writes: "One of the unquestionable virtues of the chapter that Habermas devotes to the writings of Georges Bataille is that it is focused on the problems posed by a non-Marxist [non-utilitarian] explication of modern politics" (*Barometer of Modern Reason,* 83). Descombes refers to Habermas's essay on Bataille in *Philosophical Discourse,* 211–37.

75. In the introduction to a collection of Bataille's essays that he edited under the title *Visions of Excess,* Allan Stoekl provides a fine sketch of some of these contradictions that remain unresolved in Bataille's theoretical project. "Another difficulty, implicit all along, comes to the fore at this point. To what extent has dialectics *not* been subverted in any way by Bataille, to what extent, in paying lip service to the limitlessness of this destructive tendency that constitutes man, does Bataille simply establish a new 'need' that must in turn be

recognized (at the end of history) and satisfied in order to guarantee the stability of society? Boring, useful labor—which certainly constitutes stable society—would in this case only be replaced by the safety valve of sacrificial violence or the scapegoat.... But can any one 'need' be different in kind from another, even though one is a need for construction and satisfaction, and the other is a need for destruction and loss? And if they are not fundamentally different, how radical is this 'need to expend'? How different is it from, say, a need for leisure time, or exercise? If man 'produces only in order to expend,' is expenditure different in kind from any other human value, such as religion or the family?" (xviii–xix).

76. Habermas, *Philosophical Discourse*, 235–36.

77. On this issue, see Judith Butler's brief but pointed comments on Bataille in her "Commentary."

78. "I write," Bataille says, "for one who, entering my book, would fall into it as into a black hole" (IE, 116). Would these writers, then, lure their readers to shipwreck? Karsten Harries, in "Philosopher at Sea," has argued that this may well be true of Nietzsche; in fact, Harries notes, Nietzsche often casts himself as a sailor in thought akin to the ambitious and reckless Ulysses of Dante's *Inferno* (40–43). Magnus, Stewart, and Mileur provide a fascinating discussion of the way Nietzsche's *Zarathustra* in particular, and romantic "quest" texts in general, seem to withold a secret even as they hold forth a promise (*Nietzsche's Case*, 155–85, especially 157).

79. Marx and Engels, *German Ideology*, 53, 83; Marx speaks of the "totally developed individual" in *Capital*, 1:618.

80. On the presence of romantic ideals in the young Marx, see Berman, *All That Is Solid*, 94–98, and MacIntyre, "Marxist Mask and Romantic Face," 65–66. These ideals continue to inform Marx's critical perspectives in *Capital*, particularly in chapters 13–15 of part 2 of volume 1 ("Cooperation," "The Division of Labour and Manufacture," and "Machinery and Large-Scale Industry"), chapters that guide Foucault's more recent studies of disciplinary structures at work in every sphere of modern society; the connection, though often ignored in the reception of Foucault, appears clearly in *Discipline and Punish*, 218–28, 273–85.

81. My discussion of Blake and Freud here and the map that follows are enormously indebted to Frye, *Fearful Symmetry*, "Road of Excess," "Keys to the Gates," and *Words*, 128–29 and 239–51, and Bloom, *Visionary Company*, 5–123, *Ringers in the Tower*, 55–62, and above all "Internalization," which includes a cross-mapping of Blakean romanticism and Freudian realism. Bloom characterizes the distinction between Orc and Los as a distinction between "organic" and "imaginative" energy ("Internalization," 11), associating the former with social rebellion and the latter with visionary transformation. Mark Edmundson, in *Literature against Philosophy*, 199–239, presents a capacious reading of Bloom's theory of romanticism that has also informed my discussion here.

82. Jameson, *Marxism and Form*, 103–4; cf. 105–6. These words should be read alongside Pablo Neruda's fascinating account—in a two-page essay written in 1930s Madrid—of the realm of weathered things explored in the quasi-surrealist poetry he was writing at the time ("Toward an Impure Poetry" in *Five Decades*, xxi–xxii).

83. Frye, "Drunken Boat," 205; cf. Frye, "Romantic Myth," 32–35, 46–47. Frye's account of this "downward movement" in romantic poetry rhymes with Walter Benjamin's

interpretation of the romantic-modernist dynamics of "shock" in Baudelaire and "involuntary memory" in Proust ("On Some Motifs in Baudelaire" and "The Image of Proust," in *Illuminations*, 155–215).

84. Breton, *Manifestoes of Surrealism*, 9–10.

85. Thus, too, in the second manifesto Breton recalls Blake's horizontal image of an ultimate "marriage-in-difference" of extremes: "Everything tends to make us believe that there exists a certain point of the mind at which life and death, the real and the imagined, past and future, the communicable and the incommunicable, high and low, cease to be perceived as contradictions. Now, search as one may, one will never find any other motivating force in the activities of the Surrealists than the hope of finding and fixing this point. From this it becomes obvious how absurd it would be to define Surrealism solely as constructive or destructive: the point to which we are referring is *a fortiori* that point where construction and destruction can no longer be brandished one against the other" (ibid., 123–24).

86. For a fine reading of Bataille that emphasizes his differences with surrealism, see Hollier, *Against Architecture*, especially 104–12.

87. Breton, *Manifestoes of Surrealism*, 18. Peter Bürger, in his *Theory of the Avant-Garde*, has even argued that the primary significance of the interwar avantgarde, in particular of dada and surrealism, resides in its ultimately failed effort to reintegrate art and life. Walter Benjamin seems to have found in surrealist writings what Bataille hoped was true of his own writings: "Anyone who has perceived that the writings of this [surrealist] circle are not literature but something else—demonstrations, watchwords, documents, bluffs, forgeries if you will, but at any rate not literature—will also know, for the same reason, that the writings are concerned literally with experiences, not with theories and still less with phantasms" ("Surrealism," in *Reflections*, 179).

88. Derrida, "Différance," in *Margins of Philosophy*, 21–22. See, too, *Positions*, 8–9 and 105–6 n. 35.

89. Thus Vincent Descombes, in describing this field of thought, speaks of a "melan-Hegelianism" crossed by a Nietzschean "philosophy with a hammer": "Though Habermas is certainly wrong to number Nietzsche himself among Hegel's heirs, he rightly perceives a certain Hegelian reasoning *gone wild* among Nietzsche's French interpreters. What gives this line of thought its particular flavor is not its would-be 'neo-structuralism' but its explosive mixture of dialectics and 'philosophy with a hammer.' Habermas takes pains to remind his readers that Nietzsche is not easily classified among writers who could be considered leftists. He quite effectively criticizes contradictions and ambiguities implied by a Nietzscheanism of the extreme left [un nietzschéisme rouge]. But it would have been still more accurate to speak of a dark Hegelianism [un hégélianisme noir]. Beyond the French authors taken up by Habermas, one would have to include Klossowski and Blanchot in this 'melan-Hegelian' line, if only for their interpretations of Sade and Lautréamont. Lastly, it is to be noted that even Deleuze was so preoccupied with escaping the ambient melan-Hegelianism of the time that he ended up appearing as a kind of anti-Hegel—yet another symptom of the Hegelian mania" (*Barometer of Modern Reason*, 66–67; cf. 83–92). My reading of Nietzsche in this chapter is meant to show, among other things, just how one-sided and "Bataille-like" this post-structuralist rewriting of Nietzsche is.

90. Char, "Partage formel," in *Fureur et mystère*, 73.

CHAPTER THREE. APOCALYPTIC NEGATIVITY IN KIERKEGAARD,
DICKINSON, MALLARMÉ, AND DERRIDA

My translations of Mallarmé's poems, essays, and letters in this chapter rely upon, though they often depart from, the translations by Henry Weinfield in the *Collected Poems,* Bradford Cook in *Selected Prose Poems, Essays, and Letters,* and Rosemary Lloyd in *Selected Letters;* all of these works are cited in the abbreviations preceding the text.

1. Merleau-Ponty, *The Visible and the Invisible,* 251, and Derrida, *Writing and Difference,* 248. It is perhaps worth citing this passage from one of Derrida's essays on Artaud, since this dimension of his thought, and its closeness to the thought of the later Merleau-Ponty, seem rarely recognized. It is a passage whose Nietzschean accents are also unmistakable: "For if one appropriately conceives the *horizon* of dialectics—outside a conventional Hegelianism—one understands, perhaps, that dialectics is the indefinite movement of finitude, of the unity of life and death, of difference, of original repetition, that is, of the origin of tragedy as the absence of a simple origin. In this sense, dialectics is tragedy, the only possible affirmation to be made against the philosophical or Christian idea of pure origin, against 'the spirit of beginnings'" (248). In a brief but intriguing footnote in an early essay on Levinas, "Violence and Metaphysics," Derrida recognizes in Merleau-Ponty's thought one of the fundamental claims of his own thought: "It is true that for Merleau-Ponty—differing from Levinas—the phenomenon of alterity was primordially, if not exclusively, that of the movement of temporalization" (WD, 314 n. 36).

2. See Blumenberg, *Legitimacy,* 125–226. Blumenberg's concept of "self-assertion" is not identical to the romantic theme of creative power to the extent that the latter tends toward hyperbole, granting less weight to the objective constraints on human power than do those thinkers, in particular modern scientists, whom Blumenberg primarily has in mind in constructing his concept. To be sure, it is also true than Blumenberg intends this concept of "self-assertion" to be broad enough to account for modern culture and politics as well as modern science. The provocative originality of the later Heidegger lies not least in his argument that this radical freeing of subjective power, reaching an apotheosis in Nietzsche, is not an effect of the collapse of traditional metaphysical models but an expression of their nihilist completion.

3. Foucault discusses the skewed conversation or non-conversation between Nietzsche and Mallarmé in *The Order of Things,* 303–7. "To the Nietzschean question: 'Who is speaking?', Mallarmé replies—and constantly reverts to that reply—by saying that what is speaking is, in its solitude, in its fragile vibration, in its nothingness, the word itself—not the meaning of the word, but its enigmatic and precarious being" (305).

4. On the early Heidegger's unacknowledged debts to Kierkegaard, see Schrag, *Existence and Freedom.* Levinas's criticisms of Kierkegaard are scattered throughout his writings. They are brought together in his short essay "Existence and Ethics," 26–38. For an account of Kierkegaard that stresses the affinities between Kierkegaard and Levinas, see Weston, *Kierkegaard.* These affinities are made especially clear in an essay, *The Gift of Death,* in which Derrida undertakes a Levinasian rewriting of Kierkegaard's *Fear and Trembling,* recasting Johannes de Silentio's distinction between ethical obligation and religious obligation as a

distinction between ethical obligation and a groundless response or opening to the other that cannot be justified on the basis of received ethical norms. Kierkegaard and Levinas are perhaps closer to each other than either is to Derrida in their shared conviction that this prerational or extrarational relationship to a "transcendent" other is decisively experienced by the subject as the suffering of self-sacrifice.

5. There does, however, seem to occur in time an expanded sympathy for what Climacus calls Socratic religion or Religiousness A: the sharp difference between Socratic religion and Christian religion (Religiousness B) in the *Fragments,* for example, modulates into an affinity between these two types of religion in the *Postscript,* the former coming to be conceived as a necessary, if not sufficient, stage on the way to the latter (CUP, 494).

6. Mackey, *A Kind of Poet,* 93. This is a subtle, imaginative, indeed brilliant book from which I've learned more about Kierkegaard than from any other book of commentary.

7. While a certain "return to Kant" in Kierkegaard has been noted in the past, the discussion has been raised to a whole new level of detail and cogency in Ronald M. Green's *Kierkegaard and Kant.* My understanding of Kierkegaard's relationship to Kant is greatly indebted to this book.

8. "Christianly understood," Anti-Climacus writes in a discussion of the figure of "the Way" in the Gospels, "truth is obviously not to know the truth but to be the truth" (PC, 205). Anti-Climacus's exploration of this figure in *Practice in Christianity* serves to clarify that "inwardness" in Kierkegaard's discourse should not be simply confused with an airy inner domain detached from practical action in the world: his concern is with the difficult task of "reduplicating" ideality in the concreteness of an ethicoreligious way of existing in the world. For a fine discussion of various meanings of Kierkegaard's characterization of "subjectivity as truth," see Rudd, *Limits of the Ethical,* 54–67.

9. Louis Mackey poses and engages this question in his illuminating "Ram in the Afternoon." Mackey, with a deal of irony of his own, suggests that this line may finally be a little too fine to locate surely. I'm much indebted to this essay.

10. In "Heidegger's Reading" Patricia Huntington distinguishes Kierkegaard's "dialectical" conception of ethical agency from later "oppositional" and "decisionist" conceptions like those found in the early Heidegger and in much of Sartre. Huntington writes: "Kierkegaard's ethical notion of authenticity, instead of replacing questions of normative theory and practice with the *Bildungsprozess* of interiority, maintains a sharp distinction between the ethical (sincerity of motives) and the normative (justifying a course of action). Although ethical life has a certain practical fulfillment unto itself (growth in critical awareness), this practical capacity does not dislodge, but rather prepares me for sincere participation in discourses of legitimation. . . . As dialectical, ethical agency is strictly a modal qualification for Kierkegaard, characterizing how I engage in or relate to theoretical and practical activities. It is difficult to discuss the ethical independent of actual moral and social practices because I never enter into the life of inwardness independent of real life choices" (56–57).

11. Mackey, "Ram in the Afternoon," 108–9; cf. 120. Similar claims could be made about the way a number of twentieth-century philosophers—including Heidegger, Bataille, Blanchot, Levinas, and Derrida—set in motion their discourses of "otherness" or the "other" by first positing a totalizing order of subsumptive reason (by first positing what in the second

chapter I called a hypertrophied Hegelianism). Vincent Descombes raises pointed questions about this tendency in *Barometer of Modern Reason*, 66–67, 85–88.

12. See Green, *Kierkegaard and Kant*, 75–86, and Westphal, *Kierkegaard's Critique*, 113.

13. Adorno, *Kierkegaard*, 30. Along similar lines, Walter Lowrie remarks that Kierkegaard "often reflected that if he had not been so dialectical he might have become an extravagant enthusiast like Adler and others who boast of 'new Light,' special 'guidance,' or an immediate divine call" (*Short Life of Kierkegaard*, 195). Kierkegaard's *Upbuilding Discourses* are traversed by passages that lend support to observations like these by Adorno and Lowrie. For example: "Now the moment has come. Whom should the struggler desire to resemble other than God? But if he himself is something or wants to be something, this something is sufficient to hinder the resemblance. Only when he himself becomes nothing, only then can God illuminate him so that he resembles God. However great he is, he cannot manifest God's likeness; God can imprint himself in him only when he himself has become nothing. When the ocean is exerting all its power, that is precisely the time when it cannot reflect the image of heaven, and even the slightest motion blurs the image; but when it becomes still and deep, then the image of heaven sinks into its nothingness" (EUD, 399). Climacus speaks of "the delicious quickening of that lonely wellspring which exists in every man, that wellspring in which the Deity dwells in the profound stillness where everything is silent" (CUP, 163).

14. From Kierkegaard's point of view, in other words, the inwardness of faith must steer between two shoals: if one abandons the negative theological emphasis on the Hidden God, one crashes on the shoals of superstition or fanaticism, as Kant underlines, while if one abandons the passion of the infinite, one veers toward a Kantian rational faith and thus, as Kant fails to recognize, crashes on the shoals of ethical complacency and flattened subjectivity. The task is to maintain the passion of the infinite in all its negativity. "Without risk there is no faith.... If I wish to preserve myself in faith I must constantly be intent upon holding fast the objective uncertainty, so as to remain out upon the deep, over seventy thousand fathoms of water, still preserving my faith" (CUP, 182). It should be noted, too, that the Judge William in Kierkegaard—the Protestant voice stressing the importance of a "calling" to be realized within the world—further restrains the mystical tendency in Kierkegaard's dialectic. This is also made clear in Johannes de Silentio's description of the Knight of Faith as one who, while "continually making the movement of infinity," is at the same time continually "changing the leap into life [back] into walking, absolutely expressing the sublime in the pedestrian," such that, externally, his "light and bold" step resembles that of the "philistine" (FT, 35–43).

15. Burke, *Grammar of Motives*, 511–17.

16. For fine discussions of this dimension of Plato's conception of "dialectic," see Rosen, *Limits of Analysis*, 178–79, Hadot, *Exercises spirituels*, 45–46, and Gadamer, *Plato's Dialectical Ethic*, 1–100.

17. See, for instance, Walter Lowrie's brief comments on the interplay of "spheres of existence" in his introduction to the *Postscript*, xix–xx, and Schrag's brief discussion of this interplay in "Kierkegaard-Effect," 4–5. Anthony Rudd presents a clear and concise account of this parallel between Hegel and Kierkegaard (*Limits of the Ethical*, 22–26). It is to be understood that, for Kierkegaard, the individual's movement through these stages involves not necessity but a drama of decisions (see Westphal, *Becoming a Self*, 21). And in opposition to

Hegel, of course, Kierkegaard insists that no final synthesis can ever be achieved in the realm of temporal existence: unhappy consciousness is our temporal lot; the negativity of ethico-religious striving is a wound to be healed only in eternity. It is also true, as Rudd points out, that there is in Kierkegaard an ascetic bent that at times threatens to disrupt his vision of a dialectical interpenetration of different spheres of existence: "Kierkegaard had a Manichaean streak which—especially toward the end of his life—tended to pull him towards presenting Christianity in a markedly ascetic fashion, as a negation of all 'worldly' values. But this outlook is untypical of the published writings from the 1840s" (*Limits of the Ethical*, 26).

18. Nietzsche, *Beyond Good and Evil*, 50, 229. Jaspers long ago drew attention to this affinity—a shared concern with masks—between Kierkegaard and Nietzsche (*Nietzsche*, 405–6). For an excellent discussion of ironic masks in Socrates, Kierkegaard, and Nietzsche, see Hadot, *Exercises spirituels*, 103–20.

19. At one point in *Ecce Homo* Nietzsche writes: "I do not want to be a holy man; sooner even a buffoon.—Perhaps I am a buffoon" (326). Nietzsche, in the end, is at once a buffoon and, if not exactly a holy man, certainly a religious writer of a passionate and peculiar sort. One could say the same, perhaps, about Johannes Climacus and Søren Kierkegaard.

20. Ricoeur, "Philosophy after Kierkegaard," 13.

21. Mackey, *A Kind of Poet*, 243–44.

22. Cited in Larmore, "Hölderlin and Novalis," 155.

23. In a chapter on Dickinson in *Regenerate Lyric*, "Beyond Circumference," Elisa New suggestively brings together Kierkegaard and Dickinson from a perspective very different from my own. But I do share New's sense that Dickinson's poems, animated by a severe distrust of idols, tend at their most powerful to undertake a "Puritan resignation of the vision of the eye" for the sake of "spiritual exercise beyond the limits of circumference" (177).

24. Tate, "Emily Dickinson," 223.

25. Harold Bloom, in the opening chapter of his book on Wallace Stevens, places Dickinson alongside Emerson and Whitman, characterizing all three as quasi-gnostic prophets of extravagant imaginative power (*Wallace Stevens*, 1–26). Gary Lee Stonum, in *The Dickinson Sublime*, draws attention to the ambivalence occasionally expressed in Dickinson's celebrations of power, perceptively illuminating the way she explores the "romantic sublime." His approach has affinities with that of Sandra M. Gilbert and Susan Gubar in the last chapter of *The Madwoman in the Attic*, a detailed study of Dickinson's practices of powerful indirection in relation to a patriarchal literary tradition. And, in *Emily Dickinson's Poetry*, Robert Weisbuch provides a finely nuanced account of Dickinson's connections with her major "romantic" contemporaries. The case for Dickinson as a modernist poet has been forcefully made in David Porter's insightful, if cantankerous, *Dickinson*. Porter clarifies many of the important modernist features in Dickinson's poetry, in particular the link in her texts between a radical skepticism, an inclination to voyage into groundlessness, and a radical linguistic errancy, an inclination to set loose the play of tropes: "[A]t moments in most of Dickinson's poems," he complains, wittingly or unwittingly citing Mallarmé, "language is speaking itself" (120–21). A major weakness of this book, however, is that Porter seems unable to decide whether he wishes to denounce the lyric as such (for being a compressed, elliptical, highly figurative mode of writing), modernist writing (for failing to provide the clarities and assurances of realist writing and professorial paraphrase), modern culture in general (for

lacking broadly shared conceptions of the true, the good, the beautiful, and the meaning of death), or Dickinson (for just about everything that makes her a great poet rather than another nineteenth-century versifier of Christian pieties). While it appears that Porter has an axe to grind against all these things, he does not, in my view, cogently gather the different parts of his argument. He also exaggerates the incoherence and incomprehensibility of Dickinson's poems, in part because, though he is fully aware of the way Dickinson internalizes Christian typological schemes, he often fails to bring this knowledge to bear on his readings of specific poems. The excessive claims of Porter's book are effectively refuted in both Robert Weisbuch's *Emily Dickinson's Poetry*, published six years before Porter's book, and Cynthia Griffin Wolff's more recent *Emily Dickinson*. Both Weisbuch and Wolff, extremely sensitive to the typological patterns at play in Dickinson's poetry, demonstrate that her poems are by no means incoherent provided that one not detach them from the Protestant context that supplies them with their figures. For another good discussion of Dickinson's relation to the puritan tradition, see Gelpi, *Emily Dickinson*, 55–93.

26. Wolff, in her perceptive discussion of this poem (*Emily Dickinson*, 227–33), points out that the first three stanzas describe the typical phases of a Congregationalist funeral: the visit paid by mourners, the church service, the burial.

27. This, incidentally, marks one of Dickinson's peculiar affinities with Baudelaire. For a suggestive comparative reading of Baudelaire and Dickinson, see Arac, *Critical Genealogies*, 194–214.

28. Weisbuch, in *Emily Dickinson's Poetry*, points out that it is foolish to call someone as exceptionally alive as Dickinson "morbid."

29. See Frye, *Great Code*, 79.

30. Wolff, *Emily Dickinson*, 72–73.

31. See Porter's fine discussion of Dickinson's inventive use of typological patterns in *Dickinson*, 70–71 and 167–71. Dickinson, Porter writes, "adopted this New England habit . . . to make her own brand of figuralism. . . . Her mode, even to her contemporaries, invested reality always with strangeness, indefinite meanings, and above all surprise" (70–71).

32. Frye, *Great Code*, 82–83.

33. Weisbuch, *Emily Dickinson's Poetry*, 81. In chapters 5 and 6 of his book, Weisbuch presents illuminating readings of Dickinson's poems from this perspective.

34. In the poem whose last stanza I've just cited—"At half past three a single bird" (P # 1084)—the speaker discovers a sublime reach neither in the presence nor in the song of the birds, as is sometimes claimed, but rather in the mesmerizing departure of the birds into invisibility, silence, a boundlessness akin to "the Distance / On the look of Death" (P # 258). Perhaps I can clarify my point by drawing attention to a peculiar poem of Dickinson's: "The Spider holds a Silver Ball / In unperceived Hands— / And dancing softly to Himself / His Yarn of Pearl—unwinds— // He plies from Nought to Nought— / In unsubstantial Trade— / Supplants our Tapestries with His— / In half the period— / An Hour to rear supreme / His Continents of Light— / Then dangle from the Housewife's Broom— / His Boundaries—forgot—" (P # 605). This poem has always left me a little uneasy, for its speaker, to my ear, expresses not sorrow so much as a weird, half-appalled delight over the destruction of this spider's creations and "boundaries," and of the spider himself, a figure for the artist, as well. And she does so, I think, because for Dickinson the

ruin of finite boundaries is the very motion of a "revelatory" widening of consciousness. "Thank you for the Beauty—Thank you too for Boundlessness" (L # 953). Not only is Dickinson baffled by the vastness that accompanies the ruin of the finite, then, but in a sense, too, she seems obscurely to desire, obscurely to participate in, this ruin of the finite. And it is this apocalyptic pulse that fuels the wild figural play of her poetry, as though finite reference itself had to be ruined in order to disclose the abyssal openings of the infinite. It is not that she abandons her faith—it is that she repeatedly suspends it in the darkest reaches of a possible nihilism.

35. Wilbur, "Sumptuous Destitution," 12. Wilbur presumably has all of Dickinson's vanishing birds in mind. "He stirred his Velvet Head // Like one in danger, Cautious, / I offered him a Crumb / And he unrolled his feathers / And rowed him softer home— // Than Oars divide the Ocean, / Too silver for a seam— / Or Butterflies, off Banks of Noon / Leap, plashless as they swim" (P # 328).

36. Wilbur, "Sumptuous Destitution," 11–12.

37. Weisbuch, *Emily Dickinson's Poetry*, 86.

38. Debra Fried, in a course I took with her many years ago at Cornell, drew my attention to the importance of these "sunset" poems in Dickinson's work. For a detailed exploration of a similar fascination with "the Western Mystery" in Mallarmé's work, see Davies, *Mallarmé et le drame solaire*.

39. As Wolff notes, there would seem to be a historical "allegory" at work in the poem as well, a suggestion that the "heaven" that has packed up and departed for nowhere may be a religion—a story of a carpenter, or a carpenter's son, who promised a transcendence of death—that is disappearing in nineteenth-century "North America" (*Emily Dickinson*, 303–4).

40. Emerson writes: "The eye is the first circle; the horizon which it forms is the second; and throughout nature this primary figure is repeated without end. It is the highest emblem in the cipher of the world. St. Augustine described the nature of God as a circle whose centre was everywhere, and its circumference nowhere [here, of course, is one possible source of Dickinson's notorious figure]. We are all our lifetime reading the copious sense of this first of forms. . . . Our life is an apprenticeship to the truth, that around every circle another can be drawn; that there is no end in nature, but every end is a beginning; that there is always another dawn risen on mid-noon, and under every deep a lower deep opens" ("Circles," in *Essays and Lectures*, 403).

41. I would thus want not to contradict but to qualify the broadly accepted claim that Dickinson's poems take place in an "aftermath" of moments of psychic pain or psychic intensity (see David Porter's illuminating presentation of this approach in *Dickinson*, 9–24). For the term "aftermath," I think, does not fully capture the extent to which the author of these poems, animated by an exorbitant desire for the "Missing All," repeatedly *wills herself into* these conditions of elated shock, disclosive ruin, visionary despair. Time and again she moves toward a zone of extreme, if painfully baffled, *expectation* which again is not quite captured by the term "aftermath." Hence I'm inclined to agree with Porter's argument (209–18) that the speaker of "My life had stood a loaded gun" (P # 754) is language itself: a force of creative destruction or destructive creation perilous in its extravagance.

42. Perhaps these two poets met each other on a ghostly plane unattainable by common mortals. In reading Mallarmé's prose poem "Le Nénuphar blanc," a text which could have been lifted directly from Dickinson's psychic life, I find it easy to imagine that the hidden woman who pauses in stillness and from whom the speaker of the poem rows away, lest her actual appearance disturb the reach of imaginative virtuality, is Dickinson herself who, on her side of the hedge, is playing exactly the same game of creative renunciation in relation to the rowing speaker. The poem thus becomes a clairvoyant story about the relationship in distance, the encounter in absence, of two brilliant poets of the nineteenth century who, inhabiting the spaciousness of possibility, have no need to embrace each other in the restricted domain of the finite. Dickinson's proposal: "So We must meet apart— / You there—I—here— / With just the Door ajar / That Oceans are—and Prayer— / And that White Sustenance— / Despair—" (P # 640). Mallarmé's response (about twenty years later): "Séparés, on est ensemble. . . . / Conseille, ô mon rêve, que faire? / Résumer d'un regard la vierge absence éparse en cette solitude et, comme on cueille, en mémoire d'un site, l'un de ces magiques nénuphars clos qui y surgissent tout à coup, enveloppant de leur creuse blancheur un rien, fait de songes intacts, du bonheur qui n'aura pas lieu et de mon souffle ici retenu dans la peur d'une apparition, partir avec: tacitement en déramant peu à peu sans du heurt briser l'illusion ni que le clapotis de la bulle visible d'écume enroulée à ma fuite ne jette aux pieds survenus de personne la ressemblance transparente du rapt de mon idéale fleur [Separated, we are together. . . . / Advise, oh my dream, what to do? / Condense in a glance the virginal absence dispersed in this solitude and, as one gathers, in memory of a site, one of these magically closed water lilies that suddenly spring up, enveloping in their hollow white a nothing, formed of intact dreams, of a happiness that will not take place, and of my breath that I hold here in fear of an appearance, depart with it: quietly rowing away litttle by little without breaking the illusion or permitting the plashing of the visible bubble of foam left in the wake of my flight to throw at the approaching feet of anyone the transparent resemblance of my ravished ideal flower]" (O, 286; CP, 110–13).

43. See Robert Greer Cohn's detailed discussion of the poem in *Mallarmé's Prose Poems*, 5–22.

44. Stevens, "Notes Toward a Supreme Fiction," in *Palm*, 230. Or, in the plainer terms of "Asides on the Oboe," "The prologues are over. It is a question, now, / Of final belief. So, say that final belief / Must be in a fiction. It is time to choose" (187). It is also of interest to set the letter of Mallarmé's from which I've cited alongside Nietzsche's *Birth of Tragedy*, a text first published in 1872, six years after Mallarmé's letter. In that text Nietzsche, too, evokes a nihilist abyss, "the horror or absurdity of existence" (60), the source of a "nausea" from which we can be rescued only by the "saving sorceress" of art (60). Yet in *The Birth of Tragedy* Nietzsche presents a "participatory" theory of art according to which art brings about an affirmative participation in the destructive-creative play of a primordial Dionysian flux. And while Nietzsche in *Zarathustra* places great emphasis on creative invention in response to the nihilist abyss disclosed by the soothsayer, and while in many of his later texts he speaks of the creative "fictions" that underlie all those ossified perspectives that we naively take to be "truths," in an important sense he never abandons his initial "participatory" theory of art, as is made clear, for instance, by his later tendency to evaluate art in terms of its life-affirming or life-negating force. In the letter to Cazalis, on the other hand,

Mallarmé proposes no such "participatory" theory of poetry: his "dualist" theory, rather, implies a lucid, voluntarist, stoic affirmation of the shimmering nothingness of fiction projected against the silent nothingness of the universe. For a detailed and persuasive elucidation of Mallarmé's poetry and prose from this perspective, see Marchal, *Lecture de Mallarmé* and *Religion de Mallarmé*.

45. The idea that Mallarmé surpassed his crisis by adopting some version of Hegelianism has persisted for a long time (for nuanced presentations of this point of view, see Michaud, *Mallarmé*, 51–62, and Richard, *Univers imaginaire*, 231–34). Yet all those letters of the late 1860s in which Mallarmé speaks of having become an impersonal medium of the absolute may echo not Hegel so much as the occultist discourses rampant in nineteenth-century French culture. It is important to underline that even if Mallarmé adopted some Hegelian motifs, he clearly adapted them to his own unmistakably "postreligious" poetic project. Thus I'm inclined to agree with Charles Mauron's emphasis on the poetic origin of Mallarmé's conceptions of poetry. Recurrent words like "idée" and "notion pure" in Mallarmé's adventure, Mauron points out, are drawn not from Hegel's philosophy but from Mallarmé's own experience of the evocative power of words effectively patterned in an accomplished poem (*Mallarmé par lui-même*, 69). Robert Greer Cohn, in his brilliant *Oeuvre de Mallarmé*, presents Mallarmé as among the greatest of tragic and speculative thinkers, and indeed as a thinker whose "paradoxical" and "tetrapolar" patterns surpass Hegel's "dialectical" and "triadic" patterns, yet, despite initial appearances to the contrary, Cohn is probably closer to Mauron than to, say, Michaud. Bertrand Marchal argues in detail that Mallarmé, after passing through a kind of neurosis of the absolute, comes to affirm both the silent force of nature and a "voluntarist" theory of fiction in ways that could be characterized loosely as Stevensian (*Religion de Mallarmé*, 41–100).

46. Maurice Blanchot, in his various meditations on Mallarmé, is the critic who has most persistently explored this dimension of Mallarmé's poetry: see *Part du feu*, 35–48; *Espace littéraire*, 37–52 and 135–50; *Livre à venir*, 303–32; and *Entretien infini*, 620–36.

47. For clear discussions of this issue, see Scherer's preface to "*Livre*" *de Mallarmé*, xvi–xvii, and Bonnefoy's preface to a paperback edition of Mallarmé's writings, *Igitur, Divagations, Un Coup de dés*, 7–40. I'm much indebted to Bonnefoy's essay in particular.

48. Gilles Deleuze describes and dismisses the "postreligious" character of this project in *Nietzsche and Philosophy*, 32–34. Yet any account of this project as based in "traditional dualisms" should at least be qualified. The essay "Crise de vers," as Yves Bonnefoy has underlined in the essay cited in note 47, concludes with an emphasis on a return to the world with a renewed perception brought about by the "new word" created by the poem. There is a Keatsian sensuousness and worldliness in Mallarmé—notably manifest in poems like "L'Après-midi d'un faune" or, in a different way, "Prose pour des Esseintes"—that has not always been sufficiently recognized. Bertrand Marchal has also emphasized this issue in his studies of Mallarmé, as has Leo Bersani, from a different point of view, in *The Death of Stéphane Mallarmé*.

49. In this way the romantic poetic of universal analogy, carried to an extreme, comes to disclose a kind of generative hollow of sheer relationality. As Octavio Paz writes: "Universal *correspondance* signifies perpetual metamorphosis. The text that the world is, is not a single, univocal text: every page is a translation and a metamorphosis of another one, and

so on, without end. The world is the metaphor of a metaphor. So the world loses its reality and turns into a figure of language. At the center of analogy there is a hollow: the plurality of texts implies that there is no original text. Through that hollow the reality of the world and the meaning of language, simultaneously, flow and disappear. Yet it is not Baudelaire but Mallarmé who dares to contemplate that hollow and to convert a vision of the void into the subject of his poetry" (*Hijos del limo*, 108). Richard, similarly, notes that there is in Mallarmé a tension between an "aesthetic of relationality" and "an aesthetic of absence" (*Univers imaginaire*, 331).

50. Yves Bonnefoy, in his preface to *Igitur*, underlines this derivation. So does Roger Pearson, in *Unfolding Mallarmé*, a detailed exploration of the bottomless play of rhyme, both thematic and aural, in Mallarmé's self-reflexive art.

51. As Bonnefoy underlines, at the source of Mallarmé's entire adventure is an exceptionally vivid response to the power exerted by a well-composed poem. For Mallarmé's belief in the power of poetry to surpass chance, Bonnefoy argues, resides in a simple yet forceful "observation": "The observation is that of a movement of adhesion—irrational, imperious—that draws us to certain poetic texts. Or, if one prefers, of the evidence in certain phrases (far and few between in fact) of a disposition of words whose nature is obscure but whose power is real, which Mallarmé names poetry" (preface to *Igitur*, 13). Bonnefoy also notes, though not in exactly these terms, that there is thus a paradox at the root of Mallarmé's lifelong meditation on the power of verse to vanquish "le hasard . . . mot par mot" (O, 387), a paradox that may in fact be something like the "first principle" of verse, of our fascination with rhyme and meter. The paradox is that Mallarmé's project for transmuting chance relies on chance, for, according to this project, words in their given condition are to be transmuted by being set in a resonant pattern whose phonic and rhythmic properties are, of course, wholly contingent. Yet every great poet writes *as though* there were a hidden intelligence at work in the accidental material texture of a given language— Mallarmé, occasionally skirting occultist themes of an original Language or an eschatological book, probes this paradox to the root. And yet this critical perspective needs itself to be qualified. For, as Emile Benveniste points out in "The Nature of the Linguistic Sign," the Saussurean (and, before that, the Sophist and the Lockean) thesis of the "arbitrariness" of the sign is true *only* from an abstract epistemological perspective or, as Benveniste dryly puts it, "under the impassive regard of Sirius or for the person who limits himself to observing from the outside the bond established between an objective reality and human behavior and condemns himself thus to seeing nothing in it but contingency" (44). For a speaker moving *within* any language, on the other hand, sound and sense are inextricably intertwined and could never be *simply* divided into an arbitrary relationship—if they could be so divided, we would have no way of reading either social or idiosyncratic tonal inflections, hence no way of "hearing" the subtle modulations of, say, joy or sorrow or irony, hence no way of really understanding a large part of what we say and hear. The response Bonnefoy describes, then, is entirely meaningful on an existential and historical plane, though it remains an impossible horizon, at least for a thoroughly historicist culture, on an ultimate metaphysical plane. It is a confusion of these levels, I think, that underlies the current of contemporary literary criticism that likes to find in the unruly play of sound nothing more than a *disruption of sense* by nonsensical linguistic materiality. This sort of traditional

dualism, transposed to the structure of language itself, is an unpromising way to approach texts or utterances of any sort. I would note here, too, Geoffrey Hill's acute reflections on these matters in *Style and Faith*, 136–37.

52. Blanchot, *Livre à venir*, 306. This same sort of ambiguity later appears in Eliot's discussion of artistic impersonality in "Tradition and the Individual Talent" (*Selected Prose*, 37–44). For Eliot, as for Mallarmé, the ideal of impersonality involves both a poetic technique and a spiritual vocation. Eliot may have lifted his theory at least in part from Stephen's "aesthetic manifesto" in chapter 5 of *A Portrait of the Artist as a Young Man*, a "manifesto" that concludes: "The artist, like the God of the creation, remains within or behind or beyond or above his handiwork, invisible, refined out of existence, indifferent, paring his fingernails" (209). Yet Stephen's discourse, emphasizing technical virtuosity and dramatic objectivity, would seem to owe more to Flaubert than to Mallarmé, while Eliot's ambiguous, twofold conception of impersonality would seem to be closer to Mallarmé's.

53. See Mauron, *Mallarmé*, 52–61.

54. Thus, in the same letter in which Mallarmé speaks of having finished "la première ébauche de l'Oeuvre [the first sketch of the Work]," he also writes, "[J]e n'ai créé mon Oeuvre que par *élimination*, et toute vérité acquise ne naissait que de la perte d'une impression qui, ayant étincelé, s'était consumée et me permettait, grâce à ses ténèbres dégagées, d'avancer plus profondément dans la sensation des Ténèbres Absolues. La Destruction fut ma Béatrice [I have created my Work only through *elimination*, and every truth acquired was born only through the loss of an impression that, having sparkled, burnt itself out and permitted me, thanks to the shadows thereby released, to advance more deeply into the sensation of Absolute Shadow]" (C, 348–49; L, 77).

55. I've cited Robert Greer Cohn's literal translation of the poem (*Toward the Poems of Mallarmé*, 138–46). In his discussion of the poem Cohn details many of its important parallels with *Un Coup de dés* (see especially 138–39).

56. We know from "Toast funèbre" that *le Maître* is a term for the Poet, as is also the case in *Un Coup de dés*, though in the latter it appears to refer, as well, to questing Humankind in general. It may be worth noting that in the first quatrain of the "sonnet en -yx" the root "phore," derived from the Greek word meaning "to bear" or "to carry," appears twice: perhaps it is then present in its absence in the second quatrain, the hidden "meta-phore" or "trans-position" being precisely that of the Master's passage from the tomblike room to the underworld of death. The prosopopoeic figure of Anguish in the first quatrain, a trace of the poet's kenosis, could then be said to "dedicate" her starlike fingernails to the empty night sky just as the poet "dedicates" his gleaming words and poems, his sonorous knickknacks, to the empty universe that language alone sounds. In "Crise de vers" Mallarmé speaks of the way the poet "dedicates" a distinctively shaped "instrument" not to nothingness but to language (O, 363; SPr, 37).

57. Cf. the famous letter in which Mallarmé asks Lefébure about the meaning of the word "ptyx": "Enfin, comme il se pourrait toutefois que, rythmé par le hamac, et inspiré par le laurier, je fisse un sonnet, et que je n'ai que trois rimes en *ix*, concertez-vous pour m'envoyer le sens réel du mot *ptyx*, ou m'assurer qu'il n'existe dans aucune langue, ce que je préférais de beaucoup afin de me donner le charme de le créer par la magie da la rime [Finally, as it could nonetheless happen that, rocked by the hammock and inspired by the lau-

rel, I will write a sonnet, and as I have only three rhymes in *ix*, do your best to send me the true meaning of the word *ptyx*, or to assure me that it doesn't exist in any language, which I would much prefer, for that would provide the charm of having created it through the magic of rhyme]" (C, 386; L, 85).

58. Cohn, in *Toward the Poems of Mallarmé* (passim), illuminates the tomblike, womblike "empty rooms" throughout Mallarmé's poetry, noting the way they occasionally recall the scenes of ancient mysteries.

59. I've cited from Barbara Johnson's translation in Derrida, *Dissemination*, xxii.

60. Perhaps "Mimique" also alludes to Keats's "Ode on a Grecian Urn," a poem organized around precisely a poet's translation into words of a stilled or silent ode; Mallarmé knew Keats's poetry, and the passage from "Mimique" that I've cited evokes Keats's "Ode" as much as it does Mallarmé's "Faune."

61. Wallace Stevens, "Sunday Morning," in *Palm*, 8.

62. Derrida, in fact, wavers in the way he reads this symptom. At times, sounding Heideggerian, he alludes to the constraints of an epoch that could not have been otherwise: "The privilege of the *phonè* does not depend upon a choice that could have been avoided" (OG, 7). At other times, sounding Nietzschean or Freudian, he speaks of constraints that, strongly motivated, might well have been established otherwise: "The *a* of *différance*, thus, is not heard; it remains silent, secret and discreet as a tomb: *oikesis*. And thereby let us anticipate the delineation of a site, the familial residence and tomb of the proper in which is produced, by *différance*, the *economy of death*. This stone—provided that one knows how to decipher its inscription—is not far from announcing the death of the tyrant" (MP, 4). The life of the tyrant cannot be unmotivated.

63. As Nietzsche writes: "facts is precisely what there is not, only interpretations" (WP, 267; cf. TI, 65). I would note here that Derrida's tendency to employ the word "signified" as though it were indistinguishable from the word "referent" is a peculiar decision that probably deserves more reflection than it has received. The only commentator I know of to have drawn attention to this slippage is Allan Megill: "Incidentally, it is highly significant that Foucault, Derrida, and their followers tend to blur the distinction between the 'signified' (which constitutes one half of the signified/signifier couple making up the sign) and the 'referent' (to which this signifying couple refers). The signified is expanded to cover the territory of the referent; the referent itself mysteriously disappears" (*Prophets of Extremity*, 368 n. 48). Megill reads this slippage as a minor but telling symptom of the displaced "idealism" that, in his view, characterizes the entire field of post-structuralist thought.

64. Thus one might describe Derrida's reading of Husserl in *Speech and Phenomena* as an intricate critique of the last myth, as it were, of transcending death, if nowhere else, at least in the realm of transcendental ideality. "The relationship with *my death* (my disappearance in general) thus lurks in this determination of being as presence, ideality, the absolute possibility of repetition. The possibility of the sign is this relationship with death. The determination and elimination of the sign in metaphysics is the dissimulation of this relationship with death, which yet produced signification" (SP, 54).

65. It is Derrida's ironic, paradoxical echoing of a traditional (post-Kantian, post-Husserlian) language of transcendental reflection that seems primarily to have shaped his philosophic reception in the Anglo-American world. For detailed and illuminating studies

of Derrida from this perspective, see Gasché, *Tain of the Mirror,* and Bennington, *Jacques Derrida,* especially 248–63. Richard Rorty, while attempting to ally Derrida's "playful" deconstructions with his own historicist and nominalist project, has long objected to this "canonical" voice in Derrida that would like to relaunch, under the sign of paradox, the game of transcendental reflection; see "Philosophy as a Kind of Writing," "Deconstruction and Circumvention," "Two Meanings of 'Logocentrism,'" "Is Derrida a Transcendental Philosopher?", and "Derrida and the Philosophical Tradition." Derrida's agile interweaving of Heidegger and Nietzsche has perhaps received less attention. But for a fine discussion of this interweaving, see Schrift, *Nietzsche's French Legacy,* 9–32. And for probing studies of Derrida's complex, ambivalent relationship to Heidegger, in particular as concerns the question of temporality, see Rapaport, *Heidegger and Derrida,* and Caputo, *Radical Hermeneutics.* In the latter, a study from which I've learned a great deal, Caputo provides a suggestive reading of Derrida's relationship not only to Heidegger but, more broadly, to a long hermeneutic tradition. I should note that in what follows I will concentrate on Derrida's immensely influential essays of the sixties and seventies, leaving to the side his many "quasi-Levinasian" essays of the last twenty-five years.

66. Derrida, elsewhere, seems to locate his thought on some oscillating border exactly between a "quasi-naturalist" and a "quasi-transcendental" account, suggesting that the desire for presence, or the desire for a center, is simply desire itself: "But is not the desire for a center, as a function of play, the indestructible itself? And in the repetition or return of play, how could the phantom of the center not call to us?" (WD, 297).

67. For a sharp criticism of this dimension of Derrida's work, see Dews, "Jacques Derrida." "Derrida's response to [the] collapse of Husserl's philosophical project," Dews writes, "is *not,* like that of Adorno or Merleau-Ponty, to move 'downstream' towards an account of subjectivity as emerging from and entwined with the natural and historical world, but rather to move 'upstream', in quest for the ground of transcendental consciousness itself" (19). While it is true that Derrida moves in this direction in many of his essays, in particular those written from a phenomenological angle, it is also true that in other essays, in particular those that engage Heidegger, he moves, if not downstream, at least crosscurrent in the way in which Heidegger and Merleau-Ponty themselves do. It is for this reason that at certain points in my discussion, depending on the context, I use not the term "transcendental reflection" but the broader term "transcendental argument," drawing this term from Charles Taylor's essay "The Validity of Transcendental Arguments." In this essay Taylor clarifies the way important twentieth-century philosophers—including, for example, the Heidegger of *Being and Time* and the Wittgenstein of *Philosophical Investigations*—repeat a Kantian mode of argument but attempt, not to deduce or to describe basic features of consciousness that are necessary conditions of experience or of knowledge (as in Kant or Husserl), but to describe basic "features of our experience" (for example, basic existential structures or basic linguistic practices) that are necessary conditions of any sort of knowledge. It is my sense that Derrida oscillates between these different kinds of "transcendental" argument.

68. The expression "economy of death" also appears in a somewhat riddling passage early in "Différance": "And thereby let us anticipate the delineation of a site, the familial residence and tomb of the proper in which is produced, by *différance,* the *economy of death*" (MP, 4). See, too, the thinking of such an economy, an economy of "life death," in Derrida's

"To Speculate—on 'Freud,'" a brilliant reading of Freud's *Beyond the Pleasure Principle* (PC, 257–410). Elsewhere, as if to make matters more riddling, Derrida calls this "economy of death" simply "jeu," or "play": "Play is the disruption of presence. The presence of an element is always a signifying and substitutive reference inscribed in a system of differences and the movement of a chain. Play is always play of absence and presence, but if it is to be thought radically, play must be conceived of before the alternative of presence and absence. Being must be conceived as presence or absence on the basis of the possibility of play and not the other way around" (WD, 292). Heidegger speaks in very similar terms near the end of *The Principle of Reason:* "The leap into the other tonality of the principle of reason directs a question to us which reads: does the nature of the play let itself be suitably determined in terms of being *qua* ground/reason, or must we think being and ground/reason, being *qua* abyss, in terms of the nature of play and indeed of the play which engages us mortals who are who we are only insofar as we live in proximity to death, which as the most radical possibility of existence is capable of bringing what is most elevated to the clearing and lighting of being and its truth. Death is the as yet unthought standard of measure of the unfathomable, which means, of the most elevated play in which humans are engaged on earth, a play in which they are at stake" (PR, 112).

69. This passage reads like a short version of the argument fully unfolded in another essay of great importance to Derrida, "The Onto-Theological Constitution of Metaphysics" in *Identity and Difference* (42–74). There Heidegger writes: "Thus we think Being rigorously only when we think of it in its difference with beings, and of beings in their difference with Being. The difference thus comes specifically into view.... That which bears such a name directs our thinking to the realm which the key words of [ontotheological] metaphysics—Being and beings, the ground and what is grounded—are no longer adequate to utter. For what these words name, what the manner of thinking that is guided by them represents, *originates as what differs by virtue of the difference. The origin of the difference can no longer be thought of within the scope of metaphysics*" (ID, 62, 71, my italics). For Heidegger, modern philosophy from Descartes through Nietzsche, placing the "subject" in the position once held by "substance," is the nihilist culmination of this "forgetting" of the ontic-ontological difference, a demonic effort at mastery that reduces everything on earth to a "standing reserve" made to serve a Promethean project of technical manipulation, the primordial "belonging" of human being to Being thus falling into ruin. This reading of modernity, developed in the lectures on Nietzsche given between 1936 and 1940, is clearly set forth in the essays collected in *The Question Concerning Technology*.

70. Heidegger, well aware of the danger, attempts to ward off the sort of negative theology (the indirect evocation of a hidden "emanationist" source) that he indeed approaches throughout the lecture: "There is a growing danger that when we speak of 'It,' we arbitrarily posit an indeterminate power which is supposed to bring about all giving of Being and time. However, we shall escape the indeterminacy and avoid arbitrariness as long as we hold fast to the determinations of giving which we attempted to show, if only we look ahead toward Being as presence and toward time as the realm where, by virtue of offering, a manifold presencing takes place and opens up" (OTB, 17).

71. Stevens, "An Ordinary Evening in New Haven," in *Palm*, 351. Cf. Rapaport: "From the broadest of perspectives, Derrida is also suggesting that perhaps temporality inheres in

philosophy as precisely that which cannot be thought and that philosophy poses itself historically as a resistance to the thinking through of time, despite time's attractiveness as a 'radical' in metaphysical discourse" (*Heidegger and Derrida*, 70). This is one of the guiding themes of Rapaport's book.

72. Derrida briefly discusses "On Time and Being" in the first chapter of *Given Time* (18–22). A footnote promises a future reading of this and related texts of Heidegger's (20 n. 10).

73. The same claim is made on the last two pages of "*Ousia* and *Gramme*" (MP, 66–67).

74. In "Différance" Derrida writes: "To think the ontological difference doubtless remains a difficult task, and any statement of it has remained almost inaudible. Further, to prepare, beyond our *logos*, for a *différance* so violent that it can be interpellated neither as the epochality of Being nor as ontological difference, is not in any way to dispense with the passage through the truth of Being, or to 'criticize,' 'contest,' or misconstrue its incessant necessity. On the contrary, we must stay within the difficulty of this passage, and repeat it in the rigorous reading of metaphysics, wherever metaphysics normalizes Western discourse, and not only in the texts of the 'history of philosophy'" (MP, 22–23).

75. Jameson, "Marx's Purloined Letter," 128, 134. Rapaport, in *Heidegger and Derrida*, makes a similar argument, providing a detailed map of Derrida's profoundly ambivalent approach to Heidegger over the years.

76. Derrida, "Marx and Sons," 247.

77. As, for example, in this passage from a famous essay: "If this is so, the entire history of the concept of structure, before the rupture of which we are speaking, must be thought of as a series of substitutions of center for center, as a linked chain of determinations of the center. Successively, and in a regulated fashion, the center receives different forms or names. The history of metaphysics, like the history of the West, is the history of these metaphors and metonymies [this stratospheric "identification" of the history of metaphysics with the history of the West, incidentally, is *very* Heideggerian]. Its matrix—if you will pardon me for demonstrating so little and for being so elliptical in order to come more quickly to my principal theme [this, presumably, is exactly what Jameson means when he speaks of Derrida's tendency to slip a 'minimal (Heideggerian) narrative' in the backdoor]—is the determination of Being as *presence* in all senses of this word. It could be shown that all the names related to fundamentals, to principles, or to the center have always designated an invariable presence—*eidos, arche, telos, energeia, ousia* (essence, existence, substance, subject), *aletheia*, transcendentality, consciousness, God, man, and so forth" ("Structure, Sign, and Play in the Discourse of the Human Sciences," in WD, 279–80). This passage is an exemplary instance of Derrida's characteristic "double move" with respect to Heidegger: it minimally and schematically repeats Heidegger's "problematic" while inserting an important Heideggerian term, "*aletheia*," into the list of terms forming the tradition that is to be deconstructed. Yet "*aletheia*," as Heidegger thinks it, does not refer to "an invariable presence."

78. Habermas, in his unfortunately tendentious reading of Derrida, does clearly underline this difference between Heidegger's and Derrida's "networks of metaphors" (*Philosophical Discourse*, 162). John Caputo, with far greater patience, provides a marvelously illuminating characterization of the difference-in-rapport between Heidegger and Derrida

in terms of their "different metaphorics" (*Radical Hermeneutics*, 153–206)—a characterization that my sketch above largely echoes. But see Bruns, *Heidegger's Estrangements* (especially 174–87), for a thoughtful qualification of this (Derridean) way of telling the story.

79. This "conclusion" echoes a similarly "prophetic" passage near the end of "Structure, Sign, and Play": "There are thus two interpretations of interpretation, of structure, of sign, of play. The one seeks to decipher, dreams of deciphering a truth or an origin which escapes play and the order of the sign, and which lives the necessity of interpretation as an exile. The other, which is no longer turned toward the origin, affirms play and tries to pass beyond man and humanism, the name of man being the name of that being who, throughout the history of metaphysics or ontotheology—in other words, throughout his entire history—has dreamed of full presence, the reassuring foundation, the origin and the end of play. The second interpretation of interpretation, to which Nietzsche pointed the way, does not seek in ethnography, as Lévi-Strauss does, the 'inspiration of a new humanism'" (WD, 292).

80. In *Spurs* Derrida orchestrates a dizzying version of this crossing of Heidegger and Nietzsche. Unfortunately, the crossing is entangled in a would-be "feminist" argument that, at the least, is problematic.

81. In Derrida's texts from about 1980 on, as is well known, the Nietzschean motifs considerably wane while ethical and political motifs come to the fore. One could thus speak of a quasi-Levinasian turn in Derrida's thought over the last twenty-five years (John Caputo, in *Prayers and Tears* [71], suggests that the 1980 essay "Psyche: Inventions of the Other" could be read as an early expression of this turn). Yet I discern no significant "development" or "change" in Derrida's *mode of argument* in these more recent texts. What seems to occur, rather, is an altered *thematization* of the same sorts of arguments presented in the major essays of the sixties and seventies. A reiteration of these arguments comes to be placed in the service not of a Nietzschean theme of apocalyptic "crossing over" but rather of a Levinasian theme of messianic "openness to the other." The radical alterity that is said to unsettle any "economy of the same" (PIO, 60), any seemingly bound discourse, comes to be characterized not as the violence of primordial temporality, not as the unbound spacing of death in and through life, not as the errant dissemination of textual play, but rather as the unforeseeable coming of the other (PIO, 60). And it is this deconstructive opening to the other that, in *Specters of Marx,* Derrida explicitly characterizes as a "messianic" bearing "without messianism" (SM, 59). The undoing of any regulative economy of the same is thematized as a messianic opening to the unforeseeable arrival of a wholly other always to come, or a justice always to come, or a democracy always to come, or perhaps anything you happen to like always to come (God, for example). Yet it is not entirely clear how the unbound spacing of primordial temporality has come to be reconceived in terms of an ethical openness to the other: the transition to the ethical, I think, has not been clearly developed. Put another way, the genealogy, so to speak, of this messianic ethic within Derrida's own trajectory is not the least telling sign of the extremely abstract plane on which this ethic is articulated. But in the concluding section of chapter 1, drawing on Iris Murdoch's criticism of a long tradition of post-Kantian ethical thought, I've already expressed my sense of the limits of this sort of ethical discourse. That said, I do not mean to deny here the unmistakable

ethical and political *implications* of Derrida's long, many-sided meditation on difference. For thoughtful discussions of these implications, see Richard J. Bernstein, "Serious Play: The Ethical-Political Horizon of Derrida," in *The New Constellation*, 172–98, and Drucilla Cornell, *Philosophy of the Limit*.

82. Beckett's *Watt* includes a report of an eccentric, if irrefutable, conversation between a father and son who are piano tuners. "The piano is doomed, in my opinion, said the younger. The piano tuner also, said the elder. The pianist also, said the younger." To which the narrator, a certain Sam, attaches the following commentary: "This was perhaps the principal incident of Watt's early days in Mr Knott's house. In a sense it resembled all the incidents of note proposed to Watt during his stay in Mr Knott's house, and of which a certain number will be recorded in this place, without addition, or subtraction, and in a sense not. It resembled them in the sense that it was not ended, when it was past, but continued to unfold, in Watt's head, from beginning to end, over and over again, the complex connexions of its lights and shadows, the passing from silence to sound and from sound to silence, the stillness before the movement and the stillness after, the quickenings and retardings, the approaches and the separations, all the shifting detail of its march and ordinance, according to the irrevocable caprice of its taking place. It resembled them in the vigour with which it developed a purely plastic content, and gradually lost, in the nice processes of its light, its sound, its impacts and its rhythm, all meaning, even the most literal" (72–73). In some way, I think, this glides near Mallarmé's space of meditation. "Nothing / will have taken place / but the place / except / perhaps / a constellation" (O, 474–77; CP, 143–45), a constellation that finally is only that traced by the intricately unfolded poem of shipwreck itself. Something like this could be said about *Watt*.

83. I adopt the term "change of affect," while lending it a slightly different sense, from Fredric Jameson's well-known essay "Postmodernism." Jameson, in fact, speaks of a "waning of affect."

84. On this question, see Carr, *Banalization of Nihilism*.

85. Derrida explicitly engages the question of "apocalyptic" discourse in "Apocalyptic Tone in Philosophy." This essay, close in time and spirit to *The Post Card*, is suggestive if at times evasive. On the one hand, Derrida insists that he has always distinguished between "closure" and "end" (160); on the other, he acknowledges that he has always been drawn to apocalyptic discourse (161), underlining that this is hardly a peculiar fascination in a modern culture that has produced stories of the "end" of just about everything under the sun (145). He points out, too, that any discourse calling for an end to apocalyptic discourses of the end begins to echo the very dynamic it criticizes (145)—the tradition of enlightened critique thus bears its own apocalyptic tone—and concludes with an evocation of the sort of "apocalypse without apocalypse" that has been a prominent theme in his work over the last three decades.

86. On the telling fluidity with which the "romantic," "modernist," and "existentialist" concern to foreground the "creative processes of the artist" passes into the "postmodernist" concern to foreground "the play of linguistic processes," see Christopher Butler, *After the Wake*, especially 19–20. I should perhaps note that what I've called "unmooring" throughout this chapter is related to what is often called "decentering" in contemporary culture.

But the latter is a decidedly polyvalent term, seeming to involve at least three different meanings that are often imprecisely brought together. First, it emerges out of marxist and psychoanalytic discourses of "overdetermination" and then appears in a range of "constructivist," "historicist," and "sociological" discourses. In this register it designates the "construction" of the subject by a multiplicity of social and discursive codes that can never be unproblematically synthesized in a unified subjectivity. This is a story about the intricate network of unfreedom wherein minor oscillations of freedom may occur. Second, the concept emerges out of a tradition in modern art (in particular modern poetry) of imaginative transport and metamorphic dislocation. In this register it designates the release of the subject from repressive or instrumental structures of socialization and so is experienced as a liberating crossing or departure. This is a story about the promise of extravagant passages of freedom, power, vision. Third, the concept occasionally designates the lived experience of the subjects of a thoroughly mediatized and strangely disjunctive "postmodern" social field. In this register it designates a decisive mutation in traditional modes of lived subjectivity. In short, there are, so to speak, "sociological," "aesthetic," and "historicist-phenomenological" valences to this concept that are often loosely conflated, though each of these valences brings with it a quite different intellectual history, as well as a quite different set of presuppositions and implications.

87. Silesius, *Cherubinic Wanderer*, 47.

88. See Maudmarie Clark's fine discussion of these issues in *Nietzsche on Truth*, 159–204. I borrow from Clark the expression "suicidal nihilism" (166).

89. Reactivity or *ressentiment* is, as it were, Nietzsche's version of our "original sin," the readiness with which we grow bitter amid the pain of our "thrown" lives, hence the readiness with which we spit venom (preferably from a spurious moral posture) at everything and everyone around us. We are, Nietzsche teaches, never done with overcoming this reactivity (on this important question, often neglected in readings of Nietzsche that take the opposition between "active" and "reactive" to be a happily stable one, see Pippin, "Nietzsche's Alleged Farewell," in *Idealism as Modernism*, especially 342–50). Significantly, *convalescence*, the elated passage from illness and despair toward health and hope, the passage dramatized in Zarathustra's movement through a crisis of nihilism, is an important "romantic" theme in Nietzsche's later writings (see, for example, the 1886 preface to a second edition of *The Gay Science*, especially 32).

90. For interpretations of biblical traditions that foreground the myth of Exodus and the voice of Promise—from, respectively, Jewish, Christian, secular, and Blakean points of view—see Buber, *Prophetic Faith*, Moltmann, *Theology of Hope*, Bloch, *Atheism in Christianity*, and Frye, *Great Code*. Paul Ricoeur, noting in particular the affinities between Buber and Moltmann, suggests some of the deep parallels at work in different interpretations of this sort: see "Freedom," 404–5.

91. Cited in Heschel, *Between God and Man*, 228.

92. Idel, "Jewish Apocalypticism," 207; cf. Collins, "From Prophecy to Apocalypticism."

93. Montale, "Lo sai: debbo riperderti e non posso," in *Occasions*, 42.

94. For a beautifully suggestive account of "typological images" in the Bible of creative crossings through waters of chaos, see Frye, *Great Code*, 171–98, especially 188–92.

CONCLUSION. THE DIALECTIC OF INSTRUMENTAL SOCIETY AND CREATIVE NEGATIVITY

1. Derrida, *Gift of Death*, 49. In an essay published a few years later, Derrida more emphatically places Heidegger in this field: see "Faith and Knowledge," 12. For a detailed study of philosophic "doublets" of religion in Heidegger, Derrida, Levinas, and Marion, see de Vries, *Turn to Religion*.

2. That this feature of modern poetry is so often ignored in academic literary criticism is itself, I think, a sign of a division within our culture that is at once embodied and contested in modern poetry—a division between a pragmatically secular and ironic consciousness, on the one hand, and a haunted consciousness deeply dissatisfied with the conventional social and discursive norms of a highly instrumentalized society, on the other.

3. Stevens, "The Dove in Spring," in *Palm*, 385.

4. See Charles Taylor, *Hegel and Modern Society*, especially 1–14. An antihero of one sort or another does appear to have been the most prominent protagonist in novels over the last century and a half. For a suggestive, philosophically framed reading of the modern novel as providing less an affirmative expression of the modern ideal of freedom than a critical exploration of the many ways this ideal founders, see Pippin, *Modernism*, 32–35. Both in this book and in his *Idealism as Modernism*, Pippin, attempting to recover a viable Hegelian dialectic for our time, provides an illuminating discussion of the long and troubled history in modern culture of this ideal variously invoked as freedom, autonomy, self-determination, self-reliance, and independence, among other things.

5. Char, "Pourquoi la journée vole," in *Les Matinaux*, 142.

6. Here I'm indebted to the work of Gillian Rose, who, in a far more capacious and elaborate way, has developed this sort of criticism of post-structuralist thought in general; see her *Broken Middle, Judaism and Modernity*, and *Mourning Becomes the Law*.

7. Sheppard, *Modernism—Dada—Postmodernism*, 20–21.

8. Pippin, *Idealism as Modernism*, 384.

9. Poirier, *Renewal of Literature*, 112.

10. What is sought, as William Carlos Williams says, is "the emplacement of knowledge into a living current" (*Collected Poems*, 1:225). The philosophic shift that Pippin describes as running from Nietzsche through Heidegger and beyond thus corresponds to a defining feature of literary modernism running from Rimbaud through Breton and beyond, or from Mallarmé through Eliot and beyond: the proliferation of unfamiliar languages decisively "distanced" from the shared languages and traditions of society at large. In *Discours et jeu*, a detailed study of Rimbaud, Atle Kittang sketches a suggestive "sociological" approach to this transformation that begins in the second half of the nineteenth century. Horkheimer and Adorno, exiled in 1944, write: "When examining its own guilty conscience, thought has to forgo not only the affirmative use of scientific and everyday conceptual language, but just as much that of the opposition. There is no longer any available form of linguistic expression which has not tended toward accommodation to dominant currents of thought; and what a devalued language does not do automatically is proficiently executed by societal mechanisms" (*Dialectic of Enlightenment*, xii).

11. Taylor, *Hegel and Modern Society*, 71.

12. I mean this as a "sociological" characterization, of course, not a "metaphysical" assertion. Gadamer, discussing the overwhelming extension of the contemporary capitalist economy and the waning of a vital religious presence or background in our culture, describes this process in terms that sound almost Marcusean: "In the place of Marxism, with its global denial of all forms of religion, we encounter a new type of atheism which is based on indifference. It is this indifference which increasingly seems to characterize the attitude of the younger generation in the industrialized world. Certainly, as a proportion of humankind as a whole, they still do not yet represent the majority. Moreover, the nature of this indifference varies greatly across the different Christian confessions. Nonetheless, we can no longer conceal from ourselves the fact that the industrialization of society itself sometimes takes on the form of a religion of the world economy which also prefigures future developments" ("Dialogues in Capri," 202).

13. Benjamin's essays on Baudelaire and Proust, "On Some Motifs in Baudelaire" and "The Image of Proust" (in *Illuminations*, 155–212), are perhaps the most brilliant studies of this dimension of modernism, though it has been a major theme in Fredric Jameson's criticism as well. It is briefly but suggestively addressed in Levin, "What Was Modernism?", 85–87. The romantic and later modernist search for a "lost time" or a "premodern other," of course, also belongs to the history of imperialism; on this connection see Said, *Orientalism*, 166–97, and *Culture and Imperialism*, 186–90; and Sheppard, *Modernism—Dada—Postmodernism*, 68–70, 78–82. On the complex relation between an aristocratic or feudal cultural milieu and modern art, see the suggestive reflections in both Marcuse, *One-Dimensional Man*, 55–62, and Anderson, "Modernity and Revolution," 324–26. Raymond Williams has sketched the way the dissident, bohemian, dandyistic artist emerging in the mid–nineteenth century is a figure that later branches off, so to speak, into the lonely oppositional reactionary and the bohemian oppositional revolutionary, two "artistic stances" prominent throughout the first half of the twentieth century (*Politics of Modernism*, 49–64).

14. Stevens, "Of Mere Being," in *Palm*, 398.

15. See Jameson, *Postmodernism*, 36. Jameson has two ways of making this point. One is to say that "nature" has vanished: "Postmodernism is what you have when the modernization process is complete and nature is gone for good" (ix). This is either wildly careless or, as I suspect, a tactic of provocative defamiliarization: the Bonaventure Hotel, after all, is not yet the whole of the first-world landscape. The other way, more exact, is to emphasize that modernist (and, I would argue, taking all the differences into account, also romantic) art took shape in a *semimodernized* world characterized by the coexistence of different "modes of production" and different "lifeworlds," both modernized and premodernized, a condition that generated an interplay among different sorts of existential and psychic experiences, whereas postmodernist art in the first world, at least for the last thirty years, emerges in a *thoroughly modernized* world in which the discrepant pressures of older lifeworlds are no longer present: "Modernism must be seen as uniquely corresponding to an uneven moment of social development, or to what Ernst Bloch called the 'simultaneity of the nonsimultaneous,' the 'synchronicity of the nonsynchronous': the coexistence of realities from radically different moments of history—handicrafts alongside the great cartels, peasant fields with the Krupp factories or the Ford plant in the distance. . . . What follows paradoxically as a consequence is that . . . the postmodern must be characterized as a situation

in which the survival, the residue, the holdover, the archaic, has finally been swept away without a trace. In the postmodern, then, the past itself has disappeared (along with the well-known 'sense of the past' or historicity and collective memory). Where its buildings still remain, renovation and restoration allow them to be transferred to the present in their entirety as those other, very different and postmodern things called *simulacra*. Everything is now organized and planned; nature has been triumphantly blotted out, along with peasants, petit-bourgeois commerce, handicraft, feudal aristocracies and imperial bureaucracies. Ours is a more homogeneously modernized condition; we no longer are encumbered with the embarrassment of non-simultaneities and non-synchronicities. Everything has reached the same hour on the great clock of development or rationalization (at least from the perspective of the 'West')" (307–10). Eric Hobsbawm, in a discussion of the vast movement from the country to the city in our time, writes: "The most dramatic and far-reaching social change of the second half of [the twentieth] century, and the one which cuts us off forever from the world of the past, is the death of the peasantry" (*Age of Extremes*, 289). Hobsbawm, like Jameson, describes only the thoroughly "modernized" world of the West; elsewhere, as Samir Amin says, "peasant agriculture encompasses nearly a half of humanity—three billion human beings" (*Obsolescent Capitalism*, 175).

16. See Kristeva, *Revolution in Poetic Language*, especially 19–106, as well as the essays collected in *Desire in Language*.

17. Breton, *Point du jour*, 24. For a sympathetic, but not uncritical, account of Kristeva's project, see Moi, *Sexual/Textual Politics*, 149–72. For a sharp criticism of the traditional dualisms at work in this project, see Meschonnic, *Politique du rythme*, 308–38.

18. Many contemporary accounts of "postmodernism" strike me as flawed in their impoverished accounts of earlier romantic, modernist, and avantgardist poetries and philosophies. For useful surveys of the sort of "amnesia" one often encounters in discussions of postmodernism, see Kermode, "Fragments and Ruins," and Callinicos, *Against Postmodernism*, 9–28.

19. See Huyssen, "The Search for Tradition: Avantgarde and Postmodernism in the 1970s" and "Mapping the Postmodern," in *After the Great Divide*, 160–221. I do think that Huyssen, owing to his pronounced reliance on Peter Bürger's one-dimensional account of the earlier interwar avantgarde, underestimates the "constructive" dimensions of the revived "romantic" and lasting "modernist" bearings at play in the arts of the early postwar period. For a fuller account of the "constructive" bearings of the interwar avantgarde, and especially Dada, than Bürger provides, see Sheppard, *Modernism—Dada—Postmodernism*, 171–206. For an illuminating account of the late romantic and, specifically, "Wordsworthian" and "immanentist" bearings of postwar countercultural poetries in the United States, see Altieri, *Enlarging the Temple*. And for a sharp criticism of the limits of Huyssen's approach, in particular of his tendency to underplay the "modernist" currents alive in the art and literature of the early postwar period, see Charles Bernstein, "In the Middle of Modernism," 101–5. Bernstein, I should underline, is severely critical of Huyssen's entire approach to this period.

20. This rethinking has involved, among many other things, a rethinking of the whole question of modernity, now from global or "planetary" rather than Eurocentric or "intra-European" perspectives, on the part of "world-systems" theorists and many artists and phi-

losophers working along similar lines. Such perspectives, of course, imply the need for a critical rethinking and resituating of just the sort of framework I've been working with throughout this book. For a ranging sketch of such an approach to the question of modernity, see Dussel, "Beyond Eurocentrism." For one of Wallerstein's many discussions of the new kinds of "antisystemic movements" in our time, see "1968, Revolution in the World-System," in *Geopolitics and Geoculture*, 65–83.

21. Debord, *Society of the Spectacle*, sec. 42 (unpaginated). "The spectacle is *capital* to such a degree of accumulation that it becomes image" (sec. 34).

22. For a capacious overview of the interplay among these and other factors in the emergence of postmodernity, see Best and Kellner, *Postmodern Adventure*.

23. See Jameson, *Postmodernism*, especially 1–54, and *Signatures of the Visible*. See, too, Perry Anderson's ranging overview of Jameson's work in *The Origins of Postmodernity*.

24. For a bleak account of what the second of these trends has meant for the New York art world in particular, see Suzi Gablik, *Has Modernism Failed?*, a book that might have been just as aptly titled *Has Postmodernism Failed?* And for an insightful discussion of this contradiction in general to which Jameson draws attention, see Anderson, *Origins of Postmodernity*, 110–14.

25. Jameson characterizes postmodernism as "the substitute for the sixties and the compensation for their political failure" (*Postmodernism*, xvi) and (in a sentence I've cited earlier) as the culture "you have when the modernization process is complete and nature is gone for good" (ix). He also understands it to involve a whole new level of "the becoming cultural of the economic, and the becoming economic of the cultural" ("Notes on Globalization," 60). Hence one can appeal to his own characterization of this cultural dominant that belongs to the glassy world emerging in the late sixties in order to contest his tendency to assimilate fully to this dominant the early postwar existentialisms, modernisms, and neo-avantgardes, as well as a range of post-structuralist theories. The figures at work in these different contexts and movements did not essentially form their projects or develop their thinking within (or in response to) the sort of Andy Warhol or Bonaventure Hotel world that Jameson is primarily concerned to describe. There is, then, an unclarified discrepancy in Jameson's account between his characterization of this cultural dominant that emphatically belongs to contemporary consumer society, on the one hand, and his more sweeping interpretation of an entire postwar field of history and culture, on the other. But I should at least mention in this context Jameson's ranging interpretation of the sixties in his essay "Periodizing the Sixties."

26. See, for example, the use of this term in Marjorie Perloff's well-known *Poetics of Indeterminacy*. With this term Perloff carries to an extreme the nominalist bias (the distrust of conceptual or philosophic wholes) that has always characterized a decidedly empiricist Anglo-American culture, attaching this perspective to the practices of various "experimental" writers from 1870s Europe through contemporary North America.

27. It seems significant—perhaps the sign of a broadened *fin de siècle* sensibility—that these orientations have recently passed beyond the borders of marginal or avantgarde movements. In the United States, during the first few decades after World War II, Beat, Black Mountain, and New York School poets continued to explore a range of elliptical practices developed throughout the modernist and avantgardist period. From the mid-seventies on,

Language Movement poets and others, drawing on these writers as well as earlier writers who had been marginal even within the modernist and avantgardist field (including, among others, Stein, Zukofsky, and Khlebnikov), radicalized these sorts of practices into a polemical art of the indeterminate and the dispersive. In turn, and perhaps surprisingly, these practices have in recent years been loosely assimilated by many poets working in more traditional modes and only occasionally sharing the concerns—themselves extremely diverse—of these earlier modernist and avantgardist formations. Many contemporary poets, that is, appear to have adopted a similar distrust of inherited modes of narrative and thematic patterning, though less commonly a distrust of expressive voice, and a sort of programmatic disjunction (or a parodic inversion of the old modernist imperative "Only connect") now appears to be taught in writing workshops around the country. It is true that these currents develop alongside what remains the dominant poetic in this country, namely, an attenuated neoromantic poetic that, as Altieri and others have noted, seems ultimately to derive from Coleridge's "conversation" poems: a modest, sensitive, usually elegiac art of self-expression detached from a more sweeping art of exploratory vision. Yet the poetic of indeterminate play has spread widely in the field of turn-of-the-century U.S. poetry. For a survey of similar tensions in the field of contemporary French poetry—voiced in the sardonic tone of one unhappy with the very terms of the debate—see Meschonnic, *Politique du rythme*, 572–88.

28. Frye, *Anatomy of Criticism*, 271–72.

29. Horkheimer and Adorno, *Dialectic of Enlightenment*, 126.

30. Or, as Fredric Jameson has suggested (*Signatures of the Visible*, 100, 208), ours is an age that tends to valorize what Coleridge called "fancy," the associative or digressive play of the mind, and to distrust what Coleridge called "imagination," the shaping or constructive force of the mind. The symbolist figure of "musical structure" expressed the ideal of holding these poles together.

31. Lauterbach, *On A Stair*, 31.

32. For splendid discussions of postsymbolist, early-avantgarde, and *fantaisiste* poetries around the turn of the last century, see Shattuck, *Banquet Years*, and Raymond, *De Baudelaire au surréalisme*, 217–38 and 252–66. It is of interest that many passages in Raymond's discussion could, with minor shifts in vocabulary, serve as sound commentaries on the disjunctive-digressive poetries of the last thirty years or so in both France and the United States. "The power of this sort of poetry," Raymond writes, "is not objectively demonstrable and reveals itself only to experience, that is, to individual experience. Doubtless the same can be said of any true poetry, but the engagement demanded of the reader in this case is of a particular sort: it demands that the reader yield himself to the impressions of a sensibility that is exceptionally plastic and entirely impregnated by the atmosphere of a specific age. There is nothing in this akin to the labor of gradual penetration demanded by an *oeuvre* like that of Mallarmé; the poetry of Jacob, of Cocteau, often of Apollinaire, and of many of those who have followed them, works or fails to work; it does not enclose (in any strict sense) a secret and so cannot be characterized as hermetic; it intends to be loved by virtue of a flash of lightning; and the risk to which it exposes itself—as the passing of a few years makes clear—is that of no longer finding in the future the conditions necessary for the transmission of the electricity with which it is charged. Its best

chance is to find a reader endowed with a 'sense of mystery' (as Cocteau says) similar to that of the poet himself" (258).

33. Foucault, *History of Sexuality*, 1:157.

34. Bernstein, "Semblance," 34–35.

35. See Berman, *All That Is Solid*, especially 87–129. The forces of capitalist modernity, Berman reminds us, have done at least as much to destroy the substance (as distinct from the ideological use) of religion and metaphysics as any scientific or critical theory has ever done. Perhaps the subject—or, concretely, the individual person—is but the most recent target of their tremendous movement of creative destruction. What's the point of persons, or horizons of meaning, in a thoroughly commodified world of supervised workers, machines, and consumers?

36. Jameson, in a place I've not been able to locate, says something very close to this.

37. Vallejo, *Trilce*, XLV, 116–17.

EPILOGUE. THE MIRACLE OF PLACE

1. Stevens, *Necessary Angel*, 22.

2. "The worst is not so long as we can say, 'This is the worst.' Isn't that the truth. Deepstep now baby deepstep. Bear me along your light-bearing paths. Come shining," says a voice in C. D. Wright's recent *Deepstep Come Shining* (49), a book where the extravagant is alive, bold, weird, and clairvoyant.

3. Enzensberger, *Consciousness Industry*, 14, 61. Cf. Marshall Berman's response to Perry Anderson's gloom-and-doom review of his *All That Is Solid Melts into Air:* "Doesn't he realize how much human creativity grows, and always has grown, out of disappointment?" (*Adventures in Marxism*, 154).

4. See in particular the following works: Rose, *Hegel contra Sociology*, *Broken Middle*, *Judaism and Modernity*, and *Mourning Becomes the Law*; J. M. Bernstein, *Fate of Art* and *Recovering Ethical Life*; Pippin, *Hegel's Idealism, Modernism*, and *Idealism as Modernism*; and, from an earlier generation, Taylor, *Hegel and Modern Society*, *Sources of the Self*, and *Ethics of Authenticity*. Rose, it is true, rather like Adorno in this regard, tends to assume a far more polemical stance toward other philosophic orientations than do Taylor, Pippin, and Bernstein. Yet, even then, her primary concern is to comprehend in a conceptual narrative the whole contradictory field of modernity wherein, time and again, we seem to find ourselves so divided and impeded, so uncertain of our bearings.

5. J. M. Bernstein, *Recovering Ethical Life*, 11; cf. 28. This book is a brilliant effort not only to recast Habermas's work in Hegelian terms but also to develop philosophic frames for understanding our late-modern situation in general.

6. "What is the final meaning / Of extravagance? Why are the office // Buildings, storehouses of papers, / The centers of extravagance?" (*New Collected Poems*, 64). Perhaps an ambiguity could be heard in these lines. But Oppen repeatedly voices his respect for limits, for "a limited, limiting clarity" (193), for a potentially shared world of both the "common / Place image / The initial light" (217) and a "common sense" (178). "We want

to defend / Limitation / And do not know how" (177). Oppen's *New Collected Poems* is hereafter cited in the text as CP.

    7. Vallejo, "Los nueve monstruos," in *Complete Posthumous Poems,* 172: "I, desgraciadamente, / el dolor crece en el mundo a cada rato, / crece a treinta minutos por segundo, paso a paso."

    8. See the important essay by Ricks, "Geoffrey Hill."

    9. Hill, "Annunciations, 2" in *New and Collected Poems,* 51. *Canaan* is hereafter cited in the text as C, and *The Triumph of Love* is cited as TL.

    10. My understanding of the stakes of a "testimonial" poetic owes a great deal to Charles Altieri's extraordinarily ambitious and suggestive *Act and Quality.*

    11. Hass, "One Body," 71.

    12. Hill, "Poetry," 5.

    13. Oppen, "Mind's Own Place," 133.

    14. DuPlessis, "George Oppen: 'What Do We Believe to Live With?'", 62. This is an exceptionally insightful essay on Oppen's poetry, one that provides illuminating accounts in particular of Oppen's troubled dream of community, his quiet faith in children, and his puzzled but abiding reverence for the natural world. DuPlessis, in the lines just cited, is drawing on a letter Oppen wrote to her in 1965: "The process by which sometimes a line appears, I cannot trace. It happens. Given a line, one has a place to stand, and goes further. . . . When the man writing is frightened by a word, he may have started" (*Selected Letters,* 123).

    15. Celan, "Meridian," 50.

    16. Oppen, *Selected Letters,* 67.

BIBLIOGRAPHY

Abel, Lionel. "Georges Bataille and the Repetition of Nietzsche." In Boldt-Irons, *On Bataille*, 51–60.
Abrams, M. H. "English Romanticism: The Spirit of the Age." In Bloom, *Romanticism and Consciousness*, 90–118.
———. *The Mirror and the Lamp: Romantic Theory and the Critical Tradition*. New York: Oxford University Press, 1953.
———. *Natural Supernaturalism: Tradition and Revolution in Romantic Literature*. New York: Norton, 1971.
———. "Structure and Style in the Greater Romantic Lyric." In Bloom, *Romanticism and Consciousness*, 201–29.
Adorno, Theodor. *Aesthetic Theory*. Newly translated, edited, and with an introduction by Robert Hullot-Kentor. Minneapolis: University of Minnesota Press, 1997.
———. *Kierkegaard: Construction of the Aesthetic*. Ed. and trans. Robert Hullot-Kentor. Minneapolis: University of Minnesota Press, 1989.
———. *Negative Dialectics*. Trans. E. B. Ashton. New York: Continuum, 1973.
Ahearn, Edward J. *Rimbaud: Visions and Habitations*. Berkeley: University of California Press, 1983.
Alderman, Harold. *Nietzsche's Gift*. Athens: Ohio University Press, 1977.
Allison, Henry E. *Kant's Theory of Taste: A Reading of the* Critique of Judgment. New York: Cambridge University Press, 2001.
Alloway, Lawrence. *Topics in American Art since 1945*. New York: Norton, 1975.
Altieri, Charles. *Act and Quality: A Theory of Literary Meaning and Humanistic Understanding*. Amherst: University of Massachusetts Press, 1981.
———. *Enlarging the Temple: New Directions in American Poetry during the 1960s*. Lewisburg: Bucknell University Press, 1979.
———. "The Objectivist Tradition." In *The Objectivist Nexus*, ed. Rachel Blau DuPlessis and Peter Quartermain, 25–36. Tuscaloosa: University of Alabama Press, 1999.
———. *Painterly Abstraction in Modernist American Poetry*. University Park: Pennsylvania State University Press, 1995.
———. *Self and Sensibility in Contemporary American Poetry*. New York: Cambridge University Press, 1984.

———. *Subjective Agency: A Theory of First-Person Expressivity and Its Social Implications.* Oxford: Blackwell, 1994.
———. "What Modernism Offers the Contemporary Poet." In Hank Lazer, ed., *What Is a Poet?*, 31–65. Tuscaloosa: University of Alabama Press, 1987.
Amin, Samir. *Obsolescent Capitalism: Contemporary Politics and Global Disorder.* Trans. Patrick Camiller. London: Zed Books, 2003.
Anderson, Perry. "Modernity and Revolution." In *Marxism and the Interpretation of Culture*, ed. Cary Nelson and Lawrence Grossberg, 317–33. Urbana: University of Illinois Press, 1988.
———. *The Origins of Postmodernity.* London: Verso, 1998.
Apollinaire, Guillaume. *Selected Writings.* Trans. and with an introduction by Roger Shattuck. New York: New Directions, 1971.
Arac, Jonathan. *Critical Genealogies: Historical Situations for Postmodern Literary Studies.* New York: Columbia University Press, 1987.
Aragon, Louis. *Le Mouvement perpétuel.* 1925. Reprint, Paris: Gallimard-Folio, 1970.
Ashbery, John. *Rivers and Mountains.* New York: Ecco, 1966.
Beckett, Samuel. *Watt.* New York: Grove, 1953.
Benjamin, Walter. *Illuminations.* Trans. Harry Zonh. Ed. and with an introduction by Hannah Arendt. New York: Schocken, 1969.
———. *Reflections.* Trans. Edmund Jephcott. Ed. and with an introduction by Peter Demetz. New York: Harcourt Brace Jovanovich, 1978.
Bennington, Geoffrey. "Derridabase." In *Jacques Derrida.* Paris: Seuil, 1991.
———. *Lyotard Writing the Event.* New York: Columbia University Press, 1988.
Benveniste, Emile. "The Nature of the Linguistic Sign." In *Problems in General Linguistics.* Trans. Mary Elizabeth Meek, 43–48. Coral Gables: University of Miami Press, 1971.
Berlin, Isaiah. *The Roots of Romanticism.* Ed. Henry Hardy. Princeton: Princeton University Press, 1999.
Berman, Marshall. *Adventures in Marxism.* London: Verso, 1999.
———. *All That Is Solid Melts into Air: The Experience of Modernity.* New York: Penguin, 1988.
Bernstein, Charles. "In the Middle of Modernism in the Middle of Capitalism on the Outskirts of New York." In *Poetics*, 90–105. Cambridge: Harvard University Press, 1992.
———. "Semblance." In *Content's Dream*, 34–39. Los Angeles: Sun & Moon Press, 1986.
Bernstein, J. M. *The Fate of Art: Aesthetic Alienation from Kant to Derrida and Adorno.* University Park: Pennsylvania State University Press, 1992.
———. *Recovering Ethical Life: Jürgen Habermas and the Future of Critical Theory.* London: Routledge, 1995.
Bernstein, Richard J. *The New Constellation: The Ethical-Political Horizons of Modernity/Postmodernity.* Cambridge: MIT Press, 1992.
Bersani, Leo. *The Death of Stéphane Mallarmé.* New York: Cambridge University Press, 1982.
Best, Steven, and Douglas Kellner. *The Postmodern Adventure.* New York: Guilford, 2001.
Blake, William. *The Complete Poetry and Prose.* Rev. ed. Ed. David E. Erdman, with commentary by Harold Bloom. New York: Doubleday, 1988.
Blanchot, Maurice. *L'Entretien infini.* Paris: Gallimard, 1969.

———. *L'Espace littéraire*. Paris: Gallimard, 1955.
———. "The Limits of Experience: Nihilism." In *The New Nietzsche: Contemporary Styles of Interpretation*, ed. David B. Allison, 121–27. New York: Delta, 1977.
———. *Le Livre à venir*. Paris: Gallimard, 1959.
———. *La Part du feu*. Paris: Gallimard, 1949.
Bloch, Ernst. *Atheism in Christianity: The Religion of the Exodus and the Kingdom*. Trans. J. T. Swann. New York: Herder and Herder, 1972.
Bloom, Harold. *Agon: Toward a Theory of Revisionism*. New York: Oxford University Press, 1982.
———. "The Internalization of Quest-Romance." In Bloom, *Romanticism and Consciousness*, 3–24.
———. *The Ringers in the Tower: Studies in Romantic Tradition*. Chicago: University of Chicago Press, 1971.
———. *The Visionary Company: A Reading of English Romantic Poetry*. Rev. ed. Ithaca: Cornell University Press, 1971.
———. *Wallace Stevens: The Poems of Our Climate*. Ithaca: Cornell University Press, 1977.
———, ed. *Romanticism and Consciousness*. New York: Norton, 1970.
Blumenberg, Hans. *The Legitimacy of the Modern Age*. Trans. Robert M. Wallace. Cambridge: MIT Press, 1983.
Boldt-Irons, Leslie Anne, ed. *On Bataille: Critical Essays*. Albany: State University of New York Press, 1995.
Bonnefoy, Yves. *L'Improbable et autres essais*. Paris: Gallimard-Folio, 1992.
———. Preface to *Igitur, Divagations, Un Coup de dés*, 7–40. Paris: Gallimard-Folio, 1976.
———. *Rimbaud*. Paris: Seuil, 1961.
Breton, André. *L'Amour fou*. Paris: Gallimard, 1937.
———. "For Dada, etc." In *The Dada Painters and Poets*. 2d ed. Ed. Robert Motherwell, 199–206. Cambridge: Harvard University Press, 1981.
———. *Manifestoes of Surrealism*. Trans. Richard Seaver and Helen R. Lane. Ann Arbor: University of Michigan Press, 1972.
———. *Poems*. Ed. and trans. Jean-Pierre Cauvin and Mary Ann Caws. Austin: University of Texas Press, 1982.
———. *Point du jour*. Rev. ed. Paris: Gallimard-Folio, 1970.
Bromwich, David. *Disowned by Memory: Wordsworth's Poetry of the 1790s*. Chicago: University of Chicago Press, 1998.
Bruns, Gerald. *Heidegger's Estrangements: Language, Truth, and Poetry in the Later Writings*. New Haven: Yale University Press, 1989.
Buber, Martin. *The Prophetic Faith*. Trans. Carlyle Witton-Davies. New York: Macmillan, 1949.
Bürger, Peter. *Theory of the Avant-Garde*. Trans. Michael Shaw, with a foreword by Jochen Schulte-Sasse. Minneapolis: University of Minnesota Press, 1984.
Burke, Edmund. *A Philosophical Enquiry into the Origin of Our Ideas of the Sublime and Beautiful*. Ed. and with an introduction by James T. Boulton. Notre Dame: University of Notre Dame Press, 1968.
Burke, Kenneth. *A Grammar of Motives*. Berkeley: University of California Press, 1969.

Butler, Christopher. *After the Wake: An Essay on the Contemporary Avant-Garde.* London: Oxford University Press, 1980.

———. *Early Modernism: Literature, Music, and Painting in Europe, 1900–1916.* London: Oxford University Press, 1994.

Butler, Judith. "Commentary on Joseph Flay's 'Hegel, Derrida, and Bataille's Laughter.'" In *Hegel and His Critics: Philosophy in the Aftermath of Hegel,* ed. William Desmond, 174–78. Albany: State University of New York Press, 1989.

Byrd, Don. *The Poetics of the Common Knowledge.* Albany: State University of New York Press, 1994.

Calinescu, Matei. *Five Faces of Modernity.* Durham: Duke University Press, 1987.

Callinicos, Alex. *Against Postmodernism: A Marxist Critique.* New York: St. Martins, 1989.

Caputo, John D. *The Prayers and Tears of Jacques Derrida: Religion without Religion.* Bloomington: Indiana University Press, 1997.

———. *Radical Hermeneutics: Repetition, Deconstruction, and the Hermeneutic Project.* Bloomington: Indiana University Press, 1987.

Carr, Karen L. *The Banalization of Nihilism: Twentieth-Century Responses to Meaninglessness.* Albany: State University of New York Press, 1992.

Cavell, Stanley. *The Senses of Walden.* Expanded edition. Chicago: University of Chicago Press, 1992.

Celan, Paul. "The Meridian." In *Collected Prose,* trans. Rosmarie Waldrop, 37–56. New York: Sheep Meadow Press, 1986.

Char, René. *Fureur et mystère.* Paris: Gallimard-Folio, 1967.

———. *Les Matinaux.* Paris: Gallimard-Folio, 1987.

———. *Recherche de la base et du sommet.* Paris: Gallimard-Folio, 1971.

Christ, Carol T. *Victorian and Modern Poetics.* Chicago: University of Chicago Press, 1984.

Clark, Maudmarie. *Nietzsche on Truth and Philosophy.* New York: Cambridge University Press, 1990.

Clark, T. J. *Farewell to an Idea: Episodes from a History of Modernism.* New Haven: Yale University Press, 1999.

Cohn, Robert Greer. *Mallarmé's Prose Poems: A Critical Study.* New York: Cambridge University Press, 1987.

———. *L'Oeuvre de Mallarmé: Un Coup de dés.* Paris: Librairie Les Lettres, 1951.

———. *The Poetry of Rimbaud.* Columbia: University of South Carolina Press, 1973.

———. *Toward the Poems of Mallarmé.* Enl. ed. Berkeley: University of California Press, 1980.

Coleridge, Samuel Taylor. *Biographia Literaria with Aesthetic Essays.* 2 vols. Ed. J. Shawcross. London: Oxford University Press, 1967.

———. *The Major Works.* Ed. and with an introduction by H. J. Jackson. New York: Oxford University Press, 1985.

———. "On Poesy or Art." In *Biographia Literaria with Aesthetic Essays,* 253–63.

Collins, John J. "From Prophecy to Apocalypticism: The Expectation of the End." In *The Encyclopedia of Apocalypticism.* Vol. 1. Ed. John J. Collins, 129–61. New York: Continuum, 2000.

Cook, Albert. "Point, Closure, Amplitude, and the Conditions of Utterance: Wordsworth, Whitman, and Rimbaud." In *The Reach of Poetry*, 53–72. West Lafayette: Purdue University Press, 1995.
Cornell, Drucilla. *The Philosophy of the Limit*. New York: Routledge, 1992.
Crane, Hart. *The Complete Poems*. Ed. Marc Simon, with a new introduction by Harold Bloom. New York: Liveright, 2000.
Creeley, Robert. "A Sense of Measure." In *Was That a Real Poem and Other Essays*, 13–15. Bolinas, Cal.: Four Seasons Foundations, 1979.
Dallmayr, Fred. "The Discourse of Modernity: Hegel, Nietzsche, Heidegger, and Habermas." In *Habermas and the Unfinished Project of Modernity*, ed. Maurizio Passerin d'Entrèves and Seyla Benhabib, 79–96. Cambridge: MIT Press, 1997.
Danto, Arthur. *The Philosophical Disenfranchisement of Art*. New York: Columbia University Press, 1986.
Davies, Gardner. *Mallarmé et le drame solaire*. Paris: José Corti, 1959.
Debord, Guy. *The Society of the Spectacle*. Trans. Black & Red. Detroit: Black & Red, 1977.
Deleuze, Gilles. *Nietzsche and Philosophy*. Trans. Hugh Tomlinson. New York: Columbia University Press, 1983.
de Man, Paul. "Phenomenality and Materiality in Kant." In *The Textual Sublime: Deconstruction and Its Differences*. Ed. Hugh J. Silverman and Gary E. Aylesworth, 87–108. Albany: State University of New York Press, 1990.
Derrida, Jacques, and Gianni Vattimo, eds. *Religion*. Stanford: Stanford University Press, 1998.
Descombes, Vincent. *The Barometer of Modern Reason*. Trans. Stephen Adam Schwartz. New York: Oxford University Press, 1993.
de Vries, Hent. *Philosophy and the Turn to Religion*. Baltimore: Johns Hopkins University Press, 1999.
Dews, Peter. "Jacques Derrida: The Transcendental and Différance." In *Logics of Disintegration*, 1–44. London: Verso, 1987.
Dufrenne, Mikel. "Pour une philosophie non théologique." In *Le Poétique*. 2d ed. 7–57. Paris: Presses Universitaires de France, 1973.
DuPlessis, Rachel Blau. "George Oppen: 'What Do We Believe to Live With?'" *Ironwood* 5 (1975): 62–77.
Dussel, Enrique. "Beyond Eurocentrism: The World-System and the Limits of Modernity." In Jameson and Miyoshi, *Cultures of Globalization*, 3–31.
Edmundson, Mark. *Literature against Philosophy, Plato to Derrida: A Defence of Poetry*. New York: Cambridge University Press, 1995.
Eliot, T. S. *The Complete Poems and Plays, 1909–1950*. New York: Harcourt, Brace & Co., 1967.
———. *Selected Prose*. Ed. and with an introduction by Frank Kermode. New York: Farrar, Straus & Giroux, 1975.
Emerson, Ralph Waldo. *Essays and Lectures*. Ed. Joel Porte. New York: Library of America, 1983.
Enzensberger, Hans Magnus. *The Consciousness Industry: On Literature, Politics, and the Media*. Ed. and trans. Michael Roloff. New York: Seabury, 1974.

Erkkila, Betsy. *Walt Whitman among the French: Poet and Myth*. Princeton: Princeton University Press, 1980.
Eysteinsson, Astradur. *The Concept of Modernism*. Ithaca: Cornell University Press, 1990.
Ferry, David. *The Limits of Mortality: An Essay on Wordsworth's Major Poems*. Middletown: Wesleyan University Press, 1959.
Foucault, Michel. *Discipline and Punish: The Birth of the Prison*. Trans. Alan Sheridan. New York: Random House, 1977.
———. *The History of Sexuality*. Vol. 1. Trans. Robert Hurley. New York: Random House, 1978.
———. *The Order of Things: An Archaeology of the Human Sciences*. New York: Random House, 1970.
Frye, Northrop. *Anatomy of Criticism*. Princeton: Princeton University Press, 1957.
———. "The Drunken Boat: The Revolutionary Element in Romanticism." In *The Stubborn Structure*, 200–217. London: Methuen, 1970.
———. *Fearful Symmetry: A Study of William Blake*. Princeton: Princeton University Press, 1947.
———. *The Great Code: The Bible and Literature*. New York: Harcourt Brace Jovanovich, 1982.
———. "The Keys to the Gates." In Bloom, *Romanticism and Consciousness*, 233–54.
———. "The Road of Excess." In Bloom, *Romanticism and Consciousness*, 119–32.
———. "The Romantic Myth." In *A Study of English Romanticism*, 3–49. New York: Random House, 1968.
———. *Words With Power*. New York: Harcourt Brace Jovanovich, 1990.
Gablik, Suzi. *Has Modernism Failed?* New York: Thames and Hudson, 1984.
Gadamer, Hans-Georg. "Dialogues in Capri." In Derrida and Vattimo, *Religion*, 200–211.
———. *Plato's Dialectical Ethics*. Trans. and with an introduction by Robert M. Wallace. New Haven: Yale University Press, 1991.
Gander, Forrest. *Science and Steepleflower*. New York: New Directions, 1998.
Gasché, Rodolphe. *The Tain of the Mirror: Derrida and the Philosophy of Reflection*. Cambridge: Harvard University Press, 1986.
Gelpi, Albert. *A Coherent Splendor: The American Poetic Renaissance, 1910–1950*. New York: Cambridge University Press, 1987.
———. *Emily Dickinson: The Mind of the Poet*. Cambridge: Harvard University Press, 1965.
Gilbert, Sandra M., and Susan Gubar. *The Madwoman in the Attic*. New Haven: Yale University Press, 1979.
Gill, Stephen. *William Wordsworth: A Life*. Oxford: Oxford University Press, 1990.
Gillespie, Michael Allen, and Tracy B. Strong, eds. *Nietzsche's New Seas: Explorations in Philosophy, Aesthetics, and Politics*. Chicago: University of Chicago Press, 1988.
Goldmann, Lucien. *Lukács et Heidegger*. Paris: Denoël, 1973.
Green, Ronald M. *Kierkegaard and Kant: The Hidden Debt*. Albany: State University of New York Press, 1992.
Guyaux, André. *Duplicités de Rimbaud*. Paris and Geneva: Champin-Slatkine, 1991.
Guyer, Paul. *Kant and the Experience of Freedom*. New York: Cambridge University Press, 1993.

Habermas, Jürgen. *The Philosophical Discourse of Modernity*. Trans. Frederick G. Lawrence. Cambridge: MIT Press, 1987.
———. *The Theory of Communicative Action*. 2 vols. Trans. Thomas McCarthy. Boston: Beacon Press, 1984.
Hadot, Pierre. *Exercises spirituels et philosophie antique*. With a foreword by Arnold I. Davidson. Rev. and enl. ed. Paris: Albin Michel, 2002.
Hamburger, Michael. *The Truth of Poetry: Tensions in Modern Poetry since Baudelaire*. New York: Harcourt Brace Jovanovich, 1969.
Harries, Karsten. "The Philosopher at Sea." In Gillespie and Strong, *Nietzsche's New Seas*, 21–44.
Hartman, Geoffrey. *Beyond Formalism*. New Haven: Yale University Press, 1970.
———. *The Fateful Question of Culture*. New York: Columbia University Press, 1997.
———. "Poem and Ideology: A Study of Keats's 'To Autumn.'" In *The Fate of Reading*, 124–46. Chicago: University of Chicago Press, 1975.
———. *Wordsworth's Poetry: 1787–1814*. New Haven: Yale University Press, 1964.
Hass, Robert. "One Body: Some Notes on Form." In *Twentieth-Century Pleasures*, 56–71. Hopewell, N.J.: Ecco, 1984.
Heaney, Seamus. *The Government of the Tongue: Selected Prose, 1978–1987*. New York: Farrar, Straus & Giroux, 1988.
———. *The Redress of Poetry*. New York: Farrar, Straus & Giroux, 1995.
———. *Seeing Things*. New York: Farrar, Straus & Giroux, 1991.
Heller, Erich. *The Importance of Nietzsche: Ten Essays*. Chicago: University of Chicago Press, 1988.
Hertz, Neil. "The Notion of Blockage in the Literature of the Sublime." In *The End of the Line*, 40–60. New York: Columbia University Press, 1985.
Heschel, Abraham Joshua. *Between God and Man: An Interpretation of Judaism*. Ed. and with an introduction by Fritz A. Rothschild. New York: Free Press, 1965.
Higgins, Kathleen Marie. *Nietzsche's Zarathustra*. Philadelphia: Temple University Press, 1987.
Hill, Geoffrey. *Canaan*. Boston: Houghton Mifflin, 1996.
———. *New and Collected Poems: 1952–1992*. Boston: Houghton Mifflin, 1994.
———. "Poetry as 'Menace' and 'Atonement.'" In *The Lords of Limit: Essays on Literature and Ideas*, 1–18. New York: Oxford University Press, 1984.
———. *Style and Faith*. New York: Counterpoint, 2003.
———. *The Triumph of Love*. Boston: Houghton Mifflin, 1998.
Hobsbawm, Eric. *The Age of Extremes: A History of the World, 1914–1991*. New York: Vintage, 1996.
Hollier, Denis. *Against Architecture: The Writings of Georges Bataille*. Cambridge: MIT Press, 1989.
———. "From Beyond Hegel to Nietzsche's Absence." In Boldt-Irons, *On Bataille*, 61–78.
Hollingdale, R. J. Introduction to *Thus Spoke Zarathustra*. New York: Penguin, 1969.
Hopkins, Gerard Manley. *Poems*. 4th ed., revised and enlarged. Ed. W. H. Gardner and N. H. MacKenzie. New York: Oxford University Press, 1967.
———. "Poetry and Verse." In *The Journals and Papers*, ed. Humphrey House and Graham Storey, 289–90. London: Oxford University Press, 1959.

Horkheimer, Max, and Theodor W. Adorno. *Dialectic of Enlightenment.* Trans. John Cumming. New York: Continuum, 1972.
Houston, John Porter. *The Design of Rimbaud's Poetry.* New Haven: Yale University Press, 1963.
Huizinga, Johan. *Homo Ludens: A Study of the Play Element in Culture.* Boston: Beacon, 1955.
Huntington, Patricia J. "Heidegger's Reading of Kierkegaard Revisited: From Ontological Abstraction to Ethical Concretion." In Matuštík and Westphal, *Kierkegaard,* 43–65.
Huyssen, Andreas. *After the Great Divide: Modernism, Mass Culture, Postmodernism.* Bloomington: Indiana University Press, 1986.
Idel, Moshe. "Jewish Apocalypticism: 670–1670." *The Encyclopedia of Apocalypticism.* Vol. 2. Ed. Bernard McGinn, 204–37. New York: Continuum, 2000.
Jameson, Fredric. *Marxism and Form: Twentieth-Century Dialectical Theories of Literature.* Princeton: Princeton University Press, 1971.
———. "Marx's Purloined Letter." In Sprinker, *Ghostly Demarcations,* 26–67.
———. "Notes on Globalization as a Philosophical Issue." In Jameson and Miyoshi, *Cultures of Globalization,* 54–77.
———. "Periodizing the Sixties." In *The Ideologies of Theory.* Vol. 2. 178–208. Minneapolis: University of Minnesota Press, 1988.
———. *Postmodernism, or, The Cultural Logic of Late Capitalism.* Durham: Duke University Press, 1991.
———. "Rimbaud and the Spatial Text." *Rewriting Literary History,* ed. Tak-Wai Wong and M. A. Abbas, 66–93. Hong Kong: Hong Kong University Press, 1984.
———. *Signatures of the Visible.* New York: Routledge, 1992.
———. *A Singular Modernity: Essay on the Ontology of the Present.* London: Verso, 2002.
Jameson, Fredric, and Masao Miyoshi, eds. *The Cultures of Globalization.* Durham: Duke University Press, 1998.
Jaspers, Karl. *Nietzsche: An Introduction to the Understanding of His Philosophical Activity.* Trans. Charles F. Wallraff and Frederick J. Schmitz. Baltimore: Johns Hopkins University Press, 1997.
Joyce, James. *A Portrait of the Artist as a Young Man.* New York: Bantam, 1992.
Kaufmann, Walter. *Nietzsche: Philosopher, Psychologist, Antichrist.* 4th ed. Princeton: Princeton University Press, 1974.
Keats, John. *The Complete Poems.* Ed. John Barnard. New York: Penguin, 1988.
Kermode, Frank. "Fragments and Ruins." In *History and Value,* 128–46. London: Oxford University Press, 1988.
———. *The Sense of an Ending: Studies in the Theory of Fiction.* London: Oxford University Press, 1966.
Kittang, Atle. *Discours et jeu: Essai d'analyse des textes d'Arthur Rimbaud.* Grenoble: Presses Universitaires de Grenoble, 1975.
Kristeva, Julia. *Desire in Language.* Ed. Leon S. Roudiez. Trans. Thomas Gora, Alice Jardine, and Leon S. Roudiez. New York: Columbia University Press, 1980.
———. *Revolution in Poetic Language.* Trans. Margaret Waller, with an introduction by Leon S. Roudiez. New York: Columbia University Press, 1984.

Lacoue-Labarthe, Philippe. "Où en étions-nous." In J. Derrida, V. Descombes, G. Kortian, Ph. Lacoue-Labarthe, J.-F. Lyotard, and J.-L. Nancy, *La Faculté de juger*, 165–93. Paris: Minuit, 1985.
———. "Sublime Truth." In Nancy, *Of the Sublime*, 71–108.
Langbaum, Robert. *The Poetry of Experience: The Dramatic Monologue in Modern Literary Tradition*. London: Chatto & Windus, 1957.
Larmore, Charles. "Hölderlin and Novalis." In *The Cambridge Companion to German Idealism*, ed. Karl Ameriks, 141–60. New York: Cambridge University Press, 2000.
Lauterbach, Ann. *On a Stair*. New York: Penguin, 1997.
Lawler, James. *Rimbaud's Theatre of the Self*. Cambridge: Harvard University Press, 1992.
Levinas, Emmanuel. "Existence and Ethics." In Rée and Chamberlain, *Kierkegaard*, 26–38.
———. *Otherwise than Being*. Trans. Alphonso Lingis. The Hague: Martinus Nijhoff, 1981.
———. *Totality and Infinity: An Essay on Exteriority*. Trans. Alphonso Lingis. The Hague: Marginus Nijhoff, 1969.
Levin, Harry. "What Was Modernism?" In *Refractions*, 271–95. New York: Oxford University Press, 1966.
Longinus. "On the Sublime." In *Classical Literary Criticism*, ed. and trans. T. S. Dorsch, 113–66. New York: Penguin, 1965.
Löwith, Karl. *From Hegel to Nietzsche: The Revolution in Nineteenth-Century Thought*. Trans. David E. Green, with a foreword by Hans-Georg Gadamer. New York: Columbia University Press, 1991.
———. *Martin Heidegger and European Nihilism*. Ed. Richard Wolin. Trans. Gary Steiner. New York: Columbia University Press, 1995.
Lowrie, Walter. *A Short Life of Kierkegaard*. Princeton: Princeton University Press, 1970.
Lukács, Georg. *History and Class Consciousness: Studies in Marxist Dialectics*. Trans. Rodney Livingstone. Cambridge: MIT Press, 1971.
MacIntyre, Alasdair. "Marxist Mask and Romantic Face: Lukács on Thomas Mann." In *Against the Self-Images of the Age*, 60–69. New York: Schocken, 1971.
Mackey, Louis. *Kierkegaard: A Kind of Poet*. Philadelphia: University of Pennsylvania Press, 1971.
———. "A Ram in the Afternoon: Kierkegaard's Discourse of the Other." In *Points of View: Readings of Kierkegaard*, 102–40. Tallahassee: Florida State University Press, 1986.
Magnus, Bernd. "The Deification of the Commonplace: *Twilight of the Idols*." In Solomon and Higgins, *Reading Nietzsche*, 152–81.
———. *Nietzsche's Existential Imperative*. Bloomington: Indiana University Press, 1978.
Magnus, Bernd, Stanley Stewart, and Jean-Pierre Mileur. *Nietzsche's Case: Philosophy as/and Literature*. New York: Routledge, 1993.
Mandelstam, Osip. "Conversation about Dante." In *Complete Critical Prose*, trans. Jane Gary Harris and Constance Link, 252–84. Dana Point, Cal.: Ardis, 1997.
Marchal, Bertrand. *Lecture de Mallarmé*. Paris: José Corti, 1985.
———. *La Religion de Mallarmé*. Paris: José Corti, 1988.
Marcuse, Herbert. *One-Dimensional Man: Studies in the Ideologies of Advanced Industrial Society*. Introduction by Douglas Kellner. Boston: Beacon, 1991.

Marx, Karl. *Capital*. Vol. 1. Trans. Ben Fowkes, with an introduction by Ernest Mandel. New York: Penguin, 1990.
———. *The Communist Manifesto*. Ed. Frederic L. Bender. New York: Norton, 1988.
Marx, Karl, and Frederick Engels. *The German Ideology: Part One with Selections from Parts Two and Three*. Ed. and with an introduction by C. J. Arthur. New York: International Publishers, 1970.
Matuštík, Martin J., and Merold Westphal, eds. *Kierkegaard in Post/Modernity*. Bloomington: Indiana University Press, 1995.
Mauron, Charles. *Mallarmé par lui-même*. Paris: Seuil, 1964.
Megill, Allan. *Prophets of Extremity: Nietzsche, Heidegger, Foucault, Derrida*. Berkeley: University of California Press, 1985.
Merleau-Ponty, Maurice. *The Visible and the Invisible*. Ed. Claude Lefort. Trans. Alphonso Lingis. Evanston: Northwestern University Press, 1968.
Meschonnic, Henri. *Critique du rythme: Anthropologie historique du langage*. Dijon-Quetigny: Verdier, 1992.
———. *Modernité, Modernité*. Paris: Gallimard-Folio, 1988.
———. *Politique du rythme: Politique du sujet*. Dijon-Quetigny: Verdier, 1995.
Michaud, Guy. *Mallarmé*. Trans. Marie Collins and Bertha Humez. New York: New York University Press, 1965.
Miller, J. Hillis. "Tradition and Difference." *Diacritics*. 2, 4 (winter 1972): 6–13.
Moi, Toril. *Sexual/Textual Politics*. 2d ed. New York: Routledge, 2002.
Moltmann, Jürgen. *The Theology of Hope: On the Ground and the Implications of a Christian Eschatology*. Trans. James W. Leitch. New York: Harper & Row, 1967.
Montale, Eugenio. *Cuttlefish Bones*. Trans. and with a commentary by William Arrowsmith. New York: Norton. 1992.
———. *The Occasions*. Trans. and with a commentary by William Arrowsmith. New York: Norton, 1987.
———. *The Storm and Other Things*. Trans. and with a commentary by William Arrowsmith. New York: Norton, 1985.
Munier, Roger. *L'Ardente Patience de Arthur Rimbaud*. Paris: José Corti, 1993.
Murdoch, Iris. *The Sovereignty of Good*. London: Routledge, 1970.
Nadeau, Maurice. *The History of Surrealism*. Trans. Richard Howard, with an introduction by Roger Shattuck. Cambridge: Harvard University Press, 1989.
Nancy, Jean-Luc. *The Experience of Freedom*. Trans. Bridget McDonald, with a foreword by Peter Fenves. Stanford: Stanford University Press, 1993.
———, ed. *Of the Sublime: Presence in Question*. Trans. and with an afterword by Jeffrey S. Librett. Albany: State University of New York Press, 1993.
Nehamas, Alexander. *Nietzsche: Life as Literature*. Cambridge: Harvard University Press, 1985.
———. "Who Are the Philosophers of the Future? A Reading of *Beyond Good and Evil*." In Solomon and Higgins, *Reading Nietzsche*, 46–67.
Neruda, Pablo. *Five Decades: Poems, 1925–1970*. Ed. and trans. Ben Belitt. New York: Grove, 1974.
———. *Residence on Earth*. Trans. Donald D. Walsh. New York: New Directions, 1973.
New, Elisa. *The Regenerate Lyric*. New York: Cambridge University Press, 1993.

Nicholls, Peter. *Modernisms: A Literary Guide*. Berkeley: University of California Press, 1995.
Novalis. *Hymns to the Night*. Trans. and with a foreword by Dick Higgins. Kingston, N.Y.: McPherson and Co., 1988.
Oppen, George. "The Mind's Own Place." *Montemora* 1 (1975): 132–37.
———. *New Collected Poems*. Ed. Michael Davidson, with a preface by Eliot Weinberger. New York: New Directions, 2002.
———. *Selected Letters*. Ed. Rachel Blau DuPlessis. Durham: Duke University Press, 1990.
Owen, Stephen. *Mi-Lou: Poetry and the Labyrinth of Desire*. Cambridge: Harvard University Press, 1989.
Paz, Octavio. *Los hijos del limo: Del romanticismo a la vanguardia*. Barcelona: Seix Barral, 1989.
Pearson, Roger. *Unfolding Mallarmé: The Development of a Poetic Art*. Oxford: Oxford University Press, 1996.
Perloff, Marjorie. *The Poetics of Indeterminacy: Rimbaud to Cage*. Princeton: Princeton University Press, 1981.
Pippin, Robert B. *Hegel's Idealism: The Satisfactions of Self-Consciousness*. New York: Cambridge University Press, 1989.
———. *Idealism as Modernism: Hegelian Variations*. New York: Cambridge University Press, 1997.
———. "Irony and Affirmation in Nietzsche's *Thus Spoke Zarathustra*." In Gillespie and Strong, *Nietzsche's New Seas*, 45–71.
———. *Modernism as a Philosophical Problem: On the Dissatisfactions of European High Culture*. 2d ed. Cambridge: Blackwell, 1999.
Plato. *The Republic*. Ed. G. R. F. Ferrari. Trans. Tom Griffith. New York: Cambridge University Press, 2000.
Poirier, Richard. *Poetry and Pragmatism*. Cambridge: Harvard University Press, 1992.
———. *The Renewal of Literature: Emersonian Reflections*. New Haven: Yale University Press, 1987.
Porter, David. *Dickinson: The Modern Idiom*. Cambridge: Harvard University Press, 1981.
Rapaport, Herman. *Heidegger and Derrida: Reflections on Time and Language*. Lincoln: University of Nebraska Press, 1989.
Raymond, Marcel. *De Baudelaire au surréalisme*. Paris: José Corti, 1940.
Rée, Jonathan, and Jane Chamberlain, eds. *Kierkegaard: A Critical Reader*. London: Blackwell, 1998.
Richard, Jean-Pierre. "Rimbaud ou la poésie du devenir." In *Poésie et profondeur*, 189–250. Paris: Seuil, 1955.
———. *L'Univers imaginaire de Mallarmé*. Paris: Seuil, 1961.
Richman, Michele. *Reading Georges Bataille: Beyond the Gift*. Baltimore: Johns Hopkins University Press, 1982.
Ricks, Christopher. "Geoffrey Hill: 'The Tongue's Atrocities.'" In *The Force of Poetry*, 285–318. Oxford: Oxford University Press, 1984.
Ricoeur, Paul. "Freedom in the Light of Hope." Trans. Robert Sweeney. In *The Conflict of Interpretations*, ed. Don Ihde, 402–24.
———. *Oneself as Another*. Trans. Kathleen Blamey. Chicago: University of Chicago Press, 1992.

———. "Philosophy after Kierkegaard." In Rée and Chamberlain, *Kierkegaard*, 9–25.
Rilke, Rainer Maria. *The Selected Poetry*. Ed. and trans. Stephen Mitchell, with an introduction by Robert Hass. New York: Random House, 1982.
Rivière, Jacques. *Rimbaud*. Paris: Emile-Paul Frères, 1938.
Roberts, Tyler T. *Contesting Spirit: Nietzsche, Affirmation, Religion*. Princeton: Princeton University Press, 1988.
Rorty, Richard. "Deconstruction and Circumvention." In *Essays on Heidegger and Others*, 85–106.
———. "Derrida and the Philosophical Tradition." In *Truth and Progress*, 327–50. New York: Cambridge University Press, 1998.
———. *Essays on Heidegger and Others*. New York: Cambridge University Press, 1991.
———. "Is Derrida a Transcendental Philosopher?" In *Essays on Heidegger and Others*, 119–28.
———. "Philosophy as a Kind of Writing: An Essay on Derrida." In *Consequences of Pragmatism*, 90–109. Minneapolis: University of Minnesota Press, 1982.
———. "Two Meanings of 'Logocentrism': A Reply to Norris." In *Essays on Heidegger and Others*, 107–18.
Rose, Gillian. *The Broken Middle: Out of Our Ancient Society*. Oxford: Blackwell, 1992.
———. *Dialectic of Nihilism: Post-Structuralism and Law*. Oxford: Blackwell, 1984.
———. *Hegel contra Sociology*. London: Althone, 1981.
———. *Judaism and Modernity: Philosophical Essays*. Oxford: Blackwell, 1993.
———. *Mourning Becomes the Law: Philosophy and Representation*. New York: Cambridge University Press, 1996.
Rosen, Stanley. *The Ancients and the Moderns: Rethinking Modernity*. New Haven: Yale University Press, 1989. Reprint, South Bend, Ind.: St. Augustine's Press, 2002.
———. *Hermeneutics as Politics*. 2d ed. With a foreword by Robert Pippin. New Haven: Yale University Press, 2003.
———. *The Limits of Analysis*. New York: Basic Books, 1980. Reprint, South Bend, Ind.: St. Augustine's Press, 2000.
———. *The Mask of Enlightenment: Nietzsche's* Zarathustra. New York: Cambridge University Press, 1995.
———. *Nihilism: A Philosophical Essay*. New Haven: Yale University Press, 1969. Reprint, South Bend, Ind.: St. Augustine's Press, 2000.
———. *The Quarrel between Philosophy and Poetry*. New York: Routledge, 1993.
Rosenberg, Harold. *The Anxious Object*. New York: Collier, 1966.
———. *Art on the Edge*. Chicago: University of Chicago Press, 1975.
Ross, Kristin. *The Emergence of Social Space: Rimbaud and the Paris Commune*. Foreword by Terry Eagleton. Minneapolis: University of Minnesota Press, 1988.
Rudd, Anthony. *Kierkegaard and the Limits of the Ethical*. New York: Oxford University Press, 1993.
Russell, Charles. *Poets, Prophets, and Revolutionaries: The Literary Avantgarde from Rimbaud through Postmodernism*. New York: Oxford University Press, 1985.
Said, Edward. *Culture and Imperialism*. New York: Random House, 1993.
———. *Orientalism*. New York: Random House, 1978.

Sallis, John. *Crossings: Nietzsche and the Space of Tragedy.* Chicago: University of Chicago Press, 1991.
Sartre, Jean-Paul. "Un Nouveau Mystique." In *Situations,* 1:143–88. Paris: Gallimard, 1947.
Schacht, Richard. *Making Sense of Nietzsche: Reflections Timely and Untimely.* Urbana: University of Illinois Press, 1995.
———. *Nietzsche.* London: Routledge, 1983.
Schiller, Friedrich. *On the Aesthetic Education of Man.* Trans. Elizabeth M. Wilkinson and L. A. Willoughby. London: Oxford University Press, 1967.
———. "On the Sublime." In *Naive and Sentimental Poetry and On the Sublime,* trans. Julius A. Elias, 193–212. New York: Frederick Ungar Publishing Co., 1966.
Schneider, Elisabeth. *T. S. Eliot: The Pattern in the Carpet.* Berkeley: University of California Press, 1975.
Schrag, Calvin O. *Existence and Freedom: Towards an Ontology of Human Finitude.* Evanston: Northwestern University Press, 1961.
———. "The Kierkegaard-Effect in the Shaping of the Contours of Modernity." In Matuštík and Westphal, *Kierkegaard,* 1–17.
Schrift, Alan D. *Nietzsche's French Legacy: A Genealogy of Poststructuralism.* New York: Routledge, 1995.
Sells, Michael A. *Mystical Languages of Unsaying.* Chicago: University of Chicago Press, 1984.
Shattuck, Roger. *The Banquet Years.* Rev. ed. New York: Random House, 1968.
Sheehan, Thomas. *The First Coming: How the Kingdom of God Became Christianity.* New York: Random House, 1986.
Shelley, Percy Bysshe. "A Defence of Poetry." In *Shelley's Poetry and Prose,* ed. Donald H. Reiman and Sharon B. Powers, 480–508. New York: Norton, 1977.
Sheppard, Richard. *Modernism—Dada—Postmodernism.* Evanston: Northwestern University Press, 2000.
Silesius, Angelus. *The Cherubinic Wanderer.* Trans. and with a foreword by Maria Shrady, with an introduction by Josef Schmidt. New York: Paulist Press, 1986.
Sobin, Gustaf. *By the Bias of Sound: Selected Poems, 1974–1994.* Jersey City: Talisman House, 1995.
Solomon, Robert C., and Kathleen M. Higgins, eds. *Reading Nietzsche.* New York: Oxford University Press, 1988.
Sprinker, Michael, ed. *Ghostly Demarcations: A Symposium on Jacques Derrida's Specters of Marx.* London: Verso, 1999.
Stambaugh, Joan. *The Other Nietzsche.* Albany: State University of New York Press, 1990.
Starkie, Enid. *Arthur Rimbaud.* New York: New Directions, 1961.
Steiner, George. "On Difficulty." In *On Difficulty and Other Essays,* 18–47. New York: Oxford University Press, 1978.
Stevens, Wallace. *The Necessary Angel.* New York: Random House, 1951.
———. *The Palm at the End of the Mind.* Ed. Holly Stevens. New York: Random House, 1971.
Stonum, Gary Lee. *The Dickinson Sublime.* Madison: University of Wisconsin Press, 1990.
Surette, Leon. *The Birth of Modernism: Ezra Pound, T. S. Eliot, W. B. Yeats, and the Occult.* Montreal: McGill-Queen's University Press, 1993.

Tate, Allen. "Emily Dickinson." In *The Man of Letters in the Modern World*, 211–26. London: Meridian, 1957.
Taylor, Charles. *The Ethics of Authenticity*. Cambridge: Harvard University Press, 1991.
———. *Hegel and Modern Society*. New York: Cambridge University Press, 1979.
———. *Sources of the Self: The Making of the Modern Identity*. Cambridge: Harvard University Press, 1989.
———. "The Validity of Transcendental Arguments." In *Philosophical Arguments*, 20–33. Cambridge: Harvard University Press, 1995.
Thomas, Brook. *The New Historicism and Other Old-Fashioned Topics*. Princeton: Princeton University Press, 1991.
———. "Preserving and Keeping Order by Killing Time in *Heart of Darkness*." In *Case Studies in Contemporary Criticism: Heart of Darkness*. 2d ed. Ed. Ross C. Murfin, 239–57. Boston: Bedford Books, 1996.
Thoreau, Henry David. *Walden*. Ed. and with an introduction by Stephen Fender. New York: Oxford University Press, 1997.
Vallejo, César. *The Complete Posthumous Poetry*. Trans. Clayton Eshleman and José Rubia Barcia. Berkeley: University of California Press, 1980.
———. *Trilce*. Trans. Clayton Eshleman. Middletown: Wesleyan University Press, 2000.
Vermes, Geza. *The Religion of Jesus the Jew*. Minneapolis: Fortress Press, 1993.
Wallerstein, Immanuel. *After Liberalism*. New York: The New Press, 1995.
———. *The End of the World As We Know It*. Minneapolis: University of Minnesota Press, 1999.
———. *Geopolitics and Geoculture: Essays on the Changing World-System*. New York: Cambridge University Press, 1991.
Weber, Max. *From Max Weber: Essays in Sociology*. Ed. and trans. H. H. Gerth and C. Wright Mills. New York: Oxford University Press, 1946.
———. *The Protestant Ethic and the Spirit of Capitalism*. Trans. Talcott Parsons, with an introduction by Anthony Giddens. London: Routledge, 1992.
Weisbuch, Robert. *Emily Dickinson's Poetry*. Chicago: University of Chicago Press, 1975.
Weiskel, Thomas. *The Romantic Sublime: Studies in the Structure and Psychology of Transcendence*. Baltimore: Johns Hopkins University Press, 1976.
Wesling, Donald. *The Chances of Rhyme*. Berkeley: University of California Press, 1980.
———. *The New Poetries: Poetic Form since Coleridge and Wordsworth*. London and Toronto: Associated University Press, 1985.
———. *The Scissors of Meter*. Ann Arbor: University of Michigan Press, 1996.
Weston, Michael. *Kierkegaard and Modern Continental Philosophy*. London: Routledge, 1994.
Westphal, Merold. *Becoming a Self: A Reading of Kierkegaard's Concluding Unscientific Postscript*. West Lafayette: Purdue University Press, 1996.
———. *Kierkegaard's Critique of Reason and Society*. University Park: Pennsylvania State University Press, 1991.
Whitman, Walt. *Leaves of Grass*. Ed. Schulley Bradley and Harold W. Blodgett. New York: Norton, 1973.
Wilbur, Richard. "Sumptuous Destitution." In *Responses*, 3–15. New York: Harcourt Brace Jovanovich, 1976.

Williams, Raymond. *The Politics of Modernism.* Ed. Tony Pinkney. London: Verso, 1989.
Williams, William Carlos. *The Collected Poems.* 2 vols. Ed. A. Walton Litz and Christopher MacGowan. New York: New Directions, 1986.
———. *Paterson.* New York: New Directions, 1963.
———. *Selected Essays.* New York: New Directions, 1969.
Wilson, Edmund. *Axel's Castle: A Study in the Imaginative Literature of 1870–1930.* Introduction by Hugh Kenner (1991). 1931. Reprint, New York: Macmillan, 1991.
Wittgenstein, Ludwig. *Tractatus Logico-Philosophicus.* Trans. D. F. Pears and B. F. Mcguinness. London: Routledge, 1974.
Wolff, Cynthia Griffin. *Emily Dickinson.* Foreword by R. W. B. Lewis. Reading: Perseus, 1988.
Wordsworth, Jonathan. *William Wordsworth: The Borders of Vision.* Oxford: Clarendon Press, 1982.
Wright, C. D. *Deepstep Come Shining.* Port Townsend, Wa.: Copper Canyon, 1998.

INDEX

Abel, Lionel, 338n.71
Abrams, M.H., 58, 315n.21, 316n.29, 322n.12, 323n.16
   The Mirror and the Lamp, 317n.31
   Natural Supernaturalism, 23, 59, 323n.18, 331n.25
   on Wordsworth, 26, 60, 324n.22
Adorno, Theodor, 20, 35, 36, 89, 263, 277, 280, 316n.26, 352n.67, 358n.10, 363n.4
   Aesthetic Theory, 319n.39
   vs. Bataille, 152, 153
   vs. Foucault, 294, 297
   on Kierkegaard, 189, 343n.13
   vs. Lyotard, 74, 79, 81, 269
   on mass culture, 291–92
   on modernist art, 33
   Negative Dialectics, 319n.43, 337n.69
Ahearn, Edward J., 328n.4
Alberti, Rafael, 282
Alderman, Harold, 335n.50, 336n.56
Aleixandre, Vicente, 31
alienation, 18, 51, 84, 157–59, 164, 251, 274, 275, 297, 317n.33
Alloway, Lawrence, 326n.32
alterity. *See* otherness
Althusser, Louis, 164
Altieri, Charles, 29, 314nn.14, 15, 317nn.30, 34, 318n.35, 360n.19, 361n.27, 364n.10
Amin, Samir, 359n.15
Anderson, Perry, 276, 315n.21, 328n.3, 359n.13, 361nn.23, 24, 363n.3

apocalypticism, 37, 91, 93–84, 268, 275, 315nn.21, 23, 318n.35, 322n.12, 323n.16, 328n.5
   in Christianity, 197, 199, 200, 201–2, 258
   in Heidegger, 252–53, 263
   in Marx, 44, 93, 263
   and myth of exodus, 261–64, 271
   in Nietzsche, 93–94, 135, 142–43, 147, 148, 252, 253–54, 255, 260, 261, 263
   in Rimbaud, 93–94, 95, 96, 98, 101, 106, 109, 118, 119, 135, 143, 168, 172, 270, 276
apocalyptic negativity, 39, 43–47, 176–79, 270–72
   in Derrida, 3, 43–45, 177, 178–79, 200, 252–53, 254–56, 257–58, 263, 271, 272, 356n.85
   in Dickinson, 3, 43–44, 45, 177, 178–79, 195, 196, 197, 199–200, 201–2, 203–13, 229, 253, 257, 271, 272, 345n.34, 346n.41
   in Kierkegaard, 3, 43–44, 177–79, 180, 182, 183, 186, 188, 189–90, 194, 195, 206, 212, 229, 253, 257, 262, 263, 271
   in Mallarmé, 3, 43–44, 45, 177, 178–79, 197, 209–10, 212–13, 214, 215–17, 226, 227–28, 229–30, 232, 253–54, 257, 271, 272
Apollinaire, Guillaume, 27, 293, 324n.26, 362n.32
   La Jolie Rousse, 70
   "Zone," 30
Arac, Jonathan, 3, 345n.27
Aragon, Louis, 101
Aristotle, 314n.13

380

art, avantgardist, 16, 25–26, 33, 41–42, 89, 276, 277, 281, 286–88, 289–90, 295, 324n.23, 325n.29, 361n.27
and Derrida, 235, 251, 255
See also art, modernist; dadaist art; poetry, avantgardist; surrealism
art, modern
relationship to philosophy, 8–14, 33–39, 277–78, 282, 286, 314n.14, 358n.10
See also art, modernist; art, romantic; art, symbolist
art, modernist, 16, 36, 49, 54, 281, 284–85, 286–88, 289–90, 314n.14, 318n.35, 320n.44, 356n.86, 358n.10, 361n.27
Adorno on, 33
and Derrida, 177, 235, 239, 251, 255
Lyotard on, 52, 69–71, 72, 74, 78–79, 86, 88, 89, 269, 324n.23, 325n.29, 326n.32
relationship to capitalism, 74, 279, 325n.29
relationship to romantic art, 33, 48, 274–75, 276, 277, 286, 319n.39, 359nn.13, 15
See also art, avantgardist; poetry, modernist
art, romantic, 33, 48, 274–75, 276, 277, 286, 319n.39, 359nn.13, 15
See also poetry, romantic
art, symbolist, 219, 282, 292, 319n.39, 362n.30
Ashbery, John, 273, 282, 293
Augustine, St., 187, 195, 346n.40
Confessions, 323n.18

Bacon, Francis, 11, 57, 294, 333n.44
Barthes, Roland, 290
Bataille, Georges, 149–64, 277, 285
absolute lyricism of, 151–52
vs. Adorno, 152, 153
atheistic mysticism of, 42, 95, 152, 153–57
vs. Blake, 165, 174
vs. Breton, 42, 151, 172
on capitalism, 159–60
on communism, 159–60, 171–72
on death, 150, 153, 154–57, 338nn.71, 72
and Derrida, 238, 239–43, 247, 251, 254, 255, 338n.71

on expenditure, 33, 93, 157–59, 160, 338nn.73, 75
Faustian quest in, 3, 41–42, 45, 91–96, 149–50, 162–64, 172, 174, 270
on freedom, 42–43, 45, 149–51, 152–56, 158, 159, 161, 162, 163–64, 165, 172–73, 174, 270, 272
on general economy, 94, 238, 239–41, 242
Habermas on, 161–62, 338n.74
and Hegel, 95, 151, 152–55, 157, 160, 162, 163, 172, 174, 238–39, 240–41, 247, 251, 337n.66, 338n.71, 342n.11
on history, 95, 151, 152–54, 157–58, 160, 161, 162, 163, 172, 174, 240–41, 337n.69, 338n.73
influence in France, 96
and Kojève, 152–53, 157, 337n.69
vs. Lyotard, 42, 43, 270
vs. Marx, 93
and Marxism, 95, 151–52, 157, 159–60, 171–72, 174, 240–41
on modernity, 149, 159
and negative theology, 154, 162
and negativity, 42–43, 150, 152–53, 154, 157, 158, 159–60, 162, 163, 165, 172, 173–74, 240, 255, 281–82, 283, 338n.71
vs. Nietzsche, 3, 41–42, 45, 91–96, 149, 150, 152, 153–54, 162–64, 270, 337nn.68, 70, 338n.71, 339n.78
on projects, 150–51, 152, 153, 157–58, 161, 162, 163, 165, 172, 173–74, 270
and religion, 33, 95, 153, 154, 158, 162, 263
on restricted economy, 20, 94, 240–41
vs. Rimbaud, 3, 41–42, 91–96, 149–50, 151, 156, 160, 162–64, 270
on social structures, 91, 94–95, 149–50, 153, 158–59
on sovereign subjectivity, 93, 152, 156, 157–61, 172, 240
and surrealism, 42, 151, 152, 153, 169, 171–72, 254, 337n.67, 340n.86
Bataille, Georges, works
The Accursed Share, 157–62, 338n.73
Erotism, 157, 337n.70
Guilty, 153–54

Bataille, Georges, works (cont.)
   Inner Experience, 153–54, 338n.72, 339n.78
   "The Notion of Expenditure," 338n.73
   "The 'Old Mole' and the Prefix *Sur* in the Words *Surhomme* and Surrealist," 171
   On Nietzsche, 153–54
   "The Psychological Structure of Fascism," 338n.73
   Theory of Religion, 157
Baudelaire, Charles, 13, 114, 151, 156, 281, 331n.26, 339n.83
   "Correspondences," 328n.9
   vs. Dickinson, 200, 345n.27
   vs. Mallarmé, 348n.49
   vs. Rimbaud, 100, 114, 329n.9
   "Voyage," 328n.9
beautiful, the
   Kant on, 51–52, 320n.44, 321n.5
   vs. the sublime, 29, 36–37, 52, 56, 88
Beckett, Samuel, 44, 151, 254, 255, 271, 282, 292
   Watt, 356n.82
Benjamin, Walter, 339n.83, 340n.87, 359n.13
Bennington, Geoffrey, 326n.31, 351n.65
Benveniste, Emile, 349n.51
Bergson, Henri, 10, 12
Berlin, Isaiah, 323n.16
Berman, Marshall
   on Marx, 296, 328n.3, 339n.80, 363n.3
   on modernity, 15, 92–93, 296, 312n.4, 363n.35
Bernard, Suzanne, 330n.19
Bernstein, Charles, 295–96, 360n.19
Bernstein, J. M., 35–36, 300–301, 319nn.39, 43, 363nn.4, 5
Bernstein, Richard, 315n.25, 355n.81
Bersani, Leo, 348n.48
Best, Steven, 361n.22
Bishop, Elizabeth, 293
Blake, William, 59, 65, 274, 275, 302, 320n.44, 357n.90
   vs. Bataille, 165, 174
   on doors of perception, 5, 24
   Faustian quest in, 22, 42
   vs. Freud, 168, 170, 339n.81
   Jerusalem, 57
   Los/Urthona, 88–89, 109, 166, 270, 285, 339n.81
   The Marriage of Heaven and Hell, 5, 92, 165–69, 172, 173, 174
   vs. Marx, 164
   vs. Nietzsche, 95, 165, 166, 168, 172, 270
   Orc/Devil/Luvah, 109, 165–68, 270, 285, 339n.81
   on the Poetic Genius, 42, 109–10, 166–69, 172, 174, 270
   vs. Rimbaud, 109–10, 165, 166, 168–69, 172, 174, 270, 285, 328n.4
   and surrealism, 169, 170–71, 340n.85
   Urizen, 165–68, 172
Blanchot, Maurice, 13, 81, 89, 173, 269, 277, 283, 314n.18, 332n.31, 336n.65, 340n.89, 342n.11, 350n.52
   on Mallarmé, 223–24, 348n.46
Bloch, Ernst, 263, 357n.90, 359n.15
Bloom, Harold, 315n.21, 322n.12, 328n.5
   on daemonization, 312n.6
   on Dickinson, 344n.25
   on gnosticism, 328n.5
   on hyperbole, 312n.6
   "The Internalization of Quest-Romance," 58–59, 316n.29, 320n.44, 339n.81
   on Nietzsche, 318n.36
   on romanticism, 11, 58–59, 320n.44, 323n.16, 331n.25, 339n.81
Blumenberg, Hans, 176, 315n.20, 316n.29, 341n.2
Boileau-Despreaux, Nicolas, 37
Bonnefoy, Yves, 301
   on Mallarmé, 348nn.47, 48, 349nn.50, 51
   on Rimbaud, 109, 117, 125, 329n.10, 331n.27, 332n.35
Braque, Georges, 324n.26
Breton, André, 17, 31, 44, 70, 274, 282, 285, 324n.24, 337n.67, 358n.10
   vs. Bataille, 42, 151, 172
   on imagination, 42, 170–71, 172
   on surrealism, 150, 170–71, 340n.85
Bromwich, David, 324n.22

Brooks, Gwendolyn, 301
Browning, Robert, 331n.26
  "Childe Roland to the Dark Tower
    Came," 114, 200
Bruns, Gerald, 312n.6, 354n.78
Buber, Martin, 357n.90
Bürger, Peter, 340n.87, 360n.19
Burke, Edmund, 290
  vs. Kant, 322n.11
  on the sublime, 322n.11
Burke, Kenneth, 190–91, 329n.11
Butler, Christopher, 356n.86
Butler, Judith, 339n.77
Byrd, Don, 314n.14, 318n.35
Byron, Lord, 327n.1

Cage, John, 284
Calinescu, Matei, on modernity, 14–15
capitalism, 289, 296–97, 337n.69, 359n.12, 361n.21
  Bataille on, 159–60
  consumerism, 47, 283, 288, 296, 305, 361n.25
  Lukács on, 33
  Lyotard on, 74, 79–80, 325n.29, 327n.34
  Marx on, 15, 74, 92–93, 164, 293, 301, 325n.29, 327n.34, 328n.2, 339n.80
  relationship to modernist art, 74, 279, 325n.29
  and technology, 13, 16, 79–80, 174, 278, 280, 284, 288
  See also modernity
Caputo, John, 87, 351n.65, 354n.78, 355n.81
Carlyle, Thomas, 334n.48
Catholicism, 328n.7
Cavell, Stanley
  on Emerson, 1–2, 4–5
  on Thoreau, 4–5
Celan, Paul, 301, 307
Cernuda, Luis, 292
Césaire, Aimé, 31
Char, René, 2, 30, 174, 266, 268, 301, 332n.35
  "Threshold," 22–23
Chirico, Giorgio de, 324n.26
Christ, Carol T., 317n.34

Christianity
  apocalypticism in, 197, 199, 200, 201–2, 258
  and Dickinson, 156, 178, 195–96, 197, 198, 199, 200–206, 344n.25
  dualism in, 51
  economy of desire in, 195, 196, 204–6
  Hegel on, 194–95
  Jesus, 113, 146–47, 202, 262, 264, 336nn.59, 63
  Kierkegaard on, 178, 180–81, 188–89, 192–93, 194–96, 343n.17
  Old and New Testaments in, 200–201
  Protestantism, 51, 58, 95, 96, 195–96, 200, 323n.16, 328n.7, 334n.48, 343n.14, 344n.25
  typological patterns in, 197, 199, 200–206, 344n.25, 345n.31, 357nn.90, 94
civil rights movement, 287
Clark, Maudmarie, 336n.57, 357n.88
Clark, T. J., 320n.44
Cocteau, Jean, 362n.32
Cohn, Robert Greer, 330n.19, 348n.45, 350n.55, 351n.58
Coleridge, Samuel Taylor, 32, 36, 321n.5, 361n.27
  Biographia Literaria, 306
  "The Eolian Harp," 334n.47
  on imagination, 56, 362n.30
  "Kubla Khan," 57
  on organic form, 26–27, 317n.32
  on romanticism, 24, 306
Collins, John J., 328n.5
Collins, William, 106
convention, opposition to, 33, 35, 74–75, 268, 272, 294
  in modern poetry, 17, 24, 25, 27, 29–31, 32, 58, 59, 91–92, 117–18, 149, 276, 281, 289–90, 292, 317n.33, 359n.13
Cook, Albert, 317n.33
Corbière, Tristan, 331n.26
Cornell, Drucilla, 355n.81
Crane, Hart, 31, 156, 196, 262, 318n.37
creativity
  creative destruction/destructive creation, 91–96, 162–63, 174, 206, 270, 271–72, 346n.41, 363n.35

creativity (*cont.*)
  creative power, 18–19, 30, 31, 40,
    42–43, 49, 59, 82, 86, 87–88, 95,
    97–98, 109–10, 114, 119, 124, 126,
    164, 166, 167, 168–69, 170, 172, 176,
    196, 209–10, 264, 266, 267, 268–70,
    272, 273, 274, 278, 280, 282, 285, 287,
    321n.5, 341n.2
  creative process, 24–25, 26–29, 31–32,
    266, 276, 280, 299–300, 317n.33,
    356n.86, 363n.3
  Dickinson on, 196, 197, 209–10
  of negation, 162–63, 176, 204–5, 209–10,
    212, 268, 270, 271, 290, 295
  Nietzsche on, 49, 59, 71, 72–73, 76, 80, 82,
    86, 91, 93, 99, 110, 114–15, 130, 133,
    134–35, 141–42, 144–45, 148, 164, 168,
    172, 177, 259, 260, 270, 341n.2
  See also freedom; subjectivity
Creeley, Robert, 29

dadaist art, 340n.87, 360n.19
Dallmayr, Fred, 314n.15
Dante Alighieri, 32, 263, 339n.78
Danto, Arthur, 8, 9–10
Darwin, Charles, 176
Davies, Gardner, 346n.38
death, 2, 142, 167, 179, 332n.30
  Bataille on, 150, 153, 154–57, 338nn.71, 72
  Derrida on, 231, 234, 237, 242–43,
    351nn.62, 64, 352n.68
  Dickinson on, 178, 195, 198–200, 202,
    203–4, 207–8, 212
  of God, 15–17, 18, 22–23, 134, 147, 150,
    175–76, 225, 255
  Heidegger on, 282–83, 352n.68
  Kierkegaard on, 195
  Mallarmé on, 212, 214, 215, 216, 218, 219,
    223–25, 228, 229, 230–31, 232, 233, 254,
    258, 282, 348n.46
  and truth, 217–18
Debord, Guy, 288, 361n.21
Deleuze, Gilles, 12, 324n.24, 335n.53, 340n.89,
  348n.48
de Man, Paul, 55, 312n.6

Derrida, Jacques, 12, 13, 81, 89, 176, 234–61,
  277, 316n.29, 342n.11, 351n.63
  apocalyptic negativity in, 3, 43–45, 177,
    178–79, 200, 252–53, 254–56, 257–58,
    263, 271, 272, 356n.85
  on arche-writing, 235, 237–38, 242
  and Bataille, 238, 239–43, 247, 251, 254,
    255, 338n.71
  on death, 231, 234, 237, 242–43, 351nn.62,
    64, 352n.68
  on *différance*, 33, 173, 178, 233, 234, 236–37,
    238, 240, 242, 246–47, 249–50, 253, 256,
    257–58, 351n.62, 354n.74, 355n.81
  on dissemination, 312n.6
  on errancy in Becoming, 250, 251–52,
    256, 261
  on force, 241, 243
  and freedom, 254–56, 258
  Habermas on, 354n.78
  and Hegel, 175, 235, 240, 247, 251, 253
  and Heidegger, 9, 35, 44, 180, 235, 236, 237,
    239, 241, 244–51, 252, 253, 260–62,
    314n.18, 351n.62, 65, 352n.68, 353n.69,
    354nn.72, 75, 77, 78, 355n.80, 358n.1
  on history of philosophy, 236, 239, 243,
    247–50, 251, 252, 260, 261, 265–66,
    354n.77, 355n.79
  and Husserl, 238, 241, 244, 351n.64,
    352n.67
  Jameson on, 247–49, 354n.77
  and Kierkegaard, 180, 238, 341n.4
  vs. Levinas, 238, 239, 241–42, 283, 341n.1,
    351n.65, 355n.81
  vs. Lyotard, 45, 74
  and Mallarmé, 3, 13, 43–45, 177, 178–79,
    231, 232–34, 235, 237–38, 239, 253, 254,
    255, 271
  and Marx, 238
  and modernist/avantgardist art, 177, 235,
    239, 251, 255
  on negative theology, 178
  and Nietzsche, 9, 235, 236, 237–38, 239,
    244, 250–53, 254, 255, 256, 259, 260, 261,
    319n.41, 341n.1, 351nn.62, 65, 355nn.79,
    80, 81

and nihilism, 260–61
on ontotheology, 44, 236, 240, 252
on the other, 355n.81
on play, 352n.68
on presence, 20, 231, 235, 236–37, 238, 241, 250, 251, 252, 257, 258, 261, 352nn.66, 68, 354n.77, 355n.79
and Saussure, 238
on spacing, 78, 231, 233, 237, 242, 249–50, 272
on time, 231, 236–37, 238, 239, 243, 244, 250, 251, 252, 341n.1, 353n.71
transcendental argument in, 238–43, 247, 351n.65, 352n.67
unmooring of language in, 232–34, 235–36, 237–38
on writing, 232–39, 249–50, 253, 271, 351n.62
Derrida, Jacques, works
"Apocalyptic Tone in Philosophy," 356n.85
"Circonfession," 256
"Desert of the Promise," 256
"Différance," 238, 239, 242, 246, 352n.68, 354n.74
Dissemination, 235, 254
"The Double Session," 232–33, 235, 253
"The Ends of Man," 249, 250–51, 254–55
"Faith and Knowledge," 358n.1
"Force and Signification," 241, 242, 319n.41
"From Restricted to General Economy," 240–41, 242, 338n.71
The Gift of Death, 341n.4, 358n.1
Given Time, 354n.72
"How to Avoid Speaking," 314n.18
"Implications," 242
"Letter on Humanism," 249–50
Margins of Philosophy, 238, 239, 247, 249–50, 252, 253, 254–55, 351n.62
Of Grammatology, 235, 236, 237, 238, 239, 242, 243, 253
"Positions," 239
The Post Card, 356n.85
"Psyche: Inventions of the Other," 355n.81

Specters of Marx, 247, 272, 355n.81
Speech and Phenomena, 241, 242, 243, 351n.64
Spurs, 355n.80
"Structure, Sign, and Play in the Discourse of the Human Sciences," 236, 354n.77, 355n.79
"To Speculate—on 'Freud'," 352n.68
"Violence and Metaphysics," 241–42, 341n.1
Writing and Difference, 238, 239, 240, 241–42, 243, 250, 252, 253, 255, 256, 319n.41, 335n.79, 341n.1, 352nn.66, 68, 354n.77
Descartes, René, 11, 80, 260, 333n.44, 353n.69
Descombes, Vincent, 314n.14, 327n.39, 338n.74, 340n.89, 342n.11
despair, 18, 30, 38, 188, 202, 206, 212, 215, 225, 267, 302
de Vries, Hent, 358n.1
Dewey, John, 28
Dews, Peter, 352n.67
dialectic
Hegel on, 154–55, 191, 231, 238–39, 240, 300, 358n.4
and irony, 190–91
in Plato, 343n.16
Dickinson, Emily, 31, 196–213
apocalyptic negativity in, 3, 43–44, 45, 177, 178–79, 195, 196, 197, 199–200, 201–2, 203–13, 229, 253, 257, 271, 272, 345n.34, 346n.41
vs. Baudelaire, 200, 345n.27
boundlessness in, 177, 178, 199, 200, 201, 204, 211, 345n.34
and Christianity, 156, 178, 195–96, 197, 198, 199, 200–206, 344n.25
circumference in, 201, 202, 205–6, 344n.23, 346n.40
vs. Crane, 196
on creative power, 196, 197, 209–10
on death, 178, 195, 198–200, 202, 203–4, 207–8, 212
dissolution in, 208–9
and economy of desire, 195, 196, 204–6

Dickinson, Emily (*cont.*)
  vs. Emerson, 196, 197–98, 204, 209,
    344n.25, 346n.40
  on imagination, 196, 197, 206
  and inwardness, 43–44, 195, 196, 197–200,
    201–2, 257, 258, 346n.41
  vs. Kierkegaard, 3, 43–44, 177, 178–79,
    195–96, 206, 212, 257, 258, 271, 344n.23
  vs. Mallarmé, 2, 3, 13, 24, 43–44, 44, 177,
    178–79, 196–97, 200, 206–7, 208,
    209–10, 212–13, 229, 253, 257, 258, 271,
    272, 344n.25, 346n.38, 347n.42
  vs. Nietzsche, 44, 197, 257, 271
  and nihilism, 43, 178, 197, 345n.34
  and romanticism, 196–98
  vs. Stevens, 200, 204
  sunset poems, 206–11, 346n.38
  transport in, 196, 197–200, 202
  typological patterns in poems of, 197, 199,
    200–206, 344n.25, 345n.31
  unmooring of language in, 43–44,
    212–13
  Weisbuch on, 201–2, 206, 344n.25,
    345nn.28, 33
  vs. Whitman, 196, 200, 344n.25
  Wilbur on, 204–6, 346n.35
  vs. Wordsworth, 2, 24, 206
Dickinson, Emily, letters and poems
  L # 330, 197
  L # 342, 197
  L # 562, 206
  L # 953, 201
  P # 243, 207–8
  P #, 202–4, 345n.34
  P # 266, 208, 346n.39
  P # 280, 198–99
  P # 281, 199, 200
  P # 307, 207
  P # 308, 207
  P # 328, 346n.35
  P # 378, 206
  P # 510, 212
  P # 531, 199
  P # 532, 203
  P # 605, 345n.34
  P # 628, 208–11
  P # 640, 347n.42
  P # 692, 199
  P # 745, 204
  P # 754, 346n.41
  P # 856, 210
  P # 906, 204, 211
  P # 959, 204
  P # 963, 210, 211
  P # 974, 211
  P # 985, 204
  P # 1068, 203
  P # 1084, 202, 345n.34
  P # 1349, 211
  P # 1382, 210
  P # 1512, 202, 206
Diderot, Denis, 70
Duchamp, Marcel, 281, 324n.26
Dufrenne, Mikel, 314n.18
DuPlessis, Rachel Blau, 364n.14
Durkheim, Émile, 274, 338n.71
Dussel, Enrique, 360n.20

Ecclesiastes, 138
Edmundson, Mark, 8, 9–10, 314n.13,
  339n.81
Eliot, George, 67, 324n.22
Eliot, T. S., 17–18, 99, 196, 274, 276, 292, 301,
  305, 315n.23, 317n.34, 358n.10
  "Gerontion," 18, 297
  "The Hollow Men," 18
  "The Love Song of J. Alfred Prufrock," 18
  "Tradition and the Individual Talent,"
    350n.52
Elsen, Albert E., 274
Éluard, Paul, 171
Emerson, Ralph Waldo, 49–50, 59, 101
  Cavell on, 1–2, 4–5
  "Circles," 209, 346n.40
  vs. Dickinson, 196, 197–98, 204, 209,
    344n.25, 346n.40
  "Experience," 1–2
  and Nietzsche, 276, 334n.48, 336n.59
  Poirier on, 312n.6
  "Self-Reliance," 328n.5

Enlightenment, the, 35, 57, 258
  relationship to romanticism, 2, 9, 19, 88,
    93, 126, 178–80, 273–74, 278–79
Enzensberger, Hans, 299–300
Erkkila, Betsy, 329n.16
errancy, 37, 114, 289–93, 312n.6
  Derrida on errancy in Becoming, 250,
    251–52, 256, 261
  of language, 4, 5, 43–44, 46–47, 176–77,
    178–79, 197, 212–13, 214, 232–33,
    235–36, 237–38, 257–58, 266, 271, 277,
    284–85, 289–90, 291, 295, 341n.3,
    344n.25, 349n.51, 356n.86, 358n.10
  as negative, 21, 43, 46–47, 174, 263, 268,
    270, 272, 290
  of subjectivity, 4, 43–44, 45, 176–77,
    178–79, 197, 257–58, 266, 271, 341n.3
ethics
  Kant on, 39–40, 48, 49, 50, 51, 52, 53,
    54–55, 56, 57, 58, 68–69, 72–73, 74, 78,
    80–81, 82, 83–85, 86, 88, 181, 184,
    187–88, 274
  Kierkegaard on, 179, 180, 181–82, 183–86,
    184, 188, 191, 341n.4, 342n.10, 343n.17
  Levinas on, 85, 179, 241–42, 316n.26,
    327n.39, 341nn.1, 4
  and Lyotard, 80–81, 86–87, 325n.28
  relationship to imagination, 39–40, 49,
    65–68
  relationship to the sublime, 39–40, 41,
    48–50, 65–68, 80–81, 82–85, 86–87,
    89–90
  and Wordsworth, 39–40, 49, 65–68,
    82–83, 85, 86–87, 89, 268–69, 274,
    324n.21, 324n.22
existentialism, 84, 134, 179, 184, 249, 255,
    321n.4, 327n.36
exodus, myth of, 256, 258, 261–64, 271,
    357n.90
experience
  boundaries of, 1–2, 3–5, 170–71, 272,
    274, 277
  Emerson on, 1–2
  relationship to language, 4, 9, 11–12, 33
  and romanticism, 1–2, 5, 9, 26, 331n.26
  and transcendental arguments, 352n.67
  See also imagination; subjectivity
extravagant, the
  vs. common sense, 4–5, 34
  countercurrents to, 300, 318n.35
  definition of, 2–4, 11–12
  and irony, 2, 13
  and the kerygmatic, 5–7, 24, 266
  relationship to negativity, 45–47, 280
  relationship to religion, 5–7, 11–12,
    24, 29, 38, 41, 45, 258, 265–67, 272,
    280–81
  relationship to the sublime, 3, 29, 34,
    37–38, 39, 272
  relationship to the unrepresentable, 30
  and Thoreau, 3–5, 6
  See also apocalyptic negativity;
    convention, opposition to; errancy;
    Faustian quest; hyperbole; sublime, the
Eysteinsson, Astradur, 319n.40

faith, 7, 29–30
  Kant on, 187, 343n.14
  Kierkegaard on, 177–78, 180–81, 182,
    183–84, 186, 188–90, 192, 193–94, 206,
    257, 343n.14
fantaisiste poetry, 292–93, 362n.32
Faustian quest, 37, 39
  in Bataille, 3, 41–42, 45, 91–96, 149–50,
    162–64, 172, 174, 270
  in Blake, 22, 42
  in Nietzsche, 3, 22, 41–42, 45, 91–92,
    114–15, 127, 134, 135, 147, 148,
    149–50, 162–64, 252–53, 261, 270,
    271–72, 327n.1
  in Rimbaud, 3, 41–42, 45, 91–96,
    98, 102, 103–4, 113–14, 119–20,
    135, 149–50, 162–64, 270, 271–72,
    331n.24
feminist movement, 287
Ferguson, Frances, 324n.21
Ferry, David, 324n.21
Feuerbach, Ludwig, 22, 158, 195
Flaubert, Gustave, 350n.52
Fletcher, Angus, 322n.11

Foucault, Michel, 9, 20, 273, 277, 280, 297, 351n.63
　on bio-power, 293–94
　Discipline and Punish, 43, 173, 256, 293–94, 339n.80
　The History of Sexuality, 294–95
　The Order of Things, 341n.3
　"Preface to Transgression," 173
　on transgression, 312n.6
France, 362n.32
　Catholicism in, 328n.7
　fantaisiste poetry in, 292
　French Revolution, 9, 15, 16, 17, 268, 273, 315n.21, 322n.12
　Hegelianism in, 42, 162, 173, 340n.89, 342n.11
　influence of Bataille in, 96
　Paris Commune, 329n.16
　poststructuralism in, 35–36, 43, 173, 179, 327n.39, 340n.89
　romanticism in, 41, 98–100, 323n.15
　Satanism in, 41, 98, 151, 328n.7
Frankfurt School, 301, 316n.26
freedom
　Bataille on, 42–43, 45, 149–51, 152–56, 158, 159, 161, 162, 163–64, 165, 172–73, 174, 270, 272
　and Derrida, 254–56, 258
　imaginative freedom, 39, 48–49, 57–58, 59–60, 62–68, 82, 126, 272, 274, 287, 293, 332nn.8, 30, 356n.86
　and the indeterminate, 14, 173, 269, 293
　and irony, 185
　in modernity, 12, 15, 19, 35–36, 88, 176, 263, 264, 267, 268, 273, 276, 277–78, 287, 290, 292, 294, 296, 315n.20, 356n.86, 358n.4
　moral freedom, 39, 48, 50, 51, 52, 53, 54–55, 56, 57, 58, 68–69, 80, 82, 187
　and myth of exodus, 256, 258, 261–64
　and negativity, 41, 149, 163–64, 165, 176, 185, 290, 299
　and Nietzsche, 148, 174, 321n.4
　radical freedom, 12, 51, 56, 57, 88, 149–51, 152–56, 158, 159, 162, 163, 165, 172–73, 174, 267, 270, 272, 274, 314n.16, 321n.4
　Taylor on, 12, 51, 57, 267, 314n.16, 321n.4, 358n.4
　See also creativity; subjectivity
French Revolution, 9, 15, 16, 17, 268, 273, 315n.21, 322n.12
Freud, Sigmund, 10, 11, 176, 238, 259, 309, 351n.62, 352n.68
　vs. Blake, 168, 170, 339n.81
Fried, Debra, 346n.38
Frye, Northrop
　on Christian typology, 357nn.90, 94
　on the kerygmatic, 5, 266, 313n.9
　on the plausibility-principle, 291, 292
　on romanticism, 58, 170, 316n.29, 320n.44, 323n.13, 328n.7, 339nn.81, 83

Gablik, Suzi, 361n.24
Gadamer, Hans-Georg, 283, 316n.26, 343n.16, 359n.12
Gander, Forrest, 318n.37
García Lorca, Federico, 156
Gasché, Rodolphe, 351n.65
Gaskell, Elizabeth, 67
Gelpi, Albert, 317n.34, 344n.25
Germany
　Expressionism in, 324n.26
　romanticism in, 9, 11, 27, 132, 328n.7
Gilbert, Sandra M., 344n.25
Gill, Stephen, 67, 324n.22
gnosticism, 96, 109, 161, 328n.5
God
　death of, 15–17, 18, 22–23, 134, 147, 150, 175–76, 225, 255
　Kant on, 50, 51, 56, 83, 187–88
Goethe, Johann Wolfgang von, *Faust*, 92–93, 114, 327n.1
Goldmann, Lucien, 315n.25
Green, Ronald, 187, 342n.7
Gubar, Susan, 344n.25
Guillaume de Lorris, 32
Guillén, Jorge, 292
Guyaux, André, 329n.12
Guyer, Paul, 321n.4, 322n.7

Habermas, Jürgen, 363n.5
  on art, 9–11
  on Bataille, 161–62, 338n.74
  on communication, 316n.26
  on Continental philosophy, 9–15, 277, 314n.15
  on Derrida, 354n.78
  on ideal speech situation, 36
  vs. Lyotard, 70, 73
  on modernity, 14–15, 20, 35–36, 280
  on Nietzsche, 9, 314n.15, 340n.89
  on poststructuralism, 35–36
  on reason, 9, 11, 20, 35–36, 161–62
Hadot, Pierre, 343n.16, 344n.18
Hamburger, Michael, 317n.34, 331n.26
Harries, Karsten, 339n.78
Hartman, Geoffrey, 58, 105–6, 315n.20, 330n.17
  on Wordsworth, 60–61, 63–65, 82, 83, 88, 317n.33, 322n.8
Hass, Robert, 305
H. D., 281, 292, 317n.34
Heaney, Seamus, 39, 320n.46
Hegel, G. W. F., 11, 249, 266, 274, 275, 333n.44
  on the Absolute, 175–76
  on art, 8
  and Bataille, 95, 151, 152–55, 157, 160, 162, 163, 172, 174, 238–39, 240–41, 247, 251, 337n.66, 338n.71, 342n.11
  on Christianity, 194–95
  and Derrida, 175, 235, 240, 247, 251, 253
  on dialectic, 154–55, 191, 231, 238–39, 240, 300, 358n.4
  Hegelianism in France, 42, 162, 173, 340n.89, 342n.11
  on history, 151, 152–53, 300
  on irony, 185
  vs. Kant, 176
  and Kierkegaard, 179, 181, 182, 186–87, 191, 194–95, 206, 343n.17
  and Mallarmé, 348n.45
  and Marx, 20, 175, 238, 279, 321n.4
  on master-slave dialectic, 240
  and negativity, 176, 240
  Phenomenology of Spirit, 153, 319n.43, 320n.44
  on reason, 187
  on Spirit, 175–76
  on truth, 175–76, 191
  on the unhappy consciousness, 36
Heidegger, Martin, 4–5, 12, 254, 266, 304, 342n.11
  apocalypticism in, 252–53, 263
  on Being, 20, 33, 58, 87, 88–89, 238, 239, 244–47, 250, 251, 252–53, 261, 277, 303, 316n.26, 326n.31, 353nn.69, 70, 354n.77
  on *Dasein*, 244, 247, 250
  on death, 282–83, 352n.68
  and Derrida, 9, 35, 44, 180, 235, 236, 237, 239, 241, 244–51, 252, 253, 260–62, 314n.18, 351nn.62, 65, 352n.68, 353n.69, 354nn.72, 75, 77, 78, 355n.80, 358n.1
  on *Ereignis*, 245–46, 250, 326n.31
  and Hegel, 175
  on history of philosophy, 239, 244–45, 251, 252, 260–61, 353n.69, 354n.77
  and Hölderlin, 247, 251
  and Kierkegaard, 180, 341n.4, 342n.10
  Lyotard influenced by, 40, 49, 69, 74, 78, 79, 80–81, 85, 86, 87, 88, 89, 269, 326nn.31, 32, 33
  and Nietzsche, 9, 35, 44, 180, 259, 260, 261, 333n.44, 341n.2, 353n.69, 358n.10
  and nihilism, 20, 88, 260–61, 341n.2, 353n.69
  on ontic-ontological difference, 87, 238, 244–47, 353n.69
  on ontotheology, 44, 236, 251, 252, 316n.26, 353n.69
  on presence, 58, 236, 238, 239, 244–45, 251, 252, 261, 271, 353n.70, 354n.77
  on thrownness, 142
  on time, 237, 238, 239, 244–46, 247, 251, 252, 353n.70
  on truth, 245, 246–47, 354n.77
Heidegger, Martin, works
  The Anaximander Fragment, 238, 244–45, 246–47, 251, 253
  Being and Time, 179, 275, 315n.25, 352n.67

390 • Index

Heidegger, Martin, works (*cont.*)
   Identity and Difference, 353n.69
   "Language," 326n.31
   "On Time and Being," 245–46, 353n.70, 354n.72
   "The Onto-Theological Constitution of Metaphysics," 353n.69
   "Origin of the Work of Art," 327n.38
   The Principle of Reason, 245, 352n.68
   The Question Concerning Technology and Other Essays, 251, 353n.69
   "Time and Being," 326n.31
Heraclitus, 333n.40
Herbert, George, 320n.46
Herrick, Robert, 305
Hertz, Neil, 322n.11
Higgins, Kathleen Marie, 335nn.50, 55, 336n.62
Hill, Geoffrey, 301–7, 349n.51
   "Annunciation," 364n.9, 303
   Cananan, 304
   Mercian Hymns, 302
   The Triumph of Love, 304, 306
historicism, 176, 300, 333n.44
   crisis of, 16–18, 21, 267, 276, 315nn.21, 23
history
   Bataille on, 95, 151, 152–54, 157–58, 160, 161, 162, 163, 172, 174, 240–41, 337n.69, 338n.73
   Hegel on, 151, 152–53, 300
   and negativity, 152–53, 157, 158
Hobsbawm, Eric, 359n.15
Hölderlin, Friedrich, 247, 251
Hollier, Denis, 337n.66, 340n.86
Hollingdale, R. J., 333n.42
Homer, 259
Hopkins, Gerard Manley, 31, 317n.33
Horkheimer, Max, 291–92, 358n.10
Houston, John Porter, 112–13, 330n.19, 331nn.23, 26
Huidobro, Vicente, 28
Huizinga, Johan, 329n.11
Hume, David, 51
Huntington, Patricia, "Heidegger's Reading," 342n.10

Husserl, Edmund, 78, 231, 238, 241, 244, 249, 351n.64, 352n.67
Huyssen, Andreas, 286–87, 319n.43, 360n.19
hyperbole, 4, 11–12, 31, 35, 119–20, 316n.29, 341n.2
   in Kierkegaard, 178, 180, 184, 190, 192–93, 195, 257
   in Nietzsche, 59, 133, 134, 135, 141, 148, 178, 255, 312n.6
   in Rimbaud, 148, 178

imagination, 114, 168, 299, 331n.26
   Breton on, 42, 170–71, 172
   Coleridge on, 56, 362n.30
   Dickinson on, 196, 197, 206
   imaginative freedom, 39, 48–49, 57–58, 59–60, 62–68, 82, 126, 272, 274, 287, 293, 322nn.8, 30, 356n.86
   Kant on, 52–53, 55, 73
   relationship to ethics, 39–40, 49, 65–68
   relationship to reason, 52, 55
   Wordsworth on, 39, 48–49, 58, 59, 60, 62–68, 82, 89, 322n.8
indeterminacy, 13, 37, 268, 290, 305–6, 361n.27
   of aesthetic judgment, 52, 56
   and freedom, 14, 173, 269, 293
   Lyotard on, 33–34, 40, 41, 43, 45, 49, 75–80, 86–87, 89, 269, 326nn.30, 33
   as otherness, 40, 41, 49, 76, 89, 269, 282
   Perloff on, 361n.26
irony
   and dialectic, 190–91
   Kierkegaard on, 180, 181, 184–86, 190, 191–92, 193, 194, 276, 296, 342n.9
   in modernity, 2, 13
   relationship to the extravagant, 2, 13
   in romanticism, 180, 184–86, 191–92, 296

Jacob, Max, 281, 293, 362n.32
James, Henry, 292
Jameson, Fredric, 321n.47, 339n.82, 363n.36
   on aeration of the text, 318n.37
   on Derrida, 247–49, 354n.77
   on Lyotard, 74, 325n.29

on modernity, 46, 327n.34, 359n.13, 362n.30
on nature, 284, 359n.15
on postmodernism, 74, 288–89, 296–97, 299, 356n.83, 359n.15, 361nn.23, 24, 25
on Rimbaud, 329nn.10, 16, 330n.18
on surrealism, 169–70
James, William, 10, 28
Jarry, Alfred, 293
Jaspers, Karl, 143, 336n.57, 344n.18
Jean de Meun, 32
Jesus Christ, 113, 146–47, 202, 262, 264, 336nn.59, 63
Johnson, Barbara, 351n.59
Joyce, James
  A Portrait of the Artist as a Young Man, 350n.52
  Ulysses, 319n.39

Kafka, Franz, 44, 255, 271
Kant, Immanuel, 2, 8, 10, 30, 36, 61, 266
  on the beautiful, 51–52, 320n.44, 321n.5
  vs. Burke, 322n.11
  Critique of Judgment, 50, 51–56, 57, 73, 322n.7
  Critique of Practical Reason, 50, 51, 52, 53, 54, 55–56, 73, 187
  Critique of Pure Reason, 50, 52, 187, 194
  and the ethical, 39–40, 48, 49, 50, 51, 52, 53, 54–55, 56, 57, 58, 68–69, 72–73, 74, 78, 80–81, 82, 83–85, 86, 88, 181, 184, 187–88, 274
  on faith, 187, 343n.14
  on God, 50, 51, 56, 83, 187–88
  vs. Hegel, 176
  on imagination, 52–53, 55, 73
  on immortality of the soul, 50, 51, 56, 187
  and Kierkegaard, 181, 182, 184, 187–89, 342n.7
  vs. Levinas, 85
  and Lyotard, 3, 41, 48, 49, 68–69, 70, 71, 72–73, 74, 78, 80–81, 88, 268, 324n.26
  and modernity, 50–51
  on moral freedom, 39, 48, 50, 51, 52, 53, 54–55, 56, 57, 58, 68–69, 80, 82, 187
  Murdoch on, 83–85, 327n.36
  vs. Nietzsche, 177
  Pippin on, 50, 51
  on postulates of practical reason, 50, 51, 56, 187–89
  on reason, 9, 50–51, 53, 83–84, 126, 128, 187, 194
  on subjectivity, 25, 39, 40, 41, 48, 49, 52–53, 54–56, 57, 68–69, 76, 80, 81, 82, 83, 260, 322n.11, 324n.26
  on the sublime, 3, 39–40, 41, 48, 50–56, 68–69, 70, 71, 74, 80, 81, 82, 86, 268–69, 271, 320n.44, 321n.4, 322nn.7, 11, 324n.26
  transcendental argument in, 352n.67
  vs. Wordsworth, 39–40, 41, 48, 49, 53–54, 68, 82, 83, 85, 86, 268–69, 271, 274
Kaufmann, Walter, 136, 332n.36, 334n.46
Keats, John, 56, 99, 156, 200
  "The Fall of Hyperion," 66
  vs. Mallarmé, 217–18, 348n.48
  "Ode on a Grecian Urn," 218, 351n.60
  "Ode to a Nightingale," 179, 330n.17
  "Ode to Psyche," 309, 330n.17
  vs. Rimbaud, 330n.17
  "To Autumn," 330n.17
Kellner, Douglas, 361n.22
Kermode, Frank, 315n.23, 360n.18
kerygmatic, the, 5–7, 24, 266, 313n.9
Khlebnikov, Velimir, 361n.27
Kierkegaard, Søren, 179–96, 266, 303, 304, 321n.4
  on absolute paradox, 187
  Adorno on, 189, 343n.13
  on aesthetic sphere of existence, 181, 182, 184–85, 191, 296, 343n.17
  apocalyptic negativity in, 3, 43–44, 177–79, 180, 182, 183, 186, 188, 189–90, 194, 195, 206, 212, 229, 253, 257, 262, 263, 271
  on Christianity, 178, 180–81, 188–89, 192–93, 194–96, 343n.17
  on death, 195
  and Derrida, 180, 238, 341n.4
  vs. Dickinson, 3, 43–44, 177, 178–79, 195–96, 206, 212, 257, 258, 271, 344n.23
  on ethical sphere of existence, 181–82, 184, 191, 341n.4, 342n.10, 343n.17

Kierkegaard, Søren (cont.)
  on ethicoreligious sphere of existence, 179, 180, 181–82, 183–86, 188, 343n.17
  on faith, 177–78, 180–81, 182, 183–84, 186, 188–90, 192, 193–94, 206, 257, 343n.14
  and Hegel, 179, 181, 182, 186–87, 191, 194–95, 206, 343n.17
  and Heidegger, 180, 341n.4, 342n.10
  hyperbole in, 178, 180, 184, 190, 192–93, 195, 257
  indirect communication in, 179–80, 186, 191–92
  on the individual, 179, 180–81
  on inwardness, 43, 178–79, 180, 181, 182–86, 188–90, 192, 193–94, 195, 257, 258, 342n.8, 343nn.13, 14
  on irony, 180, 181, 184–86, 190, 191–92, 193, 194, 276, 296, 342n.9
  and Kant, 181, 182, 184, 187–89, 342n.7
  vs. Levinas, 179, 341n.4
  vs. Mallarmé, 3, 43–44, 45, 177, 178–79, 229, 253, 257, 258, 271
  negative theology in, 14, 177–78, 182, 183, 186, 189–90, 194, 229, 257, 343n.14
  vs. Nietzsche, 33, 180, 191–92, 257, 271, 276, 280, 344nn.18, 19
  on passion, 188–90, 192, 193–94, 195, 258
  pseudonyms/masks used by, 179–80, 190–94
  on religious sphere of existence, 181, 188, 191, 341n.4, 342n.5, 343n.17, 344n.18
  and Socrates, 180, 185, 191–92, 193, 344n.18
  on truth as subjectivity, 182–84, 342n.8
Kierkegaard, Søren, works
  The Concept of Irony, 185–86
  Concluding Unscientific Postscript, 177–78, 180–84, 185–86, 188–90, 193, 194, 195, 342n.5
  Either/Or, 181, 185, 189
  Fear and Trembling, 181, 193, 341n.4, 343n.14
  Philosophical Fragments, 181–82, 183–84, 186–87, 193–94, 342n.5, 343n.13
  The Point of View of My Work as an Author, 193
  Practice in Christianity, 184, 342n.8
  The Sickness Unto Death, 183
  Stages on Life's Way, 181–82, 188
  Training in Christianity, 193
  Upbuilding Discourses, 343n.13
Kittang, Atle, 329n.13, 358n.10
Klossowski, Pierre, 340n.89
Kojève, Alexandre, 42, 152–53, 157, 337n.69
Kristeva, Julia, 173, 285, 290, 360n.17

Lacoue-Labarthe, Philippe, 72, 327n.38
Laforgue, Jules, 28, 331n.26
Langbaum, Robert, 26, 317nn.30, 34, 331n.26
language
  Heidegger on, 326n.31
  language games, 28–29, 76–78, 325n.28, 326n.31
  materiality of, 46, 236, 272, 284–85, 289, 349n.51
  Nietzsche on, 145–46, 177, 179, 180
  relationship to experience, 4, 9, 11–12, 33
  signifier vs. signified, 235, 351n.63
  unmooring/errancy of, 4, 5, 43–44, 46–47, 176–77, 178–79, 197, 212–13, 214, 232–33, 235–36, 237–38, 257–58, 266, 271, 277, 284–85, 289–90, 291, 295, 341n.3, 344n.25, 349n.51, 356n.86, 358n.10
Lautréamont, Comte de, 17, 31, 151, 340n.89
Lawler, James, 102, 103, 328n.9, 329nn.10, 13
Lawrence, D.H., *Women in Love*, 319n.39
Levinas, Emmanuel, 49, 89, 266
  vs. Derrida, 238, 239, 241–42, 283, 341n.1, 351n.65, 355n.81
  on ethics, 85, 179, 241–42, 316n.26, 327n.39, 341nn.1, 4
  "Existence and Ethics," 341n.4
  vs. Kant, 85
  vs. Kierkegaard, 179, 341n.4
  Lyotard influenced by, 69, 74, 79, 80–81, 269, 326n.33
  on the other, 20, 85, 179, 241–42, 283, 327n.39, 341nn.1, 4, 342n.11, 355n.81
Levin, Harry, 359n.13
Lévi-Strauss, Claude, 355n.79
Lissitsky, Lazar, 324n.26

literary criticism, 8, 10, 349n.51, 358n.2
Locke, John, 11, 57
Longinus, 37, 313n.9
Löwith, Karl, 315nn.21, 23, 338n.72
Lowrie, Walter, 343nn.13, 17
Lukács, Georg, 20, 33, 36, 275, 315n.25
Lyotard, Jean-François, 30, 277
   vs. Adorno, 74, 79, 81, 269
   vs. Bataille, 42, 43, 270
   on capitalism, 74, 79–80, 325n.29, 327n.34
   on childhood, 75–76, 326n.30
   vs. Derrida, 45, 74
   and ethics, 80–81, 86–87, 325n.28
   vs. Habermas, 70, 73
   Heidegger's influence on, 40, 49, 69, 74, 78, 79, 80–81, 85, 86, 87, 88, 89, 269, 326nn.31, 32, 33
   on indeterminacy, 33–34, 40, 41, 43, 45, 49, 75–80, 86–87, 89, 269, 326nn.30, 33
   Jameson on, 74, 325n.29
   and Kant, 3, 41, 48, 49, 68–69, 70, 71, 72–73, 74, 78, 80–81, 88, 268, 324n.26
   Levinas's influence on, 69, 74, 79, 80–81, 269, 326n.33
   on modernist art, 52, 69–71, 72, 74, 78–79, 86, 88, 89, 269, 324n.23, 325n.29, 326n.32
   on negativity, 43
   on Newman, 78–79
   Nietzsche's influence on, 40, 49, 69, 71–73, 74, 75, 77, 81, 85–86, 88, 89, 269, 324nn.24, 26, 28, 326n.32
   on paganism, 72
   on phrases/language games, 76–78, 325n.28, 326n.31
   on politics, 71–74, 77, 80–81, 86–87, 325n.28
   postmodernism defined by, 324n.26
   on reason, 20
   on subjectivity, 40–41, 49, 68–69, 78–79, 86, 87–88, 89
   on the sublime, 3, 39, 40–41, 42, 43, 45, 48, 52, 68–82, 83, 85–88, 88, 268, 269, 270, 271, 326nn.32, 33
   Wittgenstein's influence on, 40, 69, 72, 74, 78, 81, 85, 88
   vs. Wordsworth, 3, 41, 48, 49, 83, 86–87, 89, 269
Lyotard, Jean-François, works
   "Answering the Question: What is Postmodernism?", 69–71, 73
   The Differend, 69, 76–78, 325n.28, 326n.31
   "The Grip," 326n.30
   The Inhuman, 69, 74–76, 78–79, 325n.29, 326n.31
   Just Gaming, 69, 71–74, 75, 77
   Libidinal Economy, 324n.24
   Pagan Instruction, 69
   The Postmodern Condition, 69, 71, 73, 74, 75, 315n.23
   Postmodern Fables, 69, 326n.30

MacIntyre, Alasdair, 339n.80
Mackey, Louis, 186–87, 193, 342nn.6, 9, 11
Magnus, Bernd, 136, 137, 312n.6, 334n.48, 335nn.50, 51, 53, 336n.63, 339n.78
Malevitch, Kasimir M., 324n.26
Mallarmé, Stéphane, 99, 156, 213–34, 281, 350n.54, 358n.10, 362n.32
   apocalyptic negativity in, 3, 43–44, 45, 177, 178–79, 197, 209–10, 212–13, 214, 215–17, 226, 227–28, 229–30, 232, 253–54, 257, 271, 272
   vs. Baudelaire, 348n.49
   vs. Beckett, 254, 356n.82
   Blanchot on, 223–24, 348n.46
   Bonnefoy on, 348nn.47, 48, 349nn.50, 51
   on the Book, 215, 222–23, 230, 253
   on chance, 215, 218–19, 220, 221, 222–23, 224, 225, 226, 228, 229, 230, 234, 349n.51
   crisis of 1866–71, 213, 215–16, 224–26, 228, 348n.45
   on death, 212, 214, 215, 216, 218, 219, 223–25, 228, 229, 230–31, 232, 233, 254, 258, 282, 348n.46
   vs. Derrida, 3, 13, 43–45, 177, 178–79, 231, 232–34, 235, 237–38, 239, 253, 254, 255, 271
   vs. Dickinson, 2, 3, 13, 24, 43–44, 44, 177, 178–79, 196–97, 200, 206–7, 208, 209–10, 212–13, 229, 253, 257, 258, 271, 272, 344n.25, 346n.38, 347n.42

Mallarmé, Stéphane (*cont.*)
  vs. Eliot, 350n.52
  and Hegel, 348n.45
  on impersonality, 214, 219, 221, 222–24, 225, 229–30, 233, 258, 350n.52
  vs. Keats, 217–18, 348n.48
  vs. Kierkegaard, 3, 43–44, 45, 177, 178–79, 229, 253, 257, 258, 271
  on music and poetry, 292
  vs. Nerval, 230
  vs. Nietzsche, 44, 177, 226, 257, 271, 276, 341n.3, 347n.44
  and nihilism, 43, 177, 215–16, 225, 226
  poems of impasse, 114
  on poetry as fiction, 214, 215–18, 219, 220, 222–23, 226, 228, 229, 230, 231–33, 285
  on poetry as rhyme, 213–14, 219–22, 228–29, 253, 349n.50
  vs. Stevens, 216, 217–18, 348n.45
  on truth, 214, 217–18
  unmooring of language in, 212–13, 214, 228–30, 233–34, 237–38, 285
Mallarmé, Stéphane, works
  "L'Après-midi d'un faune," 231–32, 348n.48, 351n.60
  "Au seul souci de voyager,"254
  Un Coup de dés, 28, 213, 217, 218, 223, 226, 227, 228, 350nn.55, 56
  "Crises de vers," 219, 221–22, 229, 348n.48, 350n.56
  "Le Démon de l'analogie," 213–15, 230
  Hérodiade, 215–16, 218, 224, 225, 226, 231
  Igitur, 224, 225–26, 228
  "Mimique," 231–33, 351n.60
  "La Musique et les Lettres," 216–17, 219–20, 232
  "Le Nénuphar blanc," 347n.42
  "Prose (pour des Esseintes)," 312n.6, 348n.48
  "Quant au livre," 220, 221
  "sonnet en -yx," 218, 225, 226–31, 350nn.55, 56, 57
  "Ténèbres Absolues," 230
  "Toast funèbre," 216, 218, 350n.56
  "Tombeaux," 216
  Triptyche, 218, 225–26
  "Vasco," 254
Mandelstam, Osip, 313n.8
Mann, Thomas, 91
Marchal, Bertrand, 347n.44, 348nn.45, 48
Marcuse, Herbert, 20, 36, 160, 277, 280, 294, 297, 359nn.12, 13
Margueritte, Paul, *Pierrot assassin de sa femme*, 231
Marion, Jean-Luc, 266, 358n.1
Marlowe, Christopher, 91
Marxism, 18, 275, 316n.26, 320n.44, 356n.86
  and Bataille, 95, 151–52, 157, 159–60, 171–72, 174, 240–41
Marx, Karl, 11, 33, 176, 274
  apocalypticism in, 44, 93, 263
  vs. Bataille, 93
  Berman on, 296, 328n.3, 339n.80, 363n.3
  vs. Blake, 164
  Capital, 164, 301, 339nn.79, 80
  on capitalism, 15, 74, 92–93, 164, 293, 301, 325n.29, 327n.34, 328n.2, 339n.80
  The Communist Manifesto, 15, 74, 92–93, 164, 296, 328n.2
  and Derrida, 238
  The German Ideology, 164
  and Hegel, 20, 175, 238, 279, 321n.4
  Manuscripts of 1844, 164
  vs. Nietzsche, 93, 164, 301
  on reason, 93
  vs. Rimbaud, 93, 164
  and romanticism, 164, 279, 339n.80
masks
  and Kierkegaard, 179–80, 190–94
  Nietzsche on, 126, 129–30, 138, 146, 148, 191–92, 344n.18
  in Rimbaud, 102, 103, 105, 331n.26
Mauron, Charles, 225, 348n.45
Mauss, Marcel, 338n.71
Megill, Allan, 314n.14, 315n.21, 351n.63
  on art, 9–11
  on Continental philosophy, 9–14
Merleau-Ponty, Maurice, 176, 304, 341n.1, 352n.67

Meschonnic, Henri, 122, 318n.35, 332n.34, 360n.17, 361n.27
Michaud, Guy, 348n.45
Mileur, Jean-Pierre, 137, 312n.6, 334n.48, 335n.53, 336n.63, 339n.78
Miller, J. Hillis, 316n.29
Milton, John, *Paradise Lost*, 59, 84, 166
modernity
  antisystemic movements in, 287–88
  Bataille on, 149, 159
  Berman on, 15, 92–93, 296, 312n.4, 363n.35
  Calinescu on, 14–15
  chaos in, 21–22, 92–93, 274, 296, 328n.2
  crisis in, 14–22, 314n.19
  displaced religious dynamics in, 5–7, 11–12, 13–14, 22–23, 29, 38, 41, 45, 58–60, 89–90, 95, 114, 134, 135, 156, 158, 196, 197, 199, 200–206, 213, 219, 223, 226, 233, 253–54, 261, 262–64, 265–67, 271, 273, 280–81, 283, 295, 301, 309, 316n.29, 323nn.16, 18, 344n.25, 345n.31, 358n.1
  freedom in, 12, 15, 19, 35–36, 88, 176, 263, 264, 267, 268, 273, 276, 277–78, 287, 290, 292, 294, 296, 315n.20, 356n.86, 358n.4
  Habermas on, 14–15, 20, 35–36, 280
  as instrumentalized/iron cage, 14, 16, 18–22, 24, 32, 33–34, 35, 36, 38–39, 40–41, 42, 43, 45–47, 59, 75, 81, 88, 90, 93, 164, 165, 170, 171, 179, 256, 266, 267, 270, 272–73, 274–76, 278–80, 281, 284, 285, 290, 292, 293–94, 295–98, 299, 300, 316n.26, 337n.69, 356n.86, 358n.2
  irony in, 2, 13
  Jameson on, 46, 327n.34, 359n.13, 362n.30
  and Kant, 50–51
  Nietzsche on, 18, 19, 20, 71–72, 126, 149, 275–76, 277
  periodization of, 312n.4
  Pippin on, 275–76
  progress in, 16–18, 21, 176, 267
  Rimbaud on, 121–22, 124, 125, 149, 331n.28
  self-assertion in, 176, 341n.2
  self-criticism in, 24
  self-transformation in, 24

  Weber on, 19–20, 34, 42, 72, 81, 164, 171, 256, 273, 274–75, 276, 277, 297, 301
  See also capitalism; postmodernism
Moi, Toril, 360n.17
Moltmann, Jürgen, 357n.90
Montale, Eugenio, 7, 44, 281, 285, 292, 313n.10
  "Motets," 263–64
Munier, Roger, 110, 329n.10, 330nn.19, 21
Murdoch, Iris, 83–85, 327n.36, 355n.81
music, 292, 362n.30
mysticism, 13, 96, 162, 174, 189, 190, 338n.72

Nadeau, Maurice, 315n.23
Nancy, Jean-Luc, 12, 37–38
nature
  Jameson on, 284, 359n.15
  and negativity, 281–82
  otherness of, 281–82, 284
  relationship to religion, 281–82
  and romantic poetry, 282
  Schiller on, 54, 201
  Wordsworth on, 60–61, 64–67, 282, 320n.44
negativity
  as absence of foundations, 176, 197, 226, 254–55, 270–71, 272
  in Bataille, 42–43, 150, 152–53, 154, 157, 158, 159–60, 162, 163, 165, 172, 173–74, 240, 255, 281–82, 283, 338n.71
  as creative, 162–63, 176, 204–5, 209–10, 212, 268, 270, 271, 290, 295
  as disclosive, 13–14, 16, 21, 25, 38, 44–45, 202, 206, 209, 271, 299
  as errant, 21, 43, 46–47, 174, 263, 268, 270, 272, 290
  and freedom, 41, 149, 163–64, 165, 176, 185, 290, 299
  and history, 152–53, 157, 158
  Lyotard on, 43
  and nature, 281–82
  negative theology, 13, 14, 154, 162, 177–78, 182, 183, 186, 189–90, 194, 229, 257, 263, 343n.14, 353n.70
  otherness as, 33, 165, 194, 280, 282–83, 290
  and philosophy, 175–79

negativity (cont.)
   in poststructuralism, 173
   relationship to the extravagant, 45–47, 280
   of signification, 46, 284–85, 289
   See also apocalyptic negativity; death; nihilism
Nehamas, Alexander, 137, 312n.6, 334n.48, 336nn.57, 60
Neruda, Pablo, 31, 282, 339n.82
Nerval, Gérard de, 28, 151
   "El Desdichado," 230
New, Elisa, 344n.23
Newman, Barnett, 78–79, 326n.32
Newton, Isaac, 11, 57, 60
New York School poetries, 293
Nicholls, Peter, 317n.34, 332n.29
Nietzsche, Friedrich, 5, 10, 54, 84, 125–49, 169, 315n.23, 316nn.26, 29, 323n.13, 324n.25, 338n.72
   on *amor fati*, 141, 143, 147, 148, 172, 255, 259, 260, 334n.47, 335n.51, 355n.81
   apocalypticism in, 93–94, 135, 142–43, 147, 148, 252, 253–54, 255, 260, 261, 263
   on the Apollonian, 8, 127–30, 335n.55
   on art, 126, 127–32, 134, 136, 138, 141, 144–45, 146, 333n.39, 334n.46, 335n.55, 347n.44
   on the ascetic priest, 142, 258–59, 260
   vs. Bataille, 3, 41–42, 45, 91–96, 149, 150, 152, 153–54, 162–64, 270, 337nn.68, 70, 338n.71, 339n.78
   vs. Blake, 95, 165, 166, 168, 172, 270
   on convalescence, 357n.89
   on creative power, 49, 59, 71, 72–73, 76, 80, 82, 86, 91, 93, 99, 110, 114–15, 130, 133, 134–35, 141–42, 144–45, 148, 164, 168, 172, 177, 259, 260, 270, 341n.2
   on death of God, 22–23, 134, 147, 150, 255
   and Derrida, 9, 235, 236, 237–38, 239, 244, 250–53, 254, 255, 256, 259, 260, 261, 319n.41, 341n.1, 351nn.62, 65, 355nn.79, 80, 81
   on desire to be different, 30, 142–43, 259, 318n.36
   vs. Dickinson, 44, 197, 257, 271
   on the Dionysian, 8, 9, 127–30, 132, 135, 136–38, 139, 140–41, 143, 144, 146–48, 152, 153, 259, 261, 281, 335nn.53, 55, 347n.44
   and Emerson, 276, 334n.48, 336n.59
   on eternal recurrence, 129, 132, 133, 135–38, 139–41, 144, 145, 147, 218, 333n.44, 335nn.50, 51, 53, 55, 336nn.57, 58, 61
   Faustian quest in, 3, 22, 41–42, 45, 91–92, 114–15, 127, 134, 135, 147, 148, 149–50, 162–64, 252–53, 261, 270, 271–72, 327n.1
   on freedom, 148, 174, 321n.4
   Habermas on, 9, 314n.15, 340n.89
   and *Hamlet*, 129, 144, 333n.38, 335n.55
   and Hegel, 175
   and Heidegger, 9, 35, 44, 180, 259, 260, 261, 333n.44, 341n.2, 353n.69, 358n.10
   hyperbole in, 59, 133, 134, 135, 141, 148, 178, 255, 312n.6
   vs. Kant, 177
   vs. Kierkegaard, 33, 180, 191–92, 257, 271, 276, 280, 344nn.18, 19
   on language, 145–46, 177, 179, 180
   Lyotard influenced by, 40, 49, 69, 71–73, 74, 75, 77, 81, 85–86, 88, 89, 269, 324nn.24, 26, 28, 326n.32
   on lyric poetry, 333n.39
   vs. Mallarmé, 44, 177, 226, 257, 271, 276, 341n.3, 347n.44
   vs. Marx, 93, 164, 301
   on masks, 126, 129–30, 138, 146, 148, 191–92, 344n.18
   on modernity, 18, 19, 20, 71–72, 126, 149, 275–76, 277
   on nihilism, 2, 16, 18, 33, 42, 71, 88, 91, 115, 126, 127, 128–29, 130–31, 132, 133, 134, 138, 139–46, 148, 149, 150, 152, 154, 163, 176, 177, 179, 218, 226, 254, 255–56, 258–59, 260, 261, 267, 301, 333n.44, 335n.55, 336n.57, 65, 347n.44, 357n.88
   on the overman, 42, 59, 133–35, 136, 141–42, 172, 250, 334n.45, 335n.51, 336n.57
   perspectivism of, 71, 235, 238, 261, 347n.44, 351n.63
   Pippin on, 139, 142, 332n.36, 333n.44, 336n.57, 357n.89, 358n.10

and Plato, 152, 259, 313n.11, 332n.36
on reason, 315n.23
and religion, 95, 134–35, 142, 146–47,
  258–59, 260, 334n.48, 336nn.59, 63,
  344n.19
on *ressentiment,* 95, 126, 132, 336n.57,
  357n.89
vs. Rimbaud, 3, 22, 41–42, 45, 91–96,
  114–15, 134–35, 143, 148–49, 162–64,
  168, 172, 270, 271–72, 276, 328n.4
and romanticism, 334n.48, 357n.89
on science, 125–26, 131, 146
and Socrates, 127, 131–32, 145, 147, 148, 152,
  180, 344n.18
on the sublime, 129, 130
on truth, 71, 235, 238, 256, 333n.38,
  347n.44, 351n.63
on values, 125–26, 261, 333n.44
and Wagner, 127, 128, 131–32
on will to power, 25, 33, 71, 72–73, 77, 82,
  86, 94, 125–26, 132, 133, 165, 261, 315n.20,
  322n.11, 332n.36
vs. Wordsworth, 125
See also Nietzsche, Friedrich, *Thus
  Spoke Zarathustra*; Nietzsche,
  Friedrich, works
Nietzsche, Friedrich, *Thus Spoke
  Zarathustra,* 99, 110, 132–48, 174, 258,
  259, 267, 318n.37, 333n.42, 339n.78
vs. *Birth of Tragedy,* 126–27, 129, 132,
  136–38, 141, 143–45, 146, 332n.37,
  347n.44
"The Convalescent," 138, 139–41, 145–46
as crisis text, 95, 114–15, 132–33, 333n.44
eternal recurrence in, 129, 132, 133, 135–38,
  139–41, 144, 145, 147, 218, 333n.44,
  335nn.50, 51, 53, 55, 336n.57, 58, 61
"Gate of the Moment," parable in, 137
going under/crossing over in, 41, 93–94,
  134, 146, 147, 252–53, 260, 261, 355n.81
the "last men" in, 2, 18, 126, 168
"On Old and New Tablets," 139
"On Redemption," 141–42, 152
"On the Three Metamorphoses," 144
"On the Vision and the Riddle," 138, 139

the overman in, 42, 59, 133–35, 136,
  141–42, 172, 250, 334n.45, 335n.51,
  336n.57
as parody of Gospels, 146–48, 336n.63
part 1, 132–33, 146, 333n.43
part 2, 132–33, 146, 333n.43
part 3, 132, 133, 141, 146, 333n.43
part 4, 146, 333n.43, 336n.62
the soothsayer in, 126, 128, 133, 138–40,
  141, 143–44, 145–46, 218, 335n.55,
  347n.44
"The Stillest Hour," 336n.58
as tragic drama, 146, 147–48, 333n.43
Nietzsche, Friedrich, works
Beyond Good and Evil, 191–92, 334n.45,
  344n.18
Birth of Tragedy, 8, 126–32, 136–38, 141,
  143–45, 146, 332n.37, 333n.39, 347n.44
Ecce Homo, 132, 134, 147–48, 333n.38,
  344n.19
The Gay Science, 147, 357n.89
On the Genealogy of Morals, 142, 144, 250,
  258–60
"On the Uses and Disadvantages of
  History for Life," 134
"Schopenhauer as Educator," 134
Twilight of the Idols, 137
Untimely Meditations, 127
nihilism, 15, 30, 60
and Derrida, 260–61
and Dickinson, 43, 178, 197, 345n.34
and Heidegger, 20, 88, 260–61, 341n.2,
  353n.69
and Mallarmé, 43, 177, 215–16, 225, 226
and Nietzsche, 2, 16, 18, 33, 42, 71, 88, 91,
  115, 126, 127, 128–29, 130–31, 132, 133,
  134, 138, 139–46, 148, 149, 150, 152, 154,
  163, 176, 177, 179, 218, 226, 254, 255–56,
  258–59, 260, 261, 267, 301, 333n.44,
  335n.55, 336nn.57, 65, 347n.44, 357n.88
and Rimbaud, 115, 143, 149
See also negativity
nostalgia, 15, 315n.20
Novalis, 58, 195
Hymns to the Night, 57

Olson, Charles, 29
Oppen, George, 301–11
  DuPlessis on, 364n.14
  "A Narrative," 307–9, 310
  New Collected Poems, 302, 303, 304, 306–9, 310, 363n.6
  "Of Being Numerous," 307, 309
  "Route," 307
  This in Which, 364n.14
Orpheus, 113, 230
otherness, 58, 246, 266, 268, 277, 280–85, 300
  as evocative/dislocative, 24, 30, 31, 32, 33–34, 36, 39, 40, 41, 46
  as indeterminate, 40, 41, 49, 76, 89, 269, 282
  Levinas on the other, 20, 85, 179, 241–42, 283, 327n.39, 341nn.1, 4, 342n.11, 355n.81
  of natural world, 281–82, 284
  as negative, 33, 165, 194, 280, 282–83, 290
  and reason, 9, 34, 35, 51, 161–62, 239, 342n.11
  relationship to the sublime, 39, 40, 41, 49, 60, 76–79, 80
Oulipean composition, 284
Owen, Stephen, 312n.6
  Mi-Lou, 314n.13

paradox, 35, 178, 193–94, 195, 299
Pascal, Blaise, 303
Pater, Walter, 320n.44
Patocka, Jan, 265–66
Paz, Octavio, 22, 348n.49
  Hijos del limo, 314n.19, 317n.34
Pearson, Roger, 349n.50
Perloff, Marjorie, *Poetics of Indeterminacy*, 361n.26
Perse, Saint-Jean, 31
phenomenology, 176, 231, 247, 352n.67
  See also Husserl, Edmund
philosophy
  Derrida on history of, 236, 239, 243, 247–50, 251, 252, 260, 261, 265–66, 354n.77, 355n.79
  Frankfurt School, 301, 316n.26
  Habermas on, 9–15, 277, 314n.15

  Heidegger on history of, 239, 244–45, 251, 252, 260–61, 353n.69, 354n.77
  Megill on, 9–14
  and negativity, 175–79
  relationship to modern art, 8–14, 33–39, 277–78, 282, 286, 314n.14, 358n.10
  relationship to poetry, 2, 7–17, 21, 22, 33–39, 40–41, 48, 81–82, 267–68, 277–78, 282, 286, 301, 309, 313n.11, 314n.13, 319n.41, 358n.10
  relationship to religion, 11, 51, 58, 95, 253–54, 258–59, 260, 261, 263, 265–66, 281, 309, 358n.1
  relationship to writing, 179–80
  subjectivity in, 40–41, 89–90
Picabia, Francis, 324n.24
Picasso, Pablo, 324n.26
Pippin, Robert B., 300–301
  Idealism as Modernism, 321n.2, 358n.4, 363n.4
  on Kant, 50, 51
  on modernity, 275–76
  on Nietzsche, 139, 142, 332n.36, 333n.44, 336n.57, 357n.89, 358n.10
Plato, 277–78
  dialectic in, 343n.16
  and irony, 190–91
  and Nietzsche, 152, 259, 313n.11, 332n.36
  on poetry and philosophy, 7–8, 313n.11, 314n.13
  Whitehead on, 262
Poe, Edgar Allan, 212, 230
poetry
  cognitive power of, 12
  the kerygmatic in, 5–7, 24, 266, 313n.9
  and music, 292, 362n.30
  opposition to societal conventions in, 17, 24, 25, 27, 29–31, 32, 58, 59, 91–92, 117–18, 149, 276, 281, 289–90, 292, 317n.33, 359n.13
  Plato on philosophy and, 7–8, 313n.11, 314n.13
  relationship to philosophy, 2, 7–17, 21, 22, 33–39, 40–41, 48, 81–82, 267–68,

277–78, 282, 286, 301, 309, 313n.11, 314n.13, 319n.41, 358n.10
relationship to religion, 5–7, 11–12, 13–14, 22–23, 24, 29, 38, 58–60, 95, 114, 156, 196, 213, 219, 223, 226, 233, 262–64, 265, 266–67, 271, 281, 283, 309, 313n.10, 316n.29, 323nn.16, 18
relationship to truth, 7–8, 306
See also poetry, avantgardist; poetry, constructivist; poetry, modernist; poetry, romantic
poetry, avantgardist, 10–11, 25–26, 27–28, 33, 96, 360n.18
poetry, constructivist, 28–29, 318n.35
poetry, modernist
apocalypticism in, 263
creative process in, 24–25
evocative/dislocative otherness in, 24, 32, 33
the kerymatic in, 24
metamorphosis of words in, 26
negativity in, 25
processual form in, 24, 25, 26, 28–29, 31–32
relationship to philosophy, 21, 22, 33–39, 48, 81–82, 282, 319n.41, 358n.10
relationship to religion, 24, 219, 223, 226, 233, 262–64, 265, 266–67, 271, 281
relationship to romantic poetry, 7, 24, 26–28, 32, 34, 38, 44, 98–99, 196–97, 257, 258, 266, 271, 272, 275–77, 286, 317n.34, 318n.35, 319n.39, 331n.26, 344n.25
visionary/inventive power in, 24, 25, 32
poetry, romantic
apocalypticism in, 263
creative process in, 24–25, 26–27, 28, 31–32
dramatic monologue in, 317n.34
evocative/dislocative otherness in, 24, 31, 32, 33
and French Revolution, 315n.21
Frye on, 339n.83
in Germany, 27, 30
and imaginative freedom, 57–58, 82
the kerygmatic in, 5–7, 24

metamorphic departure in, 29–31, 32, 56–58, 64, 83, 86, 88, 89, 323n.13, 356n.86
metamorphosis of words in, 26
and nature, 282
negativity in, 25
otherness in, 58, 282
processual form in, 24–25, 26–27, 28, 31–32
psychic wholeness in, 29–31, 56–57, 58, 323n.13
relationship to modernist poetry, 7, 24, 26–28, 32, 34, 38, 44, 98–99, 196–97, 257, 258, 266, 271, 272, 275–77, 286, 317n.34, 318n.35, 319n.39, 331n.26, 344n.25
relationship to philosophy, 2, 8, 10–11, 22, 33–39, 48, 81–82, 282
relationship to religion, 22–23, 29, 58–60, 95, 114, 156, 196, 213, 262–64, 265, 266–67, 271, 281, 316n.29, 323nn.16, 18
situated meditation in, 26–27
and solipsism, 58, 60
visionary/inventive power in, 24, 25, 28, 29–31, 32, 88, 176
See also romanticism
poetry, symbolist, 292, 317n.34
Poirier, Richard, 312n.6, 319n.39
politics
crisis in, 16, 17
Lyotard on, 71–74, 77, 80–81, 86–87, 325n.28
relationship to modernist art, 320n.44
relationship to the sublime, 41, 49–50, 80–81, 86–87
Porter, David, 201, 344n.25, 345n.31, 346n.41
postmodernism, 72, 173, 271, 286–89, 299–300, 310–11, 312n.4, 315n.23, 319n.43, 356n.86, 360n.18, 361n.22
defined by Lyotard, 324n.26
Jameson on, 74, 288–89, 296–97, 299, 356n.83, 359n.15, 361nn.23, 24, 25
vs. poststructuralism, 43, 270, 286, 289
poststructuralism, 10, 233, 268, 272, 314n.14, 316n.26, 319n.40, 324n.25, 351n.63, 358n.6
in France, 35–36, 43, 173, 179, 327n.39, 340n.89

poststructuralism (*cont.*)
    Habermas on, 35–36
    Hegelianism in, 162, 173, 342n.11
    negativity in, 173
    vs. postmodernism, 43, 270, 286, 289
Pound, Ezra, 28, 281, 292, 305, 317n.34
presence
    Derrida on, 20, 231, 235, 236–37, 238, 241, 250, 251, 252, 257, 258, 261, 352nn.66, 68, 354n.77, 355n.79
    Heidegger on, 58, 236, 238, 239, 244–45, 251, 252, 261, 271, 353n.70, 354n.77
    and myth of exodus, 263
processual patterning, 24–25, 26–29, 31–32, 317n.33
progress, 16–18, 21, 176, 267
Protestantism, 51, 58, 95, 96, 195–96, 200, 323n.16, 328n.7, 334n.48, 343n.14, 344n.25
Proudhon, Pierre-Joseph, 17
Proust, Marcel, 206, 281, 292, 339n.83
    À la recherche du temps perdu, 323n.18
Psyche, 230–31, 309
Puritanism, 196, 200, 344n.25

Rapaport, Herman, 351n.65, 353n.71, 354n.75
Raymond, Marcel, 292, 316n.29, 317n.34, 362n.32
reason
    Habermas on, 9, 11, 20, 35–36, 161–62
    Hegel on, 187
    instrumental rationality, 2, 9, 14, 18–21, 33–34, 35, 45–46, 57, 60, 88, 89, 93, 239, 260, 267, 268, 271, 275, 277, 290, 291, 293, 295, 316n.26, 337n.69
    Kant on, 9, 50–51, 53, 83–84, 126, 128, 187, 194
    Lyotard on, 20
    Marx on, 93
    Nietzsche on, 315n.23
    and otherness, 9, 34, 35, 51, 161–62, 165, 239, 342n.11
    rational choice theory, 327n.36
    relationship to imagination, 52, 55
    and romanticism, 11, 93, 323n.16

relativism, 17, 18, 315n.23
religion
    asceticism in, 19, 142, 258–59, 260
    and Bataille, 33, 95, 153, 154, 158, 162, 263
    conversion in, 5–7, 12, 266
    displaced religious dynamics in modernity, 5–7, 11–12, 13–14, 22–23, 29, 38, 41, 45, 58–60, 89–90, 95, 114, 134, 135, 156, 158, 196, 197, 199, 200–206, 213, 219, 223, 226, 233, 253–54, 261, 262–64, 265–67, 271, 273, 280–81, 283, 295, 301, 309, 316n.29, 323nn.16, 18, 344n.25, 345n.31, 358n.1
    negative theology, 14, 153, 154, 162, 177–78, 182, 183, 186, 189–90, 229, 257, 263, 343n.14, 353n.70
    and Nietzsche, 95, 134–35, 142, 146–47, 258–59, 260, 334n.48, 336nn.59, 63, 344n.19
    redemption, 58–59
    relationship to the extravagant, 5–7, 11–12, 24, 29, 38, 41, 45, 258, 265–67, 272, 280–81
    relationship to nature, 281–82
    relationship to philosophy, 11, 51, 58, 95, 253–54, 258–59, 260, 261, 263, 265–66, 281, 309, 358n.1
    relationship to poetry, 5–7, 11–12, 13–14, 22–23, 24, 29, 38, 58–60, 95, 114, 156, 196, 213, 219, 223, 226, 233, 262–64, 265, 266–67, 271, 281, 309, 313n.10, 323nn.16, 18
    renovation, 12, 13–14, 18, 23, 58–60, 90, 96, 265, 266
    and Rimbaud, 95, 109, 331n.28
    spiritual metamorphosis, 5, 6, 12, 13, 24, 29, 41, 95, 266, 267, 271, 281
    transcendence, 12, 16, 22, 89, 95, 156, 186, 203–4, 219, 266, 283
    See also apocalypticism; Christianity; faith; God
representation
    limits of, 55–56
    relationship to subjectivity, 32–33, 70–71
Reverdy, Pierre, 27–28

Rich, Adrienne, 301
Richard, Jean-Pierre, 97, 328n.8, 329n.10, 348nn.45, 49
Richardson, Michael, 337n.67
Richman, Michelle, 338n.71
Ricoeur, Paul, 192, 266, 316n.26, 327n.39, 357n.90
Rilke, Rainer Maria, 156, 217–18, 266, 282, 292
  "Archaic Torso of Apollo," 6
Rimbaud, Arthur, 17, 24, 31, 44, 96–125, 170, 358n.10
  apocalyptic vision in, 93–94, 95, 96, 98, 101, 106, 109, 118, 119, 135, 143, 168, 172, 270, 276
  vs. Bataille, 3, 41–42, 91–96, 149–50, 151, 156, 160, 162–64, 270
  vs. Baudelaire, 100, 114, 329n.9
  vs. Blake, 109–10, 165, 166, 168–69, 172, 174, 270, 285, 328n.4
  Bonnefoy on, 109, 117, 125, 329n.10, 331n.27, 332n.35
  on disordering (*dérèglement*), 99–100, 171, 270, 285, 328n.8
  vs. Emerson, 328n.5
  Faustian quest in, 3, 41–42, 45, 91–96, 98, 102, 103–4, 113–14, 119–20, 135, 149–50, 162–64, 270, 271–72, 331n.24
  on harmony, 99–101, 270
  Houston on, 112–13, 330n.19, 331nn.23, 26
  hyperbole in, 148, 178
  impatience in, 91–92, 98, 109, 112–13, 115, 116, 119, 125, 135, 143, 174
  Jameson on, 329nn.10, 16, 330n.18
  vs. Keats, 330n.17
  Lawler on, 102, 103, 328n.9, 329nn.10, 13
  vs. Marx, 93, 164
  masks in, 102, 103, 105, 331n.26
  on metamorphosis, 2, 91, 93, 96–98, 100–102, 103–5, 106, 109, 116, 118, 119, 121–22, 124, 148–49, 162–63, 168–69
  on modernity, 121–22, 124, 125, 149, 331n.28
  vs. Nietzsche, 3, 22, 41–42, 45, 91–96, 114–15, 134–35, 143, 148–49, 162–64, 168, 172, 270, 271–72, 276, 328n.4
  and nihilism, 115, 143, 149
  otherness in, 58
  on poetry, 98–99
  prose poems of, 28
  and religion, 95, 109, 331n.28
  self-multiplication in, 30, 96–97, 102–4, 105, 118, 276, 296, 329nn.13, 14
  vs. Stevens, 110, 330n.22
  synaesthetic transport in, 99–101, 329n.10
  traversal of multiple spaces in, 104–5, 106, 329n.16
  vs. Whitman, 30, 104–5, 114, 317n.33, 329n.16
  See also Rimbaud, Arthur, *Illuminations*; Rimbaud, Arthur, *Une saison en enfer*; Rimbaud, Arthur, works
Rimbaud, Arthur, *Illuminations*, 57, 101–10, 119, 329n.12, 332n.31
  "Angoisse," 103
  "Antique," 106
  "Après le deluge," 101
  "Aube," 101, 102
  À une raison, 99, 102, 106
  "Barbare," 102, 103, 106
  "Being Beauteous," 102, 106, 330n.18
  "Bottom," 102
  "Conte," 101, 102
  "Dévotion," 103
  "Enfance," 102–3
  "Fleurs," 106
  "Génie," 6, 42, 97, 102, 106, 107–10, 113, 148, 163, 168–69, 172, 175, 285, 330nn.21, 22
  hymn/hymnal revelation in, 102, 103, 105–10
  "Jeunesse,103
  "Matinée d'ivresse," 102, 106, 114
  "Métropolitain," 103
  "Nocturne vulgaire,"102
  parable in, 101, 102, 103
  "Parade," 102, 105
  "Phrases,"102, 106
  "Les Ponts," 102, 105
  "Promontoire," 102, 105
  self-multiplication in, 102–3
  "Soir historique," 103
  spiritual autobiography in, 102

Rimbaud, Arthur, *Illuminations* (cont.)
  theatrical/carnivalesque phantasmagoria in, 102, 103–4, 105, 106, 329n.13
  "Veillées," 102, 106
  "Vies," 91–92, 102–4, 163, 329n.14, 331n.26
  "Villes II," 101, 102, 105, 106, 160
Rimbaud, Arthur, *Une saison en enfer*, 5–6, 103, 105, 109, 113–25, 143, 329n.12
  "Adieu," 121, 122–25, 169, 332n.34
  as crisis text, 95, 102, 113, 114–15, 117
  "Délires I," 116–17, 119
  "Délires II: Alchimie du Verbe," 112, 113, 119–20, 125, 330n.21, 332n.31
  "L'Éclair," 117, 118, 121–22
  "L'Impossible," 116, 117, 119, 120–21, 331n.28
  "Matin," 115, 121, 122
  "Mauvais sang," 116, 117–19, 331n.24
  "Nuit de l'enfer," 116, 119
  prologue, 115–16, 120
Rimbaud, Arthur, works
  "Le Bateau ivre," 119, 328n.9, 329n.14
  "Comédie de la soif," 112
  Dernier Vers, 94, 102, 109, 119, 125, 331n.23
  "Drunken Boat," 57
  "L'Éternité," 110–12, 163, 329n.11
  "Fêtes de la patience," 112–13
  "Soleil et chair," 97
  "voyant" letters of May 1871, 98–101
  "Voyelles," 328n.9
Rivière, Jacques, 329n.11, 330n.18
Roberts, Tyler, 134, 323n.13, 334n.47, 336n.65
Rodin, Auguste, 274
Roman de la rose, 32
romanticism, 5, 18–19, 134, 341n.2
  Bloom on, 11, 58–59, 320n.44, 323n.16, 331n.25, 339n.81
  Coleridge on, 24, 306
  crisis texts in, 95, 114–15, 331n.26
  and Dickinson, 196–98
  and experience, 1–2, 5, 9, 26, 331n.26
  in France, 41, 98–100, 323n.15
  Frye on, 58, 170, 316n.29, 320n.44, 323n.13, 328n.7, 339nn.81, 83
  in Germany, 9, 11, 27, 132, 328n.7
  irony in, 180, 184–86, 191–92, 296
  and Marx, 164, 279, 339n.80
  and Nietzsche, 334n.48, 357n.89
  and reason, 11, 93, 323n.16
  relationship to the Enlightenment, 2, 9, 19, 88, 93, 126, 178–80, 273–74, 278–79
  relationship to modernism, 24, 26–28, 32, 34, 38, 44, 98–99, 196–97, 257, 258, 271, 272, 275–77, 286, 314n.14, 317n.34, 318n.35, 319n.39, 331n.26, 344n.25
  Satanism in, 165, 328n.7
  and the sublime, 3, 39, 40, 41, 48–49, 56, 268
  synaesthetic transport in, 99–101, 329n.10
  Taylor on, 88, 278–80
  universal analogy in, 99–101, 348n.49
  See also poetry, romantic
Rorty, Richard, 236, 248, 351n.65
Rose, Gillian, 300–301, 327n.39, 358n.6, 363n.4
Rosenberg, Harold, 326n.32
Rosen, Stanley, 313n.11, 314n.14, 315n.20, 332n.36, 333n.44, 343n.16
Ross, Kristin, 328n.8, 329n.16, 332n.29
Rousseau, Jean-Jacques, 76, 253
Rudd, Anthony, 342n.8, 343n.17
Ruskin, John, 320n.44
Russell, Charles, 328n.8

Sade, Marquis de, 340n.89
Said, Edward, 332n.29, 359n.13
Sallis, John, 332n.37
Sartre, Jean-Paul, 342n.10
  on the absurd, 255
  "Nouveau Mystique," 338n.72
Saussure, Ferdinand de, 236, 238
Schacht, Richard, 332n.37, 333n.41
Schiller, Friedrich, 36, 275
  on epic poetry, 128
  on nature, 54, 281
  on play instinct, 56, 321n.5
  on the sublime, 54
Schneider, Elisabeth, 315n.23
Schopenhauer, Arthur, 126, 127, 138, 334n.48, 337n.70
Schrag, Calvin O., 341n.4, 343n.17
Schrift, Alan, 72, 351n.65

science, 11, 18–19, 26, 29, 34, 57, 60, 121, 267, 293
  Nietzsche on, 125–26, 131, 146
Sells, Michael A., 314n.18
Shakespeare, William
  Hamlet, 129, 144, 333n.38, 335n.55
  Sonnet 60, 320n.46
Shattuck, Roger, 362n.32
Shelley, Percy Bysshe, 5, 58, 320n.44
  "Defence of Poetry," 337n.69
Sheppard, Richard, 274–75, 359n.13, 360n.19
Silesius, Angelus, 44, 257
skepticism, 13, 51, 201, 212, 213, 267, 272, 344n.25
Sobin, Gustaf, "That the Universe is Chrysalid," 334n.47
Socrates, 218
  and Kierkegaard, 180, 185, 191–92, 193, 344n.18
  and Nietzsche, 127, 131–32, 145, 147, 148, 152, 180, 344n.18
solipsism, 39–40, 49, 51, 56, 58, 60, 89, 95, 114, 182, 195, 268
Sollers, Philippe, 235
Sophocles, *Oedipus at Colonnus*, 128
Soupault, Philippe, 293
Spinoza, Benedict de, 294
Stambaugh, Joan, 336n.57
Starkie, Enid, 331n.24
Steiner, George, 31–32
Stein, Gertrude, 169, 361n.27
Stevens, Wallace, 23, 30, 31, 110, 283, 285, 292, 293
  "Asides on the Oboe," 347n.44
  vs. Dickinson, 200, 204
  "The Dove in Spring," 267, 358n.3
  vs. Mallarmé, 216, 217–18, 348n.45
  "Notes Toward a Supreme Fiction," 347n.44
  "Of Mere Being," 283, 359n.14
  "An Ordinary Evening in New Haven," 246, 353n.71
  vs. Rimbaud, 110, 330n.22
  River of Rivers in Connecticut, 330n.22
  "Sunday Morning," 351n.61

Stewart, Stanley, 137, 312n.6, 334n.48, 335n.53, 336n.63, 339n.78
Stoekl, Allan, 338n.75
Stonum, Gary Lee, 344n.25
subjectivity
  Bataille on, 93, 152, 156, 157–61, 172, 240
  despair, 18, 30, 38, 188, 202, 206, 212, 215, 225, 267, 302
  Dickinson and inwardness, 43–44, 195, 196, 197–200, 201–2, 257, 258, 346n.41
  Kant on, 25, 39, 40, 41, 48, 49, 52–53, 54–56, 57, 68–69, 76, 80, 81, 82, 83, 260, 322n.11, 324n.26
  Kierkegaard on inwardness, 43, 178–79, 180, 181, 182–86, 188–90, 192, 193–94, 195, 257, 258, 342n.8, 343nn.13, 14
  Kierkegaard on truth as, 182–84, 342n.8
  Lyotard on, 40–41, 49, 68–69, 78–79, 86, 87–88, 89
  metamorphic departure, 2, 5–7, 20, 29–31, 32, 56–58, 64, 83, 86, 88, 89, 91, 93, 96–98, 100–102, 103–5, 106, 109, 116, 118, 119, 121–22, 124, 148–49, 162–63, 168–69, 272, 274, 323n.13, 356n.86
  in philosophy, 40–41, 89–90
  psychic wholeness, 29–31, 56–57, 58, 88, 126, 164, 185, 274, 276, 279, 314n.16, 321n.4, 323n.13, 339n.79
  recovery of the subject, 39, 40, 49, 52–53, 55–56, 81, 83, 88, 268–69, 271, 322n.11
  relationship to representation, 32–33, 70–71
  subject decentered/deposed, 40–41, 49, 52–53, 55–56, 68–69, 78–79, 81, 82, 83, 87–88, 89, 233, 268–69, 271, 297, 322n.11, 356n.86
  unmooring/errancy of, 4, 43–44, 45, 176–77, 178–79, 197, 257–58, 266, 271, 341n.3
  Wordsworth on, 39, 40, 41, 48–49, 82, 83
  See also creativity; freedom

sublime, the
  vs. the beautiful, 29, 36–37, 52, 56, 88
  Kant on, 3, 39–40, 41, 48, 50–56, 68–69,
    70, 71, 74, 80, 81, 82, 86, 268–69, 271,
    320n.44, 321n.4, 322nn.7, 11, 324n.26
  Longinus on, 313n.9
  Lyotard on, 39, 40–41, 42, 43, 45, 48, 52,
    68–82, 83, 85–88, 268, 269, 270, 271,
    326nn.32, 33
  and Newman, 326n.32
  Nietzsche on, 129, 130
  relationship to ethics, 39–40, 41, 48–50,
    65–68, 80–81, 82–85, 86–87, 89–90
  relationship to the extravagant, 3, 29, 34,
    37–38, 39, 272
  relationship to otherness, 39, 40, 41,
    49, 60, 76–79, 80
  relationship to politics, 41, 49–50,
    80–81, 86–87
  and romanticism, 3, 39, 40, 41, 48–49,
    56, 268
  Wordsworth on, 3, 39–40, 41, 48, 53–54,
    56–68, 81–82, 86–87, 89, 268–69, 271,
    322n.8, 323n.19
Surette, Leon, 317n.34
surrealism, 28, 98, 169–72, 282, 292–93,
  315n.23, 324n.24, 340n.87
  and Bataille, 42, 151, 152, 153, 169, 171–72,
    254, 337n.67, 340n.86
  Breton on, 150, 170–71, 340n.85
  Jameson on, 169–70

Tate, Allen, 196
Taylor, Charles, 300–301
  on freedom, 12, 51, 57, 267, 314n.16, 321n.4,
    358n.4
  Hegel and Modern Society, 273, 314n.16,
    321nn.2, 4, 358n.4, 363n.4
  on Kant, 321n.2
  on romanticism, 88, 278–80
  "The Validity of Transcendental
    Arguments," 352n.67
technology, 13, 16, 79–80, 174, 278, 280,
  284, 288

Tennyson, Alfred Lord, 331n.26
Thébaud, Jean-Loup, 73–74
Thomas, Brook, 315n.21
Thoreau, Henry David
  Cavell on, 4–5
  and the extravagant, 3–5, 6
  Poirier on, 312n.6
  Walden, 3–5, 6, 267
time
  Derrida on, 231, 236–37, 238, 239, 243, 244,
    250, 251, 252, 341n.1, 353n.71
  Heidegger on, 237, 238, 239, 244–46, 247,
    251, 252, 353n.70
  Wordsworth on spots of, 62, 63, 64,
    322n.8, 323n.19
truth, 190–91, 233
  and death, 217–18
  Hegel on, 175–76, 191
  Heidegger on, 245, 246–47, 354n.77
  Kierkegaard on, 182–84, 342n.8
  Mallarmé on, 214, 217–18
  Nietzsche on, 71, 235, 238, 256, 333n.38,
    347n.44, 351n.63
  relationship to poetry, 7–8, 306
  uncommon truth vs. common sense,
    4–5, 34

United States, 19, 286–87, 288, 360n.19,
  361nn.24, 27, 362n.32

Valente, José Ángel, 301
Valéry, Paul, 281, 292
Vallejo, César, 31, 292, 298, 301, 302, 364n.7

Wagner, Richard, 127, 128, 131–32, 334n.48
Wallerstein, Immanuel, 17, 287, 315nn.22, 23,
  360n.20
Warhol, Andy, 288, 361n.25
Weber, Max, on modernity, 19–20, 34, 42,
  72, 81, 164, 171, 256, 273, 274–75, 276,
  277, 297, 301
Weisbuch, Robert, 201–2, 206, 344n.25,
  345nn.28, 33
Weiskel, Thomas, 81, 320n.44, 322n.11

Wesling, Donald, 317n.31
  on organic form, 26–27, 317nn.32, 33
Weston, Michael, 341n.4
Westphal, Merold, 343n.17
Whitehead, Alfred North, 262
Whitman, Walt, 31, 38, 156, 179, 318n.37
  "As I Ebb'd with the Ocean of Life," 114
  vs. Dickinson, 196, 200, 344n.25
  "Out of the Cradle Endlessly Rocking," 332n.30
  vs. Rimbaud, 30, 104–5, 114, 317n.33, 329n.16
Wilbur, Richard, 204–6, 346n.35
Williams, Raymond, 359n.13
Williams, William Carlos, 358n.10
  Paterson, 71
  on poetry, 28–29, 318n.35
  Spring and All, 6–7
Wilson, Edmund, *Axel's Castle*, 292
Wittgenstein, Ludwig, 180
  Lyotard influenced by, 40, 69, 72, 74, 78, 81, 85, 88
  on meaning as use, 28
  Philosophical Investigations, 352n.67
  Tractatus Logico-Philosophicus, 1
Wolff, Cynthia Griffin, 200–201, 344n.25, 345n.26, 346n.39
Woolf, Virginia, 206, 281, 292
Wordsworth, Jonathan, 324nn.21, 22
Wordsworth, William, 22, 251, 293, 360n.19
  Abrams on, 26, 60, 324n.22
  on childhood, 60–62, 76
  vs. Dickinson, 2, 24, 206
  and the ethical, 39–40, 49, 65–68, 82–83, 85, 86–87, 89, 268–69, 274, 324n.21, 324n.22
  Hartman on, 60–61, 63–65, 82, 83, 88, 317n.33, 322n.8
  on imagination, 39, 48–49, 58, 59, 60, 62–68, 82, 89, 322n.8
  vs. Kant, 39–40, 41, 48, 49, 53–54, 68, 82, 83, 85, 86, 268–69, 271, 274
  vs. Lyotard, 3, 41, 48, 49, 83, 86–87, 89, 269
  on nature, 60–61, 64–67, 282, 320n.44
  vs. Nietzsche, 125
  on spots of time, 62, 63, 64, 322n.8, 323n.19
  on subjectivity, 39, 40, 41, 48–49, 82, 83
  on the sublime, 3, 39–40, 41, 48, 53–54, 56–68, 81–82, 86–87, 89, 268–69, 271, 322n.8, 323n.19
Wordsworth, William, works
  "Intimations of Immortality," 61, 67, 117
  Lyrical Ballads, 67
  "Ode: Composed Upon an Evening of Extraordinary Splendor," 61–62
  "Peele Castle," 67
  The Prelude, 26, 39–40, 49, 53–54, 58, 60–68, 82–83, 87, 268–69, 323nn.18, 20, 324nn.21,22
  Tintern Abbey, 323n.20
Wright, C. D., *Deepstep Come Shining*, 363n.2

Yeats, William Butler, 281, 317n.34, 320n.44

Zukofsky, Louis, 284, 292, 361n.27

ROBERT BAKER
is associate professor of English at the University of Montana, Missoula.

www.ingramcontent.com/pod-product-compliance
Lightning Source LLC
Chambersburg PA
CBHW060937230426

43665CB00015B/1973